NEW TESTAMENT APOCRYPHA
(Volume One)

E. HENNECKE

NEW TESTAMENT APOCRYPHA

edited by

W. SCHNEEMELCHER

English translation edited by
R. McL. Wilson
Lecturer in New Testament Language and Literature,
St. Mary's College, St. Andrews, Scotland

VOLUME ONE
GOSPELS AND RELATED WRITINGS

SCM PRESS LTD

This book originally appeared as E. Hennecke, *Neutestamentliche Apokryphen*, volume I, (ed. W. Schneemelcher) and was published in 1959 by J. C. B. Mohr, Tübingen, Germany. The English translation has been made by A. J. B. Higgins, George Ogg, Richard E. Taylor, and R. McL. Wilson.

334 01111 6

First published in Great Britain 1963
Second impression 1973

© J. C. B. Mohr (Paul Siebeck) Tubingen 1959
English translation © Lutterworth Press 1963

Printed in Great Britain by
Redwood Press Limited, Trowbridge, Wiltshire

NOTE TO THE SECOND IMPRESSION

SINCE THIS is a second impression and not a fresh edition, changes have been kept to a minimum and confined to the elimination of errors noticed. A few which would have entailed major disturbance of the printed text may be listed here:

A second edition of Walter Bauer's *Rechtgläubigkeit und Ketzerei* was published in 1964, with appendixes by Georg Strecker; an English translation edited by R. A. Kraft and G. Krodel appeared in 1971: *Orthodoxy and Heresy in Earliest Christianity*, London and Philadelphia.

There is an English translation of Harnack's *Entstehung des NTs* (cited on p. 29): *The Origins of the New Testament*, London 1925; also of Dibelius' *Geschichte des urchristlichen Literatur* (p. 119): *A Fresh Approach to the New Testament and Early Christian Literature*, London 1937. A revised edition of the English translation of Bultmann's *History of the Synoptic Tradition* (p. 75) appeared in 1968.

Jeremias' book *Unbekannte Jesusworte* has appeared in a third edition (1962), and an English translation of this was published in 1964. References in the present work to the second edition are not always applicable to the third.

Readers interested in the Nag Hammadi gnostic library will find a comprehensive coverage of the literature in D. M. Scholer, *Nag Hammadi Bibliography*, 1948–1969, Leiden 1971, with the annual Supplement published in *Novum Testamentum*.

St. Andrews   R. McL. W.
1973

ABBREVIATIONS

Aa	= Acta apostolorum apocrypha 1 ed. Lipsius 1891; 2, 1 & 2 ed. Bonnet 1898 & 1903
ABA	= Abhandlungen der Berliner Akademie der Wissenschaften, Phil.-hist. Klasse
Altaner	= Berthold Altaner, Patrologie [5]1958
Apa	= Apocalypses apocryphae ed. Tischendorf, 1866
Apokr. 1	= Neutestamentliche Apokryphen, hrsg. von E. Hennecke, [1]1904
Apokr. 2	= Neutestamentliche Apokryphen, hrsg. von E. Hennecke, [2]1924
AR	= Archiv für Religionswissenschaft
AThANT	= Abhandlungen zur Theologie des Alten und Neuen Testaments
Bauer	= W. Bauer, Das Leben Jesu im Zeitalter der neutestamentlichen Apokryphen, 1909
BJRL	= Bulletin of the John Rylands Library
BZAW	= Beihefte zur Zeitschrift für die alttestamentliche Wissenschaft
BZNW	= Beihefte zur Zeitschrift für die neutestamentliche Wissenschaft und die Kunde der Älteren Kirche
ChW	= Die Christliche Welt
CSCO	= Corpus scriptorum christianorum orientalium
CSEL	= Corpus scriptorum ecclesiasticorum latinorum
DB	= A Dictionary of the Bible ed. J. Hastings, 5 vols., 1898–1904
Ea	= Evangelia apocrypha ed. Tischendorf [2]1876
GCS	= Die griechisch-christlichen Schriftsteller der ersten Jahrhunderte
GGA	= Göttingische Gelehrte Anzeigen
Handb.	= Handbuch zu den neutestamentlichen Apokryphen, hrsg. von E. Hennecke, 1904
HTR	= The Harvard Theological Review
James	= The Apocryphal New Testament ed. M. R. James, 1924 (reprint 1955)
JBL	= Journal of Biblical Literature
JEH	= Journal of Ecclesiastical History
JTS	= Journal of Theological Studies
KlT	= Kleine Texte für Vorlesungen und Übungen, hrsg. von H. Lietzmann
Michaelis	= Die apokryphen Schriften zum Neuen Testament, übersetzt und erläutert von W. Michaelis, [2]1958

7

NGA   = Nachrichten der Akademie der Wissenschaften in Göttingen
NkZ   = Neue kirchliche Zeitschrift
NTS   = New Testament Studies
Or Chr   = Oriens Christianus
Orient LZ   = Orientalistische Literaturzeitung
PA   = Patrum apostolicorum opera ed. O. von Gebhardt, A. von Harnack, Th. Zahn 1, 1875 ²1876–77; 2,1876; 3,1877
PG   = Migne, Patrologia Graeca
PL   = Migne, Patrologia Latina
PO   = Patrologia Orientalis
Quasten   = J. Quasten, Patrology I & II, 1950–53
RAC   = Reallexicon für Antike und Christentum
RE   = Realencyclopädie für protestantische Theologie und Kirche
Rev. Bibl   = Revue Biblique
RGG   = Religion in Geschichte und Gegenwart ²1927ff.; ³1957ff.
RHE   = Revue d'Histoire Ecclésiastique
RHPR   = Revue d'Histoire et de Philosophie religieuses
RHR   = Revue de l'Histoire des Religions
RQS   = Römische Quartalschrift
Santos   = Los Evangelios Apócrifos ed. A. De Santos Otero, 1956
SB Berlin   = Sitzungsberichte der Berliner Akademie der Wissenschaften, Phil.-hist. Klasse
SHA   = Sitzungsberichte der Heidelberger Akademie der Wissenschaften, Phil.-hist. Klasse
ThLBl   = Theologisches Literaturblatt
ThLZ   = Theologische Literaturzeitung
ThWtb   = Theologisches Wörterbuch
TSt   = Texts and Studies, Contributions to biblical and patristic literature
TU   = Texte und Untersuchungen zur Geschichte der altchristlichen Literatur
Vig. Chr   = Vigiliae Christianae
ZDMG   = Zeitschrift der deutschen Morgenländischen Gesellschaft
ZKG   = Zeitschrift für Kirchengeschichte
ZkTh   = Zeitschrift für katholische Theologie
ZNW   = Zeitschrift für die neutestamentliche Wissenschaft und die Kunde der Älteren Kirche
ZThK   = Zeitschrift für Theologie und Kirche

PREFACE TO THE ENGLISH EDITION

THE STANDARD WORK in English on the Apocryphal New Testament has long been the admirable volume under that title edited by M. R. James. For all its merits, however, this book now suffers from two defects. In the first place, it is now more than thirty years old, and consequently takes no account of the discoveries made in that period; and secondly, it provides but little in the way of guidance to the literature devoted to these apocryphal writings.

Both these deficiencies are supplied in the third edition of the German counterpart, the *Neutestamentliche Apokryphen* originally edited by Edgar Hennecke and now, in its latest form, directed by Professor W. Schneemelcher. A proposal to make this work available to the English-speaking reader in an English translation could not but be welcomed by anyone interested in the subject, and accordingly a translation has now been prepared of the first volume, devoted to the apocryphal gospels and related works.

This book is, with certain qualifications, a direct translation from the German original. The qualifications relate in the main to the section on the Gnostic gospels, prepared by Professor H.-Ch. Puech, which was originally written in French and has been translated from the typescript and checked against the printed German text to ensure that no final corrections have been overlooked. Other modifications have been necessary to facilitate the use of the book by English-speaking readers: references to Irenaeus are given according to the divisions in W. W. Harvey's edition, and where books are available in English the fact has so far as possible been indicated. Extracts quoted from original sources in Latin, Greek, and Coptic have been checked against the text, to ensure that the translations are translations into English and not merely versions at second hand. Where the German contributor has shown a preference for a particular rendering, however, his choice has been duly respected; on occasion the German version is expressly stated to represent an eclectic text, and consequently has been followed. In short, this is an English version of Hennecke, checked and corrected to make it in every way possible an adequate tool for the use of the English-speaking reader.

At the time of its publication the German volume was as completely up to date as possible, but there have been some further studies published since that time which are relevant, particularly

9

in relation to the Nag Hammadi discovery. Opportunity has therefore been taken, in collaboration with Professor Puech, to revise this section and introduce further references to the growing literature on these texts. In addition, a complete translation of the Gospel of Thomas has been included in an appendix; for various reasons it has not been possible to include the complete text of the Gospel of Truth, but a précis has been prepared, including some further extensive extracts, and it is hoped that this will serve the purpose.

Each of the translators has been responsible for his own part of the work, but the whole has been read and revised by the editor. The portions undertaken by each are indicated in the table of contents, but may be summarized here: the Introduction and the first five sections are the work of Dr. Ogg, Section VI of Dr. Taylor, and Sections VII and IX of the editor. It was originally planned that Dr. Higgins should translate Sections VIII, IX, and X, but pressure of other duties delayed his work and rather than hold up the book as a whole he very generously offered to submit what he had completed and allow someone else to finish his part. He has accordingly been responsible for Section VIII and for part of Section X: the text of the Gospel of Nicodemus, the introduction to the Gospel of Bartholomew, and the Questions of Bartholomew. The remainder of Section X has been translated by the editor.

Acknowledgment is due to Messrs. E. J. Brill of Leiden and Messrs. Collins of London for permission to quote the extracts from the translation of the Gospel of Thomas published by them which appear in the body of the work, to the Trustees of the Griffith Institute, Oxford, for permission to quote a passage translated by P. E. Kahle in his book *Bala'izah* and to Messrs. Rascher of Zürich for permission to make use of the revised translation of the Gospel of Truth published by them in the preparation of the précis mentioned above.

Finally, the editor would express his thanks to those who have co-operated in the preparation of this book: first to his collaborators for their care and trouble in the exacting task of translation, and secondly to the staff of Lutterworth Press for their efforts in the preparation and production of the work.

It is hoped that the second volume will follow without undue delay upon the publication of the German edition.

St. Andrews
1962

R. McL. W.

PREFACE TO THE GERMAN EDITION

AFTER LONG preparation the first volume of the new edition of the *Neutestamentliche Apokryphen* can now at last be presented. Its completion, despite constant effort, has taken longer than the editor and his collaborators would have wished. As early as 1948 Dr. Edgar Hennecke approached me with the request that I should help him in the new edition of this standard work, established by him in 1904 and supervised by him in the second edition (1924), and still today a part of the indispensable equipment of every New Testament scholar or Church historian. Even in our first discussions it was clear that the work would have to be completely transformed. The chief difficulty was to find suitable collaborators for the several sections, since of the seventeen contributors to the second edition only three were still alive and many scholars were obliged to decline to take part.

In 1949 I learned, through a friendly hint from Professor O. Cullmann, of the great discovery of Coptic Gnostic documents at Nag Hammadi, and the first reports to reach Germany (at that time still largely cut off from the outside world) made it clear that this discovery would have to be taken into consideration in the *Neutestamentliche Apokryphen* if the book was not to be obsolete as soon as it appeared. Through the good offices of Professor Cullmann we succeeded in securing Professor H.-Ch. Puech of Paris as our collaborator for the whole complex subject of the Gnostic gospels and the related literature. This contribution made a few changes necessary in the original structure of the work. Since Professor Puech wished to work with a great deal of unpublished material from the Nag Hammadi discovery, certain legal difficulties had to be overcome, and this meant a considerable delay in the completion of the task, although it must be considered as justified by the richness of Puech's contribution.

On March 25, 1951, Edgar Hennecke died in Göttingen at the age of eighty-five. We must here pay grateful tribute to this man who in his day laid for the study of this literature a foundation on which many have subsequently built. His memory will long be held in honour (cf. my obituary notice in *ThLZ* 76 (1951), cols. 567f.).

Although the plans for the reorganization were often discussed between Hennecke and myself in the years 1948–51, the present arrangement is largely of later origin. My chief concern was to effect a more compact structure, with due regard for the basic considerations presented in the General Introduction. In this connection may be mentioned the fact that provision has no longer been made in the second volume for the Apostolic Fathers ("Voices of the Church" in the second edition). The material has increased to such an extent that inclusion of these writings was impossible on grounds of space. A division of the work into two volumes was in any case essential.

In the printing of the work I have had the benefit of much friendly help. In the first place I have to thank all the contributors for their trouble, and also for the patience they have often shown. To F. Scheidweiler I can no longer express these thanks. He died on October 11, 1958. To the advice of my friend, P. Vielhauer, this book owes more than I can tell. In the preparation for the press and the supervision of the printing Knut Schäferdiek and Siegfried Helmer have given untiringly of their skill. If in spite of these two faithful helpers there remain many inconsistencies in the abbreviations, etc., and even an occasional printer's error, that is not merely a sign of human insufficiency but also a result of the long history of this work. Finally, a word of thanks must also be given to the publisher, Herr H. G. Siebeck, who proposed and furthered the new edition and has met every wish of the editor with patience and understanding.

The second volume, which will contain in particular the apocryphal Acts, is in an advanced state of preparation, so that it will appear at no very great interval after the first.

Bonn,   WILHELM SCHNEEMELCHER
  22nd February, 1959

CONTENTS

13

CONTENTS

15

CONTENTS

GENERAL INTRODUCTION
(*W. Schneemelcher*)

The concept 'New Testament Apocrypha' was probably formed on the analogy of that of the 'Old Testament Apocrypha'. The latter designation is generally given to the writings of which Luther says that "whilst they are not regarded as being on an equality with Holy Writ, they yet make useful and good reading". But even for the Old Testament Apocrypha this definition by no means suffices to cover all the facts that present themselves. For the so-called 'New Testament Apocrypha' it is quite unserviceable, since here we are concerned not with writings the canonicity of which was canvassed for a long time (a part of the Old Testament Apocrypha was finally excluded from the canon proper only by the Council of Trent), but rather with a literature which very early, to a small extent even before the completion of the canon in the end of the second century and in the course of the third, was excluded from ecclesiastical use and then continued to have a separate existence among groups that were condemned as heretical. Accordingly we must cast about for another definition of the term, one that will indicate clearly what is to be understood by 'apocryphal'. In this connection the question how in general the formation of such literature came about is of course important. This question can, however, be answered only when we have the main outlines of the history of the canon before us, for it is only therewith that the exclusion of the 'non-canonical literature' becomes intelligible.

1. CANONICAL AND APOCRYPHAL

Literature: H. W. Beyer, article κανών in *ThWtb* III (1938), 600–606; R. Meyer and A. Oepke, article κρύπτω κτλ., supplement: "Kanonisch und apokryph", in *ThWtb* III, 979–999 (where further literature is given).

1. To define what has to be understood by the term *canonical* is comparatively easy.[1] The Greek word κανών is formed from κάνη, a loan-word from the Semitic with the basic meaning 'reed'; the Greek form κάννα has also documentary evidence.[2] The Hebrew קָנֶה has the meanings 'reed' and 'corn-stalk', also the further senses 'measuring-reed', 'measuring-rod' and 'measuring-stick'. The meanings 'scale-beam' and 'shaft of the candlestick' indicate further developments in the course of the history of the word. The Septuagint, however, never translates this קָנֶה by the Greek κανών, which in it appears only in three passages: Judith 13:6 (here = 'bed-post'), Micah 7:4 ("an inexplicable flaw in translation") and 4 Macc. 7:21. In the last mentioned passage it is said: Should not a man πρὸς ὅλον τὸν τῆς φιλοσοφίας κανόνα φιλοσοφῶν have control over desire? In this passage κανών is obviously used in the profane Greek sense, a sense in which, as can be shown, it is also used in Philo: κανών is the rule, the instruction, indeed almost the law (= νόμος). In profane Greek "the Semitic basic meaning 'reed' as a matter of course gives place" to the metaphorical sense, according to which κανών means a straight rod. In a further development of this sense the word is used especially in the language of carpenters to denote the measuring-tape. In this technical sense it is then transferred—as many words have been—to various spheres of life.

Among Greeks κανών thus denotes the norm, the finished condition which represents the end, the standard or the criterion which as regards their ends can be applied to all things. Consequently, by this term expression can be given to something very fundamental to Hellenism: the ideal, the perfection which is the standard by which the empirical world must be judged. What

[1] A religio-phenomenological discussion of the problem of "Holy Scriptures" is here omitted, for, profitable and legitimate as it is in itself, it is not necessary for our purpose. Cf. on it G. van der Leeuw, *Phänomenologie der Religion*, 2nd ed. (1956), 494ff.; J. Leipoldt and S. Morenz, *Heilige Schriften* (1953).
[2] Throughout this whole section see for the authorities Beyer, *op. cit.* His account has been largely used here, and word-for-word citations for which particulars are not given come from his article.

answers to the canon is what attains to "that supreme measure of accomplishment that must be aspired after", which in various ways and in diverse spheres is characteristic of Hellenism. This holds good for the departments of art, music and literature. Thus in the department of literature the Alexandrian grammarians drew up a 'canon' of authors whose Greek was regarded as standard. In view of the close connection between aesthetic and ethical ideals the carrying-over of the concept to the sphere of morals is easily understood. The moral law is described as κανών, and certain ideals are exalted as κανόνες. The taking over of the term "canon" by the philosophers is then big with significance. Epicurus and Epictetus in particular avail themselves of it. "To philosophize means nothing other than to investigate and establish standards, κανόνες" (Epict. Diss. II, 11, 24). "These κανόνες are the basic rules for the right use of the free will."

In the NT we come across the word κανών only in four passages (the variant in Phil. 3:16 may be disregarded, since it is doubtless a secondary reading). The sense of Gal. 6:15f. is clear: "For neither is circumcision anything nor uncircumcision, but a new creature. And as many as walk according to this rule, peace be upon them and mercy, upon the Israel of God." As the context shows, Paul here uses κανών in the Greek sense of standard of judgment. The attitude to circumcision and uncircumcision is the standard, the basis of cognition, on and by which it can be determined who belongs to the new creation, i.e. who is Christian. At the same time this κανών is equally the norm of action, and not merely the standard by which others are to be judged. Much more difficult to understand is the passage 2 Cor. 10:13–16, in which the word κανών is used three times:

"But we would not glory beyond measure, but according to the measure of the standard which God has apportioned us as measure, (namely) to reach even to you. For it is not the case that we (in fact) did not reach to you, and have merely enlarged our measure (by talking big), but we have actually reached to you proclaiming the Gospel of Christ. We do not boast ourselves beyond measure in other men's work, but we have the hope, when (once) your faith increases in you, to advance further to the highest height according to our standard, (namely) to proclaim the Gospel beyond you, not boasting ourselves in the province of another's standard over what has (already) been done (by another)."

That is how the passage is rendered by H. Lietzmann (*Hdb. z. NT, in loc.*). He understands κανών here as the "area of his missionary labour". But H. W. Beyer (*ThWtb* III, 603f.) and E. Käsemann (*ZNW* 41, 1942, 33ff.), with whom Kümmel (*Hdb. z. NT*

9, 4th ed., p. 209) agrees, have seen that here it is not a question of a certain territorial area which God has apportioned to Paul and that Paul does not refer to this marked-off area, but that it is a matter of his call and appointment to apostolic service, of the grace of apostleship, which for him is κανών: "on the ground of the fact that God gave grace to Paul to found the Corinthian Church the Corinthians must recognize that his claim to apostleship is justified" (Kümmel, *op. cit.*), which is to say that here also κανών has the meaning 'standard of judgment', although perhaps in a somewhat inflected sense.

With the meanings 'norm' and 'standard of judgment' the word κανών came to be used in the Church. This is bound up with the historical development of the Church from a multiplicity into a visible unity. In the early period the multiplicity of doctrines and opinions was no hindrance to faith in the one *ecclesia catholica*, which certainly was an element of the faith. But in the 2nd century, as a defence against an all-subversive syncretism, it became necessary to search for uniform norms for life and doctrine, for the compass of Scripture and for worship, and thus to make membership of the *one* Church visible and manifest.[1] In the course of this development it came about in various places and countries that what hitherto had been recognized as 'orthodox', i.e. as Christian, now all at once became 'heretical' and had to be rejected.[2] As a designation that could express unmistakably what ecclesiastically was now obligatory the word κανών presented itself.

It served in the first place quite generally to set in relief what the hard and fast ecclesiastical norm was to be, and was used in this sense in particular in a threefold connection: Rule of Truth (κανὼν τῆς ἀληθείας), Rule of Faith (κανὼν τῆς πίστεως) and Rule of the Church (or Ecclesiastical Rule, κανὼν τῆς ἐκκλησίας or ἐκκλησιαστικός). The Rule of Truth is the obligatory truth as the Church proclaims it. It takes shape in the Rule of Faith, the *regula fidei*, as it begins to come into being in the 2nd century. Both of these, the Rule of Truth and the *regula fidei*, are embraced by the κανὼν τῆς ἐκκλησίας, in which the Church is the subject, the creatress of the normalizing standard, which also fixes and formulates the *regula fidei*, even though this confession is naturally regarded as an expression of the accord (συμφωνία) of law, prophets and gospel.

"The canon is the norm to which everything in the Church accommodates itself; to canonize means to recognize as part of this norm. The Christian of *c.* 400 felt at the mention of the word

[1] Clearly the problem of the origin of the "early catholic Church" is by no means exhaustively described in this reference to it; but for our context what is said should suffice.

[2] Cf. on this W. Bauer, *Rechtgläubigkeit und Ketzerei im ältesten Christentum* (1934).

'canonical' precisely as we do when we say divine, holy, infallible, absolutely authoritative.''[1] In these words A. Jülicher has once for all summarized the development of the usage in the first centuries. Moreover, it is to be observed that κανονιζόμενος and ἐκκλησιαζόμενος are used synonymously and that this explains how the Church was made independent as the creatress of the rule. For Paul the κανών, i.e. the standard against which everything had to be measured, was Christ and the grace bestowed by Him on the apostle, but in the 3rd and 4th centuries the Church becomes the power that sets the canon. From the 4th century onwards the general use of the word 'canon' was supplemented or restricted. Certain portions of the total teaching of the Church and of the total content of its life were detached, and then these separate entities were designated κανών or κανονικός. Above all the collection of the Holy Scriptures of the Old and New Testaments was so designated from the middle of the 4th century. For instance canon 59 of the Synod of Laodicea (middle of the 4th century) ordains ὅτι . . . δεῖ . . . λέγεσθαι . . . μόνα τὰ κανονικὰ τῆς Καινῆς καὶ Παλαιᾶς Διαθήκης. This narrowing of the usage cannot be put down to a carrying-over of the terminology of the Alexandrine grammarians (see above) or to an acceptance of κανών in the sense κατάλογος (a locution which is documented), but must be understood as a phenomenon bound up with the total development of the Church; that is to say, the norm according to which Christian and ecclesiastical teaching had to be judged was fixed more and more narrowly. This usage then passed over into the Latin, where *canon* was used synonymously with *biblia*, as it has continued to be extensively down to the present time.[2]

2. Over against the canon there are now set the *Apocrypha*, i.e. those writings the canonization of which was not carried through. This usage is comparatively late. The early canon catalogues[3] know the writings about which we are here concerned in great part merely as "extra-canonical" or as "disputed" or as "writings which are to be read aloud not in the Church but in the presence of catechumens". It is true that the designation of such writings as 'apocrypha' also emerges (cf. the canon catalogues reproduced below). Here, however, the uncertainty of the usage is evident from the fact that, side by side with what we describe as apocrypha, other writings (e.g. the Epistle of Barnabas, the Epistles of Ignatius, etc.) are included under this heading. For the usage current

[1] A. Jülicher, *Einleitung in das NT*, 7th ed. (1931), p. 555.
[2] By way of comment it may be pointed out that in the Greek as in the Latin Church κανών obtained still other meanings: decree of council, roll of clergy, part of Mass, etc.: cf. Beyer, *op. cit.*, pp. 605f.
[3] Cf. the compilation in E. Preuschen, *Analecta* II, 2nd ed. 1910; a few specimens are given in translation on pp. 42ff. below.

among us today the use of the term by Karlstadt in his writing, *De canonicis scripturis*, 1520,[1] has been of great moment. It was from there that it gained a place in Luther's Bible.

In the early Church the designation ἀπόκρυφα makes its appearance from the time of Irenaeus onwards, but it has a special meaning and, in the first centuries, had a history which it is far from easy to survey.

What did ἀπόκρυφος mean originally?[2] It has been thought that ἀπόκρυφος is a translation of the Hebrew גָּנוּז, therefore of an expression by which were designated the books that were banned from those read in worship, their secular use being of course not thereby ruled out. That may be brought into accord with certain statements of the rabbis regarding such writings. But this opinion, which has been advocated above all by Th. Zahn,[3] cannot be maintained. It needs rather to be emphasized that גנז in its basic significance means 'to gather' or 'to preserve' and only in a derived sense 'to hide' or 'to withdraw from the clutches of publicity', whereas ἀπόκρυφος means in the first place 'kept hidden because of its costliness or because of the objectionable nature of its content' and then 'of hidden origin'. In any case the use of ἀπόκρυφος for certain writings cannot be explained from Judaism; rather we must turn to the Gentile-gnostic terminology for the root of this usage. Gnosis favoured esoteric and secret doctrines, it used cryptograms, and it kept its writings confidential. Thus the great Leiden magical papyrus prefaces the revelation of the Uphôr-charm with the instruction: ἔχε ἐν ἀποκρύφῳ ὡς μεγαλομυστήριον. κρύβε, κρύβε (Preisendanz, *Pap. gr. mag.* XII 321), and similar instructions are a constant element in gnostic gospels (see p. 263 below). In this connection there belongs the endeavour to carry back Greek philosophy to Oriental secret books which were designated ἀπόκρυφα βιβλία (Suidas IV 713. 16 Adler).

This terminology was decisive for the introduction of the notion 'apocryphal' into the Church. That is shown by the fact that the word 'apocryphal' first comes before us not in connection with the history of the canon, but in the Church's conflict with gnosis and other heresies. Thus according to Clement of Alexandria (*Strom.* I xv, 69, 6) certain Gnostics appealed to βίβλοι ἀπόκρυφοι.

[1] There is a reprint of Karlstadt's work in K. A. Credner, *Zur Geschichte des Kanons*, Halle 1847, pp. 316–412. It is important because of its criticism of Luther's rejection of the Epistle of James. In other respects also it presents views that are noteworthy. On the other hand it certainly involves a rigid adherence to the inspiration of all the canonical writings.
[2] Here we confine ourselves to the history of the word as a *terminus technicus* within the Church. Cf. on the whole subject Oepke, *ThWtb* III pp. 987ff.
[3] Cf. Th. Zahn, *Gesch. d. ntl. Kanons* I, pp. 123ff.

These were assuredly not books that had been removed from a Jewish or Christian lectionary, but secret books that were peculiarly precious to Gnostics. The ecclesiastical writers took over this use of the word, but, rejecting as they did the occult sciences of the Gnostics, they gave to the word a fault-finding connotation. Thus Irenaeus sets ἀπόκρυφος beside νόθος (forged), and Tertullian uses apocrypha and falsa as synonymous.[1] Writings used by the Church—whether books read in public or books for private reading—are at any rate fundamentally not 'apocryphal'. For a time another usage came into its own, when over against the gnostic 'apocrypha' the Church set as early secret books those Jewish books which the synagogue had rejected, but which had enjoyed in it an extensive popularity. It is in this sense at all events that Origen speaks of such works as 'apocrypha'.[2] As the valuation of the Old Testament 'apocrypha' went down, the expression also fell into disrepute. About 400 the depreciatory meaning of the word ἀπόκρυφος, applied now to the Jewish apocrypha as well, finally prevailed, as is clear from the following quotation from Augustine: "... de his qui appellantur apocryphi—non quod habendi sint in aliqua auctoritate secreta, sed quia nulla testificationis luce declarati de nescio quo secreto nescio quorum praesumptione prolati sunt" (C. Faust. XI, 2; CSEL 25, 314. 25—315. 3).

The withdrawal of the abundant apocryphal literature from ecclesiastical use set the term 'apocryphal' free for the writings which were not withdrawn, but were included only in the Septuagint. It is true that this use of the word prevailed only in Protestantism. In the later canon catalogues[3] these texts (in themselves permitted, but not set on an equality with the canonical writings) are still differentiated from those which were rejected. And in the catalogues only the latter are called ἀπόκρυφοι or also νόθοι καὶ ἀπόβλητοι, libri apocryphi, qui nullatenus a nobis recipi debeant (Decr. Gelasianum). At the same time the selection is still fluctuating. The Jewish pseudepigrapha and the Gospels and Acts of Apostles that did not attain to the canon are certainly rejected. But when 1 Clement, the so-called 2 Clement, the Didache, the writings of Ignatius, the Shepherd of Hermas are also designated ἀπόκρυφοι, the usage is inexact, and the notion ἀπόκρυφος is blended with that of ἀντιλεγόμενα: these writings did not belong to the canon, but the reading of them was permitted.

After all that has been said about the history of the term, it is not easy to give a straightforward definition of what is to be understood by 'New Testament Apocrypha'. It may perhaps be

---

[1] Iren., Adv. haer. i. 13. 1 Harvey; Tert., De pud. 10.12.
[2] On Origen cf. Oepke op. cit. p. 994, 21ff.
[3] Cf. the texts in Preuschen, op. cit.

formulated thus: the New Testament Apocrypha are writings which have not been received into the canon, but which by title and other statements lay claim to be in the same class with the writings of the canon, and which from the point of view of Form Criticism further develop and mould the kinds of style created and received in the NT, whilst foreign elements certainly intrude. This definition is framed very closely, and a glance at the first and second editions of the present work shows that on a strict application of it many of the writings assembled there could not be considered New Testament apocrypha. The same will hold good, if to a smaller extent, for the present edition. The first part of the definition attempted above actually refers only to works that originated up to the end of the 2nd century, since of later writings only a small portion laid claim to being in the same class with the New Testament writings. But from the point of view of Form Criticism this later literature may by all means be connected with the earlier apocryphal literature which deemed itself on a par with the New Testament writings.

Fr. Overbeck, in his fine study *Über die Anfänge der patristischen Literatur* (reprint, Basel, 1954), has defended the thesis that the NT writings cannot be regarded as the commencement of Christian literature. "Gospel, acts and apocalypse are historical forms which from a quite definite point of time disappeared within the Christian Church" (*op. cit.*, p. 23). In these writings we are concerned with Christian proto-literature, which is not literature at all in the strict sense of the word—there is such literature only onwards from the time of the apologists, actually indeed only from the time of Clement of Alexandria. Only from this time on can we speak of a Graeco–Roman literature of Christian profession and Christian interest, i.e. an actual Christian literature. Overbeck objects to the bringing of the so-called Apocrypha into the field against his thesis. "To the origin of the Apocryphal Gospels, Acts of Apostles and Apocalypses . . . there is . . . no historical frontier . . . But the designation of this literature as apocryphal shows that in history it had only what may be termed an illegitimate existence, and also that its recognition depended merely upon the fiction that its origin was very ancient or lay outside the limits of the existing literature. Thus for its part the apocryphal literature serves merely to confirm the statement that gospels, acts of apostles and apocalypse are forms which, at a time when what has continued to live as Christian literature had only begun to exist, had already ceased to be even possible" (*op. cit.*, pp. 23f.).

We shall yet have to speak of the way in which from the history of the formation of the apocryphal literature it can be shown that

Overbeck's conclusions are correct only in part (cf. pp. 63, 80f. below) and that at least a portion of this literature (e.g. the later Acts of Apostles) can equally well be designated "Graeco–Roman literature of Christian profession". But the form-historical study ("A literature has its history in its forms", *op. cit.*, p. 12) made by Overbeck is important and far-reaching, for it points the way to a correct understanding of the apocryphal literature and at the same time to a clearing up of its real relation to the sociological problem ('popular literature'!). From this we can certainly supplement the definition that has been given: When we speak of 'Apocrypha of the NT', we mean by that Gospels which are distinguished by the fact not merely that they did not come into the NT but also that they were intended to take the place of the four Gospels of the canon (this holds good for the earlier texts) or to stand as enlargement of them side by side with them. The reason of their origin will be dealt with later (cf. pp. 60ff. below). It is further a matter of particular pseudepigraphical Epistles and of elaborately fabricated Acts of Apostles, the writers of which have worked up in novelistic fashion the stories and legends about the apostles and so aimed at supplementing the deficient information which the NT communicates about the destinies of these men. Finally, there also belong here the Apocalypses in so far as they have further evolved the 'revelation' form taken over from Judaism.

Objections can of course be made to such a definition. But it is a serviceable working hypothesis and facilitates the choice of the texts that should be assembled in the present work. Our task here is not to produce a textbook on the history of the Church in the first three centuries, but to open up a literature which exhibits certain formal peculiarities and is held together by them. Our definition also suggests the reason why the so-called Apostolic Fathers have been omitted in this edition. On the other hand many texts and expositions which are necessary for the understanding of the apocryphal literature proper, although they do not belong here according to our definition, have unavoidably been included. The apocryphal literature did not originate in a vacuum, but must be seen against the background of the total development in the Church of the first centuries.

2. THE HISTORY OF THE NEW TESTAMENT CANON

Literature: In most introductions to the NT there is a brief sketch of the history of the canon. The best is still the one in A. Jülicher–E. Fascher, *Einleitung in das NT*, 7th ed. (1931), 450–558. Among older works are Th. Zahn, *Geschichte des ntl. Kanons*, I and II (1888–92); id. *Grundriss der Geschichte des ntl. Kanons*, 2nd ed. (1904); A. von Harnack,

Die Entstehung des NTs und die wichtigsten Folgen der neuen Schöpfung (1914); Hans Lietzmann, *Wie wurden die Bücher des NT heilige Schrift?* 5 Lectures (1907) (re-printed in *Kleine Schriften* ii (1958) 15ff.). For corrections of the accounts given by Jülicher, Harnack and Lietzmann see W. Bauer, *Rechtgläubigkeit und Ketzerei im ältesten Christentum* (1934).

That we may obtain an insight into the reasons that were decisive for the exclusion or non-acceptance of the 'apocryphal' literature, we shall do well to turn for a little to the formation of the NT canon. Here it must suffice to sketch this development in rough outline. Moreover, most points of the history of the canon are now so fully clarified that one can almost speak of a *communis opinio*. The hypotheses of Zahn, which must be strictly separated from his detailed *Forschungen*, have rightly failed to gain ground and today are quite widely rejected. The relevant texts are conveniently assembled in E. Preuschen, *Analecta* II, Zur Kanons-geschichte (=*Sammlung ausgew. kirchen- und dogmengesch. Quellen-schriften* 8, 2 (1910)).

1. As e.g. Gal. 6:16 shows, there is for Paul strictly speaking only one authority by which he determines what is the essential nature of a Christian—namely, Jesus Christ. Beside it there stands for him, as for the whole of early Christianity, a second entity which was also recognized as an authority, although always assuredly with Jesus Christ in view—namely, the OT as a divine revelation. Jesus, so one was persuaded, did not desire to supplement or to set aside this Holy Scripture; rather He is its fulfilment. The law and the prophets thus continue to be valid, as the many OT quotations in all the NT writings show, but the Lord stands side by side with them and as their copestone. This Lord being the Spirit (2 Cor. 3:17), it is possible to understand the OT in a new way, in the Spirit, i.e. in Christ, to interpret it christologically. On the other hand the fact that Christ is acknowledged as God's final revelation to man and that this Christ is the living Lord who in the Spirit works in the Church, provides the reason why His words are now transmitted. Thereby expression is given to the truth that this Lord now speaks to His Church and in so doing proclaims to it words of God. These words are holy not because they are written in a holy book, perhaps in a proto-gospel, but because they are words of Jesus, the Risen One, and consequently words of God. The fact that the Church then put in the mouth of Jesus words which were relevant to its own situation rests upon the same basic idea, that the living Lord is present in His Church.

Later, when the oral tradition was no longer directly at the disposal of the Church through the first generation of Jesus' disciples, and when the expansion of the Church made such an oral tradition to appear inadequate, of necessity 'attested' writings concerning Jesus and His work took its place. The Gospels, which, so far as we can see, originated in the 7th and 8th decades of the first century, are a substitute for the oral accounts, but they are also based upon them, indeed in part upon a fixation in writing of a particular portion of this tradition (the Sayings Source). Moreover, the Evangelists did not sit down with the intention of writing a canonical book, but of their own free will recorded what they knew of Jesus and what had come down to them about Him. In fixing in writing the message of Jesus Christ as it was known to them, their desire was to serve the Church. They were well aware of incompleteness (Jn. 20:30), but realized that the words of the Lord and information about His life and death had to be transmitted. The result was not the production of 'revelation documents' of one kind or another, but witness was borne to the revelation of God in Christ. And this prepared the way for documents containing this witness to become holy scriptures: whilst at first freedom was the chief characteristic of the handling of the tradition, already in Barnabas (4, 14; c. 130) the word of Jesus in Mt. 22:14 is cited with the introductory formula: *as it stands written* (cf. Köster, *TU* 65, 125f., 262). In 2 Clement the development can be seen even more clearly: the gospel changes into holy scripture.

At an early stage, however, Christendom already had a further authority beside the Lord and the OT—namely, the whole body of the apostles. Here we may recall Gal. 2:6, where reference is clearly made to the pretension of the δοκοῦντες, i.e. of those who have or claim standing and who think that they may pass judgment on Paul's preaching. It cannot be said how far they actually regarded themselves as the authentic interpreters of the revelation of God in Christ. But the discussion with Paul clearly shows that their authority was by no means unqualified and unbounded. Paul himself appears to have allowed at least as much authority to the prophets, the bearers of the Spirit. But in consequence of a certain idealizing of the first times the position of the apostles seems soon to have shifted. Both Mk. 4:11 and Mt. 28:16–20 show that it was reckoned that where the apostles were, there also was the Lord. That was then developed further in the so-called post-apostolic age, between 70 and 140. Luke already shows what part fell to the apostles. Everything that was ecclesiastically important and orthodox was carried back to them. (It is to be noted that c. 120 at the latest Paul also was included among the apostles.) Already in 1 Clement (42, 1) it can be said: "The Gospel was preached to the apostles for us by the Lord Jesus Christ; Jesus Christ was sent from God."

The remaining witnesses of the first half of the 2nd century all present the same picture. The Church is founded upon the apostles and in them has its κανών side by side with the gospel in the Gospels and with the OT. As 2 Clement shows, there is as yet no question of writings of the apostles, "the apostles" being "a purely ideal canon" (Jülicher). This state of affairs was not to last, rather there had to come a fixation in writing by which one could decide what was apostolic and what non-apostolic. Thus with the 'canon', "the Lord" and "the apostles" an evolution was begun which of necessity ended in the firm definition of an isolated circle of specific writings: certain writings were gradually advanced to the rank of holy documents.

This evolution presupposes that the writings which were raised to this rank. were in the first place much read and used. The "many" mentioned in Lk. 1:1 certainly did not write for a conventicle or for their own private use. Although we cannot speak of any regular reading aloud or of a lectionary system, it can yet be asserted that the Gospels, the Acts of the Apostles and above all the epistles of the apostles were read aloud, and that these texts were exchanged and also used in public worship. This reading aloud of the Scriptures must, however, be distinguished from canonization, although here we do have before us a first step towards that. These writings were not yet put in the same class with the revelation documents of the old covenant. But gradually the differences became effaced. Collections were made of texts that were considered important, not however with a view to setting a New Testament beside the Old Testament, for the writings are found together in the greatest variety. It is possible that the Pauline epistles were the first to be assembled; but that cannot be proved, and no firm principles governing these beginnings of the canon can be given.

2. The decisive period in the history of the canon is from c. 140 to 200. In it sources flow more copiously, and we can now determine somewhat more certainly how the canon arose. We can speak of a canonical standing of the Gospels in Justin, who certainly witnesses to the state of affairs in Rome c. 150. In his *Apology* (28, 1) he speaks of the names of the "leader of the wicked demons", the devil, which are found "in our writings" (ἡμέτερα συγγράμματα). By these he certainly means not merely the OT, but also Christian literature which now has an authoritative character. In other passages Justin speaks of the apostolic ἀπομνη- μονεύματα, which he introduces as a fixed quantity. We shall not go wrong in seeing in them the Gospels, the reading of which in public worship he also mentions. These ἀπομνημονεύματα are on an equality with the prophets, since they contain the words of

31

the Lord. But these words are now fixed in writing and so finally, i.e., the gospel is synonymous with the document (or the documents) of the written Gospel (or Gospels) from which quotations are made with the word γέγραπται (*Dial.* 100). It is questioned whether Justin knew all four Gospels and used them as Holy Scriptures. His acquaintance with and use of the Synoptics may be allowed, but it is in my opinion more than doubtful whether he used the Gospel of John.[1] But in Justin by the side of the Synoptic tradition we also come upon unknown words of Jesus concerning the origin of which it is hardly possible to give satisfactory information. The question whether he draws them from unknown gospels, i.e. gospels that have not been preserved to us, or uses unwritten tradition, must doubtless be answered in the former sense. Besides the ἀπομνημονεύματα, which for him have an authoritative significance, he knows other writings which we today find in the NT. But for him they have no proper, but only a derivative, authority.

From Justin the conclusion can at all events be drawn that at the beginning of the formation of the canon there stands a form with a single member: the writings which tell the story of the Lord, i.e. the Gospel books, first of all prevailed as canonical and authoritative, and they did so possibly not because of their apostolicity but as witnesses and attestations of the Lord. But the assertion that these Gospels which were canonized were of apostolic origin prepared the way for the later canonization of the epistles of the apostles. Whilst Papias, the Phrygian contemporary of Justin, and Hegesippus (*c.* 180) present the same picture as Justin, one in which the aversion of Papias to the 'masses of books' points to the growth of the literature which came into being beside and outside our NT texts, already in Marcion (and so almost at the same time, or perhaps somewhat earlier than Justin) we find a step taken towards the canonization of the Pauline epistles. On the grounds of his basic theological conception Marcion put another entity in the place of the 'law and prophets'—namely, the 'Gospel and Apostle', i.e. the Gospel of Luke and ten Pauline epistles, the which, however, he purged of all 'Judaistic' admixture. It can no longer be determined whether Marcion made the first collection of the Pauline epistles. But something can be said for the view that already before him there were such collections and also that the problem of the fourfold transmission of the one

---

[1] The fact hardly needs to be stressed that the logos concept in Justin comes from quite other roots than does the notion in the Gospel according to John and that therefore it may not be used as proof that Justin was acquainted with that Gospel. Cf. on the whole question W. von Loewenich, *Das Johannesverständnis im zweiten Jahrhundert* (Beiheft 13 zur *ZNW* (1932), pp. 39–50); J. N. Sanders, *The Fourth Gospel in the Early Church* (1943).

'gospel' (in the sense of the glad tidings) emerged before his time (cf. pp. 74f. below).

Marcion's Bible, which however was not the decisive ground for the Church's rupture with him, was widely disseminated. The Church followed the 'heretic' on the way of a bipartite canon, since that was obviously no strange way but one that had already been in preparation for a long time. It did not however follow him on the way of a limitation of the gospel to one book. Assuredly in the middle of the 2nd century the canon of the four Gospels was still by no means everywhere recognized. W. Bauer[1] has shown that even towards the end of the 2nd century only the Gospels of Matthew and Mark had full acceptation, that the Gospel of Luke on the other hand was only hesitatingly recognized and that there was considerable opposition to the Gospel of John. As late as 220 Hippolytus thought it necessary to contend with a man named Gaius for the acceptance of the Gospel of John. And from the assuredly rather dubious report that Epiphanius gives of the "Alogi" (*Panarion* haer. 51) it is yet quite clear that *c*. 175 there were people who rejected all the Johannine writings.

There was therefore in the second half of the 2nd century still no fixed canon of the Gospels, and indeed the plurality of the Gospels was felt as a problem.[2] This is clearly seen not least in Tatian's Gospel-harmony, the *Diatessaron*, which had great success and was able to maintain itself in Syria far into the 5th century. Tatian sought, as Marcion also did in his own way, to solve by reduction the problem that was set him. But this problem presents itself strictly speaking already in Matthew and Luke, and to some extent it called forth the extra-canonical gospel literature (see on this pp. 6off. below). To put the matter briefly, the message of Jesus Christ is recorded by men who now attempt to exhibit exhaustively what is essential. From the first the tendency here is towards multiplicity, which, however, always wars against the tendency towards unity, indeed we may say towards reduction. For to be sure the intention of the fixation of a Gospel in writing was that the gospel in its entirety should be made known. Luke and Matthew write their Gospels on the basis of two sources, but nevertheless with the purpose of thus presenting the gospel. It is true that they do not claim exclusive canonicity for their work. But as soon as the canon began to form, the problem could not but become acute. Marcion and Tatian sought to solve it. In doing so they made the same effort as we also come across in the great Church. Endeavours were made to stabilize the canon of

---

[1] W. Bauer, *Rechtgläubigkeit*, particularly pp. 187ff.

[2] O. Cullmann has investigated this question in an important study, "Die Pluralität der Evangelien als theologisches Problem im Altertum", *Theol. Zeitschrift* (Basel) I (1945), pp. 23–42 (ET in *The Early Church* (1956) 39ff.).

the Gospels and then to add to the Gospels the completed collection of the Pauline epistles. In Theophilus of Antioch (*c.* 190) the 13 Pauline epistles are on the verge of complete equality with the Gospels, whereas according to the Acts of the Scillitan martyrs (*c.* 180) in North Africa a distinction was evidently still drawn between the *libri* (i.e. the Gospels) and the *epistulae Pauli viri iusti*.

At this time Luke's Acts of the Apostles and the Revelation of John are already frequently attached to the epistles of Paul, as also is a portion of the so-called catholic epistles.

About the turn from the 2nd to the 3rd century the canon seems to have obtained its fixed primitive form. The witnesses here largely agree in the following respects: the first part, the quaternity of the Gospels, is fixed; the second part, the writings of the apostles, of which the epistles of Paul are the core but to which other writings are added, is not yet with certainty delimited in detail. That can be shown from statements in Irenaeus (d. *c.* 200), in Tertullian (d. *c.* 220) and in Clement of Alexandria (d. *c.* 220), as also from the so-called Muratori Canon, a canon catalogue composed in Rome *c.* 200 (for its text see pp. 42ff. below). It is of importance that these witnesses who have been named come from various provinces of the Church, consequently that—except for odd deviations in the *Apostolos*—a uniform kind of canon begins to make its appearance throughout the whole Church. Jülicher (*op. cit.*, p. 486) has rightly shown that the agreement of these witnesses does not mean that the great majority of the churches already thought as they did. But the way to the future is indicated. In addition to other things it is clear from the deviations that the formation of the canon was not the outcome of any synodical decision, but that it developed slowly out of the various compilations of holy writings in the several provinces of the Church. At this time there was not yet a really uniform set-up of the canon throughout the whole Church; that was first attempted in the 4th century and was accomplished later.

Irenaeus, who, although certainly bishop of Lyons, manifestly kept entirely to Roman ways in the matter of the canon, has in his principal work *Adversus haereses* (written *c.* 180) dealt in detail with the quaternity of the Gospels. For him their number is so fixed that he labours to give a 'theological' or rather a speculative reason for it (III. xi. 8). As there are four winds and four cardinal points, so there must also be a fourfold gospel. Two of the Gospels were written by apostles, the two others by disciples of apostles. More interesting is what we learn from Irenaeus about the second part of the canon. Besides the Acts of the Apostles 12 epistles of Paul certainly belong to the canon. The absence of Philemon may be accidental. 1 Peter and 1 and 2 John are put on a par with the

Pauline epistles, a thing that cannot be said of James and Hebrews, both of which are known. While the Revelation of John is also known, its canonicity is certainly not particularly emphasized.

In Tertullian the situation appears not much different from what it is in Irenaeus. To the *instrumentum evangelicum* there belong of course the four Gospels, to all of which Tertullian ascribes the same value. The Acts of the Apostles and 13 Pauline epistles, as also 1 John, 1 Peter and Jude are *instrumenta apostolica*. The Revelation of John is also recognized and is put on the same level as the Gospel of John and the First Epistle. The epistle to the Hebrews is cited but as an epistle of Barnabas. As regards its position in the canon hardly anything emerges from the passage (*de pud.* 20).

The statements of Clement of Alexandria regarding the problem of the canon are particularly copious (cf. the compilation in Preuschen, *op. cit.*). The four Gospels are cited as 'Scripture' and are sharply marked off from the apocryphal concoctions. In the apostolic portion of the canon Clement knows 14 Pauline epistles (Hebrews is regarded as a Pauline epistle), 1 Peter, 1 and 2 John, Jude and Revelation. Whether 3 John, 2 Peter and James were regarded by Clement as canonical—Eusebius (*H.E.* VI. xiv, 1) says that he had expounded these epistles—cannot be shown.

At all events it may be said in summing up that these three writers at the end of the 2nd century and the beginning of the 3rd largely agree in what they regard as canonical: the four Gospels are a sure portion of the canon, and accompanying them are the thirteen Pauline epistles, 1 Peter, 1 John, Luke's Acts of the Apostles and the Revelation of John. Opinion with regard to Hebrews and the other catholic epistles was undecided, as was also the attitude to the writings which remained outside the canon, but clearly enjoyed great popularity. 1 Clement and the Shepherd of Hermas still play a large part; in the case of Clement we must add to these writings the Epistle of Barnabas, the Preaching of Peter and other 'apocrypha'. But of a canonical authority we may speak only with the greatest reserve.

The so-called Muratori Canon largely corroborates this picture. Its text, alas but incompletely preserved, from an 8th-century manuscript (cf. pp. 42ff. below) is in manifold respects highly instructive. It shows for one thing what was reckoned to the canon in Rome at the end of the 2nd century: the four Gospels constitute a *corpus*, which is followed by the "Acts of all the Apostles" in one book. There then appear thirteen Pauline epistles, classified as epistles to churches and epistles to individuals, Jude and two epistles of John. The pseudo-Pauline epistles To the Laodiceans and To the Alexandrians are rejected. Finally, the Revelation of John is also recognized, whilst the Apocalypse of Peter is admitted only conditionally. The Shepherd of Hermas is regarded merely as a writing to be read and so is not treated as canonical.

But over and above these purely statistical statements the Muratori Canon also gives indications as to what motives had actually been at work in the shaping of the canon as on the whole it had gone on up to 200. Certainly it is difficult to gather from the expositions of the fragment the inner reasons for the formation of the canon. For obviously what the author presents is later reflection, precisely as is also what we find in Irenaeus or any other Church writer. "Of the Muratorianum it can be said that according to it want of principle was the Church's principle in the preparation of the new canon" (Jülicher, p. 495). The principal reason for this is, as Jülicher has brilliantly shown, that the canon grew and was not 'made', i.e. that it is a collection of writings which in the first place were read and loved in the churches and only then were combined in a canon. The canon is certainly a work of the Church, and the authority of the theologians and bishops in the formation of the canon ought not to be underestimated. But the decisive point would not be recognized if only these particular men were made responsible for the new creation.

Such uncertainty as we come across in the Muratori Canon and in the ecclesiastical writers regarding the principles which must be respected in the receiving of a writing into the canon, shows assuredly that at first no one rightly knew how this process, completed without reflection, might subsequently be justified. Naturally the discussions with gnosis, with Marcion and with Montanism were instrumental in the formation of a NT, but they were by no means alone decisive. In these conflicts the Church became more prudent in its judgment of particular writings which were in use. What was fundamental and apostolic was given precedence, but what was apostolic was determined by what was fundamental, i.e. by the confession and faith of the Church. That is shown by the Epistle of Serapion of Antioch, preserved in Eusebius, in which, after having previously recognized the Gospel of Peter, he now, after more accurate examination of it, perceives its heretical character and therefore forbids the public reading of it (*H.E.* VI. xii, 3–6).

The Church had once upon a time gathered itself in consequence of and around the proclamation of the risen Jesus Christ. What made this proclamation legitimate was the fact that witnesses of the resurrection preached it and in their preaching also transmitted the words of the Lord. The authority of the first witnesses rested above all on the fact that they were witnesses of the Lord and His words, and these words they 'expounded', i.e. transmitted and used in the light of the resurrection faith. With the coming to an end of the genuine authority (which in particulars was certainly many a time disputed, as the discussion in Jerusalem reported by Paul in Gal. 2 makes clear) and in addition with the discontinuance of the prophetic charisma and finally with the surprisingly rapid growth and the expansion far and wide of Christian churches, it became necessary to fix this proclamation and put it down in writing. Here lies the proper starting point of the formation of the canon, but here there must also be seen the beginnings of the association of the problem of the canon with that of apostolicity. The need of genuine authority and of certainty in the proclamation led to the formation of a canon. Only what in the opinion of the churches in the 2nd century had authority was canonized and this authority was determined by apostolicity. In this connection it is not to be overlooked that hand in hand with this striving after 'apostolic' authority there is to be detected a noteworthy trend towards a development of administration (in the clerical sense).

If these conclusions are correct, it can no longer surprise us that the process of forming a canon was by no means so much a process of elimination, a mass destruction as it were or a violent rejection of all kinds of writings. Rather it appears that in the formation of the canon there was a firm adherence with a wonderful tact to what was traditional, to what had already for internal reasons gained an authoritative place in public worship. It was indeed only rarely that in the churches a reduction of the stock of familiar writings came about: in general the process of canon formation brought an enrichment to the churches. The actual process of selection and elimination took place in the period which preceded that of the primitive form of the canon.

These conclusions must now be modified in a twofold respect. (i) They do not hold good for all areas, but only for particular regions, such as Asia Minor and Rome, in which we find at a specially early date and standing out in peculiar clearness the 'principles' of canon formation; i.e., to state once for all and strictly what they are, the distinctive marks of early catholicism. (ii) Also they hold good only for a special department of the apocryphal literature: many of the writings which are assembled in this volume never had a wide distribution, but were from the first merely the literature of sects. The conflict which from the end of the 2nd century the Church waged against this literature and which may seem to us a conflict for the purity of the canon was basically a warding-off of the 'false doctrine' which in these writings had created for itself a literature of its own. Naturally there were earlier apocryphal gospels which in certain areas occasioned serious competition for the gospels later canonized. But there was besides a whole series of gospels which originated only in the 2nd century and which are to be understood in the sense just outlined, i.e. as esoteric writings or as the propaganda literature of certain circles which in the eyes of the Church were heretical.

3. The further history of the canon is defined on the one hand by the endeavour to fix its limits uniformly throughout the whole Church, and on the other hand by reflection on the significant state of the canon thus formed. A consequence of the endeavour after fixed limits for the canon was that judgment in the sense of complete suppression was now pronounced on the 'apocrypha', i.e. on the works which had not secured a place in the canon and such as had occupied in many groups perhaps as authoritative a place as the canonical gospels had occupied in the great Church. From this development, which ran its course differently in East and West, there may here in conclusion be singled out only a few points which may be relevant to our subject. In the East, in the interval between 200 and 360 the canon was largely fixed, but there is evidence of a remarkable uncertainty in reference to several writings. The vacillation of Bishop Serapion of Antioch, which we have already mentioned, regarding the Gospel of Peter was, it is true, still possible about 200, but soon after that it was so no more. Of other writings, however, such as the epistle of Barnabas, Hermas, the Apocalypse of Peter and the Didache, we know that in the East right into the 4th century they enjoyed great esteem, if they did not sporadically have even canonical standing.

For the period that followed, the attitude of Origen to the problem of the canon was undoubtedly important. From his own writings it emerges that the books which he considered obligatory and for which, in their totality, his usual designation is ἡ καινὴ διαθήκη, were regarded as constituting a unity with the OT; they are the divinely inspired writings (cf. above all the expositions in *De princ.* IV), which are all interpreted by him in the same way. Origen has undoubtedly a very precise conception of Scripture, according to which he binds OT and NT together and regards both Testaments as portions of one Book. It is all the more remarkable that with regard to the question, What properly belongs to the NT? he seems to be uncertain.

That there are only four Gospels is assuredly for him as fixed as the fact that the Acts of the Apostles and the fourteen Pauline epistles are Holy Scripture (for Origen in spite of many doubts

Hebrews belongs to the Corpus Paulinum; cf. Eus., *H.E.* VI. xxv, pp. 53f. below). Of the so-called catholic epistles, all of which Origen uses, only 1 Peter and 1 John are for him certainly canonical. That the Revelation of John had a place in Origen's NT seems to me as clear as the fact that he used and very much valued Hermas, the Didache and Barnabas, yet did not regard them as Holy Scripture. It is also noticeable that Origen is not afraid of citing other 'apocryphal' writings (e.g. the Gospel of the Hebrews or the Acta Pauli), always insisting, however, that whilst these writings may be consulted, they are not to be put on an equality with the four Gospels. The reason for this uncertainty is, on the one hand, that he finds in existence a fixed stock of canonical literature, even though he is well informed about the differences in the various churches; and, on the other hand, that it is from the standpoint of his own theological system that he judges the writings and determines how far they belong to the canon and are of theological significance.

That he might judge the writings fairly, Origen made use of three categories to which he assigned the several canonical and non-canonical works. He thus came by a highly important classification which had consequences at a later date. In his opinion there are (i) ὁμολογούμενα, i.e. universally recognized writings; (ii) ψευδῆ, i.e. lying writings forged by heretics—the Gospel of the Egyptians, the Gospel of the Twelve, the Gospel of Basilides; (iii) ἀμφιβαλλόμενα, i.e. writings concerning which there are doubts as to their genuineness and apostolicity (e.g. 2 Peter and the other catholic epistles which are not certainly canonical, see above; Hermas.)[1] This classification is full of significance for our subject inasmuch as it shows clearly that for Origen the process of eliminating the 'apocrypha' was still going on, whereas in the churches decisions had already to a considerable extent been reached. Theoretical discussions ought not to conceal from us the fact that there was wide-ranging agreement as to what certainly ought to be excluded.

Following Origen, Eusebius took over the triple classification (*H.E.* III. xxv, see pp. 56f. below). According to him also a portion of the catholic epistles was disputed. As νόθα,, i.e. spurious, there are given the Acta Pauli, Hermas, the Apocalypse of Peter, Barnabas and the Didache, as also—if one chooses (εἰ φανείη)— the Revelation of John and the Gospel of the Hebrews. The two last named writings are then strictly speaking disputed, but in the opinion of Eusebius are not on the same level as the Gospel of

---

[1] Cf. the compilation of the passages from Origen in Th. Zahn, *RE* 9 (1901), 787f. Zahn has certainly not interpreted these passages rightly and has obscured the facts.

Peter, the Gospel of Thomas and other forgeries of the heretics. Jülicher (*Einleitung*, pp. 516ff.) has rightly underlined the fact that with his own classification Eusebius falls into considerable difficulties. Nevertheless, it is clear from his writings—and other witnesses belonging to the Greek Church of the 3rd century confirm this state of affairs—that in the East at this time the NT either consisted of twenty-six books, the writings therefore which today form the NT with the exception of the Revelation of John, or comprised only twenty-one books, the majority of the so-called catholic epistles being also wanting. For the catholic epistles a decision was soon made in the East also in favour of their canonicity, whilst the Revelation remained to a large extent excluded. But at this time whatever does not belong to the canon of the twenty-one or twenty-six writings bears upon it the label "spurious" and therefore "to be rejected", i.e. the 'apocrypha' are definitely excluded by the Church and continue to exist merely in 'heretical' circles.

The question which form of the canon, that of the twenty-one or that of the twenty-six books, should prevail in the East was decided only at a comparatively late date. It was apparently answered differently in the several divisions or patriarchates. The celebrated Easter letter of Athanasius of the year 367 (text, pp. 59f. below) presents a canon of twenty-seven books and so takes in the Revelation of John. From the second group, that of the disputed books in the classification of Eusebius, only the Didache and Hermas remain in Athanasius, everything else being rejected as heretical forgery. In the region of Antioch, however, the canon without the Revelation and with only two catholic epistles long maintained itself. Only in the 5th and 6th centuries did the seven catholic epistles win through, whilst the Revelation of John seems in part to be not fully recognized in the 9th century (cf. the so-called Stichometry of Nicephorus, p. 50 below). Now and again witnesses are also met with who reckon to the NT particular non-canonical writings (e.g. 1 Clement), but omit the Revelation. But that should not conceal from us the fact that in the East onwards from the 4th century the triple classification of Origen and Eusebius was more and more repelled: there came to be only canonical writings and over against them apocrypha, decreed as 'heretical', which were to be rejected.

The development that resulted in a canon of twenty-seven books proceeded more quickly in the West than in the East. It can be asserted that, according to the witness of Jerome and Augustine, the NT with twenty-seven books was officially recognized *c.* 400. This official decision, it is true, does not mean that this canon was now current in all churches. The Pauline derivation of Hebrews,

40

the membership of the Revelation of John in the canon, the canonicity of a portion of the catholic epistles and finally the apostolicity of the epistle to the Laodiceans are problems which in particular churches emerge again and again down into the 6th century. But on the whole the Latin Church drew earlier than did the Eastern Church a sharp dividing line between what was canonical and what was non-canonical, i.e. between what was ecclesiastical and what was to be rejected as heretical.

This short review of the history of the canon has been necessary because only against this background can the phenomenon of the 'apocryphal' literature be appreciated and understood. Indeed the history of this literature ought not to be detached from the history of the canon. Later we shall inquire into the essential factors which led to the formation of different forms of apocrypha (see pp. 60ff. below). For the present we would merely refer briefly to the fact that the history of the canon is at the same time the history of the status of the 'apocrypha' in the Church.

In the period in which the writings came into being which later found themselves together in the canon of the NT, there also came into being writings which got the name 'apocryphal' and were rejected. At first it was evidently the case, since there was no canon, that a portion of this Christian literature stood on a par with the works that were later considered canonical and was read and recognized in the several churches. That holds good, it is true, only for a small portion of the literature which is assembled in the present volume. This period of juxtaposition (peaceable or not peaceable) was superseded by a time of opposition, i.e. of conflict against the reading in worship of the non-canonical literature. A major portion of the 'apocrypha' originated in this period in which the canon came into being and hence other literature, which even only remotely claimed a semblance of authority but was now for definite reasons not taken into the canon, was severely discountenanced. The division of the literature into three classes, as seen in Origen and Eusebius, gives expression to the fact that a considerable portion of the apocryphal literature enjoyed great popularity in the churches and that the canon was not able to oust these writings in a trice. Finally, there are also so-called apocrypha which originated at a time when the canon had undisputed status and which as a matter of course were thought of only as literary fictions. That applies, e.g., to the later acts of apostles, to apocryphal epistles and to a portion of the Oriental gospel creations.

In working on the 'apocrypha' the history of the canon must undoubtedly be kept very closely in view, if the writings and their origin as also their purposes are to be rightly valued. For naturally, in judging an apocryphon, we cannot disregard the question whether it originated before the formation of the canon or side by side with and in opposition to the canon then coming into being, or afterwards and presupposing the canon. In addition the history of the canon is very significant for the fate of many of the apocrypha in the Church, as is clearly shown by the catalogues and enumerations which quite often are the only evidence of writings that have perished.

4. For the elucidation of what has been said in the above survey of the history of the canon there is given here a series of texts of which mention has already been made and which are important for the history of the compilation of the NT. It comprises (a) canon lists, i.e. texts from which the content of the canon is manifest—for various reasons such texts were drawn up from the end of the 2nd or from the 3rd century onwards—and (b) the testimonies of ecclesiastical writers who are important as witnesses for the growth of the canon and the valuation of the apocrypha. The end in view that has determined the selection of lists and texts has been that the delimitation between 'canonical' and 'apocryphal' at the various stages in the formation of the canon may be evident; texts have also been selected in which titles of apocryphal writings are given. For further texts see Th. Zahn, *Gesch. des ntl. Kanons* II, 1 (1890).

(a) CANON CATALOGUES

1. *The Muratori Canon*

In 1740 Muratori published a catalogue of the New Testament writings with comments on each of them which he had found in the Ambrosian Library in Milan, in the palimpsest manuscript Cod. Ambros. J 101 sup. of the 8th century, and which is named the Muratori Canon after its discoverer. This catalogue originated in Rome *c.* 200 (or before 200). It was originally composed in Greek and was then translated into pretty barbarous Latin (hence much in the text remains unintelligible or doubtful). The beginning and the end are mutilated. The author evidently spoke first of Matthew; this section is completely lost. Of the text devoted to Mark only one line is preserved. "The fragment seems to me a sort of introduction to the New Testament, a preliminary article like others found in numerous manuscripts of the Latin and Greek Bible" (Lietzmann, *Bücher des NT*, p. 53).

Text: Zahn, *Gesch. d. ntl. Kanons* II 1, pp. 1–143 (with commentary); H. Lietzmann, *KlT* 1, 2nd ed. (1933); Preuschen, *Analecta* II, pp. 27–35; German translation with important elucidations in Lietzmann, *Wie wurden die Bücher des NT heilige Schrift?* (1907) pp. 52ff. (*Kleine Schriften* ii (1958) 52ff.); further literature in the introductions to the NT.

. . . .
at which however he was present and so he has set it down.
The third Gospel book, that according to Luke.
This physician Luke after Christ's ascension (resurrection?),
since Paul had taken him with him as an expert in the way (of
 the teaching),
composed it in his own name   5.
according to (his) thinking. Yet neither did he himself see
the Lord in the flesh; and therefore, as he was able to ascertain it,
 so he begins
to tell the story from the birth of John.
The fourth of the Gospels, that of John, (one) of the disciples.
When his fellow-disciples and bishops urged him,   10.
he said: Fast with me from today for three days, and what
will be revealed to each one
let us relate to one another. In the same night it was
revealed to Andrew, one of the apostles, that,
whilst all were to go over (it), John in his own name   15.
should write everything down. And therefore, though various
rudiments (or: tendencies?) are taught in the several
Gospel books, yet that matters
nothing for the faith of believers, since by the one and guiding
 (original?) Spirit
everything is declared in all: concerning the birth,   20.
concerning the passion, concerning the resurrection,
concerning the intercourse with his disciples
and concerning his two comings,
the first despised in lowliness, which has come to pass,
the second glorious in kingly power,   25.
which is yet to come. What
wonder then if John, being thus always true to himself,
adduces particular points in his epistles also,
where he says of himself: What we have seen with our eyes
and have heard with our ears and   30.
our hands have handled, that have we written to you.
For so he confesses (himself) not merely an eye and ear witness,
but also a writer of all the marvels of the Lord in
order. But the acts of all the apostles

35.are written in one book. For the 'most excellent Theophilus'
   Luke
   summarizes the several things that in his own presence
   have come to pass, as also by the omission of the passion of Peter
   he makes quite clear, and equally by (the omission) of the journey
      of Paul, who from
   the city (of Rome) proceeded to Spain. The epistles, however,
40.of Paul themselves make clear to those who wish to know it
   which there are (i.e. from Paul), from what place and for what
      cause they were written.
   First of all to the Corinthians (to whom) he forbids the heresy
   of schism, then to the Galatians (to whom he forbids) circum-
      cision,
   and then to the Romans, (to whom) he explains that Christ
45.is the rule of the Scriptures and moreover their principle,
   he has written at considerable length. We must deal with these
   severally, since the blessed
   apostle Paul himself, following the rule of his predecessor
   John, writes by name only to seven
50.churches in the following order: to the Corinthians
   the first (epistle), to the Ephesians the second, to the Philippians
   the third, to the Colossians the fourth, to the Galatians the
   fifth, to the Thessalonians the sixth, to the Romans
   the seventh. Although he wrote to the Corinthians and to the
55.Thessalonians once more for their reproof,
   it is yet clearly recognizable that over the whole earth one church
   is spread. For John also in the
   Revelation writes indeed to seven churches,
   yet speaks to all. But to Philemon one,
60.and to Titus one, and to Timothy two, (written) out of goodwill
   and love, are yet held sacred to the glory of the catholic Church
   for the ordering of ecclesiastical
   discipline. There is current also (an epistle) to
   the Laodiceans, another to the Alexandrians, forged in Paul's
65.name for the sect of Marcion, and several others,
   which cannot be received in the catholic Church;
   for it will not do to mix gall with honey.
   Further an epistle of Jude and two with the title (or: two of the
      above mentioned)

44

John are accepted in the catholic Church, and the Wisdom
written by friends of Solomon in his honour.   70.
Also of the revelations we accept only those of John and
Peter, which (latter) some of our
people do not want to have read in the Church. But Hermas
wrote the Shepherd quite lately in our time in the city
of Rome, when on the throne of   75.
the church of the city of Rome the bishop Pius, his brother,
was seated. And therefore it ought indeed to be read, but
it cannot be read publicly in the Church to the people either
       among
the prophets, whose number is settled, or among
the apostles to the end of time.   80.
But we accept nothing whatever
from Arsinous or Valentinus and Miltiades(?), who have also
composed a new psalm book for Marcion,
together with Basilides of Asia Minor,
the founder of the Cataphrygians.   85.

2. *The Catalogue in the Codex Claromontanus*

In the bilingual manuscript of the Pauline epistles known under
the name *Codex Claromontanus* (Cod. D; now Paris. gr. 107, written
in the 6th century), after Philemon and before Hebrews there is
a catalogue of the Biblical writings of the Old and New Testaments with a statement of the 'lines', i.e. of the extent of the
several writings. Its NT portion is given here. According to
Jülicher (in opposition to Zahn) the catalogue belongs to the 4th
century and is of Western origin.

Text: Zahn, *Gesch. d. ntl. Kanons* II 1, pp. 157–172 (with commentary);
Preuschen, *Analecta* II, pp. 40–42.

Gospels 4	
Matthew	2600 lines
John	2000 lines
Mark	1600 lines
Luke	2900 lines
Epistles of Paul	
To the Romans	1040 lines
To the Corinthians I	1060 lines
To the Corinthians II	⟨·⟩70 lines

To the Galatians	350 lines
To the Ephesians	375 lines
(three lines seem to have fallen out here:	
Philippians, 1 and 2 Thessalonians are missing)	
To Timothy I	208 lines
To Timothy II	288 lines
To Titus	140 lines
To the Colossians	251 lines
To Philemon	50 lines
To Peter I	200 lines
To Peter II	140 lines
(Epistle) of James	220 lines
I Epistle of John	220 lines
Epistle of John II	20 lines
Epistle of John III	20 lines
Epistle of Jude	60 lines
Epistle of Barnabas (=Epistle to the	
Hebrews?)	850 lines
Revelation of John	1200 lines
Acts of the Apostles	2600 lines
Shepherd (of Hermas)	4000 lines
Acts of Paul	3560 lines
Revelation of Peter	270 lines

3. *The so-called Decretum Gelasianum*

In the so-called *Decretum Gelasianum de libris recipiendis et non recipiendis,* which upon the whole is probably of South Gallic origin (6th century) but which in several parts can be traced back to Pope Damasus and reflects Roman tradition, we have in the second part a canon catalogue, in the fourth part an enumeration of recognized synods and ecclesiastical writers, and in the fifth part a catalogue of the 'apocrypha' and other writings which are to be rejected. The canon catalogue gives all twenty-seven books of the NT, the canon being therefore settled definitely in this form. The list, already outwardly and sharply separated from it, of the 'apocrypha', i.e. of the writings to be rejected, is given here in translation (according to the edition of v. Dobschütz, see below). An identification of the several writings that are cited is dispensed with (cf. on this Dobschütz in his edition). Some of them are apocrypha which are included in the present work; and when they are discussed, reference will be made to the witness of the *Decretum Gelasianum:* but others of them are much later writings to which no further consideration can be given in this work.

Text: E. von Dobschütz, *TU* 38, 4 (1912), with commentary. Cf. also E. Schwartz, *ZNW* 29 (1930), 161–168.

The remaining writings which have been compiled or been recognized by heretics or schismatics the catholic and apostolic Roman church does not in any way receive; of these we have thought it right to cite below some which have been handed down and which are to be avoided by catholics.

Further Enumeration of Apocryphal Books:
In the first place we confess that the Synod at Ariminum which was convened by the emperor Constantius, the son of Constantine, through the prefect Taurus is damned from then and now and for ever.

Itinerary (book of travels) under the name of the apostle Peter, which is called The Nine Books of the holy Clement	apocryphal
Acts under the name of the apostle Andrew	apocryphal
Acts under the name of the apostle Thomas	apocryphal
Acts under the name of the apostle Peter	apocryphal
Acts under the name of the apostle Philip	apocryphal
Gospel under the name of Matthias	apocryphal
Gospel under the name of Barnabas	apocryphal
Gospel under the name of James the younger	apocryphal
Gospel under the name of the apostle Peter	apocryphal
Gospel under the name of Thomas, which the Manichaeans use	apocryphal
Gospels under the name of Bartholomaeus	apocryphal
Gospels under the name of Andrew	apocryphal
Gospels which Lucian has forged	apocryphal
Gospels which Hesychius has forged	apocryphal
Book about the childhood of the Redeemer	apocryphal
Book about the birth of the Redeemer and about Mary or the midwife	apocryphal
Book which is called by the name of the Shepherd	apocryphal
All books which Leucius, the disciple of the devil, has made	apocryphal

47

Book which is called The Foundation   apocryphal
Book which is called The Treasure   apocryphal
Book about the daughters of Adam: Leptogenesis(?)   apocryphal
Cento about Christ, put together in Virgilian lines   apocryphal
Book which is called The Acts of Thecla and of Paul   apocryphal
Book which is ascribed to Nepos   apocryphal
Books of the Sayings, compiled by heretics and
     denoted by the name of Sixtus   apocryphal
Revelation which is ascribed to Paul   apocryphal
Revelation which is ascribed to Thomas   apocryphal
Revelation which is ascribed to Stephen   apocryphal
Book which is called The Home-going of the holy
     Mary   apocryphal
Book which is called The Penitence of Adam   apocryphal
Book about the giant Ogias, of whom the heretics
     assert that after the flood he fought with the
     dragon   apocryphal
Book which is called The Testament of Job   apocryphal
Book which is called The Penitence of Origen   apocryphal
Book which is called The Penitence of the holy
     Cyprian   apocryphal
Book which is called The Penitence of Jamnes and
     Mambres   apocryphal
Book which is called The Portion of the Apostles   apocryphal
Book which is called The Grave-plate(?) of the
     Apostles   apocryphal
Book which is called The Canones of the Apostles   apocryphal
The book Physiologus, compiled by heretics and
     called by the name of the blessed Ambrose   apocryphal
The History of Eusebius Pamphili   apocryphal
Works of Tertullian   apocryphal
Works of Lactantius   apocryphal
     (*later addition:* or of Firmianus
               or of the African)
Works of Postumianus and of Gallus   apocryphal
Works of Montanus, of Priscilla and of Maximilla   apocryphal
Works of Faustus the Manichaean   apocryphal
Works of Commodianus   apocryphal

Works of the other Clement, of Alexandria	apocryphal
Works of Thascius Cyprian	apocryphal
Works of Arnobius	apocryphal
Works of Tichonius	apocryphal
Works of Cassian, a presbyter in Gaul	apocryphal
Works of Victorinus of Pettau	apocryphal
Works of Faustus of Riez in Gaul	apocryphal
Works of Frumentius Caecus	apocryphal
Epistle of Jesus to Abgar	apocryphal
Epistle of Abgar to Jesus	apocryphal
Passion (Martyr Acts) of Cyricus and of Iulitta	apocryphal
Passion of Georgius	apocryphal
Writing which is called Interdiction (Exorcism?) of Solomon	apocryphal
All amulets which have been compiled not, as those persons feign, in the name of the angels, but rather in that of the demons	apocryphal

These and the like, what Simon Magus, Nicolaus, Cerinthus, Marcion, Basilides, Ebion, Paul of Samosata, Photinus and Bonosus, who suffered from similar error, also Montanus with his detestable followers, Apollinaris, Valentinus the Manichaean, Faustus the African, Sabellius, Arius, Macedonius, Eunomius, Novatus, Sabbatius, Calistus, Donatus, Eustatius, Iovianus, Pelagius, Iulianus of Eclanum, Caelestius, Maximian, Priscillian from Spain, Nestorius of Constantinople, Maximus the Cynic, Lampetius, Dioscorus, Eutyches, Peter and the other Peter, of whom the one besmirched Alexandria and the other Antioch, Acacius of Constantinople with his associates, and what also all disciples of heresy and of the heretics or schismatics, whose names we have scarcely preserved, have taught or compiled, we acknowledge is to be not merely rejected but excluded from the whole Roman catholic and apostolic Church and with its authors and the adherents of its authors to be damned in the inextricable shackles of anathema for ever.

4. *The Stichometry of Nicephorus*

In the prolix version of the Chronography of Nicephorus (patriarch of Constantinople 806–818; cf. Krumbacher, *Gesch. d. Byz. Literatur*, 2nd ed. (1897), pp. 349ff.) there is a canon catalogue, the origin of which indeed has not been clearly settled, but which ought perhaps to be located in Jerusalem. Whether it is older than *c.* 850 (so Jülicher) remains open to question. It is striking that in the enumeration of the NT books the Revelation of John is wanting. Here then a canon of twenty-six books still presents itself. The catalogue of the books of the Old and New Testaments is followed by that of the 'antilegomena' and of the 'apocrypha'.

Text: C. de Boor, *Nicephori archiep. Const. opuscula historica* (1880), p. 132; Zahn, *Gesch. d. ntl. Kanons* II 1, pp. 297–301; Preuschen, *Analecta* II, pp. 62–64.

And the (writings) of the Old Testament which are gainsaid and are not recognized in the Church (ἐκκλησιάζονται = canonized) are the following:

1. 3 Books of the Maccabees	7300 lines
2. The Wisdom of Solomon	1100 lines
3. The Wisdom of Jesus Sirach	2800 lines
4. The Psalms and Odes of Solomon	2100 lines
5. Esther	350 lines
6. Judith	1700 lines
7. Susanna	500 lines
8. Tobith, also (called) Tobias	700 lines

And of the New Testament (writings) the following are gainsaid:

1. The Revelation of John	1400 lines
2. The Revelation of Peter	300 lines
3. The Epistle of Barnabas	1360 lines
4. The Gospel of the Hebrews	2200 lines

Apocrypha of the Old Testament are the following:

1. Enoch	4800 lines
2. (Testaments of the) Patriarchs	5100 lines
3. The Prayer of Joseph	1100 lines
4. The Testament of Moses	1100 lines
5. The Assumption of Moses	1400 lines
6. Abraham	300 lines
7. Eldad and Modad	400 lines
8. (Book of the) prophet Elias	316 lines
9. (Book of the) prophet Zephaniah	600 lines
10. (Book of) Zacharias, the father of John	500 lines
11. Pseudepigrapha of Baruch, Habakkuk, Ezekiel and Daniel	

Apocrypha of the New Testament are the following:

1.	The Circuit of Paul	3600 lines
2.	The Circuit of Peter	2750 lines
3.	The Circuit of John	2500 lines
4.	The Circuit of Thomas	1600 lines
5.	The Gospel of Thomas	1300 lines
6.	The Teaching (Didache) of the Apostles	200 lines
7.	The 32 (books) of Clement	2600 lines
8.	(Writings) of Ignatius, of Polycarp and of Hermas . . .	

5. *Catalogue of the 60 Canonical Books*

This list transmitted in several manuscripts (for information about these see Zahn, *Gesch. d. ntl. Kanons* II 1, pp. 289f.) reflects the view, widely held in the Greek Church at a later time, of the canon of sixty books (34 OT and 26 NT, therefore without the Revelation of John). After the enumeration of the canonical books, in which the complete silence observed regarding the Apocalypse of John is the most serious matter, there follows that of the writings 'outside the 60' and the 'apocrypha'.

Text: Zahn, *op. cit.*, pp. 290–292; Preuschen, *Analecta* II, p. 68f.

And the following (writings) outside the 60:

1. The Wisdom of Solomon
2. The Wisdom of Sirach
3. Maccabees (I)
4. Maccabees (II)
5. Maccabees (III)
6. Maccabees (IV)
7. Esther
8. Judith
9. Tobit

And the following apocryphal (writings):

1. Adam
2. Enoch
3. Lamech
4. The Patriarchs
5. The Prayer of Joseph
6. Eldad and Modad
7. The Testament of Moses
8. The Assumption of Moses

9. The Psalms of Solomon
10. The Revelation of Elias
11. The Vision of Isaiah
12. The Revelation of Zephaniah
13. The Revelation of Zechariah
14. The Revelation of Ezra
15. The History of James
16. The Revelation of Peter
17. The Circuits and Teachings of the Apostles
18. The Epistle of Barnabas
19. The Acts of Paul
20. The Revelation of Paul
21. The Teaching of Clement
22. The Teaching of Ignatius
23. The Teaching of Polycarp
24. The Gospel according to Barnabas
25. The Gospel according to Matthias

(b) TESTIMONIES OF CHURCH FATHERS FROM THE 3RD AND 4TH
CENTURIES

1. *Origen*

Eusebius in his *Church History* (*H.E.* VI. xxv, pp. 572, 10–580, 8 Schwartz) has assembled a series of observations by Origen on the canon:

In expounding the first Psalm he (Origen) gives a catalogue of the sacred Scriptures of the Old Testament. Word for word he writes: ... (there follows an enumeration of the Old Testament books). These writings he gives in the work mentioned.

In the first book of his *Commentary on Matthew*, true to the canon of the Church, he testifies that he knows only four Gospels; he writes: "Concerning the four Gospels, the only ones that meet with no opposition in the Church of God (spread out) under heaven, I have learned by tradition as follows: First was written the Gospel according to Matthew, formerly a publican and later an apostle of Jesus Christ, who published it for believers from Judaism, composed in Hebrew letters; the second is the Gospel according to Mark, who followed the instructions of Peter, who in his catholic epistle has acknowledged him as his son in the words: *The (Church) that is at Babylon, elected together with you, saluteth you; and so also doth*

Marcus my son (1 Pet. 5:13); the third is that according to Luke, who composed the Gospel commended by Paul (2 Cor. 8:18, cf. Orig., *Hom.* 1 *on Lk.*, Rauer 10. 8–14) for believers from the Gentiles; the last of all is the Gospel according to John."

And in the fifth book of his *Commentary on the Gospel of John* the same author (= Origen) speaks as follows about the epistles of the apostles: "Paul, who was enabled to be a minister *of the new testament not of the letter, but of the Spirit* (2 Cor. 3:6) and fully preached the gospel *from Jerusalem and round about unto Illyricum* (Rom. 15:19), did not write to all the churches which he had instructed; and even to those to which he wrote, he sent only a few lines. Peter, on whom the Church of Christ is built, against which the gates of hell shall not prevail (Mt. 16:18), has left one acknowledged epistle, possibly also a second, but that is disputed. What need be said of him who lay on Jesus' breast (Jn. 13:25; 21:20), of John who has left one Gospel and has confessed that he could write so many that the world could not contain them (Jn. 21:25), and who also has written the Revelation, but was commanded to keep silence and not record the words of the seven thunders (Rev. 10:4)? He has also left an epistle of only a few lines: he has possibly also left a second and third epistle, but not all consider these to be genuine. The two of them indeed do not contain a hundred lines."

Further in regard to the Epistle to the Hebrews he (= Origen) observes as follows in his Homilies upon it:

"In its style the epistle written to the Hebrews has a character which does not exhibit the rhetorical clumsiness of the apostle who confesses that he is rude in speech, i.e. in expression (2 Cor. 11:6). Rather the diction of the epistle is purer Greek, as everyone who is able to estimate differences in modes of expression must acknowledge. That on the other hand the thoughts of the epistle are wonderful and not inferior to those of the writings that are recognized as apostolic, everyone must admit to be true who gives the apostolic text his careful consideration."

After other comments he (= Origen) adds:

"Expressing my own opinion, I would say that the thoughts proceed from the apostle, but that the expression and composition are those of someone who remembered the apostle's discourses and as it were paraphrased the words of his teacher. If then a church regards this epistle as Paul's, it may in this command our assent: for not without good reason have the ancients handed it down as Paul's. But who actually wrote the epistle, God knows. According to the information that has reached us, some say that Clement, the bishop of Rome, wrote the epistle, and others that Luke, the author of the Gospel and of the Acts of the Apostles, did so."

From the first Homily on Luke (on Lk. 1:1):

According to the Latin translation of Jerome (pp. 3, 8–5, 20 Rauer)	According to the Greek fragments in Catenae (pp. 3, 4–6, 5 Rauer)
	As the attempt on the part of a man to record the teaching and discourse of God may be presumptuous, he (=Luke) with good reason justifies himself in the preface.
As once upon a time among the Jewish people	As among the ancient people

many engaged in prophetic discourse,
but some were lying prophets

(one of them was Ananias, the son of Azor)

whereas others were truthful prophets,

| and as among the people there was the gift of grace to distinguish spirits, whereby a section of the prophets was received, but some were rejected as it were by "expert bankers" (cf. Resch, *Agrapha*, 2nd ed. (1906), pp. 112–128), so now also in the new testament (*instrumentum*) have "many taken in hand" to write gospels, but not all have been accepted. | and as to the people there was granted as a gift of grace power to distinguish spirits by virtue of which they discriminated between the true and the false prophets, so also now in the new covenant many have wished to write gospels; the "efficient bankers" (cf. Resch, *Agrapha*, 2nd ed. (1906), pp. 112–128) have, however, not accepted everything, but have chosen only a few things. |

That there have been written not only the four Gospels, but a whole series from which those that we possess have been chosen and handed down to the churches, is, let it be noted, what we may learn from Luke's preface, which runs thus: "Forasmuch as many have taken in hand to compose a narrative."

The expression "they have taken in hand" (the Greek adds: forsooth) involves a covert accusation of those who precipitately and without the gift of grace (the Latin adds: of the Holy Ghost) have set about the writing of gospels.

Matthew to be sure and Mark and John as well as Luke did not "take in hand" to write, but filled with the Holy Ghost have written the Gospels. "Many have taken in hand to compose a narrative of the events which are quite definitely familiar among us." The Church possesses four Gospels, heresy a great many, of which one is entitled "The Gospel according to the Egyptians", and another "The Gospel according to the Twelve Apostles". Basilides also has presumed to write a gospel and to call it by his own name. "Many have taken in hand" to write, but only four gospels are recognized. From these the doctrines concerning the

Matthew to be sure did not "take in hand" to write, but rather has written from the Holy Ghost; so also have Mark and John and equally also Luke.

Those to be sure who have composed the gospel superscribed "The Gospel according to the Egyptians" and the one entitled "The Gospel of the Twelve" have "taken it in hand". Moreover, Basilides also has presumed to write a "Gospel according to Basilides". Thus "many have taken it in hand".

person of our Lord and Saviour are to be derived. I know a certain gospel which is called "The Gospel according to Thomas" and a "Gospel according to Matthias", and many others have we read—lest we should in any way be considered ignorant because of those who imagine that they possess some knowledge if they are acquainted with these. Nevertheless, among all these we have approved solely what the Church has recognized, which is that only the four Gospels should be accepted.

That is to say there are also in circulation the "Gospel according to Thomas" and the "Gospel according to Matthias" and some others.

These belong to those who "have taken it in hand". But the Church of God has preferred only the four. There is a report noted down in writing that John collected the written gospels in his own lifetime in the reign of Nero, and approved of and recognized those of which the deceit of the devil had not taken possession; but refused and rejected those which he perceived were not truthful.

2. *Eusebius of Caesarea*

Church History III xxv (pp. 250, 19–252, 24 Schwartz):

Here it may be in place to assemble once more the writings of the New Testament which have been mentioned. In the first place is to be set the holy quaternion of the Gospels, on which there follows the Acts of the Apostles. After this there are to be filed the epistles of the holy Paul, and then place must be given to the so-called first epistle of John and likewise to that of Peter. To these writings, provided it is considered proper, the Revelation of John may be added; the opinions with regard to it will be set out at the proper time. These belong to the recognized writings. To the disputed writings, which are nevertheless esteemed by most people, there belong the so-called epistle of James, that of

Jude, the second epistle of Peter as also the so-called second and third epistles of John, whether they belong to the Evangelist or to another person of the same name. To the writings that are spurious there must be counted the Acts of Paul, the so-called Shepherd, the Revelation of Peter, also the so-called epistle of Barnabas and the so-called Teachings (διδαχαί) of the Apostles and also, as has been said, the Revelation of John, provided that is considered proper; which some, as has been mentioned, reject but which others reckon among the recognized writings. Moreover, many have also reckoned among these writings the Gospel according to the Hebrews, in which those especially from among the Hebrews who have accepted Christ find delight.

While all these may be reckoned among the disputed writings, we have nevertheless felt ourselves called upon to draw up a catalogue of them, in which we have distinguished between the writings which according to ecclesiastical tradition are true, genuine and unanimously recognized and those which ordinarily exist side by side with them, which, although they do not indeed belong to the canon (ἐνδιάθηκος) but are disputed, yet have attention paid them by most ecclesiastics. We have felt ourselves called upon to draw up this catalogue in order that we may be in a position to know these writings as also those which have been adduced under apostolic names by the heretics, including e.g. the Gospels of Peter and Thomas and Matthias or of any others besides, or the Acts of Andrew and of John as also of other apostles. No ecclesiastical writer standing in the tradition has ever in any of his works considered any of these writings worth mentioning. Moreover their linguistic features are at variance with apostolic usage, and the thought and purpose of what is expressed in them, being in the highest degree contrary to true orthodoxy, show clearly that in them we handle the concoctions of heretics. Wherefore they ought never to be classed with the writings that are spurious, but ought to be rejected as wholly absurd and impious.

Church History II xxiii, 24f. (p. 174, 12–17 Schwartz):

This (i.e. the report given earlier by Eusebius in II xxiii) is the history of James, by whom the first of the so-called catholic epistles is said to have been written. It needs, however, to be borne in mind that it is regarded as spurious. Certainly not many of the ancients have mentioned it, and the same is true of the so-called epistle of Jude, which likewise is one of the seven so-called catholic epistles. All the same we know that these also are read publicly with the remaining epistles in most churches.

Church History III iii (pp. 188, 17–190, 27 Schwartz):

There is an epistle, the so-called first, by Peter which is generally recognized. The ancients have already used it in their writings as a work that is beyond question. As regards the so-called second epistle of Peter, it has come down to us that it does not belong to the canon (ἐνδιάθηκος); to many, however, it has appeared helpful and has been highly esteemed with the remaining writings. Certainly the Acts described as his and the Gospel bearing his name as also the Preaching ascribed to him and the so-called Revelation have, we know, by no means been handed down among the catholic writings, for no ecclesiastical writer, whether ancient or modern, has made use of testimonies drawn from them. . . . These are the writings bearing the name of Peter, of which, as I have ascertained, only one epistle is genuine and recognized by the ancients. But it is manifest and certain that the fourteen epistles of Paul come from him. It would, however, not be right to overlook the fact that some have rejected the Epistle to the Hebrews, maintaining that it is spoken against as non-Pauline in the Roman church. . . .

The so-called Acts of Paul have certainly not come down to us among the undisputed writings. Since the apostle in the closing salutations of the Epistle to the Romans has made mention among others of Hermas (Rom. 16:14) to whom the book called The Shepherd is ascribed, it is worth noting that this book also has been spoken against by some; on their account it should not be reckoned to the generally recognized writings; by others again it has been rated as extremely necessary especially for such as need introductory, elementary instruction. For that reason, as we know, it has already been read publicly in (some) churches, and, as I have ascertained, has been used by some of the very ancient writers. This may suffice as information about the divine writings, those which are not spoken against as also those which are not recognized by all.

3. *Athanasius*

From the Festal Letter XXXIX of the year 367 (Zahn II 1, pp. 210–212; Preuschen, *Analecta* II pp. 42–52; Coptic with German trans.: Carl Schmidt in *Nach. d. kgl. Gesellsch. d. Wissensch. zu Göttingen. Phil.-hist. Kl.* (1898), pp. 169–184; supplement in same journal 1901, pp. 328–330. A better edition is that of L. Th. Lefort, *CSCO* 150, pp. 15–22 and 58–62; 151, pp. 31–40).

Since, however, we have spoken of the heretics as dead but of ourselves as possessors of the divine writings unto salvation, and since I am afraid that—as Paul has written to the Corinthians (2 Cor. 11:3)—some guileless persons may be led astray from their purity and holiness by the craftiness of certain men and begin thereafter to pay attention to other books, the so-called apocryphal writings, being deceived by their possession of the same names as the genuine books, I therefore exhort you to patience when, out of regard to the Church's need and benefit, I mention in my letter matters with which you are acquainted. It being my intention to mention these matters, I shall, for the commendation of my venture, follow the example of the evangelist Luke and say (cf. Lk. 1:1–4): *Since* some *have taken in hand to set in order* for themselves the so-called apocrypha and to mingle them with the God-inspired Scripture, concerning which we have attained to a sure persuasion, according to what *the original eye witnesses and ministers of the word have delivered* unto our fathers, *I also*, having been urged by true brethren and having investigated the matter from the beginning, *have decided* to set forth in order the writings that have been put in the canon, that have been handed down and confirmed as divine, in order that every one who has been led astray may condemn his seducers and that every one who has remained stainless may rejoice, being again reminded of that.

Athanasius now in the first place enumerates the Scriptures of the Old Testament. He then proceeds:

Continuing I must without hesitation mention the Scriptures of the New Testament; they are the following: the four Gospels according to Matthew, Mark, Luke and John, after them the Acts of the Apostles and the seven so-called catholic epistles of the apostles—namely, one of James, two of Peter, then three of John and after these one of Jude. In addition there are fourteen epistles of the apostle Paul written in the following order: the first to the Romans, then two to the Corinthians and then after these the one to the Galatians, following it the one to the Ephesians, thereafter the one to the Philippians and the one to the Colossians and two to the Thessalonians and the epistle to the Hebrews and then immediately two to Timothy, one to Titus and lastly the one to Philemon. Yet further the Revelation of John.

These are the springs of salvation, in order that he who is thirsty may fully refresh himself with the words contained in them. In them alone is the doctrine of piety proclaimed. Let no one add anything to them or take anything away from them . . .

But for the sake of greater accuracy I add, being constrained to write, that there are also other books besides these, which have not indeed been put in the canon, but have been appointed by the fathers as reading matter for those who have just come forward and wish to be instructed in the doctrine of piety: the Wisdom of Solomon, the Wisdom of Sirach, Esther, Judith, Tobias, the so-called Teaching (διδαχή) of the Apostles (Coptic adds: I do not mean the Teaching of which it is said that it censures Deuteronomy) and the Shepherd. And although, beloved, the former are in the canon and the latter serve as reading matter, yet mention is nowhere made of the apocrypha; rather they are a fabrication of the heretics, who write them down when it pleases them and generously assign to them an early date of composition in order that they may be able to draw upon them as supposedly ancient writings and have in them occasion to deceive the guileless.

3. ON THE ORIGIN OF THE APOCRYPHA

In the definition given above of the writings which are known as the New Testament Apocrypha two factors are included which have to be attended to when we turn to the question how actually this literature arose. On the one hand it was stated that here we have to do with literature of the early Church which on the ground of title or other depositions claimed to be on a par with the writings of the canon. In the review of the history of the canon and its issues it became clear that this statement is in point only for a portion of the apocrypha. There was certainly an abundance of gospels, acts of apostles and apocalypses, and there has come down to us a major portion of those which were meant, on the ground of their make-up, to go side by side with, and in part even to take the place of, the New Testament books. For the earliest works of the kind still more can be said: they appear in part, as has already been said, to be almost contemporary with the canonical writings and to have been written on the basis of the same traditions, and accordingly were valued in particular districts precisely as the canonical Gospels were in other churches. But—this results from the history of the canon—a very clear distinction must be made between this earliest group and the later literary creations which deliberately operated with borrowed authority.

The second factor that has to be borne in mind is disclosed in what we have said about a connection with, and a development of, the forms and types that are present in the NT. The slant in the matter of type and form must be taken into consideration. Here also it is natural to distinguish between the earliest apocryphal writings (especially the gospels) and the later works. As regards form-history it has to be stated that the earlier works, like the canonical Scriptures, appropriated to themselves special types of style to express the faith of the churches in which they originated. The question whether we can speak of apocryphal gospels which originated in independence of the form of gospel book which we meet for the first time in Mark can hardly be answered. Whilst granting the possibility of that, we may reckon on the likelihood that the stimulus to this type nevertheless came from Mark's Gospel. For the apocrypha which were written at the time when the canon was coming into being, and above all after the closing of the New Testament collection, it holds good that in effecting connections, in taking material over and in making developments they use as means of expression the forms that are present in the New Testament writings. They are "no more than the often fantastic outgrowths of earlier forms in the direction of a romantic and legendary make-up" and let "a strong intrusion of apocalyptic and gnostic motives" appear "in the words of Jesus".[1]

Now assuredly, as later will be shown more closely, this form-historical study of the problem does not aim merely at a purely external classification of the apocryphal literature. Rather the form-historical work done on the NT has made it clear that it has also a 'sociological' aspect: the question as to 'the setting-in-life' of the small units of the material of tradition and also of the entire compendium of the tradition, the problem of the structure of the churches in which these works originated, as also of the purposes which are expressed in them, are all brought into focus by this study of forms and types. Clearly then this investigation of types

[1] G. Bornkamm in *RGG* 3rd ed., vol. II, col. 749ff.

and forms is of outstanding significance for the content of a writing and for its understanding since only by means of it is the text set in its correct context. When we inquire what reasons and motives may account for the coming into being of the literature with which we are here concerned, we shall not only keep in view the historical development of the canon—from it all that we really obtain is an answer to the question, Why were these writings declared apocryphal and not received by the Church?—but shall also have to pay particular attention to types and forms. This will have to be done in greater detail in the introductions to the several divisions (Gospels, Acts of Apostles, Apocalypses) of this book. Here there may be given in advance only a few fundamental considerations which may prove important for the whole complex.

(*a*) The apocrypha originated as developments of the forms and types present in the NT. As has been said, the earliest gospels are an exception; and here the apocryphal acts of the apostles can be named only with reserve, for whilst they are said to depend upon the canonical Acts of the Apostles by Luke, they are yet rather an independent transfer from Greek fictional and popular narrative literature.

The process which lies before us in the formation of the apocrypha, and to which the texts assembled in this book bear witness, has its earliest roots in many textual variants and textual additions in the canonical books of the NT. There we can see how the traditional text was altered, cancelled, enlarged with additions or otherwise disposed. Another way of further developing the traditional text was to choose a part of it and thereon to build something new. This can be seen most of all in certain gospels, e.g. in the gospels of the infancy, in which the meagre statements of the canonical Gospels are much elaborated, expanded and supplemented. In these texts a motive which we come across again and again is clearly manifest: the traditional writings of the NT and other early writings were no longer considered sufficient because much was lacking in them that one longed to know. E.g. with regard to the childhood of Jesus all too little was told in the Gospels, and there was a longing for further accounts of it. There were other motives: local interests such as missionary activities in certain districts had to be taken into consideration, practices that were arising had to be legalized, etc. All which leads to this, that the existing forms, especially those of the Gospels, were taken over and enlarged. We may perhaps speak briefly of a motive of supplementation.

(*b*) But the fashioning of the apocryphal literature was not restricted to this supplementing and enlarging of the forms and types met with in the NT. Rather, as we can see, there was also at the same time a streaming in of new forms. The original literature, which in great part was not literature at all in the strict sense of the word, was replaced by a literature that was influenced in the strongest possible way by the world about it.

In his article already mentioned (see p. 27 above) Overbeck makes the statement—in part an assuredly correct statement—that the beginnings of actual literature in the Church are to be seen in the apologists. Only a few portions of the apocryphal literature assembled in this book are older and may be brought into the field against his statement. We need to be very cautious in correcting Overbeck's thesis. For the fact is not to be overlooked that the apocryphal literature which can be considered literature in his sense (he himself here makes noteworthy restrictions, see pp. 27f. above) comes in the main from circles the development in which was different from, and took place in areas other than, that in the circle usually designated that of the great Church. Much of what we purpose to collect in this book appears to have had its homeland in Gnostic groups. But these groups usually entered to a much greater extent into association with the 'world'; in them, therefore, the heritage of their environment was brought into much closer connection with Christian preaching than it was in the 'ecclesiastical' groups and churches. This also is noticeable in the acceptance of literary forms. For instance in the Coptic Gnostic gospels we can see how the type of the Gnostic revelation-discourse is linked up with the traditional form of the gospel books. Similar statements can be made with regard to the acts of the apostles. This means, however, that a motive for the origin of the apocrypha is to be seen in the taking over of forms and types of pre-Christian literature into the service of the Christian proclamation of the gospel.

(c) Naturally this inflowing of strange forms and types cannot be seen from a purely formal point of view. Rather there stands behind it a further factor which was of consequence in the formation of the apocryphal literature. What has been transmitted to us in the NT as canonical scriptures is the precipitate of the proclamation of the gospel which for the time to come was to determine the aspect of the Church. But besides there also existed widely forms of proclamation of another kind. In its early period Christianity was no uniform phenomenon, and the churches which called themselves Christian in this early period, i.e. in the 1st and 2nd centuries, were quite diverse institutions especially in the matter of their doctrine. One of the motives to the formation of the apocryphal literature must be seen in this diversity of views. This diversity in doctrine and belief (which at first was not at all felt as 'splitting the Church', as some in our day would willingly

make us believe) brought with it the emergence of different presentations of the gospel and of the doings of the apostles, which
time and again tallied with the ideas of the churches concerned.
The relationships of the churches to Christ as Saviour and
Redeemer, their attitudes to the world and their dispositions towards 'history' were too different for different gospels and acts of
apostles not to come into being. Only when what had precipitated
itself in the NT as kerygma had gained ground as orthodoxy,
being interpreted uniformly in the early catholic sense, did this
literature gradually disappear or become literature of a heretical
tendency. The definition of 'tendency literature' is then applicable
to the later apocryphal creations to an extent other than it is to
the earlier works. Literary fiction was then taken into the service
of propaganda.

To many of the men who at that time composed apocryphal
literature and spread it far abroad the right to undertake that
work will not be denied. Frequently the only form of gospel they
knew was that which we today designate as apocryphal because
in the meanwhile, through the canonizing of other gospels, it has
been excluded from ecclesiastical use. But in the earliest times
they certainly acted in all good faith who transmitted this 'apocryphal' form of gospel or writings other than those which came to
be received into the canon.

We ought then in summing up to say: The question how the
formation of the apocryphal literature came about cannot be
answered in a single sentence. Different motives were operative;
motives which emerged at different times and led to the production of this literature. The form-historical study of this literature
shows that in the earliest times it underwent a development
parallel to that of the canonical scriptures and that in later times
there was a further development of the New Testament forms and
types. To this must be added differences in doctrine and belief,
which in the earlier period obtained expression in different renderings of the gospel and also of the acts of the apostles and other
works. This, however, had as its consequence that the form of
Christian proclamation which was not accepted, which was
eliminated by the early catholic Church as heretical, created for
itself an independent means of expression in a 'tendency literature'.

4. HISTORY OF RESEARCH INTO THE APOCRYPHAL LITERATURE

There is a sketch in Hennecke, *Apokr.* 1, pp. 22–28 and *Apokr.* 2, 31*f., and a valuable compilation of editions, commentaries and treatises in Hennecke, *Handb.*, pp. 5–9. This collection of titles is not repeated here: I confine myself rather to a few of the chief points in the history of the investigation.

Knowledge of a portion of the Apocrypha persisted through the Middle Ages. In particular the apocalypses appear to have been read; at all events their influence can be traced. Certain connections between the Apocalypse of Peter and also the Apocalypse of Paul and the Inferno of Dante are not to be overlooked. The Acts of Pilate also enjoyed popularity in the Middle Ages. For the most part, however, in the works that may be named here, we are concerned with late formations particular parts of which perhaps go back to earlier apocrypha. The apocryphal literature was crowded out principally because new popular devotional literature took the place which the apocrypha had occupied in the early Church. A gradual rediscovery of the whole of this literature came about through the labours of the humanists and through the art of printing.

In 1531 Friedrich Nausea published a collection of Latin lives of apostles which may be recognized as the first attempt at a collection of apocryphal literature. Like most editions of patristic writings and church histories which appeared at that time this work is casual in character: what was found in the available manuscripts was printed, and that benefited all sorts of apocrypha. There were many separate editions in those years, as e.g. that of the Protevangelium of James by Bibliander (Basel, 1552). Undoubtedly important is the edition of the apocrypha by Michael Neander, rector at Ilfeld: *Apocrypha, hoc est narrationes de Christo, Maria, Josepho, cognatione et familia Christi, extra biblia, etc.* (Basel, 1564). Neander added this edition to a miscellany which had as its principal content a Greek-Latin treatment of Luther's *Smaller Catechism* intended for school purposes. This association shows clearly that it was principally out of an historico-philological interest that Neander concerned himself with the apocrypha. The purpose of this book was to provide the humanist with material to be used in educating his pupils. The collection of the apocrypha includes besides the Protevangelium of James: the Abgar-Saga, Epistles of Pilate, a series of Sibylline books, quotations from profane and ecclesiastical writers on New Testament history and later testimonies regarding Christ.

The impetus which the investigation of Christian antiquity

received at the end of the 17th century (Cotelier, Ittig, Cave, the Bollandists) also benefited the apocrypha. In 1703 Johann Albert Fabricius, the great Hamburg compiler, published his *Codex Apocryphus Novi Testamenti*, which has retained its worth to modern times. In volume I Fabricius has collected: Infancy Gospels, the Gospel of Nicodemus and Epistles of Pilate, the Epistle of Lentulus, apocryphal Gospel Fragments. Volume II contains: "Acta, Epistolae, Apocalypses aliaque scripta Apostolis falso inscripta." Finally volume III brought liturgies under apostolic names and additions, as well as the Shepherd of Hermas. At the same time in England, Jeremiah Jones translated into English the portions of apocryphal literature that were known to him in order with his work to counter the onslaughts of the deists upon the sole authority of the New Testament. His work thus stands under the banner of polemics. For him everything depended on the proof of the spuriousness and heretical character of this literature.

As in all fields of historical theology, so in that of apocrypha investigation the 19th century brought a wealth of new editions and multifarious treatises. First there was the edition of the apocryphal gospels by Thilo, a theologian of Halle, who projected a complete edition of all apocrypha, but got only so far as volume I (*Codex apocryphus Novi Testamenti*, Leipzig, 1832). This publication inspired a series of further investigations, but also led to the apocryphal gospels coming much into the foreground as compared with other texts. Far in advance of Thilo's were the editions of apocryphal texts by Constantine Tischendorf, who strove for good manuscripts and applied the principles of philology to them (*Acta apostolorum apocrypha*, 1851; *Evangelia apocrypha*, 1852; *Apocalypses apocryphae*, 1866; the *Evangelia* in a 2nd ed., 1876, which is still indispensable; the *Acta* in a 2nd ed. by Lipsius-Bonnet, 1891–1903, likewise indispensable). Since then no complete edition of the apocryphal literature on a scientific basis has appeared. Because of the wealth of texts and above all the wide distribution of the manuscripts and also because there is almost no end of versions, it would be an arduous undertaking to gather all together in one corpus. Aurelio de Santos Otero produced in 1956 a bilingual edition of the gospels, which however, useful as it is, can be no substitute for a scientific edition of the whole of the material (Aurelio de Santos Otero, *Los Evangelios apócrifos, Colección de textos griegos y latinos, versión crítica, estudios introductorios, comentarios e ilustraciones: Biblioteca de Autores Cristianos* 148, Madrid 1956).

The historico-critical method of approach, which F. C. Baur made the possession, never to be relinquished, of evangelical theology, had a markedly fertilizing effect upon .work on the apocrypha. Particularly in the second half of the 19th century and at the beginning of our century a wealth of studies was devoted to our texts. Besides there was an unexpected multitude of new finds: manuscripts and papyri constantly brought new texts to light, which were then edited and investigated. This period of new finds is still by no means at an end, as the one at Nag Hammadi (see pp. 234f. below) shows. That in the work on the new finds and also on the texts that have been well known for a longer time the historico-critical method and also the religio-historical approach have been and must be decisive, is of course assumed. In 1904 Edgar Hennecke published the first edition of the *Neutestamentliche Apokryphen in deutscher Übersetzung*, which was followed in the same year by his *Handbuch zu den Neutestamentlichen Apokryphen*. In this collection, which soon made its way because of its scholarly importance, there were assembled the texts particularly of the 2nd and 3rd centuries. In the second edition of the work, which appeared in 1924, the notion of apocrypha was no longer so strictly adhered to. Montague Rhodes James in his English *Apocryphal New Testament* (Oxford, 1924) has kept more largely to the forms and types of the NT and has also taken later texts into consideration.

In the present revision of Hennecke's collection an endeavour is made to revert more largely to the New Testament types and at the same time to pay attention to the later texts in so far as they are important for an understanding of the phenomenon of the apocrypha. The fundamental ideas set forth in the foregoing statements of the introduction have determined the selection without securing a strict consistency. An endeavour has also been made not to neglect the Oriental versions of the apocryphal literature.

These Oriental versions come more and more largely within our purview. A clear survey of the whole stock of these translations is as yet lacking; probably the time for it has not yet come. I must content myself with giving here a few references to publications. There is a good bibliography in Santos, pp. 11–14.

Syriac texts were published by W. Wright, E. A. W. Budge, A. S. Lewis and A. Mingana and Rendel Harris; cf. A. Baumstark, *Geschichte der syrischen Literatur* (1922). Of the Coptic versions, which in more recent times have proved very important, there are many separate editions: there is a review by W. Grossouw, "Die Apocriefen van het Oude en Nieuwe Testament in de koptische Letterkunde", *Studia Catholica* X (1933–1934), 434–446 and XI (1934–35), 19–36. On the Arabic versions see Georg Graf, *Geschichte der christlich arabischen Literatur* I (=*Studi e testi*, 118) (1944), pp. 224ff. On the Latin translations: Albert Siegmund

Die Überlieferung der griechischen christlichen Literatur in der lateinischen Kirche bis zum XII. Jh. (1949), pp. 33ff. For the rest of the versions reference may be made to Santos.

The abundance of translations, which in part belong not to the time of the early Church but to the so-called Middle Ages, shows that the apocryphal literature continued to live. Moreover, this life can be traced elsewhere sometimes in literary forms (i.e. in works which develop and rearrange the apocryphal texts already in existence,[1] sometimes in the form of after-effect and stimulus (in new literary creations or in monuments of art). This problem of the 'after-life' of the apocrypha of the early Church cannot be further discussed here. In this field there is much work to be done, although on the problem of art there are already a few studies. Literature in Santos, pp. 14ff. Add U. Fabricius, *Die Legende im Bild des ersten Jahrtausends* (1956).

On the important question of the influence of the apocrypha on Islam see W. St. Clair Tisdall, *The Original Sources of the Quran* (London, 1905).

---

[1] There belongs here, e.g., the problem, fundamental both for the history of religion and for that of thought, of the effect of the apocrypha upon the Bogomils; cf. E. Turdeanu, "Apocryphes bogomiles et apocryphes pseudo-bogomiles", *RHR* 138 (1950), pp. 22–52 and 176–218; Nullo Minissi, "La tradizione apocrifa e le origini del Bogomolismo", *Ricerche Slavistiche* III (1954), pp. 97–113 (who, however, deals chiefly with the Old Testament apocrypha).

A. GOSPELS:
NON-BIBLICAL MATERIAL ABOUT JESUS

INTRODUCTION

(W. Schneemelcher)

1. GOSPEL

Literature: G. Friedrich, Art. εὐαγγελίζομαι, etc., in *ThWtb*. II (1935), pp. 705–735; J. Schniewind, *Euangelion* (1927/31); G. Bornkamm, Art. "Evangelien", "synoptische", in *RGG*, 3rd ed., Vol. II (1958), cols. 753–766; id. Art. "Evangelien", "formgeschichtlich", in *RGG*, 3rd ed., Vol. II (1958), cols. 749–753.

We are accustomed today to speak of the gospel or gospels in the sense of gospel book or gospel books. At first, however, that was not the meaning of the Greek word εὐαγγέλιον. Rather this word was an expression for something non-literary—namely, glad tidings communicated orally (and, closely connected with that, the fee for these tidings paid to him who brought them). The noun εὐαγγέλιον must be looked at in connection with the verb εὐαγγελίζεσθαι: it is assuredly to a large extent, although not exclusively, a *nomen actionis* (so G. Friedrich, *ThWtb* II 727, 2ff.). That of course is not to say that the term—as it is met with in the NT—is to be derived from the Old Testament and rabbinical usage. Rather a wealth of instances in Hellenism shows that this is where the root of the New Testament use of this word must be sought. Certainly בשׂר, the Hebrew equivalent of εὐαγγελίζομαι in the sense 'to proclaim glad tidings', is used in deutero-Isaiah (above all in Isa. 52:7) as 'a standard religious term' (Friedrich, *op. cit.*, p. 707, 14). But it is equally certain that in the Greek world εὐαγγελίζεσθαι was likewise used in a 'sacral' sense.

The question whether in late Judaism "the idea of the good news present in deutero-Isaiah continued to live" (Friedrich, *op. cit.*, p. 712, 24ff.) and whether this late Jewish (or the rabbinical) usage had an effect on the NT hardly admits of so unambiguous an answer as is often given to it. The NT is written in Greek, and the concepts used there are Greek concepts, although the influence of the OT should of course not be disregarded. At all events in attempting an explanation of the term εὐαγγέλιον its Greek provenance should not be overlooked. Friedrich points out that in the OT "a religious colloquial use of the noun is altogether lacking" (*op. cit.*, p. 719, 17f.). Also it cannot be shown that in rabbinical Judaism "the eschatological good news is called בשׂרה" (*op. cit.*, p. 723, 28f.). Rather it appears, although Friedrich asserts the opposite, that εὐαγγέλιον "was intruded into Judaism as a foreign word for the New Testament gospel" (*op. cit.*, p. 723, 48f.) and indeed for the reason that this Greek word was used by the Aramaic-speaking Jewish Christians. This means that in tracing the history of the concept we must begin in the Greek world, especially with the use of εὐαγγέλιον in the Imperial cult.

A. Deissmann for one has shown that "gospel" was an important sacral word in the Imperial cult (*Licht vom Osten*, 4th ed., p. 313, ET London 1927, p. 366). Above all Deissmann has set the celebrated Calendar Inscription from Priene of date *c.* 9 B.C. in its correct context: before him A. v. Harnack had already referred to this inscription and its importance ("Als die Zeit erfüllet war", *Reden und Aufsätze* I, 2nd ed. (1906), pp. 301–306). The decisive passage in it runs: "The birthday of the god has occasioned for the world the tidings of joy (εὐαγγέλια) associated with him."[1] And not only the news of the monarch's birthday but also the stories of the further course of his life are given the same designation. In particular the news of the enthronement of the 'saviour' was a gospel. Here it is precisely the conceptions of 'saviour' (σωτήρ) and of 'glad tidings' (εὐαγγέλιον) which belong closely together. "The Imperial cult and the Bible have this in common that for them the enthronement, which leads on a new time and gives peace to the world, is a gospel for mankind" (Friedrich, *op. cit.*, p. 722, 9ff.). The differences must not of course be overlooked. But we shall have to seek them not in the fact that in the Hellenistic world εὐαγγέλιον was to a smaller extent than in the OT an activity, i.e. a proclamation of the message of salvation which by being made was actually effective, but rather in the fact that the content of the εὐαγγέλιον, i.e. the person of whom it was declared that his doings brought salvation, was different.

The concept and many views bound up with it belong at all events to the world of Hellenistic-Oriental religions. From that world early Christianity, more particularly the Hellenistic Christianity before Paul, took over the expression εὐαγγέλιον in order therewith to denote the message of salvation in one short and comprehensive word. This, it may be added, does not exclude the possibility that very soon the deutero-Isaianic statements were associated with this Hellenistic terminology. This could readily happen, not least because the connection between the Hellenistic-Oriental conception of the redeemer and the ideology of the saviour-king that stands behind deutero-Isaiah was suggested by the subject matter itself. But Hellenistic Christianity took over the term from the speech of its own time, i.e. from

[1] That is Harnack's translation. Deissmann gives: "but (the birthday) of the god was for the world the beginning of tiding(s) of joy on his account"; similarly Friedrich.

Hellenistic piety especially as it came to expression in the Imperial cult.[1]

A glance at the use of εὐαγγέλιον in the NT confirms this view. We cannot here inquire into all the New Testament passages in which this word (and the verb εὐαγγελίζεσθαι belonging to it) occurs. Mk. 1:1 and Mk. 1:14 show that the Evangelists, or the churches in which they obtained the tradition they worked up, used εὐαγγέλιον as a comprehensive term for the message of salvation by Jesus Christ. It is striking that in Mark (apart from 1:1 and 1:14) the word constantly appears in sayings of Jesus. That of course raises the question whether Jesus Himself used this term or at least its Aramaic equivalent. This question must be answered in the negative (even for Mk. 13:10 and 14:9). It is of course not disputed that Jesus recognized His preaching of the Kingdom of God, which was to come and which had already begun in Him, as a message of joy and deliverance. Only we cannot prove that Jesus used precisely this expression as a comprehensive description of the character of His preaching. That is indeed unlikely according to what has been said about the early history of the term.

In the Pauline epistles (including Eph.) we meet with εὐαγγέλιον fifty-six times (add four times in the Pastoral Epistles). This statistical statement certainly shows what significance the concept has in Paul. Very often he uses εὐαγγέλιον absolutely, i.e. he dispenses with epithets by which the content of the Christian glad tidings may in some way be characterized (as e.g. εὐαγγέλιον τοῦ θεοῦ, εὐαγγέλιον τοῦ Χριστοῦ). The apostle can evidently dispense with such descriptive terms, because τὸ εὐαγγέλιον used absolutely seems to have been quite familiar to his readers. That in turn permits us to conclude that Paul did not introduce any such absolute use of the word into Christian usage, but took it over from the Hellenistic church. "The expressions 'to preach' and 'to hear' which are bound up with the conception and the synonymous terms 'the word' (ὁ λόγος) and 'the proclamation' (τὸ κήρυγμα) show that here gospel always means the *oral* message or its content" (Bornkamm, *RGG*, *loc. cit.*, col. 749).

Paul then does not mean some one book or document when he speaks of the gospel, but by that word seeks to characterize the preaching of salvation, which means the preaching of Jesus Christ. In the introduction to the epistle to the Romans (Rom. 1:1ff.), as also in 1 Cor. 15:1ff., he states more precisely what he understands by gospel: the salvation event in Christ, God's act of salvation in the incarnation, death and resurrection of Christ. It

[1] Otherwise R. Bultmann, *Theol. d. NT*, p. 87 (ET London 1952, i. 87), who however gives no proof of his assertion that εὐαγγέλιον was not a sacral term in the Imperial cult.

is characteristic of the Pauline view that in both passages εὐαγγέλ-ιον and the missionary preaching of the apostle, the message of Jesus Christ and the commissioning of Paul as a messenger, are set in very close connection with one another. This determines how the expression 'my gospel' (e.g. in Rom. 16:25) is to be understood. The reference is not to a special Pauline message, but to the one gospel to the service and spread of which Paul has been called. And this call is a part of the salvation event which forms the content of the preaching of the gospel. Since the 'gospel' is not a human invention (cf. e.g. Gal. 1), it has also power to work the salvation of men; certainly it also effects judgment, but this judgment is grace. The gospel is according to Pauline under-standing "God's act of revelation" (Friedrich, op. cit., p. 730, 1).

How now did it come about that εὐαγγέλιον, which in early Christianity denoted the oral preaching, the spoken word of salvation, came to designate something fixed in writing? With this another question has to be connected: How came it about that one could speak of gospels (in the plural) after early Christian-ity had spoken only of the gospel (in the singular)? A confident answer cannot be given, since we have scarcely sources at our disposal which give any evidence about the matter. Moreover, in his prologue Luke has avoided saying that the 'many' who had preceded him in the recording of the 'events' had written gospels. On the other hand Mark has manifestly set the preaching of salvation in Jesus Christ (therefore the gospel) in very close con-nection with what he has put down in writing: 'Beginning of the gospel of Jesus Christ', so he begins his gospel (Mk. 1:1). But—G. Bornkamm following M. Dibelius has rightly seen this— Mark has not yet equated his gospel with the message of salvation. What we are concerned with is rather "an interpreting leading notion": "the earthly work of Jesus is narrated as illustration of the message of Christ" (Bornkamm, RGG 3rd ed., II, col. 749). The purpose of not compromising the oneness and uniqueness of the gospel by this recording of it, is maintained in the titles of the gospel books: εὐαγγέλιον κατὰ Μάρκον, etc.

Down to the 2nd century the consciousness continues that the gospel is a unity and that it is the preaching of salvation. More-over, Irenaeus has stressed the fact that "Luke, the disciple of Paul, has recorded in a book the gospel preached by him" (adv. haer. III. 1. 2 Harvey) and further that "all have in like manner, each one of them, the gospel of God" (ib. III. 1. 1.). At any rate in the 2nd century the original sense of the term—namely, the preaching of salvation, was not lost. On the other hand, through the recognition of the written gospels as legitimate accounts of the salvation events, the term gradually became the

74

designation of the book, and so the way became open for the plural usage: τὰ εὐαγγέλια. If Clement of Alexandria adduces as ἐν τοῖς εὐαγγελίοις (*Strom.* I, 136, 1) a word which is handed down only in one gospel, it is clear that he has in mind gospel writings. When the canon was in course of formation, the Church, as we have seen, again restricted the term. Only the four recognized writings could rightly be called gospels. For they alone testify to the one gospel, to the preaching of salvation in Jesus Christ.

2. THE FORMATION OF THE GOSPELS

Literature: M. Dibelius, *Die Formgeschichte des Evangeliums*, 2nd ed. (1933) (ET *From Tradition to Gospel*, London 1935); R. Bultmann, *Die Geschichte der synoptischen Tradition*, 3rd ed. (1957, supplementary volume 1958) (ET Oxford 1963); G. Bornkamm, articles in *RGG*, 3rd ed. (see p. 71 above); E. Hirsch in his *Frühgeschichte des Evangeliums* I, II, (1941, I in 2nd ed. 1951) pursues a method different from the form-historical, but is less convincing; on Hirsch cf., e.g., Ph. Vielhauer, *Gnomon* 26 (1954), pp. 460–462 and *ThLZ* 80 (1955), cols. 647–652.

In the sketch of the history of the formation of the canon (above pp. 28ff.) reference was made to several points of view which are relevant to the question: For what reason did the gospel books come into being? These books came into being because the original bearers of the oral tradition and consequently the guarantors of the correctness and truth of this tradition were no longer within reach of the churches. But this comment, which states only indirectly the reasons for the writing of the gospels, does not cover the problem of their multiplicity.

The first three of the four gospel books which have been received into our NT belong, as we see at a glance, very closely together. In part they agree word for word, in part at least two of them have like accounts and like words and sayings. How is this connection of Matthew, Mark and Luke, the so-called Synoptics, to be explained?

Since the rise of the historico-critical investigation of the New Testament writings different solutions have been advanced (see the survey by Bornkamm in *RGG*, 3rd ed., II, col. 753f.). The two-source theory has prevailed as the clearest explanation of the matter.[1] According to this theory Mk. is the earliest gospel and was used by Mt. and Lk., who, however, utilized in addition to it another source (the so-called Sayings Source = Q) in composing

[1] This holds good in spite of Heinrich Helmbold, *Vorsynoptische Evangelien*, 1953, who has resumed the thesis of E. Hirsch, and L. Vaganay, *Le problème synoptique*, 1954; see on this P. Vielhauer in *Gnomon* 26 (1954), pp. 46off. and *ThLZ* 80 (1955), cols. 647ff.

their gospels. Further Mt. and Lk. have also worked up special material, the derivation of which in particular cases it is difficult indeed to explain. Mt. and Lk. have independently adapted this material for their special theological purposes. But Mk., to whom honour is due for composing the first written gospel, also gathered, arranged and combined earlier traditions. Whether his sources were already fixed in writing cannot be proved strictly, but that they were so must be considered likely: it has in any case to be assumed that Q was fixed in writing. The importance of this procedure in the creation of the gospel writings is underlined by the fact that the *genus* 'gospel' (understood as a literary type) represents a form which we do not elsewhere meet with in ancient literature. All attempts to connect the gospels closely with pre-Christian or non-Christian forms of literature have suffered shipwreck: the gospel as a literary type is a creation of early Christianity.

This conclusion, the significance of which for our subject will later be set out more clearly, must for the present be supplemented in two respects:

On the one hand, while it is a fact that in the matter of the form of the gospel we are concerned with a special Christian type, that does not mean that its beginnings are without parallels in pre-Christian and non-Christian literature. It can be stated "that the separate traditions of the gospels and their compilation are modelled after forms and according to laws which can also be recognized in other popular profane and religious literature" (Bornkamm, *op. cit.*, col. 750). On the other hand, the question is not to be overlooked whether this conclusion, which holds good for the three Synoptics, does not also apply to the Gospel of John. Certainly the Fourth Gospel is not to be set on one level with the Synoptics. But in its case also comparisons with the literature of the world about it very largely break down, and we must see in it a special expression of the Christian category 'gospel'. Indeed it needs in this connection to be noted that the literary interest of the author of the Gospel of John is much smaller than that of Luke.

The literary-critical work on the Synoptics has then in the two-source theory provided a basis for the understanding of the first three gospels and especially of their relations to one another. The proof that has been given of the singularity of the type 'gospel' has also shown that with this clearing up of the situation everything has not been said and that we must go further if we are to understand the genesis of the gospel literature.

Here the so-called form-historical (or tradition-historical) work affords further help. The aim in this work, which is especially associated with the names of M. Dibelius and R. Bultmann, has been to make fruitful for the NT the type-historical kind of investigation developed by H. Gunkel in the sphere of the OT. After the preliminary questions have been settled by means of the two-source theory, the question of the history of the pre-literary tradition presents itself, and that is cleared up by inquiring after the 'very small units', i.e. the building stones of which the tradition is composed. As these separate portions (and of course at the same time the means used in joining them together, i.e. in their composition) are brought into prominence, their classes or forms are also made manifest, whilst 'the situation in life', i.e. the sociological conditions which have led to the creation of these forms, is exhibited. The classes are given different names: paradigms, stories, legends and exhortations in Dibelius, who makes preaching his main starting point; apophthegmata, logia, miracle-stories and legends in Bultmann, who attaches more importance to literary analysis and the history of the tradition. But the common basis as also the common aim of the form-historical work has not been put in question by this difference in terminology. Its aim may be thus described: In this way, which is often an uphill one, an endeavour is made not only to investigate and explain the origin of the material of the tradition but also to make manifest the piety and the faith of the Church which transmitted this material and used it for preaching and mission, for public worship and life.

This means that form-history conveys information not only about the working method of the Evangelists but also about the variegated world of belief of early Christianity. "The basic hypothesis of form-history is that the origin and formation of the gospel tradition cannot be explained by source theories. The starting point of the tradition is rather pericopes which are short and self-contained, or isolated sayings" (P. Vielhauer in *Gnomon* 28 (1956), p. 31). That determines our task. The separating of the redaction from the tradition must come first, and then it is possible to investigate the tradition as it lies before us in its small units.

The result of this work can, in view of the question as to the formation of the gospels, be summarized as follows: At the outset of the development there stands the proclamation of the death and resurrection of Jesus, i.e. the stories of the passion were clearly the earliest kernel of the evangelic tradition. But this kernel was soon enriched. Upon it there supervened not merely proof from prophecy but also 'illustration' of the passion and Easter stories (as I Cor. 15:3–7 shows), and further the more profuse illustration of the life of Jesus that lies before us in the miracle stories. To that there were then added sayings of Jesus which would show the

Lord as a teacher, stories which had a saying of Jesus as their point, portions containing exhortation which would justify the Church's regulations, and much else. This does not mean, as might be assumed, that the whole tradition was merely the product of the Church; but the part of the Church in the shaping and transmitting of the material of the tradition is certainly presented as a real problem.

The form-historical work shows very clearly that Jesus Himself made use of traditional forms. On the other hand, however, the differences between the Synoptic Gospels show clearly what part the Church had in the moulding of the material. It moulded anew and transmitted in the light of the Easter happenings the tradition that had come down to it from Jesus and concerning Him.

The question how far the earliest tradition falls within the Aramaic province can hardly be answered with certainty. The method frequently practised of translating Greek concepts back into Aramaic can be used only with caution. There are of course particular paragraphs in which we cannot fail to recognize so-called Aramaisms (e.g. 1 Cor. 15), but there continues to be a considerable element of uncertainty.[1] In addition to what has been said it must now be stated that by uniting the literary-critical and form-historical work we can also explain how "the living, oral tradition which preceded the first written sources continued to exist after the latter were fixed" (Bornkamm, *op. cit.*, col. 758). This statement, which is based principally on the recognition that the literary-critical comparison of the Synoptic material does not explain all differences and that the form-historical work can show how the differences in the several portions of the tradition are to be explained, has considerable consequences for the earliest apocryphal gospels. For here the question must be asked whether the tradition of particular passages met with in the apocryphal gospels should not be explained as that of a part of the Synoptic tradition: the living oral tradition has lingered on in spite of the fixing of written sources. Assuredly this question can be raised only in regard to a small part of the apocryphal gospel literature (e.g. the Jewish Christian Gospels, the Gospel of the Egyptians, the Gospel of Thomas). But we do justice to this apocryphal literature only when we set it within the history just presented of the formation of the gospels.

In conclusion reference may be made to one other point. As has been said, the form-historical work investigates the tradition (the small units, etc.), but at the same time it pays attention to the

---

[1] See my lecture "Das Problem der Sprache in der Alten Kirche" in *Das Problem der Sprache in Theologie und Kirche*, Berlin 1959, 55ff.

composition of this tradition in the several gospels. It attempts then not merely to detach the building stones from the present fabric and to determine how they looked before they were fitted into this building, whence they were derived, etc., but seeks also to show how the material with which these stones have been connected together into the present building is to be recognized. In other words, the analytical work is followed of necessity by an attempt to understand the several gospels as wholes in their characteristic features—features which come to expression in the composition of the tradition received and worked up by the different Evangelists.

Thus in spite of its historical lay-out the Gospel of Mark is intended not merely as an "abiding remembrance of earthly things but also as vivid proclamation and address".[1] The author of the Gospel of Mark appears to have been the creator of the early Christian literary category of gospel in that he has set his account of the earthly Jesus under the leading notion of εὐαγγέλιον, i.e. under the notion of "vivid proclamation". In spite of his connection with Mk. and his use of Q, the author of Mt. has set out the history of Jesus differently and in particular from other theological angles. His gospel is determined much more largely by learned motives and is also bound more closely to Jewish-Christian traditions: Jesus is the king of Israel who expounds the law with authority. A wealth of titles of dignity indicates the start of a distinct Christology.[2] The author of the Gospel of Luke has arranged the same traditional material in yet another way. Going further than his sources, he has pushed aside the expectation of an imminent parousia—this by the way finds expression not least in the division of his literary work into Gospel and Acts of Apostles —and in the writing of his narrative his *leit-motiv* has been the history of salvation. The time of Jesus' life, the middle of time (i.e. the middle period of the three divisions of the history of salvation) is the actual time of salvation, and it is set out no longer as εὐαγγέλιον but as now understood, i.e. as history.[3]

The Gospel of John undoubtedly occupies an exceptional place among the four canonical gospels, although it is hard to define exactly this exceptional place and especially the relation of Jn. to the Synoptics. Side by side with much special material (e.g. the Story of Nicodemus, Jn. 3; the Feet-washing, Jn. 13), there

---

[1] G. Bornkamm, *RGG* ³ II, col. 760, following W. Marxsen, *Der Evangelist Markus* (1956).

[2] On Mt. cf. G. D. Kilpatrick, *The Origins of the Gospel according to St. Matthew* (1946); G. Bornkamm, "Enderwartung und Kirche im Matthäus-Evangelium", in Dodd-Festschrift (1956), pp. 222–260.

[3] On Lk. cf. H. Conzelmann, *Die Mitte der Zeit. Studien zur Theologie des Lk.* (2nd ed. 1957) (ET *The Theology of St. Luke*, London 1960).

is certainly also found Synoptic material, i.e. pericopes are found which appear to stand in closer connection with the Synoptic Gospels (e.g. the Cleansing of the Temple, Jn. 2:14ff.; the Healing of the Royal Officer's Son, Jn. 4:43ff.; the Feeding of the 5000, Jn. 6). But it is disputed and also very hard to settle how this connection is to be explained. The following possibilities have to be considered: Either the author drew directly from the Synoptics, which he knew, and from them took over portions into his own Gospel, although of course recasting them. Or the sources which the author of Jn. undoubtedly used depended in part on the Synoptics. Or these sources used by Jn. and those of the Synoptists were connected.

The question whether directly or indirectly Synoptic traditions have been used in Jn. has then to be regarded as peculiarly difficult; it must be answered, if at all, by a detailed analysis of Jn. It is, however, of significance for our subject inasmuch as a certain parallelism to the formation of the apocryphal gospels is not to be overlooked. For the same process which we cannot indeed strictly prove, but may well conjecture, to have been operative in the composition of Jn. can also be detected in the case of the early apocryphal gospels. In part they also came into being in association with traditions which were anterior to the composition of the Synoptic Gospels, and in part they likewise were fashioned in a further development of the traditional material that lies before us in the Synoptic Gospels. Consequently in the case of the apocryphal gospels also we must in detailed analysis always inquire whence their material was obtained and how that material (often very legendary) has to be judged. In doing so it will not be unimportant to pay attention to the differences in form of these gospels. For form-historical study also the apocryphal gospels are no undivided whole.

3. TYPES OF APOCRYPHAL GOSPELS

The literary form of the gospel books is a singular phenomenon in the literature of late antiquity, confined to the Christian world and having its origin in the special necessities of preaching and worship. It has already been pointed out that forms of the literature of the world round about were severally taken over, but the gospels as wholes are a Christian creation.

In his article already quoted[1] F. Overbeck has coined for the gospels the definition 'Christian proto-literature' and has shown that this proto-literature soon became extinct and was replaced by a "Graeco-Roman literature of Christian profession". In his

[1] See above p. 27.

opinion the apocryphal literature continued this proto-literature, but it was regarded as "illegitimate". We cannot wholly agree with him, but rather must here differentiate more sharply than he does. In form and in structure the apocryphal gospels are not an undivided whole. If for once we may make a broad distinction, three types of apocryphal gospels can be distinguished:

(a) Of the apocryphal gospels selected in this volume one portion, as can clearly be seen, is closely connected with the canonical Gospels, above all with the Synoptics, whether we ought to speak of a common tradition or of a dependence of the apocryphal upon the canonical Gospels. Admittedly, since for the most part the earlier works are preserved only in fragments, it can hardly be ascertained in detail how their relation to the canonical books ought to be judged. A few indications can nevertheless be gathered from the fragmentary tradition. It must be emphasized, however, that an influence of Mk., the earliest gospel, and also of Mt., which may soon have followed Mk., upon the later formation of apocryphal gospels does not seem to be out of the question, even if in the later works earlier pre-Marcan or pre-Matthaean oral traditions have been used. But that burdens this problem with considerable elements of uncertainty, and statements can be made only with the utmost caution.

Nevertheless, too much is not claimed when, e.g., the text of *Papyrus Oxyrhynchos* 840 is regarded as a fragment of a gospel of the Synoptic type (see pp. 92ff. below). How its relation to the Synoptics ought to be judged will be discussed below. Here this fragment is mentioned merely as an example: it shows that a part of the apocryphal gospel literature is closely related to the Synoptics. The question whether here we are concerned with pre-Synoptic tradition or with borrowed Synoptic material is extremely difficult to answer because of the fragmentary character of the text. But the fragment is sufficient to enable us to determine where formally it belongs. *Papyrus Egerton* 2 (see pp. 94ff. below) is interesting. Whilst the first part of it bears a Johannine character, the rest of the text points rather to the Synoptics. With regard to it J. Jeremias concludes, rightly I think: "Consequently we may have before us an instance of the overlapping of written and oral tradition: although the tradition was already fixed in writing, it was still widely reproduced from memory and in this way, enriched with extra-canonical material (IV), found new expression in writing" (p. 95 below). Thus this very text provides a particularly good illustration of the way in which the apocryphal gospels were fashioned in the earliest time: Synoptic and extra-Synoptic traditions grew together and were further developed.

It is more difficult to determine the relationship of the *Jewish-*

Christian gospels to the canonical writings, especially as the tradition consists almost entirely of scraps (cf. pp. 117ff. below). Nevertheless, these gospels also seem in part to belong to the type which lies before us in the canonical, especially in the Synoptic, gospels. Dependence on the Synoptics clearly presents itself in the case of the *Gospel of Peter* (see pp. 179ff. below); but the secondary character of this work can be inferred not from the form but only from the content of the narrative. Of the *Gospel of the Egyptians* also it may be said that it belongs to this category, although the fragments permit no far-reaching conclusions, and much in the shreds that have been handed down shows that this work belongs rather to the second category. Whether here we can speak of pre-Synoptic tradition at all is more than questionable.

All the writings that have been named belong to the earliest stratum of apocryphal literature. They hardly carry us beyond the first half of the 2nd century. But that of course does not mean that beginnings in the formation of writings of other types cannot be traced within this period.

(*b*) We have before us a second type of apocryphal gospels in the works which have to be allied with Gnosis and disseminate the doctrines of that movement, their aim being to convey revealed wisdom in the form of a "gospel". In these revelation writings we are for the most part concerned with works in which visions and dialogues of Jesus with His disciples are reported. In them Jesus is on most occasions the risen Lord, the exalted Revealer, that is to say these writings are interested primarily not in the historical Jesus but in the heavenly Redeemer. The "gnosis" which is to be imparted through such writings is revealed knowledge concerning the beginning, the course and the destination of the universe and of man.

Below (pp. 231ff.) H.-Ch. Puech has informed us in detail about the whole of this literature, and he has also more than once (cf., e.g., pp. 246f.) referred to the fact that certain peculiarities of style are common to most of these Gnostic gospels. That makes it clear that questions regarding style are by no means of a formal nature, but are bound up inseparably with the content, i.e. with the theological purpose of these writings. The dialogue form is certainly distinctive: Jesus is the person who informs the inquiring disciples. At the same time, however, there are practically no genuine dialogues, the questions merely giving occasion to the revelation discourses of the Redeemer. The setting also is frequently constructed in the same way: after His resurrection Jesus appears to the disciples on a mountain and then instructs them (details in Puech, below pp. 246f.), i.e. this type of gospel is in part bound up with the report of a vision or is determined by it.

It is significant that so important a work as the *Apocryphon of John* unites a report of such a vision with a revelation discourse (Puech, p. 320 below).

The Coptic *Gospel of Thomas* also has its place in this context: the logia which are assembled in it are words of the exalted Lord, therefore revelation discourses, and the purpose of the whole compilation is nothing other than the mediation of "gnosis" and therewith of "life". In spite then of considerable differences in style, structure and content, such works as the *Apocryphon of John* (cf. pp. 314ff. below), the *Sophia Jesu Christi* (cf. pp. 243ff. below), the *Dialogue of the Redeemer* (cf. pp. 248ff. below) and the *Gospel of Thomas* (cf. pp. 278ff. below) can be comprised as a quite definite type of gospel. They are revelation writings the purpose of which is to convey the Redeemer's words and therewith "knowledge" or "gnosis".

Here also the problem of the relationship of these writings to the canonical Gospels cannot be clearly settled. Even less than in the group of apocryphal gospels noted under (*a*) can traces of pre-Synoptic traditions be detected in these works (cf. Puech's verdict, pp. 293, 305 below). On the other hand the use of the canonical Gospels in most works of this character can be clearly shown. These "gospels" are then works which have connections with the canonical writings, develop them further and do not leave the given form of the gospel unaltered. That notwithstanding this they are styled "gospel" shows that this term was already a current literary designation and is doubtless also connected with the use of the new writings in public worship. It is significant that the *Gospel of Truth* and the *Gospel according to Philip* also have this term in their titles, although they do not so much as belong to this type of apocryphal writings; much less can they be seen to stand in any close connection with the canonical Gospels (cf. Puech, pp. 236ff., 276 below).

(*c*) As the second type was determined principally by the Gnostic tendency which found expression in the formal development, so the third type is characterized especially by the motive to supplement. Certain episodes in the life of Jesus were extracted from the canonical Gospels and further elaborated. This group, to which there belong not only the *Infancy Gospels* in particular but also the *Gospel of Nicodemus* and the literature regarding Pilate, is heavily stamped with secondary legendary elements. Christians have fastened their pious interest upon the figure of Jesus and upon the persons who in the canonical Gospels are mentioned in association with Him, and fantasy has taken possession of them. Legends of every kind normally met with in folk-literature are transferred to Jesus and these other figures. To this type there belong legendary gospels which only in part represented a distinctive tendency, but which as a rule sought to be edifying and so did not merely express the popular piety of the time when they originated, but also in their turn moulded and influenced the popular piety of later centuries.

This division of the apocryphal gospel literature into three types has of course many defects (e.g. there are also writings which both exhibit a gnostic tendency and contain legendary material). But this outline should give warning against simplification and moreover it should provide a hint of certain structural peculiarities by which the character, the provenance and in part also the age of these works may be recognized. What comes to expression in this diversity is the diversity of the Christian proclamation of the gospel in the first centuries, and because that is so it is important to recognize and classify correctly the characteristic features of each of these documents.[1]

[1] In this work it is not necessary to inquire into modern forgeries about the life of Christ and "gospel"-creations. On this see Jülicher-Fascher, "Benanbrief" in *RGG*[2] I, cols. 886–888; James, pp. 89f.; Cullmann, pp. 407f. below.

I
ISOLATED SAYINGS OF THE LORD
(*J. Jeremias*)

INTRODUCTION.

By an "isolated saying of the Lord" (agraphon) is meant a saying of Jesus which is not found in our four canonical Gospels. To avoid repetition the agrapha which in this work are discussed within the compass of the apocryphal gospels will not be quoted here in the text (cf. Introduction 3 at the end).

1. LITERATURE: (*a*) *Collections of Texts.* Standard Editions: E. Klostermann, *Apocrypha* II, Evangelien (*KlT* 8)³, Berlin 1929, and *Apocrypha* III, Agrapha, slavische Josephusstücke, Oxyrhynchos-Fragment (*KlT* 11)², Bonn-Berlin 1911. Also and still indispensable: A. Resch, *Agrapha* (*TU* 5, 4), Leipzig 1889; ²(*TU* NF 15, 3–4), Leipzig 1906 (because of its unrivalled completeness) as also J. H. Ropes, *Die Sprüche Jesu, die in den kanonischen Evangelien nicht überliefert sind* (*TU* 14, 2), Leipzig 1896 (a critical examination of Resch's material, on which Klostermann, *Apocrypha* III also relies). Santos, pp. 115–130.

(*b*) *Special Text-Editions and Source-Investigations:* On the patristic agrapha, U. Holzmeister, "Unbeachtete patristische Agrapha" in *ZkTh* 38 (1914), pp. 113–143; 39 (1915), pp. 98–118, 801–803. On Clement of Alexandria, J. Ruwet, "Les 'Agrapha' dans les oeuvres de Clément d'Alexandrie" in *Biblica* 30 (1949), pp. 133–160. On Symeon of Mesopotamia (ps. Makarius), J. Stiglmayr, "Die Agrapha bei Makarius von Ägypten" in *Theologie und Glaube* 5 (1913), pp. 634–641: H. Dörries, *Symeon von Mesopotamia* (*TU* 55, 1), Leipzig, 1941, p. 224: E. Klostermann, "Symeon und Macarius" in *ABA* 1943, No. 11, p. 13. On ps. Cyprian, M. Heer, "Pseudo-Cyprian Vom Lohn der Frommen und das Evangelium Justins" in *RQS* 28 (1914), pp. 97–186. On the inscription of Fathpur-Sikri, J. Jeremias, "Zur Überlieferungsgeschichte des Agraphon 'Die Welt ist eine Brücke'" in *NGA* 1953, No. 4, pp. 96–103; id. *Exp. Times* lxix (1957) 7–9: H. Sahlin, "Die Welt ist eine Brücke . . . " in *ZNW* 47 (1956), pp. 286f. On the Talmudic agrapha, H. L. Strack, *Jesus, die Häretiker und die Christen*, Leipzig 1910. On the Islamic agrapha, E. Sell–S. Margoliouth in Hastings, *Dictionary of Christ and the Gospels* II, Edinburgh 1908, pp. 882–886: M. Asin y Palacios, "Logia et Agrapha Domini Jesu apud Moslemicos Scriptores" in *PO* XIII, 3, Paris 1919, pp. 327–431; XIX, 4, Paris 1926, pp. 529–624.

(c) *General Disquisitions:* The modern investigation of the agrapha dates from 1889, in which year A. Resch's basic work (see above) appeared; Resch's comprehensive compilation became useful for scientific purposes only as a result of J. H. Ropes' criticism of it (see above), cf. also Ropes in *DB*, Extra Volume (1904), pp. 343–352. Also B. Jackson, *Twenty-five Agrapha*, London 1900: A. Harnack in SB Berlin 1904, pp. 170–208: E. Klostermann in *ZNW* 6 (1905), pp. 104–106 (where proof is given that several of the agrapha in Resch's list should be crossed out): Bauer, pp. 377–415 (where the critical treatment of the material is continued): E. Hennecke, *RE*³ 23, pp. 16–25 (article "Agrapha"): E. Jacquier in *Rev. Bibl.* NS, 15 (1918), pp. 93–135: L. Vaganay in *Dictionnaire de la Bible*, Supplement 1, Paris 1928, cols. 159–198 (article "Agrapha"): J. Jeremias, *Unbekannte Jesusworte*, Zürich 1948, ²Gutersloh 1951, ET *Unknown Sayings of Jesus*, London 1957: W. Michaelis, *Die Apokryphen Schriften zum NT*, Bremen (²1958), pp. 1–25.

(d) *Bibliography:* Resch, *op. cit.*², pp. 14–17: Ropes in *DB* Extra Volume (1904), p. 352: L. Vaganay, *op. cit.*, cols. 193–198 (till 1928): Santos, pp. 117–119.

2. SOURCES. (a) the NT (1 Thess. 4:16f.; Acts 20:35); (b) the peculiar readings of some New Testament manuscripts and groups of manuscripts (of special importance is Cod. D after Lk. 6:4); (c) the Christian writers from Papias of Hierapolis (on him see Iren., V. xxxiii. 3f.) as far as the Middle Ages; (d) the papyri (particularly important are Pap. Ox. 1 and 1224); (e) the Arabic agraphon of Fathpur-Sikri (India), an inscription of the year 1601; (f) the quite scanty Talmudic agrapha, which throughout bear the marks of antichristian polemic (see Literature (b) above); (g) the very numerous Islamic agrapha (see above, *loc. cit.*), of which one of the oldest recurs in the inscription mentioned under (e).

3. EXAMINATION OF THE MATERIAL. The valuation of the agrapha fluctuates between undiscriminating high esteem and extreme scepticism. The forming of a judgment that will not depend on fancy is possible only on the basis of a critical examination of the very extensive material. In the first place we must with Ropes and Klostermann exclude all texts that have been erroneously claimed as agrapha. The remaining material consists in great part:

(a) Of tendentious coinings of sayings of the Lord: (b) of barefaced legendary inventions or legendary transferences to Jesus (there belong here e.g. the Islamic agrapha [see Literature (b) above] and the sayings of Jesus in the nativity gospels): (c) of Biblical and extra-Biblical citations which, because of slips of memory, have inadvertently been transferred to Jesus: (d) of sayings of Jesus given in the Gospels, which have been remodelled and worked up: (e) of sayings the attestation of which occasions doubt.

The agrapha sorted out under these headings do not help towards an understanding of Jesus and the early Church, but merely towards an understanding of their authors or transmitters and their times. The examination and division of the material just described is the result of much work on the part of Ropes (see Literature (a) above) as also of Klostermann, Bauer, Hennecke, Vaganay and Jeremias (see Literature (c) above). There remains:

(f) a very small residue of sayings in the case of which content, form and attestation justify the opinion that they stand on a level with the sayings of our Lord (themselves historically of very differing value) contained in our four Gospels. To this last group there may be reckoned the sayings adduced below (1–11); but in the case of 6 (cited as a saying of the Lord only by Tertullian, who however gives the passion history as the place where he found it) the attestation, in the case of 7 the relationship to Mt. 6:33, in the case of 3 the content, which is broadly apocalyptic and lacking in what is specifically Christian, may give occasion for reserve in the valuation. Also the fragment of an unknown gospel Pap. Ox. 840 (see pp. 92ff. below) may belong here, and from the material of the Jewish-Christian gospels perhaps Nos. 15, 16, 23 from the Gospel of the Nazarenes and No. 5 from the Gospel of the Hebrews (see pp. 148ff. and 164). The material of the Coptic Gospel of Thomas still requires to be accurately examined from this point of view (see p. 294 below). An attempt to interpret the agrapha given under (f) was undertaken by Jeremias; see above, Literature (c).

4. ORAL OR WRITTEN TRADITION? Of the agrapha cited in what follows only the two from the NT (1 and 2) can with certainty be traced back to oral tradition. The very frequently cited saying 5 is introduced repeatedly as a word of Scripture or of the Gospel (see Resch, *op. cit.*, pp. 112–122); on 6 see 3 above; Origen found 9 in a written source ("legi alicubi") and that, in view of the parallel in the Coptic Gospel of Thomas (Logion 82, see p. 303 below) is credible, although it cannot be said which gospel Origen had before him; since Theodotus and the writer of the Acts of Peter perhaps knew the Gospel of the Egyptians, 4 and 8 may be derived from it. The compilations of sayings Pap. Ox. 1, 654, 655 also come from a gospel, as the newly discovered "Sayings Compilation", the Coptic Gospel of Thomas, suggests. At all events we may conjecture that most of the sayings given in what follows come from lost apocryphal gospels, without in so doing

saying anything as to the form of these sources (whether logia compilations like the Coptic Gospel of Thomas or gospels of the Synoptic type).

1. The Lord will descend from heaven with a loud summons, the call of the archangel and the trumpet of God.
And first will the dead in Christ arise.
Then we the living, who are left, shall together with them be caught up in the clouds to meet the Lord in the air.

(Paul, 1 Thess. 4:16–17a)

There is uncertainty as to where this "word of the Lord" (1 Thess. 4:15) begins and ends. It was perhaps spoken in connection with such a saying as Mk. 9:1 or Mt. 24:30f. (in content a development of Mt. 24:30f.?).

2. To give is more blessed than to receive.

(Paul, Acts 20:35)

3. There will be dissensions and squabbles.

(Justin, *Dial.* xxxv, 3)

Cf. the Syr. *Didasc.* vi. 5 ("As also our Lord and Saviour said, There will be squabbles and dissensions"): also the *Ps.-Clem. Hom.* twice mention that the Lord had announced squabbles (II 17: XVI 21); cf. further the Coptic Gospel of Thomas, logion 16 (below, p. 292); the sources are independent of one another. Secession and strife brought about by false prophets belong to the horrors of the time of distress that precedes the end.

4. Save thyself and thy soul (or: thy life?)!
(Theodotus apud Clem. Alex., *Exc. ex Theodoto* 2, 2)

Cf. Gen. 19:17 (summons to Lot: "Save thyself! Thy life is at stake"). Other references to the history of Sodom and Gomorrha: Mt. 10:15; 11:23f.; Lk. 17:28f., 32. A call, like the one in Mk. 13:14b–18, to flee when the end approaches.

5. Be ye competent money-changers!
(Apelles apud Epiphanium, *haer.* 44, 2)

A warning to repulse false prophets (cf. 3).

6. No one can attain the kingdom of heaven
   who has not gone through temptation.

   (Tertullian, *De baptismo* xx, 2)

The overcoming of temptation in the last days is the indispensable condition of a portion in the kingdom of God.

7. Ask for the great things,
   and God will add to you what is small.

   (Clem. Al., *Strom.* I. xxiv, 158)

The passive ("and what is small will be added unto you") para-phrases the name of God. An application of Mt. 6:33 to prayer.

8. Those who are with me have not understood me.

   (*Actus Vercellenses* 10)

9. He who is near me
   is near the fire;
   he who is far from me
   is far from the kingdom.

   (Origen, *in Jer.* hom. 20, 3 = Gospel of Thomas logion 82, pl. 95, 17–19 Labib, cf. p. 303 below)

A word of warning, like Mt. 8:19f., which will oblige a man to examine his own attachment to Jesus.

10. (He who today) stands far-off will tomorrow be (near) (to you).

    (Pap. Ox. 1224, *c.* 300)

11. When on the same day he saw a man doing work on the Sabbath, he said to him:
    Man! if thou knowest what thou doest, blessed art thou!
    But if thou knowest not, thou art cursed and a transgressor of the law.

    (Lk. 6:4 according to Cod. D)

The accent in antithetic parallelism falls on the second line. A warning against thoughtless transgression of the Sabbath com-mandment.

Because it is frequently quoted, there may be given by way of appendix the agraphon from Fathpur-Sikri (India). Often adduced from Islamic literature since the 8th century (see Intro. 1 *b*; 2 *eg*), it can hardly be included in the group Intro. 3*f*:

> Jesus, on whom be peace, has said:
> The world is a bridge.
> Go over it, but do not install yourselves upon it.

(Inscription put on the south main portal of the mosque in Fathpur-Sikri in 1601.) A warning not to forget the transitoriness of this earthly life through which we pass but once.

II

PAPYRUS FRAGMENTS OF APOCRYPHAL GOSPELS
(*J. Jeremias and W. Schneemelcher*)

INTRODUCTION (*W. Schneemelcher*):

In Egypt in recent decades there has come to light a wealth of papyri which have considerably enriched our knowledge in all departments of archaeology and also in the department of early Church history. Among others Adolf Deissmann in particular was concerned to make full use of these newly-found texts for the understanding of early Christianity, and in this endeavour he did in his own day pioneering work (*Bibelstudien*, 1895, ET ²1903; *Licht vom Osten*⁴, 1923, ET 1927). Altogether the study of papyri has been an important auxiliary science since the end of last century, and the great compilations and editions of the fragments (e.g. the series of the Oxyrhynchus papyri) are now a rich treasury for historians.

Among these papyri, besides fragments of canonical writings that are important for the history of the text of the NT (e.g. the Chester Beatty papyri of the NT, 𝔓⁴⁵⁻⁴⁷) and witnesses of literary works of the early Church that are of great value for patristics (e.g. remains of Hermas or of Origen's commentary on Romans in the papyrus find at Tura), there are also the remains of a series of apocryphal writings. In the present work reference will be made to these papyri from time to time. Here there will be assembled only important Greek papyrus fragments which appear to be either remains of unknown gospels or extracts from such gospels. Since the Fayyum fragment (see below) became known in 1885, and then the Oxyrhynchus Papyrus 1 (see below) in 1897, these being soon followed by many other texts, these fragments—often mere shreds—have time and again exercised a great attraction; almost no end of treatises have been devoted to them, and there has been attached to them a vast number of hypotheses, which often enough have quickly crumbled to dust. In this connection the lack of method, manifest over and over again and above all in "the age of discovery", is astonishing. Every fragment was immediately assigned to some one gospel, although not even the slightest clues for so doing were available. We have now become very much more cautious, particularly since new finds are continually making clearer the gaps in our knowledge of this "minor literature" of Egypt.

Several papyri which hitherto have always been mentioned in this connection may be eliminated straight away, it having been proved that they contain no gospel fragments or extracts from gospels. Thus Pap. Ox. 1081 (Greek text in Wessely, *PO* XVIII, pp. 269ff.; Klostermann, *op. cit.*, p. 25) has been identified by Puech as a fragment of the *Sophia Jesu Christi* (H.-Ch. Puech, "Les nouveaux écrits gnostiques" in *Coptic Studies in Honor of W. E. Crum*, 1950, p. 98; cf. W. Till, *Die gnostischen Schriften des kopt. Pap. Berol.* 8502, *TU* 60, 1955, pp. 216ff.; Puech, below p. 245). As regards Pap. Ox. 210 (text edited by B. P. Grenfell and A. S. Hunt, *OP* II, 1899, pp. 9f.) the editors advanced the conjecture that in it we have before us remains of or excerpts from an apocryphal gospel, possibly the Gospel of the Egyptians. But A. Deissmann (*ThLZ* 26, 1901, col. 72) pointed out that because of the fragmentary character of the scanty remains a near guess as to the provenance of this text is out of the question. That judgment still holds good. Finally, in the case of Pap. Ox. 1384 also (text: *OP* XI, 1915, pp. 238–241) the editors have indulged in guesses as to whether the texts, which here turn up between medical prescriptions, do not come from an apocryphal gospel. But its text is so short and its situation so difficult to understand that every assignation of it should be disregarded. Even if it should be the case that its source is some apocryphal writing, the latter can only be one of the later popular creations (the papyrus was written in the 5th or 6th century).

In the following survey a few important fragments are selected. An approximate completeness in bibliographical statements is just as little striven after as an exhaustive enumeration and refutation of all the conjectures that have been thrown out regarding the reconstruction or derivation of the texts. There is a compilation of Greek texts (a selection) in Klostermann, *Apocrypha* II (*KlT* 8³), 1929, pp. 19ff. and above all in Ch. Wessely, *Les plus anciens monuments du Christianisme écrits sur Papyrus*, *PO* IV, 2, Paris 1908, pp. 57ff. and XVIII, 3, Paris 1924, pp. 264ff. (with the earlier literature and a good commentary); cf. also Giuseppe Bonaccorsi, *Vangeli Apocrifi* I, Florence 1948; Santos, pp. 81–106.

1. AN UNKNOWN GOSPEL OF SYNOPTIC TYPE
(Pap. Ox. 840)
(*J. Jeremias*)

In December 1905 Grenfell and Hunt found in Oxyrhynchus (now Behnesa in Middle Egypt) a leaf of a parchment book of the smallest size (8·5 × 7 cm.) written on both sides in microscopically small letters, which had probably served as an amulet (4th or 5th century). The first seven lines contain the conclusion of a discourse of Jesus delivered in Jerusalem, in which He warns His disciples against a deceptive confidence. There follows a visit to the Temple court where a sharp discussion takes place between Jesus and a Pharisaic chief priest named Levi, who takes Jesus and His disciples to task for neglecting the purification rules laid down for the treading of the court of the Israelites (called "the place of purification"). This neglect of theirs answers to what is recorded in Mk. 7:1ff. and Mt. 15:1ff. regarding Jesus' attitude to rabbinical precept; and the severity and vigour with which in His rejoinder Jesus castigates the Pharisaic hypocrisy which sought through scrupulously careful observance of the ritual of cleanliness to delude men as to the abominable nature of what was within them, has in substance an exact parallel in Mt. 23:27f. The objections which for long were made to the historicity of this narrative, on the ground that it shows no knowledge of the Jerusalem temple and its ritual, can now no longer be sustained. On the contrary it is excellently informed, exhibits numerous Semitisms (this is taken into account in the translation) and in substance ranks as high as the Synoptic account.

First Editions: B. P. Grenfell and A. S. Hunt, *OP* V, London 1908, no. 840; id., *Fragment of an Uncanonical Gospel from Oxyrhynchus*, Oxford 1908; H. B. Swete, *Zwei neue Evangelienfragmente* (*KlT* 31), Bonn–Berlin [1]1908 = [2]1924, pp. 3–9.

Literature: A. Büchler in *The Jewish Quart. Review* 20 (1907–8), pp. 330–346; E. J. Goodspeed in *Biblical World* NS 31 (1908), pp. 142–146; A. Harnack in *Preuss. Jb.* 131 (1908), pp. 201–210 = *Aus Wissenschaft und Leben* II, Giessen 1911, pp. 237–250; E. Preuschen in *ZNW* 9 (1908), pp. 1–11; E. Schürer in *ThLZ* 33 (1908), col. 170–172; A. Sulzbach in *ZNW* 9 (1908), pp. 175f.; L. Blau, *ibid.* pp. 204–215; A. Marmorstein, *ibid.* 15 (1914), pp. 336–338; E. Riggenbach, *ibid.* 25 (1926), pp. 140–144; J. Jeremias in *Coni. Neotest.* XI in honorem A. Fridrichsen (1947), pp. 97–108: id., *Unbekannte Jesusworte*[2], Gütersloh 1951, pp. 39–49; 86f. (ET 1957, 36–49).

First before he does wrong (?) he thinks out everything that is crafty. But be ye on your guard that the same thing may not happen to you as does to them.[1] For not only among the living do evil doers among men receive retribution, but they must also suffer punishment and great torment.

And he took them (the disciples) with him into the place of purification itself and walked about in the Temple court.[2] And a Pharisaic chief priest, Levi (?) by name, fell in with them and

---

[1] Cf. Lk. 13:5.   [2] Cf. Mk. 11:27.

s⟨aid⟩ to the Saviour: Who gave thee leave to ⟨trea⟩d this place of purification and to look upon ⟨the⟩se holy utensils without having bathed thyself and even without thy disciples having ⟨wa⟩shed their f⟨eet⟩[1]? On the contrary, being defi⟨led⟩, thou hast trodden the Temple court, this clean p⟨lace⟩, although no⟨one who⟩ has ⟨not⟩ first bathed ⟨himself⟩ or ⟨chang⟩ed his clot⟨hes⟩ may tread it and ⟨venture⟩ to vi⟨ew⟩ ⟨these⟩ holy utensils! Forthwith ⟨the Saviour⟩ s⟨tood⟩ still with h⟨is⟩ disciples and ⟨answered⟩: How stands it (then) with thee, thou art forsooth (also) here in the Temple court. Art thou then clean? He said to him: I am clean. For I have bathed myself in the pool of David and have gone down by the one stair and come up by the other and have put on white and clean clothes, and (only) then have I come hither and have viewed these holy utensils. Then said the Saviour to him: Woe unto you blind that see not![2] Thou hast bathed thyself in water that is poured out, in which dogs and swine[3] lie night and day and thou hast washed thyself and hast chafed thine outer skin, which prostitutes also and flute-girls[4] anoint, bathe, chafe and rouge, in order to arouse desire in men, but within they are full of scorpions and of ⟨bad⟩ness ⟨of every kind⟩[5]. But I and ⟨my disciples⟩, of whom thou sayest that we have not im⟨mersed⟩ ourselves, ⟨have been im⟩mersed in the liv⟨ing . . . ⟩ water[6] which comes down from ⟨ . . . B⟩ut woe unto them that . . .

2. AN UNKNOWN GOSPEL WITH JOHANNINE ELEMENTS

(Pap. Egerton 2)

(J. Jeremias)

Pap. Egerton 2 (two leaves and remains of a third), before 150, London, British Museum. The text consists of the fragments of four pericopes, of which the first (ll. 1–31) bears Johannine marks, the second (ll. 32–41) and third (ll. 43–59) exhibit parallels to Synoptic stories, whilst the fourth (ll. 60–75), the text of which has been handed down in a particularly fragmentary condition, describes an apocryphal miracle wrought by Jesus on the bank of

---

[1] Cf. Jn. 13:10.   [2] Cf. Mt. 15:14; 23:16f., 19, 24, 26.
[3] Cf. Mt. 7:6; Rev. 22:15.   [4] Cf. Gospel of the Nazarenes No. 18 (p. 149 below).
[5] Cf. Mt. 23:27f.   [6] Cf. Jn. 4:14.

the Jordan. The "Johannine" fragment presents first the conclusion of a trial (*ll.* 1–5), the occasion of which was a transgression of the law on the part of Jesus; since two sayings follow from
Jn. 5, the matter dealt with may be a violation by Jesus of the
Sabbath. There follows a controversial discourse, made up of
Johannine logia, with the rulers of the people (*ll.* 5–20), which
reaches its climax in an agraphon of violent threatening. If, as is
likely, the narrative continued in *ll.* 22–31, a self-assertion of Jesus
will have followed which was felt to be blasphemous and so
provoked an attempt to stone Him, blasphemy being one of the
offences for which the punishment was stoning (cf. Jn. 8:59; 10:
31). Only very loosely connected to this, there follows the healing
of the leper.

The two Synoptic pericopes, the healing of a leper and a discourse about tribute-money (*ll.* 32–59), are distinguished by the
fact that they show contacts with all the three Synoptics; the
material is simultaneously reduced and enlarged. In five places
(see Jeremias in *Theol. Blätter* 15, 1936, cols. 40–42) there are
transitions to other Gospel passages occasioned by verbal reminiscences, and this leads to the conclusion that both stories have been
reproduced from memory. The scene at the Jordan (*ll.* 60–75)
begins with a question (by Jesus) which clearly has as its subject
the mystery of the resurrection typified in a grain of seed: Jesus
Himself answers the question by a miracle on the bank of the
Jordan, causing, as it seems, the sowing and the ripening of the
grain to follow immediately upon one another, as an index doubtless to the omnipotence of God which brings forth life out of
death.

The value which we assign to the text is determined by our
judgment as to its relation to the canonical Gospels, especially to
the Fourth. There are contacts with all four Gospels. The juxtaposition of Johannine (I) and Synoptic material (II and III) and
the fact that the Johannine material is shot through with Synoptic
phrases and the Synoptic with Johannine usage, permits the conjecture that the author knew all and every one of the canonical
Gospels. Only he had no one of them before him as a written text.
On the contrary the above-mentioned digressions in II and III,
which were occasioned by verbal reminiscences and which also
occur in I, show that the material has been reproduced from
memory. Consequently we may have before us an instance of the
overlapping of written and oral tradition: although the tradition
was already fixed in writing, it was still widely reproduced from
memory and in this way, enriched with extra-canonical material
(IV), found new expression in writing. The text shows no historical
knowledge that carries us beyond the canonical Gospels. The

reproduction of the story of the healing of the leper shows in its beginning (wandering with lepers) and at its end ("the" priests, thus plural) that Palestinian circumstances were not well known to the author; also the question about tribute-money is robbed of its typically Jewish tone through being worded in general terms.

First editions: H. I. Bell and T. C. Skeat, *Fragments of an Unknown Gospel*, London 1935; id., *The New Gospel Fragments*, London 1935 (with corrections).

Literature with suggestions as to how the text should be completed: M. J. Lagrange, *Critique textuelle* II, Paris 1935, pp. 633–649 (= *Rev. Bibl.* 44, 1935, pp. 47ff.); M. Dibelius in *Dt. Lit. Ztg.* 57 (1936), cols. 3–11; C. H. Dodd, *A New Gospel*, Manchester 1936 (= *BJRL* 20 (1936) pp. 56ff.; reprinted in *New Testament Studies*, Manchester 1953, 12ff.); K. F. W. Schmidt–J. Jeremias in *Theol. Blätter* 15 (1936), cols. 34–45 (cf. H. I. Bell, cols. 72–74); further literature in G. Mayeda, *Das Leben-Jesu-Fragment Papyrus Egerton 2*, Bern 1946 (cf. H. I. Bell in *HTR* 42, 1949, pp. 53–63); finally, J. Jeremias, *Unbekannte Jesusworte*, Gütersloh ²1951, pp. 23–25 (ET 1957, 18–20, 93f.).

f. Iv (*ll.* 1–20)

(I) ... ⟨to⟩ the lawyer⟨s " ... e⟩very one who act⟨s contrary to the l⟩aw, but not me! ... (5) ... what he does, as he does it." ⟨And⟩ having turn⟨ed⟩ to ⟨the⟩ rulers of the people he ⟨sp⟩oke the following saying; "(*Ye*) *search the scriptures* in which *ye think that ye have life; these are they* (10) *which bear witness of me.*[1] *Do not think that I* came to *accuse* ⟨*you*⟩ to my *Father! There is one* ⟨*that ac*⟩*cuses* ⟨*you*⟩, *even Moses, on whom ye have set your hope.*"[2] And when they sa(15)⟨id⟩: "*We know that God* ⟨*hath*⟩ *spok*⟨*en*⟩ *to Moses, but as for thee, we know not* ⟨*whence thou art*⟩",[3] Jesus answered and said unto them: "Now (already) accusation is raised[4] against ⟨your⟩ unbelief. (20) ⟨No one o⟩therwise ... "

f. Ir (*ll.* 22–41)

... ⟨*to gather*⟩ *stones* together *to stone him.*[5] And the ⟨rul⟩ers laid (25) their hands on him that they might arrest him and ⟨deliver⟩ him to the multitude. But they w⟨ere not able⟩ *to arrest* him *because the hour* of his betrayal ⟨*was*⟩ *not yet c*⟨*ome*⟩.[6] (30) But *he* himself, the Lord, *escaped out of* ⟨*their han*⟩*ds*[7] and turned away from them.

(II) *And behold a leper drew near* ⟨*to him*⟩ *and said:* "Master Jesus, wandering with lepers and eating with ⟨them was I?

[1] Jn. 5:39.   [2] Jn. 5:45.   [3] Jn. 9:29.   [4] Cf. Jn. 12:31.   [5] Jn. 10:31.   [6] Jn. 7:30.
[7] Jn. 10:39.

publicans art thou?⟩ (35) in the inn; I also ⟨became⟩ a le⟨per⟩.
If ⟨*thou*⟩ *therefore* ⟨*wilt*⟩, I am made *clean.*" Immediately the
Lord ⟨said to him⟩: "*I will, be thou made clean.*" ⟨And thereupon⟩
the leprosy departed *from him.* ⟨And the Lord (40) said to him⟩:
"Go ⟨thy way and show th⟩yself to the ⟨priests . . . ''¹

f. 2ʳ (*ll.* 43–59)

(III) . . . ⟨ca⟩me to him to put him to the pro⟨of⟩ and to
tempt him, whilst ⟨they said⟩: (45) "*Master* Jesus, *we know that
thou art come* ⟨*from God*⟩,² for *what* thou *doest bears a test*⟨*imony*⟩³ (to
thee) (which) (goes) beyond (that) of al(l) the prophets. ⟨Where-
fore *tell*⟩ *us*: is it *admissible* ⟨*to p*⟩*ay* to the kings the (charges)
appertaining to their rule? ⟨*Should we*⟩ *pay* ⟨*th-*⟩(50)*em or not?
But Jesus saw through* their ⟨in⟩tention,⁴ *became* ⟨*angry*⟩⁵ and said
to them; "*Why call ye me* with yo⟨ur mou⟩th Master and *yet* ⟨*do*⟩
*not what I say?*⁶ *Well has Is*⟨*aiah*⟩ *prophesied* ⟨*concerning y*⟩(55)*ou*
saying: *This* ⟨*people* honours⟩ *me with the*⟨*ir li*⟩*ps but their heart is
far from me;* ⟨*their worship is*⟩ *vain.* ⟨*They teach*⟩ *precepts* ⟨*of men*⟩."⁷

f. 2ᵛ (*ll.* 60–75)

(IV) ⟨The grain of wheat⟩ . . . (60) . . . place shut in . . . it
was laid beneath and invisible . . . its wealth imponderable?⁸
And as they were in perplexity at his strange question, (65) Jesus
on his way came ⟨to the⟩ bank of the ⟨riv⟩er Jordan, stretched
out ⟨hi⟩s right hand, ⟨fill⟩ed it with . . . and sowed . . . on the
(70) . . . And then . . . water . . . And . . . before ⟨their eyes⟩,
brought fruit . . . much . . . to the jo(75)⟨y?⟩ . . .

3. SAYINGS–COLLECTIONS ON PAPYRUS

Introduction (*W. Schneemelcher*)

As a special group among the papyrus fragments of apocryphal
gospels there must be included Pap. Ox. 1, 654 and 655, since the
sayings preserved in them come before us in a Coptic rendering
in the Gospel of Thomas, which was found in 1946 at Nag Hammadi (see pp. 278ff. below), and the Greek texts, preserved in part
in a very fragmentary condition, appear as a result of this find

---

¹ Mk. 1:40–44; Mt. 8:2–4; Lk. 5:12–14.   ² Jn. 3:2.   ³ Jn. 10:25.
⁴ Mk. 12:13–15; Mt. 22:15–18; Lk. 20:20–23.   ⁵ Cf. Mk. 1:43.   ⁶ Lk. 6:46.
⁷ Isa. 29:13 LXX; Mk. 7:6f.; Mt. 15:7f.   ⁸ Cf. Jn. 12:24.

in a new light.[1] To be sure since the three papyri do not derive from the same book, only a very guarded opinion may be expressed with regard to their homogeneousness. Nevertheless, too much is not asserted when it is said that the Greek texts preserved in these three fragments probably belonged to the Greek Gospel of Thomas, which must be assumed as the basis of the Coptic text. On the other hand, however, the fact may not be overlooked that, e.g., in Pap. Ox. 654 a saying is handed down which is attested by Clement of Alexandria for the Gospel of the Hebrews. The connections between the Gospel of Thomas and the Gospel of the Hebrews (and also between the Gospel of Thomas and the Gospel of the Egyptians) have not yet been so clarified that such a double attestation can be explained with certainty. It is indeed also quite conceivable that in the Gospel of the Hebrews and in the Gospel of Thomas (as also in the Gospel of the Egyptians) the same traditions may have been used; that would then certainly afford irrefutable proof that these texts are of very great age.

The 5th logion of Pap. Ox. 1 is presented in the Gospel of Thomas in two parts in different passages (logion 30 = P. Labib, pl. 87, 2–5; logion 77 = P. Labib, pl. 94, 22–28). That fact must warn us against seeing in the papyri simply the Greek original of the Coptic text and proceeding without the necessary caution to fill up the gaps in the papyri with the help of the Coptic text. The Coptic text will of course be a good help to the understanding of the Greek fragments, and a completion of the Greek text on the basis of the Coptic is also certainly possible for many lines. But at the same time it should never be overlooked that the Coptic text had already had a history of its own before it was written in the papyrus of Nag Hammadi (4th century). We must in the first place be content to set side by side the Greek texts (with certain cautious completions) and the Coptic rendering. This procedure has been adopted in the following translation.[2]

(a) Oxyrhynchus Papyrus 654
(W. Schneemelcher)

On the back of a property writ there were written at the end of the 2nd or beginning of the 3rd century in good uncial a series

[1] We owe the identification of the logia in question of the Gospel of Thomas with the well-known texts of the three papyri to H.-Ch. Puech, who already in 1952 had perceived the connection. Evidently in independence of Puech, G. Garitte detected that they belonged to one another (Le Muséon 70, 1957, pp. 59–73), but in a note he has acknowledged the priority of Puech's discovery.

[2] The texts from the Coptic Gospel of Thomas, then not yet published, were made available with a French translation by H.-Ch. Puech, and a German translation was prepared by W. Schneemelcher. The Gospel is cited according to P. Labib's photographic edition, Coptic Gnostic Papyri in the Coptic Museum at Old Cairo, Vol. I, Cairo 1956. See now The Gospel according to Thomas (London and Leiden 1959).

of sayings which from time to time are introduced with the formula "Jesus says". That undoubtedly ought to be assumed for all the sayings even although this formula is not everywhere legible in the fragments that have been preserved. The text has been copied from an earlier original, as can be shown from slips of the pen.

The discussion of this fragment that set in after its discovery (1903) has fostered many attempts at reconstruction (for a comparison of the attempts of White and Deissmann see Klostermann, *KlT* 8³, pp. 20ff.; cf. also the reconstruction of Ch. Wessely, *PO* IV, 2, pp. 64ff.). These restorations of the text are in part confirmed and in part seriously called in question by the Coptic Gospel of Thomas. That in this compilation of the sayings of Jesus we are not dealing with the source of a gospel (like the source Q for Mt. and Lk.) is indeed just as clear as the fact that here a fragment of a gospel lies before us. Ch. Wessely has referred to the formal parallel of the Greek maxim literature and from this has attempted to explain both Pap. Ox. 1 and Pap. Ox. 654 (*op. cit.*, pp. 57ff. and 64ff.). This reference must be taken seriously, even if in the papyri 1, 654 and 655 we are actually concerned with remains of the Greek original of the Coptic Gospel of Thomas, i.e. of a Greek Gospel of Thomas. Since the first saying is attested by Clement of Alexandria for the Gospel of the Hebrews (Clem. Alex., *Strom.* V xiv, 96), it has been thought that the whole collection is derived from this Egyptian Gospel of the Hebrews (so Waitz, *Apokr.* 2, pp. 49ff.). This assignation is, however, on various grounds just as little tenable (cf. Vielhauer, pp. 160ff. below) as Harnack's conjecture that here there lies before us a remnant of the Gospel of the Egyptians. However the problems which are set us, especially by the far-reaching agreements of our text with the Gospel of Thomas, must be solved, it may assuredly be said that the sayings handed down here show a considerable nearness to the Synoptic sayings of Jesus, but at the same time a highly characteristic tendency to further development of the Synoptic tradition.

Text: G. P. Grenfell and A. S. Hunt, *Ox. Pap.* IV, 1903, pp. 1–22; Ch. Wessely, *PO* IV, 2, pp. 64ff.; Klostermann, *op. cit.*, pp. 20–22; Bonaccorsi, *op. cit.*, pp. 48–53.

Literature: Jeremias, *Unbek. Jesusworte* (ET 1957); Puech, pp. 295ff. below; H. G. E. White, *The Sayings of Jesus from Oxyrhynchus*, Cambridge 1920 (text and commentary); cf. review by R. Reitzenstein in *GGA* 183, 1921, pp. 165–174; Reitzenstein there adduces much that contributes nothing to our understanding, but his reference to the Thomas tradition is important.

Pap. Ox. 654, lines 1–5:

> These are the words which ⟨ . . . . .
> Jesus the Living One spoke a⟨nd . . .
> and Thomas and spoke ⟨ . . . .
> these words ⟨ . . . .
>
> 5. will he not taste.

This preface, with which the first logion is connected, is no doubt the introduction to the whole series of sayings (against Waitz, *Apokr.* 2, p. 51). The translation in *l.* 3 "and Thomas" must be corrected to "who also Thomas" (*scil.* is called: Greek, ὁ καὶ Θωμᾶς). The parallel in the Coptic Gospel of Thomas runs thus:

Gospel of Thomas, Preface and Logion 1 (P. Labib, pl. 80, 10–14):

> These are the secret words which Jesus the Living One
> has spoken and which Didymus
> Judas Thomas has written. And he has said: He who
> has found the interpretation (ἑρμηνεία) of these words will
> not taste (reach) death.

Pap. Ox. 654, lines 5–9:

> 5.   ⟨Jesus says:
> Let not him cease who is se⟨eking . . . .
> has found, and when he has found ⟨ . . . .
> has been amazed (?), he will reign an⟨d . . . .
> find (?) rest.

Cf. Mt. 11:28 (perhaps also Mt. 7:7; Lk. 11:9). The saying which Clement Alex. cites as coming from the Gospel of the Hebrews is certainly very much closer; cf. p. 160 below. On the mystic-gnostic philosophy of life in which such a saying must originate see p. 162 below. The saying is directly attached to the preface, and therefore, after the analogy of the following lines, the completion 'Jesus says' in *l.* 5 is quite certain. With the saying there is to be compared

Gospel of Thomas, Logion 2 (P. Labib, pl. 80, 14–19):

> Jesus has said: he who seeks
> should not cease to seek until he
> has found, and when he has found, he will

be bewildered (beside himself), and when he is bewildered,
   he will
marvel and will
reign over the All.

Pap. Ox. 654, lines 9–21:

                    says J⟨esus . . . .
   10. who draw us ⟨ . . . . .
       the kingdom in hea⟨ven . . .
       the birds of the hea⟨ven . . .
       what is under the earth ⟨ . . . .
       the fish of the se⟨a . . . .
   15. . . . ⟩ you. And the kingdom ⟨ . . .
       is within you ⟨. . . . . . . he who?
       knows, will fi⟨nd this . . . .
       you will know yourselves ⟨. . . .
       you are of the Father, of the ⟨. . .
   20. you know yourselves in ⟨. . . .
       And you are po⟨verty?

The Greek text is so fragmentary that the gaps can be filled up
only hypothetically. For *l.* 15f. reference may be made to Lk.
17:20f., but the ἐντός here is to be rendered 'within', since it is
clearly a matter of self-knowledge (cf. *l.* 18). For *ll.* 18f. reference
may perhaps be made to Mt. 5:45, 48; Lk. 20:36 ('sons of the
father'). That is what Deissmann has supplied, and the Coptic
text suggests it.

Gospel of Thomas, Logion 3 (P. Labib, pl. 80, 19–81, 5):

                 Jesus has said: If those
who lead you say to you:
See, the kingdom is in heaven,
then the birds will
fly into the heaven in front of you. If they say to you: It is
    in the
sea, then will the fish go before you.
But the kingdom is in your inner part and
it is in your outward part. If you will know yourselves,

then you will be known,
and you will know that you
are sons of the Father, who is the Living One. If,
however, you will not know yourselves, then will
you fall into poverty. And you
are poverty.

Pap. Ox. 654, lines 21–27:

⟨Jesus says:
a m⟨an⟩ will not hesitate . . . . .
. . ⟩ to ask a ⟨child . . . .
. . . ⟩ about the place of the ⟨ . . . .
25. . . . ⟩ Then many (first) will ⟨be the last and
the last the first and ⟨ . . .
. . .

The completion of *l.* 21 has been made on the analogy of the other logia. Hitherto the sense of *ll.* 22ff. has not been clear, but the Coptic text now throws light upon it. On the other hand it is not absolutely necessary to complete *ll.* 26f. in accordance with the Gospel of Thomas. The completion 'and they will attain to life' is also possible; at all events such a reading is suggested by Mk. 10:30f.

Gospel of Thomas, Logion 4 (P. Labib, pl. 81, 5–10):

Jesus has said: The man old in his days
will not hesitate to question
a small child of seven
days about the place of life, and
he will live; for there are many among the first who will be
last

and they will become a single one.

Pap. Ox. 654, lines 27–31:

Jesus says ⟨ . . .
lies (before) thine eye and ⟨ . . . .
from thee, will be revealed ⟨ . . . nothing (?)
30. is hidden that ⟨will⟩ not ⟨be⟩ mani⟨fest,
and buried that ⟨will⟩ not ⟨be raised up (?)

Cf. with this Mk. 4:22 (Lk. 8:17) and Mt. 10:26 (Lk. 12:2). The completion of *l.* 31 is suggested by the first part of the line; it remains of course uncertain, especially since the whole of the last part of the saying is wanting in the Coptic text.

Gospel of Thomas, Logion 5 (P. Labib, pl. 81, 10–14):

> Jesus has said:
> Know that which is before thy face,
> and that which is hidden from thee will be manifested to thee;
> for nothing is hidden which will not
> be manifest.

Pap. Ox. 654, lines 32–39:

> ⟨His disciples⟩ ask him ⟨and
> s⟩ay: How should we fas⟨t and how
> should we pr⟩ay and how ⟨ . . .
> 35. . . . . . ⟩ and what should we observe ⟨of
> the traditions?⟩ Jesus says ⟨ . . . . .
> . . . . . . ⟩ do not ⟨ . . . . . .
> . . . . . . ⟩ truth ⟨ . . . . . .
> . . . . . . ⟩ hidden ⟨ . . . . . .

The saying has been handed down in a particularly sorry condition. Nevertheless it is clear from the Greek fragments that the disciples ask about right conduct (fasts, prayers?, alms?, traditions?); cf. with this perhaps Lk. 11:1; reference may also be made to Mt. 6:1–18. Jesus' answer in the second part seems to have been similar to that in the foregoing saying. At all events the Greek fragments can easily be interpreted in that way in accordance with the Coptic text.

Gospel of Thomas, Logion 6 (P. Labib, pl. 81, 14–23):

> His disciples asked him
> and said to him: Wouldst thou that we fast,
> and in what way should we pray? Should we give
> alms, and as regards food what should
> be observed? Jesus has said: Lie not, and
> do not do what you hate; for
> everything is manifest

before Heaven (before the Truth?); for nothing is hidden that
will not

be manifest; and nothing is covered over
that will not presently be uncovered.

Pap. Ox. 654, lines 40–42:

40. . . . . . . blessed is . . . . . .

. . . .

. . . .

Of this portion isolated letters are all that can be read in the
papyrus, and only in *l.* 40 can two words be completed. Hitherto
these three lines have been attached to the foregoing logion.
According to the Coptic Gospel of Thomas, however, it is to be
supposed that in the Greek text also a separate logion stood here.
But it remains questionable if it had the same wording.

Gospel of Thomas, Logion 7 (P. Labib, pl. 81, 23–28):

Jesus has said:
Blessed is the lion that
the man will devour, and the lion
will become man. And loathsome is the
man that the lion will devour,
and the lion will become man.

(*b*) Oxyrhynchus Papyrus 1

(*J. Jeremias*)

The papyrus leaf Pap. Ox. 1 (soon after 200) was discovered in
1897 in Egypt, as were similar leaves after it, and comes from
Behnesa, the ancient Oxyrhynchus in Middle Egypt; it is part of
a codex, for its verso has been provided by a later hand with the
page number 11. Since the page number was normally placed on
the right-hand page of the opened book, the content of the verso
preceded that of the recto. Further proof is afforded by the filling
out, on the verso only, of the end of short lines with an ornament,
a thing that has meaning only on the outer margin of a page.
The Coptic Gospel of Thomas confirms this conclusion: it gives
the sayings of the verso of Pap. Ox. 1 before those of the recto.
The bottom margin is broken. The whole leaf contains now

7 sayings of Jesus, or 8 sayings, since the lost bottom lines of the verso contained the beginning of a saying the last word of which can still be read in *l.* 23. In conformity with that there likewise follow one another in the Gospel of Thomas 8 sayings which on the whole correspond to the text of Pap. Ox. 1. In this connection it should however be noted that the 5th saying in Pap. Ox. 1 appears in the Gospel of Thomas in two parts in two different passages. The unvarying concise introductory formula in the present tense, 'Jesus says', is used in a similar way in Pap. Ox. 654 (see above), which goes to prove that both papyri are transcriptions from one and the same book (H. G. E. White, *op. cit.*, pp. XXIII–XXV; on the problem whether this book was the Greek original of the Coptic Gospel of Thomas, see p. 98 above). According to R. Reitzenstein (*op. cit.*, pp. 167f.) the latter was still read in the 6th–7th centuries. Three of the 7 (or 8) sayings are known from the Synoptics (cf. the references below), whilst the hitherto unknown sayings are of quite a different stamp (cf. the comments below).

Editions: B. P. Grenfell and A. S. Hunt, *Logia Jesou*[2], Oxford 1897; the same writers, *OP* I, London 1898, pp. 1ff.; E. Klostermann, *Apocrypha* II (*KlT* 8)[3], Berlin 1929, p. 19.
    Literature: F. Blass in *Hengstenbergs Evang. Kirchenzeitung* 1897, cols. 498–500; A. Harnack, *Über die jüngst entdeckten Sprüche Jesu*, Freiburg 1897; Th. Zahn in *ThLBl* 18 (1897), cols. 417–420, 425–431; C. Taylor, *The Oxyrhynchus Logia and the Apocryphal Gospels*, Oxford 1899; H. G. E. White, *The Sayings of Jesus from Oxyrhynchus*, Cambridge 1920 (with literature); R. Reitzenstein in *GGA* 183 (1921), pp. 165–170; J. Jeremias, *Unbekannte Jesusworte*, Gütersloh [2]1951, pp. 18f., 66–70, 88–91 (ET 12f., 69–74, 94–98).

Pap. Ox. 1, lines 1–4:

(Verso)   11 (Page number)
and then thou mayest see clearly
to pull out the mote
that (is) in the eye
of thy brother.

The saying answers to Lk. 6:42 with one word transposed (par. Mt. 7:5). In the Coptic Gospel of Thomas it is present in its entirety.

Gospel of Thomas, Logion 26 (P. Labib, pl. 86, 12–17):

Jesus has said: The mote
that is in thy brother's eye thou seest; but the beam
that is in thine own eye thou seest not. When
thou pullest out the beam out of thine own
eye, then thou wilt (mayest) see clearly to pull out the mote
out of thy brother's eye.

Pap. Ox. 1, lines 4–11:

Jesus says:
5. If you do not fa-
st (as to) the world, you will not
find the kingdom
of God, and if you do not
keep the Sabbath as Sab-
10. bath, you will not see the
Father.

The saying calls for a forsaking of the world and for sanctification; the use of "fasting" in a metaphorical sense is foreign to the canonical Gospels. With *ll.* 8–10 cf. Justin, *Dial.* xii, 3; with *ll.* 10f. cf. Jn. 14:9.

Gospel of Thomas, Logion 27 (P. Labib, pl. 86, 17–20):

If you do not
fast to the world, you will not find the
kingdom; if you do not observe the Sabbath as
Sabbath, you will not see the Father.

Pap. Ox. 1, lines 11–22:

Jesus says: I stood (up)
in the midst of the world,
and in the flesh I appeared
to them and found a-
15. ll drunken, and
none found I athir-
st among them, and
my soul is troubled (or: feels pain) for
the sons of men,

20. because they are blind in their heart and do ⟨not⟩ s-
   ⟨ee . . . .

With *ll.* 11–14 cf. 1 Tim. 3:16; Jn. 1:14; 1 Jn. 4:2; 2 Jn. 7; with
ll. 14f. cf. 1 Thess. 5:7; with *ll.* 16f. Jn. 7:37, with *ll.* 17f. Isa.
53:11. In its opening words the logion, a lamentation of Jesus,
approximates, in the way in which christological formulations of
the Church are put in the mouth of Jesus, to the self-testimonies of
the Fourth Gospel and to the manner of speaking of the Gnostic
redeemer; but with its reference to Isa. 53:11 and with its Semit-
izing speech (instances in Jeremias, *op. cit.*, p. 68, ET 71) it then
strikes into the Synoptic field. The lamentation reminds us of
the accusing word Mk. 9:19; its special feature is, however, that
it is grounded in the patience of Jesus with the blindness (i.e. the
stubbornness) of men. Whether the Greek rendering of the saying also had the longer conclusion which we read in the Coptic
text, cannot be said.

Gospel of Thomas, Logion 28 (P. Labib, pl. 86, 20–31):

Jesus has
said: I have stayed in the midst of the world,
and I have revealed myself to them in the flesh;
I have found them all drunken; I have found no one
among them who was athirst, and my soul has been troubled
for the sons of men, because they are blind
in their heart. And they do not see
that whilst empty they have come into the world; and
whilst they are empty they seek to go out of the world again.
But now they are drunken;
when they put away their wine, then will they
repent.

Pap. Ox. 1, line 23:

(Recto)
. . . . th⟩e poverty.

Only that one word of this saying has been preserved. But that
a complete saying which began on the verso and ended on the

recto stood here, appears to follow from the Gospel of Thomas, although naturally a completion of the papyrus is hardly possible.

Gospel of Thomas, Logion 29 (P. Labib, pl. 86, 31–87, 2):

Jesus has said: If the flesh
has existed (come to be?) for the sake of the spirit, then is that
 a marvel. If,
however, the spirit (has existed, come to be?) for the sake of
 the body, then is that a marvel
of marvels. But I marvel
at this: How so great wealth has
made its home in this poverty.

Pap. Ox. 1, lines 24–31:

⟨Jesus sa⟩ys: ⟨wh⟩erever there are
25. . . . . without?⟩ God, and
wh⟨ere on⟩e is alone,
I ⟨sa⟩y: I am with
hi⟨m⟩. Li⟨f⟩t up the stone
and there thou wilt find me;
30. cleave the wood, and I
am there.

This double saying is the most peculiar logion in the papyrus. Its first portion (*ll.* 24–28) is an expansion of Mt. 18:20 (cf. also Mt. 28:20); the second portion (*ll.* 28–31) is frequently understood as a pan-Christian word, which ascribes to Jesus a cosmic ubiquity, but in the context it is meant rather as a promise of the invisible presence of Jesus with His own; the Semitisms (instances in Jeremias, p. 89, ET 96) also suggest that the stone and the wood should be understood as the material of the hard human labour to which the Exalted One promises His presence (in contrast with the depreciation of stonebreaking and woodcutting in Eccles. 10:9?). In this case the Coptic parallel text affords little further help towards an understanding of the Greek papyrus, on the one hand because the double saying is divided into two single logia which appear in different passages, and on the other hand because both logia bear upon them clear traces of recasting at second hand.

Gospel of Thomas, Logion 30 (P. Labib, pl. 87, 2–5):

Jesus has said:
Where there are three gods, there
they are gods; where there are two or one, there **I am**
with him.

Gospel of Thomas, Logion 77 (P. Labib, pl. 94, 22–28):

Jesus
has said: I am the light that
is above them all. I am the All: the
All has emerged from me, and the All
has attained to me. Cleave a piece of wood—I
am there: lift a stone up—and you
will find me there.

Pap. Ox. 1, lines 31–36:

Jesus says:
A prophet is not acceptable
in his own country,
neither does a physician work
35. cures on those
who know him.

The saying is an expansion of Lk. 4:24 (Mk. 6:4; Mt. 13:57),
Lk. 4:23 being also drawn upon.

Gospel of Thomas, Logion 31 (P. Labib, pl. 87, 5–7):

Jesus has said: There is no proph-
et who is received in his own village; a physician is not wont
to cure those who know him.

Pap. Ox. 1, lines 37–42:

Jesus says: A city which is erected on the top
of a high ⟨m⟩ountain and firmly

109

40. stablished, can neither fal-
l⟩ nor remain hid-
d⟩en.

This saying also is known from the Synoptics. It is an expansion of Mt. 5:14b, the emphasis falling here on the invincibility of the Church.

Gospel of Thomas, Logion 32 (P. Labib, pl. 87, 7–10):

Jesus has said:
A city that has been erected
on a high mountain and which is fortified—it is not possible
that it should fall,
and also it cannot remain hidden.

Pap. Ox. 1, lines 42–44:

Jesus says: Thou hearest
i⟩n thy o⟨ne e⟩ar the

. . . .

The text being so fragmentary, no statement can be made about its content.

Gospel of Thomas, Logion 33 (P. Labib, pl. 87, 10–18):

Jesus has said: That which thou
wilt hear with thine ear, proclai⟨m⟩
it to another ear on your
roofs. For no one lights a lamp
to place it under a bushel, and one is not wont
to set it in a hidden place, but one is wont to set it on a
candlest-
ick so that every one who goes in
and goes out may see its
light.

(c) Oxyrhynchus Papyrus 655
(W. Schneemelcher)

Among the Oxyrhynchus papyri edited in 1904 by Grenfell and Hunt there were also several fragments which were the remains of a papyrus roll of the 2nd or 3rd century and the content of which proved to be a compilation of sayings of Jesus. There was subsequently much discussion as to whether these sayings come from a gospel and, if so, from which. Hennecke's opinion was that the similarity of one part to a citation in Clement (Julius Cassianus in Clem. Alex. *Strom.* III xiii, 92; cf. p. 168 below) indicates that the sayings come from the Gospel of the Egyptians (*Apokr.* 2, pp. 56ff.; so also J. Jeremias, *Unbekannte Jesusworte*[2], pp. 21f., ET 17). Apart from the fact that the same saying may have occurred in different gospels, it is here to be noted that the agreement between our text and the Clement citation is by no means word for word and that its derivation from the Gospel of the Egyptians could not be proved. In consequence of the discovery of the Gospel of Thomas it is at least suggested that these sayings also which are preserved in Pap. Ox. 655 come from the Gospel of Thomas (in its Greek original form?). But the situation is somewhat more difficult here than in the case of Pap. Ox. 654 and 1, as the text of 655 is very fragmentary.

Text: B. P. Grenfell and A. S. Hunt, *Ox. Pap.* IV, 1904, pp. 22–28; Wessely, *PO* IV, 2, pp. 83ff.; Klostermann, *op. cit.*, pp. 23f.; Bonaccorsi, *op. cit.*, pp. 34ff. Cf. also J. Jeremias, *Unbek. Jesusworte*[2], p. 81 (ET 86f.).

Pap. Ox. 655, Fragment Ia:

From early until ⟨late
nor⟩ from eveni⟨ng⟩
until⟩ early neither⟨
about food⟩ for you, what you
should eat nor⟩ about c⟨lothing
for you⟩, what you should
pu⟩t on. Much
bet⟩ter ⟨are⟩ you than ⟨the
li⟩lies which card not
neither do they spin[1].
If you have a ⟨garment⟩
. . . . . . also

Fragment Ib:

you? Who can
add to your age?
He himself will give
to you your garment.
His disciples
say to him:
When wilt thou be
manifest to us and when
shall we see thee? He says:
When you undress and
are not ashamed
. . . .

Whereas in Ib there are hardly any gaps, many of the completions in Ia are open to question. In Ib there follow about 6 lines of which single letters can be read (cf. Santos, p. 82). For the first saying, which comprises *ll.* 1–16, reference should be made to Mt. 6:25ff.; Lk. 12:22ff. With the second saying cf. the citation from Clement mentioned above.

[3] Cf. JTS 13 (1962), pp. 331f.

Gospel of Thomas, Logion 36 (P. Labib, pl. 87, 24–27):

> Jesus has said: Be not anxious from
> morning to evening and from evening
> to morning wherewith you will
> clothe you.

Gospel of Thomas, Logion 37 (P. Labib, pl. 87, 27–88, 2):

> His disciples have said: On which
> day wilt thou reveal (thyself) to us and on which
> day shall we see thee? Jesus has said: When
> you undress and are not
> ashamed, and (when) you take your garments
> and cast them upon the ground under your feet
> in the manner of little children
> and tread on them, then ⟨will
> you see⟩ the Son of him who lives, and you will
> not be afraid.

Pap. Ox. 655, Fragment II:

> they have ⟨obtained the keys
> of the ⟨kingdom and
> them they have hid⟨den, they themselves
> go ⟨not⟩ in ⟨and those
> who ⟨wish to go⟩ in ⟨ they have
> not al⟨lowed to go in. But you,
> be wise
> as ⟨serpents and without
> guile ⟨as do-
> ves . . . .
> . . . .

The translation depends largely on Santos' reconstruction (p. 83), which is indeed plausible, but, like every restoration of a text which consists merely of a series of letters, it remains hypothetical. In front there are eleven lines of which one or two letters each are preserved; there follow six lines in which still less can be read (cf. Santos, p. 83). Naturally the reconstruction is determined to a considerable extent by the parallels Mt. 23:13, Lk. 11:52 and Mt.

10:16, but is supported by logion 39 of the Gospel of Thomas. Whether logia 38 and 40 of the Coptic Gospel of Thomas were also in the Greek text of our papyrus is not certain, but that may be conjectured.

Gospel of Thomas, Logion 38 (P. Labib, pl. 88, 2–7):

Jesus has said: Many times have you
desired to hear these words of mine
which I say to you, and you have not another
from whom to hear them; there will
come days when you will seek me,
and you will not find me.

Gospel of Thomas, Logion 39 (P. Labib, pl. 88, 7–13):

Jesus has said: The Pharisees
and the scribes have obtained the keys
of knowledge. They have hidden them and have not gone in,
and those who wished to go in
they have not allowed; but you, be wise
as serpents and pure as
doves.

Gospel of Thomas, Logion 40 (P. Labib, pl. 88, 13–16):

Jesus has said: A vine has
been planted outside of the Father and has not
established itself. It will be torn up by its root, and it
will go to ruin.

4. OTHER GREEK PAPYRUS FRAGMENTS
(*W. Schneemelcher*)

Here three papyrus fragments may follow which clearly have their place in the present context, although as yet it has not been possible to assign the fragments of text which they contain to a definite gospel.

(*a*) Oxyrhynchus Papyrus 1224

The remains of a papyrus book, the writing of which points to the beginning of the 4th century, were also published by Grenfell

and Hunt (Ox. Pap. 1224 = *Ox. Pap.* X, 1914, pp. 1–10). The
pages were numbered (there can still be recognized the numbers
139, 174 and 176; with these there belong 138 or 140, 173 and
175). The condition of the pages permits only a partially trustworthy reading of them. In the present state of our knowledge the
identification of the fragments with a gospel is not possible.

Text: Wessely, *PO* XVIII, pp. 266ff.; Klostermann, *op. cit.*, p. 26;
Bonaccorsi, *op. cit.*, p. 40 (where, however, only one fragment is given).

p. 175
And the scribes and ⟨Pharisees
and priests, when they sa⟨w
him, were angry ⟨that with sinners in the midst he ⟨reclined
at table. But Jesus heard ⟨it and said:
The he⟨althy need not the physician.

p. 176
      And pray for
your enemies. For he who is not
against you⟩ is for you.
He who today⟩ is far-off—tomorrow will be
near to you⟩ . . . .

. . . .

The remaining fragments are not translated here, since they are
handed down in too poor a state. With p. 175 cf. Mk. 2:16–17
and par. With p. 176 cf. Mt. 5:44 (Lk. 6:27f.) and Mk. 9:40
(Lk. 9:50). Cf. also Jeremias, *Unbek. Jesusworte*[2], pp. 79f. (ET
85f.).

(*b*) Papyrus Cairensis 10 735

Grenfell and Hunt also claimed as a survival from a non-
canonical gospel the content of a page of papyrus of the 6th or
7th century (*Catalogue général des antiquités égyptiennes du Musée du
Caire*, vol. X, Oxford 1903, No. 10 735). But A. Deissmann brought
forward objections to this assumption and was of opinion that here
it is a matter rather of a text from a commentary or from a homily
(A. Deissmann, "Das angebliche Evangelienfragment von Kairo"
in *AR* 7, 1904, pp. 387–392; reprinted in *Licht vom Osten*[4], 1923,
pp. 368–371, ET 1927, 430–434). The objections expressed by

Deissmann still stand, although his completions and explanations are not accepted. But an identification of the text has not so far been possible. Only this is settled, that it has to do with the proclamation of the birth of Jesus and the flight to Egypt, i.e. that here material from a gospel is presented—but whether as excerpt or homily remains open.

Text: Besides in Deissmann, *op. cit.*, also in Klostermann *op. cit.*, p. 24; Bonaccorsi, *op. cit.*, pp. 32ff.

Recto
The angel of the Lord spake: Jo⟨seph, arise,
take Mary, thy w⟨ife and
flee to Egypt ⟨ . . . .
. . . .
. . . .
every gift and if ⟨ . . . . . .
his friends . . . ⟨ . . . .
of the king . . ⟨ . . . .
. . . .

Verso
  (According to Deissmann's reconstruction)
. . . ⟩ should interpret to thee. The
archistrategus however⟩ said to the virgin: Behold,
Elisabeth, thy relat⟩ive has also conceived, and it is the s⟩ixth month for her who
was called barren. In⟩ the sixth, that is ⟨in the month
      Thoth,
did his mother⟩ conceive John.
But it behoved⟩ the archistra-
tegus to an⟩nounce ⟨beforehand John, the⟩ servant who goes before his Lord's⟩ coming . . .

With the recto cf. Mt. 2:13; with the verso Lk. 1:36.

(c) The so-called Fayyum Fragment
In the collection of papyri of the Archduke Rainer at Vienna G. Bickell found in 1885 a fragment of the 3rd century which caused considerable sensation, the opinion being that it provided a first step to the formation of the Synoptic Gospels (cf. Mk.

14:27, 29f.). The publication of the papyrus (*Mittheilungen aus der Sammlung der Papyrus Erzh. Rainer* I, 1887, pp. 54–61) was followed by a wealth of hypotheses (cf. literature in *Handbuch* p. 21 and *Apokr.* 2, p. 38). But here also a secondary, indeed an abridged rendering of the Synoptic material has to be assumed, and the text must be considered an excerpt or fragment of a gospel that hitherto has been unknown to us. The brevity of the fragment forbids sure statements of any kind: the completions also remain questionable.

Text: It is also in Wessely, *PO* IV, 2, pp. 79ff.; Klostermann, *op. cit.*, p. 23; Bonaccorsi, *op. cit.*, p. 30ff.; for the literature see above.

> As⟩ he led them out, he said: ⟨All ye
> in this⟩ night will be offend-
> ed, as⟩ it is written: I will smite the ⟨shepherd,
> and the⟩ sheep will be scattered.
> When⟩ Peter ⟨said⟩: Even if all, ⟨not I,
> Jesus said:⟩ Before the cock crows twice, ⟨thrice
> wilt thou⟩ de⟨ny me today.

III

JEWISH–CHRISTIAN GOSPELS

(P. Vielhauer)

Texts and Literature: E. Preuschen, *Antilegomena*, 2nd ed. 1905; E. Klostermann, *Apocrypha* II, 3rd ed. 1929 (*KlT* 8); W. Bauer, *Das Leben Jesu im ZA der ntl. Apokryphen*, 1909; A. Schmidtke, *Neue Fragmente und Untersuchungen zu den judenchristlichen Evangelien* (*TU* 37, 1, 1911); A. Meyer, *Handb.*, pp. 21ff., 42ff. (the older literature is given here, also a sketch of the history of research); H. Waitz, *Apokr.* 2, pp. 10ff. (with literature), 17ff., 39ff., 48ff.; M. Dibelius, *Geschichte der urchristlichen Literatur* I, 1926; E. Amann, *Dictionnaire de la Bible*, Suppl. 1, 1926, 470–475; Walter Bauer, *RGG*² II, 6, 1673; IV, 473; id., *Rechtgläubigkeit und Ketzerei im ältesten Christentum* 1934; A. Schmidtke, "Zum Hebräerevangelium" in *ZNW* 35 (1936), 24ff.; H. Waitz, "Neue Untersuchungen über die sogenannten judenchristlichen Evangelien" in *ZNW* 36 (1937), 60ff.; G. Bardy, "Saint Jérôme et l'évangile selon les Hébreux" in *Mélanges de science religieuse* III (1946), 5ff.

On the History of Jewish Christianity: M. Simon, *Verus Israel*, 1948; J.-B. Colon, *Dictionnaire de la Bible*, Suppl. 4, 1949, 1298–1315; H. J. Schoeps, *Theologie und Geschichte des Judenchristentums*, 1949; id., *Aus frühchristlicher Zeit*, 1950; S. G. F. Brandon, *The Fall of Jerusalem and the Christian Church*, 1951, ²1957; J. L. Teicher, "The Dead Sea Scrolls—Documents of the Jewish Christian Sect of Ebionites" in *Journal of Jewish Studies* 2 (1951), 67ff.; H. J. Schoeps, "Ebionite Christianity" in *JTS* NS 4, 1953, 219ff.; id., "Das gnostische Judentum in den Dead Sea Scrolls" in *Zeitschr. f. Religions-u.Geistesgesch.* 1954, 1ff.; O. Cullmann, "Die neuentdeckten Qumrantexte und das Judenchristentum der Pseudoklementinen" in *Neutestamentliche Studien für Rudolf Bultmann*, *BZNW* 21 (1954), 35ff.; J. Jocz, *The Jewish People and Jesus Christ*, 1954; L. Goppelt, *Christentum und Judentum im ersten und zweiten Jahrhundert*, 1954; J. A. Fitzmyer, "The Qumran Scrolls, the Ebionites and their Literature" in *Theological Studies* 16 (1955), 335ff. (Reprinted in Stendahl, *The Scrolls and the NT* (London 1958) 208ff.); G. Strecker, *Das Judenchristentum in den Pseudoklementinen* (*TU* 70) 1958; O. Cullmann, "The significance of the Qumran texts for research into the beginnings of Christianity" in *JBL* 74 (1955), 213–226 (Reprinted in Stendahl *op. cit.* 18ff.); H. J. Schoeps, *Urgemeinde, Judenchristentum, Gnosis*, 1956; id., "Die ebionitische Wahrheit des Christentums" in *The Background of the NT and its Eschatology* (Studies in Honour of C. H. Dodd), 1956, 115ff.; Santos, pp. 32–57.

INTRODUCTION: THE TESTIMONIES OF THE EARLY CHURCH REGARDING JEWISH-CHRISTIAN GOSPELS

In the second edition of this work H. Waitz rightly described the problem of the Jewish-Christian Gospels (JG) as one of the most difficult which the apocryphal literature presents, "difficult because of the scantiness and indefiniteness of the patristic testimonies, difficult also because the results of scientific investigation are often self-contradictory" (p. 10). There are preserved, mostly as citations in the Church fathers, only small fragments from which conclusions as to the character of the whole book are difficult to draw, and also accounts which are in themselves often very vague and in their entirety make possible a whole kaleidoscope of interpretations. The Church fathers hand down the title of only one JG, that of the Gospel of the Hebrews (Gospel according to the Hebrews). On the basis of their accounts it is possible to see in this Gospel of the Hebrews either with Jerome the Gospel of the Nazaraeans or with Epiphanius that of the Ebionites or with Eusebius an independent entity and so to distinguish it from each of these. A problem in itself is the relationship of a "Gospel of the Twelve (Apostles)"—it is mentioned by Origen and identified by Jerome with the Gospel of the Hebrews—to these or to one of these JG (on this see H.-Ch. Puech, p. 264 below). Thus the number of the JG—whether there be one, two or three such Gospels—is uncertain, the identification of the several fragments is also uncertain, and finally the character and the relationship to one another of the several JG is uncertain.

Reflecting these uncertainties, investigation has led to numerous hypotheses but to no generally recognized result. Information about its position, which until now has not changed, is given in an article by Waitz (*ZNW* 36, 1937, 60ff.). The older view that there was only one JG or two adaptations of this JG has been abandoned, and now two theories are in competition, of which the one distinguishes two and the other three JG. The first of these, which depends upon some degree of confidence in the accounts of Jerome, distinguishes the Gospel of the Hebrews (= the Gospel of the Nazaraeans) and the Gospel of the Ebionites (= the Gospel of the Twelve Apostles)—so, e.g., Klostermann; the other considers that the Gospel of the Nazaraeans,[1] the Gospel of the Hebrews and the Gospel of the Ebionites are different entities— so, with differences in detail, Waitz, Dibelius and Bauer.

---

[1] The designation of this JG varies in the sources. I have on each occasion been guided by the author cited, but have myself used the designation Gospel of the Nazaraeans although the group from which the work comes was probably called the Nazoraeans.

Schmidtke's identification of the Gospel of the Ebionites with the Gospel of the Hebrews has met with violent rejection.

It seems to me that the assumption of three JG most easily does justice to the texts and accounts and their uncertainties. But as regards the state of the sources the statement of Dibelius cannot be firmly enough underlined: "Enlightenment is to be expected not from new hypotheses but only from new discoveries" (*Geschichte der urchristlichen Literatur* I, 1926, 55). How right he was the discovery at Nag Hammadi has shown (see the passage on Clement Alex. below). The following investigation concentrates on critical analysis and does not purpose to cover over the gaps in our knowledge of the JG with hypothetical constructions; it attempts to make do with a minimum of such hypotheses. Having persuaded himself of the existence of three JG, the author had to allot to the different books the fragments that have been handed down; when on this more technical ground a decision had to be taken where a *non liquet* would rather have been in order, its hypothetical character has always been made clear.

1. *Irenaeus* gives the earliest testimony—it is admittedly indirect —to the existence of a JG. He reports that the Jewish-Christian sect of the Ebionites used only one Gospel, that of Matthew (*adv. haer.* I xxii; III xi, 10 Harvey). But when in other places he says that they had eliminated the virgin birth (III xxiii; V i, 3), it is clear that the Gospel used by them cannot have been the canonical Mt., and that Irenaeus had not himself seen this book; otherwise he would not have been able to identify it with Mt. This JG had apparently no special title.

2. *Clement of Alexandria* on the other hand mentions a "Gospel according to the Hebrews" and quotes from it an apocryphal saying of Jesus (*Strom.* II ix, 45). He adduces this saying once again in *Strom.* V xiv, 96 in a longer version, but without stating where he found it. That this version gives the full text is clear from Pap. Ox. 654, in which the logion in question in its longer version occurs as the second of six sayings of the Lord. Waitz (*Apokr.* 2, 49ff.) has assigned the complete text of the papyrus to the Gospel of the Hebrews (GH). But he has done so wrongly, for this text is found in its entirety in the same sequence in the Coptic Gospel of Thomas discovered at Nag Hammadi (see pp. 97ff. above). This discovery makes it doubtful if the saying quoted by Clement should be assigned to the GH. It is, however, quite possible that it stood in both Gospels. If in this state of affairs conclusions as to the character of the GH in respect of its form and content must be reserved, Clement testifies nevertheless to

the existence of a "Gospel according to the Hebrews" that was well known in Egypt.

3. *Origen* also quotes the "Gospel according to the Hebrews" (*in Joh.* vol. II, 12) and indeed a saying of Jesus about His being carried away; His mother, the Holy Spirit, took Him by one of His hairs and carried Him to the high mountain Tabor. This account is adduced once again by Origen but without any statement as to where he found it (*in Jer.* vol. XV, 4). In this quotation we have to do with a variant of the story not of the transfiguration but of the temptation (Mt. 4:1–11 and pars.; cf. Walter Bauer, *Das Leben Jesu*, pp. 143ff.; Waitz, *Apokr.* 2, p. 13). The deviations from the canonical account are very considerable; out of the report given by the Evangelists has come an account given by Jesus Himself of His experience, the devil is replaced by the Holy Spirit, and the Holy Spirit is identified with the mother of Jesus. This last trait presupposes the Semitic conception of the Spirit, since in the Semitic tongues the Spirit is *femini generis*, but it does not imply that the GH was originally written in Hebrew or in Aramaic (Waitz, p. 52; for further particulars see Bauer, *loc. cit.*). The mythological conception of the Holy Spirit as the mother of Jesus separates the GH from the canonical nativity narratives and also from the conception of Joseph as the father of Jesus that obtained among the Ebionites of whose Gospel Irenaeus speaks; the GH cannot have been identical with that Gospel.

A further quotation from the GH occurs in the Latin revision of Origen's commentary on Matthew (*in Matth.*, vol. XV, p. 389, Benz–Klostermann), a fictional development of Mt. 19:16–24. Schmidtke (pp. 90–94) has with reason made it probable that this quotation was inserted in the commentary not by Origen himself but by the later reviser and also that it does not come from the GH used by Origen (otherwise Bardy, p. 29). Certain indications, such as the singling out of Simon ("dixit Simoni discipulo suo") connect this pericope with the Gospel fragment in Jerome *adv. Pelag.* ("dixit illi Simon discipulus eius"), whilst the address "Simon, fili Jonae" (not: Simon, son of John; so Waitz, p. 13) points rather to Mt. 16:17 than to the scholium of the Judaikon, which in this place gives "son of John" (cod. Ev. 566).

4. *Eusebius.* The accounts of the JG given by Eusebius are in his Church History (*Historia Ecclesiastica*, *H.E.*), partly in his comments on the history of the canon and partly in the information he gives about Papias and Hegesippus; he adduces direct quotations from JG only in his *Theophania*.

In his statements about the compass of the canon Eusebius mentions the GH and its constituency.

To these [i.e. to the spurious writings] some reckon the Gospel according to the Hebrews in which especially those Hebrews who have become converted to Christ find delight (*H.E.* III. xxv, 5).

The readers of the GH were above all Jewish Christians; the designation "Hebrews" indicates where they belonged as a people, but not their tongue; according to the context these Jewish Christians in the time of Eusebius used the GH side by side with the four canonical Gospels. It was otherwise with a special school of thought among the Ebionites: the members of this school, in contrast to the ordinary Ebionites, recognized the virgin birth of Jesus although they called His pre-existence in question (*H.E.* III. xxvii, 1–3).[1]

. . . as they use only the so-called Gospel according to the Hebrews, they attach little value to the rest (*H.E.* III. xxvii, 4).

Since two fragments of the GH assume the pre-existence of Jesus, this Ebionite group either did not dispute it or did not read the GH. But apart from this question, this note shows that for Eusebius the GH was not identical with the gospel which according to Irenaeus was used by the ordinary Ebionites.

The note of Papias of Hierapolis (*c.* 150) quoted by Eusebius, that Mt. collected the sayings of the Lord in "the Hebrew tongue" and that every one interpreted them as he was able (*H.E.* III. xxxix, 16), was meant to defend the Gospel of Matthew from being used improperly, as in the opinion of this churchman of Asia Minor heretics were using it (W. Bauer, *Rechtgläubigkeit*, pp. 187ff., 207f.); but it is at most an indirect witness for a specifically Jewish-Christian Gospel, if Schmidtke's conjecture should be right (46f.), that the statements of Papias were occasioned by accounts of an Aramaic revision of the Gospel of Matthew.

After observing that Papias also used 1 Jn. and 1 Pet., Eusebius says:

And he has adduced another story of a woman who was accused of many sins before the Lord, which is contained in the Gospel according to the Hebrews (*H.E.* III. xxxix, 17).

The statement of the place where this story was found clearly comes not from Papias but from Eusebius (Schmidtke, pp. 149ff.; Waitz, *Apokr.* 2, p. 11; id. in *ZNW* 36, 1937, p. 68). What story is meant is uncertain. As it cannot be identical with Lk. 7:36–50 —otherwise Eusebius would not have assigned it to the apocryphal GH—it has since Rufinus been readily equated with the *pericope*

[1] This information comes from Origen (*c. Celsum*, V, 65, p. 68 Koetschau). There is dispute as to what sort of a group we are here concerned with (cf. Schoeps, *Theologie und Geschichte des Judenchristentums*, p. 16).

adulterae (Jn. 7:53—8:11), which originally did not belong to Jn. and is found there for the first time in codex D; but it is already attested earlier by the Syriac *Didascalia* (Achelis-Flemming, *TU* 25. 2, 1904, 38f.), and here the woman is not called an adulteress but a sinner, as in Jn. 8:3 D (cf. W. Bauer, *Das Johannesevangelium*, 3rd ed. 1933, 115ff.). But this evidence does not suffice either for the identification of the story adduced by Papias with the pseudo-Johannine pericope in the version of cod. D or for conclusions as to the literary character of the apocryphal gospel. That the story adduced by Papias lies before us in Jn. 7:53ff. is merely a possible hypothesis; if Eusebius localizes it in the GH, he must have found it there; and nothing justifies our assigning it to the Gospel of the Nazaraeans and fixing its original position between Mt. 22:22 and 23 (against Waitz, *Apokr.* 2, 11f.; 18).

Regarding Hegesippus and his "Memoirs" Eusebius reports:

> He quotes both from the Gospel according to the Hebrews and from the Syriac (Gospel) and in particular some words in the Hebrew tongue, showing that he was a convert from the Hebrews (*H.E.* IV. xxii, 8).

The attempts frequently undertaken to equate the GH and the "Syriac Gospel" with one another are abortive; because of the Greek syntax Eusebius' sentence can only be understood as meaning that Hegesippus quoted two different Gospels, the GH and a Syriac one, i.e. one written in Aramaic, and that Eusebius also distinguishes these. The "Hebrew tongue" is as elsewhere in Eusebius the Aramaic, the "mother-tongue" of the "Hebrews"; the quotations "in the Hebrew tongue" come therefore not from the GH but from the "Syriac Gospel". That Eusebius designated this as "Syriac" contrary to his usage elsewhere, may be put down to Hegesippus' account (Schmidtke, pp. 51ff.). Although Eusebius speaks frequently elsewhere of the "Hebrew" proto-Matthew (III xxiv, 6; xxxix, 16; V viii, 2; x, 3; VI xxv, 4), he nowhere identifies it with the "Syriac" Gospel known to Hegesippus; this identification therefore ought not to be ascribed to him (against Schmidtke, *op. cit.*); the early Church historian was more sparing of such hypotheses than the moderns. From the fact that in the *H.E.* he gives no quotations from either of the two JG it ought not to be concluded that at the time he wrote the *H.E.* he did not know them (against Schmidtke and Waitz): he at least knew the GH if he identified the Papias story of the woman that was a sinner, and of the Syriac Gospel he knew at any rate the quotations in the Memoirs of Hegesippus.

In the *Theophania* (c. 333) Eusebius adduces two quotations from JG and introduces them in a peculiar way:

... as we have found somewhere or other in the Gospel which is (in circulation) among the Jews in the Hebrew tongue ... (*Theoph.* IV 12).

Since the Gospel that has come down to us in the Hebrew script turns the threat not against him who ... , I put myself the question whether according to Matthew ... (Mai, *Nova Patr. Bibl.* IV, 1, 155).

In this JG it is clearly not a matter of the GH, for this is regularly given the fixed designation "Gospel according to the Hebrews", but of a Gospel of no fixed name; Eusebius characterizes it by its tongue, script and constituency as an Aramaic gospel. He clearly puts a space between it and the Greek Mt., to which on both occasions he adduces it as a parallel; but nothing indicates that he considered it as its Aramaic original (against Schmidtke, pp. 55ff.). If in the *H.E.* he treats the "Hebrew" Mt. as a bygone entity and as a curious fact records that an exemplar of it had survived among the Indians down to the time of Pantaenus (V x, 3), then in the *Theophania* he would assuredly have underlined the new appearance of the original Matthew otherwise than by the phrase "the Gospel that has come down to us in the Hebrew script", had he seen the former in the latter. Again, he does not connect it with the Syriac Gospel known to Hegesippus; it is uncertain whether he regarded the two as identical, but likely that they were identical; for of the existence of two JG in the Aramaic tongue nothing is otherwise known.

Eusebius thus knew two JG: first the GH also mentioned by Hegesippus, Clement and Origen, which was already known to Papias and which was supposed to have been used as their only gospel by a particular group of the heretical Ebionites; and second an Aramaic gospel from which Hegesippus and he himself quote.

5. *Epiphanius* in his "Panarion" enlarges at great length regarding the Jewish-Christian sects of the Nazoraeans and Ebionites. *Haer.* 29 is devoted to the history and teaching of the Nazoraeans, the Syrian Jewish-Christians; Schmidtke (pp. 95–126) has analysed this conglomerate of tradition and phantasy and with regard to the home of this sect has come to the conclusion (pp. 98ff.) that the only substantiated piece of information is "this sect dwells in Beroea in Coelesyria" (29, 7.7). Their canon comprised not merely the New but also the whole of the Old Testament, and the latter the Nazoraeans read in Hebrew (29, 7. 2. 4). In conclusion Epiphanius speaks of the Gospels:

They have the Gospel according to Matthew complete and in Hebrew. For this is evidently still preserved among them, as it was originally written, in Hebrew script. But I do not know whether they have removed the genealogy from Abraham to Christ (*Haer.* 29, 9. 4).

Two points are here worthy of note: (1) the Gospel of the Nazoraeans is the complete Hebrew original Matthew; (2) as his last observation shows, Epiphanius had not himself seen the book, and also he had not heard of anything (such as misrepresentation or abridgment) against it.

How is this note to be judged against the background of what has already been said? Eusebius had sharply distinguished between the "Hebrew" original of Matthew, which he knew merely as a forgotten entity of the past, and the "Gospel (written) in Hebrew letters which has come down to us", the "Gospel which is (in circulation) among the Jews in the Hebrew tongue". If we are unwilling to assume that there were different "Hebrew" Gospels among the Jewish-Christian sects, then nothing stands in the way of the assumption that the "Jews" of Eusebius are the Nazoraeans of Epiphanius and that the Gospel composed in "Hebrew" of these latter is the Gospel composed in the Hebrew script and tongue of the former. The identification, which Eusebius has avoided, of this JG with the Hebrew original Matthew occurs for the first time in Epiphanius, but is probably to be accredited to his tradition. Since he can impute to it nothing heretical or non-Matthaean, the Gospel of the Nazoraeans must have been an Aramaic version of Mt. (and was possibly identical with the Syriac Gospel known to Hegesippus). It is to be underlined that Epiphanius as little as Eusebius designates this "Hebrew", i.e. Aramaic JG as GH.

Epiphanius gives more numerous accounts of the Gospel of the Ebionites (*Haer.* 30), and he also communicates a few fragments from it. After relating a little about Ebion, the alleged founder of the sect, and his Christology, he says with regard to the Ebionites:

> And they too receive the Gospel according to Matthew. For this they too use, as do the followers of Cerinthus and Merinthus, to the exclusion of all others. But they call it (the Gospel) according to the Hebrews, for, to speak truthfully, Matthew alone of New Testament writers presents and proclaims the gospel in Hebrew and in the Hebrew script (*Haer.* 30, 3. 7).

In the opinion of this Church father the only Gospel which the Ebionites use is the Gospel of Matthew; but evidently they call it not the Gospel of Matthew but the Gospel according to the Hebrews and do so, as he adds in an aetiological comment, because Matthew wrote his Gospel "in Hebrew". It is striking that in giving this description he does not identify the Gospel of the Nazoraeans with that of the Ebionites; he neither states that the latter was still read in Hebrew as he has said of the former, nor does he call the former GH as he names the latter. That the two cannot be identical and are not so for Epiphanius, is shown by another note on the Gospel of the Ebionites:

> In the Gospel used by them, that called "according to Matthew", which however is not wholly complete but falsified and mutilated–they call it the "Hebrew (Gospel)"—it is recorded . . . (*Haer.* 30, 13. 2).

As title Epiphanius no longer gives GH but the Hebrew Gospel. But both mean the same thing: the book composed originally in Hebrew in accordance with *Haer.* 30, 3. 7. All the same as regards the Gospel of the Ebionites it is not a question of the Hebrew original Matthew; whilst the Gospel of the Nazoraeans is the Hebrew and complete Mt., that of the Ebionites is merely a "so-called Matthew" and as compared with the real Mt. is falsified and abridged. Over these abridgments and falsifications the Church father very much loses his temper in the following:

> They have cut away the genealogy in Matthew and, as has already been said, have let the Gospel begin in this way: It came to pass, it is said, in the days of Herod, the king of Judaea, when Caiaphas was high priest, that there came a certain man John by name and baptized with the baptism of repentance in the river Jordan (*Haer.* 30, 14. 3).

Since the Gospel begins with the appearance of the Baptist, it lacks the whole nativity narrative Mt. 1 and 2. The fragments adduced below may convey an impression of the distortions.

The statements of Epiphanius regarding the Gospel of the Ebionites agree with those of Irenaeus in this, that the Ebionites use only a single Gospel and that this is a Gospel of Matthew; further in this, that this sect denies the virgin birth. That the Gospel in question cannot then have been the canonical Mt., Irenaeus does not indeed say, but Epiphanius does so all the more clearly. New in Epiphanius as compared with Irenaeus is the communication of the title, the Gospel of the Hebrews or the Hebrew Gospel, and the aetiology of the Church father for this title. That the Ebionites themselves gave it that name is, however, more than doubtful. For on the one hand the earlier ecclesiastical writers never associate the GH with Mt. On the other hand Epiphanius bestows this title (GH) even on Tatian's Gospel Harmony which was rejected by the great Church:

> It is said that from him [Tatian] there comes the Diatessaron, which is also called the Gospel according to the Hebrews (*Haer.* 46, 1).

On the motive of this identification see Schmidtke, pp. 167f. This assuredly false statement casts suspicion on the entitling also of the Gospel of the Ebionites; it certainly does not rest on trust-worthy tradition, but is a combination made by Epiphanius. He may have been inspired to associate the two documents by the comment of Eusebius (*H.E.* III. xxvii, 4) that a special school of thought among the Ebionites used only the GH; a further link in the equation is his own aetiological explanation of the title.

Whence Epiphanius obtained his knowledge of the Gospel of the Ebionites, is disputed. The assumption that he had it in his hands and made excerpts from it (Waitz, *Apokr.* 2, 14f.) is the one nearest at hand and least cumbered with hypotheses. Whilst he knows the Gospel of the Nazoraeans only from hearsay and with regard to the GH is aware of little more than the title, the Gospel of the Ebionites is familiar to him, as his citations show. This last must be differentiated in accordance with his own statements from the Gospel of the Nazoraeans and also for the reasons already mentioned from the GH. We are concerned here with three different entities.

6. *Jerome.* The most numerous citations and the most numerous but also the most perplexing accounts of JG have been handed down by Jerome. Critical investigations have not yet led to any generally recognized result. It is above all uncertain how far the statements of this Church father ought to be trusted and how far conclusions ought to be drawn from them as to the tongue, compass and literary character of the JG. The identification of the several fragments is a further problem; in the present state of research no complete certainty can be obtained in regard to either of these two questions. Only this is certain, that Jerome has always only one JG in mind. The styling varies: he calls it on seven occasions the Gospel according to the Hebrews, on two occasions the Gospel of the Hebrews, on three occasions the Hebrew Gospel, on two occasions the Hebrew Gospel according to Matthew, and on two occasions he tells us that this designation is an hypothesis of others; also on one occasion he calls it the Gospel according to the Apostles. Thus he means always the GH and regards it as the Hebrew original Matthew.

Jerome cites his JG for the first time in his *Commentary on Ephesians* (on 5: 4), which appeared in 386–387, and does so with the introductory formula: "As we also read in the Hebrew Gospel", without describing it more closely as later he always does; that seems to indicate that he took the citation not from the Gospel itself, but from one of his exegetical texts, which however can no more be identified. The next citation—the report by Jesus, adduced also by Origen, of His being carried away by His mother, the Holy Spirit—is found in the *Commentary on Micah* (on 7:6) written between 390 and 392 and is introduced:

> He who . . . believes in the Gospel according to the Hebrews which I have recently translated.

This translation must therefore have appeared shortly before 390. In spite of the certainty with which Jerome speaks of it, doubt cannot be suppressed; for Origen cites this passage of the GH twice without giving any hint that the GH was not composed originally in Greek, and it cannot be understood why Jerome should have translated a book that already for a long time had been available in Greek.

In the *de viris inlustribus* (392–393) he speaks repeatedly of the GH.

> Also the Gospel which is called "according to the Hebrews" and which was recently translated by me into Greek and Latin speech, which Origen also used frequently . . . (*vir. inl.* 2).

According to that the original of the GH was composed in a Semitic tongue. The reference to Origen indicates that Jerome took the citation from him and not from the GH itself (Schmidtke 135; Bardy 9f.). The Semitic original is for him the "Hebrew" proto-Matthew.

> Matthew in Judaea was the first to compose the gospel of Christ in the Hebrew character and speech for the sake of those who came over to the faith from Judaism; who he was who later translated it into Greek is no longer known with certainty. Further the Hebrew text itself is still preserved in the library at Caesarea which the martyr Pamphilus collected with great care. The Nazaraeans in Beroea, a city of Syria, who use this book, also permitted me to copy it. In it it is to be noted that wherever the evangelist adduces testimonies from the OT—be this done by himself or by our Lord and Saviour— he follows not the Septuagint translation but the Hebrew original text (*vir. inl.* 3).

Jerome can hardly have seen the Hebrew original of Mt. in the library at Caesarea, for Eusebius never says anything about such a treasure in his library and never identifies an unknown JG with the Hebrew original of Matthew. What we are concerned with here must be an Aramaic Gospel—the one from which come the citations in the *Theophania*—and this Jerome equates with the original Matthew. Whether he knew the Caesarean exemplar from having himself seen it, is open to question. At all events he does not imply that he derives his information from it. For he notes—in order of course to show his familiarity with this work— that this Gospel was used by the Nazaraeans in Beroea and that he had copied it with their permission. Since in his citations from JG he again and again refers to the Nazaraeans (or Nazarenes), he obviously implies that he obtained his information amongst them. The Coelesyrian Beroea near Aleppo was in fact a centre of the Nazoraeans, i.e. of the Syrian Jewish-Christians (Epiphanius, *Haer.* 29, 7. 7; 30, 2. 7; Bardy 11). Jerome can have had contact with them only during his stay in the desert of Chalcis, i.e. between 373 and 376 (Bardy 11); but then it is altogether inconceivable that he kept the Gospel of the Nazaraeans so long to himself and was silent about it, and cited it for the first time in 386. It is equally inconceivable that the differences between the Gospel of the Nazaraeans and the canonical Matthew can have struck him so little that he could consider the latter to be the translation of the former. The conclusion is inevitable that it was not the Nazaraeans who communicated to him his knowledge of this Gospel.

In critical examination of the JG the paragraph *de viris inlustribus* 16 has played a decisive rôle. In it Jerome asserts that Ignatius quotes the GH in his *Epistle to Polycarp*:

> Ignatius . . . writes in particular (an epistle) to Polycarp . . . , in which he also adduces a testimony about the person of Christ from the Gospel which was recently translated by me; he says: "And I have also seen him in the flesh after the resurrection and believe that he is. And when he came to Peter and to those who were with Peter, he said to them: Behold, handle me and see that I am no bodiless demon. And forthwith they touched him and believed."

Years later (in 408–409) in his *Commentary on Isaiah* (XVIII, preface) he cites the saying about the bodiless demon, but without reference to Ignatius:

> Since that is to say the disciples took him for a spirit or according to the Gospel of the Hebrews, which the Nazaraeans read, for a bodiless demon . . .

The statement of *de viris inlustribus* 16 is much disputed; whilst it serves Waitz as basis for far-reaching constructions, Bardy categorically calls its accuracy in question. The fact cannot be denied that in this passage Jerome makes two solid mistakes. In the first place the passage cited from Ignatius stands not in his epistle to Polycarp but in that to the Smyrnaeans; and then Jerome understands the first sentence ("and I have also seen him in the flesh after the resurrection" etc.) as part of the fragment said to be quoted by Ignatius, whereas it is actually an avowal on the part of Ignatius. Ignatius writes:

> And I know and believe that even after his resurrection he was in the flesh. And when he came to those about Peter, he said to them:

Lay hold, handle me and see that I am no bodiless demon. And forthwith they touched him and believed, being closely joined to his flesh and spirit (*Smyrn.* 3, 1f.).

The statement of the Church father that the passage stood in the Gospel of the Nazaraeans which he had translated is wrecked on the fact that the decisive notion "bodiless demon" cannot be the translation of a Semitic original.[1] That eliminates an Aramaic gospel as source; a Greek text, perhaps the GH as such, is at most what can be considered. Moreover it has long been recognized and acknowledged that when writing the *de viris inlustribus* Jerome had before him neither the text of the apocryphal Gospel nor that of the epistles of Ignatius, but the *Ecclesiastical History* of Eusebius who (III. xxxvi, 11) adduces Ign. *Smyrn.* 3, 1f.; Jerome cites the text only as far as Eusebius gives it; his assigning of it to the epistle to Polycarp finds its explanation in cursory reading, and his misunderstanding of the first sentence in the fact that he did not take in the context of the Ignatian expositions. Two points tell against the derivation of *Smyrn.* 3, 2 from a JG:

(i) Eusebius says expressly that he did not know the source of the Ignatian sentence (*H.E.* III. xxxvi, 11); since he knew the GH and an Aramaic JG and the latter according to Jerome was at hand in the library at Caesarea, Eusebius could have identified the passage in question without more ado, had it stood in a JG; that he came to know the Aramaic JG only after he had written the *H.E.* is a way out of the difficulty with which Schmidtke and Waitz would vindicate Jerome's statement about the source and make Ignatius a witness of the Gospel of the Nazaraeans. (ii) Origen (*de princ.* I prooem. 8) says that the word of the risen Jesus "I am no bodiless demon" stood in an apocryphal "Teaching of Peter". That speaks decisively against Jerome's statement about the source and eliminates also the GH known to Origen and cited by him. We may leave aside the question whether the expression "Petri doctrina" is Rufinus' rendering of κήρυγμα Πέτρου (so above all Bardy, 13f.); the attribution of the sentence to this Kerygma or to a lost Teaching of Peter remains an assumption.

What makes the identification of the Ignatian sentence uncertain is simply the expression "bodiless demon"; otherwise Eusebius would not have hesitated to see in *Smyrn.* 3, 2 a free rendering of Lk. 24:36–41, where the risen Jesus says: "Handle me and see, for a spirit hath not flesh and bones as ye see me have"

---

[1] Neither in Hebrew nor in Aramaic is there an equivalent for the Greek ἀσώματος. On the other hand this Greek vocable, as a loan word ('asomata' = incorporalia and 'asomataja' = incorporalis) taken over into the Syriac, is attested for the first time in Ephraem and in the *Breviarium Chaldaicum* (Brockelmann, *Lexicon Syriacum* 2nd ed., 1928, 35b). Cf. also on this logion H. Köster, *Synoptische Überlieferung bei den Apostolischen Vätern* (*TU* 65), 1957, pp. 50ff.

(vs. 39). It is true that Walter Bauer also is of opinion that Ignatius does not formulate *Smyrn.* 3, 2 independently but follows here a strange context, since he connects vs. 2 to what goes before it with 'and when' instead of, as the logical procedure would have been, with 'then when' (Lietzmann, *Handb. zum. NT, Die Apostolischen Väter* 1920, 266). Nevertheless, as argument for the derivation of the tradition cited by Ignatius this not quite correct linkage seems to me to have less weight than the similarity of the passage with Lk. 24:36ff.; the situation is the same, and the emphasis on Peter answers to the estimate of him in the 2nd century and is besides justified by Lk. 24:33f. The word of the risen Jesus in vs. 39b: "Handle me and see, for a spirit has not flesh and bones as ye see me have" is given a Greek formulation in *Smyrn.* 3, 2 and above all, as the context shows, is pointed against Docetism. Immediately before (in *Smyrn.* 2) Ignatius calls the docetic heretics "bodiless and demonic". The latter term is a polemical distortion of the term "pneumatic" which the Gnostics applied to themselves, and the former refers to the Gnostic understanding of redemption as the liberation of the spirit from the matter of corporeality. The characterization of the Docetics in *Smyrn.* 2 and the logion in *Smyrn.* 3, 2 harmonize terminologically the one with the other, and this they do in using and distorting the Gnostic terminology.

In my opinion the antidocetic tendency of Ignatius and the actual front-line in which he stood sufficiently explain the formulation of the saying of the Lord and make the assumption of any source other than Lk. 24:36ff. unnecessary. In the Ignatian rendering, which was easier to remember and of greater striking power than the Lucan, the logion passed into the Teaching of Peter. The dominating position of Peter and the absence of any reference to doubt on the part of the disciples do not in any way show that the Ignatian text is original, but that from the point of view of tradition-history it is secondary as compared with Luke (against Waitz, *Apokr.* 2, 10f. and *ZNW* 36, 1937, 67). Jerome was led to make his false identification simply through the uncanonical formulation of the saying and through the comment of Eusebius that he did not know Ignatius' source. Ignatius, *Smyrn.* 3, 2 drops out as a fragment of an apocryphal JG and therefore as an index to its dating.

In the *Commentary on Matthew* written shortly before 398 Jerome adduces the majority of his quotations from his JG. Of the formulae of introduction only the one to the story of the healing of the man with the withered hand is noteworthy:

> In the Gospel which the Nazarenes and the Ebionites use, which we recently translated out of the Hebrew tongue into the Greek and which is called by most people the authentic (Gospel) of Matthew...

In contrast to *de vir. inl.* 2 and 3 there is no more mention of a translation into Latin, and that this JG is to be equated with the "Hebrew" proto-Matthew is no longer described as an individual opinion but as that of "most people", who these are being left open; and this change in emphasis occurs later still (*In Ps. cxxxv tract.*: in the Hebrew Gospel according to Matthew; *adv. Pelag.* III, 2: . . . as most assume, according to Matthew; see below). The mentioning of the Ebionites as readers of this Gospel is singular in Jerome and probably a literary reminiscence from his reading of Epiphanius.

In his writings composed after the *Commentary on Matthew* Jerome no longer states that he had translated the JG. The introductory formulae characterize it as "written in Hebrew letters" (*Epist.* 120, 8 *ad Hedib.*) or as composed "in the Hebrew speech" (*Com. in Is.* on xi. 2) and usually also as read among the Nazaraeans. The most detailed citation formula is found in the *Dial. adv. Pelag.* III, 2, which appeared towards the end of 415; it introduces two citations:

> In the Gospel according to the Hebrews, which is in the Chaldaean and Syriac tongue, but written in Hebrew letters, and which the Nazarenes use to this day as (the Gospel) according to the Apostles or, as most people suppose, according to Matthew, which is also in stock in the library of Caesarea, the story tells . . .

after the citation:

> And in the same volume: . . .

What in these statements goes beyond what Jerome has already said about his JG is first the precise statement regarding the tongue and secondly the identification of it with a "Gospel according to the Apostles". As the original tongue he no longer gives Hebrew but the "Chaldaean and Syriac dialect", by which he clearly means Aramaic; in these different statements we are concerned not with a fundamental antithesis or with an indication that Jerome was informed only in 415 about the actual tongue of the JG, but with a terminological difference which finds its explanation in the fact that where Jerome speaks of a "Hebrew Gospel" he makes use of the inexact, popular designation (Bardy 19)—by the "Gospel according to the Apostles" he certainly understands the Gospel according to the Twelve Apostles which he also mentions in the prologue to his *Commentary on Matthew* side by side with other apocryphal gospels, which Origen in his *Homily on Lk. i* calls the "Gospel of the Twelve" (in Jerome's translation: "Juxta duodecim apostolos"), which is also mentioned elsewhere (by Ambrose and Theophylact) but never cited.

The statement that the Aramaic Gospel of the Nazaraeans was identical with this is supported, however, by no other evidence and is for that reason unreliable. Also we do not know whether Jerome knew more than the name of the Gospel of the Apostles and therefore we have no occasion to assign the two citations or one of them to a Gospel other than that of the Nazaraeans, and we had better renounce the conjecture that he had these fragments of the Gospel of the Twelve from the writings of Origen; for there is no citation of the kind in the preserved portions of his writings and their lost portions are no proper basis for a credible hypothesis. The mention of the Gospel of the Apostles rests in all likelihood upon the Church father's wish to let his erudition shine forth "en disant tout ce qu'il savait ou croyait savoir au sujet de l'ouvrage qu'il allait citer. Il en a trop dit et sa mémoire l'a trompé" (Bardy, 27f.).

This detailed review made in chronological order of the learned framework within which Jerome sets his citations has been necessary in order to find out what measure of confidence ought to be put in the Church father's statements. It is a very small measure. But the recognition of this should give no occasion to daring hypotheses; these can only increase the confusion which Jerome has brought about. In the following summary it is a question merely as to what can in a measure be counted as certain.

It is clear that Jerome has always only one Gospel in mind, that he designates this as the GH and that he equates it with the Aramaic Gospel of the Nazaraeans. But this equation is false and does not make head against the clear distinction between the GH (drafted in Greek) and an Aramaic JG, particularly since Clement and Origen say nothing of a Semitic original form of the GH. Jerome thus reluctantly confirms the existence of two JG, the GH and an Aramaic Gospel.

That the latter was at hand in the library in Caesarea, is not to be disputed; it is at any rate likely on the ground of the citations of Eusebius in his *Theophany*. It will likewise be correct that the Nazaraeans used such an Aramaic Gospel, since Epiphanius also testifies to this. That the Aramaic Gospel, evidence of which is given by Hegesippus and Eusebius, is identical with this Gospel of the Nazaraeans, is possible, even very probable, but not absolutely certain.

The following statements of Jerome are, however, open to question: first that he got to know the Gospel of the Nazaraeans among the Nazaraeans of the Syrian Beroea, secondly that he copied it there and thirdly that he translated it "recently", i.e. between 386 and 390. As has already been said, the chronology tells against the first two of these assertions. He must have got to know the book at another time and in another way; Bardy even thinks that he did not actually know the Nazaraeans, for he speaks of them almost in stereotyped phrases and what he records about them he may have read in Epiphanius (so Schmidtke also). Several arguments tell against the third assertion. No one has seen or mentioned the translation, and Jerome himself mentions it only between 390 and 397 and thereafter no more. It is true that the different statements regarding the original tongue (Hebrew, Chaldaean, Syriac) do not prove that he was not quite certain about that; the fact, however, that in 392–393 he speaks of a translation into Greek and Latin but in 397 only of a translation into Greek, is puzzling. The fact that in the texts which he demonstrably came upon in Greek and assuredly did not translate out of Aramaic he speaks of a translation, must intensify to scepticism our doubt as to his statements. It is therefore widely recognized that Jerome did not translate the Gospel of the Nazaraeans. He had obviously only purposed to translate it; and although unable to carry out this purpose, he spoke of it as an accomplished fact (Bardy, 32f.).

The erroneous equation of the Greek GH and the Aramaic Gospel of the Nazaraeans shows at all events that Jerome knew accurately neither of these two Gospels, for otherwise the differences in their content and character must have struck him. Apparently he worked only with fragments, a fact which also explains how he could ascribe them all to one and the same book. Whence he had the fragments cannot be said with certainty. It is disputed whether he himself had looked into the Aramaic GN and had made a note of some things that he found in it (so Waitz, *Apokr.* 2, 15) or had not done so (so Schmidtke, 66ff.; 246ff.); this question cannot by any means be settled. On his visit to Caesarea the opportunity was at all events afforded him of examining the exemplar in the library there. He certainly drew citations from literature of second rank, especially from commentaries. Origen can be identified as the source of some of his citations; as regards the others no certain or probable statement of their source can be made; all conjectures which would assert more about it are futile. That holds good in particular of the hypothesis, brought forward with as much drive as constructive power by Schmidtke, that Jerome borrowed the fragments of the GH from the commentaries of Origen and those of the GN from the commentaries of Apollinaris of Laodicea; for in the first place in the literary remains of Apollinaris nothing is found which justifies such a conjecture (Bardy, 6 note 2; 30), and besides in no citation does Jerome appeal to him as his authority, as anyhow he appeals once to Origen. The fact that he had heard and read Apollinaris is no cogent reason for the assertion that he had from him the citations in question. At all events the thesis of Schmidtke, which many have accepted, is not indisputable because the opposite cannot be proved; even as a working hypothesis it is not suitable.

Such being the state of affairs, no complete certainty can be arrived at in the matter of the identification of the several fragments. The canon drawn up confidently by Waitz (*Apokr.* 2, 15): "The question merely is in what cases Jerome has followed either Origen or Apollinaris or has obtained them on his own", does not suffice, after what has just been adduced, for a decision as to whether a fragment belongs to the GH or to the GN. It has already been said that the citation twice repeated about the "bodiless demon" is to be eliminated since it did not originate in any JG. As this instance shows, the possibility must be reckoned with that Jerome has also elsewhere attested certain texts which appealed to him and handed them down as coming from a JG; this element of uncertainty cannot be eliminated.

The trustworthy testimony of Origen must pass as evidence of membership in the GH. According to it the story of the carrying away of Jesus by His mother, the Holy Spirit (*in Mich.* vii. 7; *in Is.* xl. 19; *in Ezek.* xvi. 13), belongs assuredly to the GH, and also in all likelihood the appearance of Christ to James (*vir. inl.* 2), for which Jerome refers to the authority of the Alexandrian.

Criteria for derivation from the Aramaic GN must be: (*a*) indications that the text has a Semitic basis and (*b*) the Synoptic character of the text or its affinity in particular with Mt., since the GH, according to all that we know of it, diverged very much from the Synoptic type. According to (*a*) we shall be inclined to refer to the GN the Aramaic readings and the corrections of evangelic OT-citations made to bring them into accord with the original text of the OT. But here also a warning must be given against a too great certainty: the explanation of the name Barabbas as "son of their teacher" is in a Semitic text extremely questionable (Waitz, *Apokr.* 2, 19f.); the assertion that instead of ἐπιούσιος in the petition for bread in the Lord's Prayer there stood "maḥar" *crastinus* may be a conjecture on the part of Jerome; and that at the time of Jesus' death according to the GN it was not the veil of the temple that was rent but the lintel that collapsed is according to Schmidtke "Jerome's own invention" (p. 80), according to Bardy a gleaning by Jerome from Eusebius' *Chronicon* (19–22). If, however, the tradition in question comes from a JG, it may be ascribed to the GN rather than to the GH, for the collapse of the lintel can be understood as a coarsening of the Synoptic motif of the rending of the veil of the temple.

In view of its Synoptic character one will ascribe the story of the man with the withered hand (*in Matth.* on xii. 13) to the GN. So also in the case of the two citations in *adv. Pelag.* III 2 we do well to handle them as variants of Synoptic and indeed Matthaean texts. The first, the conversation of Jesus with His mother and brethren before His baptism, is connected in theme (the baptism of Jesus in spite of His sinlessness) with the conversation with the Baptist in Mt. 3:14f. The second, the conversation about forgivingness, is, as the dialogue form shows, a colouring of the dialogue in Mt. 18:21f. (and not of the single saying Lk. 17:4); moreover the last sentence has been handed down in Greek as the version of the Judaikon (see No. 7 below). Since there are neither formal nor material reasons for a different derivation of the two fragments, they are to be referred to the GN.

Ordinarily the other baptism story (*in Is.* on xi. 2) is also reckoned to the GN. For that Jerome's statement that the story came from the Gospel composed "in the Hebrew speech" is not a sufficient reason, particularly as it is wanting in his *Commentary on Matthew,* in which he cites the GN five times; but a characteristic trait—the sounding forth of the voice *after* Jesus has left the water—which is found only here and in Mt. 3:16, goes to prove the derivation of the passage from the GN. But there are also considerable differences: the "resting" of the Spirit on Jesus has no parallel in the Synoptics, although it has one in the "abiding" of the Spirit upon Him in Jn. 1:32f.; further it is not a voice from heaven that speaks but the Spirit resting on Jesus, and it speaks not in the third person as in Mt., but in the second person as in Mk. and Lk. And above all the content of the saying is a great deal more mythological than it is in the Synoptics; it assumes the notions of the pre-existence and the transfiguration of the Redeemer and in its motif of the eschatological "rest" ("that I may rest in thee": "thou art my rest") it points to the GH (cf. Clem. Alex. *Strom.* II ix, 45; V xiv, 96). These peculiarities make it in my opinion questionable whether this passage belongs to the same baptism story as does the conversation of Jesus with His mother and His brethren (*adv. Pelag.* III 2); accordingly I would—with reserve—assign it to the GH.

The derivation of the citations *in Eph.* v. 4 and *in Ezek.* xviii. 7 is altogether uncertain. Jerome has probably taken the first—it is also the earliest which he adduces—from one of his exegetical sources, but from which cannot be made out, and for that reason it cannot be concluded to which JG the fragment belongs (Schmidtke, 75–79: Apollinaris and the GN; Bardy, 5f.: Origen and the GH); since on the one hand the association of Apollinaris with the GN rests solely upon conjectures on the part of Schmidtke

which admit of no proof, and since on the other hand Jerome can
have obtained his knowledge of an Aramaic GN only after the
writing of his *Commentary on Ephesians* (Bardy, 7ff.), the assignation
proposed by Bardy has a little more likelihood. Since moreover
the saying exhibits no Semitisms and shows no close relationship
to a Synoptic saying of the Lord, it may be entered among the
fragments of the GH. For the identification of the second citation
no evidence that is at all likely can be adduced. Only because
actual Synoptic parallels are wanting, because Jerome in his
Commentary on Ezekiel (on xvi. 13) gives a genuine GH-citation,
and because of the material relationship of this saying to the one
just discussed, it may be assigned with it to the GH.

7. The so-called *"Zion Gospel Edition"*. In the *subscriptiones* of
thirty-six Gospel manuscripts dating from the 9th to the 13th
centuries there is a reference to a Gospel described as τὸ Ἰουδαϊκόν,
and two of these manuscripts (codices 566 and 899) adduce
readings of the Judaikon as marginal notes to Mt. Codex 1424,
which does not have the subscriptions, presents the largest number, namely ten of the thirteen Judaikon readings on Mt., and
for eight of them it is the sole witness. The subscriptions refer
to the standard exemplar on the "holy mount", Zion, in
Jerusalem.

Schmidtke (1–32) has investigated this group and shown that
it goes back to a Gospel edition that was preserved in a basilica
on Zion in Jerusalem and which he has accordingly called the
"Zion Gospel Edition". He puts its origin in 370–500 (this is
disputed by Ernst von Dobschütz in Nestle's *Einführung in das
griechische NT*, 4th ed. 1923, 51). His statement that the Judaikon-
readings given in this Gospel edition go back to the lost *Commentary
on Matthew* by Apollinaris of Laodicea, cannot be proved. The
designation τὸ Ἰουδαϊκόν characterizes the book as a JG which
cannot be one of the four canonical Gospels. But neither can it
be identified with the GH, for otherwise the latter common title
would certainly have been given. Since it is nowhere characterized as heretical, we cannot here be concerned with the Gospel of
the Ebionites. Moreover it is nearly related to Mt. and is clearly a
variant of the Gospel of Matthew. The title Judaikon may also
point to the "Jewish" speech, the Aramaic. The Greek citations
from the Judaikon are certainly ad hoc renderings. The relationship to Mt. and to many JG-citations in Jerome (especially the
identity of the reading for Mt. 18:22 with the concluding sentence
of the second fragment in *adv. Pelag.* III 2) suggests the conclusion
that the Judaikon and the GN were closely related to one another,
if not identical.

8. *Cyril of Jerusalem.* In the Coptic translation of a discourse of Cyril of Jerusalem he (Cyril) puts a citation from the GH into the mouth of a heretical monk from "the neighbourhood of Maiôma near Gaza" (ed. by E. A. W. Budge, *Miscellaneous Coptic Texts* 1915, Coptic p. 60, English p. 637). We are concerned here with a fragment of the story of the birth of Jesus: When Jesus wished to come into the world, God the Father entrusted Him to a mighty power which was called Michael; this came into the world and was named Mary. In the Greek writings of Cyril this discourse is not preserved; V. Burch (*JTS* 21, 1920, 310ff.) regards it as a sort of excursus on the twelfth Catechesis. But it is questionable whether it actually goes back to Cyril, and above all whether the citation really comes from the GH. This question forces itself upon us in view of the different conceptions of the mother of Jesus in the GH fragment on the carrying away of Jesus (Origen and Jerome) and in the present passage. Whilst there the mother is designated the Holy Spirit, here she passes as the incarnation of a "mighty power" which in its pre-existence is called Michael; our hesitations are strengthened if Burch's thesis is correct, that the "mighty power" denotes a star and that Michael is to be understood as a star angel.[1] But we know the GH too little to be able to deny this fragment to it; we are possibly concerned here with a corrupted fragment of the GH or with a fragment of a corrupted GH.

9. *Nicephorus.* In the Stichometry of Nicephorus (*Nicephori opusc. hist.* ed. de Boor 1880, 134; see pp. 49ff. above) it is recorded under the rubric New Testament Antilegomena: "4. The Gospel according to the Hebrews: 2200 lines". For the Gospel of Matthew there are reckoned 2500 lines.

10. *Testimonies from the Middle Ages.* References are also found in writers of the Middle Ages to the GH or the GN. Haimo of Auxerre (*c.* 850) in his *Commentary on Isaiah* (on 53:12) cites the word of Jesus: "Father, forgive them" (Lk. 23:34) and adds: "For as it is said in the Gospel of the Nazaraeans", many thousands of the Jews who were standing round the cross became believers. Here it is deserving of notice that what is spoken of is a Gospel of the Nazaraeans, therefore one with a title which Jerome never uses. It is questionable whether this citation actually comes from the GN; the GN is clearly a working up of Mt., but Haimo's citation

[1] Burch certainly does not examine this difficulty. The main fault of his religio-historical investigation consists in his giving to affinity of motives the value of literary dependence. His statement that the Cyril fragment represents the beginning, the *Gospel of Peter* and Ignatius, *Smyrn.* 3, 2 the conclusion of one and the same book, the GH, is altogether inept.

is based on Lk. 23:48 and *Petr. Ev.* VII. 25. It is certain that another apocryphal dictum which according to Haimo's *Commentary on Hebrews* (on 13:4) "the blessed apostle Matthew" gives "somewhere" (Klostermann p. 12, No. 28), does not belong to a JG.

In a 13th-century English ms. of the "Aurora" of Peter of Riga, a Bible put in verse (12th cent.), a marginal note on the cleansing of the temple gives a citation which may "be read in the books of the Gospels which the Nazarenes used".[1]

In the "Celtic Catechesis" of the Breton Vaticanus Regin. lat. 49 of the 9th century a statement is made according to the "Gospel of the Hebrews" about the day of the last judgment (Dom A. Wilmart, "Analecta Reginensia" in *Studi e Testi* 59, 1933, 58). More recently Bernhard Bischoff has published two unknown fragments of the GH from Irish commentaries (*Sacris erudiri* VI, 1954, 189ff.): (i) a "Historical Commentary on Luke" mentions that the "Gospel according to the Hebrews" gave the miracles that Jesus had wrought in Bethsaida and Chorazin; (ii) in his *Commentary on Matthew* Sedulius Scotus adduces from the "Gospel which is entitled according to the Hebrews" a fictional expansion of the episode of the Magi. Fictional development of Mt. is generally characteristic of the GN; we have before us a case such as we have many a time in Jerome, a text being ascribed to the GH which according to its literary character should be assigned rather to the GN. Moreover Bischoff conjectures that the statements regarding names in an Irish commentary on Matthew (in Bischoff, p. 252) and in the "Historical Commentary on Luke" (*ibid.* p. 262) go back to the same apocryphal passage.

Finally in a theological miscellany manuscript (saec. XIV–XV) of German origin Bischoff has discovered a "historia passionis domini" (saec. XIV, first half), in which the latest authority adduced is Nicolas de Lyra and which contains several citations from the "Gospel of the Nazaraeans". In a letter Bischoff has in an extremely friendly and kindly way put the relative passages at our disposal.

As far then as into the 14th century we come across citations from the JG; the designation alternates between GH and GN. Whether this alternation should be appraised as evidence for our distinction between the two JG seems to me to be open to question. For it is quite possible that we have to do not with direct citations from such Gospel books but rather with borrowings from catenae or commentaries. But the influence of Jerome on this exegetical tradition is unmistakable. This tradition was evidently carried

[1] Cf. GN No. 25 below. This observation is hardly a citation from the GN, but a literary reminiscence on the part of the scholiast from Jerome, *Com. on Mt.* on 21:12: "A certain fiery and starry light radiated from his eyes and the majesty of Godhead gleamed in his face" (cf. James, *The Apocryphal NT*, p. 8).

on in particular by the Irish, and Bischoff thinks probably rightly that the citation in Haimo of Auxerre and the scholion in the Aurora go back to Irish intervention. How far these citations and references are trustworthy testimonies for the content of the GN and the GH must remain open.

11. The result which the foregoing investigation gives is in agreement so far as concerns the number of the JG with that of H. Waitz, M. Dibelius and W. Bauer. According to it three JG have to be distinguished:

(1) *The Gospel of the Nazaraeans*, a Gospel read in a Semitic speech (Aramaic or Syriac), which is attested by Hegesippus and Eusebius, Epiphanius and Jerome, which according to the latter was in use among the Nazaraeans, the Syrian Jewish Christians, and which showed a close relationship to the canonical Matthew.

(2) *The Gospel of the Ebionites*, the Gospel of heretical Jewish Christians composed in Greek, of which Irenaeus knew and from which Epiphanius quotes, which was related more to Mt. than to any other of the canonical Gospels, but differed from it in essential respects.

(3) *The Gospel of the Hebrews*, the JG that is mentioned most often, was perhaps already used by Papias and in the time of Eusebius still belonged to the Antilegomena; its most important witnesses are Clement of Alexandria and Origen. The few fragments that have been preserved indicate no special relationship to one of the canonical Gospels, but contain syncretistic elements and show the heretical character of the Jewish Christian users of the GH.

In the present state of research it is not yet possible to fit these JG into place in the history of Jewish Christianity or in the history of its theology. G. Strecker's analysis of the pseudo-Clementines has shown how complex an entity Jewish Christianity was; the relevant accounts of the early Church heresiologists have not yet been sufficiently investigated; the clarification of the connection between the Qumran sect and the primitive Church and Jewish Christianity is still in full swing; it would then be premature to attempt to fix the JG historically. Here our only or main concern must be the clearing up of the literary question which these books occasion.

1. THE GOSPEL OF THE NAZARAEANS

INTRODUCTION.

1. *Content and Compass*. In content and compass the GN was closely related to Mt. That is shown first and foremost by the readings of the Judaikon, but also by the other fragments that

have been preserved. If the observation of Jerome, *de vir. inl.* 3 (GN 1) refers not merely to Mt. 2:15, 23 but also to the GN, then the latter contained the Matthaean nativity narrative, with the lack of which even Epiphanius could not charge it. Also its story of the baptism had as its basis the Matthaean report. Moreover the GN contained the story of the temptation, the sermon on the mount, the mission discourse, the discourse about the Baptist together with the cry of jubilation, the healing of the withered hand, the sayings against a mania for marvels, about the washing of hands, and about the demand for signs, the confession of Peter, the discourse to the disciples, the story of the rich man, the discourse to the Pharisees, the parable of the entrusted pounds, the denial of Peter, the release of Barabbas, the miracles at the time of the crucifixion, the watchmen at the grave. Since in the fragments only peculiarities that are more or less striking are handed down, it may be concluded that the content of the GN was roughly identical with that of Mt. and consequently that the GN was merely a secondary form of Mt., the character of which has still to be discussed. The Easter stories must have been similar to those in Mt., for the Christophany in Ign. *Smyrn.* 3, 2 does not belong to the GN. That the *pericope adulterae* (Jn. 7:53–8:11) does not belong to it, has already been said. So also the encounter of Jesus with the high priest (Pap. Ox. 840; see pp. 93f. above) belongs to another context.

Waitz finds traces of and citations from the GN in the Epistle of Barnabas, in Justin and in the Didascalia; but he has failed to give either a compelling or a likely proof of his thesis. It is a question of fictional developments of stories or of new formations or recastings of sayings of the Lord, of documents of "rampant" tradition, which may have been transmitted in writing, but also orally, and to identify which with certainty is meanwhile a hopeless undertaking.

2. *Language.* According to the testimony of Hegesippus and Eusebius, of Epiphanius and Jerome, the GN was written in Syriac or Aramaic. Among scholars, however, it is disputed whether the GN was originally drafted in Aramaic or was a translation from the Greek. Closely bound up with this is the question whether the GN represents or discloses an earlier tradition than the canonical Gospel of Matthew, but this question cannot be decided on philological grounds alone. The Aramaic or Hebrew expressions which are handed down in the fragments are adduced both for Aramaic (Hebrew) and for Greek as the original tongue of the GN, but the scantiness and uncertainty of the material permit of no conclusion that is absolutely sure.

The fragments in question are Nos. 5, 12 and 20; in addition two observations of Jerome must also be taken into account, and these we will consider first.

> (On Bethlehem of Judaea) . . . that is an error on the part of the copyist. We believe i.e. that, as we read in the Hebrew, 'Judah' and not 'Judaea' was originally written by the Evangelist (Jerome, *Com. on Mt.*, on 2:5).

The question is whether in this conjecture regarding the original text of Mt. 2:5 the Church father meant by the expression "in ipso Hebraico" the Hebrew text of the citation (Micah 5:1) or the "Hebrew Gospel" (=GN). In favour of the first there is the immediate impression and then Jerome's statement that Mt. in his Old Testament citations follows the Hebrew text. Since, however, in both the Hebrew and the Septuagint text "Judah" does not stand in immediate connection with Bethlehem—"And thou Bethlehem-Ephrath, thou least among the districts of Judah" (Massoretic text, and so also the LXX)—it is often supposed that the note refers not to the Hebrew text of Micah 5:1 but to the "Hebrew Gospel". In that case, however, Jerome would certainly have expressed himself more clearly (cf. the formulae of citation in his *Commentary on Matthew* Nos. 5, 10, 17, 20), especially as this would then be his first reference to the JG in his *Commentary on Matthew*. But since in his opinion this JG represents the original Mt. and therefore all the more in the matter of its Old Testament citations must follow its original text, the same perplexity confronts us. It is best solved by the assumption that Jerome referred to the original text of the OT, but did not accurately remember it.

The other observation is found in the Epistle to Damasus, in which he answers a question of his as to the meaning of "Hosanna to the son of David":

> Finally Matthew, who composed the Gospel in the Hebrew speech, has written: "Osanna barrama", i.e. Hosanna in the highest (Jerome, *Epist.* XX, 5; Klostermann, p. 9 No. 12).

The old question whether by the Hebrew Mt. Jerome means the JG that he usually values so much (cf. A. Meyer, *Handb.*, pp. 31f.), is settled by a reference to the chronology; Damasus addressed his question to Jerome in 383, the latter mentions a JG for the first time in 386–387 and speaks of a "Hebrew" JG first in 390–393; thereby another question, whether "Hosanna in the highest" stood in the place of or side by side with "Hosanna to the son of David", is decided in the latter sense. And finally yet another question, whether Jerome had read or merely conjectured the expression "Osanna barrama" in a Hebrew Gospel text, falls to the ground; moreover the retranslation is wrong: for "height of heaven" is *rama* neither in Hebrew nor in Aramaic, but in Hebrew *marom* or *meromim* and in Aramaic *marom* or *meroma*.[1] This therefore like the foregoing observation of Jerome drops out so far as concerns the question as to the original tongue of the GN.

No. 12 provides no decision on the matter. If the Judaikon in Mt. 15:5 read Corban instead of "offering", as does the parallel Mk. 7:11, it here used a Hebrew-Aramaic *terminus technicus* which must of necessity have stood in a Hebrew or Aramaic rendering of this saying, whether we have here the original text or the Aramaic translation of the Greek word.

The situation is different in No. 5, the rendering of the petition for bread in the Lord's prayer: "Give us today our bread of tomorrow." The *maḥar* given by Jerome as the text of the GN cannot be the original Aramaic or Hebrew text of this petition; otherwise this vocable would not have been rendered in like manner in Mt. and Lk. by ἐπιούσιος, a rare expression and one hard to interpret. Jerome himself understands ἐπιούσιος as *super-substantialis*, and so not as equivalent to *maḥar*; accordingly he has not himself translated back into Aramaic and given out his retroversion as the original text. If the GN actually contained the vocable *maḥar* in the petition for bread—and that there is no reason to doubt—then the conclusion is inevitable that this reading is "merely an erroneous translation, resting on a misunderstanding, of the original epiūsiŏs" (Waitz, *Apokr.* 2, 19; so also A. Meyer, *Handb.* 28f.). The rendering of the petition for bread in the GN is the earliest attempt to explain it. The Aramaic GN thus assumes, at least here, the Greek text of Matthew.

Jerome's statement in No. 20 that in the GN the name Barabbas was "interpreted" as "son of their teacher" is difficult to grasp. For *bar-abba* is a frequent personal name (cf. Strack-Billerbeck 1, 1031) and means "son of the abba" or "son of the father"; if "father" is understood as "teacher", it then means "son of the teacher"; for the latter meaning there may also be assumed *bar-rabba* or *bar-rabban* (the name being written then with two r's). But in either case the translation "son of *their* teacher" is wrong. It is obscure why a name that was so well-known and the meaning of which was so obvious should have had to be "interpreted" in an Aramaic Gospel, and what this interpretation can have looked like ("*bar-abba*, i.e. *bar-rabba*"? But what sense would this explanation have had?); and it is altogether incredible that a person who spoke Aramaic translated this name as "son of *their* teacher" and so wrongly. Accordingly Waitz postulates a Greek original for the Aramaic GN, in which there stood (similarly as in Acts 4:36) this

[1] Cf. Köhler/Baumgartner, *Lexicon* 893b, 565b; Dalman, *Aram-Neuhebr. Handwörterbuch*, 3rd ed. 1938, 252b. In the Syriac the word for it is *merauma*, and that is precisely what the Syriac has in our passage. *Rama* in the sense 'heaven' is first documented in Ephraem; cf. Brockelmann, *Lexicon Syriacum*, 2nd ed. 1928, 720b.

wrong explanation of the name, and from that he concludes that the original tongue of the GN was Greek and therefore that the Aramaic GN was a translation; "in an original Greek GN such an addition had a meaning: in an original Aramaic GN it would have been meaningless" (*Apokr.* 2, p. 20).

This thesis assumes, however, (i) that the writer of the Greek GN read the name only in the accusative (Βαραββᾶν) and did not understand it as such; (ii) that in consequence of an imperfect acquaintance with Aramaic he misunderstood the termination of the word, and (iii) that the Aramaic translator accepted this wrong translation of the Aramaic name and retranslated it into the Aramaic. This hypothesis is burdened by so many improbabilities that it collapses under them. Now Jerome also brings forward the interpretation of the name in his *Onomasticon* (Lagarde, *Onomastica sacra*, 2nd ed., p. 93):

> *barraban*, the son of their teacher. That is Syriac, not Hebrew.

There is here no reference to the Aramaic JG as the place where this translation was found. In the *Onomasticon* it is a question simply of the traditional interpretation of Semitic names. In a Greek Origen-scholion of unknown date (in Gallandi, *Bibliotheca*, vol. XIV app. p. 81, cited in Klostermann, *KlT* 8, p. 10, note on lines 9ff.) it is said:

> For clearly the brigand bore a patronymic, Barabbas, which being interpreted is 'son of the teacher'. Conformably the name Barabban means 'son of our teacher'.

In the second interpretation the termination "an" is understood as a personal suffix of the first person. A similar scholion is found in the Codex S (028) and in other manuscripts on Mt. 27:17:

> Barabbas, which being interpreted is 'son of the teacher'

(cf. Tischendorf, *NTG* octava *loc. cit.*). These scholia testify to a tolerably extensive onomastic tradition which manifestly does not go back to Jerome, since it is nowhere carried back to him and since it nowhere contains the objectionable personal pronoun "their" given by him. In his remark about the name Barabbas it may be a question of such a tradition and not of a citation from the GN. Since it is questionable whether Jerome had had the GN actually in his hands, since it is established that his commentaries are compilations, and since it is certain that he attributed to the esteemed JG much that he had found elsewhere, no absolute certainty is to be attributed to his statement of the place where he found this meaning of the name. Rather we must reckon with the possibility of an error. He probably found the interpretation 'son of the teacher' or 'son of our teacher' in one of the commentaries which he used, of his own accord inserted the personal pronoun "their" in order to distinguish this "teacher" from the "teacher" of Christians, and localized the whole in his JG. At all events the interpretation of the name given by Jerome is linguistically so impossible that it can have stood neither in an Aramaic original nor in an Aramaic translation; this note does not suffice as a basis capable of bearing the postulate of a Greek GN as the original of the Aramaic.

After what has been said in the introduction to the JG under Nos. 4 and 6 the further arguments of Waitz for the existence of a Greek GN anterior to the Aramaic (Ign. *Smyrn.* 3, 2; Jn. 7:53–8:11; *Apokr.* 2, p. 19) are futile.

The fragments Nos. 5 and 7 certainly assume a Greek text, but no other than that of the canonical Mt. The GN was clearly an Aramaic version of the Greek Mt., but, as the fictional enlargements of canonical scenes, many corrections and deletions and the insertion of new sayings of the Lord show, it was no accurate translation, but a targumistic rendering of the canonical Gospel of Mt.

3. *Literary Character.* So far as can be discovered from the fragments the GN was a gospel of the Synoptic type. Alike in its narratives and in its discourse material it proves itself for the most part secondary in comparison with Mt.

In the narratives a fictional development of the tradition can often be detected. Especially significant is the Nazaraean variant in No. 16 of the story of the rich young man (Mt. 19:16–30). The one rich man has become two; such doublings, which can also be observed e.g. in Mt. (cf. Mt. 20:29ff. with Mk. 10:46ff.), are signs of a later stage of the tradition. The situation is fictionally delineated (Jesus and Peter are seated; the rich man who has been spoken to scratches his head); Joachim Jeremias (*Unbekannte Jesusworte* 1948, 35f.; ET 1957, 35) points out "Palestinian colouring": the phrase "sons of Abraham"; "brother" in the sense of fellow-countryman; the animation of what is inanimate (nothing "comes forth" from the goods that are in the house); such traits show the Semitic character of this JG. The saying of Jesus is more detailed; with a graphic description of the prevailing misery it comments upon the requirement to fulfil the law and the prophets. Here there is a suggestion of a social motive which is not yet present in Mt. 19:16ff. Whilst in Mt. vs. 21 the giving away of one's goods to the poor expresses how extremely serious a thing it is to follow Christ, in the GN it is motivated by charity; the transformation of eschatological into ethical ideas, so characteristic of the development of the tradition, is evident.

No. 10 shows a similar secondary character. The story of the healing of the withered hand is fictionally enlarged by a request from the sick man, and further it is given a different point through a social motive.

The conversation of Jesus with His mother and His brethren (No. 2) is a variant of the conversation with the Baptist and is determined by the dogmatic idea of the sinlessness of Jesus.

If the passion story told in the GN (No. 21) actually reported the collapse of the lintel instead of the rending of the veil of the temple—a trait which recurs in the mediaeval *Historia passionis domini* (No. 36)—then here also we have to do with a fictional development, which has perhaps been influenced by the account in Josephus of calamitous omens of the destruction of the temple (*Bell. Jud.* VI, 293–300) or by Eusebius (*Chronicon*, ad annum 32, ed. Helm 2nd ed. 1956, 175; cf. Bardy, 19ff.).

The mediaeval fragments of the JG show the growth of fictional and legendary interests. These determine the working up of the Magi episode, No. 28 (the introduction of Joseph, who is wanting in the Matthaean Magi legend; the colourful description of the circumstances; on a cave as the place of Jesus' birth cf. Justin, *Dial.* 78 and *Protev. Jacobi* 18, 19, 21. 3 and W. Bauer, *Leben Jesu*, pp. 61ff.; the dress described characterizes the Magi as Persians, more accurately as servants of Mithras, as they are also characterized in representations of this scene in Christian art; cf. A. Dieterich in *ZNW* 3, 1902, pp. 4f.). A legendary interest in secondary characters is also found in Nos. 29, 30, 33, edifying traits in the martyrdom style in Nos. 24 and 35.

As regards the discourse material of the GN there are occasions when a late stage of the tradition history can clearly be recognized in it. No. 18 can claim no originality in comparison with Mt. 25: 14ff. In the saying on forgivingness (No. 15) the sin of the brother is, as compared with Mt. 18:21f., limited to sins of the tongue, to insulting language. The saying in No. 23 has no Synoptic parallel, but on the other hand it contains two "Johannine" expressions: "I choose" (cf. Jn. 6:70; 13:18; 15:16, 19) and "whom my Father giveth me" (cf. Jn. 6:37, 39; 17:2, 6, 24). At all events we can see here, as already in Q (Mt. 11:25ff. and parallels) an infiltration of "Johannine" motifs. The Judaikon reading of Mt. 7:5 (No. 6), which is actually a variant of Mt. 7: 21f., has an apocryphal parallel in 2 Clem. 4. 5:

> Though ye be gathered together in my bosom and do not my commandments, I will cast you away and will say to you: Depart from me, I know you not whence ye are, ye workers of iniquity.

On the tradition-history of this saying cf. Bultmann, *Die Geschichte der synoptischen Tradition* 1931, 98, 122f. (ET 1960). It is a point of importance that in place of the original "Lord, Lord" saying there appears "to be in my bosom", that the "symbol of the cultic-legal piety" (Dibelius) is replaced by a formula of mystical communion (on this term cf. W. Bauer, *Das Johannesevangelium*, 3rd ed. 1933, on 1:18); Dibelius rightly sees here "the intrusion of exotic expressions" (*Geschichte der urchristlichen Literatur* 1, 1926, 56).

Its literary character shows the GN secondary as compared with the canonical Mt.; again, from the point of view of Form Criticism and the history of tradition, as well as from that of language, it presents no proto-Matthew but a development of the Greek Gospel of Matthew (against Waitz). "Such an Aramaic Gospel, unoriginal in character but closely related to our Matthew, can hardly be put down to independent development of the earliest Aramaic traditions, but is rather to be explained as retranslation of developed Greek Gospel material" (Dibelius, *op. cit.*, p. 57).

4. *Time and Place of Origin*. The terminus a quo is accordingly the writing of Mt., the terminus ad quem is Hegesippus (180), who is the first to testify to the existence of the GN. It will have appeared in the first half of the second century.

The place of its origin is uncertain. We must think of regions in which Aramaic-speaking Jewish Christian churches continued down to the time of Jerome. It is quite possible that the GN originated where according to the testimony of Epiphanius and Jerome it was in use as the Gospel, in Beroea (Aleppo) in Coelesyria.

The circles in which it arose, those of Syrian Jewish Christians (Nazaraeans), were clearly not "heretical" but belonged, so far as the GN permits us to make out, to the great Church; "in content and character it was not more Jewish Christian than Mt." (Waitz, *Apokr.* 2, 28). A closer characterization of Nazaraean Christianity is not yet possible, since what is dark in the history and theology of Jewish Christianity has not yet been sufficiently cleared up.

Fragments:

1. To these [*namely the citations in which Mt. follows not the Septuagint but the Hebrew original text*] belong the two: "Out of Egypt have I called my son"[1] and "For he shall be called a Nazaraean".[2]

(Jerome, *vir. inl.* 3)

2. Behold, the mother of the Lord and his brethren[3] said to him: John the Baptist baptizes unto the remission of sins,[4]

[1] Cf. Mt. 2:15; Hos. 11:1. [2] Cf. Mt. 2:23 (Lev. 21:12; Jud. 13:5; Isa. 11:1; 53:2).
[3] Cf. Mt. 12:46 and pars. [4] Cf. Mk. 1:4; Lk. 3:3.

let us go and be baptized by him.[1] But he said to them: Wherein have I sinned that I should go and be baptized by him?[2] Unless what I have said is ignorance (a sin of ignorance).[3]

(Jerome, *adv. Pelag.* III 2)

3. The Jewish Gospel has not "into the holy city"[4] but "to Jerusalem".[5]

(Variant to Mt. 4:5 in the Zion Gospel Edition)

4. The phrase "without a cause"[6] is lacking in some witnesses and in the Jewish Gospel.

(Variant to Mt. 5:22, *ibid.*)

5. In the so-called Gospel according to the Hebrews instead of "essential to existence" I found "*maḥar*", which means "of tomorrow", so that the sense is:

Our bread of tomorrow—that is, of the future—give us this day.[7]

(Jerome, *Com. on Mt.* on 6:11 and *Tract. on Ps. cxxxv*)

6. The Jewish Gospel reads here as follows:

If ye be in my bosom and do not the will of my Father in heaven, I will cast you out of my bosom.[8]

(Variant to Mt. 7:5, or better to Mt. 7:21ff., in the Zion Gospel Edition)

7. The Jewish Gospel: [wise] more than serpents.

(Variant to Mt. 10:16, *ibid.*)

8. The Jewish Gospel has: [the kingdom of heaven] is plundered.

(Variant to Mt. 11:12, *ibid.*)

9. The Jewish Gospel: I thank thee.

(Variant to Mt. 11:25, *ibid.*)

10. In the Gospel which the Nazarenes and the Ebionites use, which we have recently translated out of Hebrew into Greek, and which is called by most people the authentic

---

[1] Cf. Mt. 3:13; Mk. 1:9. [2] Cf. Mt. 3:14. [3] Cf. Lev. 4:2; 5:18b.
[4] Cf. Mt. 4:5. [5] Cf. Lk. 4:9. [6] Cf. Mt. 5:22 D W Θλφα it sy sa bo.
[7] Cf. Mt. 6:11 (Lk. 11:3). [8] Cf. Mt. 7:21, 23; 2 Clem. 4. 5.

[Gospel] of Matthew, the man who had the withered hand[1] is described as a mason who pleaded for help in the following words:

I was a mason and earned [my] livelihood with [my] hands; I beseech thee, Jesus, to restore to me my health that I may not with ignominy have to beg for my bread.

(Jerome, *Com. on Mt.*, on 12:13)

11. The Jewish Gospel does not have: three d[ays and nights].
(Variant to Mt. 12:40 in the Zion Gospel Edition)

12. The Jewish Gospel: corban is what you should obtain from us.
(Variant to Mt. 15:5, *ibid.*)

13. What is marked with an asterisk[2] is not found in other manuscripts, also it is not found in the Jewish Gospel.
(Variant to Mt. 16:2f., *ibid.*)

14. The Jewish Gospel: son of John.[3]
(Variant to Mt. 16:17, *ibid.*)

15a. He [*namely Jesus*] said: If thy brother has sinned with a word and has made thee reparation, receive him seven times in a day.[4] Simon his disciple said to him: Seven times in a day? The Lord answered and said to him: Yea, I say unto thee, until seventy times seven times.[5] For in the prophets also after they were anointed with the Holy Spirit, the word of sin [*sinful discourse?*][6] was found.
(Jerome, *adv. Pelag.* III 2)

15b. The Jewish Gospel has after "seventy times seven times": For in the prophets also, after they were anointed with the Holy Spirit, the word of sin [*sinful discourse?*] was found.
(Variant to Mt. 18:22 in the Zion Gospel Edition)

16. The other of the two rich men said to him:[7] Master, what good thing must I do that I may live? He said to him: Man, fulfil the law and the prophets. He answered him: That

---

[1] Cf. Mt. 12:9ff. and pars.
[2] Cf. Mt. 16:2f. (onwards from "When it was evening"); the saying is also lacking in S B φ sy^es sa.
[3] Cf. Mt. 16:17; Jn. 1:42; 21:15ff.   [4] Cf. Lk. 17:4.   [5] Cf. Mt. 18:21f.
[6] Cf. Jas. 3:2.   [7] Cf. Mt. 19:16–24.

have I done. He said to him: Go and sell all that thou possessest and distribute it among the poor, and then come and follow me. But the rich man then began to scratch his head and it [*the saying*] pleased him not. And the Lord said to him: How canst thou say, I have fulfilled the law and the prophets? For it stands written in the law: Love thy neighbour as thyself;[1] and behold, many of thy brethren, sons of Abraham, are begrimed with dirt and die of hunger— and thy house is full of many good things and nothing at all comes forth from it to them! And he turned and said to Simon, his disciple, who was sitting by him: Simon, son of Jona, it is easier for a camel to go through the eye of a needle than for a rich man to enter into the kingdom of heaven.

(Origen, *Com. on Mt.* XV 14 on 19:16ff. in the Latin rendering)

17. In the Gospel which the Nazarenes use, instead of "son of Barachias"[2] we have found written "son of Joiada".[3]

(Jerome, *Com. on Mt.* on 23:35)

18. But since the Gospel [*written*] in Hebrew characters which has come into our hands enters the threat not against the man who had hid [*the talent*], but against him who had lived dissolutely[4]—for he [*the master*] had three servants: one who squandered his master's substance with harlots and flute-girls,[5] one who multiplied the gain, and one who hid the talent; and accordingly one was accepted (with joy), another merely rebuked, and another cast into prison—I wonder whether in Matthew the threat which is uttered after the word against the man who did nothing may refer not to him, but by epanalepsis to the first who had feasted and drunk with the drunken.

(Eusebius, *Theophania* on Mt. 25:14f.: Klostermann, p. 9 No. 15; not in Gressmann, *GCS*)

19. The Jewish Gospel: And he denied and swore and damned himself.

(Variant to Mt. 26:74 in the Zion Gospel Edition,

[1] Cf. Lev. 19:18.   [2] Cf. Mt. 23:35; Zech. 1:1.   [3] Cf. 2 Chron. 24:20ff.
[4] Cf. Mt. 25:14–30.   [5] Cf. P. Ox. 840.

20. Barabbas . . . is interpreted in the so-called Gospel according to the Hebrews as "son of their teacher".
                              (Jerome, *Com. on Mt.* on 27:16)

21. But in the Gospel which is written in Hebrew characters we read not that the veil of the temple was rent, but that the lintel of the temple of wondrous size collapsed.
(Jerome, *Epist.* 120 *to Hedibia* and *Com. on Mt.* on 27:51)

22. The Jewish Gospel: And he delivered to them armed men that they might sit over against the cave and guard it day and night.
                    (Variant to Mt. 27:65 in the Zion Gospel Edition)

23. He (Christ) himself taught the reason for the separations of souls[1] that take place in houses, as we have found somewhere in the Gospel that is spread abroad among the Jews in the Hebrew tongue, in which it is said:
I choose[2] for myself the most worthy[3]: the most worthy are those whom my Father in heaven has given me.[4]
(Eusebius, *Theophania*—In Syriac—IV 12 on Mt. 10:34–36)

Examples from the Middle Ages:

24. As it is said in the Gospel of the Nazaraeans:
At this word of the Lord[5] many thousands of the Jews who were standing round the cross became believers.[6]
                              (Haimo of Auxerre, *Com. on Is.* on 53:12)

25. In the Gospel books which the Nazarenes use we read:
Rays went forth from his eyes, by which they were affrighted and fled.[7]
                    (Marginal note in a manuscript of the *Aurora* of
                                                      Peter of Riga)

26. These eight days of the Passover at which Christ, the Son of God, rose again[8] signify eight days after the recurrence [?] of the Passover[9] at which all the seed of Adam will be judged,[10] as is proclaimed in the Gospel of the Hebrews; and

[1] Cf. Mt. 10:34ff.   [2] Cf. Jn. 13:18; 15:16, 19.   [3] Cf. Mt. 10:13.
[4] Cf. Jn. 6:37, 39; 17:2, 6, 9; Mt. 11:27.   [5] Cf. Lk. 23:34.
[6] Cf. Lk. 23:48; Gospel of Peter 7,25; GN 35.   [7] Cf. Mt. 21:12ff.
[8] Cf. Mk. 16:1–8 and pars.   [9] Cf. Rom. 4:25.   [10] Cf. Rev. 20:11ff.

for this reason the learned believe that the day of judgment will be at Easter time, because on that day Christ rose again, that on that day also the saints should rise again.

(From the *Catéchèse celtique* of the Breton Vaticanus Regin. lat. 49; *Studi e Testi* 59, 1933, p. 58)

27. In these cities (namely Chorazin and Bethsaida) many wonders have been wrought,[1] as their number the Gospel according to the Hebrews gives 53.

("Historical Commentary on Luke" on Lk. 10:13; MS: Clm. 6235, fol. 56r: cited by Bischoff in *Sacris Erudiri* VI, 1954, p. 262)

28. For thus the Gospel which is entitled "According to the Hebrews" reports:

When[2] Joseph looked out with his eyes, he saw a crowd of pilgrims who were coming in company to the cave,[3] and he said: I will arise and go out to meet them. And when Joseph went out, he said to Simon[4]: It seems to me as if those coming were soothsayers, for lo, every moment they look up to heaven and confer one with another. But they seem also to be strangers, for their appearance differs from ours; for their dress is very rich and their complexion quite dark; they have caps on their heads and their garments seem to me to be silky, and they have breeches on their legs. And lo, they have halted and are looking at me, and lo, they have again set themselves in motion and are coming here.

From these words it is clear that not merely three men, but a crowd of pilgrims came to the Lord, even if according to some the foremost leaders of this crowd were named with the definite names Melchus, Caspar and Phadizarda.

(Sedulius Scotus, *Com. on Mt.*; MSS: Berlin, Phill. 1660, saec. IX, fol. 17v; Vienna 740, saec. IX, fol. 15r.v.; cited by Bischoff in *Sacris Erudiri* VI, 1954, 203f.)

29. on Mt. ix. 20 [a woman with an issue of blood] named Mariosa.

[1] Cf. Lk. 10:13; Mt. 11:20f.   [2] Cf. Mt. 2:9ff.
[3] Justin, *Dial.* 78; *Protev. Jacobi* 18, 19, 21.   [4] Cf. Mk. 6:3?

on Mt. xii. 10 "a man" by name Malchus and he was a
mason.

on Mt. xii. 42 "the queen", namely Meroe, "of the south",
that is Aethiopia.

(*Com. on Mt.*; MS: Würzburg, M. p. th. fol. 61, saec.
VIII–IX, cited by Bischoff in *Sacris Erudiri* VI, 1954,
252)

30. on Lk. viii. 42 "the daughter", that is the synagogue, whose
name is Mariossa.

on Lk. xi. 31 "the queen of the south" whose name is
Meruae.

("Historical Com. on Lk."; MS: Clm. 6235 fol. 55ᵛ
and 57ᵛ, cited by Bischoff, *op. cit.*, 262)

From the "Historia passionis Domini", MS: Theolog. Sammel-
handschrift saec. XIV–XV, foll. 8–71 (saec. XIV):

31. [And he wiped their feet.[1]] And as it is said in the Gospel of
the Nazaraeans: He kissed the feet of each one of them.[2]

(fol. 25ᵛ)

32. And how the angel strengthened Christ in his struggle in
prayer,[3] is told in the Gospel of the Nazaraeans. And the
same is also adduced by Anselm in his lamentation: Be
constant, Lord, for now comes the time in which through
thy passion mankind sold in Adam will be ransomed.[4]

(fol. 32ʳ)

33. In the Gospel of the Nazaraeans the reason is given why
John was known to the high priest.[5] As he was the son of
the poor fisherman Zebedee,[6] he had often brought fish to
the palace of the high priests Annas and Caiaphas. And
John went out to the damsel that kept the door and secured
from her permission for his companion Peter, who stood
weeping loudly before the door, to come in.

(fol. 35ʳ)

34. We read in the Gospel of the Nazaraeans that the Jews
bribed four soldiers to scourge the Lord[7] so severely that

[1] Cf. Jn. 13:5 [2] Cf. Lk. 7:38–45. [3] Cf. Lk. 22:43ff. [4] Cf. Gal. 3:13.
[5] Cf. Jn. 18:15ff. [6] Cf. Mk. 1:19f. [7] Cf. Mk. 15:15–20; Mt. 27:27–31; Jn. 19:1-3.

the blood might flow from every part of his body. They had also bribed the same soldiers to the end that they crucified him as it is said in Jn. xix . . .

(fol. 44[r])

35. [Father, forgive them, for they know not what they do.[1]] Note that in the Gospel of the Nazaraeans we have to read that at this virtuous discourse of Christ eight thousand were later converted to the faith; namely three thousand on the day of Pentecost as stated in the Acts of the Apostles ii,[2] and subsequently five thousand about whom we are informed in the Acts of the Apostles x [?].[3]

(fol. 55[r])

36. Also in the Gospel of the Nazaraeans we read that at the time of Christ's death the lintel of the temple, of immense size, had split[4] (Josephus says the same and adds that overhead awful voices were heard which said: Let us depart from this abode[5]).

(fol. 65[r])

2. THE GOSPEL OF THE EBIONITES

INTRODUCTION.

1. *Testimony*. Epiphanius testifies to a JG which was used by the Jewish Christian sect of the Ebionites, which must have been an abridged and falsified Gospel of Matthew, and which he incorrectly entitles the "Gospel of the Hebrews" and the "Hebrew Gospel" (see pp. 123ff. above). What title it actually bore is unknown. In the rest of the treatises on the heresies it is neither attested nor quoted. For our knowledge of it we are dependent on the accounts and quotations in Epiphanius.

Origen (*Hom. on Lk.* 1:1) and Jerome (Introduction to his *Com. on Mt.* and *adv. Pelag.* III 2) mention a "Gospel according to the Twelve" or "according to the Apostles", which the latter identifies with the Aramaic GH read among the Nazaraeans (see pp. 126ff. above). Since now in a GE-fragment in Epiphanius the apostles themselves appear as narrators (No. 1) and so are put forward as authorities for what is reported, the GE has frequently been identified with the Gospel of the Twelve (cf. Waitz, *Apokr.* 2, 39). On the other hand Schmidtke (pp. 173f.) wants to see in the

---

[1] Cf. Lk. 23:34; GN 24. [2] Cf. Acts 2:41. [3] Cf. Acts 4:4.
[4] Cf. GN 21. [5] Cf. Josephus, *Bell. Jud.* VI, 293–300.

"Gospel of the Twelve" the Gospel of the national Syrian sect of the Quqājē (against this see Waitz in *ZNW* 14, 1913, 46). Nevertheless the equating of the GE with the Gospel of the Twelve remains questionable and contributes nothing to increase the number of the fragments, for the assigning by Waitz of the account of the baptism (GN 2 = Jerome, *adv. Pelag.* III 2) to the GE is unsupported. For fuller information about the "Gospel of the 12 (Apostles)" and the Gospel of the Quqājē see VII D 1 and 2 below (pp. 263ff.).

2. *Content and Compass.* Waitz has sought to reconstruct the content and compass of the GE by assigning to it Gospel citations from the *Kerygmata Petrou* and another source-document of the pseudo-Clementines (*ZNW* 14, 1913, 48ff., *Apokr.* 2, 39f.). But G. Strecker has in my opinion shown convincingly that no JG is cited in the pseudo-Clementines (*Das Judenchristentum in den Pseudoklementinen*, (*TU* 70) 1958, section D, pp. 117–136). Also the two citations from Origen, *de Princ.* IV, 22 and Clement Alex., *Strom.* V x, 63, which Waitz adduces (*Apokr.* 2, 47f. Nos. 37 and 59b) cannot with certainty be carried back to the GE. There remain only the fragments that have been handed down by Epiphanius.

These have to do with John the Baptist and his work, the call of the disciples and the baptism of Jesus, and contain a parallel to Mt. 12:46–50, one to Mt. 5:17 and one to Mt. 26:17ff.; Lk. 22:15. The GE began, as Epiphanius states emphatically, not with the nativity narrative but with the appearance of the Baptist; it contained an account of the Last Supper and also a history of the passion and Easter, about which, however, we know nothing in detail. It may be that No. 6 comes from a kind of Sermon on the Mount from which Epiphanius cites this one saying merely because of its peculiarity.

The structure of the GE is not quite clear. No. 3 forms the beginning; but it is quite uncertain whether No. 2 or No. 1 came after it and whether in No. 1 two fragments are united or a coherent text lies before us; it is also open to question whether the call of the twelve was recorded before or after the baptism of Jesus; the schema of the canonical account favours the latter view, whilst the context of No. 1, the close connection with No. 2 and the introductory remark of Epiphanius in No. 4 "and after many words" favour the former. In view of these obscurities I have, in reproducing the fragments, retained the sequence which they have in Epiphanius and have dispensed with an arrangement of my own.

3. *The Language.* The GE was originally composed in Greek. Proof of that is furnished by the account of the food of the Baptist

(No. 2) in which locusts (ἀκρίς Mk. 1:6; Mt. 3:4) are missing and only "wild honey, the taste of which was as manna, as a cake (ἐγκρίς) dipped in oil" is mentioned. This characterization of the honey is borrowed from Num. 11:8 where the taste of the manna is so described; "but without the similarity of the Greek words the author would hardly have lighted here on the manna" (Dibelius, *Geschichte der urchristlichen Literatur* 1, 60). Dibelius also points out that the GE adheres considerably to the text of the Synoptic Gospels, and that goes to prove a composition in Greek.

4. *Character*. In literary character the GE is a Gospel of the Synoptic type. It may be especially related to Mt. (No. 6 has a parallel in Mt. alone), but it also assumes the two other Synoptics. The chronological and biographical statements in the account of the Baptist, the statement about the age of Jesus and the saying No. 7 come from Lk. (cf. the notes to the fragments). In the story of the baptism of Jesus all the three Synoptic accounts are utilized: it gives the voice from heaven three times, according to Mk. 1:11, Lk. 3:22 D it and Mt. 3:17. The dependence of the GE on the GN asserted by Waitz (*Apokr.* 2, 42f.) and after him by Schoeps does not exist, for it is not proved that the passages adduced in support of this thesis belong to the GE.

The alterations of the Synoptic tradition made in the GE are in part of a literary and in part of a dogmatic sort. To the former there belongs the story of the call of the twelve apostles. It is Jesus Himself who narrates it. And this narration of Jesus is framed in an account by the apostles in the "we" style ("He chose us"). But it can no longer be made out whether and, if at all, how far the we-account determined the form of the GE, nor whether elsewhere also Jesus came forward as narrator. The we-account was assuredly intended to set the GE under the authority of the twelve apostles and the emphasis on Matthew to make him known as the writer of the GE.

To a dogmatic tendency there goes back the striking-out of the nativity narrative Mt. 1 and 2. The Ebionites denied the virgin birth of Jesus; according to their christology the divine sonship of Jesus rests not upon His divine begetting and wonderful birth, but on the union of the Holy Spirit with Him at the time of His baptism (No. 4). This "entry" of the Holy Spirit is clearly something other than his descent upon Jesus (Mk. 1:10; Mt. 3:16; Lk. 3:22); it is not adoption or inspiration, but a union of a heavenly being with the man Jesus resulting in the Christ, the Son of God. In this trait there is to be discerned a Gnostic characteristic of the Ebionite christology (cf. Dibelius, *op. cit.* p. 61). The task of Jesus is to annul the "sacrifices" (No. 6); in this saying the enmity of the Ebionites against the temple cult registers itself. No. 7 and also the account of the food of the Baptist (the cutting-out of the locusts) point to vegetarianism. The ordaining of the twelve apostles for Israel underscores the Jewish character of this Gospel.

A gnosticizing christology, a hatred of cult, and vegetarianism —these dogmatic elements distinguish the Jewish Christianity of the Ebionites from that of the Nazaraeans and characterize it as different from the Christianity of the great Church, as "heretical". A closer description of this Jewish Christianity is not possible on the basis of the GE fragments.

5. *Time and Place of Origin.* Since the GE pre-supposes the Synoptics, it can have originated at the earliest in the beginning of the 2nd century. Irenaeus (*c.* 175) knew of its existence, although only from hearsay. Accordingly the origin of the GE is to be dated in the first half of the 2nd century.

The place of origin is uncertain. It was possibly composed in the region east of Jordan, where according to the accounts of the Church fathers the Ebionites had their headquarters and where Epiphanius will have seen the book and made excerpts from it.

Fragments:

1. In the Gospel that is in general use amongst them, which is called according to Matthew, which however is not whole (and) complete but forged and mutilated—they call it the Hebrew Gospel—it is reported:

There appeared a certain man named Jesus of about thirty years of age,[1] who chose us.[2] And when he came to Capernaum,[3] he entered into the house of Simon[4] whose surname was Peter,[5] and opened his mouth and said: As I passed along the Lake of Tiberias,[6] I chose John and James the sons of Zebedee, and Simon and Andrew and Thaddaeus and Simon the Zealot and Judas the Iscariot,[7] and thee, Matthew, I called as thou didst sit at the receipt of custom, and thou didst follow me.[8] You therefore I will to be twelve apostles for a testimony unto Israel.[9]

(Epiphanius, *Haer.* 30. 13, 2f.)

[1] Cf. Lk. 3:23.   [2] Cf. Lk. 6:13.   [3] Cf. Mk. 1:21; Lk. 4:31.
[4] Cf. Mk. 1:29; Lk. 4:38.   [5] Cf. Mt. 4:18.   [6] Cf. Mk. 1:16; Mt. 4:18.
[7] Cf. Mt. 10:2-4 and pars.   [8] Cf. Mt. 9:9.
[9] Cf. Mt. 10:2, 6; Mk. 3:14; Lk. 6:13; Barn. 8:3.

2. And

It came to pass that John was baptizing[1]; and there went out to him Pharisees and were baptized,[2] and all Jerusalem.[3] And John had a garment of camel's hair and a leathern girdle about his loins, and his food, as it saith, was wild honey,[4] the taste of which was that of manna, as a cake dipped in oil.[5]

Thus they were resolved to pervert the word of truth into a lie and to put a cake in the place of locusts.

(*ibid.* 30. 13, 4f.)

3. And the beginning of their Gospel runs:

It came to pass in the days of Herod the king of Judaea,[6] ⟨when Caiaphas was high priest,[7]⟩ that there came ⟨one⟩, John ⟨by name,⟩ and baptized with the baptism of repentance in the river Jordan.[8] It was said of him that he was of the lineage of Aaron the priest, a son of Zacharias and Elisabeth;[9] and all went out to him.[10]

(*ibid.* 30. 13, 6)

4. And after much has been recorded it proceeds:

When the people were baptized,[11] Jesus also came and was baptized by John.[12] And as he came up from the water, the heavens were opened and he saw the Holy Spirit in the form of a dove that descended[13] and entered into him. And a voice (sounded) from heaven that said: Thou art my beloved Son, in thee I am well pleased.[14] And again: I have this day begotten thee.[15] And immediately a great light shone round about the place.[16] When John saw this, it saith, he saith unto him:

Who art thou, Lord? And again a voice from heaven (rang out) to him: This is my beloved Son in whom I am well pleased.[17] And then, it saith, John fell down before him and said: I beseech thee, Lord, baptize thou me. But he prevented

[1] Cf. Mk. 1:4 (Mt. 3:1).   [2] Cf. Mt. 3:7.   [3] Cf. Mt. 3:5; Mk. 1:5.
[4] Cf. Mt. 3:4; Mk. 1:6.   [5] Cf. Exod. 16:31; Num. 11:8.   [6] Cf. Lk. 1:5.
[7] Cf. Lk. 3:2.   [8] Cf. Mk. 1:4f.; Lk. 3:3.   [9] Cf. Lk. 1:5-18; 3:2.
[10] Cf. Mt. 3:5; Mk. 1:5.   [11] Cf. Lk. 3:21.   [12] Cf. Lk. 3:21; Mt. 3:13; Mk. 1:9.
[13] Cf. Mt. 3:16 and pars.   [14] Cf. Mk. 1:11.   [15] Cf. Lk. 3:23 D; Ps. 2:7.
[16] On the shining of a light at the baptism of Jesus cf. Walter Bauer, *Leben Jesu*, 134-139.
[17] Cf. Mt. 3:17.

him and said: Suffer it; for thus it is fitting that everything should be fulfilled.[1]

(ibid. 30. 13, 7f.)

5. Moreover they deny that he was a man, evidently on the ground of the word which the Saviour spoke when it was reported to him: "Behold, thy mother and thy brethren stand without", namely:

Who is my mother and who are my brethren? And he stretched forth his hand towards his disciples and said: These are my brethren and mother and sisters, who do the will of my Father.[2]

(ibid. 30. 14, 5)

6. They say that he (Christ) was not begotten of God the Father, but created as one of the archangels . . . that he rules over the angels and all the creatures of the Almighty, and that he came and declared, as their Gospel, which is called *(according to Matthew? according to the Hebrews?),* reports:

I am come to do away with sacrifices,[3] and if ye cease not from sacrificing, the wrath of God will not cease from you.[4]

(ibid. 30. 16, 4f.)

7. But they abandon the proper sequence of the words and pervert the saying,[5] as is plain to all from the readings attached, and have let the disciples say:

Where wilt thou that we prepare for thee the passover? and him to answer to that:

Do I desire with desire at this Passover to eat flesh with you?

(ibid. 30. 22, 4)

3. THE GOSPEL OF THE HEBREWS

INTRODUCTION.

1. *Content and Compass.* It is not known how the GH began; but if the Cyril-fragment (No. 1) belonged to it, then in its introduction the pre-existence and birth of Jesus must have been recorded, and indeed largely otherwise than they are in the prologue to Jn.

[1] Cf. Mt. 3:14f.   [2] Cf. Mt. 12:47–50.   [3] Cf. Mt. 5:17f.
[4] Cf. Jn. 3:36b   [5] Cf. Mt. 26:17ff. and par.; Lk. 22:15.

and in the nativity narratives of Mt. and Lk.; No. 1, the account of the descent of Jesus, seems to be a fragment which belongs essentially between the two accounts. No. 3 belongs obviously to a story of the temptation. It is not clear into what context the sayings (4, 5, 6) should be fitted, since Synoptic parallels are wanting.

At its end or somewhere near its end the GH told the story of an appearance of Christ to James; in it two lost accounts are assumed, which however we can still trace by inference: the one was an account of the Last Supper according to which James the brother of the Lord had been present and had vowed to abstain from food until he had seen Jesus risen from the dead—a pledge which assumes that at the Last Supper Jesus had spoken of His death and resurrection; the other was an account of the resurrection according to which it must have taken place in the sight of those who guarded the sepulchre, for Jesus gives the linen cloth to the priest's servant; and this trait presupposes an account of the burial. It is clear that the account of Easter given in the GH departed considerably from those of the canonical Gospels (cf. Waitz, *Apokr.* 2, 58f.).

The fragments of the GH that have been preserved give us no idea of its compass. According to the stichometry of Nicephorus it comprised 2200 lines, therefore only 300 fewer than the canonical Mt.

2. *Character.* As literature and in substance the GH differs considerably from the canonical Gospels and also from the GN and the GE. Its stories and sayings scarcely permit of their being understood as developments of Synoptic or Johannine texts.

The appearance of the risen Christ to James is an independent legend, which has formed round an historical kernel of which the oldest witness is 1 Cor. 15:7. But that the first appearance of the risen Christ was to James, and that he was present at the Last Supper, contradicts the New Testament tradition; the target of the account is the setting free of the Lord's brother from his promise to abstain from food; here a special interest in the person of James is evident. This interest gives the christophany of the GH the character of a personal legend. The handing-over of the linen cloth to the priest's servant points to a legendary working up of the resurrection story; if, as is probable, the linen cloth was intended to be to the "priest" (the high priest) a proof of the reality of Jesus' resurrection, then an apologetic motive here makes its appearance. The account of the baptism (No. 2) is hardly a fictional or legendary development of the Synoptic parallels, but a mythical variant (see below).

It is interesting that Jesus Himself tells the story of the temptation (No. 3), as in the GE He tells of the choice of the apostles;

possibly this was intended to explain how the disciples came to know about Jesus' temptation (Dibelius, *Geschichte der urchristlichen Literatur* 1, 62); but as the example from the GE shows, in the I-form of the narrative we may have to do with a popular expedient in composition.

Among the sayings No. 4 is cast in a form that is worthy of note, the form of a rhetorical "chain" which in the New Testament occurs above all in Paul and in the epistle of James and to which Dibelius has devoted an instructive study (*Der Brief des Jakobus*, 8th ed. 1956, 92–95). The chain in No. 4 is a *climax* and portrays the way of salvation (seek—find—marvel—reign—rest). The saying has been handed down in four versions; it has already been said (p. 119) that the version which Clement first presents (No. 4a) is, as P. Ox. 654 shows, abbreviated compared with the later version (4b); the version of P. Ox. may be the more original since it is less polished, while on the other hand that of the Coptic Gospel of Thomas (see VII E, p. 297 below) presents a different chain: seek—find—be bewildered—marvel—reign. To the question which this difference occasions no answer can yet be given in the present state of investigation (on the relation of the Gospel of Thomas to the Gospel of the Hebrews see below p. 297).

The Jewish-Christian character of the GH is indicated not merely by the title (as to that see below) but above all by the emphasis on James the brother of the Lord, who according to the reports of the NT (Gal. 2; Acts 15; 21:18f.) and of Hegesippus (Eusebius, *H.E.* II. xxiii, 4–18) was the champion of a strict Jewish Christianity and leader of the early Jerusalem church. Since contrary to the historical facts he is distinguished as a participant at Jesus' Last Supper and as the first witness and consequently the most important guarantor of the resurrection, it is clear that for the GH he is the highest authority in the circle of Jesus' acquaintances. This trait also has a striking parallel in the Coptic Gospel of Thomas (cf. logion 12, p. 290 below). The understanding of the Holy Spirit as a female is also Jewish or Semitic.

But this Jewish Christianity comprises syncretistic-gnostic elements. The account of the carrying away of Jesus (No. 3) shows a strong mythological trait, the Holy Ghost being designated the mother of Jesus; what form was taken by the speculation here pre-supposed with regard to Jesus' birth is uncertain. But if, in spite of the objections urged in the introduction No. 8, the Coptic Cyril-fragment belongs to the GH, then the Holy Spirit is to be identified with the "mighty power in heaven" and Mary to be understood as the incarnation of the heavenly power. Not merely for Jesus but also for His mother the pre-existence and incarnation myth may have been assumed. That the mighty power in heaven was called Michael is not surprising, in view of his importance in Egyptian magical texts and in the *Pistis Sophia* (cf. W. Bauer, *Rechtgläubigkeit*, p. 57) and in the last analysis is no decisive objection to the identification of the "mighty power" with the Holy Spirit. In the Coptic Epistle of James of the Cod. Jung, Jesus describes Himself as "son of the Holy Spirit" (H.-Ch. Puech and G. Quispel in *Vig. Chr.* 8, 1954, p. 12).

The story of the baptism (No. 2) also bears upon it mythical imprints. In the first place what happens is presented as inspiration and adoption. But the fact that it is not the voice (of God) which speaks out of the opened heaven as in the Synoptic story of the baptism, but the Holy Spirit that has come down, and also the content of the words tell against the view that not until His baptism was Jesus inaugurated as Son of God. It is true that the last sentence has the ring of an adoption formula, but that ring is as faint as it is in Lk. 3:22 (contrasted with Mk. 1:11); for the two foregoing sentences assume Jesus' sonship, as the address "my Son" shows, and they characterize it otherwise than as Messianic dignity ("thou art my rest"). The Holy Spirit waits for the coming of his Son, clearly for his coming forth from pre-existence; he has waited for him in all the prophets, but till now in vain; he waits for him that he may "rest" upon him. This "resting" of the Spirit upon his Son is clearly something other than the resting of the Spirit of the Lord upon the Messiah (Isa. 11:2), and is not inspiration but complete and final union of the Spirit with his Son ("the whole fount of the Spirit" comes down upon him; "thou art my rest"). The Holy Spirit speaks here as does the hypostatized divine Wisdom in the Jewish Wisdom Literature. As the Spirit waited in vain to find "his rest" in all the prophets until the Son came, so Wisdom "seeks" her "rest" in vain in all peoples until she finds it in Israel.

> With all these I sought rest (ἀνάπαυσις);
> And in whose inheritance shall I lodge? (Ecclus. 24:7)

And as the Spirit knows rest in no prophet, so from primaeval times Wisdom passes into ever new souls.

> From generation to generation passing into holy souls
> She maketh (men) friends of God and prophets. (Wisd. 7:27)

The "rest" that the Holy Spirit waits for and finally finds in his Son is the eschatological rest. This is also the objective of the pre-existent Redeemer who, according to the Jewish-Christian-gnostic *Kerygmata Petrou*, after endless change in form becomes incarnate in Jesus:

From the beginning of the world he runs through the ages, changing his form at the same time as his name, until in his time, anointed of God's mercy for his toil, he shall find his rest for ever.

(ps. Clem. *Hom.* III 20, 2; cf. *Rec.* II 22, 4)

To the circle of such Gnostic speculations belongs the christology of the baptism pericope of the GH.

The chain-saying No. 4 with its *climax* "seek—find—marvel—reign—rest" points to the same religious milieu. It is not in the least an equivalent of Mt. 7:7, but with its notion of "rest" has a New Testament parallel only in Mt. 11:28f. But even this passage is a foreign body in the Synoptic tradition (cf. Dibelius, *Die Formgeschichte des Evangeliums* 1933, 279ff.; ET 1934, 279ff.). Our saying describes the steps of the revelation of salvation and of the way of salvation. This description is characteristic of the Hermetic gnosis, as Dibelius has pointed out (*op. cit.*, 285 note 2; ET 284 n. 2); here also "to marvel" is found as a step (*Corp. Hermet.* IV 2; XIV 4) and the "rest" as eschatological salvation (*Corp. Hermet.* IX 10; XIII 20). The Jewish-Christian pseudo-Clementines speak in different ways of the "rest" as eschatological salvation: according to the *Kerygmata Petrou* the true prophet makes known "the word of rest" (*Hom.* III 26, 5), and instruction as to who the true prophet is and as to how he is found is said "to bring to rest" (*Hom.* I 20, 1); according to the basic writing one reaches "the haven of rest" (*Ep. Clem.* 13, 3; 16, 3), and in a prayer which goes back to the homilist "rest" is the last and highest of many affirmations about God ("Lord and Master of all, Father and God . . . thou art rest": *Hom.* III 72, 1f.). In Clement of Alexandria there occurs the sentence: "For I shall take you up into rest (and into the enjoyment) of inexpressible and ineffable good things . . ." (*Quis dives salvetur* 23, 3, cited by Dibelius *op. cit.* 283 note 2). These examples of Gentile, Jewish-Christian and churchly gnosis may make plain the atmosphere out of which there arose the "mystic" piety that reveals itself in our saying.

Because of the scantiness of the material we cannot say how strongly this mystic-gnostic religiosity has influenced the GH, whether it is an essential or merely an infused element. The two other sayings (5 and 6) with their demand for brotherly love stand much closer to the preaching of Jesus.

3. *Title, Country and Time of Origin.* The GH is the only JG the title of which ("the Gospel according to the Hebrews") has been handed down. "When it is a matter of marking their nationality Greek-speaking Jews also are called Hebrews" (W. Bauer,

Rechtgl. u. Ketz. 56). The title characterizes the book as the Gospel of Greek-speaking Jewish-Christian circles, and that in distinction from and in contrast with the Gospel of other and Gentile-Christian circles—for a distinction from the Gospels according to Matthew or Luke can hardly be implied in such a title. An analogous instance presents itself in the "Gospel according to the Egyptians". W. Bauer has made it probable that these two designations were provided to distinguish the Gospels of two churches existing in the same area, and that the Gospel of the Egyptians was the Gospel of the Egyptian Gentile-Christians, the GH the Gospel of the Egyptian Jewish-Christians (*op. cit.* 54–57). If the GH was used in Egypt and given that name there, then it may also have originated there. Egypt is indicated as its place of origin also by the fact that its principal witnesses are the Alexandrians Clement and Origen, by the religio-historical character of the fragments Nos. 1 and 4, and also by the conception of Jesus as the Son of the Holy Spirit, which is documented for Egypt by the Coptic Epistle of James (Puech-Quispel, *op. cit.* pp. 7–22). The GH was known to Hegesippus and must therefore have originated, as did the two other JG, in the first half of the second century. Since a literary dependence upon one of the other JG cannot be made out, the time of origin of the GH cannot be determined more closely.

Fragments:

1. It is written in the Gospel of the Hebrews:

    When Christ wished to come upon the earth to men, the good Father summoned a mighty power in heaven, which was called Michael, and entrusted Christ to the care thereof. And the power came into the world and it was called Mary, and Christ was in her womb seven months.

    (From the Coptic translation of a discourse ascribed to Cyril of Jerusalem, edited by E. A. W. Budge, *Miscellaneous Coptic Texts* 1915, Coptic p. 60, English p. 637)

2. According to the Gospel written in the Hebrew speech, which the Nazaraeans read, the whole fount of the Holy Spirit shall descend upon him . . . Further in the Gospel which we have just mentioned we find the following written:

    And it came to pass when the Lord was come up out of the water,[1] the whole fount of the Holy Spirit descended

---

[1] Cf. Mt. 3:16.

upon him and rested on him[1] and said to him: My Son,[2] in all the prophets was I waiting for thee that thou shouldest come and I might rest in thee.[3] For thou art my rest;[4] thou art my first-begotten Son[5] that reignest for ever.[6]

(Jerome, *Comm. on Is.* IV on Is. 11:2)

3. And if any accept the Gospel of the Hebrews—here the Saviour says:

Even so did my mother, the Holy Spirit,[7] take me by one of my hairs and carry me away[8] on to the great mountain[9] Tabor.

(Origen, *Com. on Jn.* II, 12; *Hom. on Jer.* XV, 4; Jerome, *Com. on Micah* 7:6; *Com. on Is.* 40:9; *Com. on Ezek.* 16:13)

4a. As also it stands written in the Gospel of the Hebrews:

He that marvels shall reign, and he that has reigned shall rest.

(Clem. Alex., *Strom.* II ix, 45)

4b. To those words[10] this is equivalent:[11]

He that seeks will not rest until he finds; and he that has found shall marvel; and he that has marvelled shall reign; and he that has reigned shall rest.[12]

(Clem. Alex. *Strom.* V xiv, 96; cf. P. Ox. 654 and the Coptic Gospel of Thomas p. 297 below)

5. As we have read in the Hebrew Gospel, the Lord says to his disciples:

And never be ye joyful, save when ye behold your brother with love.[13]

(Jerome, *Com. on Eph.* 5:4)

[1] Cf. Isa. 11:2; 61:1.

[2] In the Coptic Epistle of James of the cod. Jung the risen Christ says to James and the disciples: "Soyez Élus, ressemblez au Fils de l'Esprit Saint" (Puech-Quispel, *Vig. Chr.* 8, 1954, p. 12).

[3] Cf. Ecclus. 24:7.   [4] Cf. Ps. 132:14.

[5] Cf. Ps. 2:7; Lk. 3:22 D; Mk. 1:11; Exod. 4:22; Jer. 31:9; Col. 1:15; Hebr. 1:6.
[6] Cf. Ps. 89:29f.; Lk. 1:33.   [7] Cf. Mk. 1:12; Mt. 4:1.
[8] Cf. Ezek. 8:3; Bel and the Dragon 36.   [9] Cf. Mt. 4:8.   [10] Plato, *Timaeus* 90.
[11] Cf. Mt. 7:7; Lk. 11:9.
[12] Cf. Mt. 11:28f.; Clem. Alex. *Quis dives salvetur* 23, 3; *Corp. Hermet.* 13, 20.
[13] Cf. Lk. 15:31f.

6. In the Gospel according to the Hebrews, which the Nazaraeans are wont to read, there is counted among the most
grievous offences:

He that has grieved the spirit of his brother.[1]

(Jerome, *Com. on Ezek.* 18:7)

7. The Gospel called according to the Hebrews which was
recently translated by me into Greek and Latin, which
Origen frequently uses, records after the resurrection of the
Saviour:

And when the Lord had given the linen cloth to the servant
of the priest, he went to James and appeared to him.[2] For
James had sworn that he would not eat bread from that hour
in which he had drunk the cup of the Lord until[3] he should
see him risen from among them that sleep. And shortly thereafter the Lord said: Bring a table and bread! And immediately it is added: he took the bread, blessed it and brake it
and gave it[4] to James the Just and said to him: My brother,
eat thy bread, for the Son of man is risen from among them
that sleep.[5]

(Jerome, *vir. inl.* 2)

[1] Cf. Mt. 18:6.   [2] Cf. 1 Cor. 15:7.   [3] Cf. Mk. 14:25 and pars.
[4] Cf. Mk. 14:22 and pars.; 1 Cor. 11:23f.   [5] Cf. Mk. 8:31 and pars.

IV

THE GOSPEL OF THE EGYPTIANS
(*W. Schneemelcher*)

In his first Homily on Lk., along with other apocryphal gospels, Origen also mentions a Gospel of the Egyptians (for the text see p. 55 above). From the text nothing emerges regarding the content and character of this Gospel, only it is clear that in Origen's time it was already no longer recognized by the Church. Almost nothing of it has been preserved, and the few lines that have been handed down scarcely permit of any far-reaching conclusions, although learned phantasy has time and again attempted to close these gaps in our knowledge. The Greek Gospel of the Egyptians is not identical with the "Gospel of the Egyptians" recently found at Nag Hammadi (see VII H below).

1. *Fragments and Reports.* The chief source of the little knowledge that we have is Clement of Alexandria, who evidently knew the Gospel of the Egyptians and cites it. In *Stromateis* III, which is devoted to the discussion of marriage questions and of sexuality in general, Clement has to join issues with Encratites and others. In doing so he states that these groups (he mentions in addition the name of Julius Cassianus) use the Gospel of the Egyptians, but nothing is said as to the sort of use they made of it.

To refute those who object to marriage and the begetting of children Clement adduces what follows:

(*a*) When Salome asked, "How long will death have power?" the Lord answered, "So long as ye women bear children" —not as if life was something bad and creation evil, but as teaching the sequence of nature.

(*Strom.* III 45; Stählin II 217, 6–10)

There is a reference to this saying in a later passage in which Clement again turns against the Encratites and gives the source of the saying:

(*b*) Those who are opposed to God's creation because of continence, which has a fair-sounding name, also quote the words addressed to Salome which I mentioned earlier. They are handed down, as I believe, in the Gospel of the Egyptians. For, they say: the Saviour himself said, "I am

166

come to undo the works of the female", by the female meaning lust, and by the works birth and decay.

(*Strom.* III 63: Stählin II 225, 1–6)

The Lord—so Clement proceeds—has indeed actually made an
end of lust, but birth and decay, i.e. the system of the world,
persist.

(c) Since then the Word has alluded to the consummation,
Salome saith rightly, "Until when shall men die?" Now
Scripture uses the term 'man' in the two senses, of the visible
outward form and of the soul, and again of the redeemed
man and of him who is not redeemed. And sin is called the
death of the soul. Wherefore the Lord answers advisedly,
"So long as women bear children", i.e. so long as lusts are
powerful.

(*Strom.* III 64; Stählin II 225, 15–21)

After further counter-arguments (with quotations from Scripture)
it is said:

(d) Why do they not also adduce what follows the words
spoken to Salome, these people who do anything but walk
by the gospel rule according to truth? For when she said,
"I have then done well in not bearing children", as if it
were improper to engage in procreation, then the Lord
answered and said, "Eat every plant, but that which has
bitterness eat not".

(*Strom.* III 66; Stählin II 226, 11–16)

Clement's concern is to make it clear that marriage and child-
bearing are just as little sinful as is continence. In this connection
he combats a false interpretation of Mt. 18:20:

(e) For they declare that the Lord meant to say: with the
greater number there is the Creator, God, the primal cause
of existence, but with the one, the elect one, there is the
Redeemer, the Son of another, to wit the good God.

(*Strom.* III 68: Stählin II 227, 2–5)

Although the context suggests that this last saying, which may of
course have been taken from any writing of the opponents, should
be associated with the previously used Gospel of the Egyptians,
yet that cannot be done, since Clement gives no indication that

that is where it belongs. For the whole polemic he has used, it is clear, only the dialogue of Salome with Christ on death and on the problem of sexuality (on Salome see below). To this dialogue, however, there must also be reckoned a passage which appears in Clement in another context: in his polemic against Julius Cassianus (on him see Hilgenfeld, *Ketzergesch. d. Urch.* pp. 546ff.), whom he looks upon as the founder of the doctrine of Docetism, he quotes from his writing 'On Continence or on Castration':

> (*f*) If such an arrangement [*namely, the institution of different sexes*] were of God, to whom we aspire, then he would not have praised eunuchs and the prophet would not have said that they are no unfruitful tree (*Isa.* 56:3) . . .
>
> Contending further for the impious doctrine he adds: 'And how could a charge not be rightly brought against the Saviour, if he has transformed us and freed us from error, and delivered us from sexual intercourse?' In this matter his teaching is similar to that of Tatian. But he emerged from the school of Valentinus. Therefore Cassianus now says, When Salome asked when what she had inquired about would be known,[1] the Lord said, "When you have trampled on the garment of shame and when the two become one and the male with the female (is) neither male nor female". Now in the first place we have not this word in the four Gospels that have been handed down to us, but in the Gospel of the Egyptians. Further he seems to me to fail to recognize that by the male impulse is meant wrath and by the female lust.
>
> (*Strom.* III 91ff.; Stählin II 238, 14–30)

We also come across a portion of Jesus' answer to Salome in the so-called 2nd Epistle of Clement, an early Christian sermon from the middle of the 2nd century. But only a fragment of the answer is preserved there, and the wording is new:

> (*g*) Let us now every hour expect the kingdom of God in love and righteousness, since we know not the day of God's appearing. For the Lord himself, on being asked by some one when his kingdom should come, said: When the two shall be one and that which is without as that which is

[1] Zahn, *Gesch. d. ntl. Kanons* II 2, p. 634, suggests: when . . . would come to pass. But the alteration is needless, since for the author of the Gospel of the Egyptians 'to know' is more important than 'to come to pass'.

within, and the male with the female neither male nor female.

(2 Clem. 12. 1–2)

The preacher then expounds this saying, which is doubtless identical with or at least closely related to the one quoted by Clement and assigned by him to the Gospel of the Egyptians. The question whether on this ground the other non-synoptic gospel citations in 2 Clem. should also be assigned to the Gospel of the Egyptians will be discussed below.

It has been conjectured (O. Stählin, ed. *in loc.*) that the Gospel of the Egyptians has been used in yet another passage:

(*h*) Again the Lord says: He who has married should not repudiate his wife, and he who has not married should not marry.

(*Strom.* III 97; Stählin II 241, 3f.)

But Clement does not indicate that here he uses some apocryphon. One easily assumes a free use of 1 Cor. 7:27, 32–36.

It is clear then from the texts given thus far that Clement knew the Gospel of the Egyptians and that he did not regard it as being on a par with the four canonical Gospels, yet did not wholly disapprove of it; cf. (*a*), (*c*) and (*d*). He is aware of the use of this Gospel by the Encratites and Julius Cassianus. From yet another text it is clear that Theodotus, from whom Clement made excerpts, used this Gospel:

(*i*) And when the Saviour says to Salome that death will reign as long as women bear children, he does not thereby slander procreation, for that indeed is necessary for the redemption of believers.

(*Exc. ex Theod.* 67; Stählin III 129, 3–6)

Here use is made of the same discourse which we came across in the passages given above, but we are told nothing more about it.

The Gospel of the Egyptians must also have been used by the Naassenes, a Gnostic group whom Hippolytus attacks in his *Refutatio* (after 222):

(*k*) They inquire yet further what the soul is, whence it originates and of what nature it is . . . This, however, they search for not in the Scriptures but in esoteric doctrines [*or teachers of esoteric doctrine?*]. Now they say that the soul is very hard to find and to perceive. For it does not always remain in the same fashion or form or in one condition. . .

And these various changes [*of the soul*] they find recorded in the so-called Gospel of the Egyptians.

(Hippol. *Ref.* V 7, 8f.; Wendland 80, 15–81, 2)

Since Hippolytus does not quote literally but contents himself with this general reference to the use and interpretation of the Gospel of the Egyptians by the Naassenes, there is not much that one can do with his statements. In particular they provide no basis for a reconstruction of this lost Gospel or for assigning other fragments to it. Some (e.g. Zahn, *Gesch. d. ntl. Kanons* II 2, p. 630 n. 1) have been minded to derive yet other sayings in Hippolytus from this Gospel, but scarcely with reason (cf. the compilation of the passages in Preuschen, *Antilegomena* p. 12f.). Certainly we have no means of proving that any such assigning of these sayings is correct.

J. Doresse, "Hermès et la Gnose" in *Novum Testamentum* I (1956), p. 66 conjectures that Hippolytus perhaps knew the Coptic Gospel of the Egyptians (see VII H below). Since the text of this Gospel has not yet been edited, nothing can be said regarding this hypothesis.

Finally Epiphanius of Salamis (4th century) refers to the fact that the Sabellians used the Gospel of the Egyptians:

(*l*) Their whole error, however, and the strength of it they derive from some apocrypha, above all from the so-called Gospel of the Egyptians, as some name it. For in it many such mysterious things are handed down as having come secretly from the Saviour, as that he had revealed to the disciples that the Father, the Son and the Holy Spirit are one and the same person.

(Epiph. *Haer.* 62, 2; Holl II 391, 4ff.)

Let alone that Epiphanius gives no literal quotation, his statement is in other respects also not very illuminating. For it is quite possible that here he merely brings together his description of the heterodox teaching of the Sabellians and the Gospel of the Egyptians, which for him was of course also heretical. The Sabellians may as a matter of fact have used this Gospel. But any drawing of conclusions as to its character from the notice in Epiphanius is forbidden.

The possibility that the Coptic work which was current under the same name (see VII H below) was in use among the Sabellians merits consideration, but that it was so cannot at present be proved.[1]

1 Suggestion of M. Hornschuh.

2. *The Gospel of the Egyptians and other Apocrypha*. Various attempts have been made to identify the Gospel of the Egyptians with other apocryphal writings, to prove its use in them or to establish a connection between it and them. Thus in his time M. Schnecken-burger (*Über das Evangelium der Aegyptier*, Berne 1834) imagined that he could prove "that the Gospel of the Egyptians stood in a close inner relationship to the Gospel of the Ebionites, and therefore also to its basis, the Gospel of the Hebrews" (*op. cit.*, p. 38). Now this venture was very closely bound up with the basic notion of the "Ebionites" entertained by the Tübingen School and likewise therefore cannot be sustained. For Schneckenburger the fact that a saying in 2 Clement is quoted also in Clement of Alexandria as coming from the Gospel of the Egyptians plays an important part in the proof. But only a fragment of 2 Clement was known to him. When the whole text became known, all the gospel citations in this homily were claimed by many for the Gospel of the Egyptians, and in this connection the passage (*g*) adduced above has to bear the burden of proof. The citations in 2 Clement cannot in fact all be referred to the canonical Gospels:

> 2, 4. And another Scripture says: I am not come to call the righteous, but sinners.

Cf. Mk. 2:17 and parallels.

> 3, 2. But he himself says: He who confesses me before men, him will I confess before my Father.

Evidently a free quotation of Mt. 10:32 = Lk. 12:8.

> 4, 2. For he says: Not every one who says to me 'Lord, Lord' will be saved, but he who does righteousness.

As compared with Mt. 7:21, with which the premise agrees, the conclusion has 'salvation' in place of 'entrance into the kingdom of God' and 'righteousness' in place of the 'will of the heavenly Father'. That scarcely permits us to trace a tendency; either then the citation is from memory or it is a free remodelling; if it is extra-canonical tradition, then we cannot go further and determine which tradition it is.

> 4, 5. Wherefore, if you do this, the Lord says: Though you should be joined to me in my bosom and keep not my commandments, I will cast you out and say to you: Depart from me, I know you not, whence you are, you doers of lawlessness.

No direct parallels to this saying can be adduced from the canonical Gospels. Reminiscences of Lk. 13:27 and Mt. 7:23 can in any case be found only in single words; the altered form of these passages in Justin, *Apol.* I xvi. 11 and *Dial.* lxxvi. 5 cannot be drawn upon in explanation. Here extra-canonical tradition must indeed be assumed, but the source must have been very similar to the Synoptic tradition. Cf. also the Gospel of the Nazarenes, No. 6, p. 147 above.

> 5, 2–4. For the Lord says: You will be as sheep in the midst of wolves. But Peter answered him and said: What if the wolves tear the sheep in pieces? Jesus said to Peter: Let the sheep not fear the wolves after death; you also fear not them who kill you, but otherwise cannot do anything to you; but fear him who after your death has power over body and soul to cast (them) into hell-fire.

In spite of reminiscences of Mt. 10:16 and 10:28 and parallels, as also of such later passages as Justin, *Apol.* I xix. 7; Clem. Alex., *Exc. ex Theod.* 14, 3 and 51, 3; Iren., *Adv. haer.* III, xix. 4 Harvey, a special tradition can be traced here: the form of the dialogue between Jesus and Peter certainly points to a special form of the evangelic tradition; the fact that the saying 2 Clem. 12, 2 [= (*g*) above] also has the form of a dialogue cannot however be brought forward in support of the view that 5, 2–4 is also derived from the Gospel of the Egyptians.

> 6, 1. But the Lord says: "No servant can serve two masters". If we desire to serve God and mammon, that is without profit for us.

The first part = Lk. 16:13; what is added is the writer's own free extension of it.

> 6, 2. For what is the profit if one gain the whole world and lose his soul?

A free modelling of Mt. 16:26 and parallels.

> 8, 5. For the Lord says in the gospel: If you have not kept what is little, who will give you what is great? For I say to you: He who is faithful in what is least, is faithful also in much.

The saying is closely connected with Lk. 16:10; it can also, it is true, come from another source, since the expression 'gospel' is used as a comprehensive term for the whole Christian message of salvation: there is only one gospel, although different gospels are used.

> 9, 11. For the Lord also says: My brethren are those who do the will of my Father.

This saying is best explained as a free application of Mk. 3:35 and parallels.

12, 1–2. See (g) above.

13, 4. For when they hear from us that God says: There is no favour for you if you love those who love you, but there is favour for you if you love your enemies and them that hate you.

Probably to be explained from Lk. 6:32, 35; cf. also Didache 1. 3; at all events hardly to be considered special tradition from another gospel.

To these sayings there ought perhaps to be added 2 Clem. 11, 2–4 and 11, 7. In both passages use is made of apocryphal traditions which are also met with in 1 Clem., but nothing further can be stated regarding their origin. And this seems to me to be characteristic: even if the author must have taken the saying in 12, 1–2 from the Gospel of the Egyptians, that cannot prove that the other citations are also derived from it. That possibility must indeed be taken into account. Since the Gospel of the Egyptians belongs to the earliest non-canonical gospels, it would not be astonishing if material from the Synoptic tradition was also contained in it side by side with the pronouncedly gnostic-encratite conversation between Christ and Salome. This thesis is however unlikely, since the typically Gnostic form of the dialogue (cf. below VII, p. 246 and elsewhere) was probably a characteristic trait of the Gospel of the Egyptians. But that also is conjecture.

Zahn was of opinion that there was a connection between the Gospel of the Egyptians and the Gospel of Peter (*Gesch. d. ntl. Kanons* II, 2, pp. 635f.). In particular he supposed that Cassianus had used not the Gospel of the Egyptians but another and that indeed the Gospel of Peter, but that the material in both was very closely connected. D. Völter then changed into an identity the relationship which Zahn had conjectured, but not proved, between the Gospel of the Egyptians and the Gospel of Peter (D. Völter, *Petrusevangelium oder Ägypterevangelium?* 1893; id., "Petrusevangelium oder Ägypterevangelium" in *ZNW* 6 (1905), pp. 368–372). But this venture has rightly met with no approval. For the surviving fragments of the two apocryphal writings permit no such conclusion.

Just as questionable is also the assigning of the various texts preserved in papyri to the Gospel of the Egyptians (for the texts of these papyri see II above). When in 1897 Pap. Ox. 1 appeared, Harnack attempted in a short study (*Über die jüngst entdeckten Sprüche Jesu,* 1897) to show that "the new sayings are excerpts from the Gospel of the Egyptians" (p. 34). Harnack stays his proof on seven passages from 2 Clem. and on the dialogue between Jesus and Salome, i.e. on one sure passage and seven highly questionable pieces of evidence. Further he wants to use as proof the statement of Epiphanius: "The Gospel of the Egyptians had a more highly pneumatic Christology that even approximated to modalism" (p. 33). That also in my opinion admits of no proof, the fragments being too scanty to establish such a far-reaching statement.[1]

Still more questionable is the suggestion of Grenfell and Hunt (*P. Ox.* II, 1899, p. 9) that the fragment in P. Ox. 210 may have belonged to the Gospel of the Egyptians or that here a quotation from this gospel may lie before us. The passage has come down to us in so fragmentary a condition that any conjecture which stays itself solely on the use of particular words must lead us astray.

The ascription to the Gospel of the Egyptians of the fragment contained in P. Ox. 655, which Hennecke (*Apokr.* 2, pp. 56ff.) proposed because of the consonance and material connection of its last lines, also remains very disputable. There it is said:

His disciples say to him: When will you be manifest to us and when shall we see you? He says: When you have undressed and are not ashamed.

This problem appears in a new light owing to the fact that this saying also recurs in the Coptic Gospel of Thomas. On the one hand, the close connection of the texts of P. Ox. 1, 654 and 655 with the Gospel of Thomas is manifest (see pp. 97ff. above); on the other hand, H.-Ch. Puech (pp. 298f. below; cf. among others the logia 22, 37 and 114) conjectures that between the Gospel of Thomas and the Gospel of the Egyptians also there are connections that cannot at present be closely determined but are not to be overlooked. The similarity of the passage just quoted from P. Ox. 655 to fragment (*f*) may also be accounted for on the assumption that the Gospel of the Egyptians and the Gospel of Thomas use the same traditions (Puech, p. 299 below). Moreover it is striking that according to the passages from Clement of Alexandria cited above Salome played a part in the Gospel of the Egyptians and that in the Gospel of Thomas also she appears as an important person (see below p. 298, especially logion 61; cf. also the instances in W. Bauer, *Rechtgläubigkeit*, p. 55).

Hennecke (*Apokr.* 2, p. 56) was willing to assign with 'great

[1] With it there are also to be dismissed the theses of Waitz (*Apokr.* 2, p. 51) which as a whole are in any case questionable. The conjecture of Hennecke (*Apokr.* 2, p. 56) that the Fayyum fragment (cf. II 4c., pp. 115f. above) should be connected with the Gospel of the Egyptians is also not tenable.

likelihood' two sayings from the Acts of Peter to the Gospel of the Egyptians:[1]

Concerning this the Lord says in a mystery: Unless you make what is on the right hand as what is on the left and what is on the left hand as what is on the right and what is above as what is below and what is behind as what is before, you will not recognize the kingdom.

(Acts of Peter ch. 38, *Aa.* I 94; the same saying with small differences—'to enter into the kingdom of heaven' instead of 'to recognize'—is also in the Acta Philippi 140, *Aa.* II 2 p. 74; cf. also the Acta Thomae 147, *Aa.* II 2 p. 256; Coptic Gospel of Thomas, logion 22, Puech, p. 298 below.).

I have heard, that is to say, that he has said this: Those who are with me have not understood me.

(Actus Petri c. Simone 10, *Aa.* I p. 58)

But as regards these words also not even a probability that they belong to the Gospel of the Egyptians can be established. The fact that we are concerned with a peculiar saying is no indication that it belongs to that gospel. The same applies to the passages from the so-called Apostolic Church Order which Hennecke (*Apokr.* 2, pp. 56 and 59), following Harnack and Baumstark, claimed for this gospel.

Finally, we must inquire into the apocryphal sayings of the Lord in the so-called Epistle of Titus (text edited by De Bruyne in *Revue Bénédictine* 37, 1925, pp. 47–72; cf. A. von Harnack, "Der apokryphe Brief des Paulusschülers Titus 'De dispositione sancti-monii'" in SB Berlin 1925, pp. 180–213; cf. vol. II, B XII 5). Hennecke suggested for them also a derivation from the Gospel of the Egyptians. But that cannot be proved, even though in the case of this tractate of the Priscillianists, in which the preference of this group for apocryphal writings is clearly in evidence, the possibility is not excluded that it used the (a?) Gospel of the Egyptians.[2]

Here four apocryphal logia are our concern:

1. . . . as the voice of the Lord says: O what manner of maid, what manner of woman! Such a mystery of the resurrection have you indicated to me, you who in the beginning of the world did institute vain feasts for yourselves and have taken

---

[1] So also Jeremias, *Unbek. Jesusworte*[2] p. 73 (ET 77).
[2] E. Hennecke, "Zur christlichen Apokryphenliteratur" in *ZKG* 45, 1927, p. 312 n.3. Zahn, *op. cit.*, p. 629 n. 2, had already pointed to possible connections between Priscillian and the Gospel of the Egyptians (the older literature on this question is also given there).

delight in popular revelries and done like those who let themselves be amused.

(De Bruyne, *ll.* 69ff.)

Perhaps there belongs to this the continuation:

See, what youths are among you! But come and consider, because he is here who considers (the soul?) and because the last day of persecution and punishment is here.

2. When the Saviour Christ saw the deeds of this offence multiplying (in, till?, the end) he was grieved and said: Precious to me are those who despise their souls (conscientiously?), for I see that some allow their souls to grow cold unto vanity and surrender themselves to the unclean age and turn above all to the devil (?). But I can assist them and can say to them: O you souls, who abandon yourselves to voluptuousness and the fear of God is not in you.

(De Bruyne, *ll.* 355ff.)

3. In encouragement given by the Lord (?) he said: Hear me, you whom I have chosen as lambs, and fear not the wolves.

(De Bruyne, *l.* 492f.)

4. For in particular the cypress is a mystery of pious conduct (?) according to the Lord Christ's question and answer.

(De Bruyne, *l.* 502f.)

A satisfactory interpretation of these sayings is scarcely possible, since they are wrenched from their context and above all because many linguistic and textual questions remain unsolved; the fact that the tractate has been transmitted in barbarous Latin adds to the difficulty of our problem. No. 3 is the most easily understood, since in it use is made of the well-known figure of the sheep and wolves (cf. Mt. 10:16). But whether this saying comes from the same source as the others and whether this source was the Gospel of the Egyptians cannot be ascertained. Even if Harnack's conjecture (*op. cit.*, p. 195 n. 3) were correct, that No. 4 and indeed Nos. 1 and 2 also are derived from a conversation of Jesus with His disciples, apparently after His resurrection (a conjecture for which there is scarcely a clue in the texts), that would not carry us further so far as the Gospel of the Egyptians is concerned. For there are dialogues of Jesus with His disciples in diverse forms and in many writings.[1]

[1] It may also be mentioned that A. Jacoby wanted to ascribe to the Gospel of the Egyptians the Strasbourg Coptic fragment edited by him (for its text see VI 3, pp. 227ff. below), a thing that has already been proved to be absurd by C. Schmidt (*GGA* 1900,

The outcome of this review is then that apart from the fragments in Clement which are expressly declared to be portions of the Gospel of the Egyptians almost nothing can with certainty be claimed for this apocryphal gospel.

3. *Name, Character, Time of Composition.* Such being the outcome, it is well-nigh futile to attempt any precise statements regarding the content, structure, character and time of the Gospel of the Egyptians. Only the following may be said:

In the 2nd century there was in Egypt a gospel which was named after the land in which it was used or after its inhabitants. In its construction the Greek title Εὐαγγέλιον κατ' Αἰγυπτίους is, like the headings of the canonical Gospels, a substitute for the genitive. But this means—as Bauer, *Rechtgläubigkeit* p. 54, observes —that the Gospel of the Egyptians reaches back to a time "in which the Christians of Egypt made use of this gospel and indeed of it alone as their life of Jesus". In contra-distinction to the Alexandrian and Jewish-Christian Gospel of the Hebrews,[1] it was the gospel of the Gentile-Christian Egyptians. Moreover for our subject it is not very important whether the title was given to the work in Egypt itself or outside it (Rome?; cf. A. Schmidtke, *TU* 37. 1, 1911, p. 140 n. 1). Still, if the title originated in Rome, that would throw some light on the use of the Gospel in 2 Clement (see above), which may also belong to Rome, but at the same time we should be referred for its origin to an Encratite circle of the first half of the 2nd century which cannot have comprised the whole body of the Egyptian Gentile Christians, i.e. Bauer's thesis would have to be somewhat modified.[2]

Bauer is undoubtedly right in his opinion that the Christianity of the Nile valley was already at its outset influenced by Gnosticism. It is therefore not astonishing that the few fragments which can with likelihood be assigned to this gospel show sturdy Gnostic traits. The rôle of Salome, who in these circles was evidently an important personality, may also be accounted for in this way. At all events it is not in the least so 'strange' as Bardenhewer thinks (*Lit.-gesch.* I 522 n. 1) that this gospel became popular in Egypt earlier than did the canonical books. Further, if the suggestion of

481–506). The Account of the Baptism edited by Jacoby (A. Jacoby, *Ein bisher unbeachteter apokrypher Bericht über die Taufe Jesu nebst Beiträgen zur Geschichte der Didaskalie der 12 Apostel*, Strasbourg 1902) was claimed for the Gospel of the Egyptians by A. Baumstark (*Oriens Christianus* II, 1902, p. 466). But this hypothesis could hold its ground only if as a matter of fact we knew so much of the Gospel of the Egyptians as Baumstark thinks we do, which, however, is not the case. At any rate I cannot follow these profusely fanciful statements.

[1] That the Gospel of the Egyptians "used the Gospel of the Hebrews as a source and worked it up", as G. Quispel, *Vig. Chr.* 11, 1957, p. 143, supposes, is in my opinion not capable of proof because our information is so fragmentary. On the Gospel of the Hebrews see pp. 158ff. above.

[2] Suggestion of M. Hornschuh.

H.-Ch. Puech (see p. 249 below) proves right—and I see nothing
that can be said against it—that many logia of the Coptic "Dialogue of the Redeemer" (Cod. I of the library from Nag Hammadi) are derived from the Gospel of the Egyptians, that would
to a certain extent confirm the view that this writing enjoyed great
popularity in different Gnostic groups—to be sure because it was
intimately connected with their doctrines. As the time of its
composition one can only mention the 2nd century, probably the
first third; a closer definition cannot be given.

V

THE GOSPEL OF PETER

(Chr. Maurer)

1. *Tradition.* Down to 1886 one was aware of the existence of a
"Gospel according to Peter", but not so much as a single quotation from it was known. Whether Origen had a knowledge of its
contents is very much open to question. According to his account
(*Com. in Mt.* x. 17) some who maintained that the brethren of
Jesus sprang from a first marriage of Joseph (cf. Protevangelium
of James, viiif.) relied on a tradition in the Gospel according to
Peter or in the Book of James. Eusebius also, who reckons it among
the heretical forgeries, discloses no direct knowledge of this Gospel
(*H.E.* III, 3; III, 25), and just as little do Jerome and the Decretum Gelasianum, both based on Eusebius. The most important
and at the same time the earliest witness is Serapion of Antioch
(*c.* 200), from whose writing on the Gospel of Peter Eusebius
quotes a few sentences (*H.E.* VI, 12). According to them, when
Serapion was in the church at Rhossus, he at first decided, without having read the Gospel, that to meet the requirement of some
of the church members it might (should?) be read. Later, however, he himself read it through and as refutation of it made a
collection of its Gnostic statements.

In the winter of 1886–87 a fragment of the Gospel of Peter was
found at Akhmîm in Upper Egypt. With fragments of the Greek
Apocalypse of Peter and of the Greek Book of Enoch it lay in the
grave of a Christian monk of the 8th to the 12th century and is
now in the Cairo Museum. The manuscript is of the 8th or 9th
century. The account begins with Pilate's washing of his hands
and then proceeds to the condemnation and death of Jesus and to
a peculiar description of His resurrection. The thread of the
narrative breaks off at the beginning of the description of the
first appearance of the risen Jesus at the sea (of Tiberias). Ornaments at the beginning and end of the manuscript indicate that
the copyist knew no more than the text that is known to us. Accordingly conjectures as to the compass and contents of the whole have
no foundation. On the conjecture of Zahn, James etc. that the
Greek Apocalypse of Peter represents a portion of the original
Gospel, see the introduction to that Apocalypse. The present text
is divided by Harnack into sixty verses and, independently of these,
by Robinson into fourteen chapters.

2. *The Relationships of the Writing.* Although Peter himself is indicated as the author (v. 26f., 60), what lies before us is a further development of the traditional material of the four canonical Gospels. These are used as remembered, whilst the oral transmission of the material in the preaching of the gospel has also told upon it (Dibelius).

Whilst the different sources, often as far as particular expressions, are woven into one another, the impression made upon us is that of a completely new account. What alterations have resulted are in part unintentional and in part have known theological motives hid behind them. Mt. with its special material forms the basis of the composition (washing of hands v. 1; guarding and sealing of the grave v. 29ff.; attempt to hush up the resurrection of Jesus by influencing the Roman soldiers and Pilate v. 47ff.). To Jn. there go back the dating of the day of the death (v. 5), the crurifragium (v. 14), the appearance of the risen Jesus at the sea (v. 60), as also many particular traits. Lk. contributes the participation of Herod in the condemnation of Jesus (v. 2ff.) and the episode of the thief (v. 13f.). The time of writing is thus at the earliest that of the existence of the canonical Gospels, and at the latest the second half of the 2nd century, since Serapion dates this gospel back about a generation at least. We may then accept the middle of the 2nd century as the time when it came into being. A connection with Justin is questionable and contributes nothing to the dating. Since the "Unknown Gospel" (edited by H. I. Bell and T. C. Skeat, 1935; see pp. 94ff. above) makes a similar use of the four Gospels already in the first half of the 2nd century, the Gospel of Peter also may possibly be carried further back.

As Serapion reports, the Gospel of Peter was read by heretical Christians of his diocese. He himself obtained it that he might read it from "successors of those who compiled it", who were Docetics. Its origin is then to be sought in Syria, probably in Gnostic circles. Into this conclusion there fits the fact that the Syriac *Didascalia*, especially in its 21st chapter, is connected with our Gospel (Jesus is executed by order of Herod, v. 2, 5; fasting of the disciples until the Sabbath, v. 27; resurrection of Jesus in the night, v. 35; special mention of Levi, v. 60). Possible traces in Cyril of Jerusalem and others are also to be appraised as having emanated from Syria. The connections with the epistle of Pilate to Claudius (cf. pp. 477f.), in which it is stated that Pilate was guiltless of the death of Jesus and that the Jews alone were answerable for it, are of no consequence, since the different strata within the Pilate literature cannot be clearly delimited.

3. *Character.* The most important question is whether, how far and in what sense the Gospel of Peter is to be regarded as Gnostic,

how in consequence Serapion is to be understood when he says, "We were able . . . to find most things in accordance with the true doctrine of our Redeemer, but some things (commandments and doctrines) added to it . . .".

Passages have been pointed out which disclose special Gnostic speculation on divine things. But precisely these particular traits of the christology may be construed "more simply". The silence of Jesus on the cross (v. 10) can indeed, but need not, point to a merely apparent passion. The statement, "He was taken up" (v. 19) may be simply a turn of expression, of which there are other instances, for "to die", in which case we do not need to think of an ascension from the cross. The substitution of "power" for the name of God in the same verse may be a mere toning down of Jesus' cry of despair and here no thought of a separation of the "supreme" Christ from the body of flesh may be involved. The walking and speaking cross (v. 39, 42) stands most easily in closer connection with the later Gnostic speculation about the cross, yet here also (cf. K. L. Schmidt, pp. 66ff.; 71) the literary starting point must be sought in Mt. 24:30 (cf. Aeth. Apocalypse of Peter, 1). All these odd statements are at most to be regarded as finger-holds upon which the Gnostic remodelling of the Gospel accounts could get a grip, and later did very thoroughly. The crucial problem, however, lies in the fact that in their entirety the statements of the Gospel of Peter have an undertone which already indicates a climate that is strange to the NT. At the same time it may be conceded to the author that he deliberately purposes to keep to the line of the hitherto existing Gospels. He means, as they do, to prove through all details that Christ is Lord.

What, however, distinguishes it from the New Testament Gospels is its massive apologetic reasoning. What in them emerges on the fringe is here at the centre. The testimony of belief is replaced by apparently direct proof of truth. This purpose is served above all by the professedly ocular testimony of the apostle Peter (v. 26f., 59f.), side by side with the fantastic accounts of wonders. Here, however, special mention must be made of the resurrection, which, in enlargement of Mt's account and in contrast to all Christian and Gnostic presentations, takes place openly before the heathen soldiers and Jewish authorities, therefore before the enemies of Jesus (v. 35ff.). That by this means the apologetic aim, despite the minutely recorded details, is simply not attained, is clear. Rather the passion and resurrection of Jesus, yea He himself, are loosened out of the soil of real history and transferred to the realm of legend and myth. This evaporation is underlined by vague presentations of the circumstances obtaining in Palestine in the time of Jesus. Ignorance of the political relationships, the

religious groups, the feast-calendar etc. likewise result in the real
figure of Jesus being allowed to become more and more hazy.

The difference in climate is apparent in the second place in the
misunderstanding of the scriptural proofs in the Gospels. There
the passion and resurrection of Jesus are presented as the eschatological fulfilment of the old covenant. This decisive element of the
presentation is not perceived by the author of our Gospel. Evidence of this is provided by the strange motivation of particular
traits, which primarily are to be evaluated only against the background of scriptural proof. Thus the crurifragium (in spite of a
harsh construction v. 14 ought in my opinion to be connected with
Jesus) is provided with an irrelevant foundation. What in the
Gospel of John is referred to the fulfilment of the scripture (Jn.
19:28–30) is in the Gospel of Peter given a new interpretation and
referred to the accomplishment of the sins of the Jews (v. 17). The
like holds good of the silence of Jesus (v. 10). Also the one citation
from the OT, Deut. 21:23 (v. 5, 15), is torn out of the context in
which it is used in Jn. 19:31. In Jn. the taking down from the
cross in the evening of the Sabbath day stands in connection with
the proof that Jesus is the passover lamb: in the Gospel of Peter
on the other hand this eschatological anchorage is abandoned, the
citation serving merely to characterize the formalism of the Jews.
Thus here also the revelation-history of the Gospels, which points
to Christ, is resolved into a happening which can have taken place
anywhere.

In the third place those traits are lacking through which the
death of Jesus is shown to be an expiatory passion for the world
(Barabbas, the word to the thief, the word of forgiveness on the
cross, Jesus as the passover lamb). Likewise the author suppresses
the denial of the disciples (cf. v. 26f.), through which the relation
of Jesus to His Church is brought within the point of view of forgiveness. Only with an eye on the Jews is mention made of guilt,
and this quite bluntly (v. 2, 6ff., 13, 17, 25, 47f. and often). The
heathen Pilate is completely exonerated (v. 1, 3f., 46), indeed
hallmarked as a positive witness of the Lord's divinity (v. 46).
This playing down of the problem of guilt betrays a conception
of the redemption wrought in Christ for fallen mankind which is
foreign to the NT.

All these references show no articulated Gnostic theology, but
they indicate that such a theology is already on the way, since
the representation is taken out of the framework of the divine act
of revelation and set in that of a Gnostic myth. Thus the Gospel
of Peter stands on the one hand through its comparative sobriety
nearer to the canonical Gospels than to the later Gnostic embel-
lishments, but on the other hand it prepares a way for them.

4. From the literature the following works may be mentioned:

(a) *Editions:* Editio princeps: U. Bouriant, *Mémoires publiés par les membres de la mission archéologique française au Caire*, tom. IX, Paris, 1892—With a reproduction of the manuscript: A. Lods, *ibid.*, 1893; O. v. Gebhardt, 1893—Also H. B. Swete, *The Akhmîm Fragment of the Apocryphal Gospel of St. Peter*, London 1893; E. Preuschen, *Antilegomena*, ²1905; E. Klostermann in *KlT* No. 3, 1903; ²1908 and reprint.

(b) *Studies* (almost all with text and translation): J. A. Robinson and M. R. James, *The Gospel according to Peter and the Revelation of Peter*, London, 1892; A. v. Harnack, *Bruchstücke des Evangeliums und der Apokalypse des Petrus* (*TU* 9, 1893); H. v. Schubert, *Die Composition des pseudopetrinischen Evangelien-Fragments*, 1893; Th. Zahn, *Das Evangelium des Petrus*, 1893 (*NkZ* IV, pp. 143ff.); M. Dibelius, "Die at.lichen Motive in der Leidensgeschichte des Petrus- und Johannesevangeliums" (*BZAW* 33, 1918, pp. 125ff. = *Botschaft u. Geschichte, Gesammelte Aufsätze von M. Dibelius†*, edited by G. Bornkamm, Vol. I, 1953, pp. 221–247); A. Stülcken, see *Handb.* pp. 72ff. and *Apokr.* 2, 1924, pp. 59ff.; P. Gardner-Smith, "The Gospel of Peter" in *JTS*, 1926, pp. 225–271; id., "The Date of the Gospel of Peter" (it is dated A.D. 90–100) in *JTS*, 1926, pp. 401–407; L. Vaganay, *L'évangile de Pierre*, 1930 (with an extensive bibliography); K. L. Schmidt, *Kanonische und apokryphe Evangelien und Apostelgeschichten* (*Abhandlungen z. Theol. d. AT u. NT*, 5), 1944, pp. 37–78; J. Quasten, *Patrology*, Vol. I, *The Beginnings of Patristic Literature*, 1950, pp. 114–115 (with bibliography); Santos, pp. 68–71 and 398–417.

Fragment:

1. 1. But of the Jews none *washed their hands*,[1] neither Herod nor any one of his judges. And as they would not wash, Pilate arose. 2. And then Herod the king commanded that the Lord should be marched off, saying to them, "What I have commanded you to do to him, do ye".

2. 3. Now there stood there *Joseph*, the friend of Pilate and of the Lord, and knowing that they were about to crucify him *he came to Pilate and begged the body of the*[2] Lord for burial. 4. And Pilate sent to Herod and begged his body. 5. And Herod said, "Brother Pilate, even if no one had begged him, we should bury him, since the *Sabbath is drawing on*.[3] For it stands written in the law: The *sun* should not *set* on one that has been put to death".[4]

[1] Cf. Mt. 27:24.   [2] Mk. 15:43 and par.   [3] Cf. Lk. 23:54.
[4] Cf. Jn. 19:31; Deut. 21:22ff.; Josh. 8:29; 10:27.

And *he delivered*[1] him to the people on the day before the *unleavened bread*,[2] their feast. **3.** 6. So they *took* the Lord and pushed him in great haste and said, "Let us hale the Son of God now that we have gotten power over him". 7. And they *put upon him a purple robe* and set him on the judgment seat and said, "Judge righteously, *O King of Israel!*".[3] 8. And one of them brought a *crown of thorns and put it on the Lord's head.* 9. And others who stood by spat on his face, and others buffeted him on the cheeks, others nudged him with a *reed*,[4] and some scourged him, saying, "With such honour let us honour the Son of God".

4. 10. And they brought *two malefactors and crucified* the Lord *in the midst between them.*[5] But he *held his peace*,[6] as if he felt no pain. 11. And when they had set up the cross, they wrote upon it: *This is the King* of Israel.[5] 12. And they laid down his garments before him and *divided* them among themselves and *cast the lot* upon them.[5] 13. *But one of the malefactors* rebuked them, saying, "*We* have landed in suffering for the deeds of wickedness which we have committed, *but this man,* who has become the saviour of men, what wrong has he done you?".[7] 14. And they were wroth with him and commanded that his *legs* should not be broken,[8] so that he might die in torments.

5. 15. Now it was *midday* and a *darkness* covered all Judaea. And they became anxious and uneasy lest the sun had already set, since he was still alive. ⟨For⟩ it stands written for them: the *sun* should not *set* on one that has been put to death.[9] 16. And one of them said, "Give him to drink *gall* with *vinegar*". And they mixed it and gave *him to drink.*[10] 17. And they fulfilled all things and completed the measure of their sins on their head.[11] 18. And many went about with lamps, [and] as they supposed that it was night, [they went to bed *or* they stumbled].[12] 19. And the Lord *called out and cried,* "My power, O power, *thou hast forsaken me!*"[13] And having said this he was taken up. 20. And at the same hour *the veil of the temple* in Jerusalem was rent *in two.*[14]

[1] Cf. Mk. 15:15 and par.   [2] Cf. Mk. 14:12 and par.
[3] Cf. Justin, *Apol.* I. xxxv; Jn. 19:13.
[4] To v. 6–9 cf. Mk. 14:65; 15:16–20 and par.
[5] Cf. Mk. 15:24ff. and par.   [6] Cf. Mk. 14:61 and par.; 15:5 and par.
[7] Cf. Lk. 23:39ff.   [8] Cf. Jn. 19:31ff.
[9] Mk. 15:33 and par.; Am. 8:9; cf. note 4, p. 183.   [10] Cf. Mt. 27:34, 48 and par.
[11] Cf. Jn. 19:28, 30.   [12] Cf. Jn. 11:10.   [13] Cf. Mk. 15:34 and par.
[14] Mk. 15:38 and par.

6. 21. And then the Jews drew *the nails*[1] from the hands of the Lord and laid him on the earth. And the whole *earth shook* and there came a *great fear*.[2] 22. Then the sun shone ⟨again⟩, and it was found to be the ninth hour.[3] 23. And the Jews rejoiced and gave his body to Joseph that he might bury it, since he had seen all the good that he (=Jesus) had done. 24. And he took the Lord, washed him, *wrapped him in linen*[4] and brought him into his own sepulchre, called Joseph's *Garden*.[5]

7. 25. Then the Jews and the elders and the priests, perceiving what great evil they had done to themselves, began to lament and to say, "Woe on our sins, the judgment and the end of Jerusalem is drawn nigh".[6] 26. But I mourned with my fellows, and being wounded in heart we hid ourselves, for we were sought after by them as evildoers and as persons who wanted to set fire to the temple. 27. Because of all these things *we were fasting* and sat *mourning and weeping* night and day until the Sabbath.[7]

8. 28. But the scribes and Pharisees and elders, being assembled together and hearing that all the people were murmuring and beating their breasts, saying, "If at his death these exceeding great signs have come to pass, behold how *righteous* he was!",[8]— 29. were afraid and came *to Pilate*,[9] entreating him and saying, 30. "Give us soldiers that we may watch his sepulchre *for three days, lest his disciples come and steal him away* and the *people* suppose that he *is risen from the dead*, and do us harm". 31. And Pilate gave them Petronius the centurion with soldiers to watch the sepulchre. And with them there came elders and scribes to the sepulchre. 32. And all who were there, together with the centurion and the soldiers, *rolled* thither a great stone and laid it against the entrance to the sepulchre 33. and *put* on it seven *seals*, pitched a tent and kept watch.[10] **9.** 34. Early in the morning, when the Sabbath dawned, there came a crowd from Jerusalem and the country round about to see the sepulchre that had been sealed.

35. Now in the night in which the Lord's day dawned, when the soldiers, two by two in every watch, were keeping guard, there rang out a loud *voice in heaven*, 36. and they saw the *heavens*

---

[1] Jn. 20: 25, 27.   [2] Mt.27:51, 54.   [3] Cf. Mk. 15:33 and par.
[4] Cf. Mk. 15:46 and par.   [5] Jn. 19:41.   [6] Cf. Lk. 23:48 var. lect.
[7] Cf. Mk. 2:20 and par.; 16:10.   [8] Cf. Lk. 23:47f.
[9] With v. 29–33 cf. Mt. 27:62–66.   [10] Cf. Mk. 15:46 and par.; Mt. 27:66.

opened[1] and two men *come down* from there in a great brightness and draw nigh to the sepulchre. 37. That *stone* which had been laid against the entrance to the sepulchre started of itself *to roll* and gave way to the side, and the sepulchre was opened, and both the young men entered in.[2] **10.** 38. When now those soldiers saw this, they awakened the centurion and the elders—for they also were there to assist at the watch. 39. And whilst they were relating what they had seen, they saw again three men come out from the sepulchre, and two of them sustaining the other, and a cross following them, 40. and the heads of the two reaching to heaven, but that of him who was led of them by the hand overpassing the heavens. 41. And they heard a voice out of the heavens crying, "Thou hast preached to them that sleep",[3] 42. and from the cross there was heard the answer, "Yea". **11.** 43. Those men therefore took counsel with one another to go and report this to Pilate. 44. And whilst they were still deliberating, the heavens were again seen to open, and a man descended and entered into the sepulchre. 45. When those who were of the centurion's company saw this, they hastened by night to Pilate, abandoning the sepulchre which they were guarding, and reported everything that they had seen, being full of disquietude and saying, *"In truth* he was *the Son of God".*[4] 46. Pilate answered and said, "I am clean *from the blood* of the Son of God, upon such a thing have you decided."[5] 47. Then all came to him, beseeching him and urgently calling upon him to command the centurion and the soldiers to tell no one what they had seen. 48. "For *it is better* for us", they said, "to make ourselves guilty of the greatest sin before God than to fall into the hands of the people of the Jews and be stoned".[6] 49. Pilate therefore commanded the centurion and the soldiers to say nothing.[7]

12. 50. *Early in the morning* of the Lord's day *Mary Magdalene,*[8] a woman disciple of the Lord—for *fear* of the *Jews,*[9] since (they) were inflamed with wrath, she had not done at the sepulchre of the Lord what women are wont to do for those beloved of them who die—took 51. with her her women friends and came to the sepulchre where he was laid. 52. And they feared lest the Jews should see them, and said, "Although we could not weep and

---

[1] Cf. Mt. 3:16f. and par.   [2] With v. 35–37 cf. Mt. 28:1f.   [3] Cf. 1 Pet. 3:19.
[4] Mk. 15:39 and par.   [5] Cf. Mt. 27:24.   [6] Cf. Jn. 11:50.
[7] With v. 47–49 cf. Mt. 28:11–15.   [8] Cf. Mt. 28:1 and par.   [9] Cf. Jn. 20:19.

lament on that day when he was crucified, yet let us now do so at his sepulchre. 53. *But who will roll away for us the stone* also that is set *on the entrance to the sepulchre,* that we may go in and sit beside him and do what is due?—54. For *the stone was great,*[1]—and we fear lest any one see us. And if we cannot do so, let us at least put down at the entrance what we bring for a memorial of him and let us weep and lament until we have again gone home".
13. 55. So they went and found the sepulchre opened. And they came near, *stooped down* and saw there *a young man* sitting in the midst of the sepulchre, comely and *clothed with a brightly shining robe,* who said to them, 56. "Wherefore are ye come? *Whom seek ye?* Not him that *was crucified? He is risen* and gone. But if ye believe not, stoop this way and *see the place where he lay, for he is not here.* For he is risen and is gone thither whence he was sent". 57. Then the women *fled affrighted.*[2]

14. 58. Now it was the last day of unleavened bread and many went away and repaired to their homes, since the feast was at an end. 59. But we, the twelve disciples of the Lord, wept and mourned, and each one, very grieved for what had come to pass, went to his own home. 60. But I, Simon Peter, and my brother Andrew took our nets and went to the sea.[3] And there was with us Levi, the son of Alphaeus, whom the Lord—(had called away from the custom-house (?), cf. Mk. 2:14).

[1] Cf. Mk. 16:3f.   [2] With v. 55–57 cf. Mk. 16:1–8.   [3] Cf. Jn. 21:1ff.

VI

CONVERSATIONS BETWEEN JESUS AND HIS DISCIPLES AFTER THE RESURRECTION

1. THE FREER LOGION: [Mk.] 16:14 W

(*J. Jeremias*)

The Gospel ms. W (4th or 5th century) has, like most manuscripts, the longer spurious ending after Mk. 16:8 (i.e. verses 9–20), but inserts into it a dialogue between the disciples and the risen Lord, the beginning of which is also transmitted by Jerome (*c. Pelag.* II. 15). In the longer ending of Mark it is described how the risen Lord, early on the first day of the week, appeared first to Mary Magdalene and then in another form "to two of them" as they walked; then follows the appearance to the eleven as a third occasion. While the corresponding passage in Lk. (24:41f.) records that their unbelief is overcome when the risen Lord eats before them, Mk. 16:14 simply mentions a reproach and immediately goes on to the mission charge. In the Freer Logion this gap is eliminated by the insertion of a dialogue between the risen Lord and the disciples. There the disciples charge Satan and the unclean spirits with responsibility for their unbelief and ask about the immediate parousia. To this request the risen Lord replies that the power of Satan has truly reached its end, but that certain signs must yet be fulfilled; then follows the mission charge.

Although an apocryphal amplification, the piece shows itself ancient by the highly eschatological tone (which comes out in the request of the disciples) and by its Jewish-apocalyptic terminology. The striking designation of the parousia as a revealing of the "righteousness" of Christ is related to Old Testament usage, for there the righteousness of God and triumph of God are connected (Jud. 5:11, Isa. 5:16; cf. Mt. 6:33, Jn. 16:8, 1 Tim. 3:16).

Text: H. A. Sanders in *Biblical World*, NS, 31 (1908), 140–142, and in *American Journal of Archaeology*, ser. II, 12 (1908), 52–54; H. B. Swete, *Zwei neue Evangelienfragmente* (*KlT* 31), Bonn, ¹1908 = ²1924.
Literature: E. J. Goodspeed in *Biblical World*, NS, 31 (1908), 220–226; C. R. Gregory, *Das Freer-Logion*, Leipzig, 1908; A. Harnack in *ThLZ* 33 (1908) 168–170; C. Schmidt in *ThLZ* 33 (1908), 359f.; H. von Soden in *ChW* 22 (1908), 482–486; E. Helzle, *Der Schluss des Markusevangeliums* (*Mk. 16:9–20*) *und das Freer-Logion* (*Mk. 16:14 W*),

ihre Tendenzen und ihr gegenseitiges Verhältnis. Eine wortexegetische Untersuchung. Phil. Diss. Tübingen 1959.

[*Mark 16:14:* Afterward he appeared to the eleven as they reclined at table and reproached them for their unbelief and hardness of heart, for they had not believed those who had seen him after he arose.] And they excused themselves with the words, "This eon (age) of lawlessness and unbelief[1] is under Satan,[2] who through the unclean spirits[3] does not allow the true power of God[4] to be comprehended. Therefore," they said to Christ, "reveal your righteousness[5] now." And Christ replied to them, "The measure of the years of Satan's power[6] is filled up.[7] But other fearful things draw near, also (for those) for whom I, because they have sinned, was delivered to death, that they might turn back to the truth and sin no more[8] in order to inherit the spiritual and imperishable glory of righteousness (preserved) in heaven.[9]

[*Verse 15:* Now then, go into all the world," *etc.*]

[The whole is contained in the Gospel ms. W (4th–5th cent.) from Egypt, now in the Freer Museum in Washington; the words of the apostles are also in Jerome, *c. Pelag.* II. 15.]

2. EPISTULA APOSTOLORUM
(*H. Duensing*)

INTRODUCTION.

1. *Transmission and attestation.* This unusual apocryphon is nowhere mentioned in the literature of early Christianity. Nothing was known of its existence until 1895, when Carl Schmidt discovered fifteen leaves with the Coptic text of the work in the Institut de la Mission Archéologique in Cairo. He reported his find the same year, but twenty-four years passed before he was able to bring out an edition of the work. Meanwhile, a few small Latin fragments were recognized by Bick in a Vienna palimpsest and edited. An Ethiopic translation containing the entire work was edited by Guerrier in 1913. On the basis of this material Schmidt, with the assistance of Wajnberg as collaborator on the Ethiopic text, published the work in 1919. Harnack discovered a

[1] Cf. 2 Cor. 4:4; Gal. 1:4.   [2] Cf. Jn. 14:30; Eph. 2:2.
[3] Cf. Mk. 1:23, 26, etc.   [4] Cf. Mk. 12:24; 1 Cor. 6:14; Eph. 1:19f.
[5] Cf. Mt. 6:33; Jn. 16:8; 1 Tim. 3:16.   [6] Cf. Lk. 10:18; Jn. 12:31; 16:11.
[7] Cf. Mk. 1:15.   [8] Cf. Jn. 5:14; 8:11.   [9] Cf. 1 Pet. 1:4; 2 Tim. 4:8.

trace of its use in the writing edited by de Bruyne, "De dispositione sanctimonii," which presents an apocryphal letter of Paul's follower Titus (see below, p. 213). Whether the citation from Commodian (below, p. 197) comes, as James thinks, from the *Epistula Apostolorum* appears questionable.

2. *Contents and significance.* The eleven disciples, in a letter addressed to the Christians of the four regions of the earth, present a dialogue between Christ and themselves that took place after His resurrection, and in which He gave them revelations concerning various heavenly things. His coming to earth is said to have come about when He entered into the womb of Mary in the disguise of the angel Gabriel. After His resurrection also He sent His power in the form of Gabriel to free Peter from the prison for one night. The reality of Christ's body is strongly maintained (against Cerinthus and Simon, whom the apostles warn against), but at the same time the unity of the Son and the Father is so strongly emphasized that one could justifiably speak of identity. During Christ's descent He took on, in each of the heavenly spheres, the form of the angel residing there, in order to reach the earth without being recognized (as also described in the *Ascension of Isaiah*). As the Logos took on real flesh and also after the resurrection appears to His disciples with flesh that can be felt (so that Peter as well as Thomas can put his fingers into the nailprints of His hands), so too will His redeemed rise again in the flesh, "a garment that will not pass away". Christ has also proclaimed the message of salvation in the underworld. His disciples receive the commission to preach. At their request the disciples receive instruction about the future, as contained also in other apocalypses.

The writing is a remarkable document from the time of the battle between Christianity and Gnosticism. It shows how the young Christianity prevailed against this opponent but at the same time experienced a change of its thought forms. And it must have been these strange forms, arising not from the soil of ordinary Christianity but from Gnosticism, which caused the writing to be dropped in a later period. It was too heavily loaded with strange views and no longer had any contemporary significance. But the writing also shows the terrific moral fervour and the unrelenting strictness of moral judgment evident in other early Christian writings. The poor man should censure even his benefactor without fear if he sees him sin. In the day of judgment the Son will not fear the rich nor have pity on the poor, as required by the Father who commands that He deliver to eternal punishment every one according to his sins.

3. *Date of composition.* The opposition against a Gnosticism that

still exercises a strong influence puts the writing in the 2nd century. The free and easy way with which the author uses and treats the New Testament writings could point to the first half of that century. The questions concerning the end of the world and the Lord's return still have very immediate significance. That also points to an early period. On the other hand the writing poses a question in that it presupposes a liturgical service celebrated daily on the altar in heaven.[1] The Logos who left heaven furnishes the archangels with a wondrous voice, that they may perform the service at the altar in His place until His return. Is this a projection into heaven of a practice of the Christian community? And if so, from what time may we suppose the existence of such a religious service performed daily without qualification?

4. Literature: Carl Schmidt, *Gespräche Jesu mit seinen Jüngern nach der Auferstehung* (*TU* 43), Leipzig, 1919. Hugo Duensing, *Epistula Apostolorum*, Bonn, 1925 (*KlT* 152). Louis Guerrier, *Le Testament en Galilée*, Paris, 1913 (*PO* IX, 3). Hennecke, in *Apokr.* 2, pp. 146–150, gave a detailed account of the contents with useful notes. Cf. also H. Lietzmann, *ZNW*, 1921, pp. 173–176 and H. Duensing, *GGA*, 1922, pp. 241–252, and the reply of Schmidt in *Orient.LZ*, 1925, pp. 855–859. The orthodoxy of the work is questioned in *Rev. Bibl.* 30 (1921), pp. 110–134. M. R. James gave an English translation based upon Schmidt and Guerrier in *The Apocryphal New Testament*, pp. 485–503. L. Gry, in *Rev. Bibl.* 49 (1940), pp. 86–97, discusses the divergent dates of the parousia in the two texts. Anyone wanting information concerning the textual basis of the following translation must refer to my small edition in Lietzmann's *Kleine Texte* 152.

Where the two versions deviate markedly from one another the text is printed in parallel columns, Ethiopic on the left and Coptic on the right.

EPISTULA APOSTOLORUM
[The title is not transmitted but can be inferred.]

1. (*Chaps. 1–6 in Eth. only.*) What Jesus Christ revealed to his disciples as a letter, and how Jesus Christ revealed the letter of the council of the apostles, the disciples of Jesus Christ, to the Catholics; which was written because of the false apostles Simon and Cerinthus, that no one should follow them—for in them is deceit with which they kill men—that you may be established and not

[1] Seidensticker in a review of the German edition (*Franzisk. Studien* 1960, p. 91) contests the idea that in Ep. Apost. 13 (24) anything is said of a divine service in heaven. The passage cannot be understood as the projection of Christian practice into heaven.

waver, not be shaken and not turn away from *the word of the Gospel*[1] that you have heard. As we have heard (it),[2] kept (it), and have written (it) for the whole world, so we entrust (it) to you, our sons and daughters, in joy and in the name of God the Father, the ruler of the world, and in Jesus Christ. May Grace increase upon you.

2. (We,) John and Thomas and Peter and Andrew and James and Philip and Bartholomew and Matthew and Nathanael and Judas Zelotes and Cephas,[3] we have written (*or*, write) to the churches of the East and West, towards North and South, recounting and proclaiming to you concerning our Lord Jesus Christ, how we have †written† and *heard* and *felt* him after he had risen from the dead,[4] and how he has revealed to us things great, astonishing, real.

3. We know this: our Lord and Saviour Jesus Christ (is) God, Son of God who was sent from God, the ruler of the entire world, the maker and creator of what *is named with every name*,[5] who is over all authority (as) *Lord of lords and King of kings*,[6] the ruler of the rulers, the heavenly one who is over the Cherubim[7] and Seraphim and sits *at the right hand of the throne* of the Father,[8] who by his word commanded the heavens and built the earth and all that is in it and bounded the sea that it should not go beyond its boundaries,[9] and (caused) deeps and springs to bubble up and flow over the earth day and night; who established the sun, moon, and stars in heaven and separated light from darkness;[10] who commanded hell, and in the twinkling of an eye summons the rain for the wintertime, and fog, frost, and hail, and the days (?) in their time; who shakes and makes firm; who has created man according to his image and likeness;[11] who spoke in parables through the patriarchs and prophets and in truth through him whom the apostles declared and the disciples touched.[12] And God, the Lord, the Son of God—we believe that *the word*, which *became flesh*[13] through the holy virgin Mary, was carried (con-

---

[1] Acts 15:7. [2] Cf. 1 Jn. 1:1.
[3] On the list of apostles, cf. the *Apostolic Church Order*, where Peter and Cephas are regarded as different disciples.
[4] 1 Jn. 1:1; Jn. 20:27. [5] Eph. 1:21. [6] 1 Tim. 6:15; Rev. 17:14; 19:16.
[7] Dan. 3:54 LXX.
[8] Cf. Mt. 22:44; 26:64; Mk. 16:19; Acts 2:33; Heb. 1:3; 8:1; 12:2.
[9] Job 38:10f.; 1 Clem. 20:6f. [10] Gen. 1:14; 1 Clem. 20:2f.
[11] Gen. 1:26f. [12] Cf. Hebr. 1:1. [13] Jn. 1:14.

ceived) in her womb by the Holy Spirit, and was born not by the lust of the flesh but by the will of God,[1] and was wrapped (in swaddling clothes)[2] and made known at Bethlehem; and that he was reared and grew up, as we saw.

4. This is what our Lord Jesus Christ did, who was delivered by Joseph and Mary his mother to where he might learn letters. And he who taught him said to him as he taught him, "Say Alpha". He answered and said to him, "First you tell me what Beta is".[3] And . . . true . . . a real thing which was done.

5. Then *there was a marriage in Cana of Galilee.*[4] And he was invited with his mother and his brothers.[5] And he made water into wine and awakened the dead and made the lame to walk;[6] for him whose hand was withered, he stretched it out again,[7] and the *woman who suffered twelve years from a haemorrhage touched the edge of his garment* and was immediately whole; and while we reflected and wondered concerning the miracle he performed, he said to us, "*Who touched me?*" And we said to him, "O Lord, the crowd of people touched you". And he answered and said to us, "*I noticed that a power went out from me*". Immediately that woman came before him, answered him and said to him, "Lord, I touched you". And he answered and said to her, "Go, *your faith has made you whole*".[8] Then he made the deaf to hear and the blind to see, and he exorcized those who were possessed,[9] and he cleansed the lepers.[10] And the demon Legion, that a man had, met with Jesus, cried and said, "Before the day of our destruction has come You have come to turn us out". But the Lord Jesus rebuked him and said to him, "Go out of this man without doing anything to him". And he went into the swine and drowned them in the sea, and they were choked.[11] Then he walked on the sea, and the winds blew, and he rebuked them, and the waves of the sea became calm.[12] And when we, his disciples, had no denarii,

[1] Cf. Jn. 1:13.   [2] Lk. 2:7.
[3] Infancy *Gospel of Thomas* 6:3; 14:2; *Pseudo-Matt.* 31:2; 38:1; *Arabic Infancy Gospel* 49.
[4] Jn. 2:1ff.   [5] Brothers: cf. Jn. 2:12.
[6] Lk. 7:14f. 8:49ff; Mk. 5:35ff; Jn. 11:39ff.; Mk. 2:3ff.; Mt. 9:2ff.
[7] Mt. 12:10ff.; Mk. 3:3ff.   [8] Mt. 9:20ff.; Mk. 5:25ff.; Lk. 8:43ff.
[9] Mt. 11:4f.; 15:30; Lk. 7:22; Mt. 9:32f.; Mk. 7:32ff.; 8:22ff.; Jn. 9:1ff.; Mt. 4:24; 8:16; Mk. 1:34.
[10] Mt. 8:2f.; Mk. 1:40ff.; Lk. 5:12ff.   [11] Mk. 5:1–20; Lk. 8:26–39.
[12] Mt. 14:23ff.; Mk. 6:47ff. in connection with Mk. 4:35ff. and par.

we said to him, "Master, what should we do about the tax-collector?" And he answered and said to us, "One of you *cast the hook*, the net, into the deep and draw out a fish, and he will find a denarius in it. Give that to the tax-collector for me and for you".[1] Then when we had no bread *except five loaves and two fish, he commanded* the people *to lie down*, and their number amounted to *5000 besides children and women*, whom we served with pieces of bread; *and they were filled*, and there was (some) left over, and we carried away *twelve baskets full* of pieces,[2] asking and saying, "What meaning is there in these five loaves?" They are a picture of our faith concerning the great Christianity; and i.e. in the Father, the ruler of the entire world, and in Jesus Christ our Saviour, and in the Holy Spirit, the Paraclete, and in the holy Church and in the forgiveness of sins.

6. And these things our Lord and Saviour revealed and showed to us, and likewise we to you, that you, reflecting upon eternal life, may be associates in the grace of the Lord and in our service and in our glory. Be firm, without wavering, in the knowledge and investigation of our Lord Jesus Christ, and he will prove gracious and will save always and in all never ending eternity.

7. (*Here begins the Coptic.*) Cerinthus and Simon have come to go through the world. But they are the enemies of our Lord Jesus Christ,

who in reality alienate those who believe in the true word and deed, i.e. Jesus Christ. Therefore take care and beware of them,[3] for in them is affliction and contamination and death, the end of which will be destruction and judgment.

for they pervert the words and the object, i.e. Jesus Christ. Now keep ⟨yourselves⟩ away from them,[3] for death is in them and a great stain of corruption—these to whom shall be judgment and the end and eternal perdition.

8. Because of that we have not hesitated

with the true testimony of our Lord and Saviour Jesus Christ, how he acted while we saw him,

to write to you concerning the testimony of our Saviour Christ, what he did when we were

---

[1] Mt. 17:24ff.   [2] Mt. 14:17ff.; Mk. 6:38ff.; Jn. 6:9ff.
[3] Cf. Ignatius, *Trall.* 7:1; *Smyrn.* 7:2; *Trall.* 11:1.

and how he constantly both explained and caused our thoughts within us.

9. He of whom we are witnesses we know as the one crucified in the days of Pontius Pilate and of the prince Archelaus, who was crucified between two thieves[1] and was taken down from the wood of the cross together with them, and was buried in the place called qarānejō (κρανίου),[2] to which three women came, Sarah, Martha, and Mary Magdalene. They carried ointment to pour out

behind him watching ⟨and yet?⟩ again in thoughts and deeds,

he concerning whom ⟨we⟩ bear witness that the Lord is he who was crucified by Pontius Pilate and Archelaus between the two thieves[1]

⟨and⟩ who was buried in a place called the ⟨place of the skull⟩.[2] There went to that place ⟨three⟩ women: Mary, she who belonged to Martha, and Mary ⟨Magd⟩alene. They took ointment to pour

upon his body,[3] weeping and mourning[4] over what had happened.

And they approached the tomb and found the stone where it had been rolled away from the tomb,[6] and they opened the door

But when they had approached the tomb they looked inside[5]

and did not find his (*Coptic*: the) body.[7]

10. And (*Copt.*: But) as they were mourning and weeping, the Lord appeared to them and said to them, "(*Copt.*: For whom are you weeping? Now) do not weep;[8] I am he whom you seek.[9] But let one of you go to your brothers and say (*Eth.*: to them),[10] 'Come, our (*Copt.*: the) Master has risen from the dead'."[11]

And Mary came to us and told us. And we said to her, "What have we to do with you, O

Martha came and told it to us. We said to her, "What do you want with us, O woman? He

---

[1] Mt. 27:38; Mk. 15:27; Jn. 19:18.
[2] Place of the skull; Mt. 27:33; Mk. 15:22; Lk. 23:33; Jn. 19:17.
[3] Mk. 16:1; Lk. 24:1. [4] Mk. 16:10. [5] Jn. 20:11; *Gospel of Peter* 55.
[6] Lk. 24:2; Mk. 16:4. [7] Lk. 24:3. [8] Jn. 20:14f.; Mk. 16:6.
[9] Cf. Jn. 20:15 (18:4). [10] Mt. 28:7. [11] Mt. 28:10; Jn. 20:17.

woman? He that is dead and buried, can he then live?" And we did not believe her,[1] that our Saviour had risen from the dead.

who has died is buried, and could it be possible for him to live?" We did not believe her,[1] that the Saviour had risen from the dead.

Then she went back to our (*Copt.:* the) Lord and said to him,

"None of them believed me concerning your resurrection". And he said to her,

that you are alive". He said,

"Let another one of you go (*Copt.:* to them) saying this again to them".

And Sarah came and gave us the same news, and we accused her of lying. And she returned to our Lord and spoke to him as Mary had.

Mary came and told us again, and we did not believe her. She returned to the Lord and she also told it to him.

11. Then (*Eth.:* And then) the Lord said to Mary and (*Copt.:* and also) to her sisters, "Let us go to them." And he came[2] and found us inside, veiled.

And we doubted and did not believe. He came before us like a ghost[3] and we did not believe that it was he. But it was he. And thus he said to us, "Come, and

He called us out. But we thought it was a ghost,[3] and we did not believe it was the Lord. Then ⟨he said⟩ to us, "Come,

do not be afraid.[4] I am your teacher (*Copt.:* ⟨master⟩) whom you, Peter, denied three times (*Eth.:* before the cock crowed);[5] and now do you deny again?"

And we went to him, thinking and doubting[6] whether it was he. And he said to us,

But we went to him, doubting[6] in ⟨our⟩ hearts whether it was possibly he. Then he said to ⟨us⟩,

[1] Mk. 16:11ff.; Lk. 24:11–41.   [2] Jn. 20:19, 26; Mk. 16:14.
[3] Cf. Lk. 24:37, 39.   [4] Mt. 28:10.   [5] Mt. 26:34, 96ff. and par.
[6] Mt. 28:17 (14:31).

"Why do you (*Copt.*: still) doubt and (*Eth.*: why) are you not believing?[1] (*Eth.*: believing that) I am he who spoke to you concerning my flesh, my death, and my resurrection.

And that you may know that it is I, lay your hand, Peter, (and your finger) in the nailprint of my hands; and you, Thomas, in my side;[2] and also you, Andrew, see whether my foot steps on the ground and leaves a footprint.

That you may know that it is I, put your finger, Peter, in the nailprints of my hands; and you, Thomas, put your finger in the spear-wounds of my side;[2] but you, Andrew, look at my feet and see if they do not touch the ground.

For it is written in the prophet,

'But a ghost, a demon, leaves no print on the ground'."[3]

'The foot of a ghost or a demon does not join to the ground'."[3]

12. But now we felt him,[4] that he had truly risen in the flesh. And then we fell on our faces before him, asked him for pardon and entreated him because we had not believed him. Then our Lord and Saviour said to us, "Stand up and I will reveal to you what is on earth, and what is above heaven, and your resurrection that is in the kingdom of heaven, concerning which my Father has sent me, that I may take up[6] you and those who believe in me".

But we ⟨touched⟩ him[4] that we might truly know whether he ⟨had risen⟩ in the flesh, and we fell on our ⟨faces⟩ confessing our sin, that we had been ⟨un⟩believing. Then the Lord our redeemer said, "Rise up, and I will reveal to you what is above heaven and what is in heaven, and your rest that is in the kingdom of heaven.[5] For my ⟨Father⟩ has given me the power to take up[6] you and those who believe in me".

13. And what he revealed is this, as he said to us,[7] "While I was coming from the Father

But what he revealed is this that he said,[7] "But it happened, as I was about to

---

[1] Jn. 20:27; Mk. 16:14.   [2] Cf. Jn. 20:20, 27.
[3] Cf. Commodian, Apol. V. 564 ed. Dombart p. 152: Vestigium umbra non facit (a shadow does not make a mark); cf. also *Acts of John* c. 93.
[4] Lk. 24:39; 1 Jn. 1:1; Ignatius, *Smyrn.* 3:2.   [5] 2 Clem. 5:5; 6:7.
[6] Jn. 12:32.   [7] On the following cf. *Ascension of Isaiah* 10:7ff.

† of † all, passing by the heavens, wherein I put on the wisdom of the Father and by his power clothed myself in his power, I was † in † the heavens. And passing by the angels and archangels in their form and as one of them, I passed by the orders, dominions, and princes, possessing the measure of the wisdom of the Father who sent me. And the archangels Michael and Gabriel, Raphael and Uriel followed me (*Lat. adds:* secretly) until the fifth firmament of heaven, while I appeared as one of them. This kind of power was given me by the Father. Then I made the archangels to become distracted with the voice and go up to the altar[1] of the Father and serve the Father in his work until I should return to him. I did this thus in the likeness (*or, form?*) of his wisdom. For I became all in all with them, that I, having . . . the will of the mercy of the Father and perfected the glory of him who sent me, might return to him.[3]

14. Do you know that the angel Gabriel came and brought the message to Mary?"[4] And we said to him, "Yes, O Lord". And he answered and said to us, "Do you not remember

come down from the Father of all, I passed by the heavens; I put on the wisdom of the Father and the power of his might (?). I was in the heavens, and I passed by the angels and archangels in their form, as if I were one of them among the dominions and powers. I passed through them, possessing the wisdom of him who sent me. But the chief leader of the angels is Michael, and Gabriel and Uriel and Raphael, but they followed me to the fifth firmament, thinking in their hearts that I was one of them. But the Father gave me power of this nature. And in that day I adorned the archangels with a wondrous voice that they might go up to the altar[1] of the Father and serve and complete the service until I should go to him. Thus I did it through the wisdom of the likeness. For I became all things in everything that I might . . . the plan[2] of the Father and perfect the glory of him who sent me, and might go to him.[3]

For you know that the angel Gabriel brought the message to Mary".[4] We answered, "Yes, O Lord". Then he answered and said to us, "Do you not then remember that a little

---

[1] Rev. 8:3f.   [2] Col. 1:25; Eph. 1:10.   [3] Jn. 14:12, 28.   [4] Lk. 1:26ff.

that I previously said to you that I became like an angel to the angels?" And we said to him, "Yes, O Lord". And he said to us, "At that time I appeared in the form of the archangel Gabriel to (the virgin) Mary[1] and spoke with her, and her heart received (me); she believed and laughed;[2] and I, the Word, went into her and became flesh;[3] and I myself was servant[4] for myself, and in the form of the image of an angel; so I will do †after† I have gone to my Father.

while ago I told you I became an angel among angels and I became all things in everything?" We ⟨said⟩ to him, "Yes, O Lord". Then he answered and said to us, "On that day, when I took the form of the angel Gabriel, I appeared to Mary[1] and ⟨spoke⟩ with her. Her heart received me and she believed; I formed myself and entered into her womb; I became flesh,[3] for I alone was servant[4] to myself with respect to Mary in an appearance of the form of an angel. So will I do, after I have gone to the Father.

15. And *you* therefore celebrate the remembrance of my death,[5] i.e. the passover;

And *you* remember my death.[5] If now the passover takes place,

then will one of you (*Eth.*: who stands beside me) be thrown into prison for my name's sake,[6] and he will

be very grieved and sorrowful, for while you celebrate the passover he who is in custody did not celebrate it with you. And I will send my power in the form of my angel, and the door of the prison will open, and he will come out and come to you to watch with you and to rest. And when you complete my Agape and my

⟨be⟩ in sorrow and care that you celebrate ⟨the⟩ passover while he is in prison and ⟨far⟩ from you; for he will sorrow that he does not celebrate the passover ⟨with⟩ you. I will send my power in the ⟨form⟩ of the angel Gabriel, and the doors of the prison will be opened. He will go out and come to you; he will spend a

---

[1] Cf. Reitzenstein, *Zwei religionsgeschichtliche Fragen*, pp. 119ff.
[2] Laughed: *Orac. Sibyll.* viii, 466ff.   [3] Jn. 1:14.
[4] Cf. Pistis Sophia p. 80, l.31 (ed. Schmidt, *Koptisch-Gnostische Schriften* vol. I (Berlin, 1954); ET by G. Horner (London, 1924) p. 61, 4 lines from bottom).
[5] 1 Cor. 11:26.   [6] Acts 12:3ff.; Lk. 21:12; Rev. 2:3; cf. Jn. 15:21.

remembrance[1] at the crowing of the cock,[2] he will again be taken and thrown in prison for a testimony,[3] until he comes out to preach, as I have commanded you". And we said to him, "O Lord, have *you* then not completed the drinking of the passover?[4] Must we, then, do it again?" And he said to us, "Yes, until I come from the Father with my wounds".

16. And we said to him, "O Lord, great is this that you say and reveal to us. In what kind of power and form are you about to come?" And he said to us, "Truly I say to you, I will come as the sun which bursts forth; thus will I, shining seven times brighter than it in glory,[6] while I am carried on the wings of the clouds in splendour with my cross going on before me,[7] come to the earth to judge *the living and the dead*".[8]

17. And we said to him, "O Lord, how many years yet?" And he said to us, "When the

night of the watch with ⟨you⟩ and stay with you until the cock crows.[2] But when you complete the remembrance[1] that is for me, and the Agape, he will again be thrown into prison for a testimony,[3] until he comes out from there and preaches what I have delivered to you". And we said to him, "O Lord, is it perhaps necessary again that we take the cup and drink?" He said to us, "Yes, it is necessary until the day when I come with those who were killed for my sake".[5]

We said to him, "O Lord, what you have revealed to us beforehand is great. In a power of what sort or in an appearance of what order will you come?" But he answered, saying, "Truly I say to you, I will come as does the sun that shines, and shining seven times brighter than it[6] in my brightness; with the wings of the clouds ⟨carry⟩ing me in splendour and the sign of the cross before me,[7] I will come down to the earth to judge *the living and the dead*".[8]

But we said to him, "O Lord, after how many years yet will this happen?" He said to us,

[1] Lk. 22:19; I Cor. 11:24f.   [2] Mk. 13:35.
[3] Testimony: Mk. 13:9.   [4] Mt. 26:27f.; Mk. 14:23; I Cor. 11:25.
[5] Rev. 6:9; 20:4; *Didache* 16:7; *Apoc. of Elias* 43:10, Steindorff, p. 105.
[6] *Apocalypse of Peter* 7.   [7] *Apoc. Elias* 87:32; *Apoc. Peter* 7.
[8] Acts 10:42; I Pet. 4:5; 2 Tim. 4:1.

hundred and fiftieth year is completed, between Pentecost and Passover will the coming of my Father take place". And we said to him, "O Lord, now you said to us, '*I* will come', and then you said, 'he who sent me will come'." And he said to us, "*I am* wholly *in the Father and the Father in me*".[1] Then we said to him, "Will you really leave us until your coming? Where will we find a teacher?" And he answered and said to us, "Do you not know that until now I am both here and there with him who sent me?" And *we* said to him, "O Lord, is it possible that you should be both here and there?" And he said to us, "I am wholly in the Father and the Father in me † after † his image and after his form and after his power and after his perfection and after his light, and I am his perfect word".[2]

18. This is, when he was crucified, had died and risen again, as he said this, and the work that was thus accomplished in the flesh, that he was crucified, and his ascension—this is the fulfilling of the number. "And the wonders and his image and everything

"When the hundredth part and the twentieth part is completed, between Pentecost and the feast of unleavened bread, will the coming of the Father take place". But we said to him, "Here now, what have you said to us, 'I will come', and how do you say, 'It is he who sent me who will come'?" Then he said to us, "*I am* wholly *in* my *Father and* my *Father is in me*[1]

with regard to the resemblance of form and of power (?) and of perfection and of light and of full measure and with regard to voice. I am the word.[2]

I have become to him a thing, i.e. . . . . completed according to the type; I have come into being on the eight(h day) which is the day of the Lord.[3] But the whole completion of the completion you will see through the redemption that has happened to me, and you will see me,

---

[1] Jn. 10:38; 14:10, 11–20; 17:21, 22, 23; Cf. *Acts of John* c. 100   [2] Jn. 1:1.
[3] *Barnabas* 15:8; Justin, *Dial.* cc. 24, 41, 138; Clement of Alexandria, *Exc. Theod.* 63:1; *Strom.* vii, 57:5 and v, 106:2–4.

perfect you will see in me with respect to redemption which takes place through me, and while I go to the Father and into heaven.[1] But look, *a new commandment I give you, that you love one another*[2]

how I shall go to heaven to my Father who is in heaven.[1] But look now, *I give you a new commandment; love one another*[2] and [One leaf missing in the Coptic.]

and obey each other and (that) continual peace reign among you. *Love your enemies, and what you do not want done to you, that do to no one else.*[3]

19. And both preach and teach this to those who believe in me, and preach concerning the kingdom of my Father,[4] and as my Father has given me the power (ms. *C:* so I give it to you) that you may bring near the children of the heavenly father. Preach, and they will believe. You (it is) whose duty is to lead his children into heaven". And we said to him, "O Lord, it is possible for you to do what you have told us; but how will we be able to do (it)?" And he said to us, "Truly I say to you, preach and teach, as I will be with you.[5] For I am well pleased to be with you, that you may become *joint heirs* with me[6] of the kingdom of heaven of him who sent me. Truly I say to you, you will be my brothers and companions, for my Father has delighted in you and in those who will believe in me through you. Truly I say to you, such and so great a joy has my Father prepared (for you) that angels and powers desired and will desire to view and to see it, but they will not be allowed to see the greatness of my Father".[7] And we said to him, "O Lord, what kind (of thing) is this that you tell us?"

And he said to us, "You will see a light brighter than light and more perfect than perfection. And the Son will be perfected through the Father, the light—for the Father is perfect—(the Son) whom death

⟨He said to us,⟩ "You will see a light ⟨that⟩ is more exalted than all that shines . . .

the accomplishment that accomplishes in . . . I am fully the ⟨right hand⟩ of the ⟨Father

---

[1] Mt. 7:21 *et passim.*   [2] Jn. 13:34.
[3] Mt. 5:44; Lk. 6:27, 35; Tob. 4:15; Acts 15:20, 29 Cod. D; *Didache* 1:2; *Apostolic Constitutions* vii. 1 (ed. Lagarde, London, 1862, p. 198); Syriac *Didascalia.*
[4] Lk. 9:2.   [5] Mt. 28:18ff.   [6] Cf. Rom. 8:17.   [7] Cf. 1 Peter 1:12.

and resurrection make perfect, and the one accomplishment surpasses the other. And I am fully the right hand of the Father; I am in him who accomplishes". And we twelve said to him, "O Lord, in all things you have become to us salvation and life. Do you speak (or, while you speak) to us of such a hope?" And he said to us, "Have confidence and be of good courage. Truly I say to you,[1] such a rest will be yours where there is no eating and drinking and no mourning and singing (or care) and neither earthly garment nor perishing. And you will not have part in the creation of below, but will belong to the incorruptibility of my Father, you who will not perish. As I am continually in the Father, so also you (are) in me".[2] And we said again to him, "In what form? Of an angel or that of flesh?" And for this he answered and said to us, "I have put on your flesh, in which I was born and died and was buried and rose again through my heavenly Father, that it might be fulfilled that was said by the prophet David[3] concerning my death and resurrection: '*O Lord, how numerous have they*

who . . . ⟩ me (? or, than I) who is perfection". But we said ⟨to him, "O Lord,⟩ in all ⟨things⟩ you have become to us ⟨salvation and⟩ life, proclaiming to us such a ⟨hope⟩". He said to us, "Have confidence and be of a peaceful heart. Truly I say to you,[1] your rest will be ⟨above?⟩ in the place where there is (neither) eating nor drinking, neither ⟨rejoicing⟩ nor mourning nor perishing of those who are ⟨in it. You⟩ have no part in . . . , but you will receive of the ⟨incorruptibility of my Father. As I⟩ am in him, so ⟨you will be⟩ in me".[2]

Again ⟨we said to him, "In what⟩ form? In the manner of angels, or also ⟨in flesh?"⟩ He answered and said to us, ⟨"Look. I have⟩ put on ⟨your⟩ flesh, in which ⟨I⟩ was born and crucified ⟨and⟩ rose again through my Father who is ⟨in heaven⟩, that the prophecy ⟨of the⟩ prophet David might be fulfilled[3] concerning what he ⟨foretold⟩ about me and ⟨my⟩ death and my resurrection,

---

[1] Synoptic introductory formula.　　[2] Cf. Jn. 14:20; 15:4f.　　[3] Cf. Lk. 24:44f.

become that oppress me; many have risen up against me. Many say to my soul, "He has no salvation by his God." But you, O Lord, are my refuge, my glory, and he who lifts up my head. With my voice I cried to God, and he heard me from the mount of his sanctuary. I lay down and fell asleep; and I rose up, for God raised me up. I was not afraid of thousands of people who surrounded me and rose up against me. Arise, O Lord my God, and save me. For you have smitten (S adds: trodden down) all who show me enmity without cause; and you have shattered the teeth of sinners. Deliverance is of God, and your blessing (be) upon your people'.[1]

All that was said by the prophets was thus performed and has taken place and is completed in me, for I spoke in (or, by) them;[2] how much more will what I myself have made known to you really happen, that he who sent me may be glorified[3] by you and by those who believe in me".

saying, 'O Lord, numerous have they become that ⟨oppose⟩ me, and many have risen up against me. Many say to my soul, There is no ⟨deliverance for him⟩ with God. ⟨But you, O Lord, are⟩ my protector; ⟨you are my glory and he who lifts up⟩ my head. With my ⟨voice I cried out to the⟩ Lord, and he heard me. I lay down and fell asleep; I rose up, for you, O Lord, are my protector. I will not be afraid of tens of thousands of people who set themselves against me round about. Rise up, O Lord; save me, my God. For you have cast down all who are my enemies without cause; the teeth of sinners you have broken. To the Lord is salvation and his delight in his people'.[1]

But if all the words that were spoken by the prophets are fulfilled in me—for I was in them[2]—how much more will what I say to you truly [what I say to you (dittography)] happen, that he who sent me may be glorified[3] by you and by those who believe in me".

20. (Copt.: But) After he had said this to us, we said to him, "O Lord, in all things you have shown yourself merciful to us and have saved us; you have revealed all (Eth.: all this) to us. Yet (Eth.: Yet one thing) might we ask you, if you permit us". (Eth.: And) He answered and said to us, "I know

[1] Ps. 3:1-8.   [2] Cf. Hebr. 1:1 and 1 Pet. 1:10f.   [3] Cf. Jn. 13:31f.

that you are listening and long to listen; concerning what you wish, †ask† me. Look; †ask† me and keep in mind what you hear, and it will be agreeable with me to speak with you.

that you will †carry† and your heart is pleased when you hear me. But ask me concerning what you wish, and I will speak well with you.

21. (*Copt.*: For) Truly I say to you, as the (*Copt.*: my) Father awakened *me* from the dead, in the same manner *you* also will arise[1]

in the flesh, and he will cause you to rise up above the heavens to the place of which I have spoken to you from the beginning (*or*, already), which he who sent me has prepared for you. And for this cause have I perfected all mercy: without being begotten I was born (*or*, begotten) of man, and without having flesh I put on flesh and grew up, that (I might regenerate) you who were begotten in the flesh, and

and be taken up above the heavens to the place of which I have spoken to you from the beginning (before), to the place which he who sent me has prepared for you. And thus will I complete all arrangements (for salvation): being unbegotten and (yet) begotten of man, being without flesh (and yet) I have worn flesh,[2] for on that account have I come, that you . . .

(*Coptic lacks about 10 lines.*)

in regeneration you obtain the resurrection in your flesh,[3] a garment that will not pass away, with all who hope and believe in him *who sent me*;[4] for my Father has found pleasure in you; and to whoever I will I give the hope of the kingdom". Then we said to him, "It is great, how you cause to hope, and how you speak". He answered and said to us, "Believe (*must mean,* Do you believe) that everything I say to you will happen". And we answered him and said to him, "Yes, O Lord". And he said to us, "Truly I say to you that I have received all power[5] from my Father that I may bring back those in darkness into light[6] and those in corruptibility into incorruptibility and those in error into righteousness and those in death into life, and that those in captivity may be loosed, as what is impossible on the part of men

[1] Cf. Jn. 5:21; 2 Clem. 9:5.　　[2] Ignatius, *Eph.* 7:2.　　[3] 2 Clem. 9:5.
[4] Jn. 5:24.　　[5] Cf. Mt. 28:18.
[6] 1 Pet. 2:9; Cf. *Odes of Solomon* 21:3 and 42:16.

is possible on the part of the Father.[1] I am the hope of the hopeless, the helper of those who have no helper, the treasure of those in need, the physician of the sick, the resurrection of the dead".[2]

22. After he had said this to us, we said to him, "O Lord, is it really in store for the flesh to be judged (together) with the soul and spirit,[3] and will (one of these) (*Copt.*: really) rest in heaven and the other (*Copt.*: however) be punished eternally while it is (still) alive?[4]" And (*Copt.*: But) he said to us, "How long do you still ask and inquire?"

23. And (*not in Copt.*) we said again to him, "O Lord,

but it is necessary, since you have commanded us to preach, prophesy, and teach, that we, having heard accurately from you, may be good preachers and may teach them, that they may believe in you. Therefore we question you".

there is a necessity upon us to inquire through you, for you command us to preach, that we ourselves may learn with certainty through you and be profitable preachers, and (that) those who will be instructed by us may believe in you. Therefore we question you frequently".

24. He answered and said to us, "Truly I say to you, the flesh of every man will rise with his soul [alive] and his spirit".

He answered us, saying, "Truly I say to you, the resurrection of the flesh will happen while the soul and the spirit are in it".

And we said to him, "O Lord,

then can what is departed and scattered become alive? Not as if we deny it do we ask; rather we believe that what you say has happened and will happen". And he said to us, being angry, "You of little faith,[5] how long yet do you

is it then possible that what is dissolved and destroyed should be whole? Not as unbelieving do we ask you—[nor is it impossible for you]—rather we really believe that what you say will happen". And ⟨he⟩ was angry with us, saying to us, "O

[1] Mt. 19:26 and par.
[2] *Acts of Paul and Thecla* c. 37; *Liturgy of Mark* (in Brightman, *Liturgies*, p. 124, *ll.* 2ff.).
[3] Cf. 1 Thess. 5:23.   [4] Cf. 2 Clem. 9:1.   [5] Ct. Mt. 6:30; 8:26; 14:31; 16:8.

ask me? And inquire (only)
without anguish after what you
wish to hear. *Keep*

you of little faith,[1] until what
day do you ask? But what you
wish, say to me, and I will tell
it to you without grudging.
Only *keep*

my commandments,[2] and do what I tell you,

without delay and without reserve and without respect of
persons;[3] serve in the strait,
direct, and narrow way.[4] And
thereby will the Father in every
respect rejoice concerning you".

and do not turn away your face
from anyone, that I also may
not turn my face away from
you; rather without delay and
without reserve . . . (and) without respect of persons[3] serve
in the way that is direct and
strait and oppressed (narrow).[4] So it is also with my
Father. He will rejoice concerning you".

25. And we said again to
him, "O Lord, look; we † have
you to derision † with the many
questions". And he said to us,

Again ⟨we⟩ said to him,
"O Lord, already we are
ashamed that we repeatedly
question and trouble ⟨you⟩".
Then ⟨he⟩ answered and said
to us,

"I know that in faith and with (*Copt.:* from) your whole heart
you question me. Therefore (*Eth.:* And) I am glad because of you.
(*Copt.:* For) Truly I say to you

I am pleased, and my Father in
me[5] rejoices, that you thus
inquire and ask. Your boldness
makes me rejoice, and it affords yourselves life". And when
he had said this to us, we were
glad, for he had spoken to us in
gentleness. And we said again
to him, "Our Lord, in all

I am ⟨glad⟩, and my Father
who is in me,[5] that ⟨you⟩
question me. For your boldness
⟨affords me⟩ rejoicing and
gives yourselves ⟨life⟩". But
when he had said this to us we
were ⟨glad that⟩ we asked him.
And we said to him, ⟨"O
Lord, in⟩ all things you make

[1] *Ibid.*   [2] Jn. 14:15, 21; 15:10.
[3] Cf. Rom. 2:11; Eph. 6:9; Col. 3:25; Jas. 2:1; Lk. 20:21.
[4] Mt. 7:14; Lk. 13:24.   [5] Cf. Jn. 14:10.

things you have shown yourself gracious toward us and † grant † us life; for all we have asked you you have told us". Then he said to us, "Does the flesh or the spirit fall away?" And we said to him, "The flesh". And he said to us, "Now what has fallen will arise, and what is ill will be sound, that my Father may be praised therein; as he has done to me, so I (will do) to you and to all who believe in me.

us alive and pity ⟨us. Only⟩ now will you make known to us what we will ask ⟨you⟩?" Then he said to us, ⟨"What is it⟩ then ⟨that pa⟩sses away? Is it ⟨the flesh⟩ or the spirit?" We said to him, "The flesh is perishable". ⟨Then⟩ he said to us, "What has fallen will ⟨arise⟩, and what is lost will be found and what is ⟨weak⟩ will recover, that in what is thus done ⟨may be revealed⟩ the glory of my Father. As ⟨he⟩ has done to me, so will I do to all ⟨of you⟩ who believe.

26. (*Copt.:* But) Truly I say to you, the flesh will rise alive with the soul, that

they may confess and be judged with the work

their accounting may take place ⟨on⟩ that ⟨day⟩, concerning what

they have done, *whether it is good or bad,*[1] in order that

it may become a selection[2] and exhibition for those who have believed and have done the commandment of my Father who sent me. Then will the righteous judgment take place; for thus my Father wills, and he said to me, 'My son, on *the day of judgment*[3] you will not fear the rich and not spare (mss. BC: pity) the poor; rather deliver each one to eternal punishment[4] according

⟨a⟩ selection[2] may take place of believers who have done the ⟨commandments of my⟩ Father who sent me. And thus will the judgment take place in severity. For my Father said to me, 'My son, on *the day of judgment*[3] ⟨you will neither fear⟩ the rich nor will you ⟨have pity on⟩ the poor; rather according to the sin of each one will you ⟨de-⟩ liver him to eternal punishment'.[4] But ⟨to my⟩ beloved

[1] Cf. 2 Cor. 5:10.   [2] Cf. 1 Thess. 1:4; 2 Pet. 1:10.
[3] Mt. 10:15; 11:22, 24; 2 Pet. 2:9; 3:7; 1 Jn. 4:17; Jude 6.   [4] Cf. Mt. 25:46.

to his sins'. But to those who have loved me and do love me and who have done my commandment I will grant rest in life in the kingdom of my heavenly Father.[1] Look, see what kind of power he has granted me, and he has given me, that . . . what I want and as I have wanted . . . and in whom I have awakened hope.

27. And on that account I have descended and have spoken with Abraham and Isaac and Jacob, to your fathers the prophets, and have brought to them news[3] that they may † come † from the rest † which is † below into heaven, and have given them the right hand of the baptism of life and forgiveness[4] and pardon for all wickedness as to you, so from now on also to those who believe in me. But whoever believes in me and does not do my commandment[5] receives, although he believes in my name, no benefit from it. He has run a course in vain.[6] His end is determined for ruin and for punishment of great pain, for he has sinned against my commandment.

28. But to you I have given

ones who have done the commandments ⟨of my Fa⟩ther who sent me I will grant rest of life in the kingdom of my ⟨Father who is in⟩ heaven,[1] and they will see what he has granted me; and he has given me power ⟨that I may⟩ do what I wish, and that I may give to . . . and to those whom I have determined to give and to grant.

On that account I have descended to ⟨the place of⟩ Lazarus,[2] and have preached ⟨to the righteous and⟩ to the prophets,[3] that they may come forth from the rest which is below and go up to what is ⟨above⟩ . . . right ⟨hand⟩ to them . . . of life and forgiveness and deliverance ⟨from⟩ all ⟨evil⟩, as I have done to you and ⟨to those who⟩ believe in me. But if someone believes ⟨in me and⟩ does not do my commandments,[5] although he has acknowledged my name he receives no benefit from it and has ⟨run a⟩ futile course.[6] For such will be in error and in ⟨ruin, since they have⟩ disregarded my commandments.

⟨But so much more you,⟩ the

---

[1] Cf. 2 Clem. 5:5; 6:7. [2] Cf. Lk. 16:23. [3] Cf. 1 Pet. 3:19.
[4] Cf. *Barnabas* 11:1. [5] Cf. 1 Jn. 2:4. [6] Cf. Gal. 2:2; Phil. 2:16.

that you should be children of the light in God and should be pure from all wickedness and from all power of the †judgment† (*probably should be:* rulers, *or* archons); and to those who believe in me through you I will do the same, and as I have said and promised to you, that he should go out of prison and should be rescued from the chains and the spears (*probably should be:* archons) and the terrible fire".[2] And we said to him, "O Lord, in every respect you have made us rejoice and have given us rest; for in faithfulness and truthfulness you have preached to our fathers and to the prophets, and even so to us and to every man". And he said to us, "Truly I say to you, you and all who believe and also they who yet will believe in him *who sent me*[3] I will cause to rise up into heaven, to the place which the Father has prepared for the elect[4] and most elect, (the Father) who will give the rest[5] that he has promised, and eternal life.[6]

29. But those who have sinned against my commandment, who teach something else, subtract from and add to

children of life, I have redeemed from all evil and from ⟨the power of the⟩ archons,[1] and all who through you will believe ⟨in⟩ me. For what I have promised ⟨you I⟩ will also give to them, that they may come ⟨out of⟩ the prison and the chains of the archons and the powerful fire".[2] We answered and said to him, "O Lord, you have given rest of ⟨. . . us⟩ and have given . . . in wonders to . . . of faith; will you yourself now preach these things . . . , after you have preached to the fathers and to the prophets?" Then he said to ⟨us⟩, "Truly I say to you, ⟨all⟩ who have believed in me ⟨and who will⟩ believe in him *who sent me*[3] I will ⟨lead⟩ up to heaven, to the place ⟨which⟩ my Father has ⟨prepared⟩ for the elect,[4] and I will give you the chosen kingdom in rest,[5] and eternal life.[6]

But those who have transgressed ⟨my⟩ commandments and have taught another teaching, while they . . . what is

[1] Archons: cf. 1 Cor. 2:6, 8.
[3] Cf. Jn. 5:24; 12:44.
[5] Cf. 2 Clem. 5:5; 6:7.
[2] Mt. 3:10; Lk. 3:17 and often elsewhere.
[4] Mt. 24:22, 24, 31; Mk. 13:20.
[6] Jn. 10:28; 17:2.

and work for their own glory, alienating those who rightly believe in me, (*ms. S adds:* I will deliver them to ruin)."[1] And we said to him, "O Lord, will there exist another teaching and grievance (?)?" And he said to us, "As those who fulfil what is good and beautiful, so (also) the wicked shall be manifest.[2] And then a righteous judgment will take place according to their work, how they have acted;[3] and they will be delivered to ruin". And we said to him, "Blessed are we, for we see and hear you as you speak to us, and our eyes have seen such mighty deeds that you have done".[4] And he answered and said to us, "But much more *blessed* will they be *who do not see* me *and* (*yet*) *believe* in me,[5] for they will be called children of the kingdom[6] and (will be) perfect in the perfect one;[7] to these I will become eternal life in the kingdom of my Father".[8] And we said again to him, "O Lord, how will it be possible to believe that you will leave us, as you said: There is coming a time and an hour[9]

written and add to . . . own . . . teaching with other words ⟨those who⟩ believe in me rightly, if ⟨they⟩ are brought to ruin by such . . . eternal punishment". ⟨But⟩ we said ⟨to him,⟩ "O Lord, then ⟨will⟩ there exist teaching from ⟨others⟩, besides what ⟨you⟩ have told us?" ⟨ . . . ⟩ us, "It is necessary that they exist, that ⟨what is⟩ evil and what is good should be manifest.[2] And thus will.the judgment of those who do these works be revealed, and ⟨according to their⟩ works[3] will they be judged and delivered to death". ⟨We⟩ said again to him, "O Lord, blessed are we, ⟨ . . . ⟩ you and hear you as you ⟨preach⟩ such things, for our eyes have seen these great wonders that you have done".[4] He ⟨answered and said⟩ to us, "Much more *blessed* are they *who have not seen and* (*yet*) *have believed*,[5] for such will be called ⟨children⟩ of the kingdom,[6] ⟨and they⟩ will be perfect ⟨in⟩ the perfect one[7] ⟨and⟩ I will be life ⟨to them⟩ in the kingdom of my Father".[8] Again ⟨we said to him,⟩ "O Lord, in what way

---

[1] Mt. 25:46.   [2] 1 Cor. 11:19; 1 Jn. 2:19; Lk. 17:1.
[3] Rom. 2:6.   [4] Mt. 13:16f.
[5] Cf. Jn. 20:29.   [6] Cf. Mt. 13:38.
[7] Cf. Mt. 5:48.   [8] Mt. 26:29.
[9] Cf. Jn. 5:25, 28; 16:25, 32.

when it is in store for you to go to your Father?"[2]

30. He answered and said to us, "Go and preach[3] to the twelve tribes of Israel[4] and to the Gentiles and Israel and to the land of Israel towards East and West, North and South;[5] and many will believe in me, the son of God".[6] And we said to him, "O Lord, who will believe us and who will listen to us and how can we do and teach and tell the wonders and signs and mighty deeds,[7] as you have done?" And he answered and said to us, "Go and preach [and teach] concerning [the coming and] the mercy of my Father. As my Father has done through me, I will also do through you in that I am with you, and I will give you my peace and my spirit[8] and my power, [that it may happen to you] that they believe. Also to them will this power be given and transmitted that they may give it to the Gentiles.

will one be able to believe ⟨that you⟩ will go and leave us, as you ⟨said⟩ to us, 'A day will come ⟨and an hour⟩[1] when I shall go up to my Father'?"[2] But ⟨he⟩ said to ⟨us⟩, "Go you and preach[3] to the twelve tribes[4] and preach also to the Gentiles and to the whole land of Israel from ⟨sunrise⟩ to sunset and from ⟨South to⟩ North,[5] and many will believe ⟨in the⟩ son of God".[6] But we said to him, "⟨O Lord,⟩ who will believe us or ⟨who⟩ will listen to us while we do, teach, and tell the powers and the signs that ⟨you⟩ have done, and the ⟨wonders⟩?"[7] Then he answered and said to us, "⟨Go⟩ and preach the mercy ⟨of my⟩ Father; and what he has done through me ⟨will I my⟩self do through you in that I am in you, ⟨and⟩ I will give you my peace, and from my spirit I will give you a power that you may prophesy to them to eternal life. But to the others will I † myself † also give my power, that they may teach the other nations.

(Coptic lacks 6 leaves.)

[1] Cf. Jn. 5:25, 28; 16:25, 32. [2] Jn. 16:10, 17 etc.
[3] Cf. Mt. 28:19; Mk. 16:15.
[4] Mt. 19:28; Lk. 22:30; Acts 26:7; Jas. 1:1; Rev. 21:12.
[5] Lk. 13:29; Mk. 16 (second ending). [6] Cf. Jn. 9:35; 12:37.
[7] Acts 2:22; 2 Cor. 12:12; 2 Thess. 2:9; Hebr. 2:4.
[8] Jn. 14:27; 20:21, 22; Acts 1:8; 2:17f.

31. And look; you will meet a man whose name is Saul, which being interpreted means Paul.[1] He is a Jew,[2] circumcised according to the command of the law;[3] and he will hear my voice from heaven[4] with terror, fear, and trembling; and his eyes will be darkened[5] and by your hand be crossed with spittle. And do all to him as I have done to you. Deliver (?) (him?) to others. And this man—immediately his eyes will be opened,[6] and he will praise God, my heavenly Father. And he will become strong among the nations and will preach and teach, and many will be delighted when they hear and will be saved. Then will he be hated and delivered into the hand of his enemy, and he will testify before mortal (*mss. AU:* and perishable) kings,[7] and upon him will come the completion of the testimony to me; because he had persecuted[8] and hated me, he will be converted to me and preach and teach, and he will be among my elect, a chosen vessel and a wall that does not fall.[9] The last of the last will become a preacher to the Gentiles,[10] perfect in (*or,* through) the will of my Father. As you have learned from the Scriptures that your fathers the prophets spoke concerning me, and it is fulfilled in me"—this certain thing he said—"so you must become a leader to them. And every word which I have spoken to you and which you have written concerning me, that I am the word of the Father[11] and the Father is in me,[12] so you must become also to that man, as it befits you. Teach and remind (him) what has been said in the Scriptures and fulfilled concerning me, and then he will be for the salvation of the Gentiles".[13]

32. And we said to him, "O master, do we have together with them *one* hope of the inheritance?"[14] He answered and said to us, "Are the fingers of the hand alike or the ears of corn in the field? Or do the fruit-bearing trees give the same fruit? Do they not bring forth fruit according to their nature?" And we said to him, "O Lord, are you speaking again in parables to us?" And

---

[1] Acts 13:9. [2] Acts 21:39; 22:3. [3] Phil. 3:5.
[4] Acts 9:4; 22:7; 26:14. [5] Acts 9:8f.; 22:11. [6] Acts 9:18.
[7] Acts 9:15; 1 Clem. 5:7. [8] Acts 9:5; 22:7f.; 26:14f.; Gal. 1:13; 1 Cor. 15:9.
[9] Acts 9:15. Cf. Harnack, *Der apokryphe Brief des Paulusschülers Titus* "De dispositione sanctimonii", SB Berlin 1925, p. 198: vas eleccionis—inexpugnabilis murus. Cf. Jer. 1:18; 15:20.
[10] Gal. 1:16; 2:8f.; Acts 26:17. [11] 1 Jn. 1:1. [12] Jn. 10:38; 14:20.
[13] Acts 13:47; 26:18; 28:28. [14] Cf. Eph. 3:6; Acts 26:6.

he said to us, "Do not be grieved. Truly I say to you, you are my brothers, companions in the kingdom of heaven with my Father, for so has it pleased him. Truly I say to you, also to those whom you shall have taught and who have become believers in me will I give this hope".

33. And we said again to him, "When, Lord, will we meet that man, and when will you go to your Father and to our God and Lord?" And he answered and said to us, "That man will set out from the land of Cilicia[1] to Damascus in Syria[2] to tear asunder the Church[3] which you must create. It is I who will speak (to him) through you, and he will come quickly. He will be (*ms. C:* strong) in his faith, *that the word of the prophet may be fulfilled*[4] where it says,[5] 'Behold, out of the land of Syria I will begin to call a new Jerusalem, and I will subdue Zion and it will be captured; and the barren one who has no children will be fruitful[6] and will be called the daughter of my Father, but to me, my bride; for so has it pleased him who sent me'. But that man will I turn aside, that he may not go there and complete his evil plan. And glory of my Father will come in through him. For after I have gone away and remain with my Father, I will speak with him from heaven;[7] and it will all happen as I have predicted to you concerning him".

34. And we said again to him, "O Lord, such meaningful things you have spoken and preached to us and have revealed to us great things never yet spoken, and in every respect you have comforted us and have shown yourself gracious to us. For after your resurrection you revealed all this to us that we might be really saved. But you told us only that signs and wonders would happen in heaven and upon earth before the end of the world comes.[8] Teach us, that we thus may recognize it". And he said to us, "I will teach you, and not only what will happen to you, but (also) to those whom you shall teach and who shall believe;[9] and there are such as will hear [this man?] and will believe in me. In those years and in those days this will happen". And we said

[1] Acts 21:39; 22:3; 23:34.　　[2] Acts 9:2; 22:5; 26:12 and often elsewhere.
[3] Gal. 1:13, 23.　　[4] Jn. 12:38 and often elsewhere.
[5] Source unknown. Cf. Rev. 3:12; 21:2–10; Hebr. 12:22; Gal. 4:26.
[6] Cf. Gal. 4:27; Isa. 54:1.　　[7] Acts 9:4; 22:6f.; 26:14.
[8] Cf. Mt. 24; Mk. 13; Lk. 21.　　[9] Cf. Jn. 17:20.

to him again, "O Lord, what is it then that will happen?" And he said to us, "Then will the believers and also they who do not believe see a trumpet in heaven, and the sight of great stars that are visible while it is day, and a dragon (so *mss. AS; BL have:* stars or wonders) reaching from heaven to earth, and stars that are like fire falling down[1] and great hailstones of severe (?) fire;[2] and how sun and moon fight against each other, and constantly the frightening of thunder and lightning, thunderclaps and earthquakes,[3] how cities fall down and in their ruin men die,[4] constant drought from the failing of the rain, a great plague and an extensive and often quick death, so that those who die will lack a grave; and the going out (*or*, carrying out) of children and relatives will be on *one* bed (*or*, bier). And the relative will not turn toward his child, nor the child to his relative; and a man will not turn toward his neighbour. But those forsaken who were left behind will rise'up and see those who forsook them when they brought (*Patr. Or.* ix, p. 40: did not bring) them out because (there was) plague. Everything is hatred and affliction and jealousy, and they will take from the one and give to another; and what comes after this will be worse than this. (*Patr. Or.* ix, p. 40: Mourn those who have not listened to his commandment.)

35. Then my Father will become angry because of the wickedness of men; for their offences are many and the horror of their impurity is much against them in the corruption of their life". And we said to him, "What, Lord, what (is allotted) to those who hope in you?" And he answered and said to us, "How long are you still slow of heart?[5] Truly I say to you, as the prophet David has spoken concerning me and my people, so will it also be concerning those who shall believe in me. But there will be in the world deceivers and enemies (*mss. AL:* blasphemers) of righteousness,[6] and they will meet the prophecy of David who said, '*Their feet are quick to shed blood*[7] and their *tongue weaves deceit*,[8] and *the venom of serpents is under their lips.*[7] And I see you as you *wander* with a *thief and your share* is *with a fornicator.*[9] *While you sit there* furthermore *you slander your brother, and set a trap for the*

---

[1] Cf. Rev. 6:13; 8:10; 9:1.   [2] Cf. Rev. 8:7; 11:19; 16:21.
[3] Cf. Rev. 8:5; 11:19; 16:18.   [4] Rev. 11:13; 16:19.   [5] Cf. Lk. 24:25.
[6] Cf. Acts 13:10.   [7] Ps. 13:3 LXX   [8] Ps. 49:19b LXX.   [9] Ps. 49:18 LXX.

son of your mother.[1] What do you think? *Should I be like you?*[2] And now see how the prophet of God has spoken concerning everything, that all may be fulfilled that was said before".

36. And we said to him again, "O Lord, *will the Gentiles then not say, 'Where is their God?'*"[3] He answered and said to us, "Thus will the elect be revealed, in that they go out after they have been afflicted by such a distress". And we said to him, "Will their exit[4] from the world (take place) through a plague that has tormented them?" And he said to us, "No, but if they suffer torment, such suffering will be a test for them, whether they have faith[5] and whether they keep in mind these words of mine and obey my commandment.[6] They will rise up, and their waiting will last (only a) few days, that he who sent me may be glorified, and I with him.[7] For he has sent me to you. I tell you this. But you tell (it) to Israel and to the Gentiles, that they may hear; they also are to be saved and believe in me and escape the distress of the plague. And whoever has escaped the distress of death, such a one will be taken and kept in prison, under torture like that of a thief". And we said to him, "O Lord, will they be like unto the unbelievers, and will you likewise punish those who have escaped the plague?" And he said to us, "Believing in my name they have done the work of sinners; they have acted like unbelievers".[8] And we said again to him, "O Lord, have they who have escaped in this part no life?" He answered and said to us, "Whoever has done the glorification of my Father, he is the dwelling-place of my Father".[9]

37. And we said to him, "O Lord, teach us what will happen after this". And he said to us, "In those years and days there shall be war upon war, and the four corners of the world will be shaken and will make war upon each other. And then a disturbance of the clouds (will take place), darkness and drought[10] and persecution of those who believe in me, and of the elect. Then dissension, conflict, and evil of action against each other. Among them there are some who believe in my name and (yet) follow evil and teach vain teaching. And men will follow them and will submit them-

---

[1] Ps. 49:20 LXX.   [2] Ps. 49:21b LXX.   [3] Ps. 78:10 LXX.
[4] Exit: cf. Wisdom of Solomon 3:2.   [5] Cf. Jas. 1:3; 1 Pet. 1:7.
[6] Jn. 14:15; 15:10.   [7] Cf. Jn. 13:31f.; 14:13.   [8] Cf. 1 Jn. 2:4.
[9] Cf. Jn. 14:23.   [10] Cf. Lk. 21:10f.

selves to their riches, their depravity, their mania for drinking, and their gifts of bribery; and respect of persons will rule among them.

38. But those who desire to see the face of God and who do not regard the person of the sinful rich and who do not fear the men who lead them astray, but reprove them, they will be crowned (*text:* wounded) in the presence of the Father, as also those who reprove their neighbours will be saved. This is a son of wisdom and of faith. But if he does not become a son of wisdom, then he will hate and persecute and not turn towards

his brother, and will despise (him) and cast him away.

his neighbour, will turn against him and . . . him.

But those who walk in truth and in the knowledge of faith[1]

in me and have the knowledge of wisdom and perseverance for righteousness' sake, in that men despise those who strive for poverty and they (nevertheless) endure—great is their reward. Those who are reviled, tormented, persecuted,[2] since they are destitute and men are arrogant against them and they hunger and thirst and because they have persevered—blessed will they be in heaven, and they will be there with me always.[3] Woe to those who hate and despise them! And their end is for destruction".[4]

possessing love for me—for they have endured abuse—they will be proud, walking in poverty and tolerating those who hate them ⟨and⟩ revile them.[2] They have been ⟨tormented⟩, being destitute, since men were arrogant against them while they walk in hunger and thirst; but because they have persevered . . . the blessedness of heaven, they also will be with me eternally.[3] But woe to those who walk in pride and boasting, for *their end is destruction*".[4]

39. And we said to him, "O Lord, will all this happen?" And he said to us, "How will the judgment of righteousness

But we said to him, "O Lord, what is yours is this, that you do not let us come upon them". But he answered and said to us,

[1] Cf. Acts 23:1; Phil. 1:27; 2 Jn. 4; 3 Jn. 4; 1 Tim. 2:7.
[2] Lk. 6:22–27; Jn. 15:18; 1 Jn. 3:13; Mt. 5:11.
[3] Cf. 1 Thess. 4:17.   [4] Cf. Phil. 3:19.

take place for the sinners and the righteous?"[1] And we said to him, "Will they not in that day say to you, 'You caused to lead toward righteousness and sin and have separated (*ms. L:* created) darkness and light, evil and good'?" And he said to us, "Adam was given the power that he might choose what he wanted from the two;[2] and he chose the light and stretched out his hand and took (it) and left the darkness and withdrew from it (*perhaps should be:* put it away from himself). Likewise every man is given the ability to believe in the light;[3] this is the life[4] of the Father who sent me. And whoever has believed in me will live,[6] if he has done the work of light. But if he acknowledges that it is light and does what is (characteristic) of darkness, then, he has neither anything that he can say in defence nor will he be able to raise his face and look at the son, which (Son) I am. And I will say to him, 'You have sought and found, have asked and received.[9] What do you blame us for? Why did you withdraw from me and my kingdom? You have acknowledged me

"How will the judgment come about? Either of the righteous or of the unrighteous?"[1] But we said to him, "O Lord, in that day they will say to you, 'You did not pursue ⟨righteousness⟩ and unrighteousness, light and darkness, evil and good'." Then he said, "I will answer them saying, 'Adam was given the power to choose one of ⟨the⟩ two.[2] He chose the light and put his hand upon it; but he forsook the darkness and cast it from him. So have all men the power to believe in the light[3] which is ⟨life⟩[4] and which is the Father[5] who sent me'. But everyone who believes (and) does the works of light will live in them.[6] But if there is someone who acknowledges that he is reckoned to the light, while he does the works of darkness[7]—such a one has no defence to make, nor will he be able to lift up his face to ⟨look at the⟩ son of God, which (Son) I am.[8] I will say to him, 'As you sought you have found, and as you asked you have received.[9] In what do you condemn me, O man? Why did you leave me and deny me? Why did you acknowledge me and (yet) deny

[1] Cf. Acts 24:15.　　[2] Cf. Ecclus. 15:16ff.　　[3] Jn. 12:36.
[4] Cf. Jn. 1:4.　　[5] Cf. 1 Jn. 1:5.　　[6] Cf. Gal. 3:12; Rom. 10:5.
[7] Cf. Rom. 13:12; Eph. 5:11.　　[8] Cf. Jn. 10:36.　　[9] Cf. Mt. 7:7; Lk. 11:9f.

and (yet) denied'.[1] Now therefore see that each one is able to live as well as to die. And whoever does my commandment and keeps it[2] will be a son of the light,[3] i.e. of my Father. And for those who keep and do (it), for † their † sake I came down from heaven; I, the word, became flesh[5] and died, teaching and guiding, that some shall be saved, but the others eternally ruined, being punished by fire in flesh and spirit".

40. And we said to him, "O Lord, we are truly troubled on their account". And he said to us, "You do well, for so are the righteous anxious about the sinners, and they pray and implore God and ask him". And we said to him, "O Lord, does no one entreat you?" And he said to us, "Yes, I will hear the requests of the righteous concerning them".[7] And we said to him, "O Lord, all this you have taught us, and have stimulated us and have proved gracious toward us. And we will preach it to those to whom it is fitting. But will there be for us a reward with you?"[8]

me?[1] Does not every man have the power to live or to die?' Now whoever has kept my commandments[2] will be a son of light,[3] i.e. of the Father who is in me.[4] But on account of those who pervert my words I have come down from heaven. I am the Logos; I became flesh,[5] labouring and teaching that those who are called will be saved,[6] and the lost will be lost eternally. They will be ⟨tormented⟩ alive and will be scourged in ⟨their⟩ flesh and in their soul".

But we said to him, "O Lord, truly we are anxious on their account". But he said to us, "You do well, for the righteous are anxious about the sinners, and pray for them, asking my Father". Again we said to him, "O Lord, now why is no one afraid of you?" But he said to us, "Yes, I will hear the prayer of the righteous that they make for them".[7] But when he had said this to us, we said to him, "O Lord, in all things you have taught us [. . .] and pitied us and saved us, that we may preach to those who are worthy to be saved, and that we may earn a reward with you".[8]

---

[1] Cf. Tit. 1:16.   [2] Cf. Jn. 14:15 and frequently.
[3] Lk. 16:8; Jn. 12:36; Eph. 5:8; 1 Thess. 5:5.   [4] See above, p. 201 n. 1.
[5] Cf. Jn. 1:14.   [6] Mt. 22:8; Lk. 14:24; Rev. 17:14.
[7] Cf. Jas. 5:16.   [8] Cf. Mt. 5:12 and frequently.

41. And he said to us, "Go and preach and be good ministers and servants". And we said to him, "O Lord, you are our father".[2] And he said to us, "Are all fathers and all servants, all teachers?" And we said to him, "O Lord, did you not say, 'Do not call (anyone) on earth father and master, for one is your father and teacher, he who is in heaven'?[3] Now you say to us that we should like you become fathers to many children[4] and also teachers and servants". And he answered and said to us. "You have rightly said. Truly I say to you, all who have listened to you and have believed in me will receive the light of the seal that is in my hand, and through me you will become fathers and teachers".

42. And we said to him, "O Lord, how is it possible for these three to be in one?" And he answered and said to us, "Truly, truly I say to you, you will be called fathers, for you, full of love and compassion, have revealed to them what (is) in heaven (. . . for) by my hand they will receive the baptism of life and forgiveness

⟨But⟩ he answered and said to us, "Go, and preach; thus you will become workers[1] . . . and servants". But we said to him, "You it is who will preach through us". Then he answered us saying, "Do not be all fathers nor all masters". We said to him, "O Lord, it is you who said, 'Do not call (anyone) father upon earth, for one is your father who is in heaven[3] and your master'. Why do you now say to us, 'You will be fathers of many children[4] and servants and masters'?" But he answered and said to us, "As you have said. For truly I say to you, whoever will hear you and believe in me, he ⟨will receive from⟩ you the light of the seal through ⟨me⟩ and baptism through me; you will ⟨become⟩ fathers and servants and also masters".

But we said to him, "O Lord, how now (is it possible) that each one of us should become these three?" But he said to us, "Truly I say to you, you will first of all be called fathers, for you have revealed to them with seemly hearts and in love the things of the kingdom of heaven. And you will be called servants, for they will receive

---

[1] Mt. 9:37 and frequently.
[3] Mt. 23:8f.
[2] Cf. Jn. 12:26.
[4] Cf. 1 Cor. 4:15.

of sin.[1] And teachers, for you have delivered to them my word without anguish and have warned them and they have turned back in the things for which you rebuked them. And you were not afraid of their riches and did not respect the face (*or*, the person), but you kept the commandment of the Father and did it. And you have a reward with my heavenly Father;[2] and they shall have forgiveness of sins and eternal life and a share of the kingdom". And we said to him, "O Lord, if they had a ten-thousandfold mouth[3] they would not be able to give thanks to you as it is fitting". And he answered and said to us, "I say this to you that you may do as I have done to you;[4]

43. and be as the wise virgins who kindled the light and did not slumber and who went with their lamps to meet the lord, the bridegroom, and have gone in with him into the bridegroom's chamber. But the foolish ones who talked with them were not able to watch, but fell asleep."[5] And we said to

by my hand through you the baptism of life and the forgiveness of their sins.[1] And you will be called masters, for you have given them the word without grudging and have warned them; and when you warned them they turned back. You were not afraid of their riches ⟨and of⟩ their face, but you kept ⟨the commandments⟩ of my Father and performed them. And you will have ⟨a⟩ great reward with my Father[2] who is in heaven, and they shall have forgiveness of sins and eternal life, and will have a part in the kingdom of heaven". But we said to him, "O Lord, even if each one of us had ten thousand tongues[3] to speak with, we would not be able to give thanks to you, for you promise us such things". Then he answered, saying, "Only do what I say to you, as I myself have also done;[4] and you will be like the wise virgins who watched and did not sleep, but ⟨went⟩ out to the lord into the bride-chamber. But ⟨the foolish⟩ were not able to watch, but fell asleep".[5] But we said to him, "O Lord, who are the wise and who are the foolish?" He said to us, "Five wise and five foolish,

[1] See above, p. 209 n. 4.
[3] Cf. Theoph. *ad Autol.* 2:12.
[2] Cf. Mt. 5:12; Lk. 6:23; Mt. 10:41f.
[4] Cf. Jn. 13:15.　　[5] Mt. 25:1ff.

him, "O Lord, who are the wise and who the foolish?" And he said to us, "The wise are these five, who are called by the prophet daughters of God,[1] whose names let men hear". But we were sad and troubled and wept for those who had been shut out. And he said to us, "The five wise are these: Faith, Love, Joy, Peace, Hope. As soon as they who believe in me have these, they will be leaders[2] to those who believe in me and in him who sent me. I am the Lord and I am the bridegroom; they have received me and have gone with me into the house of the bridegroom, and laid themselves down (at table) with the bridegroom and rejoiced. But the five foolish slept, and when they awoke they came to the house of the bridegroom and knocked at the doors, for they had been shut; and they wept, because they were shut".[3] And we said to him, "O Lord, now these their wise sisters who (are) in the house—do they not open to them and are they not sorrowful on their account?" And he said to us, "Yes, they are sorrowful and concerned on their account and entreat the bridegroom and are not yet

these with respect to whom the prophet said, 'They are children of God.'[1] Now hear their names". But we wept and were sad about those who had fallen asleep. He said to us, "The five wise are Faith and Love and Grace, Peace and Hope. Among those who believe they who have these will be guides[2] to those who have believed in me and in him who sent me. I am the Lord and I am the bridegroom whom they have received, and they have gone into the house of the ⟨bridegroom⟩ and have laid themselves down with me in my ⟨bride⟩chamber ⟨and rejoiced⟩. But the five foolish, when ⟨they⟩ had fallen asleep(?), they awoke, came to the door of the bridechamber and knocked, for they had been shut out.[3] Then they wept and grieved that it was not opened for them". But we said to him, "O Lord, and their wise sisters who were within in the house of the bridegroom, did they remain in there without opening to them, and did they not grieve on their account or did they not pray the bridegroom to open to them?" He answered saying, "They were not yet able to find grace on

[1] Cf. Ps. 81:6 LXX.   [2] Cf. Mt. 15:14; 23:24.   [3] Mt. 25:10.

able to obtain (anything) on their account". And we said to him, "O Lord, when will they go in for their sisters' sakes?" And he said to us, "Whoever is shut out is shut out". And we said to him, "O Lord, is this thing definite? Who now are these foolish ones?" And he said to us, "Listen: Insight, Knowledge, Obedience, Endurance, Mercy. These have slept in those who have believed and acknowledged me.

44. And since those who slept did not fulfil my commandment, they will be outside the kingdom and the fold of the shepherd;[1] and whoever remains outside the fold will the wolf eat.[2] And although he hears he will be judged and will die, and much suffering and distress and endurance will come upon him; and although he is badly pained and although he is cut into pieces and lacerated with long and painful punishment, yet he will not be able to die quickly."

45. And we said to him, "O Lord, you have revealed everything to us well". And he said to us, "Understand and apprehend these words".[4] And we

their behalf". We said to him, "O Lord, on what day will they go in for their sisters' sakes?" ⟨Then⟩ he said to us, "Whoever ⟨is shut out⟩ is shut out". But we said to him, "O Lord, is this ⟨. . . ?⟩ Now who are the foolish?" He said to us, "Hear their names. They are Knowledge and Insight, Obedience, Forbearance, and Mercy. These are they which slept in those who have believed and acknowledged me.

But my commandments were not fulfilled by those who slept. Consequently they will remain outside the kingdom and the fold of the ⟨shepherd⟩ and his sheep.[1] But whoever remains outside ⟨the fold⟩ of the sheep will the wolves eat,[2] and he will . . . , dying in much suffering. ⟨Rest⟩ and perseverance will not be ⟨in⟩ him, and he ⟨will⟩ be badly (?) tormented that he . . . ⟨and they will punish⟩ him in great ⟨punishment, and he will⟩ be under tortures".[3]

⟨But we said to him,⟩ "O Lord, you have revealed everything ⟨to us⟩ well". Then he answered ⟨say⟩ing to us, "Do you not apprehend these

---

[1] Jn. 10:1f. [2] Cf. Mt. 7:15; 10:16; Jn. 10:12; Acts 20:29.
[3] Cf. Rev. 14:10f. [4] Cf. Mk. 8:17.

said to him, "O Lord, these five it is through which they (*fem.*) have the expectation of going into your kingdom; and five who are shut out through which they will be outside your kingdom. Yet they who have watched and who have gone in with the Lord, the bridegroom, will not rejoice because of those who slept". And he said to us, "They will rejoice that they have gone in with the Lord, and will be grieved on account of those who slept; for they are their sisters. And these daughters of God are ten". And we said to him, "O Lord, it suits your greatness that you show grace to their sisters". And he said to us, "This thing is not yours, but his who sent me, and I also agree with him.

46. But you, as you go, preach and teach truly and rightly, respecting and fearing the person of no one, but especially (not) that of the rich, among whom (something) will be found, who do not do my commandment,[1] who revel in their riches".[2] And we said to him, "O Lord, do you speak to us only of the rich?" And he said to us, "Also of him who is not rich; as soon

words?" We said to him, "Yes, O Lord; through the five will they come into your kingdom. Yet they who watched and were with you, the Lord and bridegroom, will nevertheless not rejoice because of those who slept". He said to us, "They ⟨will rejoice⟩ that they have gone in with the bridegroom, the Lord; and they are troubled on account of those who ⟨slept⟩, for they are their sisters. The ten are the daughters of God the Father". We ⟨then said⟩ to him, ⟨"O Lord,⟩ it is yours that you . . ." He said to us, ". . . , but his who sent me, and ⟨I⟩ agree with him.

But you preach and teach in uprightness (and) well, hesitating before no one and fearing no one, but especially (not) the rich, for they do not do my commandments,[1] but revel(?) in their riches".[2] But we said to him, "O Lord, if ⟨it⟩ is the rich ⟨alone⟩?" He answered saying ⟨to us, "If⟩ anyone who is not rich and possesses ⟨a little⟩ property gives to the needy ⟨and to the

---

[1] Cf. Mt. 19:23f. and par.; Lk. 6:24; 18:24; 12:15f.; Jas. 1:10f.; 2:1f.; *Hermas* Sim. 9:20.
[2] Cf. *Hermas* Vis. i.1.8; iii.9.6.

as he gives and does not deny to him who has nothing, of such a one (I say this:) he will be called by men a doer.

47. But if someone should fall bearing his burden, i.e. the sin he has committed against the person of his neighbour, then his neighbour should admonish him (in return) for what (good) he has done to his neighbour. And when his neighbour has admonished him and he has returned, then he will be saved,[1] and he who has admonished him will obtain eternal life. But if he sees how this one who renders him (service) sins, and encourages him, such a one will be judged in a great judgment. *For a blind man who leads a blind man, both will fall into a ditch.*[2] Even so the one who encourages, who respects the person, and also the one whom he encourages and whose person he respects, will both be punished with *one* punishment, as the prophet said, 'Woe to those who encourage, who speak fair to the sinner for the sake of a bribe,[3] *whose God is* their *belly*'.[4] You see how the judgment is? Truly I say to you, in that day I will not fear the rich and will have no pity for the poor.

poor), then men will call him a bene⟨factor.⟩

But if ⟨someone⟩ should fall ⟨under the⟩ load because of the sins he has ⟨committed, then let⟩ his neighbour admonish him for ⟨the good that⟩ he has done to his neighbour. Now if his neighbour ⟨has admonished⟩ him and he returns he will be saved;[1] (and) he who admonished him will receive a reward and live for ever. For a needy man, if he sees someone sinning who has done him good, and does not admonish him, then he will be judged in an evil judgment. But a blind man who leads a blind man, ⟨both⟩ fall into ⟨a⟩ ditch.[2] And whoever regards the person for ⟨their⟩ sake, ⟨he will be like⟩ the two, as the pro⟨phet said,⟩ 'Woe to those who regard the person and ⟨*justify the ungodly*⟩ *for the sake of gifts*,[3] *whose ⟨God is⟩* their *belly*.'[4] See now that a judgment ⟨is appointed for them.⟩ For truly I say ⟨to you, in⟩ that day I will neither fear ⟨the⟩ rich nor have sympathy with the ⟨poor⟩.

[1] Cf. Jas. 5:19f. [2] Mt. 15:14; Lk. 6:39. [3] Cf. Isa. 5:23. [4] Phil. 3:19.

48. If you have seen with your eyes how (someone) sins, then correct him, you alone (or, under four eyes). *If he listens to you, then you have won* him. *But if he does not listen* to you, then come out with one or at the most two others; correct your brother. But if he (even then) does not listen to you, *so shall he be to you as a Gentile and a tax collector.*[1]

If you see a sinner, then ⟨*admonish him*⟩ *between yourself and him. But if he does not listen* to ⟨you, *then take*⟩ *with you* another up to three and instruct your brother. If he will not listen to you again, then set him before you as . . ."[1]

(Here the Coptic text breaks off.)

49. If you hear something, then do not give any belief against your brother and do not slander and do not love to listen to slander. For it is written, 'Let your ear listen to nothing against your brother, but (only) if you have seen, censure, correct, and convert him'." And we said to him, "Lord, you have taught and exhorted us in everything. But, Lord, among the believers who among them believe in the preaching of your name should there be dissension and dispute and envy and confusion and hatred and distress? For you have nevertheless said, 'They will find fault with one another and have not regarded the person (or, without regarding the person)'. Do these sin who hate the one who has corrected them?" And he answered and said to us, "Now why will the judgment take place? That *the wheat may be put in its barn and* its *chaff* thrown into the fire.[2]

50. . . . . Who thus hate, and he who loves me and finds fault with those who do not do my commandments,[3] these will thus be hated and persecuted, and men will despise and mock (them). They will also deliberately say what is not (true), and there will come a conspiracy against those who love me. But these will rebuke them that they may be saved. And those who will find fault with them and correct and exhort them will be hated and set apart and despised; and those who wish (to) do good to them will be prevented (from it). But those who have endured this will be as martyrs with the Father, for they were zealous concerning

[1] Mt. 18:15f.   [2] Cf. Lk. 3:17; Mt. 3:12; 13:30.
[3] Cf. Mt. 5:11; 10:22.

righteousness and were not zealous with corruptible zeal". And we said to him, "Will such, Lord, also happen in our midst?" And he said to us, "Do not fear what will happen not with many, but (only) with few". And we said to him, "Tell us in what way". And he said to us, "There will come another teaching and a conflict;[1] and in that they seek their own glory[2] and produce worthless teaching an offence of death will come thereby, and they will teach and turn away from my commandment even those who believe in me and bring them out of eternal life. But woe to those who use my word and my commandment for a pretext,[3] and also to those who listen to them and to those who turn away from the life of the teaching, [to those who turn away from the commandment of life,] they will be eternally punished with them".

51. And after he had said this and had ended the discourse with us, he said again to us, "Look. After three days and three hours he who sent me will come that I may go with him". And as he spoke there was thunder and lightning and an earthquake, and the heavens divided and a bright *cloud* came and *took him away*.[4] And (*ms. C:* we heard) the voice of many angels as they rejoiced and praised and said, "Assemble us, O priest,[5] in the light of glory". And when he (*mss. ACS:* they) had come near to the firmament of heaven, we heard him say, *"Go in peace"*.[6]

3. A GOSPEL FRAGMENT FROM THE STRASBOURG COPTIC PAPYRUS

(*W. Schneemelcher*)

On shreds of papyrus from the 5th or 6th century, which in 1899 came into the possession of the Strasbourg Landes- und Universitätsbibliothek, were found, as Carl Schmidt recognized, the remains of an apocryphal gospel. The first attempt to set the small pieces in order and restore a coherent text was undertaken by Adolf Jacoby, W. Spiegelberg being responsible for the Coptic part (Adolf Jacoby, *Ein neues Evangelienfragment*, Strasbourg 1900). This effort met with a justly severe criticism from C. Schmidt

[1] Cf. Rom. 16:17.   [2] Cf. Jn. 7:18.
[3] Mt. 24:5ff.; Rom. 16:18.   [4] Acts 1:9.
[5] Cf. Hebr. 8:1; 10:11–12; 1 Clem. 36·1.   [6] Mk. 5:34; Acts 16:36; Jas. 2:16.

(*GGA* 1900, 481–506), who for his part advanced a reconstruction of his own for almost all the lines, and thereby made it possible to read with comprehension. The shreds indeed are preserved in such a sorry condition that any reconstruction must remain subject to considerable uncertainty (cf. the illustrations in Jacoby).

The two leaves, remains of an extensive manuscript, are designated Copt. 5 and Copt. 6. The recto of Copt. 5 contains a prayer of Jesus, in which there may be distant echoes of John 17. Certainly the text of the verso, which is separated from the recto only by two or three broken-off lines (which must have contained the end of the prayer), shows that the situation in which this prayer of Jesus is supposed to have been uttered is that of His farewell to the disciples (before the Passion or after the Resurrection?). The prayer is cast in the form of brief sentences, rounded off from time to time by an Amen (cf. the hymn in the Acts of John c. 94–95). On the verso the quotations from Matthew are remarkable, while on the recto there is evidently a reference to 1 Cor. 15. Unfortunately it cannot be said how Copt. 6 is to be related to Copt. 5, since only 6 and not 5 shows any pagination. From the few lines it is however clear that in Copt. 6 we have to do with the end of this apocryphal gospel. Possibly the whole passage is to be explained on the basis of this ending: it may be that in this "gospel" also we have to assume that the content was a dialogue of Jesus with His disciples, who here characteristically are described with emphasis as apostles. Whether this dialogue took place 'on the mountain' (Copt. 6 recto, line 8), and whether by this mountain was meant the place of the Ascension (or of the Transfiguration?), we cannot say. Even in explanation of the content we cannot pass beyond conjecture. The Synoptics are used, John seems to be known, and reference is made to Paul. The form shows acquaintance with Gnostic constructions. We might therefore think, for the original milieu, of a Gnostic group which stood not very far apart from the great Church. But this remains pure conjecture!

All attempts to assign these fragments to a particular gospel have proved abortive. Jacoby maintained that it was a question of a fragment from the Gospel of the Egyptians; Schmidt conjectured (very cautiously!) that the text belonged to the (Jewish-Christian!) 'Gospel of the Twelve', since the apostles here speak in the plural. But F. Haase rightly rejected all speculations of the kind (*Literarkritische Untersuchungen zur orientalisch-apokryphen Evangelienliteratur*, 1913, pp. 1–11; further literature there). Equally unanswerable is the question of the original language: the number of Greek loan-words is in this text rather smaller than greater than in the other Coptic texts. The age of the apocryphon can scarcely be established, but in view of the use of the NT we can hardly go back beyond the beginning of the 3rd century.

The translation is given according to the text revised by C. Schmidt (*Apokr.* 2, p. 66), with a few variations resulting from a fresh examination of the Coptic text.

I.

Copt. 5 (Recto):

⟨that⟩ he may be recognized by ⟨his hospitality? . . . . . . ⟩ and be praised through his fruits, for (since?)

. . . . . many of . . .
. . . Amen. Give me now thy ⟨power⟩, O Father, that ⟨they⟩ with me may endure ⟨the world⟩. Amen. ⟨I have⟩ received the diadem (sceptre?) of the kingdom⟨. . . the⟩ diadem of him who is
. . . ⟨while men despise them ⟨in their⟩ lowliness, since they have not ⟨recognized them⟩. I am become king ⟨through thee⟩, Father. Thou wilt make ⟨all⟩ subject to me.

⟨Amen⟩. Through whom will

⟨the last⟩ enemy be destroyed? Through
⟨Christ⟩. Amen. Through whom is
the sting of death ⟨destroyed⟩?[7]
⟨Through the⟩ Only-begotten. Amen. To whom belongs ⟨the⟩ dominion?

(Verso):

⟨When⟩ now ⟨Jesus had⟩ completed all ⟨the praise? of his Father⟩[1]
then he turned to us and spake ⟨to us⟩:

The hour is nigh,[2]
when I shall be taken from you.[3]
The Spirit ⟨is⟩ willing,
but the flesh ⟨is⟩ weak.[4] *⟨Wait⟩*
now *and watch ⟨with me⟩.*[5]
But we, the apost⟨les, we⟩ wept, ⟨and⟩ said ⟨to him⟩:

. . . . ⟨Son⟩
of God . . . . . . ⟨will⟩
himself . . . .

He answered and said ⟨to us⟩:

Fear ye not the
destruction (of the body) but ⟨*fear ye*⟩
rather . . . . [6]

the power ⟨of darkness?⟩

Be mindful of all that ⟨I⟩ have said unto you: ⟨if⟩ they have persecuted ⟨me⟩, ⟨they will⟩

[1] ⟨cf. Mt. 26:30?⟩   [2] Mt. 26:45.   [3] Mt. 9:15 and par.
[4] Mt. 26:41.   [5] Mt. 26:38.   [6] Cf. Mt. 10:28.   [7] Cf. 1 Cor. 15:25f., 55.

⟨It belongs to the Son⟩. Amen.   also persecute you . . .[1] ⟨Ye(?)⟩
  ⟨Through

whom has all come into being?   now rejoice, that I have
  Through⟩

· · · · · · · · · · · ·   ⟨overcome⟩ the world,[2] and I
                         have · · · · · · ·

(2–3 lines missing)

2.

Copt. 6 (Recto):   p. 157 (Verso):   p. 158
(that I) may reveal to you all   Our eyes penetrated all places,
  my glory and show you   we beheld the glory[3] of his
all your power and the secret   godhead and all the glory of
of your apostolate · · · · ·   ⟨his⟩ dominion. He clothed
                             ⟨us⟩

· · · · · · · · · ·   ⟨with⟩ the power ⟨of our⟩
                             apostle⟨ship⟩

· · · · · · · · · ·   · · · · · · · · · · ·
· · · · · · · · · ·   · · · · · · · · · · ·
· · · · ⟨on the⟩ mountain   · · · · · · · · · · ·
· · · · · · · · · ·   · · · · · · · · · · ·

[1] Jn. 15:20.   [2] Cf. Jn. 16:33.   [3] Jn. 1:14.

VII

GNOSTIC GOSPELS AND RELATED DOCUMENTS*
(*Henri-Charles Puech*)

A. GOSPELS UNDER GENERAL TITLES

1. *The Gospel of the Four Heavenly Regions or of the Four Corners of the World*

A document of this title is mentioned, in connection with the Simonians, in the catalogue of heresies drawn up by Marūtā, bishop of Maiperkat (d. before 420), in his *De sancta synodo Nicaena*;[1] "And they (those godless men) made for themselves a gospel, (dividing it into four volumes, and called it) the Book of the regions of the world." Arabic version and Latin translation by Abraham Ecchellensis:[2] "Sibi autem perfidi isti evangelium effinxerunt, quod in quattuor tomos secantes librum quattuor angulorum et cardinum mundi appellarunt."

Marūtā's notice is not of great value. Nevertheless Harnack[3] and Haase[4] are inclined to consider 'trustworthy' what is there said about the Gospel of the four regions. It might, in fact, be a question of one of the works which according to Const. Apost. VI. 16 were current "under the name of Christ and His disciples", and which were alleged to have been composed by Simon Magus and his followers. The title recalls the famous theory of Irenaeus (*adv. haer.* III. 11.11 Harvey) on the fourfold Gospel: "It cannot be admitted that there are either more or less than four Gospels. For since there are four regions of the world (quattuor regiones mundi, τέσσαρα κλίματα τοῦ κόσμου) in which we live, and four winds from the four cardinal points (quattuor principales spiritus, τέσσαρα καθολικὰ πνεύματα), and since on the other hand the Church is spread over all the earth, and the Gospel and the Spirit of life are the pillar and foundation of the Church, it follows that this Church has four pillars, which from every part breathe out

---

* The French version of this section was completed in September 1957, apart from a few additions at the proof-stage. The present English translation has been made, with the consent of Prof. Puech, from a photo-copy of the original French, and has been checked throughout against the German version to ensure completeness in all respects.

[1] O. Braun, *Kirchengeschichtliche Studien* IV, 3 Münster 1898, p. 47; A. Harnack, *TU* 19, 1b, 1899, p. 7; F. Haase, *Altchristliche Kirchengeschichte nach orientalischen Quellen*, Leipzig 1925, p. 324.

[2] Mansi II, col. 1057b, and Harnack *op. cit.* p. 15.

[3] p. 7 n. 2.   [4] p. 324 n. 2.

incorruptibility and quicken men to life." Perhaps also we may recall certain passages of Pistis Sophia, e.g. ch. 136, p. 232, 14–26 (Jesus with His disciples turns to face the four corners of the world), or p. 254, 10–17 (the twelve apostles going in threes to the four quarters of heaven, and preaching the Gospel of the kingdom in the whole world). However that may be, the title of the document and its division into four books, each corresponding to one of the four cardinal points, seem to indicate that the apocryphon ascribed to the Simonians claimed to be a universal Gospel, if not *the* universal Gospel. We know nothing more, nor can we guess anything further; whether the book ever existed at all remains doubtful.

2. *The Gospel of Perfection*

All we know of this gospel goes back to a single source, the *Panarion* of Epiphanius (26.2.5, vol. 1, p. 277, 13–17 Holl). It is also mentioned by Filastrius of Brescia (*Haer.* 33. 7, p. 18, 18 Marx), but this is from Epiphanius, as the immediate context shows (it derives from *Pan.* 26. 2. 6–3. 2). The two heresiologues are content to name the work (εὐαγγέλιον τελειώσεως, *evangelium consummationis*) and to condemn it. Epiphanius attributes its fabrication to the 'Gnostics', Filastrius to the Nicolaitans (discussed in Epiph. *Pan.* 25), whom he confuses with the *Gnostici*. Harnack (*Litg.* I, p. 167f.) and Hennecke (*Apokr.* 2, p. 69) propose (not without reservations) to explain title and content by the aid of a Naassene saying quoted by Hippolytus (*Ref.* V. 6. 6; V. 8. 38, cf. X. 9): "The beginning of perfection (ἀρχὴ τελειώσεως) is the knowledge of man, the knowledge of God is complete perfection (ἀπηρτισμένη τελείωσις)". This suggestion remains doubtful. It would be as plausible to appeal to Irenaeus (*adv. haer.* I. 28. 7 ad fin. Harvey) and conjecture that the gospel related to the 'future consummation' (*consummationem futuram*), which is to take place when all the dispersed spiritual 'seed of light' is finally gathered together (*quando tota humectatio spiritus luminis colligatur*).

This theme of the σύλλεξις recurs in other Gnostic gospels, notably the Gospel of Eve and the Gospel of Philip (see below, pp. 241ff. and 271ff.). By concentration, by focusing himself upon himself, the Gnostic regains knowledge and possession of himself, recovers his perfection and his state of being saved: on each such occasion, a morsel or part of the spiritual substance now scattered among the elect (the men of the superior race, who are 'born from above') is recovered, and at the same time is detached from its admixture of matter and brought back to the transcendent place of its origin; thus the greater part of this 'light-substance' is progressively restored. When in course of time the process of collection is complete, the final 'consummation' will take place: the visible world will pass away, the perfecting of the πνευματικοί will be brought to a close, and the universal salvation of the 'spiritual race' will be finally assured. It is possible that our document described the manner, theoretical and practical, of this process. In more general and less specific terms, it must have been either a gospel teaching an ideal of perfection and the means of attaining thereto, or a gospel destined for the 'perfect', the τέλειοι, i.e. the πνευματικοί, the 'elect', or a gospel perfect in itself, the supreme Gospel containing in itself the sum total of revelation or of *gnosis*. However, owing to the paucity of our sources, all hypotheses can only be inadequate. For the same reason it is pure conjecture to date its composition, as Harnack does (*Litg.* II, 2, 178f.), in the 2nd century.

3. *The Gospel of Truth*

Until recently the only witnesses to an apocryphon under this name were Irenaeus and pseudo-Tertullian. Irenaeus (*adv. haer.* III. 11. 12 Harvey) reports that lately—i.e. not long before the composition of his work (*c.* 180)—the Valentinians had dared to produce a kind of fifth Gospel, entirely different from the Gospels of the apostles and entitled *veritatis evangelium*: "The Valentinians, again, outstep all bounds of reverence in producing their own writings, and boast that they possess more Gospels than there really are. Indeed they have advanced to such a pitch of audacity that they give the title 'Gospel of Truth' to a work composed by them not long ago, which agrees in no respect with the Gospels of the apostles, so that among them not even the Gospel is without blasphemy. For if what they produce is the 'Gospel of Truth', yet is different from those handed down to us by the apostles, then any who will may learn (as is manifest from the writings themselves) that what has been handed down by the apostles is not the 'Gospel of Truth'".

Pseudo-Tertullian writes (*adv. omnes haer.* 4, p. 221, 9–13 Kroymann): "He (Valentinus) approves some parts of the law and the prophets, but rejects others. Also he has a gospel of his own in addition to these of ours. After him arose Ptolemaeus and Secundus". There is perhaps a further allusion to this same writing in Tertullian (*de praescr. haer.* 25, p. 30, 15–31, 15 Kroymann), who has certain unnamed Gnostics in view: "They (the Gnostics) will not admit that they (the apostles) revealed all things to everyone; for some they delivered openly and to the world at large, some in private and to a few, because Paul makes use of this saying to Timothy (*2 Tim. 1:14*): 'O Timothy, that which was committed to thee, keep . . .' But not even the fact that he wished him 'to commit these things to faithful men, who may be fit to teach others also' (2 Tim. 2:2) is ground for interpreting that also as proof of a hidden gospel". Equally uncertain and much more debatable are the references to the Valentinian gospel which Zahn (*Geschichte des ntl. Kanons*, I, 2 Erlangen 1889, p. 749) suspected in Origen (*in Luc. hom.* XXIX, p. 179, 14–22 Rauer; *c. Cels.* II. 27, vol. I, p. 156, 5–8 Koetschau).

Since the document was so poorly attested, the efforts of scholars to gain some idea of its form and content were doomed to failure from the outset. Numerous hypotheses were nevertheless advanced, all of which today are to be regarded as more or less worthless or erroneous. The fragment of the Valentinian epistle quoted by Epiphanius (*Pan.* 31. 5–6), despite the statement in Migne's *Dictionnaire des Apocryphes* (II, Paris 1858, col. 1065), cannot in any sense represent the beginning of the Gospel of Truth. Zahn (*op. cit.* I, 2, p. 749f.) rightly denied that the Gospel of Truth, like that of Marcion, was a redaction of the canonical Gospels, since according to Irenaeus it was entirely different; but he was mistaken when he supposed it to be a complement to a book containing the secret traditions of the Valentinian school, in particular the traditions which according to Clement of Alexandria (*Strom.* VII. 106. 4) had been transmitted from Paul to Valentinus by a disciple of the apostle, Theodas or Theodotus. Perhaps he was also wrong in holding the apocryphon to be a complement to the Church's Gospel. The Gospel of Truth, again, is not "a selection of the words of the Saviour", as Liechtenhan imagined (*Die Offenbarung im Gnosticismus*, Tübingen 1901, p. 69f.), although this view was followed, with some reserve, by Hennecke (*Apokr.* 2, p. 68). The latter however added that the work was "perhaps identical with the Sophia Jesu Christi", a hypothesis which in its turn is to be disputed, since in the Gnostic library of Nag Hammadi the Sophia Jesu Christi (see below pp. 243ff.) and the Gospel of Truth are two clearly distinct writings. As for the theory of Kreyenbühl (*Das Evangelium der Wahrheit* I, Berlin 1901, II, 1905), who went so far as to identify the Gospel of Truth with that of John, it is quite untenable, and belongs to the realm of fantasy.

The situation is entirely different now that we possess what may be the complete text of the Gospel of Truth, translated from Greek into Coptic (Subachmimic). It is the second of the four or five writings contained in the 'Codex C. G. Jung' (middle of 4th century), one of the volumes discovered about 1945 near Nag Hammadi (= Codex II of the classification which I have suggested for the discovery as a whole) and the only one to have been brought out of Egypt. Acquired in 1946 by the antiquary Albert

Eid, it was taken to the U.S.A., then to Belgium, and finally on May 10, 1952 passed into the possession of the Jung Institute in Zürich.

Literature: H.-Ch. Puech and J. Doresse, Communication of Feb. 20, 1948 in *CR Acad. Inscrr. et Belles-Lettres*, Institut de France, 1948, p. 89. – Togo Mina, "Le papyrus gnostique du Musée Copte" (*Vig. Chr.* 2 (1948) 129). – J. Doresse, "Nouveaux textes gnostiques coptes décou-verts en Haute Égypte. La bibliothèque de Chénoboskion" (*Vig. Chr.* 3 (1949) 132f. and 137). – id., "Une bibliothèque gnostique copte découverte en Haute-Égypte" (*Académie Royale de Belgique. Bulletin de la classe des Lettres et des Sciences morales et politiques*, 5ème série, t. XXXV, 1949, 438f. and 444). H.-Ch. Puech, "Les nouveaux écrits gnostiques découverts en Haute-Égypte. Premier inventaire et essai d'identifica-tion" (in *Coptic Studies in Honor of W. E. Crum = Bulletin of the Byzantine Institute* 2, Boston 1950, 103f.). – G. Quispel, "Note on an unknown gnostic codex" (*Vig. Chr.* 7 (1953) 193). – H.-Ch. Puech and G. Quispel, "Les écrits gnostiques du Codex Jung" (*Vig. Chr.* 8 (1954) 1–51). – id., "Le quatrième écrit gnostique du Codex Jung" (*Vig. Chr.* 9 (1955) 65–102). – G. Quispel, "Neue Funde zur valentinianischen Gnosis" (*Zeitschr. f. Religions- u. Geistesgesch.* 6 (1954) 289–305). – W. Foerster, "Neue Literatur über die gnostischen Papyri von Cheno-boskion" (*ThLZ* 79 (1954) 377–384). – H.-Ch. Puech, G. Quispel, W. C. van Unnik, *The Jung Codex. A Newly Recovered Gnostic Papyrus*, London, 1955. – H.-Ch. Puech, "Découverte d'une bibliothèque gnostique en Haute-Égypte", in *Encyclopédie Française*, t. XIX, Paris, 1957, fasc. 19. 42-7-19. 42-8. S. Schulz, *Theol. Rundschau* 26 (1960) 248, 250ff. – F. M. Braun, *Jean le Théologien et son Évangile*, Paris 1959, 112ff.

The Gospel of Truth, as it is now thus restored to us, has been more specially studied and analysed by H.-Ch. Puech and G. Quispel (in *Vig. Chr.* 8 (1954) 22–39, and *Op zoek naar het Evangelie der Waarheid*, Nijkerk, 1954), by W. C. van Unnik (*Het kortgeleden ontdekte "Evangelie der Waarheid"* en het *Nieuwe Testament*, in *Mededelingen der Koninklijke Nederlandse Akademie van Wetenschappen*, Afd. Letterkunde, Nieuwe Reeks, Deel 17, No. 3, Amsterdam, 1954 = The 'Gospel of Truth' and the New Testament, in *The Jung Codex* (London, 1955), 79–129), and by G. Quispel ("The Jung Codex and its Significance", in *The Jung Codex*, 47–54 and 72–78). – F. M. Braun, "L'énigme des Odes de Salomon" (*Rev. Thomiste* 1957, 577–627), J. Leipoldt, *ThLZ* 82 (1957) cols. 825ff., L. Cerfaux, *NTS* v (1958/9) 103ff., A. Orbe, *Hacia la primera Teologia de la procesion del Verbo*, Rome 1958, esp. pp. 68ff., M. Cramer, in *Studia Biblica et Orientalia* 1959, 48–56. Edition of Coptic text with introduction, notes and indices by M. Malinine, H.-Ch. Puech, G. Quispel: *Evangelium Veritatis* (Studien aus dem C. G. Jung Institut VI), Zürich 1956; see further W. C. Till, "Bemerkungen zur Erstausgabe des 'Evangelium Veritatis'," *Orientalia* N.S. 27 (1958) 269–286.

The text covers pages 16, 31–43, 29 of the Codex but when it was bought by the Jung Institute two folios (fol. XVII and XVIII, i.e. four pages, 33–36) were missing. These have however been found in the Coptic Museum in Old Cairo among a pile of detached leaves, likewise belonging to the Nag Hammadi discovery, and have been published in a photographic edition by Pahor Labib, *Coptic Gnostic Papyri in the Coptic Museum at Old Cairo*, vol. 1, Cairo 1956: p. 33 ($\overline{\lambda\gamma}$) =plate 9; p. 34 (wrongly numbered $\overline{\lambda\epsilon}$=35 in the manuscript) =plate 10; p. 35 (wrongly numbered $\overline{\lambda s}$=36) =plate 6; p. 36 ($\overline{\lambda s}$) =plate 5 (cf. Puech, *RHR* 151 (1957) 267–270). We thus possess the complete text of the gospel. German translation of these four pages by H. M. Schenke in *ThLZ* 83 (1958) cols. 497–500; edition of Coptic text by W. C. Till in *Orientalia* 28 (1959) 170–185; edition with introduction, notes and indices by Malinine, Puech, Quispel and Till in *Evangelium Veritatis* (Supplementum), Zürich and Stuttgart 1961. Complete translations of the whole text by H. M. Schenke, *Die Herkunft des sogenannten Evangelium Veritatis* (Berlin 1958) 33ff. and in *Evangelien aus dem Nilsand* (Frankfurt am Main 1960) 174ff., and W. C. Till, *ZNW* 50 (1959) 165ff. (both German), and K. Grobel, *The Gospel of Truth*, London 1960 and W. W. Isenberg, in *Gnosticism. An Anthology* (ed. R. M. Grant), London 1961, 146ff. (English).

The work bears no title, but one is nevertheless suggested (*p̆euaggĕlion ᵉntmēĕ* = τὸ εὐαγγέλιον τῆς ἀληθέιας) by the first words of the text:

The Gospel (εὐαγγέλιον) of Truth is joy for those who have received from the Father of Truth the grace of knowing him through the power of the Logos, which has come forth from the Pleroma (πλήρωμα), (the Logos) which is in the thought and mind (νοῦς) of the Father, which is he whom men call the Redeemer (σωτήρ), since that is the name of the work which he must do for the redemption of those who knew not the Father, since the name of the Gospel (εὐαγγέλιον) is the revelation of hope (ἐλπίς), since it is a discovery for those who seek him.

(Codex Jung, p. 16, 31–17, 4)

In spite of the title—which might be merely traditional and in any case is here supplied only by implication—the treatise does not belong to the ordinary type of a Gospel, whether canonical or Gnostic. It contains no account of the life or works of Jesus, nor any mention of the words or sayings of the Lord. On the contrary, it presupposes acquaintance with the Synoptics, of which it expounds episodes and parables, and with the Gospel of John. In addition it makes use of the Apocalypse and of the Pauline Epistles, and probably also of some narrative of the infancy of the Saviour (Biblical citations and allusions in W. C. van Unnik, *op.*

cit., and in the critical notes to the edition, pp. 51–60). Some few passages only are a little more concrete and less allusive than the rest of the text, e.g.:

He made his appearance in a school, he spoke the word as a master (*Lk. 2:46–49? Infancy Gospel?*) There came to him those who were wise (σοφός) in their own hearts (*Isa. 5:21, Rom. 12:16*) tempting him (πειράζειν; *Mt. 16:1; 19:3; 22:18, 35; Mk. 8:11; 10:2; 12:18; Lk. 11:16; Jn. 6:6*). But he convinced them that they were empty. They hated him (*cf. Jn. 7:7, 15:18*), because they were not truly wise. After all these there came also the little children, of whom is the knowledge of the Father (*Mt. 11:25, 18:2–6, 10; Lk. 10:21*) . . . They knew, they were known (*cf. 1 Cor. 8:2–3, 13:12; Gal. 4:9*), they were glorified, they glorified (*cf. Rom. 8:30*).

(Codex Jung, p. 19, 18–34)

or:

None could be revealed of those who have believed in the redemption, so long as this book had not appeared (*sc. the living book of the living: Ps. 69:28; Phil. 4:3; Rev. 13:8*). Therefore this merciful, this faithful (πιστός) Jesus (*Hebr. 2:17, 3:2, Rev. 19:11*) was patient, in that he took upon himself suffering, until he had received this book (*Rev. 5:9, 12; 13:8*), since (ἐπειδή) he knew that his death was life for many (*cf. Mk. 10:45*). Just as the fortune (οὐσία) of the dead master of the house remains concealed so long as his will (διαθήκη; *cf. Hebr. 9:16?*) is not opened, so also (δέ) the All remained concealed so long as the Father of All was invisible (ἀόρατος), since he is a self-existent being out of whom come all ways. For this reason Jesus appeared, he took this book for himself. He was nailed to a cross of wood; he affixed the decree (διάταγμα) of the Father upon the cross (σταυρός; *cf. Col. 2:14*). O what a great doctrine! He humbled himself even to death, although he was clothed with eternal life (*cf. Phil. 2:8; 1 Cor. 15:53f.; 2 Cor. 5:2–4; perhaps Col. 2:14f.?*). After he had stripped off these transitory rags, he put on immortality, something none can take from him (*cf. Jn. 10:29?*). After he had penetrated into the empty spaces of horror he passed over to those who were

237

stripped by forgetfulness, since he became Knowledge and Perfection . . .

(Codex Jung, p. 20, 6–39)

One might further cite the arithmological interpretation of the Parable of the Lost Sheep (Mt. 18:12–13, Lk. 15:4–7), which is to be compared with the exposition supplied for these verses by the Valentinians (Marcosians), of which Irenaeus (*adv. haer.* I. 1. 17; I. 9. 1–2; II. 36. 4 Harvey) gives an account:

He is the shepherd who left the ninety-nine sheep that did not go astray, (but) went and sought for the one that was lost, (and) rejoiced when he found it. For ninety-nine is a number which (is reckoned) on the left hand, which contains it. But as soon as the one is found, the whole number goes over to the right (hand). Even so he who lacks the one, that is, the entire right hand, which draws to itself that which was missing, and takes from it the left side and transfers it to the right: and so the number becomes a hundred . . . He laboured even (κἄν) on the Sabbath (σάββατον) for the sheep, which he found fallen into the well (*Mt. 12:11–12*). He saved the life of this sheep, because he drew it out of the well, that you may know in (your) hearts—you, the children of the knowledge of the heart—what is the Sabbath (σάββατον) on which the work of redemption may not remain inactive, that you may say—of this day from above, which has no night, and of the light which does not pass away (*cf. Isa. 60:19f.; 5 Esd. 2:35*), because it is perfect. Say therefore in your hearts, that you are this perfect day, and that it dwells in you, this light which does not grow dim . . .

(Codex Jung, p. 31, 35–32, 34)

On the other hand, the work is not constructed on the pattern usual in Gnostic gospels. It does not profess to record, in the form of a vision or a dialogue, the sublime teaching imparted by Christ to some privileged person, an apostle, a group of disciples, or the disciples and the holy women as a body. It has on the contrary the character of a public address, a lecture, interrupted by admonitions to the audience, present or imagined, (the "children of the knowledge of the heart" (see above), the πνευματικοί), and closing with a personal statement (p. 42, lines 39ff.). An initiate, who possesses the authority of a master and the warmth and unction of a preacher, here speaks to his 'brethren', offering them a kind of meditation or devotional homily on the Gospel.

His purpose—and also the object of the treatise—is to define, describe and commend what the evangelic message essentially is, in its purest and profoundest significance: the complete manifestation of the Truth, the unforeseen and gracious revelation of their true selves and of God, brought to the Elect, the πνευματικοί, the 'living', by a 'messenger' who is thereby a 'saviour'; the awakening to knowledge and to 'light' of the man who has hitherto been plunged in the thick fog of ignorance and error, buried in the night of a world which is illusion, nightmare, anguish, and from whom suddenly the senselessness, the deceptive emptiness, the nothingness have been dispersed (cf. p. 17, 10–37 and above all p. 28, 24–30, 16). In other words, the essence of the Gospel, the content of the 'good and joyful tidings' revealed by Jesus, is summed up completely in 'Gnosis': the Son by revealing himself has opened the 'book of life' or 'of the living'; he has drawn men out of their 'forgetting' of themselves and of their true nature, has delivered them from the 'terror', the 'sleep' the 'drunkenness' in which they lay as prisoners, ignorant that they were of God, the Father, ignorant of their real situation; he has made them to know God, or to recover their knowledge of him, and at the same time to recover the knowledge of themselves; he has awakened them, enlightened them, and thereby restored them to their primal state and brought them once more into possession of their true and permanent being, which he has made it possible for them to rediscover.

He who, thanks to Jesus and the Gospel, has found Knowledge and thus possesses Gnosis 'knows', in fact, who he is, "whence he is come and whither he goes" (p. 22, 13–15; cf. *Exc. ex Theod.* 78, 2), and this knowledge frees him from 'deficiency' (ὑστέρημα), the condition of existence which hitherto was his in the Cosmos, the world here below, a condition of incompleteness, insufficiency, and emptiness (κένωμα). It enables him to ascend to the 'Pleroma' (πλήρωμα), to the 'fulness' of being and of his own existence, i.e. to 'Rest' (ἀνάπαυσις) or to the 'place of rest' (cf. p. 21, 8–25; 22, 2–19; 24, 9–25, 3; 36, 1–34; 41, 3–19).

What is commended here under the name of the 'Gospel' is thus in fact Gnosis, and the whole work could be regarded as a kind of hymn to Knowledge, expanded or reinforced in its second part (p. 36, lines 39ff.) by expositions of the relations which unite the Father and the Son, and more particularly concerning the Son as the 'name' (ὄνομα) of the Father.[1]

[1] On this and on the possible relations between this theory and certain Jewish speculations and the Fourth Gospel, cf. G. Quispel, *The Jung Codex*, 64–76.—id., "Christliche Gnosis und jüdische Heterodoxie", in *Evang. Theol.* 1954, 474–484.—id., "Het Johannesevangelie en de Gnosis", *Ned. Theol. Tijdsch.* 11, 173ff.

It seems, accordingly, that we must abandon the idea that our treatise is a 'gospel' in the proper sense, or that it was intended to be a kind of fifth Gospel, beside the four canonical Gospels or in opposition to them, designed to correct or complete them, to be 'the true Gospel', an authentic, genuine and perfect gospel. There is no reason for allowing ourselves to be influenced in this respect by the testimony of Irenaeus, who may well have had no more than a superficial or indirect knowledge of the work[1] and may not have read it himself.[2] On the basis of the title alone, or the little he knew of the book, he may have been led to think of it as a gospel (in the exact and technical sense of the term) fabricated over and above the fourfold Gospel in order to complete or perhaps replace it, a gospel of which the very name seemed to express the view that here Truth was opposed to Error, to falsehood and inaccuracy.

In my opinion we have to do rather with a homily which might be reckoned among the pieces of the same kind which, according to Clement of Alexandria (*Strom.* IV. 13. 89. 1–3; VI. 6. 52, 3–4), belonged to the literary work of Valentinus. Far from pretending to be a new gospel, the character or quality of which would be that it was true, this discourse treats only of the truth of the Gospel; its purpose is only to unfold and explain the significance and the bearing of this message of truth, this revelation and exposition of the truth, which is the Gospel (in the original and etymological sense of the word): the 'Good News' proclaimed by Christ, which came into the world with Him (cf. W. C. van Unnik, in *The Jung Codex*, pp. 104–106).

The document is probably of Valentinian origin, and earlier than 180.[3] It is even possible that it should be ascribed to Valentinus himself, rather than to his disciple Marcus, and that it was composed towards the middle of the second century. W. C. van Unnik (*op. cit.* 97–104) would be still more precise: Valentinus wrote the Gospel of Truth in Rome between 140 and 145, shortly before or after his breach with the catholic community of the city. The interest of the document would in that case be considerably increased: not only should we now possess at last a complete work by the founder and head of the Valentinian school, but also we should be in a position to comprehend the first efforts towards the formation of the system of this heresiarch, still only in part detached from the more orthodox Christian envelope in which he had first tried to formulate it. Moreover the numerous and diverse Biblical citations would make the work a very valuable witness

[1] Cf. Harnack *Litg.* 1.176.
[2] Hennecke *Apokr.* 2, 68; A. Loisy, *La naissance du christianisme*, Paris 1933, 65 n. 3.
[3] Cf. H.-Ch. Puech—G. Quispel, *Vig. Chr.* 8 (1954) 27–32, and the critical notes of the edition.

for the state of the New Testament canon at that date. However, some of the arguments which van Unnik has advanced are open to question,[1] and one may well still hesitate to adopt in their entirety the conclusions which he draws. On the other hand Schenke and others have claimed that the Gospel of Truth shows nothing specifically Valentinian, and that its central ideas represent a theory of *gnosis* akin to that of the Odes of Solomon. Nevertheless we still believe that the document should rather be linked with Valentinianism.[2]

B. GOSPELS UNDER THE NAME OF AN OLD TESTAMENT FIGURE

The only example which we have is the Gospel of Eve (εὐαγγέλιον Εὔας). The title is mentioned in connection with the Gospel of Perfection (see above, pp. 232f.) by Epiphanius (*Pan.* 26. 2. 6; I, p. 277, 17–278, 6 Holl), who ascribes the work to the Gnostics. He also gives the only certain quotation:

I stood upon a high mountain and saw a tall man, and another of short stature, and heard as it were a sound of thunder and went nearer in order to hear. Then he spoke to me and said: I am thou and thou art I, and where thou art there am I, and I am sown in all things; and whence thou wilt, thou gatherest me, but when thou gatherest me, then gatherest thou thyself.

(Pan. 26. 3. 1; I, p. 278, 8–13)

This passage, which apparently belonged to the beginning of the work, ought to allow us to form some conception of its structure. Unfortunately it is very difficult to identify the narrator of the vision here related, and the mythical interlocutor. Is Eve herself the speaker, or a seer, to us anonymous? Do the two figures, the one tall, the other short and stunted, represent "the Urmensch and his dwarfish earthly likeness"?[3] Perhaps indeed they are in reality one, seen at one and the same time under different aspects, as is frequently the case in narratives of this type (cf. e.g. the beginning of the Apocryphon of John, or visions of Christ or other

[1] E.g. the argument from the method of finger-reckoning referred to in the gospel (see H. I. Marrou, *Vig. Chr.* 12 (1958) 98ff.), which van Unnik himself has now withdrawn (*Newly Discovered Gnostic Writings*, London 1960, p. 64 n. 1.) See also H. Jonas in *Gnomon* 32 (1960) p. 333.

[2] That the Gospel of Truth is of Valentinian origin is also the opinion of A. D. Nock (*JTS* 9 (1958) 323) H. Jonas (*Gnomon* 32 (1960) 327ff.), F. M. Braun, A. Orbe, R. M. Grant, K. Grobel and others.

[3] Hennecke, *Apokr.* 2, p. 69; cf. perhaps a picture in Cubiculum I of the hypogaeum of the Aurelii, in C. Cecchelli, *Monumenti cristiani-eretici di Roma*, Rome 1949, pl. II right.

beings, divine or demoniac, in manifold embodiments). Or is it 'Man' (ὁ ἄνθρωπος, the Urmensch) and the Son of Man?[1] Or do they represent "God the Father and Barbelo, who is stunted because the power has been taken from her"?[2] Or Christ in His double form, as transcendent Son of God and as incarnate and humiliated man? Or is some other being intended?

We cannot say with confidence. All that is certain is that we have to do with a revelation, an apocalypse, constructed after the usual pattern and employing the normal motifs of this kind of literature: the setting of the scene upon a mountain, the appearance of a figure of very great or gigantic stature, an address by this figure to the seer. The revealer, or divine being, discloses to his interlocutor his identity with him, by an almost stereotyped formula (ἐγὼ σὺ καὶ σὺ ἐγώ) which is often employed in Gnostic, Hermetic, magic or alchemical texts.[3] This identity implies that the one is everywhere and always present to the other, and that there is a consubstantiality between them. "To gather oneself" (ἑαυτὸν συλλέγειν), i.e. to gather the substance of one's spiritual 'light-nature' which is dispersed in the body and in matter, to recover and save one's 'ego' by disengaging it from the diversity of the world and restoring it to its original unity, is equivalent to saying that the one at the same time gathers and saves the substance, or a part of the substance, of the other, which is likewise scattered, dispersed and imprisoned in the world. There is a solidarity and a collaboration between the Saviour and the saved. Here again the theory and the language are Gnostic.[4] They recur in Manicheism.[5]

On the other hand a reference in Epiphanius (*Pan.* 26. 2. 6; I p. 278, 1–2 Holl: αὐτῆς (sc. Εὔας) δῆθεν ὡς εὑρούσης τὸ βρῶμα τῆς γνώσεως ἐξ ἀποκαλύψεως τοῦ λαλήσαντος αὐτῇ ὄφεως) suggests that the writing had for its subject the discovery by Eve, in consequence of a revelation received from the mouth of the serpent, of the 'food' or 'fruit of Gnosis', the saving knowledge.[6] It would then set forth the Gnostic doctrine of salvation thus revealed. The encounter with the serpent and the latter's speech were probably reported either by Eve herself or by the narrator,

[1] Holl in his edition of the Panarion, vol. I, p. 278, note to line 8.
[2] H. Leisegang, *Die Gnosis*[4], Leipzig 1955, p. 190.
[3] Cf. Reitzenstein, *Poimandres* 236–244; A. Dieterich, *Mithrasliturgie*, 3rd ed, 97, 240; K. Holl in his edition of the Panarion, I.278, note to line 11; A. J. Festugière, *Corpus Hermeticum* I. 68 note 33.
[4] Cf. Epiphanius, *Pan.* 26. 10. 9; Gospel of Philip, in Epiph. *Pan.* 26. 13. 2 (see below, p. 273); L. Fendt, *Gnostische Mysterien*, Munich 1922, 4–32, 76f.; H. Jonas, *Gnosis und spätantiker Geist I*, Göttingen 1934, [2]1954, p. 139f.; R. Bultmann, *ZNW* 24, 1925, 118f.; id., *Das Evangelium des Johannes*[11], Göttingen 1950, 41 n. 2.
[5] Cf. SB Berlin 1933, 308, and 1934, 877 and 891.
[6] Cf. Iren. *adv. haer.* I.28.4 Harvey; ps.-Tertullian *adv. omnes haer.* 2; Filastrius 1; Epiphanius *Pan.* 37. 3. 1: Ophites; Hippol. *Ref.* V.16.8: Peratae.

who would have learned of it in the course of his vision. Since it contained the announcement made by Eve, or at least to Eve, of this 'good tidings' which is Gnosis, the true knowledge, and perhaps also because it took the form of a dialogue with a redeemer (Christ Himself?), the work could in a sense be taken as a kind of 'gospel', transmitted by Eve, or with her as the central figure. The rather peculiar title would be much better explained in this way than on the assumption that Eve was a witness to the earthly life and teaching of Christ. The Armenian Infancy Gospel (chap. IX) relates how Eve was present with Joseph at the first suckling of Jesus, and testified to the virgin birth, so that this interpretation would not be entirely arbitrary. In the present case, however, it seems excluded.

It is much less certain that, as is commonly supposed,[1] a second extract from the Gospel of Eve is preserved by Epiphanius:

I saw a tree which bore twelve fruits in the year, and he said to me: This is the Tree of Life.

(*Pan.* 26. 5. 1; I p. 281, 17–19)

The context adds that the 'Gnostics' read these lines 'in apocrypha' (ἐν ἀποκρύφοις) and saw in them a symbolic reference to menstrual blood. But it is more probably a case of a very free quotation of Rev. 22:2 (K. Holl in his edition of the Panarion, I.281, note to line 17). Even if it be maintained that ἀπόκρυφα here indicates an esoteric writing of Gnostic origin, it would seem that the passage ought rather to be connected with "The Great Questions of Mary" (below p. 339), where we find a theory of menstrual blood, based on allegorical interpretation of other Biblical passages, which is analogous to that which our quotation is held to presuppose (Epiph. *Pan.* 26. 8. 7 and 9. 2).

Harnack (*Litg.* I p. 166 and 168) believed it possible to find traces of the Gospel of Eve in the Pistis Sophia (chap. 96) and among the Peratae (Hippol. *Ref.* V.16.8 and 13–14), but the evidence on which he relies admits of several opinions. On the other hand one may agree with him in the assumption (*op. cit.* II. 1.539) that the work was written in the 2nd century.

C. GOSPELS CURRENT, DIRECTLY OR INDIRECTLY, UNDER THE NAME OF JESUS, AND SIMILAR WORKS

1. *The Sophia Jesu Christi*

The text of a writing of this name is preserved complete in Coptic (Sahidic) in two manuscripts:

[1] E.g. Harnack, *Litg.* I, p. 166; Bardenhewer, *Litg.* I², p. 347.

(*a*) Papyrus Berolinensis 8502 (5th cent. or beginning of 5th cent.), from the region of Akhmîm, bought in Cairo in 1896 by Dr. C. Reinhardt for the Egyptian Department of the Berlin Museum and now in the papyrus collection of this museum. The work there appears on pages 77.8 to 127.12 as the third piece in the collection, which begins with the Gospel of Mary (see below, pp. 340ff.), between the Apocryphon of John (short version: see below, pp. 314ff.) and part of the Acts of Peter. The title—*Tsophia* *eniēsous pĕchristos*—is given at the beginning (77.8) and at the end (127.11f.).

On the manuscript: C. Schmidt, "Ein vorirenäisches gnostisches Originalwerk in koptischer Sprache" = SB Berlin, 1896, 839–847; id., *Die alten Petrusakten*, *TU* 24. 1, 1903, p. 1f.; W. C. Till, "Die Berliner gnostische Handschrift": *Europäischer Wissenschafts-Dienst* 4, 1944, 19–21. Summary or partial translation of beginning of text: R. Liechtenhan, "Die pseudepigraphe Litteratur der Gnostiker", *ZNW* 3, 1902, 229; E. Hennecke, *Apokr.* 2, 69f.; translation of a passage (after Schmidt) in E. Norden, *Agnostos Theos*, 1913, p. 72; translation of another passage, wrongly given both times as from the Apocryphon of John, in C. Schmidt, *Pistis Sophia*, Leipzig 1925, XXIff. and *ZNW* 24, 1925, 235; some examples of the text in W. E. Crum, *A Coptic Dictionary*, Oxford 1929–1939. Analysis of the document: W. C. Till, "Die Gnosis in Ägypten", *La Parola del Passato*, 12, 1949, 239. Complete edition with introductory analysis, critical apparatus, German translation, notes and index: W. C. Till, *Die gnostischen Schriften des koptischen Papyrus Berolinensis* 8502 = *TU* 60, 1955, 52–61 and 194–295.

(*b*) The second manuscript (middle or second half of 4th cent.) is in one of the volumes of the Coptic Gnostic Library discovered about 1945 near Nag Hammadi (Codex I of my classification). This volume was bought in 1946 for the Coptic Museum in Old Cairo, where it now is. The work occupies pages 90.14 to 119.18. Preceded by the Apocryphon of John (short version), the Sacred Book of the Great Invisible Spirit or Gospel of the Egyptians (see below, p. 362) and the Epistle of Eugnostos, it is the fourth in the volume and is followed by the Dialogue of the Redeemer (see below, pp. 248ff.). In the superscription (90.14) it is named *tsophia* *eniēsous pĕchristos*, and in the colophon (119.18) more simply *tsophia eniēsous*. The text is parallel to that of the Berlin papyrus and presents only slight differences. Two leaves however (four pages: 109f. and 115f.) are missing. This second exemplar is still unpublished (edition in preparation), but its peculiar readings and variants are taken into account in the critical apparatus of Till's edition of the Berlin text.

General description and brief examination: H.-Ch. Puech and J. Doresse, *CR Acad. Inscrr. et Belles-Lettres* (Institut de France) 1948, 90–

92; Togo Mina, "Le papyrus gnostique du Musée Copte", *Vig. Chr.* 2, 1948, 129ff; J. Doresse, "Trois livres gnostiques inédits", *Vig. Chr.* 2, 1948, 146–160; id., *Les livres secrets des gnostiques d'Égypte*, Paris 1958, 215–218 (ET 1960, 198–200); H.-Ch. Puech, "Les nouveaux écrits gnostiques" in *Coptic Studies in Honor of W. E. Crum*, Boston 1950, 102 and 104; id., "Découverte d'une bibliothèque gnostique", in *Enc. Fr.*, t. XIX, Paris 1957, fasc. 19. 42–47.

In addition I have shown that P. Ox. 1081 (3rd cent. or beginning of 4th cent.) contains two pages of the Greek text of this work (these correspond to pages 88.19–91.17 of P. Berol. 8502 = 97. 16–99.13 of the Cairo Codex).[1] This papyrus was first published, with inaccurate restorations, by A. S. Hunt (*The Oxyrhynchus Papyri* VIII, London 1911, 16–19), then by C. Wessely (*PO* XVIII, Paris 1924, 493–495); it was printed as the remains of an anonymous gospel or a Gnostic fragment by E. Klostermann (Apokrypha II[3] = *Kleine Texte* 8, Berlin 1929, 25), and again by A. de Santos Otero (Santos 87–89). It is thereby proved[2] that the Sophia Jesu Christi was originally composed in Greek, and not in Coptic as J. Doresse has maintained[3] and W. Förster expressly repeats.[4]

Some scholars,[5] following Carl Schmidt (who however in *Pistis Sophia*, Leipzig 1925, p. LXXXIV, showed himself very sceptical), had proposed, admittedly with hesitation or with great reserve, to identify the Sophia Jesu Christi with a work of Valentinus which was supposed to have been entitled Sophia, but the discovery of the document itself makes this proposal quite untenable. In the passage of Tertullian invoked in support of the hypothesis (*adv. Val.* 2: Sophia herself teaches, not that of Valentinus but that of Solomon), Sophia denotes an aeon, not the title of a book (cf. Bardenhewer, *Litg.* I, 2nd ed., 359); but above all the content of the Sophia Jesu Christi as it is now known shows nothing that recalls the Valentinian Gnosis (contrary to the view of Hennecke, *Apokr.* 2, 70 and A. de Santos Otero 112). So also we must reject Hennecke's proposal (*Apokr.* 2, 68), to identify the Sophia Jesu Christi with the (Valentinian) Gospel of Truth (see above, pp. 233ff.).

The title of the work may be explained in two different ways. Either we may translate it as "The Wisdom of Jesus Christ" (Hennecke, Doresse, Puech), and understand it as announcing a writing which professes to contain the teaching of Jesus, His

---

[1] H.-Ch. Puech, Communication at 6th International Congress for Papyrology, 1949; *Coptic Studies in Honor of W. E. Crum*, 1950, 98 n. 2.
[2] H.-Ch. Puech, *op. cit.* 98 n. 2; W. C. Till, *Die gnostischen Schriften*, 54.
[3] *Vig. Chr.* 2, 1948, 151f. and 189; *La Nouvelle Clio* 1, 1949, 66.
[4] *Th LZ* 79, 1954, 379.
[5] Harnack, *Litg.* I.176; B. Altaner[2], 1950, 108; Quasten I.276.

'wisdom' revealed and imparted to the disciples; or with W. C. Till (*Die gnost. Schriften*, 55) we may retain the term Sophia without translation, and see in it "rather the name of the celestial being Sophia", who in fact as "the female aspect of the creative power" plays here an important rôle.

However that may be, the writing has all the appearance of a gospel and corresponds to the usual type of Gnostic works of this category. It begins with the customary setting: the scene is laid on a mountain, after the Resurrection; the Saviour appears in supernatural, luminous form; those present (here the twelve disciples and the seven holy women) are struck with astonishment and terror; then begins immediately a dialogue in the course of which the risen and glorified Christ imparts to His hearers the most sublime revelations, expounds all the mysteries and resolves all the problems the profundity, obscurity and difficulty of which still perplex them. Here is the characteristic introduction:

After he had risen from the dead, when they came, the twelve disciples (μαθητής) and seven women who had followed him as disciples (μαθητεύειν), into Galilee, to the mountain which is called "the place of ripeness and joy", where they were now (οὖν) at a loss (ἀπορεῖν) in regard to the true nature (ὑπόστασις) of the universe, the plan of salvation (οἰκονομία), the holy providence (πρόνοια), the excellency (ἀρετή) of the powers (ἐξουσία), about all that the Redeemer (σωτήρ) did with them, the secrets (μυστήριον) of the holy plan of salvation (οἰκονομία), then there appeared to them the Redeemer (σωτήρ), not in his original form (μορφή) but (ἀλλά) in the invisible (ἀόρατον) spirit (πνεῦμα). But (δέ) his appearance was the appearance of a great angel (ἄγγελος) of light. But (δέ) his form I cannot describe. No mortal flesh (σάρξ) could bear it, but (ἀλλά) a pure (καθαρόν) and perfect (τέλειος) flesh (σάρξ) in his kind (=as formerly), as he showed himself to us on the mountain which is called "that of the Olives", in Galilee (*cf. Lk. 19:29; 21:37*). He said: Peace (εἰρήνη) (be) with you! My peace (εἰρήνη) give I unto you (*cf. Lk. 24:36, Jn. 20:19, 21, 26; 1 Pet. 5:14*). And they all wondered and were afraid. The Redeemer (σωτήρ) smiled and spake to them: Of what are you thinking, or (ἤ) about what are you at a loss (ἀπορεῖν), or (ἤ) what are you seeking?

(P. Berol. 77.9–79.18)

A series of doctrinal expositions follows, presented—again in correspondence with the scheme of Gnostic gospels—as so many replies by Jesus to questions posed in turn by His hearers: now by Philip or by Thomas, by Matthew or Bartholomew, now by the twelve 'disciples' or 'apostles' as a whole, now by Mary (Magdalene), the only one of the holy women present who is expressly named. The teaching thus transmitted by the Saviour concerns the origin of the transcendent and of the visible world, as well as the salvation of man. Christ sums it up in conclusion as follows:

Behold, I have taught you the name of the Perfect One (τέλειος), the whole will of the holy angels (ἄγγελος) and of the Mother, that the manly host may here be made perfect, that they may appear in all aeons (αἰών) from the Unlimited up to those which have arisen in the unsearchable riches of the great invisible Spirit (πνεῦμα); that they all may receive of his goodness (—ἀγαθός) and of the riches of his place of rest (*Cod. I Nag Hammadi*, 118.15: ἀνάπαυσις) above which there is no dominion. But (δέ) I am come from the First, who was sent that I might reveal to you that which was from the beginning, because of the arrogance of the ἀρχιγενέτωρ and his angels (ἄγγελος) who say of themselves that they are gods. But (δέ) I am come to lead them out of their blindness, that I may make known to everyone the God who is over the All. But you, trample down their graves, suppress their πρόνοια, break their yoke asunder, and awaken (or: raise up) that which is mine! For (γάρ) I have given you power (ἐξουσία) over all things as (ὡς) children of the light, to trample their might with your feet.

(P. Berol. 124.9–126.16)

After the dialogue has thus come to an end, the document closes with the following words:

Thus said the blessed (μακάριος) Redeemer (σωτήρ) and vanished from their sight. But they fell into great and indescribable joy in the Spirit (πνεῦμα). From that day on his disciples began (ἄρχεσθαι) to preach the Gospel (εὐαγγέλιον) of God, the eternal Father of him who is immortal for ever.

(P. Berol. 126.17–127.10)

Such a conclusion is normal in other Gnostic gospels also, and the Sophia Jesu Christi seems therefore to be constructed from beginning to end according to a conventional and stereotyped model.

Artificial in itself, this gospel form is artificial also in the sense

247

that it seems to have been added to and imposed upon a writing which originally had nothing to do with a 'gospel'. The text of the Sophia is in fact almost throughout and in its main points closely parallel to that of the work which immediately precedes it in Codex I of the Coptic Museum (70.1–90.13), and of which another fragmentary version appears at the beginning of Codex VII of the Nag Hammadi collection: a dogmatic epistle, without any distinct Christian features, addressed to his people by a Gnostic teacher here named 'Eugnostos the Blessed'.[1] Apart from slight differences in the sections common to them, the two writings diverge only in the following points: The Sophia is a little longer than the Epistle of Eugnostos and contains here and there passages which are peculiar to it; its prologue and epilogue have the form of a narrative, not of a letter; the doctrinal exposition is in the Sophia presented not in the form of a continuous discourse but in that of a dialogue.

It would therefore seem that the Sophia is only a simple re-casting of the letter: its author has taken over the content of the letter, broken it into sections, and divided it, almost without variants and with only a few additions, among the answers put in the mouth of Jesus. By slight alterations, by placing the content of the epistle in a fictitious frame, by a setting as artificial as the questions posed by the characters introduced, he has transformed a treatise written for a correspondent of the author or for his pupils into a dialogue of the risen Saviour with His disciples. So at least I believe, as does Doresse, that we must explain the evident connection between the two works. W. C. Till[2] however expresses an opposing view: it seems to him "much more probable that SJC was the source of Eug and not the contrary". But he has not yet advanced his arguments, and for the present the first hypothesis appears the better and more natural. Were it accepted, it would have the advantage of providing us with direct insight into the process of the fabrication of a Gnostic gospel.

The present state of research does not yet allow us to determine exactly the sect from which the Sophia Jesu Christi derived. For the composition of its Greek original we can give only an approximate date: perhaps the second half of the 2nd century, or at latest the 3rd century.

2. *The Dialogue of the Redeemer*

This document, preserved only in Coptic (Sahidic), appears in Cod. I of the Nag Hammadi library (above, p. 244), after the

[1] Cf. J. Doresse, *Vig. Chr.* 2, 1948, 143–146 and 150–159; id., *Les livres secrets des gnostiques d'Égypte*, Paris 1958, 209–214 (ET London 1960, 192–197); H.-Ch. Puech, *Coptic Studies in Honor of W. E. Crum*, 102 and 106.
[2] *Die gnost. Schriften*, 54.

Sophia Jesu Christi. The fifth and last work in the volume, it occupies pages 120 to the end. The title (*pdialogos ᵉmpsōtēr*) appears at the beginning and (partly mutilated) at the end. The text is in poor condition; several pages are missing and the original order of the extant leaves, between which there are frequent lacunae, has not yet been satisfactorily restored.

Literature: H.-Ch. Puech and J. Doresse, *CR Acad. Inscrr. et Belles-Lettres* (Institut de France) 1948, 88, 90, 93; Togo Mina, "Le papyrus gnostique du Musée Copte", *Vig. Chr.* 2, 1948, 132; H.-Ch. Puech, "Les nouveaux écrits gnostiques", *Coptic Studies in Honor of W. E. Crum*, Boston, 1950, 103; id. "Découverte d'une bibliothèque gnostique", *Enc. Fr.*, t. XIX, Paris 1957, fasc. 19. 42–47.

The apocryphon belongs to the same type as the Sophia Jesu Christi, but begins much more abruptly:

The Saviour (σωτήρ) said to his disciples (μαθητής): Already the moment has come, my brothers, for us to leave our troubles behind and to abide in the Rest (ἀνάπαυσις). Verily, he who abides in the Rest (ἀνάπαυσις) shall rest eternally. But now I say unto you (. . .)

(120.2–9)

The discourse by Jesus is continued and is only interrupted some time later by frequent questions from certain disciples (now Judas, now Matthew), or in two cases from all the disciples or the 'twelve' or from holy women (Maria, Mariham, Marihamme). At one point Judas, Matthew and Marihamme all ask together; at another a dialogue develops between Judas and Matthew. In each case the Saviour takes pains to satisfy the demands of his interlocutors. His explanations are introduced by the stereotyped formula: "And the Lord said" or "replied".

We have thus to do with a 'gospel' in dialogue form, in which however some symbolic episodes and visions have apparently been inserted. The content is none the less dogmatic: the conversation ranges over very diverse problems, cosmological, anthropological and, towards the end, eschatological and soteriological. Here and there occur echoes of the Synoptics or of John. Logia are cited, e.g. "The labourer (ἐργάτης) is worthy of his food (τροφή)" (Mt. 10:10; cf. Lk. 10:7 and Resch, Agrapha[1], Log. 3, p. 97 and 140f.) and "The disciple (μαθητής) is not like his master" (cf. Mt. 10:24); and probably also use is made of words of Jesus from apocryphal gospels. The following might derive from the Gospel of the Egyptians: "He who has come forth from the Truth does not die; but he who has come forth from woman dies"; "Blessed (shall ye be) when you are all unclothed"; "Pray in a place where

there is no woman, that ye may destroy the works of womankind".
Perhaps also there may be some relation to the Gospel of Thomas.

It is too early to say more about the Dialogue of the Redeemer,
or to attempt to resolve the questions of the date of its composition (2nd or 3rd century) and its origin (Egypt? A Gnostic milieu
with encratite tendencies?). The writing, very imperfectly
restored, is still too little and too badly known.

3. *The Pistis Sophia*

The work, or more precisely group of works, traditionally known
by this name is contained in a Coptic version (almost pure
Sahidic, slightly influenced by Fayyumic) in a parchment manuscript of the second half of the 4th century,[1] the Codex Askewianus.
Bought in a London book-shop in 1773 by the English collector
Dr. A. Askew, it passed in 1785 to the British Museum, where it
is now preserved as Ms. Add. 5114. Attention was first drawn to
it in 1778 by C. G. Woide, under the title "Pistis Sophia", and
the text of the codex was published, with a Latin translation, in
the posthumous work of M. G. Schwartze.[2] Later it was published
again, without a translation, by Carl Schmidt,[3] and in addition
has been translated into several languages.[4]

Following the analysis of K. R. Köstlin,[5] the results of which
were adopted and more precisely stated by C. Schmidt, it is today almost unanimously agreed that the four sections of the
manuscript must be divided into two distinct groups. The first
three sections correspond to the three books of one and the same
work, probably composed between 250 and 300: the first book
(pp. 1–81 of the Schmidt-Till translation) has neither superscription nor colophon; the second (pp. 82–162) has at the beginning the title (added later) "The second book ($\tau\acute{o}\mu os$) of the
Pistis Sophia", but is designated at the end as "A part ($\mu\acute{e}\rho os$) of
the books (or rolls: $\tau\epsilon\acute{v}\chi\eta$[6]) of the saviour ($\sigma\omega\tau\acute{\eta}\rho$)"; the third

---

[1] According to Carl Schmidt, who had originally opted for the 5th century; for an
earlier date cf. L.Th.Lefort, "La littérature égyptienne aux derniers siècles avant
l'invasion arabe", *Chronique d'Égypte* 6, 1931, 321.
[2] *Pistis Sophia. Opus gnosticum Valentino adiudicatum e codice manuscripto coptico Londinensi
descripsit et latine vertit M. G. Schwartze. Edidit J. H. Petermann, Berolini, 1851.
[3] *Pistis Sophia* = Coptica 2, Copenhagen 1925.
[4] English: G. R. S. Mead, *Pistis Sophia*, London 1896, 2nd ed. 1921, reprinted
1947, 1955; G. Horner, *Pistis Sophia*, London 1924. French: "Le livre de la fidèle
Sagesse", in Migne, *Dictionnaire des Apocryphes*, vol. I, Paris 1856, 1191–1286; E.
Amélineau, *Pistis Sophia, ouvrage gnostique de Valentin*, Paris, 1895. German: C. Schmidt,
Koptisch-gnostische Schriften I = GCS 13, Leipzig 1905, 1–254; 2nd ed. revised by W. C.
Till, Berlin 1954; id., *Pistis Sophia. Ein gnostisches Originalwerk des 3 Jahrhunderts aus
dem Koptischen übersetzt*, Leipzig 1925.
[5] "Das gnostische System des Buches Pistis Sophia", *Theol. Jahrbücher* 13, 1854,
1–104 and 137–196.
[6] On the meaning of $\tau\epsilon\hat{v}\chi os$, see C. H. Roberts, "The Codex" (*Proc. Br. Acad.* xl

(pp. 164. 20–231. 9), separated from the second by an independent fragment, the end of a lost book, is likewise entitled in the colophon "A part (μέρος) of the books (or rolls: τεύχη) of the saviour (σωτήρ)". On the other hand the fourth section (232. 1–254. 8), which has no title, is in reality a distinct work, composed in the *first* half of the 3rd century and thus older than those which precede it. Accordingly only the work contained in the first three books merits the name "Pistis Sophia".

Again, this is only a late title, added subsequently on one page of the manuscript, and strictly speaking is appropriate only to that part of the treatise which extends from the beginning to page 118. 36. It would seem better to give preference to the more primitive but less significant and rather technical title "Books (Rolls) of the Saviour" (τὰ τεύχη τοῦ σωτῆρος). Pistis Sophia is moreover a title the meaning of which was long in dispute. K. R. Koestlin (*op. cit.* 9) explained it in relation to the main theme of the first part of the work: Sophia, fallen and repentant, expresses her hope of deliverance from the chaos into which she has fallen, her faith in her salvation. For Renan,[1] Pistis (perhaps read πιστή) Sophia was to be translated 'the faithful Wisdom'. R. Eisler[2] thinks that Sophia is here regarded as Wisdom, present at the side of God and intervening as Fidelity, Confidence and Faith in the work of creation. As Carl Schmidt has shown,[3] the true explanation seems to be supplied by a passage in the Sophia Jesu Christi (above, pp. 243ff.: BG 102. 15–103. 9 = CG I 106. 16–23), which Schmidt however wrongly ascribes to the Apocryphon of John (below, pp. 314ff.): "The Son of Man agreed (συμφωνεῖν) with Sophia, his consort (σύζυγος) and revealed himself in a [great light] as bisexual. His male nature (μέν) is called 'the Saviour (σωτήρ), the begetter of all things', but (δέ) his female 'Sophia, mother of all' (παγγενέτειρα), whom some call Pistis". The same appears in the Epistle of Eugnostos, the probable source of the Sophia Jesu Christi (above, pp. 247f.; CG I, 81. 21–82. 6), which further states that Pistis Sophia is at once the name of the consort of the Saviour and the female designation of the sixth of the emanations manifested by Him.

Several authors have proposed to identify the Pistis Sophia proper, or parts thereof, with the "little Questions of Mary", an apocryphon mentioned by Epiphanius (*Pan.* 26. 8. 1–3) in connection with the Gnostics (see below, pp. 338ff.), but this hypothesis

---

(1954), p. 176 n. 1): sometimes mistakenly thought the equivalent of *codex*; in the glossographers the standard equivalent of *volumen*. Cf. Liddell-Scott-Jones, Lexicon s.v.

[1] *Marc-Aurèle*, 12th ed. Paris 1905, 120, n. 3.

[2] "Pistis Sophia und Barbēlō", *Angelos* 3, 1930, 93–110.

[3] *Pistis Sophia*, Leipzig 1925, p. XXIf., and "Die Urschrift der Pistis Sophia", *ZNW* 24, 1925, 235.

appears untenable.[1] Nor can we admit the view of Liechtenhan,[2] for whom Book I of Pistis Sophia might once have been called "the Gospel of Philip" (below, pp. 271ff.), and Book II the "Questions of Mary"; in the latter case it would not be a question either of the "little" or of the "great Questions of Mary" mentioned by Epiphanius. Whether an anonymous apocalypse, the sixth treatise in one of the Gnostic volumes from Nag Hammadi (Codex III in my classification), may be taken as a partial source of the Pistis Sophia,[3] it is still too early to determine.

All critics agree in regarding Egypt as the land of origin of the two writings of the Codex Askewianus. The attempt, made at the beginning, to claim them as the work of Valentinus or a Valentinian author has long been abandoned. They are much more probably to be ascribed to the 'Gnostics' (of Epiphanius), although it is not possible to determine more precisely whether they were Sethians or, as Schmidt for a time supposed, Severians.[4] That in these writings we have to do with translations of Greek originals seems certain; the suggestion that they were directly composed in Coptic[5] is exposed to objections and arguments of fact which appear to be decisive.[6]

Literature: H. Leisegang, "Pistis Sophia", in Pauly–Wissowa, 1 Reihe, 40 Halbbd., 1950, cols. 1813–1821. – Further literature in *Koptisch-gnostische Schriften I*, ed. Carl Schmidt, 2nd ed. revised by W. C. Till (= *GCS* 45), Berlin 1954, p. IX–XV.

The Pistis Sophia and the separate work which follows it in the manuscript have both the form of a gospel of the common Gnostic type: they profess to contain the esoteric teaching revealed by the risen Christ to His disciples in response to their questions and in the form of a dialogue.

The first book of the Pistis Sophia begins as follows:

But (δέ) it came to pass, after Jesus was risen from the dead, that he spent 11 years discoursing with his disciples (μαθηταί),

[1] References in H. Leisegang, Pauly-Wissowa 1 Reihe, 40 Halbbd., 1950, cols. 1820. 62–1821.11.

[2] "Untersuchungen zur kopt.–gnost. Literatur", *Zeitschr. f. wissenschaftl. Theol.* 44, 1901, 236–253.

[3] J. Doresse, "Nouveaux écrits gnostiques coptes", *Vig. Chr.* 3, 1949, 134; id., "Une bibliothèque gnostique", *Acad. Royale de Belgique. Bull. de la classe des Lettres*, 5ème série, t. XXXV, 1949, 440; cf. H.-Ch. Puech in *Coptic Studies in Honor of W. E. Crum*, Boston 1950, 105.

[4] Cf. however the reservations of E. de Faye, *Gnostiques et Gnosticisme*[2], Paris 1925, 273–275.

[5] So F. Granger, *JTS* 5, 1904, 401; F. C. Burkitt, "Pistis Sophia", *JTS* 23, 1921/2, 271–280; id., "Pistis Sophia again", *JTS* 26, 1924/5, 391–399; id., "Pistis Sophia and the Coptic Language", *JTS* 27, 1925/26, 148–157.

[6] C. Schmidt, *Pistis Sophia*, Copenhagen 1925, p. XXII; id., "Die Urschrift der Pistis Sophia", *ZNW* 24, 1925, 218–240; R. Eisler, "Pistis Sophia und Barbēlō", *Angelos* 3, 1930, 110.

and taught them only as far as the places (τόποι) of the first commandment and as far as the places (τόποι) of the first mystery (μυστήριον).

(Pistis Sophia c. 1, Schmidt-Till 1. 2–6)

So wonderful was the teaching given that the disciples believed that everything had been revealed to them, not realizing that this was but the lowest of a series of mysteries still more sublime.

The supreme mystery, of which the disciples as yet are entirely ignorant, is to be revealed to them in the course of the twelfth and last year of the Saviour's sojourn among His followers between the Resurrection and the final Ascension on the 15th of the moon in the month of Tōbe or Tybi (January). This date is perhaps to be connected with that on which, according to Clement of Alexandria (*Strom.* I. 21. 146. 2), some of the Basilidian Gnostics celebrated annually the Baptism of Jesus (τὴν πεντεκαιδεκάτην τοῦ τυβὶ μηνός: the 15th Tybi). The scenery here employed (action set upon a mountain, appearance of the Revealer in luminous and supernatural form, the terror of the spectators, the salutation, the promise of a direct and comprehensive revelation of the truth) is so characteristic, so completely typical, that despite its length this second introduction must be cited in full:

Now it came to pass, that the disciples (μαθηταί) were sitting together on the Mount of Olives, speaking these words and rejoicing greatly (lit. with a great joy), and being very glad and saying to one another: Blessed (μακάριοι) are we above (παρὰ) all men on earth, since the Saviour (σωτήρ) has revealed these things to us, and we have received the fulness (πλήρωμα) and complete perfection—this they were saying to one another, while Jesus sat a little way apart from them.

But (δέ) it came to pass on the 15th of the moon in the month Tybi, which is the day on which the moon becomes full, on that day now, when the sun was come out upon its path (βάσις), there came forth behind it a great power (δύναμις) of light, gleaming very bright, and the light that was in it was beyond measure. For (γάρ) it came out of the Light of lights, and it came out of the last mystery (μυστήριον), which is the 24th mystery (μυστήριον) from within outwards—those (=the 24 mysteries) which are in the orders (τάξεις) of the second space (χώρημα) of the first mystery (μυστήριον). But (δέ) that power of light descended upon Jesus and surrounded him entirely, while he sat apart from his disciples (μαθηταί), and he shone exceedingly, and the light that was upon him was beyond measure. And the disciples (μαθηταί) did not see Jesus because of the great light in which he was, or (ἤ) which was upon him, for (γάρ) their eyes were darkened because of the great light in which he was, but (ἀλλά) they saw only the light, which sent forth many beams (ἀκτῖνες) of light. And the beams (ἀκτῖνες) of light were not like unto one another, and the light was of different kinds, and it was of different form (τύπος) from below upwards, since one (sc. beam) was more excellent than the other [. . .] in a great and boundless splendour of light; it extended from beneath the earth as far as the heaven.—And when the disciples (μαθηταί) saw that light, they were in great fear and agitation.

Now it came to pass, when that power of light descended upon Jesus, it gradually surrounded him wholly; then (τότε) Jesus rose up or (ἤ) flew into the heights, since he was become exceeding shining in an immeasurable light. And the disciples (μαθηταί) followed him with their eyes, and none of them spoke, until he reached the heaven, but (ἀλλά) they were all in great silence (σιγή). This now came to pass on the 15th of the moon, on the day on which it becomes full in ᴜᴉe month Tybi.

Now it came to pass, when Jesus went up into the heaven, after three hours, all the powers of heaven were troubled, and they all trembled together, they and all their aeons (αἰῶνες) and all their places (τόποι) and all their orders (τάξεις), and the whole earth was moved, and all that dwell upon it. And all men in the world (κόσμος) were troubled, and the disciples (μαθηταί) also, and all thought: Perhaps the world (κόσμος) will be rolled up. And all the powers that are in the heaven ceased not from their agitation, they and the whole world (κόσμος), and they were all moved one against the other from the third hour of the 15th of the moon ⟨in the month⟩ Tybi until the ninth hour of the following day. And all the angels (ἄγγελοι) and their archangels (ἀρχάγγελοι) and all the powers of the height all praised (ὑμνεῖν) the Inmost of the Inmost, so that (ὥστε) the whole world (κόσμος) heard their voice, without ceasing until the ninth hour of the following day.

But (δέ) the disciples (μαθηταί) sat together, in fear, and they were exceedingly troubled; but (δέ) they were afraid because of the great earthquake which took place, and wept with one another, saying: What then (ἄρα) will happen? Perhaps the Saviour (σωτήρ) will destroy all places (τοποί).

While they now said this and wept to one another, then the heavens opened, about the ninth hour of the following day, and they saw Jesus descend, shining very bright, and the light in which he was was beyond measure. For (γάρ) he shone more than at the hour when he ascended up to the heavens, so that (ὥστε) the men in the world (κόσμος) could not describe the light that was upon him, and it sent forth many beams (ἀκτῖνες) of light, and its beams (ἀκτῖνες) were beyond number, and its light was not like one to the other, but (ἀλλά) it was of different kind and of different form (τύπος), since some (sc. beams) surpassed the others countless times; and the whole light was together, it was of three different kinds, and one surpassed the others countless times; the second, which was in the midst, was superior to the first, which was beneath; and the third, which was above them all, was superior to both those which were beneath; and the first beam, which was beneath them all, was like the light which came upon Jesus before he ascended into the heavens, and was like only to itself in its light. And the three lights were of different kinds of light, and they were of different form (τύπος), whereby some surpassed others countless times.

But (δέ) it came to pass, when the disciples (μαθηταί) saw this, they were exceedingly afraid, and were troubled. Jesus now, the merciful and kind-hearted, when he saw that his disciples (μαθηταί) were greatly troubled (lit. troubled with a great troubling), spoke to them, saying: Be of good cheer; it is I, be not afraid (cf. Mt. 14:27, Mk. 6:50).

Now it came to pass, when the disciples (μαθηταί) heard these words, they said: O Lord, if it be thou, draw to thyself thy glorious light, that we may be able to stand, else are our eyes darkened and we are troubled, and also the whole world (κόσμος) is troubled because of the great light that is in thee.

Then (τότε) Jesus drew to himself the splendour of his light; and when this had come to pass all the disciples (μαθηταί) took courage, stood before Jesus, and all fell down together and worshipped him, rejoicing with great joy; they said to him: Rabbi, whither didst thou go, or (ἤ) what is thy service (διακονία) to which thou didst go, or (ἤ) why rather were all these upheavals and earthquakes which have taken place?

Then (τότε) spoke Jesus, the merciful, to them: Rejoice and be glad (cf. Mt. 5:12) from this hour on, for I went to the places (τόποι) out of which I came. From henceforth will I speak with you openly (παρρησία) from the beginning (ἀρχή) of the truth (ἀλήθεια) unto its completion, and I will speak with you face to face without parable (παραβολή: cf. Jn. 16:25); I will not hide from you from this hour anything of the things of the height and of the things of the place (τόπος) of the truth (ἀλήθεια). For (γάρ) to me is given by the Ineffable and by the first Mystery (μυστήριον) of all mysteries (μυστήρια) the power (ἐξουσία: cf. Mt. 28:18), to speak with you from the beginning (ἀρχή) to the fulfilment (πλήρωμα) and from within to without, and from without to within. Hear now, that I may tell you all things.

(Pistis Sophia c. 2–6; Schmidt-Till 3. 8–6. 5)

Jesus begins by relating the journey which He has just accomplished through the aeons, in the course of which He has met Pistis Sophia 'quite alone', 'distressed and mourning', 'beneath the thirteenth aeon'. At the request of Mary He recounts at length the adventures and the lamentations of this being, who has fallen from the thirteenth aeon into matter (ὕλη), and whom He has finally restored to her original abode. Then follows a dialogue on other themes: the mysteries of light, especially the most sublime among them, those of the Ineffable and of the first mystery; the origin of sin and evil in the world of men; the necessity of repentance; the punishments which await the sinner after death.

The revelations by Jesus are interrupted by questions from the disciples and the holy women, to which the Saviour replies, each of His answers being followed by demonstrations of joy or of adoration, which mark the gratitude of those present. Sometimes also one of the disciples or one of the women supplies the explanation; Jesus encourages them to speak and inspires them, illuminating the 'man of light' who dwells within each. The following intervene in turn and on several occasions: Mary the mother of Jesus, Mary Magdalene, Philip, Peter, Martha, John, Andrew, Thomas, Matthew, James, Salome. A prominent place is reserved for Mary Magdalene and for John, 'the maiden' (παρθένος), of whom the Saviour declares:

But (ἀλλά) Mary Magdalene and John, the maiden (παρθένος), will surpass all my disciples (μαθηταί) and all men who shall receive mysteries (μυστήρια) in the Ineffable, they will be on my right hand and on my left, and I am they and they are I, and they will be equal with you in all things, save (ἀλλὰ πλήν) that your thrones (θρόνοι) will surpass theirs, and my own throne (θρόνος) will surpass yours[1] and those of all men who shall find the word of the Ineffable.

(Pistis Sophia c. 96; Schmidt-Till 148. 25–33)

It has been reckoned[2] that of the 46 questions here put to Jesus 39 fall to the lot of Mary Magdalene.

The content of the Pistis Sophia is too varied and extensive to be summarized here or evaluated in detail. As an example the following passage, already discussed by Hennecke,[3] Leisegang[4] and Marmorstein,[5] may be selected:

But (δέ) Mary answered and said: My Lord, concerning the word which thy power prophesied (προφητεύειν) through David (*Ps. 84:11f. LXX*): "Grace and Truth met one another, Righteousness (δικαιοσύνη) and Peace (εἰρήνη) kissed each other. Truth sprouted forth from the earth, and Righteousness (δικαιοσύνη) looked down from heaven", thy power prophesied (προφητεύειν) this word at this time concerning thee. When thou wast small, before the Spirit (πνεῦμα) was come upon thee, thou wast in a vineyard with Joseph. The Spirit (πνεῦμα) came out of the height and came to me in my house, in thy likeness, and I knew him not, and I thought that it was thou. And the Spirit (πνεῦμα) said to me: Where is Jesus my brother, that I may meet him (ἀπαντᾶν)? And when he said this to me, I was at a loss (ἀπορεῖν), and thought it was a spectre (φάντασμα), to tempt (πειράζειν) me. But (δέ) I took him and bound him to the foot of the bed which was in my house, until I could go out to you in the field, you and Joseph, and found you in the vineyard, while Joseph was fencing the vineyard. Now it came to pass, when thou didst hear me speak the word to Joseph, thou didst understand (νοεῖν) the word, and didst rejoice and say: Where is he, that I may see him, else I await him in this

---

[1] A footnote remarks that the text must be corrupt and should read: "save that their throne will surpass yours, and my own throne will surpass theirs".

[2] C. Schmidt, *Koptisch-gnostische Schriften* 1, Leipzig 1905, p. XV; H. Leisegang, *Die Gnosis*, 4th ed., Leipzig 1955, p. 353.

[3] *Apokr.* 2, pp. 102f.

[4] "Der Bruder des Erlösers", *Angelos* 1, 1925, 24–33.

[5] "Ein Wort über den Bruder des Erlösers", *Angelos* 2, 1926, pp. 155f.

place (τόπος)? But (δέ) it came to pass, when Joseph heard thee say these words, he was perturbed, and we went off at once, entered into the house, and found the Spirit (πνεῦμα) bound to the bed. And we looked on thee and on him, and found thee like unto him; and he that was bound to the bed was set free, he embraced thee, and kissed thee, and thou also didst kiss him, and ye became one.

(Pistis Sophia c. 61; Schmidt-Till 77. 33–78. 20)

In the second treatise of the Codex Askewianus, contained in the fourth and last section of the manuscript, we have to do likewise with a gospel in dialogue form, but the episodes here narrated are set at a time and in a framework different from those of the previous work. Here the action takes place on the day after the Resurrection, and in the first instance on the shore of the ocean:

Now it came to pass, when our Lord Jesus was crucified (σταυροῦν) and on the third day was risen from the dead (cf. Synoptics, Acts, 1 Cor. 15:4), then his disciples (μαθηταί) gathered round him, and entreated him, saying: Our Lord, have mercy upon us, for we have forsaken father and mother and the whole world (κόσμος) and have followed thee (cf. Mt. 10:37; 19:27, 29; Mk. 10:28f.; Lk. 14:26; 18:28f.; Apokryphon Jacobi (below, pp. 333ff.) 4:25–28 of Codex Jung; the Books of Jeu c. 2 (258. 5–9 Schmidt-Till) and c. 44 (306. 3–6)).

Then (τότε) Jesus stood with his disciples (μαθηταί) by the water of the ocean (ὠκεανός) and called aloud (ἐπικαλεῖσθαι) this prayer (προσευχή), saying: Hearken to me, my Father, thou Father of all Fatherhood, thou boundless (ἀπέραντος) Light: αεηιουω· ιαω· αωϊ· ωϊα· ψινωθερ· θερνωψ· νωψιτερ· ζαγουρη· παγουρη· νεθμομαωθ· νεψιομαωθ· μαραχαχθα· θωβαρραβαυ· θαρναχαχαν· ζοροκο-θορα· ϊεου· σαβαωθ.

But (δέ) while Jesus was saying this, Thomas, Andrew, James and Simon the Canaanite (κανανίτης) were in the west, with their faces turned towards the east, but (δέ) Philip and Bartholomew were in the south (with their faces) turned towards the north, but (δέ) the other disciples (μαθηταί) and the women disciples (μαθητρίαι) stood behind Jesus. But (δέ) Jesus stood beside the altar (θυσιαστήριον).

And Jesus cried out, turning towards the four corners of the world (κόσμος) with his disciples (μαθηταί), who were all clothed in linen garments, and said: ϊαω, ϊαω, ϊαω. This is its interpretation (ἑρμηνεία): Iota, since the All is gone forth—Alpha, since it will turn back again—Omega, since the perfection of all perfections will take place.

But (δέ) when Jesus had said this, he said: ϊαφθα· ϊαφθα· μουναηρ· μουναηρ· ερμανουηρ· ερμανουηρ· i.e. Thou Father of all Fatherhood of the Infinite (ἀπέραντος) hearken unto me for my disciples' (μαθηταί) sake; whom I have brought before Thee, that they may believe (πιστεύειν) on all the words of Thy truth (ἀλήθεια), and grant all whereof I cry to Thee, for I know the name of the Father of the treasure (θησαυρός) of light.

(Pistis Sophia c. 136: Schmidt-Till 232. 1–233. 5)

The scene changes in the course of the narrative, and the action is set successively in an 'aëry' region on the way of the Midst (233. 29–30), in an 'air' of very strong light (242. 6), on the mount of Galilee (243. 12), and in *Amente* (253. 36f.).

Whatever the external frame, the speeches of Jesus, which give the writing its unity, all centre on the same theme. As K. R. Köstlin has put it (*Theol. Jahrbücher* 13, 1854, p. 6): "One might describe the whole precisely . . . as a treatise περὶ μετανοίας (in the Gnostic sense)". Jesus, here also called Aberamentho,[1] relates to His disciples the story of the Archons of destiny, and sets forth the terrible punishments which they inflict upon men. To calm the fears of His audience, He celebrates before them the mysteries which purify from sin; but here only the lesser mysteries, of which the manuscript, here defective, describes only the first, the baptism of water. The revelation then continues and concludes with an exposition of the fate which awaits the soul of the sinner after death.

As in the Pistis Sophia, the disciples and the holy women intervene in turn, either in groups or as individuals, to ask questions of the Saviour. The following appear in succession: Mary, Salome, Peter, Andrew, Thomas, Bartholomew, Thomas (a second time), John and once again Mary.

4. *The Two Books of Jeu*

This work, like an anonymous dogmatic treatise which follows it, is contained in the Codex Brucianus, the date of which is much

---

[1] On this name see S. Eitrem, *Papyri Osloenses* I, Oslo 1925, pp. 34 and 55; F. C. Burkitt, *Church and Gnosis*, Cambridge 1932, pp. 39 and 82f.; Campbell Bonner, *Studies in Magical Amulets*, Ann Arbor 1950, p. 203.

disputed (9th or 10th cent.? 7th, 6th, 5th or 4th cent.? 3rd cent.?). The manuscript was bought in 1769 in Thebes, or more probably in Medinet Habu, by the Scottish traveller James Bruce, and since 1848 has been in the Bodleian Library, Oxford, as Bruce Ms 96. The treatise begins with the words:

This is the book of the knowledges (γνώσεις) of the invisible (ἀόρατος) God through the medium of the hidden mysteries (μυστήρια) which show the way to the chosen race (γένος), (leading) into rest to the life of the Father . . .

(Schmidt-Till 257. 5–8)

The title is implicitly mentioned towards the end of the first part (301. 27), and is given in a colophon to this part (302): "the book of the great κατὰ μυστήριον λόγος".

Despite the objections of E. Preuschen[1] and R. Liechtenhan[2] it is now generally admitted, as a result of the work of Carl Schmidt,[3] that the document thus described and transmitted is identical with the "two books of Jeu" twice mentioned in the Pistis Sophia (158. 18f., and 228. 35). The text is written in Coptic (Sahidic), and shows only at the beginning some dialectic peculiarities which in Till's opinion betray an influence from Subachmimic. There is no doubt, however, that we have to do with the translation of a Greek original, probably composed in Egypt in the first half or at the beginning of the 3rd century. The writing, which especially in its second part is closely related to those of the Codex Askewianus, must derive from the same milieu: a circle of 'Gnostics' (in the narrow sense) or Barbelognostics with Encratite tendencies.

Literature: Edition and French translation: E. Amélineau, "Notice sur le Papyrus gnostique Bruce", *Notices et extraits des manuscrits de la Bibliothèque Nationale*, 29, Paris 1891, 82–305 (the text combined with that of the second writing in the Codex). – Coptic text and German translation: C. Schmidt, *Gnostische Schriften in koptischer Sprache aus dem Codex Brucianus* (*TU* 8, Leipzig 1892). – German translation only: C. Schmidt, *Koptische-gnostische Schriften I* (= *GCS* 13), Leipzig 1905, 257–329; 2nd ed., revised by Walter Till (= *GCS* 45), Berlin 1954 (with Bibliography, pp. IX–XV).

"The two books of Jeu" or "The great λόγος κατὰ μυστήριον" appears in its present form (perhaps artificially imposed) as a

---

[1] *ThLZ* 7, 1894, 184f.

[2] "Untersuchungen zur koptisch-gnost. Literatur", *Ztschr. f. wissenschaftl. Theol.* 44, 1901, 236–253.

[3] "Die in dem koptisch-gnostischen Codex Brucianus enthaltenen 'beiden Bücher Jeu' in ihrem Verhaltnis zu der Pistis Sophia", *Ztschr. f. wissenschaftl. Theol.* 37, 1894, 555–585.

gospel of the Gnostic type; otherwise it would be more readily compared with a didactic treatise in the form of a revelation. This work also professes to record the conversations of Jesus with His disciples and the holy women, either with all the apostles (ἀπόστολοι), "Matthew and John, Philip and Bartholomew and James", as it is precisely stated on p. 258. 26f., or with the "Twelve" or "twelve disciples (μαθηταί)" and the female disciples (μαθητρίαι), as it is put elsewhere (303.3–6; cf. 308.4f.). As in the Gospel of Thomas (below, pp. 285ff.), in Manicheism and elsewhere, Jesus is designated as "the living", i.e. as the "risen" or as the "life-giving".[1] The revelations which He imparts to His disciples in response to their questions (here very few in number) are introduced in the following terms:

Jesus, the living one, answered and said to his apostles (ἀπόστολοι): Blessed is he who has crucified the world (κόσμος), and has not allowed the world (κόσμος) to crucify him (*cf. Gal. 6:14*). The apostles (ἀπόστολοι) answered with one voice, saying: Lord, teach us the way to crucify the world (κόσμος), that it may not crucify us, and we perish and lose our life. Jesus, the living one, answered and said: He who has crucified the world (κόσμος) is he who has found my word, and has fulfilled it after the will of him who sent me (*cf. Mt. 10:40, etc.*) The apostles (ἀπόστολοι) answered, saying: Speak to us, Lord, that we may hear thee. We have followed thee with all our heart, have left father and mother, have left vineyard and field, have left our goods (κτῆσις), have left the king's glory and have followed thee, that thou mightest teach us the life of thy Father who hath sent thee (*cf. Mt. 10:37; 19:27, 29; Lk. 14:26; 18:28–30; Apocryphon Jacobi (below, pp. 333ff.) 4:25–28 of Codex Jung; the second document of the Codex Askewianus, 232.4–6 Schmidt-Till*). Jesus, the living one, answered and said: This is the life of my Father, that ye receive your soul (ψυχή) from the race (γένος) of reason (νοῦς), and it cease to be earthly (χοϊκός) and become wise (νοερός) through that which I say unto you in the course of my words, that ye may complete it and be delivered before the Archon (ἄρχων) of this aeon (αἰών; *cf. Jn. 12:31 etc.*) and his snares, which have no end. But (δέ) you

[1] Cf. Rev. 1:18; Irenaeus, *adv. haer.* I.14.2 Harvey; the anonymous work in the Codex Brucianus, p. 362.11 Schmidt-Till (cf. Baynes, *A Coptic Gnostic Treatise*, Cambridge 1933, 180, 188f.); Acts of Thomas c. 60, c. 129, c. 169; E. Waldschmidt and W. Lentz, *Die Stellung Jesu in Manichäismus*, Abh. d. preuss. Akad. d. Wissensch. 1926, no. 4, p. 41; F. J. Dölger, *Ichthys* I², Münster 1928, 6*–8*; M. Kropp, *Ausgewählte koptische Zaubertexte* III, Brussels 1930, p. 64.

are my disciples (μαθηταί), make haste to receive my word carefully to yourselves, that ye may know it, that the Archon (ἄρχων) of this aeon (αἰών) may not strive with you, he who hath found none of his commands in me (cf. Jn. 14:31), and that ye yourselves, O my apostles (ἀπόστολοι), may fulfil my word in relation to me, and I myself may make you free, and ye may become whole through a freedom (–ἐλεύθερος) wherein is no blemish. As the Spirit (πνεῦμα) of the Comforter (παράκλητος) is whole, so shall ye also become whole through the freedom of the Spirit (πνεῦμα) of the holy Comforter (παράκλητος) (cf. Jn. 14:16, 26; 15:26; 16:7). All the apostles (ἀπόστολοι) answered with one voice, Matthew and John, Philip and Bartholomew and James, saying: Lord Jesus, thou living one, whose goodness (–ἀγαθός) is spread abroad upon those who have found his wisdom (σοφία) and his form, in which he shines—O Light, that is in the light which has illumined our heart until we received the light of life—O true word (λόγος), which through knowledge (γνῶσις) teaches us the hidden knowledge of the Lord Jesus, the living one. Jesus, the living one, answered and said: Blessed is the man who knoweth this, and has brought the heaven down, and carried the earth and sent it to heaven, and he became the Midst, for it (sc. the Midst) is nothing. The apostles (ἀπόστολοι) answered, saying: Jesus, thou living one, O Lord, explain to us in what way one may bring down the heaven, for (γάρ) we have followed thee, that thou mightest teach us the true light.

(c. 1–3; Schmidt-Till 257. 17–259. 8)

In the first part of the work the answer of Jesus consists essentially in revealing how the Father projected from his bosom Jeu ('Ιεου) the "true God", and in what manner there issued from him in turn 28 emanations, whose form, mystic name and number (ψῆφος) are noted each time with great precision. In the second part Jesus bestows upon those present "the three baptisms" (with water, with fire, and with the Holy Spirit), and then the "mystery" destined to remove from them the "wickedness (κακία) of the Archons", which must be followed by "the mystery (μυστήριον) of the spiritual unction" (χρῖσμα πνευματικόν). Then is described the ascension which will lead the souls of the disciples, thus purified, initiated and saved, through the aeons of the transcendent world to the place of "the great invisible (ἀόρατος) God", "the great virginal Spirit" (παρθενικὸν πνεῦμα) and the 24 "emanations

```
              $   08.95Sa A
              $   00.72CT A
EE10 > 10 *$  09.67TL A
```

THANK YOU

(προβολαί) of the invisible God". Here also are imparted the secret names of the aeons, their several numbers (ψῆφος), the "seals" (σφραγίδες) and "pass-words", the formulae (ἀπολογίαι) which allow free passage through each of their spheres, one after the other, and ensure escape from their grasp and power.

The esoteric character of such teaching is so evident that it is unnecessary to enter into detail. Note should be taken, however, of the typical expressions employed by Jesus to instruct or admonish the disciples, the initiates, to keep His revelations secret and to transmit or divulge them only to the élite, i.e. to those only who are worthy to receive them and capable of understanding them:

These mysteries (μυστήρια) which I shall give you, preserve, and give them to no man except (εἰ μήτι) he be worthy of them. Give them not to father nor (οὐδέ) to mother, (οὐδέ) to brother or (οὐδέ) to sister or (οὐδέ) to kinsman (συγγενής), neither (οὐδέ) for food nor (οὐδέ) for drink, nor (οὐδέ) for woman-kind, neither (οὐδέ) for gold nor (οὐδέ) for silver, nor (οὐδέ) for anything at all of this world (κόσμος). Preserve them, and give them to no one whatsoever for the sake of the good of this whole world (κόσμος).

(c. 43; Schmidt-Till 304. 6–13)

The two formulae, or double formula: to keep hidden, securely and in secret (ἀσφαλῶς, ἐν ασφαλείᾳ ἔχειν), the teaching of the Master received orally or in writing; to preserve the tradition (παράδοσις) and impart it only to those who by initiation are worthy of it (ἄξιοι, digni)—these are almost technical in the language of the occult sciences and apocalyptic literature of the first centuries of our era;[1] but a still closer connection can be established between this passage and the epilogue of the Apocryphon of John (below, pp. 327ff.).

D. GOSPELS ATTRIBUTED TO THE TWELVE AS A GROUP

1. *The Gospel of the Twelve* (or: *of the Twelve Apostles*)

Origen (*In Luc. hom.* I, p. 5.2–4 Rauer) mentions, immediately after the Gospel according to the Egyptians (above, pp. 166ff.) and before the Gospels of Basilides, Thomas and Matthias (below, pp. 346ff., 278ff., 308ff.), a heterodox writing entitled "the Gospel

[1] Cf. A. J. Festugière, *L'idéal religieux des Grecs et l'Évangile*, Paris 1932, p. 305 n. 6; id., *La Révélation d'Hermès Trismégiste* I, Paris 1944, pp. 309–354, esp. 345 and n. 6, and 352.

of the Twelve" (τὸ ἐπιγεγράμμενον τῶν Δώδεκα εὐαγγέλιον) or, according to Jerome's translation (adduced by Rauer ad loc.), "the Gospel according to the Twelve Apostles" ("aliud (*sc.* evangelium) iuxta Duodecim Apostolos"). Echoes of this testimony are to be found in Ambrose (*Expositio euangelii Lucae* I. 2, p. 10. 18 Schenkl: "euangelium, quod duodecira scripsisse dicuntur"), Jerome (*Comm. in Matt.*, Prol., *PL* XXVI. 17A: "duodecim apostolorum euangelium"), Philip of Side (*Hist. eccl.*, in *TU* 5, 2, 1888, p. 169 no. 4), the Venerable Bede (*In Lucae euangelium expositio* I, Prol., *PL* XCII. 307C), and in Theophylact (*Enarratio in Evangelium Lucae*, Prol., *PG* CXXIII. 692A: τὸ ἐπιγραφόμενον τῶν Δώδεκα).

The context in which Origen sets the work might lead one to think of a Gnostic gospel. On the basis of a wrongly interpreted passage in Jerome (*Dial. adv. Pelag.* III 2) an abortive attempt was made to link the Gospel of the Twelve with the Gospel of the Hebrews, but the majority of critics today are inclined to identify it with the Gospel of the Ebionites (fragments collected in Preuschen, *Antilegomena*, 2nd ed., 9–12, or Klostermann, *Apokrypha* II, 3rd ed. 12–15: cf. Vielhauer, above, pp. 153ff.); according to Bardenhewer (*Litg.* I², 519), the complete title would have been Εὐαγγέλιον τῶν Δώδεκα (or δεκαδύο) ἀποστόλων διὰ Ματθαίου.[1] The document consequently has probably nothing to do with Gnosticism, or at most is to be connected with gnosticizing Jewish Christianity. The contrary opinion of A. Schmidtke (*Neue Fragmente und Untersuchungen zu den judenchristlichen Evangelien* = *TU* 37. 1, Leipzig, 1911, 170–174), who saw in it a Gentile Christian Gnostic gospel, has been criticized and refuted by H. Waitz.

The question however remains open whether there may not have existed, under the same or a similar title, another work, or perhaps even several distinct works, whose Gnostic origin and character would be less in dispute.

2. *The (Kukean) Gospel of the Twelve*

Marūtā of Maiperkat reports in his catalogue of heresies,[2] on the subject of the Kukeans (Quqājē) of the region of Edessa: "With the names of the Twelve Apostles [they imagine] for themselves twelve Evangelists. Also they corrupt [the New Testament], but not the Old". Abraham Ecchellensis writes[3] with reference to the same sect, whom he calls 'Phocalites': "They have done

---

[1] On the whole question cf. Bardenhewer *Litg.* I, 2nd ed., 518–521; H. Waitz, "Das Evangelium der zwölf Apostel (Ebionitenevangelium)": *ZNW* 13, 1912, 338–348; above pp. 117ff.

[2] O. Braun, *De sancta synodo Nicaena*, Münster 1898, p.49; Harnack *TU* 19, 1b, 1899, p. 10.

[3] Mansi, *Conc.* II, 1058E; Harnack *op. cit.* p. 16; F. Haase, *Altchristliche Kirchengeschichte nach orientalischen Quellen*, Leipzig 1925, p. 322.

away with the New Testament and forged for themselves another. On the twelve apostles they impose barbarous names, but they retain the Old Testament intact".

For Harnack (*op. cit.* 11) and Zahn (*Forschungen zur Gesch. d. ntl. Kanons* VI, 279 n. 1), this referred to a work called "the Gospel of the Twelve Apostles", which was no other than the gospel of the same title in use among the Ebionites. Appealing to certain ritual practices ascribed to the sect in Marūtā's notice (strict and scrupulous purification observances, abstinence from pork, abhorrence of all unclean contact, etc.), Harnack in fact held the Kukeans to be 'Jewish-Christian Gnostics' who lived in Edessa alongside the Bardesanites, who would represent a 'pagan-Christian' Gnostic group. On the other hand, apart from the Syrian recension of the text of Marūtā published by I. E. Rahmani (*Studia Syriaca* IV, Rome 1909, p. 78) and the version of Abraham Ecchellensis, where they are more or less brought into relation with the Samaritans, the Kukeans are either mentioned only in association with the Marcionites, the Valentinians and the Bardesanites,[1] or are said to have separated themselves by a schism from the Valentinians,[2] or finally are accused of professing a system of Gnosis which in certain features recalls Bardesanism but was crudely mythical and even pagan in character.[3]

In the circumstances, one might be inclined to prefer the view of Schmidtke (*Neue Fragmente und Untersuchungen, TU* 37. 1, 1911, 173f.), who proposed to link the name of the sect with that of the 'Koddiani' (Epiphanius, *Pan.* 26. 3. 6–7), and thus identified the Quqājē with "Gentile Christians strongly influenced by Parsism"; this would involve regarding their "Gospel of the Twelve Apostles" as a Gnostic production, and distinguishing it from that of the Ebionites. On the other hand Waitz (*ZNW* 14, 1913, 46ff.) has produced evidence that the reference in Marūtā's catalogue concerns not a gospel but the Gnostic system of the Qūqājē, and affords no proof of the Gentile Christian character of the "Gospel of the Twelve".

3. *The Memoria Apostolorum*

A work of this title (Tradition, Statement, History or Memoirs

---

[1] Ephraem, *adv. haer. hymn.* 22.2f., *CSCO* 169, pp. 78f., and vol. 170, pp. 77f.; beside the Sabbatians, however, *hymn.* 2.6, vol. 169, p. 7 and 170, p. 8; cf. also 24.16, vol. 169, p. 95 and 170, p. 89 and the Testament of Ephraem in *Journal Asiatique*, 9. Série, 18, 1901, p. 298.

[2] James of Edessa, Ep. XIII, to John the Stylite of Litharba; Syr. text: W. Wright, *Journal of sacred Literature and Biblical Record* X, 1876, p. 24; French translation: F. Nau, *Revue de l'Orient chrétien* 10, 1905, pp. 278f.; German translation: A. Rücker, *BKV* 61, pp. 13f.

[3] Theodore bar Konai, *Liber scholiorum* XI: H. Pognon, *Inscriptions mandaïtes des coupes de Khouabir*, Paris 1898, pp. 144 and 209–212, or *CSCO*, Script. syr., ser. II, tom. LXVI, pp. 333f., ed. A. Scher.

of the Apostles? ὑπόμνημα?) is mentioned about 440 by Turribius of Astorga in his letter to the bishops Idacius and Ceponius (c. 5, *PL* LIV. 694D), among the apocryphal literature common to the Manicheans and the Priscillianists, beside the Acts of Andrew, John, Thomas and others (see vol. II: XIII). The notice is somewhat vague:

"From these (*sc.* the Acts and apocryphal books) the Manicheans and Priscillianists, or whatever sect is akin to them, strive to establish all their false doctrine; and principally from that most blasphemous book which is called the *Memoria Apostolorum*, in which to the great authority of their perversity they falsely claim a doctrine of the Lord, who destroyed the whole law of the Old Testament and all that was divinely revealed to the blessed Moses concerning the diversity of creature and Creator; besides the other blasphemies of this same book, to recount which is vexatious".

There is every reason to believe[1] that Turribius borrowed everything he knew and here says from an earlier document, which is in any case our primary source on this question: the *Consultatio* or *Commonitorium de errore Priscillianistarum et Origenistarum* composed, probably in 414, by Paulus Orosius (ed. Schepss, *CSEL* 18, 1889). It is there said of Priscillian:

And this very thing (*sc.* his dualistic doctrine of the eternity of Hell, from which the 'prince of the world' has come forth) he establishes from a certain book entitled *Memoria Apostolorum*, wherein the Saviour appears to be questioned by the disciples in secret, and to show from the Gospel parable which has 'The sower went forth to sow' (*Mt. 13:3*) that he was not a good sower, asserting that if he had been good he would not have been neglectful, or cast seed 'by the wayside' or 'on stony places' or 'in untilled soil' (*Mt. 13:4f.*); wishing it to be understood that the sower is he who scatters captive souls in diverse bodies as he wills. In which book also many things are said about the prince of dampness and the prince of fire, which is meant to signify that it is by art and not by the power of God that all good things are done in this world. For it says that there is a certain virgin light whom God, when he wishes to give rain to men, shows to the prince of dampness, who since he desires to take possession of her perspires in his excitement and makes rain, and when he is deprived of her causes peals of thunder by his roaring.

[1] Cf. E.-Ch. Babut, *Priscillien et le Priscillanisme*, Paris 1909, p. 239.

(Orosius c. 2, p. 154.4–18 Schepss; corrections on the basis of a manuscript in Milan: G. Mercati, "Note di letteratura biblica e cristiana antica" = *Studi e Testi* 5, Rome 1901, 136.)

Here it is certainly a question of a gospel, Gnostic both in form and in content. Jesus is presented as conversing in secret (*secreto*) with His disciples, revealing His teaching in answer to their questions, and in particular supplying the esoteric interpretation of a parable. The doctrinal content of the book was anti-biblical, dualistic, and contained a cosmogony which introduced certain mythical beings (among others, the Archons of water and of fire). More precisely, the figure of the 'Virgin of light' (παρθένος τοῦ φωτός, Iōēl) and the erotic myth relating to the production of rain appear also in other accounts of the opinions which Priscillian and his disciples were accused of holding (First Priscillianist Tractate of Würzburg, p. 24. 13–17 Schepss; ps. Jerome, *Indiculus de haer*. 6, I p. 287f. Oehler, *Corpus haereseologicum*); but they belong also to the common stock of the Nicolaitans, Borborians, 'Gnostics' (cf. e.g. Epiph. *Pan*. 25. 2. 4) and Manicheans (Acta Archelai IX. 1–4; Titus of Bostra, *c. Manich*. II 56 ed. P. de Lagarde; Ephraem, *Hymn. contra haer*. 50. 5f.: *CSCO* vol. 169, pp. 196f. and 170 pp. 172f.).[1]

The Gnostic origin of the *Memoria Apostolorum* seems therefore beyond question.[2] Lipsius indeed has maintained that this apocryphon is "a specifically Manichean writing" (*Aa* I, p. 74 n. 1). The attempt has been made[3] to identify the Memoria with the Gnostic gospel (?) referred to in Irenaeus (*adv. haer*. I.20.3 Harvey = Theod. Cyr., *Haer. fab. comp*. I. 5): "In their writings (*sc*. of the Carpocratians or the Gnostics) it is written, and they themselves thus explain: saying that Jesus spoke in secret (*in mysterio*) and apart to His disciples and apostles, and that they requested that they might transmit these things to those who were worthy and agreed with them". Since the relationship is far from clear, this is too bold. P. Alfaric[4] also goes too far in his assertion that the *Memoria Apostolorum* is identical with the gospel which according to Theodor Abū Qurra and al-Biruni was in use among the Manichees (below, pp. 268f.), and ultimately with the Gospel of the Twelve Apostles (above, pp. 263ff.), here itself identified with the Gospel of the Ebionites.

[1] Cf. F. C. Baur, *Das manichäische Religionssystem*, Tübingen 1831, pp. 214–225; F. Cumont, *Recherches sur le Manichéisme* I, Brussels 1908, pp. 54–68; K. Holl, edition of the Panarion of Epiphanius, vol. III p. 60, note to line 12.

[2] A. Dufourcq, *Étude sur les Gesta Martyrum romains* IV, Paris 1910, p. 162 n. 3.

[3] G. Schepss, note to p. 154 line 5 of his edition of Priscilliani quae supersunt; J. A. Davids, *De Orosio et Sancto Augustino Priscillianistarum adversariis commentatio*, Dissertation Nimwegen, The Hague 1930, p. 239.

[4] *Les écritures manichéennes* II, Paris 1919, pp. 173–177.

All that is certain is that the writing was not a narrative about the apostles or, as A. Dufourcq writes (*op. cit.* IV, p. 162), "a pretended history of Christ and the apostles", and that it has nothing to do with the apocryphal Acts of the collection attributed to Leucius.[1] It was a work of the ordinary type of Gnostic gospels and professed to relate either the secret conversations of Jesus with the apostles or, perhaps more exactly, the recollections of these conversations preserved and reported by the apostles themselves. The date of its composition—before the middle of the 4th century—cannot be exactly determined.

4. *The (Manichean) Gospel of the Twelve Apostles*

In the second part of the 8th century, Theodor Abū Qurra, Melchite bishop of Harran (Carrhae), writes in par. 24 of his Tractate on the Creator and the true Religion: "I separated myself from these, and there met me people of the Manicheans. These are they who are called the Zanādiqa, and they said: Thou must attach thyself to the (true) Christians and give heed to the word of their gospel. For the true Gospel is in our possession, which the twelve apostles have written, and there is no religion other than that which we possess, and there are no Christians apart from us. No one understands the interpretation of the Gospel save Mani, our Lord".[2]

It is possible that the work here mentioned is a "Gospel of the Twelve Apostles", but is it, as P. Alfaric holds,[3] a question of the Ebionite gospel of this name? One will hesitate also to ascribe to it, with the same scholar (p. 175), two extracts from a writing of Mani (The book of the 'Mysteries' or 'Secrets') quoted by al-Biruni:

The apostles asked Jesus about the life of inanimate nature, whereupon he said: If that which is inanimate is separated from the living element which is commingled with it, and appears alone by itself, it is again inanimate and is not capable of living, whilst the living element which has left it, retaining its vital energy unimpared, never dies.

(India I, p. 48, trans. E. Sachau)

Since the apostles knew that the souls are immortal, and that in their migrations they array themselves in every form, that they are shaped in every animal, and are cast in the mould of every

---

[1] Lipsius *Aa* I, p. 74 n. 1, against the view of Zahn, *Acta Johannis*, p. 204 n. 1.

[2] Translation from German of G. Graf, "Des Theodor Abû Kurra Traktat über den Schöpfer und die wahre Religion", *Beiträge zur Geschichte der Philosophie des Mittelalters* XIV. 1, Münster, 1913, p. 27.

[3] *Les écritures manichéennes* II, pp. 173 and 177.

figure, they asked Messiah what would be the end of those souls which did not receive the truth nor learn the origin of their existence. Whereupon he said: Any weak soul which has not received all that belongs to her of the truth perishes without any rest or bliss.

(India I, pp. 54–55 Sachau; German trans. in A. Adam, *Texte zum Manichäismus* (*Kleine Texte* 175), Berlin 1954, p. 10)

Perhaps we may here adduce a little-known testimony from Shenute of Atripe (d. 466), who reproaches the heretics for having said that there are 'twelve Gospels' (Coptic text in C. Wessely, *Studien zur Paläographie und Papyruskunde* IX, Leipzig 1909, p. 143). The heretics in question must in fact have been Manicheans.[1] But it would be unwise to attach much value to an apparently analogous account in al-Jaqūbī (in Kessler, *Mani* I, Berlin 1889, pp. 206 and 329), who names among the books composed by Mani 'twelve gospels', "of which" he adds, "he (Mani) named each after one of the letters of the alphabet, and in which he expounded the prayer and what must be employed for the freeing of the spirit". 'Twelve' is here an error for 'twenty-two'; from the context, it is evidently a reference to Mani's 'Living Gospel', which was divided into twenty-two chapters or sections, corresponding to the twenty-two letters of the Syriac alphabet (below, pp. 350ff.).

5. *The Gospel of the Seventy*

The only testimony we possess is that of al-Biruni: "Everyone of the sects of Marcion, and of Bardesanes, has a special Gospel, which in some parts differs from the Gospels we have mentioned (*sc.* the orthodox Gospels previously discussed). Also the Manicheans have a Gospel of their own, the contents of which from the first to the last are opposed to the doctrines of the Christians; but the Manicheans consider them as their religious law, and believe that it is the correct Gospel, that its contents are really that which Messiah thought and taught, that every other Gospel is false, and its followers are liars against Messiah. Of this Gospel there is a copy, called 'The Gospel of the Seventy', which is attributed to one *Balāmīs* (var.: *Iklāmīs*), and in the beginning of which it is stated, that Salām ben Abdallāh ben Salām wrote it down as he heard it from Salmān Alfārisī. He, however, who looks into it, will see at once that it is a forgery; it is not acknowledged by Christians and others" (*Kitāb al-Athār al-bāqiya*; English translation from E. Sachau, *The Chronology of Ancient Nations* (London

[1] Cf. W. E. Crum, *Journal of Egyptian Archaeology* 19, 1933, 198.

1879) p. 27; partial German translation in K. Kessler, *Mani* I, Berlin 1889, pp. 207f.).

The interpretation of such a testimony is exceptionally difficult. Kessler (*Mani*, p. 208) thinks it refers to Mani's 'Living Gospel' (below, pp. 350ff.). But in that case the writing al-Biruni mentions in the sequel, which he apparently considers a very different recension of the Manichean Gospel, must have been an independent work, a late apocryphon which, although perhaps placed under the authority of Clement of Rome (Iklāmīs), could not be dated earlier than the first half of the 7th century. Salmān of Fārs and 'Abd Allāh b. Salām, the Jew of Medina whose (fictitious?) son is alleged to have written the work at the dictation of the former, were contemporaries of Mohamed, with whom they are brought into relation by traditions more or less legendary. P. Alfaric, however, advances another interpretation.[1] The gospel in question would, in his view, be the Gospel of the Twelve Apostles. In his own words:

"The exemplar which Salām ben Abdallah transcribed . . . is here mentioned only because he did not confine himself to the reproduction of the text previously described. In Biruni's view, it was not a slavish 'copy', but an adaptation. It is for that reason that it bears a separate title: the Gospel of the Seventy. Instead of purporting to be the work of the *twelve* apostles, it professes to be that of the *seventy* disciples of Christ, to whom the Gnostics appealed. Just as the Gospel of the Twelve Apostles is said to have been composed by Matthew, so that of the seventy is derived from Balāmīs. In place of the latter name, which occurs in no list of disciples in the Christian literature of the early centuries, one manuscript offers that of Iklāmīs, the Arabic form of the name of the most famous among them, Clement of Rome. This last ascription seems very natural. Clement of Rome in fact enjoyed a very great popularity in Gnostic circles, and particularly those in which the Gospel of the Twelve Apostles was current. The Homilies and Recognitions which have come down to us under his name show, despite numerous catholic revisions, the evident marks of Ebionite origin . . . It can be readily understood that in the same circles, and later among the Manicheans, there should have been a Gospel of Clement". Alfaric's argument is however open to question in several of its details, and his theory can scarcely be said to carry conviction.

The same reserve is necessary in regard to another conjecture by this scholar, who thinks that we possess a fragment of the Gospel of the Seventy in a Uyghur text, perhaps translated from Syriac, which was discovered at Bulayīq, in the north of Turfan:

[1] *Les écritures manichéennes* II, Paris, pp. 177–180.

... my son, thy way is (evil?) Hear now the (command) of God. Go not upon this way. For if thou dost go without hearing, thou shalt fall into the great ditch (or: fire?). If thou ask Why?, the Adversary lies in wait for thee, he thinks to destroy thee utterly.

18th saying: This is good (to hear?): thus says Zavtai the Apostle (Zebedee, Zabdai in the Syriac list of the seventy disciples?): Thou art, O Son of man, like the cow which lowed from afar after her calf, which had gone astray. When that calf ... heard the voice of its mother, it came running quickly (?) ... to meet its mother, it became free from suffering. So also thy (?) which ... afar will (?) quickly (?) with great joy.

19th saying: This is bad (to hear?): thus says Luke the Apostle: Son of man, wash thy hands clean; before the evil (one?) have no fear; think pure thoughts; what thou dost possess of love for God, carry fully into effect. ...

(A. von le Coq, *Ein christliches und ein manichäisches Manuskript-fragment*, SB Berlin 1909, pp. 1205–1208)

6. Other "Gospels of the Twelve Apostles"

The gospel published by J. Rendel Harris from a Syriac manuscript of the 8th (?) century (*The Gospel of the Twelve Apostles, with the Apocalypses of each of them, edited from the Syriac ms. with a translation and introduction*, Cambridge 1900), and said to have been translated from Hebrew into Greek and from Greek into Syriac, does not belong in this section of the New Testament apocrypha. This document has nothing to do with the Gospel of the Twelve, and is shown by the doctrines which it contains to be a forgery of very late date (cf. E. Nestle, *ThLZ* 1900, 557–559).

The pretended Gospel of the Twelve Apostles published by E. Revillout (*PO* ii. 2, Paris 1904, pp. 117–198) is only a collection of sixteen independent Coptic fragments, likewise of late date, arbitrarily grouped under a fictitious title (cf. A. Baumstark, "Les apocryphes coptes", *Rev. Bibl.* NS 3, 1906, 245–265; P. Ladeuze, "Apocryphes évangéliques coptes: Pseudo-Gamaliel, Évangile de Barthélemy", *RHE* 7, 1906, 245–268).

E. GOSPELS UNDER THE NAME OF AN APOSTLE

1. The Gospel of Philip

Describing an incident alleged to have taken place after the Resurrection, the Pistis Sophia (c. 42) introduces Philip as "the

writer of all the words which Jesus spake, and of all that he did"
(Schmidt-Till 44. 21f.). Jesus says to Philip:

"Hear, Philip, thou blessed one (μακάριος), that I may speak
with thee, for you and Thomas and Matthew are they to whom
the charge is given by the first mystery (μυστήριον), to write down
all the things which I shall say and do, and all the things which
ye shall see. But (δέ) so far as thou art concerned, the number
(ἀριθμός) of the things which thou shalt write is not yet complete;
when they are complete, thou shalt go forth and preach that which
pleases thee. But now shall ye three write down all the things that
I shall say and do, and (all the things) which ye shall see, that ye
may testify to all the things of the kingdom of heaven" (Pistis
Sophia c. 42; Schmidt-Till 44. 33–45. 3).

These words are explained in the following chapter by Mary:
"With regard to the word which thou (sc. Jesus) hast said to
Philip: 'Thou and Thomas and Matthew are the three to whom
the charge is given by the first mystery (μυστήριον), to write down
all the things of the kingdom of light, and to testify thereto', hear
now, that I may proclaim the interpretation of this word—this is
what thy power of light once prophesied (προφητεύειν) through
Moses (*Deut. 19:15; cf. Mt. 18:16*): 'Through two and three
witnesses shall every thing be established'; the three witnesses are
Philip and Thomas and Matthew" (Pistis Sophia, c. 43; Schmidt-
Till 45. 12–19).

In point of fact, Jesus shortly afterwards commands Philip:
"Well done (εὖγε), Philip, thou beloved one. But now come, sit
down and write thy share (μέρος) of all the things that I shall say
and do, and all the things which thou shalt see."—And straightway Philip sat down and wrote (Pistis Sophia c. 44; Schmidt-
Till 47. 5–8).

This account, or the tradition on which it draws, presupposes—
or is intended to create the impression—that the Apostle Philip
should be considered, beside Thomas and Matthew (perhaps
Matthias: below, pp. 312f.), as the author of one of the three chief
gospels held in honour in certain Gnostic schools. As a matter of fact,
a 'Gospel of Philip' or 'according to Philip' was in use among the
Gnostics (Epiphanius, *Pan.* 26. 13. 2, I p. 292. 13–14 Holl: εἰς
ὄνομα Φιλίππου τοῦ ἁγίου μαθητοῦ εὐαγγέλιον πεπλασμένον) and
among the Manichees (Timotheus of Constantinople, *De receptione
haereticorum, PG* LXXXVI, 1, 21 C; Pseudo-Leontius of Byzantium (Theodore of Raithu?), *De sectis* III, 2, *PG* LXXXVI, I,
1213 C; in both cases the work is called τὸ κατὰ Φίλιππον
εὐαγγέλιον, and is named immediately after the Gospel of Thomas).

Literature: Theodor Zahn, *Gesch. des ntl. Kanons* II, 2, Erlangen 1892,
761–768. – id., *Forschungen zur Gesch. des ntl. Kanons* VI, Leipzig 1900,

24–27. – Harnack, *Litg.* I. 14–15 and II. 1. 592f. – P. Alfaric, *Les écritures manichéennes* II, Paris 1919, 182–184. – E. Hennecke, *Apokr.* 2, 69. – Santos 67f. (with bibliography).

Up to recent years the content of the Gospel of Philip was known only by one express citation:

The Lord (ὁ κύριος) revealed (ἀπεκάλυψεν) to me what the soul must say in its ascent to heaven, and how it must answer each of the powers above (τῶν ἄνω δυνάμεων): "I have recognized myself (ἐπέγνων ἐμαυτήν) and gathered myself together from all sides (καὶ συνέλεξα ἐμαυτὴν ἐκ πανταχόθεν) and have not sown children to the Archon (καὶ οὐκ ἔσπειρα τέκνα τῷ ἄρχοντι) but have uprooted his roots (ἀλλὰ ἐξερρίζωσα τὰς ῥίζας αὐτοῦ) and have gathered the scattered members (καὶ συνέλεξα τὰ μέλη τὰ διεσκορπισμένα), and I know thee who thou art; for I belong to those from above (ἐγὼ γὰρ τῶν ἄνωθέν εἰμι)". And so it is set free (ἀπολύεται). But if it should prove that the soul has borne a son, it is kept beneath (κάτω) until it is in a position to recover its children and bring them back to itself (ἕως ἂν τὰ ἴδια τέκνα δυνηθῇ ἀναλαβεῖν καὶ ἀναστρέψαι εἰς ἑαυτήν).

(Epiphanius *Pan.* 26. 13. 2–3; I, p. 292. 14–293. 1 Holl)

The gospel must therefore have contained revelations imparted by Jesus to another person (probably Philip) and reported by him. The instruction here bears upon a subject familiar to Gnosis: the manner of the ascent of the soul. By means of ritual formulae, which are at the same time passwords (ἀπολογίαι), the soul ascending after death to its heavenly fatherland obtains from the planetary Archons, the hostile 'powers' of destiny who oppose its return, free passage through the seven successive spheres of the visible firmament.[1] The soul boasts that it possesses 'Gnosis': above all, that it knows or has recognized itself (γνῶσις or ἐπίγνωσις ἑαυτοῦ),[2] and in consequence knows that it derives its origin from the transcendent world (τῶν ἄνωθεν εἶναι),[3] that it is of a 'race' (γένος) superior to that of the Archons, whose inferior and contemptible nature it has at the same time come to know. This knowledge of the self, through which the soul has found itself

[1] Cf. Irenaeus, *adv. haer.* I.14.4H; Origen, *c. Cels.* VI. 31; Gospel of Mary, Pap. Berol. 8502 (ed. W. C. Till, *TU* 60 = 5 Reihe V, 1955), pp. 15.1–17.7; W. Bousset, "Die Himmelsreise der Seele", *Archiv f. Religionswissensch.* 4, 1901, pp. 136–169 and 229–273.
[2] Cf. for example Bultmann, *ThWtb* I, pp. 688–719.
[3] Cf. Jn. 3:31 and 8:23, also Bultmann *Das Evangelium des Johannes*, 11th ed., Göttingen 1950, p. 95 n. 6; Gospel of Truth, p. 22. 3f.; ritual formula of the Valentinians in Irenaeus *adv. haer.* I.14.4: ἐγὼ οἶδα ἐμαυτὸν καὶ γινώσκω ὅθεν εἰμί.

once more in its true and original condition of being saved from all eternity, is a recovery of the self by the self, a 'gathering' (σύλλεξις) to the self and in the self of the spiritual, luminous substance of the 'ego' or of the soul, dispersed here below in the body and in matter. The particles of the psychic substance, scattered and imprisoned in the world, represent the 'members' (μέλη) of the 'living soul', which are thus collected, set in order, and restored to their organic unity.

The concentration, collection and consequent deliverance of this soul, regarded as consubstantial with that of Christ and compared by the Gnostics combated by Epiphanius (*Pan.* 26) with sperm (in the biological sense), are achieved either by ascetic continence or by libertine practices.[1] In any case, each of these attitudes has as its object the complete deliverance of the imprisoned soul. It must not become shackled again to the flesh by conception and generation, and thereby continue as the slave of the wicked or inferior god of creation, the Archon or Cosmocrator (in Manicheism, of matter or concupiscence personified).

The Gnostic may then, in the formula quoted, boast that he has left nothing of himself in the world, that he has not there scattered his seed, that he has not begotten children, either with demonic beings (Ascension of Elias, in Epiphanius *Pan.* 26. 13. 5) or for the benefit of the Archon or the principle of evil. On the contrary, he has wrested all power from his grasp by destroying his domination to its very 'roots'. In contrast, he who in his earthly life has committed the error of procreation has given the Archon power over him; his soul must be re-incarnated in order to rejoin the particles of itself which it left imprisoned in the material bodies of the children begotten, to recover possession of them, and to gather them anew into complete integration.

This theory of the liberation of the soul through a ritual or purely intellectual act, which is at the same time a gathering of the self (σύλλεξις ἑαυτοῦ) or of its 'members' and knowledge of the self (γνῶσις or ἐπίγνωσις ἑαυτοῦ), occurs frequently among the Gnostics (Gospel of Eve, in Epiphanius *Pan.* 26. 3. 1; fragment of a prayer appended to the Books of Jeu, pp. 330. 3–332. 37 Schmidt-Till; cf. generally H. Jonas, *Gnosis und spätantiker Geist* I, Göttingen 1934, 139f.). The closest parallel to the passage in the Gospel of Philip is provided by the remark of a libertine Gnostic in Epiphanius: "If anyone, he says, attains to this knowledge and gathers himself out of the world . . . he is no longer held there in prison, but surpasses the afore-mentioned Archons" (*Pan.* 26. 10. 9). The same conception, expressed in almost identical terms and imagery, recurs in Manicheism (cf. for example the Turfan

[1] Cf. L. Fendt, *Gnostische Mysterien*, Munich 1922, pp. 3–29 and 76f.

fragments M 49, SB Berlin, 1933, 308; M 33 and M 21, ib. 1934, 877 and 891). But it appears also here and there in the apocryphal Acts of the Apostles (cf. Acts of Andrew 6; Acts of Thomas 43 and 48). It may take a more or less mythical form, but may also be philosophical and relate to the inward composure, the spiritual *recollectio* (e.g. Plotinus, *Enn.* I. 6. 5; Marinus, *Vita Procli* c. 21; Ambrose, *De bono mortis* 10; cf. W. Theiler in *Gnomon* 25, 1953, 115).

The most remarkable fact, however, is that, as Reitzenstein has noted (*Historia Monachorum und Historia Lausiaca*, Göttingen 1916, 97–100), the expressions used in the fragment quoted from the Gnostic Gospel of Philip are almost exactly the same as those employed by the Neo-Platonist philosopher Porphyry in his Epistle to Marcella: "If thou study to ascend into thyself, gathering from the body all thy scattered members which have been scattered into a multitude from the unity which up to a point held sway" (c. 10; pp. 281. 1–2 Nauck[2]). These expressions are Platonic:[1] they come from Plato (*Phaedo* 67c: "to separate so far as possible the soul from the body, and accustom it to gather and consolidate itself to itself from every part of the body"; and 83a: "to gather and consolidate itself to itself"). The only difference is that instead of employing, like Porphyry, the expression τὰ διασκεδασθέντα μέλη, the author of the gospel writes τὰ μέλη τὰ διεσκορπισμένα, thus using (or substituting?) a Johannine term (Jn. 11:52: ἵνα καὶ τὰ τέκνα τοῦ θεοῦ τὰ διεσκορπισμένα συναγάγῃ εἰς ἕν).

According to Zahn,[2] Clement of Alexandria (*Strom.* III. 4. 25) was influenced by the Gospel of Philip when in connection with Marcion and the Marcionites he identified as Philip the man (in the Synoptics anonymous) to whom Jesus turns in Lk. 9:60 (= Mt. 8:22). But the hypothesis remains 'questionable' (Harnack *Litg.* I. 15).

The whole problem is today re-opened, and is dominated by the discovery of a Gospel according to Philip among the documents of the Gnostic library found near Nag Hammadi in 1945.[3] The work, translated into Coptic (Sahidic), is contained in one

---

[1] Cf. A. J. Festugière, *Personal Religion among the Greeks*, Los Angeles 1954, p. 59 and *La Révélation d'Hermès Trismégiste* IV, Paris 1954, p. 215 and n. 1, who however does not mention the passage in the Gospel of Philip.

[2] *Gesch. des ntl. Kanons* II, pp. 761–768, and *Forschungen zur Gesch. des ntl. Kanons* VI, 26f.

[3] Cf. J. Doresse, "Nouveaux textes gnostiques", *Vig. Chr.* 3, 1949, pp. 134 and 138; id., "Une bibliothèque gnostique copte", *Acad. Royale de Belgique, Bull. de la classe des Lettres*, 5 série, vol. 35, 1949, pp. 440 and 444; id., *Les livres secrets des gnostiques d'Egypte*, Paris 1958, pp. 239–243 (ET London 1960, 221–225); H.-Ch. Puech, "Les nouveaux écrits gnostiques", in *Coptic Studies in Honor of W. E. Crum*, Boston 1950, pp. 104 and 117–119; id., "Découverte d'une bibliothèque gnostique", in *Enc. Fr.*, t. XIX, Paris 1957, fasc. 19.42–9.

GNOSTIC GOSPELS AND RELATED DOCUMENTS

of the volumes, Codex III of my classification, now preserved in the Coptic Museum in Old Cairo. The manuscript was at first dated in the middle or the first half of the 3rd century, but seems rather to belong to the 4th or 5th, and the document occupies pages 53 (?). 29–88 (?). 19. It is the third text in the volume, in which it follows immediately on the Gospel of Thomas (below, pp. 278ff.) and precedes a dogmatic tractate, "The Hypostasis of the Archons". The latter is related to the Book of Norea, which Epiphanius likewise mentions in his section on the 'Gnostics' (*Pan.* 26. 1. 3–9). The title is given in the colophon: *peuaggelion pkata philippos*.

Photographic reproduction of the text (under the designation "Codex II Part A") in Pahor Labib, *Coptic Gnostic Papyri in the Coptic Museum at Old Cairo*, vol. I, Cairo 1956, plates 99. 29–134. 19; German translation by H. M. Schenke, *ThLZ* 84 (1959) col. 1ff. and in Leipoldt-Schenke, *Koptisch-gnostische Schriften aus den Papyrus-Codices von Nag-Hamadi*, Hamburg-Bergstedt 1960, 33ff. – E. Segelberg, *Numen* 7 (1960) 198ff. – R. M. Grant, *Vig. Chr.* 15 (1961) 129ff.

Unfortunately the study of the new document is still not sufficiently advanced to allow us at the moment to form and present a satisfactory and reasonably certain idea of it. The first impression is somewhat disconcerting: the writing has not the appearance of a 'gospel', and the name of Philip (*Philippos papostolos*) occurs only once (pl. 121. 8) in a phrase in the third person. Apparently we have to do with a continuous discourse, an exposition (or exhortation) addressed now to several people, now to one only, and delivered by a group who present themselves as Hebrews converted to Christianity (pl. 100. 21–24: "When we were Hebrews (ἑβραῖος) we were orphans (ὀρφανός), and we had (only) our mother. But since we became Christians (χριστιανός) we have again both father and mother"); these 'Hebrews' are "those who have not yet received the Lord" (110. 5–6). Cf. 103. 29–30, where the apostles appear as Hebraioi.

The themes discussed in this long exposition are very varied: the fate and redemption of the soul in the world; sacrifice; the substitution for animal nourishment of the 'heavenly bread' (Jn. 6:26–58) brought by Christ, the 'perfect Man'; the different natures and significance of the names given to the Son (Jesus, Christ or Messiah, Ναζαρηνός or Ναζωραῖος: pl. 104. 3–13 and 110. 7–17); the resurrection; the glorification of the 'children of God'; the work of salvation accomplished by Christ, etc. The author appears to have a certain fondness for such themes as the sacraments (Baptism of water and of fire, Eucharist with wine and water) and their interpretation, or for terms, or groups of terms, like 'truth', 'knowledge', 'love' (pl. 127. 24–31), or γνῶσις, πίστις, ἐλπίς, ἀγάπη.

A Gnostic influence, traceable here and there in the vocabulary (e.g. πλήρωμα, ἀνάπαυσις, ἄρχοντες, εἰκονικός, εὐγένεια), comes to light especially in pl. 108. 10–15 ("Ekhamoth is one thing, Ekhmoth another. Ekhamoth is simply (ἁπλῶς) Sophia; Ekhmoth is the Sophia of death, i.e. the one who knows death, whom they call 'the little Sophia' "); it is also to be seen in the frequent use of the metaphysical and mystical symbols of the 'bridal chamber' (παστός, νυμφών), the 'bridegroom' (νύμφιος) and the 'bride' (νύμφη). Allusions however are not wanting to episodes or persons in the Gospels: the Transfiguration (pl. 106. 5–12); the Virgin Mary (pl. 103. 23 and 27); Philip (pl. 121. 8); Joseph (pl. 121. 9). Reference is made (pl. 107. 6–9) to the 'three' holy women "who walked continually with the Lord: his mother Mary and her sister (Mary the wife of Cleopas? cf. Jn. 19:25) and Magdalene, whom men called his companion (κοινωνός)". In addition, words of Jesus are occasionally related, some canonical (pl. 105. 4–5: "He who does not eat my flesh and drink my blood hath not life in him", cf. Jn. 6:53), others uncanonical (pl. 107. 23–27: "A disciple one day asked the Lord about something worldly. He replied: Ask thy mother, and she will give thee strange (ἀλλότριον) things").

Taking it as a whole it seems to me, after the pioneer work of Schenke, that the 'gospel' is a collection of sayings and short meditations, of Valentinian origin, which are of great importance as a document of mysticism and for the development of the Gnostic theology of the sacraments. Some of the theories presented are close in thought and language to the Gospel of Thomas (e.g. pl. 121. 19–26 and 118. 9–17: cf. Gospel of Thomas log. 11; 112. 9–11: cf. log. 19; 115. 30–34: cf. log. 22). We cannot yet however attempt to resolve all the problems which it poses. It is not yet possible for example to determine whether or not it is identical with the Gospel of Philip mentioned in the Panarion. At most, the fact that it evidently does not have the form of a gospel, and that the text cited by Epiphanius does not seem to occur in it, suggests a negative answer, or the provisional conjecture that we have here on one side and on the other two revised versions of one and the same document. In any case, the solution must be reserved for future study.

At all events it may be assumed that the Gospel of Philip in Codex III from Nag Hammadi, like the Gospel of Thomas which precedes it in that volume, is in fact the apocryphon of the same name which was in use among the Manichees. The 'Sophia of death' (pl. 108. 12) is to be brought into relation as much with the 'ἐνθύμησις of death' in Manicheism[1] as with the 'ἐπιθυμία', the 'greed of death' in the Apocryphon of John (p. 57. 4f. Till).

It is possible that, as Zahn thought,[2] the gospel quoted by Epiphanius "emanated from early Gnostic circles in Egypt in the first decades of the 2nd century". The original of the Nag Hammadi text, which quite evidently was composed in Greek, could likewise be dated in the 2nd century, or at latest in the beginning or the middle of the 3rd.

Further Literature: English translation by C. J. de Catanzaro, *JTS* 13, 1962, pp. 35ff.; English translation with introduction and notes by R. McL. Wilson, *The Gospel of Philip*, London 1962; edition of Coptic text with revised German translation by W. C. Till (in the press).

2. *The Gospel of Thomas*

As we have just seen, a tradition echoed in chapters 42 and 43 of the Pistis Sophia (pp. 44. 33–36 and 45. 12–19 Schmidt-Till) declares that Jesus after His Resurrection charged the apostle Thomas as well as Philip and Matthew to commit to writing "all His words", and thus appointed him as one of the three attested witnesses to His message. This means however that Thomas must be regarded as the author or guarantor of a gospel—or more exactly: of one of the three gospels considered primary by the Gnostics, and in use in certain Gnostic circles. A work entitled "the Gospel of Thomas" (τὸ κατὰ Θωμᾶν ἐπιγραφόμενον εὐαγγέλιον) is in fact mentioned and quoted by Hippolytus about 230 in his account of the Naassenes (*Ref.* V. 7. 20). Some years later, shortly after 233, Origen in the first of his homilies on Luke (*in Luc. hom.* I, p. 5. 13–14 Rauer) mentions the Gospel of Thomas (τὸ κατὰ Θωμᾶν εὐαγγέλιον), alongside that of Matthias, among the heterodox gospels which 'many' had had the presumption to compose. His testimony, translated or paraphrased into Latin, is repeated by Jerome (trans. of Origen's homilies on Luke, p. 5. 11–13 Rauer: "euangelium, quod appellatur secundum Thomam"; *Comm. in Matth.*, Prol., *PL* XXVI. 17 A: "euangelium iuxta Thomam"), Ambrose (*Expositio euangelii Lucae* I. 2, p. 10. 20–11. 1 Schenkl) and the Venerable Bede (*In Lucae euangelium expositio* I Prol., *PL* XCII. 307 C: "euangelium Thomae").

On the Greek side Eusebius of Caesarea (*H.E.* III. 25. 6), probably under the influence of Origen, assigns a Gospel of Thomas (Θωμᾶ εὐαγγέλιον) to the category of apocrypha of a frankly heterodox character, "commended by the heretics under

---

[1] Cf. C. Schmidt–H. J. Polotsky, "Ein Mani-Fund in Ägypten", SB Berlin, 1933, pp. 78–80, and H. J. Polotsky, Art. "Manichäismus" in Pauly-Wissowa, Suppl. VI, 1934, 254.1–18.
[2] *Gesch. d. ntl. Kanons* II, 768.

the name of the apostle"; he inserts it between the Gospel of Peter and that of Matthias. Following Eusebius, Philip of Side towards 430 declares in a fragment of his history (preserved in the Codex Baroccianus 142; C. de Boor, *TU* 5, 2, 1888, p. 169 no. 4) that "the majority of the ancients" ($\pi\lambda\epsilon\hat{\iota}\sigma\tau\omicron\iota$ $\tau\hat{\omega}\nu$ $\grave{\alpha}\rho\chi\alpha\hat{\iota}\omega\nu$) had completely ($\tau\epsilon\lambda\epsilon\hat{\iota}\omega\varsigma$) rejected the so-called Gospel of Thomas ($\tau\grave{\omicron}$ $\lambda\epsilon\gamma\acute{\omicron}\mu\epsilon\nu\omicron\nu$ $\Theta\omega\mu\hat{\alpha}$ $\epsilon\grave{\upsilon}\alpha\gamma\gamma\acute{\epsilon}\lambda\iota\omicron\nu$), as well as those of the Hebrews and of Peter, "saying that these writings were the work of heretics". These belong to the "false gospels" ($\epsilon\grave{\upsilon}\alpha\gamma\gamma\acute{\epsilon}\lambda\iota\alpha$ $\psi\epsilon\upsilon\delta\hat{\eta}$) of which he gives other examples: the Gospel of the Egyptians, the Gospel of the Twelve, the Gospel of Basilides.

On the other hand a series of Greek witnesses (Cyril of Jerusalem, *Cat.* IV. 36 and VI. 31, *PG* XXXIII 500 B and 593 A, followed by Peter of Sicily, *Hist. Manich.* 16, *PG* CIV 1265 C and by ps. Photius *c. Manich.* I. 14, *PG* CII 41 B; ps. Leontius of Byzantium (Theodore of Raithu?), *De sectis* III. 2, *PG* LXXXVI, 1 1213 C; Timotheus of Constantinople, *De recept. haeret.*, *PG* LXXXVI, 1 21 C; Acts of the Second Council of Nicaea (787), Act VI 5, Mansi XIII 293 B) include a Gospel of Thomas ($\tau\grave{\omicron}$ $\kappa\alpha\tau\grave{\alpha}$ $\Theta\omega\mu\hat{\alpha}\nu$ $\epsilon\grave{\upsilon}\alpha\gamma\gamma\acute{\epsilon}\lambda\iota\omicron\nu$) among the writings in use among the Manichees or even, as it is occasionally affirmed, composed by them. Cyril and those who copied him identify the author not of course as an apostle but as a disciple of Mani who was also called Thomas.

The notices of ps. Leontius and Timotheus are particularly interesting: both link the Gospel of Thomas closely with the Gospel of Philip (above, pp. 271ff.), which they mention immediately afterwards; and Timotheus expressly distinguishes the Gospel of Thomas and another apocryphon, the Infancy of the Lord ($\pi\alpha\iota\delta\iota\kappa\grave{\alpha}$ $\tau\omicron\hat{\upsilon}$ $\kappa\upsilon\rho\acute{\iota}\omicron\upsilon$), classifying them in his list of Manichean Scriptures under the numbers 9 and 13. The pseudo-Gelasian Decree (E. von Dobschütz, *Das Decretum Gelasianum*, *TU* 38, 4, 1912, p. 11, commentary p. 295) inserts in its catalogue of *libri non recipiendi* an "Evangelium nomine Thomae quibus Manichaei utuntur, apocryphum". It is however difficult here to decide whether the work in view is the Gospel of Thomas properly so called, or the Infancy Gospel attributed to Thomas, which was also read by the Manichees. The same ambiguity occurs in the case of two other references to the $\epsilon\grave{\upsilon}\alpha\gamma\gamma\acute{\epsilon}\lambda\iota\omicron\nu$ $\kappa\alpha\tau\grave{\alpha}$ $\Theta\omega\mu\hat{\alpha}\nu$, found in the Stichometry of Nicephorus (*PG* C 1060 B) and in the 'Synopsis' of ps. Athanasius (*PG* XXVIII 432 B). Since these passages contain no allusions to the Manichees, it would seem that they refer rather to the $\pi\alpha\iota\delta\iota\kappa\acute{\alpha}$.

Until recently all that was known of this Gnostic gospel, finally adopted by the Manicheans also, was a single passage quoted by

Hippolytus (*Ref.* V. 7. 20, p. 83, 10–16 Wendland). This gives, on the basis of one of their writings, a summary of the doctrine of the Naassenes concerning "the blessed nature, at once hidden and revealed, of things past, present and to come" (τὴν τῶν γεγονότων καὶ γινομένων καὶ ἐσομένων ἔτι μακαρίαν κρυβομένην ὁμοῦ καὶ φανερουμένην φύσιν), a nature compared by them with "the kingdom of the heavens which is within man, and is sought after" (ἥνπερ φησὶ <τὴν> ἐντὸς ἀνθρώπου βασιλείαν οὐρανῶν ζητουμένην). Hippolytus writes:

Of this nature (or: this kingdom) they (the Naassenes) speak expressly (διαρρήδην παραδιδόασι) in the gospel entitled 'according to Thomas' (ἐν τῷ κατὰ Θωμᾶν ἐπιγραφομένῳ εὐαγγελίῳ), saying: "He who seeks me will find me in children of seven years upward, for there hidden in the fourteenth aeon am I revealed" (ἐμὲ ὁ ζητῶν εὑρήσει ἐν παιδίοις ἀπὸ ἐτῶν ἑπτά. ἐκεῖ γὰρ ἐν τῷ τεσσαρεσκαιδεκάτῳ αἰῶνι κρυβόμενος φανεροῦμαι.

(Hippol. *Ref.* V. 7. 20, Wendland p. 83. 13–16)

It is evidently a question of a saying attributed to Jesus, a *logion* the meaning of which remains obscure. The attempt has been made (*Handb.* p. 90) to explain it with the help of a passage from the second Book of Jeu (c. 52, pp. 327. 23f. Schmidt-Till), in which "the great God, who . . . is called the great and righteous" (χρηστός) is sought "in the 14th aeon". H. H. Schaeder (*Gnomon* 1933, p. 353 n. 2) proposed to connect it with the "fourteen great aeons (of light)" about which according to the Manichean Kephalaia (*Keph.* X, p. 42. 24–43. 21) "Sethel has spoken in his prayer". The most plausible interpretation however appears to be that advanced by Hippolytus himself (*Ref.* V. 7. 21) and adopted by Leisegang (*Die Gnosis*, 4th ed., 1955, p. 136; cf. also, in one sense, Hennecke *Apokr.* 2, p. 68): that the idea underlying the words quoted belongs to a Hippocratic theory preserved by the Stoics (Zeno, Diogenes of Babylon, Cleanthes). Up to the seventh year, i.e. to the loss of the milk-teeth, a child has neither understanding nor λόγος. It is in the period from the seventh to the fourteenth year that the λόγος develops, and the process is complete with puberty and the breaking of the voice. Finally, in the fourteenth year, the divine λόγος takes the place of the human reason, and the invisible presence of Christ, the perfect Man, and thereby of the kingdom of heaven, becomes effective in us.

This explanation is to some extent confirmed, in my opinion, by a later passage in Hippolytus (*Ref.* V. 8. 19–21): "This entrance and this gate Jacob saw when he betook himself to Mesopotamia, i.e. when he passed from childhood to youth and manhood; for this is the meaning of the expression: 'He betook himself to Mesopotamia' (Gen. 28:7). Mesopotamia, the Naassene explains, is the current of the great ocean, which flows from the midst of the perfect Man (τέλειος ἄνθρωπος). Looking in admiration at the gate of heaven, Jacob cried out: 'How dreadful is this place! This is none other than the house of God, and this is the gate of heaven' (Gen. 28:17). That is why, he continues, Jesus said: 'I am the true door' (Jn. 10:9). But he who thus speaks is the perfect Man (ὁ τέλειος ἄνθρωπος), who has received a form from above, from the Being whom no form can define (ἀπὸ τοῦ ἀχαρακτηρίστου). The perfect Man, then, can only be saved by entering through this gate to be born again to a new life".

This quotation Hippolytus or his source very probably borrowed from the Gospel of Thomas. It seems, however,[1] that it ought also to be brought into association with a passage in one of the Latin versions of the Infancy Gospel related to the παιδικὰ τοῦ κυρίου, of which Thomas is alleged to be the author: in ps. Matthew 30:4 (*Ea* p. 100; cf. below, p. 406) Jesus says: "I have been among you with the children, and ye have not recognized me. I have spoken with you as with people of understanding, and ye have not recognized my voice".

This would seem to support the hypothesis now generally accepted, that the Gospel of Thomas mentioned in these testimonies was itself an Infancy Gospel, and should be brought into relation with the original form of the legendary narratives indicated by this name.[2] As a matter of fact most scholars have agreed in ascribing to the Gospel of Thomas a narrative from the childhood of Jesus recorded by Irenaeus (*adv. haer.* I.13.1H) as derived from one of the numerous apocryphal books fabricated by the Gnostics.[3] Here the Lord explains the meaning of the letters of the alphabet to the teacher entrusted with His education. The episode seems to have a connection, more or less loose, with the text quoted by Hippolytus, and occurs also in chapter 14 of the παιδικά in its present form (below, p. 397). These scholars accordingly were led to suppose that the Gospel of Thomas in use among the Gnostics and the Manichees was a primitive, and decidedly heterodox, version of the "Narrative of the Infancy of the Lord, by Thomas the Israelite philosopher" which has come down to us. In the words of Bardenhewer (*Litg.* I, p. 532) and James (p. 14),

---

[1] Cf. Hennecke, *Apokr.* 2, p. 68; A. Meyer, *ibid.*, p. 94.

[2] Zahn, *Gesch. des ntl. Kanons* I, pp. 746–748 and II, pp. 768–773; Harnack, *Litg.* II.1, pp. 593–595; Bardenhewer, *Litg.* I, pp. 530–532; James pp. 14–16; Altaner, p. 57; Quasten, I, pp. 123–125; for a contrary opinion, P. Alfaric, *Les écritures manichéennes* 11, Paris 1919, pp. 184f.

[3] Probably here the Marcosians, despite Sagnard, *Irénée de Lyon, Contre les hérésies, livre III*; Paris–Lyon 1952, p. 66 n. 2.

it was "a shortened and expurgated form of the original Gospel of Thomas", "the skeleton of the old one—the stories retained and the unorthodox discourses cut out". Against this the following objections could already be raised: (1) there is no proof that the legend reported by Irenaeus was part of a gospel or any other writing attributed to Thomas (cf. Santos p. 64); (2) it appears also in chapter 4 of an apocryphon which can be dated approximately between 140 and 170, the *Epistola Apostolorum*,[1] where Thomas is no more mentioned than in the *Adversus Haereses*.

Such was the situation not long ago. Today however it is completely changed: we now possess the complete text of the Gospel of Thomas. One of the volumes of the Coptic Gnostic library found about 1945 near Nag Hammadi, Codex III of my classification (4th or 5th cent., rather than in the middle or first half of the 3rd, as was thought at first), now preserved in the Coptic Museum at Old Cairo, contains on pages 32. 10–51.28 (according to Doresse) a short work whose title, according to the colophon, runs: *peuaggelion pkata thomas*. Like all the other pieces in this manuscript, it is written in Sahidic. The work is the second in the volume, in which it follows the Apocryphon of John (long recension, below, pp. 314ff.). Apart from a few unimportant lacunae, mostly easy to make good, the text is in perfect condition.

Literature: J. Doresse, "Nouveaux textes gnostiques", *Vig. Chr.* 3, 1949, p. 134 and 138; id., "Une bibliothèque gnostique copte", *Acad. Royale de Belgique, Bull. de la classe des Lettres*, 5ème série, t. XXXV, 1949, p. 440 and 444; H.-Ch. Puech, "Les nouveaux écrits gnostiques", *Coptic Studies in Honor of W. E. Crum*, Boston 1950, 104 and 117–119; id., "The Jung Codex and the other Gnostic documents from Nag Hammadi", in H.-Ch. Puech, G. Quispel, W. C. van Unnik, *The Jung Codex*, London 1955, pp. 21f.; id., "Un logion de Jésus sur bandelette funéraire", in *RHR* 147, 1955, pp. 126–129; id., lecture in the University of Utrecht, 10th April 1956; id., "Découverte d'une bibliothèque gnostique", *Enc. Fr.*, t. XIX, Paris 1957, fasc. 19. 42–8 and 9; id., in *Annuaire du Collège de France*, 1957, pp. 231–238; 1958, 238–239; 1959, 255–264; id., in *CR Acad. Inscrr. et Belles-Lettres* 1957, pp. 146–166; G. Garitte, *RHE* 52, 1957, pp. 221f.; id., "Le premier volume de l'édition photographique des manuscrits gnostiques coptes et l'Évangile de Thomas", *Le Muséon* 70, 1957, pp. 59–73.
Coptic text in photographic reproduction in Pahor Labib, *Coptic Gnostic Papyri in the Coptic Museum at Old Cairo*, vol. I, Cairo 1956, plates 80. 10 to 99. 28. Editions with English, French and German translations by A. Guillaumont, H.-Ch. Puech, G. Quispel, W. Till and Yassa 'abd al-Masīh (London, Leiden etc., 1959); a full critical edition with commentary is in preparation. German translations by J. Leipoldt (*ThLZ* 83 (1958) 481ff. and in Leipoldt–Schenke, *Koptisch-gnostische*

[1] *TU* 43 = 3 Folge, XIII, 1919, p. 29; above, p. 193.

Schriften aus den Papyrus-Codices von Nag-Hamadi, Hamburg-Bergstedt 1960) and H. Quecke (in van Unnik etc., *Evangelien aus dem Nilsand*, Frankfurt am Main 1960, 161ff., and Grant-Freedman, *Geheime Worte Jesu*, Frankfurt 1960, 206ff.); French by J. Doresse, *L'Évangile selon Thomas*, Paris 1959 (English version in Doresse, *The Secret Books*, London 1960, pp. 333ff.); English by W. R. Schoedel in Grant-Freedman, *The Secret Sayings of Jesus*, London and New York 1960. There are also versions in other languages. Further literature in Prigent, *RHPR* 39 (1959) 39ff., *Evangelien aus dem Nilsand* 217–221, and *Geheime Worte* 224–226. Reference may also be made to the bibliographies published periodically in *Biblica* and in *Orientalia*. The extracts here quoted are given according to the above-mentioned English translation, by permission of the publishers.

My personal study of this work, the true character of which I identified in 1952, has led to the following conclusion: contrary to the view at present in favour, the Gospel of Thomas, although ascribed to the same author, has nothing to do with the παιδικὰ τοῦ κυρίου, or with any other Infancy Gospel. It is a quite independent apocryphon, of an entirely different type. It recounts no episodes from the life of Jesus, and contains scarcely any narrative; it is in no respect a gospel of narrative character. On the other hand it is certain that it is identical with the document of the same title which our ancient authorities number among the Manichean Scriptures. Not only do we find it, both in Codex III of Nag Hammadi and in the lists drawn up by ps. Leontius of Byzantium and Timotheus of Constantinople, linked with the Gospel of Philip and in the same order, but also, and more important, one or another of the sayings of Jesus which it contains recurs, exactly or with some variations, in the Manichean texts found in Central Asia and in the Fayyum, in some of the Turfan fragments as well as in the Coptic Kephalaia and Psalmbook (below, pp. 299ff.).

For convincing proof that the founder of Manicheism knew our document and was occasionally influenced by it, we need only compare the beginning of Mani's *Epistula Fundamenti* (in Augustine, *c. Epist. Fundam.* 11 and *c. Felicem* I. 1; cf. T II D II 134 in SB Berlin 1934, p. 856) with the Prologue to the Gospel of Thomas as it is now restored to us. On the other hand, it is much more difficult to determine the relation of the new document to the Gospel of Thomas mentioned by Hippolytus in connection with the Naassenes. What seems to be a quotation in the *Refutation* does not occur in the Nag Hammadi text, or rather there are only very distant echoes of it. At most we might compare Logion 4:

Jesus said: "The man old in days will not hesitate to ask a little child of seven days about the place of Life, and he will live. For many who are first shall become last, and they shall become a single one".

(Logion 4, pl. 81. 5–10)

This logion occurs, again in a divergent form, in the Coptic Manichean Psalm-book (p. 192. 2–3 Allberry): "The grey-haired old men, the little children instruct them. They that are six years old instruct them that are sixty years old". The similarities are so slight and the differences so great that one is almost tempted to deny any connection between the two gospels. I do not think however that we must go so far. The passage from the Naassene work which Hippolytus summarizes or paraphrases before introducing his quotation seems to me in fact to have a fairly close relation to the words of Jesus which in the Nag Hammadi document immediately precede or follow the logion to which I have appealed. The themes and expressions are in both cases related: the subject is the search for a truth mysterious and sublime; the heavenly kingdom is said to be at once within us and outside of us; it is affirmed that there is nothing hidden which shall not be revealed. I should therefore be inclined to believe that it is a question in both cases of the same Gospel of Thomas, but that the Naassenes employed a version which at some points had undergone revision.

It is equally possible that the saying preserved in the *Refutation* does not literally reproduce a passage from this particular version but was very freely quoted and modified by the writer who served as source for Hippolytus. One thing at any rate seems certain: when the Naassenes, again according to the same heresiologue (*Ref.* V. 8. 32), said: "If you ate dead things and made them living, what will you do if you eat living things?", there is every reason to believe that here again they were influenced by the Gospel of Thomas, and moreover by a version of this gospel identical with the one now rediscovered. We need only compare this Naassene saying with a brief 'word' of Jesus, logion 11 of the Coptic text:

"In the days when you devoured the dead, you made it alive; when you come into light, what will you do?"

(Logion 11, pl. 82. 19–22)

Taken in itself, as it has now finally come down to us, thanks to the Nag Hammadi discovery, the Gospel of Thomas is not a 'gospel' in the proper sense, or at least it is not a work of the usual type of the canonical, apocryphal or Gnostic gospels: it is no other and no less than a collection of 114 logia, the most extensive collection of sayings of Jesus, or sayings attributed to Jesus, that has yet

284

come down to us independently of the New Testament tradition. The structure is as follows: the collection begins with a brief pre-amble of four and a half lines, already containing a first logion; thereafter follow sayings and dialogues only, independent of each other and mechanically arranged without any narrative or systematic framework. For the most part they are introduced by the stereotyped formula 'Jesus said' (*pedsche īs dsche*: Greek: ἔλεγεν —elsewhere λέγει—or εἶπεν, εἴρηκεν, ἔφη 'Ιησοῦς) or 'He said' (*pedschaf dsche*).[1] The collection is thus apparently a more or less artificial conglomeration of diverse elements, preceded by an introduction which itself seems equally artificial, and may have been added later. Including logion 1, it runs:

These are the secret words (*schadsche ethēp*) which the Living Jesus spoke and Didymus Judas Thomas wrote (Δίδυμος 'Ιούδας Θωμᾶς). And he said: "Whoever finds the explanation (ἑρμηνεία) of these words will not taste death".

(pl. 80. 10–14; cf. Jn. 8:51f.)

In several respects this passage is of the greatest importance. In the first place, it coincides exactly with the first five lines of the famous Oxyrhynchus Papyrus 654 (3rd cent.; above, pp. 99f.), the further content of which moreover corresponds, apart from a few details, to the six logia which in the Coptic text follow immediately upon the introduction, in the same wording and in the same order. The correspondence is not apparent at first sight because of the lacunae of the Greek text, the more especially if we persist in the effort to restore them, as a large number of scholars have hitherto sought to do in very various ways.[2] Nevertheless it becomes clear beyond question once we set aside the conjectural restorations of earlier editors and restore the wording of the Oxyrhynchus Papyrus correctly with the aid of the Coptic version. Apart from the possibility of restoring the text in its complete integrity, this leads to two interesting results.

POx 654 is not to be connected, at least not directly, with the Gospel according to the Hebrews, as had been generally assumed, nor does it belong, as was also maintained, to the Gospel according to the Egyptians; nor does it represent, as others have supposed, the remains of an anthology of sayings, its first lines corresponding to "the conclusion and epilogue to other sayings, which somehow must have preceded".[3] Rather does it belong to the Gospel of

---

[1] On these formulae see A. Resch, *Agrapha*[1], *TU* 5, 4, 1889, pp. 83–86; H. G. Evelyn White, *The Sayings of Jesus from Oxyrhynchus*, Cambridge 1920, pp. XXIX–XXXIII and LXXIII–LXXVI.

[2] Cf. for example H. G. E. White, *op. cit.*, p. 1.

[3] Cf. White, *op. cit.*, pp. XLII–LXVII; H. Waitz, *Apokr.* 2, pp. 49–52.

Thomas, of which it reproduces the beginning; of this Gospel it preserves the Greek version, or one of the Greek versions, i.e. versions original in comparison with the Coptic. The preamble, in the second place, warns us as to the nature of the work which it introduces: a collection of sayings, of λόγοι, spoken or alleged to have been spoken by Jesus and written down by the Apostle Thomas. It defines the character or the purpose of the document: it is esoteric, or intended to be so considered, and contains secret utterances, concealed from the uninitiate, the interpretation of which, to him who is capable of discovering it, ensures eternal life; but above all, by revealing the identity of its ostensible author or redactor 'Didymus Judas Thomas', 'Judas the twin' (in Greek, Δίδυμος; in Aramaic, *tauma*, *toma*), it supplies a very valuable clue. The name in fact is not only redundant, but also very peculiar. The apostle, who in the canonical Gospels and in the Western tradition is commonly called simply Thomas or Thomas Didymus (Θωμᾶς ὁ λεγόμενος Δίδυμος), seems in the Eastern tradition, and especially in authors or works of Syriac language and origin, to have been named Judas Thomas.[1] In particular, the apocryphal Acts of Thomas frequently bestow on their hero the name Ἰούδας ὁ καὶ Θωμᾶς, and even, in the first chapter (p. 100. 4f. Bonnet), exactly as in the prologue to our gospel, that of Ἰούδας Θωμᾶς ὁ καὶ Δίδυμος.

But there is still more to be said. These same Acts of Thomas here and there (c. 10, p. 114. 11–13; c. 47, p. 163. 21–164. 1; c. 78, p. 193. 5–7) refer to the privilege the apostle is alleged to have enjoyed, of being the confidant of the most secret teachings of Jesus. Notably in chapter 39 (p. 156. 12–15) Thomas is addressed in the following terms: "Twin brother of Christ, Apostle of the Most High and fellow-initiate in the hidden word of Christ, thou who didst receive his secret sayings (ὁ δίδυμος τοῦ Χριστοῦ, ὁ ἀπόστολος τοῦ ὑψίστου καὶ συμμύστης τοῦ λόγου τοῦ Χριστοῦ τοῦ ἀποκρύφου, ὁ δεχόμενος αὐτοῦ τὰ ἀπόκρυφα λόγια)"; or, in the Syriac version (W. Wright, *Apocryphal Acts of the Apostles*, London 1871, vol. I, p. 208, translation vol. II, p. 180): "Twin brother of Christ and apostle of the Most High, thou who hast had part in the secret word (*melleteh kesita*) of the Lifegiver (*demehyana*) and hast received the hidden mysteries (*razawi kasye*) of the Son of God." This means that here as in our prologue Judas Thomas or Judas Thomas Didymus is considered as the custodian of the mysterious or esoteric words of Christ, the *schadsche ethēp* (Coptic text from Nag Hammadi), the λόγοι ἀπόκρυφοι (POx. 654), the λόγος ἀπόκρυφος or ἀπόκρυφα λόγια (Acts of Thomas), which have been revealed to

---

[1] W. Bauer, vol. II 3 pp. 59f.: XI; U. Monneret de Villard, *Le leggende orientali sui Magi evangelici = Studi e Testi* 163, Rome 1952, p. 46 n. 1.

him by the 'Life-giver' (Acts of Thomas, Syr.) or 'the Living Jesus' (Gospel of Thomas). It is therefore clear that either the prologue of our gospel is echoed in the Acts of Thomas or both are influenced by the same tradition. Such a relation between the Acts and the Gospel of Thomas is confirmed by the only other passage in the Coptic document in which the Apostle Thomas appears, to play moreover a prominent part:

Jesus said to his disciples: "Make a comparison to me and tell me whom I am like". Simon Peter said to him: "Thou art like a righteous angel (or: messenger, ἄγγελος)". Matthew said to him: "Thou art like a wise man of understanding". Thomas said to him: "Master, my mouth will not at all be capable of saying whom thou art like". Jesus said to him: "I am not thy Master, because thou hast drunk, thou hast become drunk from the bubbling spring which I have measured out" (*cf. Act. Thom. c. 37, p. 155. 16–17; c. 39, p. 157. 6–7; c. 147, p. 256. 8f.*). And he took him, he withdrew (cf. Lk. 9:10), he spoke three words to him (*cf. Act. Thom. c. 47, p. 164. 1–4*). Now when Thomas came to his companions, they asked him: "What did Jesus say to thee?" Thomas said to them: "If I tell you one of the words which he said to me, you will take up stones and throw at me; and fire will come from the stones and burn you up".

(Logion 13, pl. 82. 30–83. 14)

It would be possible to establish further but less distinct connections between the Acts and the Gospel of Thomas (e.g. c. 136, p. 243. 8–10 and Logion 2, pl. 80. 14–19 parr.; c. 147, p. 256. 11–13 and Logion 22, pl. 85. 20–35 parr.; c. 170, p. 286. 1f., 7f. and Logion 52, pl. 90. 12–18). In particular, certain episodes in the Acts seem to have been composed as explanations of this or that Logion in the gospel (cf. c. 14 with Logion 37, pl. 87. 27–88. 2 parr.; c. 92 with Logion 22, pl. 85. 20–35 parr.). On the whole we may conclude from all these connections that the Acts are dependent on the gospel.

The Acts of Thomas appear to have been composed in Edessa or a neighbouring district, towards the beginning or in the first half of the 3rd century. If this be so, it might allow us to determine approximately at least the date of the composition of our gospel, if not its place of origin.

Passing from the prologue to the body of the work, one is immediately struck by the inorganic arrangement of the great mass of the logia of which it is entirely composed. Each of the sayings is an independent unit, and one follows upon another without any connection. Only rarely can one observe a certain coherence in the grouping of some among them, when key-words or relation to the same or a similar theme link one to another. In any case it is for the present difficult to discover a plan in the work as a whole, or to avoid the impression that the elements from which it is composed are heterogeneous in character or of diverse origin.

The logia themselves belong to very different categories. All are more or less short (the longest does not exceed 26 lines), and the majority consist of words spoken by Jesus alone. They take different forms: some are proverbs, precepts, maxims, terse aphorisms or short exhortations. The following may be adduced as examples:

Jesus said: "Whoever has in his hand, to him shall be given; and whoever does not have, from him shall be taken even the little which he has" (cf. Mt. 13:12).

(Logion 41, pl. 88. 16–18)

Jesus said: "Whoever has known the world has found a corpse ($\pi\tau\tilde{\omega}\mu\alpha$), and whoever has found a corpse, of him the world is not worthy."

(Logion 56, pl. 90. 29–33)

Jesus said: "Whoever has known the world has found the body ($\sigma\tilde{\omega}\mu\alpha$), and whoever has found the body, of him the world is not worthy."

(Logion 80, pl. 95. 12–15)

Jesus said: "Whoever knows the All but fails to know himself lacks everything."

(Logion 67, pl. 93. 19f.)

Or:

Jesus said: "Love thy brother as thy soul (=thyself), guard him as the apple of thine eye."

(Logion 25, pl. 86. 10–12)

Jesus said: "Become passers-by" (etet^en^erparage).

(Logion 42, pl. 88. 19)

Jesus said: "Come to me, for easy ($\chi\rho\eta\sigma\tau\acute{o}s$) is my yoke and my lordship is gentle, and you shall find repose for yourselves" (cf. Mt. 11:28–30).

(Logion 90, pl. 96. 16–20)

Jesus said: "Seek and you will find (*cf. Mt. 7:7 and Lk. 11:9*), but those things which you asked me in those days, I did not tell you then; now I desire to tell you, but you do not inquire after them."

(Logion 92, pl. 96. 25–30)

Other logia are beatitudes, or the contrary, e.g.:

Jesus said: "Blessed are the solitary (μοναχός) and elect, for you shall find the Kingdom; because you come from it, (and) you shall go there again."

(Logion 49, pl. 89. 27–30)

Jesus said: "Blessed is the man who has suffered, he has found the Life."

(Logion 58, pl. 91. 7–9)

Jesus said: "Blessed are those who have been persecuted in their heart; these are they who have known the Father in truth. Blessed are the hungry, for the belly of him who desires will be filled" (i.e. "for they will fill their belly with what they desire").

(Logion 69, pl. 93. 24–29)

Jesus said: "Wretched is the body which depends upon a body, and wretched is the soul which depends upon these two."

(Logion 87, pl. 96. 4–7)

Jesus said: "Woe to them, the Pharisees, for they are like a dog sleeping in the manger of oxen, for neither does he eat nor does he allow the oxen to eat."

(Logion 102, pl. 98. 2–5)

Jesus said: "Woe to the flesh which depends upon the soul; woe to the soul which depends upon the flesh."

(Logion 112, pl. 99. 10–12)

Logia of this kind include finally parables, of which I here give a few examples:

Jesus said: "The Kingdom of the [Father] is like a woman who was carrying a jar full of meal. While she was walking (on a) distant road, the handle of the jar broke. The meal streamed out behind her on the road. She did not know (it), she had noticed no accident. After she came into her house, she put down her jar, she found it empty."

(Logion 97, pl. 97. 7–15)

Jesus said: "The Kingdom of the Father is like a man who wishes to kill a powerful man (μεγιστᾶνος). He drew the sword in his house, he stuck it into the wall, in order to know whether his hand would carry through; then he slew the powerful man."

(Logion 98, pl. 97. 15–20)

Beside such sayings there are others—less numerous—which we find inserted at the end of dialogues or in fragmentary conversations. These are replies by Jesus to a question posed by one or more of those present, or find their place in a discussion provoked by a remark of Jesus. For example:

The disciples said to Jesus: "We know that thou wilt go away from us. Who is it who shall be great over us?" Jesus said to them: "Wherever you have come, you will go to James the righteous, for whose sake heaven and earth came into being."

(Logion 12, pl. 82. 25–30)

The disciples said to Jesus: "Tell us how our end will be". Jesus said: "Have you then discovered the beginning, so that you inquire about the end? For where the beginning is, there shall be the end. Blessed is he who shall stand at the beginning, and he shall know the end and he shall not taste death."

(Logion 18, pl. 84. 9–17)

His disciples said to him: "Who art thou that thou shouldst say these things to us?" ⟨Jesus said to them⟩: "From what I say to you, you do not know who I am, but you have become as the Jews, for they love the tree, they hate its fruit, and they love the fruit, they hate the tree" (*cf. Mt. 7:16–20; 12:33; Lk. 6:43f.*).

(Logion 43, pl. 88. 20–26)

His disciples said to him: "Is circumcision profitable (ὠφελεῖ, *cf. Rom. 2:25 and 3:1*) or not?" He said to them: "If it were profitable, their father would beget them circumcised from their mother. But the true circumcision in Spirit has become profitable in every way."

(Logion 53, pl. 90. 18–23)

⟨They saw⟩ a Samaritan carrying a lamb on his way to Judea. He said to his disciples: "(Why does) this man (carry) the lamb with him?" They said to him: "In order that he may kill it and eat it." He said to them: "As long as it is alive, he will not eat it, but (only) if he has killed it and it has become a corpse." They said: "Otherwise he will not be able to do it." He said to them: "You yourselves, seek a place for yourselves in Repose (ἀνάπαυσις), lest you become a corpse (πτῶμα) and be eaten."

(Logion 60, pl. 91. 12–23)

The other speakers are generally the disciples, taken as a body and not identified by name. Here and there however—but very rarely—there occur the names of Simon Peter, Matthew and Thomas (Logion 13, pl. 82. 30–83. 14), or Simon Peter and Mary (*Mariham*: Logion 114, pl. 99. 18–26). One logion begins with a question from Mary (*Mariham*: Logion 21, pl. 84. 23–85. 19). Another consists of an exchange of words between Jesus and Salome (Logion 61, pl. 91.23–34). Two others finally contain the replies of Jesus to the exclamation of an anonymous woman in the crowd (Logion 79, pl. 95. 3–12) and to the request of a man likewise anonymous (Logion 72, pl. 94. 1–6).

In addition, it is convenient to make among the logia here collected a less formal distinction. Many are more or less identical with, or related to, sayings in the canonical Gospels. Nevertheless, with very few exceptions, even those which are most closely related to the canonical logia do not reproduce them literally; they show variations of detail, or are formulated in a very different way, and sometimes the situation too is altered. Some are more developed than the corresponding Synoptic sayings or parables, and may therefore be no more than amplifications, e.g. Logion 47:

Jesus said: "It is impossible for a man to mount two horses and to stretch two bows, and it is impossible for a servant to serve two masters, otherwise he will honour the one and offend the other" (*cf. Mt. 6:24; Lk. 16:13*).

(Logion 47, pl. 89. 12–17)

Or Logion 64:

Jesus said: "A man had guest-friends, and when he had prepared the dinner, he sent his servant to invite the guest-friends. He went to the first, he said to him: 'My master invites thee.' He said: 'I have some claims against some merchants; they will come to me in the evening: I will go and give them my orders. I pray to be excused from the dinner.' He went to another, he said to him: 'My master has invited thee.' He said to him: 'I have bought a house and they request me for a day. I will have no time.' He came to another, he said to him: 'My master invites thee.' He said to him: 'My friend is to be married and I am to arrange a dinner; I shall not be able to come. I pray to be excused from the dinner.' He went to another, he said to him: 'My master invites thee.' He said to him: 'I have bought a farm (κώμη), I go to collect the rent. I shall not be able to come. I pray to be excused.' The servant came, he said to his master: 'Those whom thou hast invited to the dinner have excused themselves.' The master said to his servant: 'Go out to the roads, bring those whom thou shalt find, so that they may dine. Tradesmen and merchants shall not [enter] the places of my Father'." (*cf. Lk. 14:16–24, Mt. 22:1–9*).

(Logion 64, pl. 92. 10–35)

In contrast to these examples, other sayings are shorter and more concise than their Synoptic parallels, e.g.:

Jesus said: "There was a rich man who had much money. He said: 'I will use my money that I may sow and reap and plant and fill my storehouses with fruit, so that I lack nothing'. This was what he thought in his heart. And that night he died. Whoever has ears, let him hear" (*cf. Lk. 12:16–21*).

(Logion 63, pl. 92. 2–10)

In other cases, diverse Synoptic elements appear to have been combined together. A curious example is provided by Logion 16 (pl. 83. 31–84. 5), of which the second half, apart from an expansion at the end, is an obvious abbreviation of Lk. 12:52f., so much so indeed that it is scarcely comprehensible without reference to the Lucan passage:

Jesus said: "Men possibly think that I have come to throw peace upon the world (*cf. Mt. 10:34 and Lk. 12:51*), and they do not know that I have come to throw divisions upon the earth (*Lk. 12:51*), fire (*Lk. 12:49*), sword (*Mt. 10:34*), war. For there shall be five in a house: three shall be against two and two against three, the father against the son and the son against the father (*cf. Lk. 12:52f.*) and they shall stand as solitaries (μοναχός)."

(Logion 16, pl. 83. 31–84. 5)

At other points logia seem to be grouped and combined which in a Synoptic Gospel appear separately and in a different context. Among others, this is the case in logion 79:

A woman from the multitude said to him: "Blessed is the womb which bore thee and the breasts which nourished thee". He said to (her): "Blessed are those who have heard the word of the Father (and) have kept it in truth (*cf.* Lk. *11:27f.*). For there will be days when you will say: 'Blessed is the womb which has not conceived and the breasts which have not suckled' " (*cf. Lk. 23:29*).

(Logion 79, pl. 95. 3–12)

It is not possible here to examine in detail and in all their aspects the differences of this kind which exist between the Logia of our collection and their canonical parallels.[1] Nor is it possible for the moment to suggest a solution for the very difficult problems raised by these differences: are they all the result of revision undertaken by the redactor or compiler of the Gospel of Thomas? Are the sayings in question only more or less free adaptations of the Synoptic logia and therefore, as would appear certain for some of them, composed later than the Gospel of Luke or even, as some indications, less numerous and less obvious, would suggest, than the Gospel of John? Or are they drawn from the same source as the canonical logia, reproducing these sayings more faithfully and in a better or more primitive form? Or do they represent a parallel tradition? This question can and must be raised at least for some of them because of the archaic stamp and the Aramaisms which appear to lie behind them.[2] An answer can only be attained when the long and careful investigations now in process, which must put into application the accepted methods of textual criticism and of Form Criticism, have been completed.

The researches undertaken by G. Quispel have shown that the text of our logia belongs to the 'Western' tradition.[3] He has indicated contacts with the Clementines and the various versions of the Diatessaron, and also with the Saxon Heliand (but on this last cf. Krogmann, *ZNW* 51 (1960) 255ff.), and has argued that the sayings in the Gospel of Thomas derive from a tradition independent of the Synoptics which may go back to the Gospel according to the Hebrews.

[1] Cf. G. Quispel, "The Gospel of Thomas and the New Testament", *Vig. Chr.* 11, 1957, pp. 189–207; G. Garitte–L. Cerfaux, "Les Paraboles du Royaume dans l'"Évangile de Thomas' ", *Le Muséon* 70, 1957, pp. 307–327.

[2] See A. Guillaumont, *Journal Asiatique* ccxlvii (1958) 113ff.

[3] G. Quispel, *Vig. Chr.* 11 (1957) pp. 189ff; 12 (1958) pp. 181ff.; 13 (1959) pp. 87ff.; 14 (1960) pp. 225ff.; *NTS* v (1959) pp. 276ff. But cf. the criticisms of A. F. J. Klijn, *Nov. Test.* 3 (1959) pp. 161ff.

Some of Quispel's arguments have however been subjected to criticism by H. W. Bartsch (*NTS* vi (1960) 249ff.), while on the question of the relation between Thomas and our Gospels the opinions of scholars have differed widely. W. Michaelis and K. Th. Schäfer have emphasized the secondary character of the sayings in Thomas as compared with the Synoptics.[1] C. H. Hunzinger however justly observes[2] that the fact that our present document is a Gnostic work does not preclude the possibility that the author may have made use of genuine early tradition; the structure of the gospel, the variation in the order of the sayings as compared with the Synoptics, and the fact that sayings separate in our Gospels are here re-grouped, all suggest an independent tradition. Moreover some sayings are apparently more primitive, and elements recognized as secondary by Synoptic criticism are here missing.

O. Cullmann (*ThLZ* 85 (1960) cols. 321ff.) had already argued that the collection has passed through a process of development: the final redactor was a Gnostic, who made use not of two independent sources but of an earlier collection and also of the source from which it drew. The earlier collections underlying our present document were already Gnostic, although their Gnosticism was not so strongly marked, and the earliest probably derived from Jewish-Christian circles. That particular sayings go back to a tradition independent of the Synoptics cannot be proved, although there are various factors to suggest it; each must be tested by itself. In Britain R. McL. Wilson has argued independently that the gospel has a history behind it,[3] and that the process may have been more complex than has sometimes been supposed; while there are grounds for assuming some measure of independence, the sayings in Thomas appear often to reflect a later stage in the development of the tradition, and the relationship may indeed vary from one saying to another. The theological ideas of the document have been specially studied by Bertil Gaertner.[4]

All the other logia collected in the Gospel of Thomas are uncanonical, alien to the New Testament writings. Among them are Agrapha already known, or which might have been known, some of them long ago noted, discussed and collected, others hitherto unobserved or ill-identified. These also, thanks to our document, we may now recognize—and this has been my own concern for

[1] W. Michaelis, *Das Thomasevangelium*, Stuttgart 1960; K. Th. Schäfer, *Bible und Leben* 1 (1960), pp. 62ff. A similar position has been taken in America by R. M. Grant, *Vig. Chr.* 13 (1959) pp. 170ff., and in *The Secret Sayings of Jesus* (1960), and by H. K. McArthur, *Exp. Times* lxxi (1960) cols. 286f.

[2] In *Judentum, Urchristentum, Kirche* (Beiheft 26 zur *ZNW*, 1960), pp. 209ff.; also *ThLZ* 85 (1960) cols. 843ff.

[3] R. McL. Wilson, *Studies in the Gospel of Thomas* (London 1960).

[4] B. Gaertner, *The Theology of the Gospel of Thomas* (London 1961).

some years past—in ancient and even mediaeval literature, be it patristic or Manichean, orthodox or heterodox.

For example, apart from a few details and with due regard for the reservations imposed by the serious lacunae in these papyri, all the sayings of Jesus of which the Greek text, more or less incomplete, was provided by the three famous Oxyrhynchus papyri (POx 654, 3rd cent.; POx 1, beginning of 3rd cent.; POx 655, 3rd cent.; 654 and 655 discovered in 1903, 1 in 1897) are to be found, in the same order and arrangement, at the beginning and at two other points in the Coptic collection. Since the text of these logia has been given and the parallels indicated in an earlier section of this work (above, pp. 97ff.), it is sufficient here to present a synoptic table of the corresponding passages:

POx 654 (B. P. Grenfell—A. S. Hunt,   *Gospel of Thomas*
    The Oxyrhynchus Papyri IV, London
    1904, p. 1–22)

1– 3: Prologue	pl. 80. 10–12: Prologue
3– 5: Logion 1	12–14: Logion 1
6– 9: Logion 2	14–19: Logion 2
9–21: Logion 3	pl. 80. 19–81. 5: Logion 3
21–27: Logion 4	pl. 81. 5–10: Logion 4
27–31: Logion 5	10–14: Logion 5
32–39 (40?): Logion 6	14–23: Logion 6
39(40?)–42: Logion 7	23–28: Logion 7
and beyond	

POx 655
    fr. d, col. I. 24–28   pl. 86.   7–10: Logion 24 [1]

POx 1 (Grenfell-Hunt, *Ox. Pap.* I,
    1898, p. 1–3)

verso	1– 4: Logion 1 (beginning	
	missing)	pl. 86. 12–17: Logion 26
	4–11: Logion 2	17–20: Logion 27
	11–21 (and beyond): Logion 3	20–31: Logion 28
recto	1 end of Logion 4	pl. 86. 31–87. 2: Logion 29
	2– 9: Logion 5 (first part)	87. 2– 5: Logion 30
	9–14: Logion 6	5– 7: Logion 31
	15–20: Logion 7	7–10: Logion 32
	20–21 (and beyond): Logion 8	10–18: Logion 33

It should be noted that only the first part of Logion 5 of POx 1 corresponds to Logion 30 of the Gospel of Thomas:

[1] Kasser, *Rev. Théol. et Phil.* 1959, 367 n. 1.

Jesus said: "Where there are three gods, they are gods; where there are two or one, I am with him".

(Logion 30, pl. 87. 2–5)

The second part of the Oxyrhynchus logion however occurs, separated from the first part and combined with a different context, at a later point in the Coptic collection, logion 77:

Jesus said: "I am the Light that is above them all, I am the All, the All came forth from me and the All attained to me. Cleave a (piece of) wood, I am there; lift up the stone and you will find me there."

(Logion 77, pl. 94. 22–28)

POx 655 (Grenfell-Hunt IV, 1904, p. 22–28)	Gospel of Thomas
Col. I. 1–17: Logion 1 (beginning missing)	pl. 87. 24–27 (shorter) : Logion 36
Col. I. 17–23: Logion 2	pl. 87. 27–88. 2: Logion 37
Col. II. 30(?)–38 (and beyond): Logion 3	pl. 88. 2–7: Logion 38
Col. II. 39(?)–50: Logion 4	pl. 88. 7–13: Logion 39
POx 1 recto 6–9: Logion 5 (second part)	pl. 94. 26–28: Logion 77 (second part)

The parallelism between the Greek and the Coptic versions now permits a reconstruction, more or less certain, of the Greek text (cf. the studies of Fitzmyer, *Theol. Studies* 20 (1959) 505ff., and O. Hofius, *Evang. Theol.* xx (1960) 21–42 and 182–192). The differences however make it necessary to believe that we have to deal with two different recensions. It is generally recognized that the Coptic text of Nag Hammadi is based upon a Greek version, but G. Garitte (*Muséon* 73 (1960) 151ff.) has advanced the theory that the Greek version now represented by POx is a translation from the Coptic. This however appears debatable, and has in fact been opposed by Guillaumont (*Muséon* 73 (1960) 325ff.) and J. B. Bauer (in Grant-Freedman, *Geheime Worte Jesu*, Frankfurt am Main 1960, esp. 185–194); but Garitte maintains his position (*Muséon* 73 (1960) 335ff.).

On the basis of the correspondence and agreement which manifestly exist between the two versions, we can now take up a position in regard to the discussion which has hitherto divided scholars on the subject of the three Oxyrhynchus papyri. It was generally admitted that either the papyri 654, 1 and 655 were fragments of

three independent writings or, if papyri 654 and 1 together belonged to the same work, papyrus 655 must be separated from
them and ascribed to a distinct document. Only V. Bartlet maintained that the three papyri were parts of a single work, which he
identified with "an Alexandrine *Gospel according to the Hebrews*".

On the other hand there was disagreement as to the identity of
the work from which the content of each of these papyri might
derive. To mention only the more important hypotheses: in a
sense, B. P. Grenfell and A. S. Hunt, and incidentally V. Taylor,
had already thought of the Gospel of Thomas; nevertheless,
papyrus 654 was connected by some scholars with the Gospel
according to the Hebrews (P. Batiffol; H. Waitz; M. J. Lagrange;
H. G. E. White etc.), by others with the Gospel according to the
Egyptians (Harnack; F. P. Badham; A. Robinson; C. Taylor;
E. Preuschen, etc.). Papyrus 1 in turn was considered to be a
fragment either of the Gospel according to the Hebrews (Batiffol;
White) or of the Gospel according to the Egyptians (Harnack;
Preuschen) or of the Gospel of the Ebionites (Zahn), or of a
florilegium consisting of extracts from various non-canonical
gospels (G. Esser; Hennecke); as for papyrus 655, which was
occasionally connected with the Gospel according to the Hebrews
(Bartlet) or the Gospel of the Egyptians (Hennecke), it was
considered rather to belong to an independent and unidentifiable
collection.[1] The solution now appears quite evident: compared
with the Nag Hammadi collection, the three Oxyrhynchus papyri,
whose mutilated text, thanks to the Coptic parallels, can now be
restored, must be linked together and ascribed to one and the
same work, the Gospel of Thomas.[2]

Other extra-canonical logia in the collection must have been
drawn from apocryphal gospels and in any case recur in the extant
portions of writings of this kind. Logion 2 must certainly be
linked with the Gospel according to the Hebrews:

Jesus said: "Let him who seeks, not cease seeking until he finds,
and when he finds, he will be troubled, and when he has been
troubled, he will marvel and he will reign over the All".

> (Logion 2, pl. 80. 14–19 = POx 654, lines 6–9; cf.
> Clem. Alex., *Strom.* II. 9. 45. 5 and V. 14. 96. 3; in the
> first passage Clement expressly cites the Gospel accord-
> ing to the Hebrews; cf. above, pp. 160ff.)

[1] On all these points cf. H. G. E. White, *The Sayings of Jesus from Oxyrhynchus*,
pp. XLII–LXVII; *Apokr.* 2, pp. 36f.; 49–52; 56.
[2] The connection of the three POx and the Gospel of Thomas had already been
suggested by I. H. A. Michelsen, in *Theologisch Tijdschrift* III, 3 (1905) pp. 153ff. and
VII, 2 (1909) pp. 214ff.

There is probably ground also for assigning to the same Gospel logion 12, already quoted, concerning James the Just, and it seems quite possible that a number of other logia have the same provenance. On the other hand, the following sayings may be ascribed, with more or less certainty, to the Gospel of the Egyptians:

Jesus saw children who were being suckled. He said to his disciples: "These children who are being suckled are like those who enter the Kingdom" (cf. Mt. 18:3; 19:14 and par.). They said to Him: "Shall we then, being children, enter the Kingdom?" Jesus said to them: "When you make the two one, and when you make the inner as the outer and the outer as the inner and the above as the below, and when you make the male and the female into a single one, so that the male will not be male and the female (not) be female, when you make the eyes in the place of an eye, and a hand in the place of a hand, and a foot in the place of a foot, (and) an image (εἰκών) in the place of an image (εἰκών), then shall you enter the Kingdom."

> (Logion 22, pl. 85. 20–35; cf. Clem. Alex., after Julius Cassianus, *Strom*. III. 13. 92; 2 Clem. 12:2–6; Acta Petri 38; Acta Philippi 140; Testamentum Domini p. 65)

His disciples said: "When wilt Thou be revealed to us and when will we see Thee?" Jesus said: "When you take off your clothing without being ashamed, and take your clothes and put them under your feet as the little children and tread on them, then [shall you behold] the Son of the Living (One) and you shall not fear."

> (Logion 37, pl. 87. 27–88. 2 = POx 655, lines 17–30; cf. Clem. Alex. (after Julius Cassianus), *Strom*. III. 13. 92: ὅταν τὸ τῆς αἰσχύνης ἔνδυμα πατήσητε, where however the question is put by Salome; cf. above, p. 168)

Jesus said: "Two will rest on a bed: the one will die, the one will live" (cf. Lk. 17:34). Salome said: "Who art thou, man, and whose son? Thou didst take thy place upon my bench and eat from my table." Jesus said to her: "I am He who is from the Same, to me was given from the things of my Father." ⟨Salome said⟩: "I am thy disciple." ⟨Jesus said⟩: "Therefore I say, if he is the Same, he will be filled with light, but if he is divided, he will be filled with darkness."

(Logion 61, pl. 91. 23–34; cf. the rôle played by Salome as interlocutor of Jesus in the Gospel of the Egyptians)

Jesus said: "When you make the two one, you shall become sons of Man, and when you say: 'Mountain, be moved', it will be moved" (*cf. Mt. 17:20; 21:21; Mk. 11:23*).

(Logion 106, pl. 98. 18–22)

Simon Peter said to them: "Let Mary go out from among us, because women are not worthy of the Life." Jesus said: "See, I shall lead her, so that I will make her male, that she too may become a living spirit (πνεῦμα), resembling you males. For every woman who makes herself male will enter the Kingdom of Heaven."

(Logion 114, pl. 99. 18–26)

Here also it is possible that many other sayings of this kind were borrowed from the Gospel of the Egyptians, or are common to this gospel and that of Thomas.

Finally, I append a list of those logia which are found, in whole or in part, in traces or in echoes, scattered here and there in the works of the Fathers, in Manichean writings, and in the remains of Gnostic or heretical literature. This list is deliberately incomplete, and of necessity provisional; I include only the most certain results of an investigation entirely personal, and one which must be continued. The content of this list will certainly require to be enlarged, by myself or by others. Moreover I would observe that in setting out these sayings, or parts of sayings, which are common to our collection and to other documents, I do not mean to indicate or suggest that they must all, when they recur elsewhere, be considered to derive from the Gospel of Thomas. We must also reckon with the possibility, which in some cases amounts to a certainty, that on one side and on the other there has been borrowing from the same sources.

Prologue and Logion 1 (pl. 80. 10–14; cited above, p. 285): cf. Mani, *Epistula Fundamenti*, in Augustine, *c. Epist. Fundam.* 11 and *c. Felicem*. I. 1; fictitious letter of Mani to Mār Ammō, Turfan fragment T II D II 134, in SB Berlin 1934, p. 856.

Logion 2 (pl. 80. 14–19; cited above, p. 297): cf. 2 Clem. 5:5 (?); POx 654, lines 6–9; Clem. Alex. *Strom.* II. 9. 45. 5 and V. 14. 96. 3; Acts of Thomas c. 136, p. 243. 8–10 Bonnet; Pistis Sophia c. 100, p. 161. 24–28 Schmidt-Till, and c. 102, p. 164. 23–27.

Logion 4 (pl. 81. 5–10; cited above, pp. 283f.): cf. Hippol. (after the Naassenes), *Ref.* V. 7. 20; Coptic Manichean Psalm-book p. 192. 2–3 Allberry.

Logion 5:

Jesus said: "Know what is in thy sight, and what is hidden from thee will be revealed to thee. For there is nothing hidden which will not be manifest"

(pl. 81. 10–14): cf. POx 654, lines 27–31 (where the saying is expanded by another clause: "and nothing buried which will not rise again"); Coptic Manichean *Kephalaia* LXV, vol. I, p. 163. 28f. (without reference to resurrection); Christian burial shroud (5th or 6th cent.) from Behnesa (ancient Oxyrhynchus), acquired in 1953 and in my possession (v. H.-Ch. Puech, *RHR* 147, 1955, 126–129): it reproduces the final clause of POx 654 (λέγει 'Ιησοῦς· οὔκ ἐστιν τεθαμμένον ὃ οὔκ ἐγερθήσεται†).

Logion 11 (pl. 82. 19–22; cited above, p. 284): cf. the Naassenes in Hippolytus *Ref.* V. 8. 32; Ev. Philip. 121. 19–28 Labib.

Logion 13, end (pl. 83. 13–14: cited above, p. 287): cf. (?) Gospel of Bartholomew (Greek version) II. 5.

Logion 17:

Jesus said: "I will give you what eye has not seen and what ear has not heard and what hand has not touched and (what) has not arisen in the heart of man"

(pl. 84. 5–9): cf. 1 Cor. 2:9, but here attributed to Jesus. Cf. A. Resch, *Agrapha*, 1st ed., 102f. (Logion 16), 154–167, 281f.; E. Haenchen, "Das Buch Baruch", *ZThK* 50, 1953, 139 note 2; and especially Acts of Peter 39 (10) (*Aa* 1, p. 98. 7–10), where the saying is likewise ascribed to Jesus. An exact parallel occurs in the Manichean Turfan fragment M 789 (*Abh. pr. Akad. d. Wissensch.* 1904, *Anhang, phil.-hist. Abh.* II, p. 68): "I will give you what you have not seen with your eyes, nor heard with your ears, nor grasped with your hand" (cf. M 551, ib. p. 67f.). Cf. Prigent, *Theol. Zeitschr.* 14 (1958) 416ff.

Logion 19 begins:

Jesus said: "Blessed is he who was before he came into being" (pl. 84. 17–19): cf. Irenaeus, *Demonstratio* c. 43 (J. P. Smith, *St. Irenaeus, Proof of the Apostolic Preaching*, Westminster–London 1952, translation p. 75, commentary p. 182; A. Resch, *Agrapha*, 2nd ed., p. 285f.); Lactantius, *Div. Inst.* IV. 8. On these two passages cf. Hennecke *Apokr.* 2, p. 386.

Logion 22 (pl. 85. 20–35: cited above, p. 298): cf. 2 Clem. 12:2–6; Julius Cassianus, in Clem. Alex., *Strom*. III. 13. 92; Acts of Peter 38; Acts of Philip 140; Acts of Thomas 147; Testamentum Domini p. 64. 16–18; Did. Syr. xxvi (136. 28–30 Achelis); Ev. Philip. 115. 30–34 Labib. On this logion, see Resch, *Agrapha*, 1st ed., 109 (logion 30), 195–204, 287, 416f. (Apocryphon 44).

Logion 27 begins:

"If you fast (νηστεύειν) not from the world (κόσμος), you will not find the Kingdom"

(pl. 86. 17–19) POx 1 verso, lines 4–8: cf. Clem. Alex., *Strom*. III. 15. 99. 4 and *Eclog. proph*. 14. 1. On this logion see J. Jeremias, *Unknown Sayings of Jesus* (ET London 1957) p. 13, 25.

Logion 30 (pl. 87. 2–5; cited above, p. 296) =POx 1 recto, lines 2–6: cf. (??) Clem. Alex., *Strom*. III. 10. 68; Ephraem, *Evangelii concordantis expositio* XIV. 24, p. 144. 13–16 Leloir (A. Resch, *Agrapha*, 1st ed., 295f.; H. G. E. White, *The Sayings of Jesus* 36–38).

Logion 38:

Jesus said: "Many times have you desired (ἐπιθυμεῖν) to hear these words which I say to you, and you have no other from whom to hear them. There will be days when you will seek me (and) you will not find me"

(pl. 88. 2–7): the first part of this logion occurs in three different forms, which all presuppose the same original: 1) Irenaeus, *adv. haer*. I. 13. 2 H, on the Marcosians ("Often have I desired to hear one of those words, and have had none to tell it to me") =Epiph. *Pan*. 34. 18. 13 (πολλάκις ἐπεθύμησα ἀκοῦσαι ἕνα τῶν λόγων τούτων, καὶ οὐκ ἔσχον τὸν ἐροῦντα) (on this text cf. Resch, *Agrapha*, 1st ed., 397, Apocryphon 25; Harnack SB Berlin 1904, 187f.); 2) Acta Johannis c. 98 (Jesus to John on the Mount of Olives at the moment of the Crucifixion: "John, some-one must hear this from me; for I have need of one who will hear it"); 3) Psalm of Heraclides in the Coptic Manichean Psalm-book, p. 187. 28f. (words spoken by Jesus to Peter on the Mount of Olives, of which Mary Magdalene is to remind him: "I have something to say, I have none to whom to say it").

On the second part of the logion cf. Cyprian, *Testimoniorum libri tres ad Quirinum* III. 29, p. 143. 2–4 Hartel (a witness contained only in Cod. Würzburgensis 145): Likewise in Baruch (ms.: barach): "For a time will come, and ye shall seek me, both you and those who shall come after you, to hear the word of wisdom and of insight, and shall not find" (cf. Hennecke *Apokr*. 2, p. 390).

Logion 48:

Jesus said: "If two make peace with each other in this one house, they shall say to the mountain: 'Be moved', and it shall be moved" (pl. 89. 24–27): cf. the peculiar reading of Mt. 18:19 in H. Achelis and J. Flemming, *Die syrische Didaskalia* (*TU* 25, 2 = NF 10. 2), Leipzig 1904, p. 345: "Duo si convenerint in unum et dixerint monti huic: tolle et mitte te in mari, fiet".

Logion 52:

His disciples said to him: "Twenty-four prophets spoke in Israel and they all spoke about (lit.: in) thee". He said to them: "You have dismissed the Living (One) who is before you and you have spoken about the dead" (*cf. Lk. 24:5*)

(pl. 90. 12–18): This logion is reproduced by Augustine in his *Contra adversarium legis et prophetarum* II. 4. 14 (*PL* XLII 647), from an anonymous Marcionite or neo-Marcionite tractate widely read about 420 on the *Piazza Maritima* of Carthage; its provenance he says he does not know (testimonium de scripturis nescio quibus apocryphis): "But when the apostles (so he said) asked what was to be thought of the Jewish prophets who, as men assumed, announced His coming as something relating to the past" (so Jeremias, *Unknown Sayings of Jesus* p. 74 and n. 1; usual translation: who, as men assumed, in the past proclaimed His coming), "our Lord answered, under the impression that they still cherished such opinions: 'You have rejected the Living One who stands before you, and talked fables (prattled) about the dead'". On this logion see Jeremias, *Unknown Sayings of Jesus* (ET London 1957) p. 74ff.; cf. Hennecke, *Apokr.* 2, p. 65; James p. 20; Santos p. 72.

Logion 62:

Jesus said: "I will tell my mysteries to those [who are worthy of my] mysteries. [What] thy right (hand) will do, let not thy left (hand) know what it does" (*cf. Mt. 6:3*)

(pl. 91. 34–92. 2); cf. (?) Logion 17 in Resch, *Agrapha*, 1st ed., 103f. and 282.

Logion 69 (pl. 93. 24–29): cf. "Epistle of Mani", in Böhlig, *Bull. soc. arch. copte* xv (1958–60) 57 n. 5.

Logion 74:

He said: "Lord, there are many around the cistern, but nobody in the cistern"

(pl. 94. 9–11): cf. the (Ophite?) Heavenly Dialogue in Orig. *c.*

apGGsefires

Cels. VIII. 15 (II p. 232. 14–15 Koetschau) and 16 (II p. 233. 26–27): "How are there so many about the well, and no one in the well!" On this text see Resch, *Agrapha*, 1st ed., p. 444 (Apocryphon 79).

Logion 82:

Jesus said: "Whoever is near to me is near to the fire, and whoever is far from me is far from the Kingdom"

(pl. 95. 17–19) = Orig. *in Jerem. hom.* XX. 3 in Jerome's translation (*PG* XIII 531 D–532 A): "I have read somewhere an alleged word of the Saviour, and I ask whether someone imagined the figure of the Saviour or called the words to mind, or whether the saying is true. The Saviour at any rate said: 'He who is near to me is near the fire; he who is far from me, is far from the Kingdom'"; Didymus of Alexandria (after Origen), in Ps. 88:8 (*PG* XXXIX 1488 D); διό φησιν ὁ σωτήρ· ὁ ἐγγύς μου ἐγγὺς τοῦ πυρός. ὁ δὲ μακρὰν ἀπ' ἐμοῦ μακρὰν ἀπὸ τῆς βασιλείας; Syrian anti-Marcionite explanation of parables, preserved in Armenian (German translation in J. Schäfers, *Eine altsyrische anti-markionitische Erklärung von Parabeln des Herrn*, Münster 1917, p. 79): "That is what our life-giving Redeemer said: 'He who draws nigh to me, draws nigh to the fire; he who moves away from me, moves away from life'". On this logion see Resch, *Agrapha*, 1st ed. p. 98 and 142 (logion 5); Harnack, *Der kirchengeschichtliche Ertrag der exegetischen Arbeiten des Origenes*, *TU* 42, 3, 1918, p. 20 and 42, 4, 1919, p. 41; Hennecke, *Apokr.* 2, p. 35; Jeremias, *Unknown Sayings of Jesus* (ET 1957) 54ff.; J. B. Bauer, *Theol. Zeitschr.* 15 (1959) 446–450.

Logion 114 (pl. 99. 18–26; cited above p. 299): cf. *Excerpta ex Theodoto* 21. 3 (cf. 79) and Heracleon in Orig., in Joh. VI. 20 (12) § 111; the mediaeval Cathari, in Döllinger, *Beiträge zur Sektengeschichte des Mittelalters*, Zweiter Theil, Munich 1890, pp. 151f., 176f., 191, 219. On the (conjectured) use of certain apocryphal gospels among the Cathari in the Middle Ages see F. P. Badham and F. C. Conybeare, "Fragments of an Ancient (?Egyptian) Gospel used by the Cathars of Albi", *Hibbert Journal* 11, 1913, 805–818.

If we subtract from the logia collected in the Gospel of Thomas those which were in this way already known or may now be more or less clearly rediscovered elsewhere, there remains a good number which in the present state of research deserve to be described as unpublished and completely new. Some examples of these hitherto unknown sayings have been presented above. Some are aphorisms or parables in the style of the Synoptic Gospels; others present traits or presuppose doctrines of a much more esoteric or Gnostic character, e.g. logion 19:

303

Jesus said: "Blessed is he who was before he came into being (see above, p. 300). If you become disciples to me and hear my words, these stones will minister (διακονεῖν) to you (*cf. Mt. 3:9; Lk. 3:8?*). For you have five trees in Paradise, which are unmoved in summer (or) in winter and their leaves do not fall"

(Cf. C. Schmidt-W. Till, *Koptisch-Gnostische Schriften*, 1 Bd., 2nd ed., Berlin 1954, index p. 402 s.v. "Bäume, die fünf im Lichtschatze"; Fragment of a dialogue between Jesus and John, below, pp. 331ff.; for Manicheism, references in H.-Ch. Puech, *Le Manichéisme*, Paris 1949, p. 159 n. 285).

"Whoever knows them will not taste death" (*cf. Mt. 16:28; Mk. 9:1; Lk. 9:27; Jn. 8:52*).

(Logion 19, pl. 84. 17–25)

Or Logion 50:

Jesus said: "If they say to you: 'From where have you originated?', say to them: 'We have come from the Light, where the Light has originated through itself. It [stood] and it [revealed itself] in their image'. If they say to you: '(Who) are you?', say: 'We are His sons and we are the elect of the Living Father'. If they ask you: 'What is the sign of your Father in you?', you say to them: 'It is a movement and a rest (ἀνάπαυσις)'."

(Logion 50, pl. 89. 30–90. 7)

Or again, logia 83 and 84, which follow the same line as that just mentioned:

Jesus said: "The images are manifest to man and the Light which is within them (*sc. the images*) is hidden in the Image of the Light of the Father. He will manifest himself and his Image is concealed by his Light".

(Logion 83, pl. 95. 19–24)

Jesus said: "When you see your likeness, you rejoice. But when you see your images which came into existence before you, (which) neither die nor are manifested, how much will you bear!"

(Logion 84, pl. 95. 24–29)

Or Logion 111, the strange construction of which is remarkable:

Jesus said: "The heavens will be rolled up (*cf. Isa. 34:4; Rev. 6:14*) and the earth in your presence, and he who lives on the Living (One) shall neither see death nor ⟨fear⟩, because Jesus says 'Whoever finds himself, of him the world is not worthy'."

(Logion 111, pl. 99. 6–10)

The number of these unpublished logia is however too great for them all to be cited here; nor is it possible at the moment to deal in other than summary and conjectural fashion with the numerous problems raised by the new document and the analysis which has just been given.

It is difficult to assign any very precise date to the Gospel of Thomas or, more exactly, to the collection of 'oracles' or words of Jesus transmitted under this title from a period which cannot be determined, at latest the beginning of the 3rd century.

The work gives the impression of a compilation or anthology incorporating diverse elements, which were borrowed probably from sources of varying origin and of different ages, or perhaps in part composed, or at any rate revised, by the author of the apocryphon. The composition of collections of this kind, which may be readily enlarged, compressed or altered at the whim of the compiler, is subject, or at least was probably subject, to constant change. We have in fact the proof that there were different recensions of our work, and we cannot consider that which we now possess, thanks to the Nag Hammadi papyrus, as either the first or the final version. It is hazardous, and probably indeed misguided, to seek to visualize its original form and determine its origin. At most one will be inclined to place the earliest redaction of our gospel about 140, or perhaps even a little later.

This question is however secondary. More important than the dating of the collection itself is that of its constituent elements, or more generally of the sources and the documents from which the groups of sayings here combined and utilized may derive. Only when we have first attempted to distinguish, enumerate, and more or less hypothetically identify these sources or documents, shall we be in a position to pronounce with less uncertainty on the subject of the date of a collection which, taken as a whole, appears to be neither entirely original nor completely homogeneous. It is for the researches now in progress, or still to be undertaken, to solve the problem or facilitate its solution. At the moment it would appear that beside logia of comparatively late formation our collection contains others of which the origin might go very far back.

With the same reserves I should say that the Gospel of Thomas does not seem to me to be either exclusively or originally the work of a Gnostic. Undoubtedly some passages have a Gnostic ring, and there is scarcely anything which could not be adapted, or has not been adapted, to Gnostic doctrine. Nevertheless we must take account of a fact which I have been able to establish on the basis of certain indications, slight but of sufficient weight: there existed at least two recensions, two versions, of this work, one of which was read by orthodox Christians—as late as the 5th or 6th century, as the inscription on the shroud from Oxyrhynchus mentioned above suggests—while the other circulated in Gnostic and Manichean circles.

So far as we can compare the two versions, the 'heterodox' seems to have differed from the 'Christian' in changes of detail and in certain omissions designed to remove the inconsistency between a saying attributed to Christ and this or that Gnostic dogma. In particular, as we have noted above in passing, logion 5 has been curtailed both in the Coptic text from Nag Hammadi and in one of the Manichean *Kephalaia* in which it is quoted: as is shown by the two Greek parallels (POx 654 and the shroud from Behnesa), it affirmed the resurrection of the body. On the other hand, the copyist of Nag Hammadi has allowed certain details to stand which would be difficult to explain if the document had originally been composed by a pure Gnostic: the exaltation of James the Just (Logion 12), several Jewish-Christian traits, perhaps also the statement that Jesus 'appeared in the flesh' (Logion 28, pl. 86. 22 = POx 1, verso, line 13).

These points, it is true, are open to question: James occupies a prominent place in several of the writings of the Gnostic library of Nag Hammadi; one might think of a Judaizing or Jewish-Christian Gnosis; the statement of logion 28, instead of asserting the reality of the incarnation, might possibly, as P. Batiffol thought (*Rev. Bibl.* 6, 1897, 507f.), imply on the contrary a Docetic conception. Again, perhaps we might reverse the relation between the two versions and suppose that it was the 'orthodox' redactor who corrected the 'heterodox' version with the help of additions. Despite all this the interpretation of the facts which I have suggested seems to me more probable. This does not mean of course that the 'Gnostic' redactor confined himself to a few omissions here and there. He must at other points have inserted phrases, revised a passage more or less completely, or introduced into the collection logia forged by himself or by his fellow-believers. Even if these modifications were more important and the inter-polations more numerous than appears to be the case, it remains probable, taking everything into account, that the 'heterodox' version of the Gospel of Thomas, as it is presented by the Nag Hammadi manuscript and the Manichean quotations, is only a revision of the 'orthodox' or 'more orthodox' version. It must therefore be the later. Perhaps there is ground for associating this first version in some sense with a group which professed that rather bizarre Christianity, strongly tinged with Encratism, which was widespread in Syria and Egypt in the 2nd century.

I leave aside the question of the 'authenticity' of the words of Jesus transmitted by the new collection;[1] it can be raised only for some among them, after the mass of the material has been sifted and each saying closely studied in regard to its origin and form. Beyond a doubt many even now appear spurious.

It cannot be too often repeated: the complete text of this gospel has only recently become accessible and made known, and all the problems to which it gives rise are still in the balance. What has been said here is intended simply to show the complexity of these problems and the interest which they merit, and to emphasize the immense importance of the document which the Nag Hammadi discovery has now presented to us.

Additional literature: E. Haenchen, *Th. Rundschau* 27 (1961) 147ff. – H. W. Montefiore, *New Testament Studies* 7 (1961) 220ff. – A. J. B. Higgins, *Novum Testamentum* 4 (1960) 292ff. – A. F. J. Klijn, *Vig. Chr.* 15 (1961) 146ff. – B. Gärtner, *The Theology of the Gospel of Thomas*, London and New York 1961. – E. Haenchen, *Die Botschaft des Thomasevangeliums*, Berlin 1961. – R. Kasser, *L'Évangile selon Thomas*, Neuchâtel 1961.

3. *The Book of Thomas the Athlete*

In the volume of the Nag Hammadi library (Codex III of my classification) which contains as its second and third works the Gospel of Thomas and that of Philip, the seventh and last place is occupied by a document described in the colophon as "The Book of Thomas the Athlete which he wrote for the Perfect" (*pdschōme ᵉnthōmas pathlētēs efschai ᵉnᵉteleios*); it begins as follows:

The secret words (*ᵉnschadsche ethēp*) spoken by the Saviour (σωτήρ) to Judas Thomas ('Ιούδας Θωμᾶς), and which I have written down, I, Matthew (Ματθαῖος), who heard them while they spoke together.

Literature: J. Doresse, "Nouveaux écrits coptes", *Vig. Chr.* 3, 1949, p. 134; id., "Une bibliothèque gnostique copte", *Acad. Royale de Belgique, Bull. de la classe des Lettres*, 5ème série, t. XXXV, pp. 440f.; id., *Les livres secrets des gnostiques d'Égypte*, Paris 1958, p. 243f. (ET 1960, 225f.); H.-Ch. Puech, "Les nouveaux écrits gnostiques", *Coptic Studies in Honor of W. E. Crum* (=*Bull. of the Byzantine Institute* 2), Boston 1950, p. 105 and 117–120; id., "Découverte d'une bibliothèque gnostique", *Enc. Fr.*, t. XIX, Paris 1957, fasc. 19. 42–9.

Unfortunately this work has so far remained almost inaccessible, and the little that is known of it is not enough to allow us to form

[1] Cf. J. B. Bauer in *Verbum Domini* 37 (1959) 129–146 and in van Unnik, etc., *Evangelien aus dem Nilsand* (Frankfurt 1960) 108ff.

a satisfactory idea of its character and content. We can only say that it consists of a dialogue between Jesus and Thomas (so at least the opening suggests). From the first the Saviour turns to His 'brother' Thomas, who is called His 'twin brother' (*soeisch*) and 'companion' (*schbᵉr*).[1] He promises him certain revelations, and the apostle requests Him to impart them to him before His Ascension (ἀνάλημψις). The dialogue therefore takes place, as in the gospels of a Gnostic type, between the Resurrection and the Ascension; but for the present the continuation remains unknown. Towards the end the work deals with eschatological questions. The last two pages reproduce a long discourse by Jesus, which closes with an "Amen!" It is divided into two parts, of which the first contains threats and maledictions ("Woe to you who . . .") and the second benedictions ("Blessed are ye who . . ."). The style is rather Gnostic and the theme Encratite: condemnation of the flesh, of womanhood, of sexuality; promise of a future rest in the kingdom of heaven, an ἀνάπαυσις, which will be ἀπάθεια, impassibility. It has been suggested that the Book of Thomas should be identified with the Gospel or Traditions of Matthias, but this is open to dispute. On this see below, pp. 312f.

4. *The Gospel according to Matthias. The traditions of Matthias*

A Gospel according to Matthias or of Matthias (τὸ εὐαγγέλιον κατὰ Ματθίαν, *Euangelium secundum Matthiam, Euangelium nomine Matthiae*) stands beside the Gospel according to Thomas on the list of heterodox works drawn up by Origen (*in Luc. hom.* I, p. 5. 14 Rauer) and Eusebius of Caesarea (*H.E.* III. 25. 6). It is also mentioned by Ambrose (*Expositio euangelii Lucae* I. 2, p. 11. 1 Schenkl), Jerome (*Comm. in Matth.* prol., PL XXVI 17A), the Venerable Bede (*In Luc. evang. expos.* I, prol., PL XCII 307C), the so-called Decretum Gelasianum 3. 1 (*TU* 38, 4, p. 11), and the seventh-century Byzantine Index known as "The Index of the sixty books" (above, pp. 51f.). On the other hand we know of "Traditions" (παραδόσεις) ascribed to Matthias or current under his name; these were probably recorded in a separate document.

Three quotations from these "Traditions" are preserved by Clement of Alexandria:

1. The beginning thereof (*sc. of the knowledge of the truth*) is to wonder at things, as Plato says in the Theaetetus and Matthias in the Traditions when he warns "Wonder at what is present"

---

[1] Cf. in Manicheism and according to the Fihrist al-'Ulum of Ibn an-Nadim (G. Flügel, *Mani*, Leipzig 1862, p. 84): "at-Ta'um, which in Nabatean means the same as companion" = Coptic *saïsch*, Arabic *qurīn*: C. Schmidt–H. J. Polotsky in SB Berlin 1933, p. 72; H. H. Schaeder in *Gnomon* 1933, pp. 351f.; G. Widengren, *The Great Vohu Manah and the Apostle of God*, Uppsala–Leipzig 1945, pp. 25–29.

GOSPELS UNDER THE NAME OF AN APOSTLE

(θαύμασον τὰ παρόντα), establishing this as the first step to the knowledge of things beyond (τῆς ἐπέκεινα γνώσεως).

> (Clem. Alex., *Strom.* II. 9. 45. 4; II, p. 137. 1–3 Staehlin)

2. They (the Gnostics) say that Matthias also taught as follows: "To strive with the flesh and misuse it (σαρκὶ μάχεσθαι καὶ παραχρῆσθαι), without yielding to it in any way to unbridled lust, but to increase the soul through faith and knowledge (διὰ πίστεως καὶ γνώσεως)".

> (Clem. Alex., *Strom.* III. 4. 26. 3; II, p. 208. 7–9 Staehlin = Euseb. *H.E.* III. 29. 4, where the Syriac version has the variant *Tholmai* instead of Matthias)

3. They say that Matthias the Apostle in the Traditions explains at every turn: "If the neighbour of one of the chosen (ἐκλεκτοῦ) sin, then has the elect sinned; for if he had so conducted himself as the Word (ὁ λόγος) commends, the neighbour would have had such awe at his way of life that he would not have fallen into sin".

> (Clem. Alex., *Strom.* VII. 13. 82. 1; III, p. 58. 20–23 Staehlin)

Perhaps we should follow the suggestion of Zahn (*Gesch. d. ntl. Kanons* II pp. 752f.), and assign to the Traditions a further passage from Clement of Alexandria: a parallel to Luke 19:1–10, in which the tax-gatherer is named not Zacchaeus but Matthias:

4. (?) Zacchaeus then (but some say Matthias), a chief tax-gatherer, when he heard that the Lord had seen fit to be with him, (said) "Behold, the half of my goods I give in alms, O Lord; and if I have extorted anything from any man, I restore it fourfold". Whereupon the Saviour also said "The Son of man is come today, and has found that which was lost".

> (Clem. Alex., *Strom.* IV. 6. 35. 2; II, p. 263. 30–264. 3 Staehlin)[1]

Apart from the second, these citations have manifestly no marked Gnostic character. The word *gnosis* indeed appears in the first and second fragments, but in the first it belongs to the context, where it has been introduced by Clement, and in the second,

---

[1] It would be hazardous to link with these citations, as Klostermann suggests, with great reserves (*Apokrypha* II, *KlT* 8, 3rd ed., Berlin 1929, p. 18), a passage from Haimo of Auxerre, *in Hebr.* 13:4 (*PL* CXVII 930 A): "Hence the blessed Matthew (l. Matthias?) the Apostle says in a certain place that lawful wedlock and the bed undefiled (Heb. 13:4) have in a sense something vile, in the mingling of seed, but that they do not have the stain of sin".

309

where it is linked with πίστις, it need not strictly speaking have the specific technical sense. The theory presupposed by the first fragment, which makes of admiration or astonishment (θαῦμα) the first step or first stage in the progressive advance to contemplation or to the supreme knowledge, is more or less commonplace, a τόπος of ancient philosophy (cf. for example, in addition to Plato, *Theaetetus* 155 D, to which Clement appeals, *Epinomis* 986 C–D; Aristotle, *Metaph.* A 2, 982b; Plotinus, *Enn.* III. 8. 10). At most one might observe that it occurs in Gnostic writings, or works read by Gnostics: in the Corpus Hermeticum (IV. 2; XIV. 4; cf. Asclepius 13) and in the Gospel of Thomas (Logion 2, pl. 80. 14–19 Labib = POx 654 lines 6–9: "Let him who seeks, not cease seeking until he finds, and when he finds, he will be troubled, and when he has been troubled, he will marvel").

Nevertheless, it should be noted that Clement (*Strom.* II. 9. 45. 5, more fully in V. 14. 96. 3) quotes a saying which corresponds to Logion 2 of the Gospel of Thomas, and compares it with our fragment 1 of the Traditions; now of this logion he says expressly that it derived from the Gospel of the Hebrews. The editor of the sayings-collection current under the name of Thomas seems therefore to have taken it from the Gospel according to the Hebrews; thus it need not necessarily be of Gnostic origin. Further, the precept cited by Clement from the Traditions of Matthias ("Wonder at what is present") recalls logion 5 of the Gospel of Thomas (pl. 81. 10–14 = POx 654. 27–31; Manichean *Kephalaia* LXV, pp. 163. 28f.): "Know what is in thy sight, and what is hidden from thee will be revealed to thee. For there is nothing hidden which will not be manifest". Perhaps this logion also derives from the Gospel according to the Hebrews, and thus proves nothing for the Gnostic origin of the Traditions.

In the third fragment of the Traditions ἐκλεκτός (elect) is indeed probably a Gnostic term (Valentinian or Basilidian: cf. Clem. Alex., *Strom.* VI. 6. 53. 4); but it might here just as well be a synonym for 'Christian' (cf. 1 Pet. 2:9). In the second fragment the interpretation of παραχρῆσθαι remains ambiguous. The verb means either (construed, as in our passage, with the dative) 'to make a bad use of', 'to misuse', or (with the genitive or accusative) 'to make little of', 'to despise'. If we take it in the first sense, the maxim would recommend carnal freedom, and in particular sexual licence. It would then conform to the libertine doctrines ascribed, among other Gnostics, to the Basilidians (Agrippa Castor, in Euseb. *H.E.* IV. 7. 7; Irenaeus *adv. haer.* I. 19. 3 H.; Clem. Alex., *Strom.* III. 1. 1–3, 4; Epiphanius *Pan.* 24. 3. 7; Filastrius *haer.* 32. 7) and the Nicolaitans, who according to Clement of Alexandria (*Strom.* II. 20. 118. 2f.; III. 4. 26. 3 =

Euseb. *H.E.* III. 29. 2) appealed precisely to the text of the Traditions of Matthias now in question.

But the fact that Gnostics employed this text and understood it in such a way proves neither the Gnostic origin of the passage nor the correctness of such an interpretation, the more so since Clement himself considers it a mis-use. Just as he recognizes (*Strom.* III. 3. 3–4) that the libertinism of the Basilidians of his own time was a deviation from the original and strictly moral doctrine of the founder of the sect, so he maintains in the texts mentioned that the Nicolaitans had falsely interpreted a saying of Nicolaus in such a way as to favour their ethical licentiousness, whereas Nicolaus himself understood it in an ascetic sense, as a command to despise the things of the flesh and abstain therefrom. The ambiguity therefore remains. To declare, as for example do Bardenhewer (*Litg.* I, 2nd ed. p. 530) and A. de Santos Otero (Santos p. 62), that the Traditions of Matthias, of which our four fragments are, with varying degrees of certainty, the only known extracts, derive from Gnostic circles, is to go beyond the evidence; it is only possible, or at most probable.

Finally, Clement of Alexandria and Hippolytus of Rome speak of a certain secret tradition inherited from Matthias by the Basilidians. The first testimony is somewhat obscure. Clement (*Strom.* VII. 17. 108. 1; III p. 76. 20–24 Staehlin), quoting examples of heresies which bear the name of their founders, writes: "Of the sects, some are called from a (personal) name, as that of Valentinus and of Marcion and of Basilides, even if they boast to present the doctrine of Matthias; for as there was (only) one doctrine of all the apostles, so (there is only) the (one) tradition". Hippolytus (*Ref.* VII. 20. 1, p. 195. 19–24 Wendland) is more precise and much more instructive: "Basilides and Isidore, the true son and disciple of Basilides, say that Matthias spake to them secret words (λόγοι ἀπόκρυφοι) which he heard from the Saviour when he was taught in private (cf. VII. 20. 5, p. 196. 13f.: 'something of the secret words of Matthias'). Let us see, then, how manifestly Basilides and Isidore also and all their crew calumniate not simply Matthias only but also even the Saviour Himself". Probably these secret teachings, transmitted presumably under the name of Matthias, should be linked with the traditions vouched for by the same apostle.

The problem is thus to know whether or not these alleged Traditions are identical with the Gospel of Matthias mentioned in other sources. The most widely different solutions have been proposed. Harnack (*Litg.* II. 1, pp. 595–598) believed that two distinct works were involved. On the contrary, Zahn (*Gesch. d. ntl. Kanons* II, pp. 751–761), Bardenhewer (*Litg.* I, 2nd ed., pp. 529f.), James (p. 12) and G. Bonaccorsi (*Vangeli Apocrifi* I, Florence 1948, pp. XVIf. and 23–31) decide more or less confidently for their identity. Others, like O. Stählin ("Die altchristliche griechische Literatur", in W. C. Christ, *Gesch. der griech. Literatur*, II Teil, 2 Hälfte, 6th ed., Munich 1924, p. 1192 n. 3) or J. Tixeront (*Précis de Patrologie*, Paris 1928, p. 83), would incline rather towards distinguishing the works. Finally, some (e.g. A. Puech, *Histoire de la littérature grecque chrétienne* I, Paris 1928, p. 169) are content to express their hesitation.

Zahn and Bardenhewer draw their chief argument from fragment 4: its parallelism with Lk. 19:1–10 proves that the Traditions contained accounts after the fashion of the Gospels. But still we should require to be certain that the fragment really did belong to the παραδόσεις. It would perhaps be tempting to recall the Gnostic tradition reported by the Pistis Sophia (c. 42f.; p. 44. 19–45. 19 Schmidt), according to which Jesus after His Resurrection entrusted to Matthew—or rather, as Zahn conjectures (II, pp. 758f.) to Matthias—as well as to Philip and to Thomas the task of reporting all His acts and recording all His words. If we accept Zahn's suggestion (approved by Bardenhewer *Litg.* I, 2nd ed., p. 530, but rejected by Harnack, *Litg.* II. 1, pp. 597f.), then Matthias would appear as the author of a gospel, or better still of a gospel parallel to those of Philip and of Thomas (now re-discovered: above, pp. 271ff. and 278ff.), which like the latter of these may have contained sayings or 'secret words' of Jesus, transmitted in secret 'Traditions'. This would agree fairly well with the testimony of Hippolytus, but remains nevertheless uncertain.

May we hope that—as has already been suggested[1]—one of the writings found at Nag Hammadi will reopen the question, and allow us to reach a better solution? The opening words of the Book of Thomas the Athlete, according to the translation communicated by J. Doresse, run: "Secret words, spoken by the Saviour to Judas Thomas and written down by Matthias (sic!)". This would in fact lead us to believe the work to be no other than a collection of the λόγοι ἀπόκρυφοι mentioned by Hippolytus, the gospel whose compilation Christ entrusted, according to the Pistis Sophia, to Matthias. It would stand beside the Gospels of Philip and Thomas, which are after all bound up in the same codex with it. It might in consequence be identical with the Traditions or the Gospel of Matthias. To confirm or disprove such a hypothesis, however, we should require to be in a position to establish whether the passages quoted by Clement occur in the new document. Unfortunately it remains as yet entirely unpublished, and I know only a few pages of it. The reading of these,

[1] H.-Ch. Puech, in *Coptic Studies in Honor of W. E. Crum*, Boston 1950, pp. 119f.

and a very superficial and incomplete examination of the part of the manuscript which contains the work, would make me inclined today to abandon the hypothesis. One argument is particularly decisive: In the opening words of the Coptic text of the Book of Thomas the ostensible editor of the sayings here recorded is named Matthew and not, as Doresse has declared and still maintains,[1] Matthias.

However that may be, the Gospel or Traditions of Matthias could only have been composed before the beginning of the 3rd century. There seems to be nothing against Bardenhewer's dating (*Litg.* I, 2nd ed., p. 530), which is followed by Altaner (p. 52): the first decade or the first half of the 2nd century. We must probably also assume, with the same scholars, that the apocryphon originated in Alexandria, or at any rate in Egypt.

5. *The Gospel of Judas*

The most important and oldest source here is Irenaeus (*adv. haer.* I. 28. 9 H = Theodoret of Cyrus, *Haereticorum fabularum compendium* I. 15, *PG* LXXXIII 368 B): certain Gnostic sectaries possessed in addition to other works of their own composition, a 'gospel' under the name of the traitor Judas (*Iudae euangelium*, εὐαγγέλιον Ἰούδα); these sectaries are elsewhere identified with the Cainites, and reckoned among the 'Gnostics' of Epiphanius, the Nicolaitans, Ophites, Sethians, or Carpocratians. The existence and title of the document (εὐαγγέλιον τοῦ Ἰούδα) are also attested by Epiphanius (*Pan.* 38. 1. 5; II p. 63. 13f. Holl).

It would be rash to ascribe to the Gospel of Judas a quotation derived by Epiphanius from a Cainite book (*Pan.* 38. 2. 4; II, p. 64. 17–19 Holl: "This is the angel who blinded Moses, and these are the angels who hid the people about Korah and Dathan and Abiram, and carried them off"). Still less reason is there for ascribing to this gospel a formula reproduced by Irenaeus (*loc. cit.*) and Epiphanius (38. 2. 2), which accompanied the sexual rite practised by the sect for the attainment of the 'perfect gnosis'. As to the subject and content of the apocryphon, we are reduced to simple conjecture, supported at best by some characteristics of Cainite doctrine as it is known from the notices of the heresiologues. It is possible, but far from certain, that this 'gospel' contained a Passion story setting forth the 'mystery of the betrayal' (*proditionis mysterium*, μυστήριον προδοσίας) and explaining how Judas by his treachery made possible the salvation of all mankind: either he forestalled the destruction of the truth proclaimed by Christ, or he thwarted the designs of the evil powers, the Archons, who wished to prevent the Crucifixion since they knew that it

---

[1] *Les livres secrets des gnostiques d'Égypte*, Paris 1958, p. 243 (ET London 1960, p. 225).

would deprive them of their feeble power and bring salvation to men (ps. Tertullian, *adv. omn. haer.* 2; Epiphanius *Pan.* 38. 3. 3–5; Filastrius *haer.* 34; Augustine, *de haer.* 18; ps. Jerome, *Indiculus de haer.* 8; cf. Bauer p. 176). However that may be, the work was probably in substance an exposition of the secret doctrine (licentious and violently antinomian in character) ostensibly revealed by Judas, a summary of the Truth or of the superior and perfect Gnosis which he was supposed to possess in virtue of a revelation (Irenaeus, *loc. cit.*; Epiph. *Pan.* 38. 1. 5; Filastrius *haer.* 34).

The Gospel of Judas was of course composed before 180, the date at which it is mentioned for the first time by Irenaeus in *adv. haer.* If it is in fact a Cainite work, and if this sect—assuming that it was an independent Gnostic group—was constituted in part, as has sometimes been asserted,[1] in dependence on the doctrine of Marcion, the apocryphon can scarcely have been composed before the middle of the 2nd century. This would however be to build on weak arguments. At most we may be inclined to suspect a date between 130 and 170 or thereabouts.

6. *The Apocryphon of John*

The text of the Apocryphon of John, in a Coptic (Sahidic) version, is preserved in four copies in the following manuscripts:

(*a*) Pap. Berol. 8502 (5th cent. or beginning of 5th cent.). The papyrus derives from the cemetery of Akhmîm or from the neighbourhood of that town, and was acquired in Cairo in 1896 by Dr. C. Reinhardt for the Egyptian section of the Berlin Museum. On this manuscript, see above, p. 244, and also the introductions by H. Ibscher to the editions of *A Manichean Psalm-book*, Part II, Stuttgart 1938, pp. XIIf., and of the *Kephalaia* I, Stuttgart 1940, pp. VIIf. The Apocryphon of John stands on pages 19. 6–77. 7, between the Gospel of Mary (below, pp. 340ff.) and the Sophia Jesu Christi (above, pp. 243ff.). The title (*papokruphon* *eniōhannēs*) is given in the colophon (pp. 77. 6f.).

The writing was long known only through this papyrus, and very imperfectly at that. It was briefly described in 1896 by Carl Schmidt,[2] but at that time confused with the Gospel of Mary, an error which passed into several histories of early Christian literature. The same scholar then in 1907 made it the subject of a more careful and more detailed study, and published the first part in translation with a commentary.[3] The beginning of this translation was reproduced with a brief introduction by Hennecke

---

[1] E.g. E. de Faye, *Gnostiques et Gnosticisme*, 2nd ed., Paris 1925, p. 371.

[2] *Ein vorirenäisches gnostisches Originalwerk in koptischen Sprache*, SB Berlin 1896, pp. 839–847.

[3] "Irenäus und seine Quellen in adv. haer. 1.29", in *Philotesia. Paul Kleinert zum 70 Geburtstag dargebracht*, Berlin 1907, pp. 317–336.

in his New Testament Apocrypha (*Apokr.* 2, p. 70). The proofs of a first edition of the Coptic text were accidentally destroyed in 1912. Schmidt took up the work afresh, and dedicated to the Apocryphon some pages of his later publications[1]—but at some points confused it with the Sophia Jesu Christi. Only with the work of Walter Till were complete and accurate analyses provided of the document as it is presented in the Berlin papyrus,[2] as well as a full edition with a German translation: *Die gnostischen Schriften des koptischen Papyrus Berolinensis 8502* (*TU* 60=5 Reihe V, Berlin 1955. pp. 33–51 and 79–195). (English translation of the text in *Gnosticism. An Anthology* (ed. R. M. Grant), London 1961, pp. 69ff.).

(*b*) Codex I of the Gnostic library of Nag Hammadi (middle or second half of 4th century). The codex was found about 1945 in the neighbourhood of Nag Hammadi, and acquired in 1946 by Togo Mina for the Coptic Museum in Old Cairo, where·it has since been preserved. The Apocryphon occupies pages 5. 1–40. 11 of the volume, of which it is the first writing; it is immediately followed by *The sacred Book of the Great Invisible Spirit* or *Gospel of the Egyptians* (below, p. 362). The first pages are missing, as are pages 19 and 20. The title is given on the first leaf (not numbered) and as a conclusion (40. 10f.): *papokruphon ᵉniōhannēs*. The text is parallel even to details with that of the Berlin papyrus, without however corresponding to it word for word. The two documents represent, as W. C. Till has explained (*TU* 60 p. 10), independent translations of Greek versions of the work which here and there were distinct. The text of Codex I is still unpublished, although an edition has been long in preparation. Since all its variant readings are noted in the critical apparatus to the edition of the Berlin papyrus it is easy to reconstitute the text in full.

Literature: H.-Ch. Puech and J. Doresse, "Nouveaux écrits gnostiques" (communication read on February 20 1948): *CR Acad. Inscrr. et Belles-Lettres* (Institut de France) 1948, 87–95; L.-Th. Lefort, "Note": *Acad. Royale de Belgique, Bull. de la classe des Lettres*, 5ème série, t. XXXIV, 1948, pp. 100–102; Togo Mina, "Le papyrus gnostique du Musée Copte", *Vig. Chr.* 2, 1948, pp. 129–136; id., "Un papyrus gnostique du IVe siècle", *Bull. de l'Institut d'Égypte* XXX, 1949, pp. 325f.; H.-Ch. Puech, "Nouveaux écrits gnostiques découverts à Nag Hammadi", *RHR* 134, 1947–48, p. 244f.; id., "Les nouveaux écrits gnostiques", *Coptic Studies in Honor of W. E. Crum* (=*Bull. of the Byzantine Institute* 2), Boston 1950, 101f. and 112f.; id., "Découverte d'une bibliothèque gnostique": *Enc. Fr.* XIX, Paris 1957, fasc. 19. 42–6 and 19. 42–7; J. Doresse, "Trois livres gnostiques inédits", *Vig. Chr.* 2, 1948, pp. 157–160; id., "Nouveaux aperçus historiques sur les gnostiques coptes: Ophites

[1] *Pistis Sophia*, Leipzig 1925, pp. xxi and xc f.; "Die Urschrift der Pistis Sophia", *ZNW* 24, 1925, p. 235.
[2] "Die Gnosis in Ägypten", *La Parola del Passato* 12, 1949, pp. 231–250; "The Gnostic Apocryphon of John", *JEH* 3, 1952, pp. 14–22.

et Séthiens", *Bull. de l'Institut d'Égypte* XXXI, 1948–49, pp. 409–419.

(*c*) Codex III of the Gnostic library of Nag Hammadi (first dated in the middle or first half of the 3rd century, but rather to be assigned to the 4th or 5th century; now in the Coptic Museum in Old Cairo). Here also the writing appears at the beginning of the volume, of which it occupies pages 1–34 (?). 9, immediately before the Gospel of Thomas (above, pp. 278ff.). Of the first three leaves only fragments or shreds remain; the two following leaves are seriously impaired by lacunae, but these soon become fewer and scarcely occur at all on the remaining pages. The work bears in the colophon a title slightly different from that given in the two manuscripts already mentioned: *kata iōhannēn ᵉnapokruphon*. By and large the text is parallel to that of the Berlin papyrus and Codex I; here and there however it presents fairly considerable divergences: passages displaced, peculiar or supplementary developments, a longer and less incoherent conclusion.

Literature: Photographic edition (under the designation Codex II, part a): Pahor Labib, *Coptic Gnostic Papyri in the Coptic Museum at Old Cairo*, vol. I, Cairo 1956, plates 47–80. 9. – J. Doresse, "Nouveaux écrits coptes", *Vig. Chr.* 3, 1949, pp. 133f.; id., "Une bibliothèque gnostique copte", *Acad. Royale de Belgique. Bull. de la classe des Lettres*, 5ème série, t. XXXV, 1949, p. 440; id., "Une bibliothèque gnostique copte", *La Nouvelle Clio* 1, 1949, p. 63; id., "Les Apocalypses de Zoroastre, de Zostrien, de Nicothée. . . . ," *Coptic Studies in Honor of W. E. Crum*, Boston 1950, pp. 262f.; H.-Ch. Puech, "Les nouveaux écrits gnostiques", *Coptic Studies in Honor of W. E. Crum*, p. 104; id., "Découverte d'une bibliothèque gnostique", *Enc. Fr.*, t. XIX, 1957, fasc. 19. 42–8.

(*d*) Codex VIII of the Gnostic library of Nag Hammadi (end of 3rd or beginning of 4th century? Now in the Coptic Museum in Old Cairo). Here again the Apocryphon is the first writing in the volume, and as in Codex I it is followed by the *Sacred Book of the Great Invisible Spirit* or *Gospel of the Egyptians*. The work, like the volume as a whole, is in very bad condition. The leaves are broken, and their remains would require to be restored to their proper order. The title (here somewhat fragmentary) is the same as in Codex III, and is given likewise at the end: *kata iōh[annē]n [ᵉn]apokr[u]phon*. So far as can be ascertained, this fourth exemplar like the third contains, but in a fragmentary form, a version of the Apocryphon more developed than that represented in the other two.

Literature: J. Doresse, *Vig. Chr.* 3, 1949, p. 136; id., *Acad. Royale de Belgique, Bulletin de la classe des Lettres*, 5ème série, t. XXXV, 1949, p. 442; id., *La Nouvelle Clio* 1, 1949, p. 63; H.-Ch. Puech, *Coptic Studies in Honor of W. E. Crum*, 1950, p. 107; id., *Enc. Fr.*, t. XIX, 1957, fasc. 19. 42–10; W. C. Till, *TU* 60, 1955, pp. 10f. and 34.

Examination of the indirect tradition is extremely instructive. As Carl Schmidt established long ago,[1] the first part, or more exactly the beginning of the dogmatic section of the Apocryphon, was used by Irenaeus (*adv. haer.* 1. 27 H)[2] for his account (written between 180 and 185) of the 'Barbelo-Gnostics' or, if we accept Harvey's suggestion (vol. 1, p. 221 n. 2 of his edition), the 'Gnostics' properly so called. The fact is beyond dispute. There are however certain differences between the text of the Apocryphon as it is now known and the notice in Irenaeus (who does not mention the title of the work). These differences may go back to errors in the Coptic translation or to mistakes due to Irenaeus, but they may also be explained on the assumption that the model reproduced by Irenaeus corresponds to an older and more primitive form of the work (perhaps not yet ascribed to John, and possibly pre-Christian), a form, that is, more or less distinct from that in which the Apocryphon has come down to us (J. Doresse, *Vig. Chr.* 2, 1948, pp. 157f.).

It is, moreover, rather surprising that Irenaeus at first follows step by step the cosmological exposition provided by his source, but then suddenly breaks off and follows it no longer, while the Apocryphon goes on to develop a complete anthropological system and to sketch, on the basis of the Old Testament, a history of mankind. This difference has been variously interpreted. According to Doresse, the Apocryphon in its original form, or the underlying document, the 'Grundschrift', contained only the part summarized by Irenaeus. Carl Schmidt held that there was indeed in Irenaeus' source an anthropological exposition identical with that of our present Apocryphon, but that Irenaeus observed that its content corresponded to the myths of the Gnostic sect whose doctrines he analyses at greater length in the following chapter (*adv. haer.* I. 28); not wishing to repeat himself, he deliberately refrained from using in *adv. haer.* I. 27 those parts of the Apocryphon which might give the impression of repetition. However that may be, the testimony of Irenaeus remains of the first importance for the questions of the date, the language and the origin of our document.

Very doubtful, on the other hand, is the testimony to our Apocryphon which one might be tempted to find in a Coptic sermon of John of Parallos (6th century) against the heretics (Text in A. van Lantschoot, "Fragments coptes d'une homélie de

[1] SB Berlin 1896, pp. 839–847; above all, *Philotesia. Paul Kleinert . . . dargebracht*, Berlin 1907, pp. 317–336.
[2] Theodoret of Cyrus has preserved in part the original Greek text, which he assigns to sects which, as he believed, sprang from Valentinianism(?): the Barbeliotae or Borborians, the Naassenes, the Stratiotics, or again the Phemionites (*haer. fab. comp.* I.13, *PG* LXXXlII 361C–364C).

Jean de Parallos", *Miscellanea Giovanni Mercati*, vol. 1 = *Studi e Testi* 121, Rome 1946, pp. 296–326).[1] John, Bishop of Parallos, cites the titles of five 'blasphemous' writings disseminated in his time by the heretics in the orthodox churches. Beside the *Investiture of Michael*, the *Jubilation* (?) *of the Apostles*, the *Teachings of Adam*, and the *Counsel of the Saviour*, he mentions the 'Preaching of John' (*pkĕrekma ᵉniōhannes* = τὸ κήρυγμα Ἰωάννου; text, p. 303, translation, p. 319). But is it a question of our Apocryphon? Of most of the documents mentioned in the context we know nothing. At most we might link the *Teachings of Adam*—but this is pure conjecture—with some apocryphon of similar title, in particular the *Revelations of Adam to his son Seth* contained in Codex VII of the Nag Hammadi library,[2] and the *Counsel of the Saviour* with the *Dialogue of the Saviour* which belongs to the same collection (above, pp. 248ff.). In any case what we know of the *Investiture of Michael*, the character of which seems legendary rather than heterodox or specifically Gnostic, does not favour the identification of the *Kerygma* and the Apocryphon of John.

A positive testimony, and one of the greatest importance, is provided by the Nestorian Theodore bar Konai, "the teacher of the land of Kashkar", in Mesopotamia (probably end of 8th century), in section XI of his Book of Scholia in a chapter about the Odaje or Audians.[3] Originally simply schismatics, these sectaries appear in the later heresiological tradition as Gnostics (Syriac text and French translation in H. Pognon, *Inscriptions mandaïtes des coupes de Khouabir*, Paris 1898, p. 132. 9–133. 23 and 194–196; new edition in Addai Scher, *CSCO* 69 = Script. Syri, ser. II, t. LXVI, p. 319. 6–320. 20). Theodore cites the titles and a few passages from some of the apocryphal works employed in large numbers by the Audians. Among others he mentions an 'Apocalypse in the name of Abraham' (*geljūnā dabᵉšem Abrāhām*) and an 'Apocalypse' or 'Book of the Strangers' (*geljūnā* or *kᵉtābā dᵉnukrājē*). The former is identical with the ἀποκάλυψις ἐξ ὀνόματος Ἀβραάμ, which according to Epiphanius (*Pan.* 39. 5. 1) was employed by the Sethians. The second Apocalypse is to be linked with the following: the ἀποκάλυψις Ἀλλογενοῦς of the Gnostics combated in Rome towards the middle of the 3rd century by Plotinus (Porphyry, *Vita Plotini* 16); the βίβλοι ἀλλογενεῖς, the βίβλος or βίβλοι Ἀλλογενοῦς (=Seth) of the 'Gnostics' proper (Epiphanius, *Pan.* 26. 8. 1), the Sethians (ib. 39. 5. 1) and the Archontics (ib. 40. 2. 2 and 7. 4; that the writing was the common property of these three sects in Egypt in the first half of the 4th

[1] Cf. C. D. G. Müller, *Die alte koptische Predigt*, Diss. Heidelberg, 1954, p. 151.
[2] Cf. H.-Ch. Puech, *Enc. Fr.*, t. XIX, fasc. 19.42–10.
[3] H.-Ch. Puech, Art. "Audianer", *RAC* I, col. 910–915.

century, cf. ib. 40. 7. 5); the ἀλλογενὴς ὕψιστος, the text of which in a Sahidic version has been recovered through the discovery of Nag Hammadi.[1]

In addition to these two apocrypha Theodore mentions the 'Revelation' or 'Apocalypse in the name of John' (geljūnā dabᵉšem Jōhannān), from which he quotes two extracts: "And in the Revelation which is in the name of John he (Audi, the founder of the sect) said: 'These powers (šaliṭāne) which I have seen, from them comes my body'. And he enumerates these holy creators ('abudē) which he says: 'My Wisdom made the hair (sa'rā), Understanding (bintā) the skin. Elohim made the bones, and my Sovereignty (malkuthi) made the blood. Adonai made the nerves, and Zeal (qenetā) made the flesh (besrā), and Thought (maḥsabtā) made the marrow'."

Already in 1936 I had suspected that the Apocryphon of John was identical with the Revelation under the name of this Apostle mentioned here by Theodore.[2] At that time only the first part of the work contained in the Berlin papyrus was known, and a relationship between the two works could only be suggested as a hypothesis which could not be controlled. When the complete text of the Apocryphon became better known, although still imperfectly, through Codex I of the Nag Hammadi library, I was able to maintain the conjecture with more assurance.[3] Today the identity of the two works seems to me absolutely certain and definitely proved: the passage relating to the creation by the seven Archons of the seven parts of the body of Adam, which the Syriac author extracted from the (Audian) Revelation of John, has an almost exact parallel in three of the four copies of the Apocryphon now accessible to us: PBerol. 8502, p. 43. 11–44. 4 and 49. 9–50. 4; Coptic Museum, Codex I, p. 19 (missing) and 22. 18–23. 6; Codex III, pl. 60. 15–25 and pl. 63. 13–23 ed. Labib. This conclusion is of great interest for the history and indeed for the establishing of the text of the Apocryphon. It shows the remarkable prestige which the work enjoyed from the 2nd to the 8th century, as far afield as Mesopotamia; at the very least, if Theodore bar Konai is here only copying an older source, it was highly esteemed for a long time, and elsewhere than in the West and in Egypt.

There is not the slightest reason for considering as a later remoulding of our Apocryphon one of the very few writings

[1] Cf. H.-Ch. Puech, *Coptic Studies in Honor of W. E. Crum*, p. 106 and 126–132; id., *Enc. Fr.*, t. XIX, fasc. 19.42–10.

[2] H.-Ch. Puech, "Fragments retrouvés de l' 'Apocalypse d'Allogène' ", *Mélanges Franz Cumont = Ann. Inst. Phil. et Hist. or. et slav.* IV, Brussels 1936, p. 942 n. 2 and p. 952 n. 4.

[3] *Coptic Studies in Honor of W. E. Crum*, 1950, p. 113.

preserved from the literature common to the Bogomils and the mediaeval Cathari: the 'Interrogatio Iohannis et apostoli et evangelistae in cena secreta regni coelorum de ordinatione mundi istius et de principe et de Adam' (Latin text in its two versions in R. Reitzenstein, *Die Vorgeschichte der christlichen Taufe*, Leipzig–Berlin 1929, pp. 299–311).[1] The work was brought about 1190 from Bulgaria to North Italy by Nazarius, later Bishop of the Cathar community in Concorezzo, and passed thence to Languedoc; but we cannot say with any certainty whether it does not presuppose a Greek rather than a Slavonic prototype, or whether it was not already known between 1111 and 1118 to Euthymius Zigabenus (*Pan. dogm.*, tit. XXVII, *PG* CXXX 1293D–1296B).

This work also is a 'secretum' (cf. Reitzenstein *op. cit.* p. 309; "Tractatus de haereticis", ed. A. Dondaine, *Archivum Fratrum Praedicatorum* XX, 1950 p. 311. 6–8 and 319. 29f.) and professes likewise to reproduce the revelations made by Jesus in reply to questions from John. Nevertheless it differs in framework and in scenery from the Apocryphon, and the doctrines expounded in the two writings, although dealing by and large with the same themes, have nothing in common. The *Interrogatio Johannis*, which moreover is related to the Apocalypse of John published by Tischendorf (*Apa* p. 87; cf. *Interrog.*, Version B, p. 308 Reitzenstein), belongs apparently among the apocrypha of the ordinary type. It is therefore difficult to understand why J. Doresse has thought it possible to write, with reference to this work (*Bull. de l'Inst. d'Égypte* XXXI, 1949, p. 418): "The Audians were to modify the Book of John a little further, and perhaps in their turn hand it on, in its mediaeval form of the *Interrogatio Iohannis*, to the different Manichean groups of the Balkans and the West".

The structure of the Apocryphon of John is that of the classic Gnostic gospels. One might even say that it corresponds to both the types which may be broadly distinguished in writings of this kind. Especially in its first part, the work is a 'visionary narrative': the narrator relates the vision with which he has been favoured and the teaching he has received, imparted to him alone in the form of a continuous discourse from the lips of the heavenly Revealer who has appeared to him. Gradually, however, and ever increasingly, the Apocryphon takes on the form of a dialogue, but here between two persons only, in the course of which the visionary is transformed into a participant who interrupts the Revealer to speak himself, and then receives instruction from him in the form of successive replies to his questions.

[1] A more recent study in E. Tardeanu, "Apocryphes bogomiles et apocryphes pseudo-bogomiles", *RHR* 138, 1950, pp. 204–213.

The beginning is in full conformity with the rules of this literary genre. It combines the traits characteristic of the majority of the Gnostic gospels and handles the conventional stereotyped themes which we find generally in these gospels and in this revelation-literature, and in the visionary or esoteric writings of the period: the scene is laid after the Resurrection; the vision and revelation take place upon a mountain (here as elsewhere the Mount of Olives); extraordinary phenomena accompany the appearance of the Revealer; the seer is at first alarmed, but is then reassured at the first words of the supernatural being who has just manifested himself to him; the heavenly being (who here, be it noted, is only later identified with Christ) appears in luminous form and in varied and contradictory aspects, constantly changing and therefore bewildering (cf. the πολύμορφος Christ in many apocryphal Acts).[1] Here is the beginning of the Apocryphon, from the Berlin Papyrus (the passage is missing from Codex I in Cairo, at this point mutilated):

But it came to pass one day, when John the brother of James was come up—these are the sons of Zebedee—when he was come up to the Temple, there came to him a Pharisee (φαρισαῖος) named A.manias (= Arimanios in Codex III in Cairo, pl. 47.9 Labib), and said to him: "Where is thy master, in whose train thou wast?" He said to him: "Whence he came, thither is he returned again" (cf. Jn. 16:5, 28; Ev. Petri 56; Apokryphon Jacobi—see below, pp. 333ff., 2.24f. and 14.20–22). Then spake the Pharisee (φαρισαῖος) to him: "Through deceit (πλάνη) hath he led you astray (πλανᾶν), this Nazarene (Ναζωραῖος), [. . .] He hath hardened [your hearts and] turned you away [from] the traditions (παράδοσις) of your [fathers]". When I heard this, I turned away from the sanctuary (ἱερόν) to the mountain (cf. Mk. 13:3, Acts 1:12), to a solitary place, and with great sorrow (λυπεῖσθαι) in my heart I thought: "How (πῶς) then was the Saviour (σωτήρ) appointed (χειροτονεῖν) and why was he sent into the world (κόσμος) by his Father who sent him? And who is his Father? And of what kind is that aeon (αἰών) to which we shall go? He said to us: 'This aeon (αἰών) hath assumed the form (τύπος) of that everlasting aeon (αἰών).' But he did not teach us about it, of what kind it is". Straightway, as I thus

[1] Cf. thereon, e.g., E. Peterson, "Einige Bemerkungen zum Hamburger Papyrusfragment der Acta Pauli", Vig. Chr. 3, 1949, pp. 149–159 (Frühkirche, Judentum und Gnosis, Freiburg 1959, pp. 183ff.); but the theme, influenced by a certain conception of the αἰών which is applicable to any divine being, is much more comprehensive, and would require a systematic study.

thought, the heavens opened and the whole creation shone forth
in a light that [is not earthly] and the [whole] world (κόσμος)
[began to tremble]. I was afraid, and [cast] myself [down]. And
lo, there [appeared to me] a child. But (δέ) [I saw] the form as
an old man, in [whom] is light. [I looked] upon him (and)
[understood] not [this] marvel. If [it is] a [unity (?)] with many
forms (μορφή) [in consequence of this (?)] light, do their forms
(μορφή) [appear] through their . . . [(or: through one another)
or] if it is one, [how then does it have] threefold appearances?
[He said to me]: "John, why art [thou] in doubt, when I [. . .]
to thee? For (γάρ) indeed [this is not] strange [to thee]. But be
not faint-[hearted (For)] I am he who [is] with [you] alway (cf.
Mt. 28:20). I am [the Father]; I am the Mother, I [am the Son].
I am the eternally Existing, the Unmixable, [since there is none
who] mingles himself with him. [Now am I come] to reveal to
thee [what] is, what [was], and what [shall] be, that [thou mayest
know] the invisible things like [the] visible, and [to instruct thee]
concerning the perfect (τέλειος) [man] (cf. Wisd. Sol. 7:17–21;
Manichean Kephalaia I, p. 15.1–23 and II, p. 16.19–21). But now
lift up thy [countenance (?) and] come (?), hear and [under-
stand what] I shall say today, [that] thou for thy part may proclaim it [to thy fellow-]spirits (ὁμόπνευμα), who are of the race
(γενεά) that does not [waver, of the per]fect (τέλειος) Man, and
to [those who are able] to perceive (νοεῖν)".

(PBerol. 8502, p. 19.6–22. 17; pp. 79–85 Till)

Thereupon the Revealer (who receives the name Christ for the
first time only at p. 45.6, Till p. 131) begins as promised to reveal
to John this mysterious and sublime doctrine. At first, and for a
long time, indeed right up to page 45.5 of the Berlin papyrus
(Till p. 131 = Cod. III in Cairo, pl. 61.17), i.e. up to the very
point at which the extract in Irenaeus ends, this teaching is given
in the form of a monologue, in the course of which, after an
introduction bearing on the divine μοναρχία which is in fact an
epitome of negative, apophatic theology, the speaker expounds,
methodically and in succession according to the systematic order
of a dogmatic treatise, the constitution of the transcendent world
and the emanation of the beings or aeons who compose it (notably
Barbelo, Christ, and the four great lights—Harmozēl, Ōroiaēl,
Daveithe, Hēlēlēth—which are destined to support the Son or
θεὸς αὐτογενής, the Perfect Man or Adamas, who is established

in Harmozēl; the other three lights are respectively the abodes of Seth, the son of Adamas, of the 'souls of the saints', who are the descendants, the seed, of Seth, and of all the souls which after some hesitation or delay, and as a result of their repentance, come to knowledge of themselves thanks to *gnosis* and find themselves again in their fulness).

Then is described the lapse of the last aeon, the third of the aeons associated with the fourth light, namely Sophia 'our sister', who gives birth to a monster, the πρωτάρχων, the future Demiurge, Ialdabaoth-Saklas. Finally he relates how Ialdabaoth created the firmament, the material world and its masters or kings, the angels, powers or archons. In conclusion he tells of the arrogant declaration of the Demiurge (inspired by Exod. 20:5; Deut. 4:35; Isa. 44:6; 45:5f., 15; 46:9), who proclaims himself the only God, and of the repentance and anguished disquiet of his mother, 'the Mother', Sophia who becomes conscious of the state of humiliation and deficiency (*šta, ὑστέρημα, labes, deminoratio*) into which she has fallen through her presumptuous attempt to act and to produce without the consent of her σύμφωνος or σύζυγος, her consort.

The exposition, hitherto continuous, is here interrupted by a first question from John, who asks Christ about the meaning of ἐπιφέρεσθαι, 'move upon', in Gen. 1:2. Instead of an explanation he learns that the term is to be understood not in the sense of the Mosaic text but in relation to the unrest and uncertainty by which Sophia is tormented, tossed to and fro in the darkness of ignorance. From this point the monologue passes into a dialogue, or kind of dialogue, of a more or less artificial character. We must however wait a considerable time before John puts a second question (PBerol. p. 58.1, Till p. 157 = Cairo, Cod. I, p. 28.17 = Cairo, Cod. III, p. 70.9). In the interval the dogmatic exposition continues: first the redemption of Sophia on the ground of her μετανοία; the revelation to Ialdabaoth of the existence of 'Man' and the 'Son of Man' (cf. Iren. *adv. haer.* I. 28. 3H, where the following paragraph also offers parallels to the immediate sequel in the Apocryphon); the creation of Adam by the seven planetary Archons, in imitation of the 'image' of the first Man, the 'perfect Father'.

Here it is related in detail how first his 'psychic' body and the seven members which compose it (bones, nerves, flesh, marrow, blood, skin, hair)[1] were created. The body thus formed being incapable of movement (cf. Saturninus in Irenaeus, *adv. haer.* I. 18H; Hippol., *Ref.* VII. 28.3; Tertullian, *de anima* 23; Epiphanius, *Pan.* 23. 1. 8f.—the Ophites, in Irenaeus, *adv. haer.* I.

---

[1] See above p. 319, and cf. H.-Ch. Puech, "Fragments retrouvés de l' 'Apocalypse d'Allogène' ", *Mélanges F. Cumont*, 1936, p. 938 n. 2.

28. 3H; ps. Tertullian, *adv. omn. haer.* 2; Epiphanius, *Pan.* 37.4.1–3.—the Quqājē in Theodore bar Konai, Scholia, tr. Pognon, *Inscriptions mandaïtes*, p. 210.—the Naassenes in Hippolytus *Ref.* V. 7.6.—the Mandeans, Ginza R. III, p. 108.4–113.16 Lidzbarski, and Ginza L., II. 1, p. 454. 18–23), Ialdabaoth at the instigation of Sophia breathes into Adam his spirit, his πνεῦμα, i.e. the power which he possesses from his mother. The Archons recognize the superiority of Adam, to whom out of pity the blessed Father sends to support and help him (ὑπουργεῖν, pl. 68. 19 Cod. III Cairo) the ἐπίνοια of light, ζωή (cf. Gen. 2:18, 20; 3:20 = Eve).

The psychic man is now imprisoned in a material body made of the four elements (air, earth, water, fire), mixed together by the four winds blowing from the four cardinal points (cf. *Slav. Enoch* XXX. 13f.; *Or. Sibyl.* III. 24–26; VIII. 321 and cf. II. 195; XI. 3; ps. Cyprian, *De montibus Sina et Sion,* 4; Augustine, *in Joh. tract.* 9.14 and 10.12; Zosimus of Panopolis in Berthelot-Ruelle, *Collection des anciens alchimistes grecs,* Paris 1888, III, XLIX, 6, p. 231.1–14 and Olympiodorus, II. IV. 32, *ibid.,* p. 89.2–4, etc.: ADAM = A[νατολή], Δ[ύσις], Ἄ[ρκτος], Μ[εσημβρία]; Const. Apost. VII. 34. 6: "Adam, formed of the four elements"; Pirke of Rabbi Elieser in J. Dreyfus, *Adam und Eva nach der Auffassung des Midrasch,* Diss. Strasbourg 1894, p. 12, and Zohar in S. Karppe, *Étude sur les origines et la nature du Zohar,* Paris 1901, pp. 503f.: Adama Kadmon, formed by the assembling of the four elements drawn from the four cardinal points). Adam is then settled in the pretended paradise of delight (τρυφή), which is in reality only a deception (ἀπάτη). Reference is made to the Tree of Life, whose fruit is the desire (ἐπιθυμία) of death (cf. Manicheism); it represents the ἀντίμιμον πνεῦμα, the deceitful counterfeit spirit who hinders men from ascending to *gnosis* and to their fulness.

The conclusion deals with the Tree of the Knowledge of Good and Evil, which symbolizes the ἐπίνοια of light; despite the prohibition of the Demiurge, Christ incites Adam to eat of its fruit.[1] This long discourse, however, supposed as always to be directed to John, presents an anomaly: speaking of the Tree of Life and of the Archons whose instrument or creation it is, Christ declares: "I will make known to you (not: to thee!) the secrets (μυστήριον) of your life" (PBerol. 8502, p. 56.12f., Till p. 153 = Cairo Cod. I, p. 27.15–17 = Cairo Cod. III pl. 69.26).

In the sequel, questions become more frequent and follow more closely on one another. John asks if it was not the serpent, as Genesis relates, which advised Eve; the reply is that the serpent

[1] Studies on these sections and episodes in K. Rudolph, "Ein Grundtyp gnostischer Urmensch-Adam-Spekulation", *Zeitschr. f. Religions- u. Geistegesch.* 9, 1957, pp. 1–20; S. Giversen, "Johannes' apokryfon og Genesis", *Dansk Teologisk Tidsskrift,* 1957, pp. 65–80.

taught only the generation of the appetite for defilement and corruption (PBerol. p. 58.1–14, Till p. 153 = Cairo Cod. I, p. 28.17–29 = Cairo Cod. III, pl. 70.9–21). A further question about the meaning of ἔκστασις in Gen. 2:21 leads Christ to explain (in the light of Isa. 6:10) that it was not a question of a physical sleep but of a state of unconsciousness (ἀναισθησία), an overclouding of the spirit, the νοῦς, plunged by the Demiurge into ἄγνοια or ἀγνωσία, ignorance or lack of knowledge. Christ then develops at length a remarkable interpretation of the birth of Eve, then of that of Cain and Abel (Jave, the unrighteous, with the features of a bear, and Elohim, the righteous, with those of a cat), the offspring of the union of Eve with Ialdabaoth. Only Seth is begotten of Adam and has the same substance as he; he possesses therefore an οὐσία which the Spirit, the πνεῦμα, comes to awaken out of its incapacity for knowledge and its depravity and restore to its fulness (perfection) (PBerol. p. 58.14–64.13 = Cairo Cod. I, p. 29.2–32. 22 = Cairo Cod. III, pl. 70.21–73.16).

Parallel or similar myths occur among the anonymous Gnostics (Ophites?) in Irenaeus (*adv. haer.* 1.28. 4H), in Justin the Gnostic (Hippol. *Ref.* V. 26.23), among the Cainites (Filastrius, *haer.* 2), the Sethians (Epiph. *Pan.* 39.2.1–7), and the Archontics (Epiph. *Pan.* 40.5.3; 6.9; 7.1); among the Audians (*Mélanges F. Cumont*, p. 939; cf. "The Hypostasis of the Archons" in Labib, *Coptic Gnostic Papyri* I, pl. 137; German trans. by Schenke *ThLZ* 83 (1958) 665, and in Leipoldt-Schenke, *Kopt.-gnost. Schriften*), the (Manichean?) heretics in view in the first Priscillianist tractate of Würzburg (p. 18.31–19.4 Schepss: express mention of Saclas!), the Manichees (Ibn an-Nadim in G. Flügel, *Mani*, Leipzig 1862, pp. 91f., and remains of the same legend in the Turfan fragments M 528 II and T II D 79 V, *Abh. d. pr. Akad. d. Wissensch.* 1936, No. 10, p. 48 and 101, where the Archon is called Saqlōn), the Bogomils (cf. H.-Ch. Puech and A. Vaillant, *Le Traité contre les Bogomiles de Cosmas le Prêtre*, Paris 1945, p. 201 and n. 3), and in certain Jewish authors (cf. M. Grünbaum, "Beiträge zur vergleichenden Mythologie aus der Hagada," *ZDMG* 31, 1877, pp. 231f., V. Aptowitzer, *Kain und Abel in der Agada*, 1922, pp. 128–131).

The dialogue however only becomes more lively towards the end. John persists in questioning Christ, who on each occasion briefly furnishes the explanation sought, at the same time congratulating him on the relevance and depth of his questions. So gradually it is revealed: that salvation and access to perfection are assured to men of 'the unshakeable race' through the descent of the Spirit (πνεῦμα) of life and his presence among them (PBerol. p. 64.13–66.12, Till pp. 169–173 = Cairo Cod. I, p. 32.22–33.

23 = Cairo Cod. III, pl. 73.16–74. 7); that on the contrary those into whom the 'counterfeit spirit' (ἀντίμιμον πνεῦμα) enters are drawn into error and enticed to evil (PBerol. 66.13–67.18, Till pl. 173–175 = Cod. I, p. 33.23–34. 18 = Cod. III, pl. 74.7–22); that after death the souls of the redeemed will attain to the place of rest (ἀνάπαυσις) of the Aeons (PBerol. 67.18–68.13, Till pp. 175–177 = Cod. I, p. 34.18–35.2 = Cod. III, pl. 74.22–32), while the souls of sinners, those 'who have not recognized the All', will have to undergo new incarnations until they attain to *gnosis*, the saving knowledge (PBerol. 68.13–69.13, Till pp. 177–179 = Cod. I, p. 35.2–18 = Cod. III, pl. 74.32–75.11). John is assured that the soul of him who listens to the Spirit of life will be saved, and no longer bound to the flesh (PBerol. p. 69.14–70.8, Till pp. 179–181 = Cod. I, p. 35.18–36.4 = Cod. III, pl. 75.11–21), and is then informed of the eternal punishment which awaits those who have sinned against the Holy Spirit (cf. Mt. 12:31f. and par.: Gospel of Thomas, log. 44, pl. 88.26–31), i.e. who having once possessed knowledge have turned away from it (PBerol. 70.8–71.2, Till pp. 181–183 = Cod. I, p. 36.4–15 = Cod. III, pl. 75.21–31).

The last of his questions, relating to the origin of the ἀντίμιμον πνεῦμα, once more elicits, on the other hand, a very detailed reply, which seems in a sense to reach back across the preceding soteriological dialogue and take up again the earlier dogmatic exposition, and continues to the end of the work (PBerol. 71.2–76.6, Till pp. 173–193, (from which p. 75.14–76.1, Till pp. 191–193, must be removed) = Cod. I, p. 36.15–39.22 (except 39.13–18) = Cod. III, pl. 75.21–79.25, with variants and a different conclusion). Here it is reported: that Ialdabaoth, knowing that men were superior to himself, resolved to aggravate their captivity and their unconsciousness by shackling them to fate; that universal εἱμαρμένη was produced; that vexed and smitten by remorse the Demiurge repented of all that had come into being through him (cf. Gen. 6:6),[1] and sought to destroy mankind by the flood. A peculiar interpretation of Gen. 6:11–9:19 follows, according to which Noah was warned by the 'ἐπίνοια of light' (cf. Iren. *adv. haer.* I. 28.5 H), and took refuge, in company with the people of 'the race that does not flinch', not in an ark but under a cloud of light. Then is related how the angels of Ialdabaoth and his powers were sent to the 'daughters of men' (cf. Gen. 6:4); on the failure of this new attempt to corrupt and enslave the human race there follows the creation of the ἀντίμιμον πνεῦμα. The same angels descend again to earth, bringing gold, silver, gifts, copper, iron, and all kinds of metals (cf. Enoch VIII. 1f.; on the whole passage,

[1] Cf. G. Quispel, "Die Reue des 'Schöpfers' ", *Theol. Zeitschr.* 5, 1949, pp. 157f.

Enoch VI. 1f.; VII. 1; Jub. X. 1–3) and pour this ἀντίμιμον πνεῦμα into the bosom of the women, with whom they unite in the guise of their husbands; from them it passes into the children thus conceived (cf. Pistis Sophia c. 111 and 131f.).

As it is preserved in the Berlin Papyrus and Codex I of the Coptic Museum, the end of the exposition, obviously mutilated and rendered incoherent by the insertion of a fragment detached from the epilogue, is scarcely comprehensible. At most we may presume that it dealt with the providential and merciful action of the Mother, Sophia, in favour of her descendants, the 'spirituals' or πνευματικοί, perhaps also with the coming of Christ. At any rate the promise of the Revealer: "I will make known to you (sic!) what shall come to pass" (PBerol. pp. 76.5f., Till p. 193 = Cod. I, p. 39.21f.) is not fulfilled. The corresponding passage in Codex III is longer, better constructed, and in many respects more satisfactory. It is a poetic piece of lyrical style, formed apparently of three strophes in which the same expressions recur in turns, and set (contrary to all expectation) in the mouth of the 'perfect πρόνοια of the universe' or 'πρόνοια of light'. Three times, she recalls, she has advanced, unknown to the powers of evil, into the depths of darkness, even to the foundations of Chaos, to the bosom of Amente, the inferno, to seek out in their prison the celestial beings held captive in the body and to deliver them. The third time the prisoner awoke in tears from his heavy slumber at her call; he rose up, remembered again his origin, and recovered consciousness and possession of himself. She sealed him with 'five seals', thus protecting him against the angels of deficiency, the demons of chaos and all those who were holding him back, and so withdrew him for ever from the power of death.

The piece recalls a passage in the Latin translation of Ecclus. 24:32 (*Apokr.* 2, p. 388: "I (Wisdom!) will penetrate all regions deep beneath the earth, and will visit all that sleep, and will enlighten all that hope upon the Lord"), as well as one passage or another in the *Descensus ad Inferos* and finally the version of the Manichean myth of the awaking and salvation of Adam reproduced by Theodore bar Konai (A. Adam, *Texte zur Manichäismus, KlT* 175, Berlin 1954, pp. 22f.). There will be room for discussion as to whether this is an example of early or late Gnostic literature, and whether it is to be considered an integral part of the original version of the Apocryphon, or on the contrary supplementary, a later edition.

In the Berlin Papyrus (p. 75.14–76.1 and 76, 7–77.5, Till pp. 191–195) and in the Cairo Codex I (p. 39.13–18 and 39.22–40.9) the epilogue is unfortunately interrupted by the interpolation of some lines which properly belong to the preceding exposition.

Codex III however (p. 79.25–80.6) offers an uninterrupted text which except for a supplementary phrase and slight variants is exactly parallel to the other two. Like the prologue, it conforms to the type of conclusion usual in Gnostic gospels, and employs themes and expressions familiar in esoteric literature. It is devoted to instructions relating to the transmission, the παράδοσις, of the revelations which the work is supposed to contain. It is ordained that these 'mysteries' be consigned to writing, and that the book be not communicated to any save the initiate, the πνευματικοί, the other members of the same spiritual brotherhood, i.e., to use the terms employed elsewhere, those who are capable and worthy (ἄξιοι, digni) of receiving it and understanding its content. Whosoever shall traffic with the book, transmit it to any 'profane' person for money or any material goods is threatened with a curse, (a corresponding formula in the second Book of Jeu c. 43; above, p. 263, with commentary).

Thus written down, transmitted privately or in secret (h^em ppēthēp, PBerol. p. 75. 18f.; h^en ouhōp, Cairo Cod. III, pl. 79. 30), and kept in security (h^en outadschro, PBerol. p. 76.8f. and Cod. III, pl. 79.33f.; h^en ouasphalia, Cod. I, p. 39.24; cf. ἀσφαλῶς ἔχειν, Kyranis, proem. 3, p. 3. 10 Ruelle; ἀσφαλῶς, Kore Kosmou 5),[1] the work is guaranteed against any attack on its integrity, preserved from any profanation, and its authenticity and sacred character confirmed. At the end a few lines of the epilogue describe how the Revealer, vanishing from the sight of the seer, returns to heaven, and how the content of the vision is transmitted to the other disciples. In this the text corresponds to the majority of gospels of this type, which however speak more clearly of the Ascension properly so called and of the communication to the world of the message of the risen Christ, which immediately follows.

It will suffice to translate these concluding pages, taking account of and, especially at the beginning, occasionally preferring the readings of Codex III of the Coptic Museum.

"And lo, now I am about to ascend to the perfect Aeon. I have perfected thee in all things through thine ears. As for me, I have told thee this, that thou mayest write it down and give it in secret to thy kindred spirits (ὁμόπνευμα). For it is the secret (μυστήριον) of the race (or: For this secret belongs to the race) which does not flinch. For (καὶ γάρ) I have given this to thee to write it down, and it shall be securely deposited" (Cod. III: and the Saviour gave me this, that I might write it down and place it in security).

---

[1] On this see A. J. Festugière, La Révélation d'Hermès Trismégiste I, p. 345 and n. 6.

Then (τότε) said he to me: "Cursed is any man who imparts this for a gift (δῶρον), or (ἤ) for food or (ἤ) for drink or (ἤ) for clothing, or (ἤ) for anything else of the kind". He committed to him (=to John) this secret (μυστήριον) (and) forthwith vanished from him (cf. Lk. 24:31). And he (John) came to his fellow-disciples (μαθητής) and began (ἄρχεσθαι) to tell them what had been said to him by the Saviour (σωτήρ).

> (PBerol. 8502, p. 75.14–77.5, Till pp. 191–195 = Cairo
> Cod. I, p. 39.22–40.9 = Cairo Cod. III, pl. 79.25–80.6)

It is not possible here to summarize in detail the content of the Apocryphon and its teachings. Further analyses in: W. C. Till, "Die Gnosis in Ägypten", *La Parola del Passato* 12, 1949, pp. 233–238; id., "The Gnostic Apocryphon of John", *JEH* 3, 1952, pp. 16–22; id., *Die gnostischen Schriften des koptischen Papyrus Berolinensis 8502*, Berlin 1955, pp. 35–51; J. Doresse, *Les livres secrets des gnostiques d'Égypte*, Paris 1958, pp. 218–237, 274–276 (ET 201–218; several elements derived from my lectures in the École des Hautes-Études, November 1956 to June 1957). More succinct surveys in: J. Doresse, Ophites et Séthiens, *Bull. Inst. Ég.* 31, 1949, pp. 412–419, and G. Quispel, *Gnosis als Weltreligion*, Zürich 1951, pp. 13–15.

The majority of the problems raised by the Apocryphon are in a sense overshadowed by two questions of special importance, which it has not yet been possible to investigate in full. There are, as we have seen, two distinct versions of the Apocryphon, designated in the manuscripts, moreover, by somewhat different titles: the one, commonly called the 'short version', is represented by the Berlin papyrus and Codex I of the Nag Hammadi library; the other, in some passages more detailed, is preserved in volumes III and VIII of the same library, and has been labelled the 'long version'.

What relation can we establish between the two versions? Is the first only an abbreviation of the second, which would then be the older, or the reverse? J. Doresse[1] considers the 'long' version 'visibly older' than the 'short'. This is not my opinion, but the question would appear to be much more difficult: besides developments which are 'visibly' later additions and amplifications (in particular the whole section in Cod. III, pl. 63. 29–67.10, an interminable dissertation—which refers to the 'Book of Zoroaster'!—about the demons which preside over the parts of the body, diseases and the passions), the long version might comprise,

[1] *Vig. Chr.* 3, 1949, pp. 133f.; *Acad. Royale de Belgique. Bull. de la classe des Lettres*, 5ème série, t. XXXV, 1949, p. 440.

e.g. towards the end, portions of the primitive text. Nevertheless, so long as the recension contained in Codex VIII of the Coptic Museum remains unknown, and the two versions have not been minutely and carefully compared, we cannot reach a decision. On the other hand, if the short version is held to be the older, it would in my opinion be difficult to identify it with the original version of the work; its composition presents too many anomalies, its content is too heterogeneous, not to leave the impression of a redaction.

It would therefore be important to form some conception of the original document, the *Grundschrift*, which underlies our present versions, and which, modified, enlarged and transformed, has become our Apocryphon. But can we go so far as to conceive of this *Grundschrift* as a short treatise on the 'higher cosmogony', identical with the source which Irenaeus followed from beginning to end (*adv. haer.* I.27 H), on the basis of which the first part of the Apocryphon was constructed?[1] Or can we, still more boldly, consider it as a document of 'non-Christian character' or 'non-Christian origin'?[2] Here again it will be well to reserve our opinion.

However that may be, the Apocryphon of John, either in one of its present forms or in one more primitive and under a different title, saw the light before 180, the date at which it was quite certainly used by Irenaeus. It is scarcely too much to assume that it was composed in the first half of the second century. It is also certain that the original was composed in Greek: Irenaeus could have known it only in that language. The Coptic text is evidently only a translation, and Greek terms are particularly numerous in the long version of Cairo Codex III. Long ago Carl Schmidt[3] declared that the Apocryphon was a product of the $\Gamma\nu\omega\sigma\tau\iota\kappa oi$, the Gnostics properly so called, and more particularly of the Sethians, a branch of this sect whose different groups were widely spread in Syria, Palestine and Egypt. In Egypt the Sethians had developed from a religious society into a school, and also they had had contacts with the Valentinians; it was from Egypt that the document originated.

Everything points, it seems, to the conclusion that Schmidt was right: Irenaeus appeals to the Apocryphon in order to expound the doctrines of the Barbelo-Gnostics or 'Gnostics'; the Audians, to whom Theodore bar Konai ascribes the use of a 'Revelation

[1] J. Doresse, *Vig. Chr.* 2, 1948, p. 158.

[2] J. Doresee, "Nouveaux textes gnostiques découverts en Égypte: Le livre secret de Jean" (unpublished communication at the VIIIth international Byzantine Congress, Brussels 1948); cf. *Vig. Chr.* 3, 1949, p. 149 and *Acad. Royale de Belgique. Bull. de la classe des Lettres*, 5ème série, t. XXXV, 1949, p. 440.

[3] *Philotesia. Paul Kleinert . . . dargebra·ht*, Berlin 1907, pp. 334–336; *Pistis Sophia*, 1925, p. XCI.

of John' identical with our document, can be assimilated, as I have shown, to the Sethians and, what comes to more or less the same, to the Archontics; three of the Coptic exemplars belong to a collection formed for the most part of Sethian works and deriving probably from an Archontic or Sethian community in Upper Egypt; some features of the system expounded in the writing, in particular the place of Seth and those of his race, the 'spiritual' members of the sect—in other words, the Sethians—likewise favour the hypothesis. It seems therefore in high degree preferable to that recently advanced by Robert M. Grant:[1] according to Grant the Apocryphon might have had as its author Saturninus (Saturnilus of Antioch), and have been composed in Syria at the beginning of the second century. Schmidt (*Philotesia* p. 318) further proposed to interpret and translate the title as "The secret Teaching of John", and with this W. C. Till agrees (*TU* 60, 1955, p. 38). But it is not excluded that ἀπόκρυφον, in conformity with the usage of the period,[2] may here have rather the sense of 'secret Book'.

The importance of the document is of course generally admitted, and is well-grounded. It rests on the age of the Apocryphon, and the coherence, simplicity and relative purity of the complete system of *gnosis* here developed, as well as on the prestige and authority which it earned. This prestige is shown not only by the number of copies which have been preserved but also by the enduring success which it consistently enjoyed from the 2nd to the 8th century in different Gnostic communities. Moreover scholars are today inclined[3] to admit or to suggest that it represents a form of Gnosticism earlier than Valentinus, a *gnosis* still archaic and not far advanced in the development of myths; from this, according to the testimony of Irenaeus (*adv. haer.* I.5.1 H) and Tertullian (*adv. Valent.* 4), Valentinus drew his inspiration, accommodating it to his own ideas. If this be so, the importance of the Apocryphon would be even more considerable.

7. *Fragments of a Dialogue between John and Jesus*

In the first part of his article "Coptic Anecdota" in *JTS* (44, 1943, pp. 176–182), W. E. Crum published on pp. 176–179, under the title "A Gnostic Fragment", a parchment leaf (paginated 41 and 42) found at Deir el-Bala'izah (probably the ancient monastery of Apa Apollo) to the west of Assyut, and two small fragments

---

[1] "The Earliest Christian Gnosticism", *Church History* 22, 1953, pp. 88–90.
[2] Cf. for example F. Cumont, *L'Égypte des Astrologues*, Brussels 1937, pp. 152–158; G. Bardy, Art. "Apokryphen", in *RAC* I, 1942, col. 516–520; see below p. 335, beginning of *Apocryphon of James*.
[3] F. M. M. Sagnard, *La gnose valentinienne et le témoignage de saint Irénée*, Paris 1947, pp. 445f.; G. Quispel, *Gnosis als Weltreligion*, Zürich, 1951, p. 11.

of other leaves belonging to the same manuscript. This leaf and the fragments were published again, with an improved translation, by Paul E. Kahle (*Bala'izah. Coptic Texts from Deir el-Bala'izah in Upper Egypt*, vol. 1, London 1954, pp. 473–477, text no. 52).

The manuscript, dated by Crum in the 5th or 4th century, by Kahle in the 4th, is written in Sahidic (with some archaic forms). The Gnostic character of the work of which it contains the remains is beyond doubt: the Biblical themes treated are familiar in Gnostic literature (Adam, Paradise, the trees of Eden; Abel and Cain, Noah, the ark and the flood: *Apocryphon of John* (above, pp. 322ff.); Abel and Cain: Epiphanius, *Pan.* 38.2.6–7; 39.2.1–7; 40.5.3–4; Noah and the flood: *Hypostasis of the Archons*, Nag Hammadi Codex III. 4, and *Book of Noria*, cf. Epiphanius *Pan.* 26.1.3–9, the fourth document of Codex VII and the fifth of Codex XI of Nag Hammadi, etc.; Melchizedek: cf. C. Schmidt, *Koptische-gnostische Schriften*, Leipzig 1905, index s.v., p. 397); some expressions and details belong to the terminology and mythology of Gnosis (the five powers; the 'sealing' of these five powers: cf. perhaps the 'five seals': *Apocryphon of John* long version, in Labib, Coptic Gnostic Papyri, vol. 1, pl. 79.24; *The Sacred Book of the Great Invisible Spirit*, Nag Hammadi Codex I p. 55. 11, 63. 3, 66. 2–4; anonymous work in the Codex Brucianus, c. 4, p. 339.30 Schmidt (Baynes, *A Coptic Gnostic Treatise*, 1933, p. 70); the five trees: C. Schmidt-W. C. Till, *Koptisch-gnostische Schriften*, 2nd ed., index s.v. Bäume, p. 402; Logion 19 of the Gospel of Thomas, in Labib, *Coptic Gnostic Papyri* I, pl. 84.21–25: "You have five trees in Paradise, which are unmoved in summer (or) in winter and their leaves do not fall. Whoever knows them will not taste death"; cf. also the "five trees of light" in Manicheism).

To judge from what remains, the writing must have been a 'revelation', an ἀποκάλυψις, in which John himself was presumed to relate the secret teaching which he had received from the Saviour in the course of a conversation with Him. The apocryphon consisted of a series of questions posed by the apostle, to each of which Christ replies. Both for this reason and because of its themes it is to be linked with the Apocryphon of John (above, pp. 314ff.); it is not however to be identified with it, or considered as one of its different versions. On the other hand, it has no connection with the various other apocrypha ('Apocalypse', 'Mysteries of John' etc.) current under the name of the same apostle.

". . .] the body (σῶμα) [. . .] naked [. . .] without sin [. . .] the spiritual (? λογικός) power, ere it (she) had been revealed, its (her) name was not this, but its (her) name was Σιγή. For (ἐπειδή) all they that (were) in the heavenly Paradise (παράδεισος) were sealed in silence. But such as shall partake thereof (Paradise, or the tree of knowledge?) will become spiritual (?λογικός), having known all; they shall seal the five powers in silence. Lo, I have explained (ἑρμηνεύειν) unto thee, O Johannes, concerning Adam and Paradise (παράδεισος) and the Five Trees, in an intelligible allegory (σύμβολον νοερόν)". When I, Johannes, heard these (things), I said: "I have made a good beginning (ἄρχεσθαι, ἀρχή); I have completed knowledge (γνῶσις) and a hidden mystery (μυστήριον) (cf. Rom. 15:14; 1 Cor. 13:2) and allegories (σύμβολον) of truth, having been encouraged (προτρέπειν) by Thy love (ἀγάπη). Now I desire further to ask Thee that Thou wouldst explain (ἑρμηνεύειν) unto me in Thy will concerning Cain and Abel: according to what fashion (τύπος) did Cain slay Abel? And not this only, but he was asked by him (that) spoke with him, saying, Where is Abel, thy brother? But Cain denied (ἀρνεῖσθαι), saying, Am (μή) I the keeper . . ." (Gen. 4:9).

". . .] of the fullness (πλήρωμα) he (or: it) being completed. Lo, I have explained (ἑρμηνεύειν) unto thee, O Johannes, concerning Noah and [his?] ark (κιβωτός) and [. . ."

". . .] Now I desire further to [ask Thee what Thou wouldst] explain (ἑρμηνεύειν) [unto me] concerning Melchizedek. Is it not (μή) said [concerning him]: being without [father, being without] mother, his generation (γενεά) [was not mentioned], having no beginning [of days], having no end of life, [being] like to the Son of God, being a priest for ever (Heb. 7:3). It is also said concerning him . . .[. . ."

(Papyrus from Deir el-Bala'izah: Oxford, Bodl. Ms. Copt. d54, ed. P. E. Kahle, Bala'izah, pp. 473–477. By permission of the Trustees of the Griffith Institute, Oxford)

8. The Apocryphon of James (Apocryphon Jacobi)

There is no express testimony to justify us in saying that there was ever a Gnostic Gospel attributed to James (whether the James in view was the brother of the Lord, or James the son of Alphaeus, or James the son of Zebedee). Books have indeed been handed down under the name of James, such as the Book or Protevangelium of James (see below, pp. 370ff.); but this account of the life of the Virgin and of the nativity of Jesus is to be regarded as pious fancy. Again, two Coptic fragments dealing with the

Resurrection and the incident at Emmaus have been published by E. Revillout, in *Journal Asiatique* (série 10, vol. VI, 1905, pp. 113–120) under the title: "Un nouvel apocryphe copte: le Livre de Jacques"; they have nothing to do with the Protevangelium. But these writings cannot be considered purely heterodox. Nor can we attach any importance at all to the series of very late apocryphal writings found in 1597 in leaden boxes in the Sacro Monte de Grenada and designated "The Gospel of James the Elder" (Santos p. 27). Hippolytus however (*Ref.* V. 7. 1, p. 78. 22–79. 1 Wendland) speaks in a note about the Naassenes of a secret teaching transmitted to Mariamme (probably Mary Magdalene) by James the brother of the Lord ("These are the chief heads of a great mass of words which, they say, James the brother of the Lord delivered to Mariamme").

We may therefore suspect that these 'Traditions' of James, like those of Matthias (above, pp. 308ff.), were written down in a document which perhaps had more or less the form of a gospel. But there is nothing to prove that this was so, or that this gospel—assuming that it ever existed—bore the name of James rather than that of Mariamme or Mary, who has given her name to more than one Gnostic writing of this kind (below, pp. 338ff.). It is equally possible that these παραδόσεις were composed in the form of an ἀποκάλυψις and given out as a 'revelation' disclosed by James in the course of a conversation or by the channel of a message, a letter. In this case one would be inclined to think of a writing identical with or similar to one of the three works in the Gnostic library of Nag Hammadi which are placed under the aegis of James.

Unfortunately, of two of these we know as yet practically nothing, namely the third and fourth writings of Codex VII.[1] Of these documents all that can be said at the moment is that both, perhaps a little hastily, have been designated 'Apocalypses of James'.[2] It is also known that in the first the stage is set for a dialogue between Jesus and James (Jesus declares: "In the morning they will arrest me . . ." James replies "Rabbi . . ."), and that the second begins with the following words: "These are the sayings which James the Just uttered at Jerusalem. . . . They were written down by Mereim, one of the priests". On the other hand, the third document, also still unpublished, is much better known.

[1] H.-Ch. Puech, "Les nouveaux écrits gnostiques", *Coptic Studies in Honor of W. E. Crum*, Boston 1950, p. 106; id., "Découverte d'une bibliothèque gnostique", *Enc. Fr.*, tome XIX, Paris 1957, fasc. 19. 42–10.

[2] J. Doresse, "Nouveaux écrits gnostiques coptes", *Vig. Chr.* 3, 1949, pp. 132 and 135f.; id., "Une bibliothèque gnostique copte", *Acad. Royale de Belgique. Bull. de la classe des Lettres*, 5ème série, tome XXXV, 1949, pp. 438 and 442; id., *Les livres secrets des gnostiques d'Égypte*, Paris 1958, p. 252 (ET London 1960, pp. 236–7).

The document in question is the first in Codex II, the Codex C. G. Jung, of which it occupies pages 1. 1–16. 29, preceding the Gospel of Truth (above, pp. 233ff.). On this work cf.: H.-Ch. Puech and G. Quispel, "Les écrits gnostiques du Codex Jung", *Vig. Chr.* 8, 1954, pp. 7–22; G. Quispel, "The Jung Codex and its Significance", in H.-Ch. Puech, G. Quispel, W. C. van Unnik, *The Jung Codex*, London 1955, pp. 45–47; W. C. van Unnik, "The Origin of the recently discovered 'Apocryphon Jacobi'," *Atti del VIII Congresso internazionale di Storia delle Religioni*, Florence 1956, pp. 407f., and in *Vig. Chr.* 10, 1956, pp. 149–156; H.-Ch. Puech, in *Enc. Fr.* tom. XIX, Paris 1957, fasc. 19. 42–7.

The work, in the Coptic (Subachmimic) version which we now possess, bears no title; after a greeting and a benediction of which only a few words remain, it begins as follows:

Since thou hast prayed me to send thee a secret book (ἀπόκρυ-φον) of which the revelation was given to me, as well as to Peter, by the Lord, I have not been able to refuse thee nor to keep silence to thee-ward, but I have written it in Hebrew (ἑβραῖος) characters and send it to thee—but to thee alone. However, since thou art a servant (ὑπηρέτης; *cf. Lk. 1:2, Acts 26:16, 1 Cor. 4:1*) of the holy salvation, strive to beware of communicating to many people this book which the Saviour did not wish to entrust (indiscriminately) to all of us, his twelve disciples. And blessed (μακάριος) shall they be, who shall be saved through faith (πίστις) in this word (λόγος). Moreover I have sent thee, ten months ago, another secret writing (ἀπόκρυφον), which the Saviour hath revealed to me. But in regard to this, think thereon, and on that which hath been revealed to me, James, who . . .

(p. 1. 8–35 of Ms.; translation after M. Malinine, H.-Ch. Puech, G. Quispel)

We have therefore to do not with a gospel in the proper sense but, as these lines make clear, with an ἀπόκρυφον, an esoteric revelation, supposed to have been composed in Hebrew by James (the brother of the Lord?) and apparently transmitted by him in the form of an epistle to a recipient whose name—assuming that it occurred in the preamble of the writing, now mutilated—remains unknown. In spite of this it deserves, like the Apocryphon of John (above, pp. 314ff.), to be ranked among the writings related to the Gnostic gospels or referring to one episode or another of the Gospel narrative.

As in the Gospels of this type, the special teachings which

James relates in confidence to his correspondent are supposed to have been delivered by the risen Christ on the eve of His Ascension. The scene is described as follows:

And after 550 days which followed his resurrection from the dead, we (the twelve disciples) said to him: "Thou hast gone, and thou hast departed from us". And Jesus said: "No, but I am about to go to the place (τόπος) whence I am come (*cf. also p. 14. 20–22 and Jn. 16:5, 28; Evang. Petri 56; Apocryphon Johannis p. 19:15f., Till p. 79*). If ye wish to come with me, come". They all answered and said: "If thou dost command us, we shall come". He said: "Verily, I say unto you, that no one (*of you*) shall ever enter into the Kingdom of Heaven because I have commanded him, but inasmuch as ye (*i.e. only when ye*) have been perfected in fulness (*lit.: filled up*). Leave me James and Peter, that I may perfect them (*lit.: fill them up*) in fulness". And when he had called them both, he took them aside, commanding the others to attend to their tasks.

(p. 2. 19–39)

Two things should be noted: in the first place, the 550 days here mentioned correspond to the period assigned—contrary to Acts 1:3 (40 days)—by the Valentinians (Iren. *adv. haer.* I. 1. 5 H: 18 months), the Ophites (Iren. I. 28. 7: 18 months) and the Ascension of Isaiah (9. 16: 545 days) to the sojourn of Jesus among His disciples between the Resurrection and the Ascension.[1] Secondly, the place and privileged rôle accorded to James and Peter recall a tradition reported by Eusebius of Caesarea (*H.E.* II. 1. 3–4) after Clement of Alexandria, according to which the Lord after His Resurrection imparted 'Gnosis' first to these same two apostles and to John.

In the sequel, the Saviour instructs James and Peter, answering questions posed now by one, now by the other. The principal themes are the attitude to be adopted in the face of persecution (πειρασμός), and the possibility of prophecy. A series of long exhortations, interrupted by threatening warnings, ends with the announcement of the Ascension and the account of its accomplishment. Here Peter and James are the only witnesses, and not as in Acts 1:9 all the apostles:

"Here must I stop (*cease to tell you these things*). And now I ascend again to the place (τόπος) whence I came . . . Be ye attentive

[1] On this cf. A. Harnack, *Chronologische Berechnung des 'Tags von Damaskus'*, SB Berlin, 1912, pp. 673–682.

(προσέχειν) to the glory which awaits me, and when you have opened your heart, hear the hymns which await me in the heavens. In fact, I must today betake myself to the right hand of my Father. The supreme word, I have spoken it unto you. I am going to separate myself from you. For the chariot (ἅρμα) of the Spirit (πνεῦμα) carries me into the heights, and from this moment I must strip myself to clothe myself again. But pay ye heed! Blessed are they who have spread abroad the good news (εὐαγγελίζειν) of the Son before he is descended to earth . . . Thrice blessed are they who have preached these things before they are accomplished . . .". When he had thus spoken, he went away. But we knelt down, Peter and I; we gave thanks and lifted up our heart to the heavens (cf. Acts 1:10f.). We heard with our ears and saw with our eyes the noise of war (πόλεμος: cf. Mt. 24:6; Mk. 13:7?) and the sound of the trumpet (cf. 1 Cor. 15:52?) and a great tribulation. Nay more, we lifted up our understanding (νοῦς) higher still, and saw with our eyes and heard with our ears hymns and the prayers of angels. And the angels and the eminences of the heavens rejoiced. They sang hymns, and we too rejoiced. Then we wished to lift up our spirit (πνεῦμα) beyond (?) the heaven, nigh to the Greatness, but as we ascended up it was not given to us to see or to hear any thing. The other disciples called us and asked: "What have ye heard from the mouth of the Master? What did he say to you, and whither has he gone?" And we answered them: "He is ascended up, and hath greeted us with the right hand (δεξιά), and he hath promised us, to all of us, Life".

(p. 14. 29–15. 37)

Such a description—which is in a sense to be compared with the account of the same incident given in chapters 42–51 of the *Epistula Apostolorum* (above, pp. 220ff.)—combines reminiscences of Biblical material (farewell discourse in Jn. 16, assumption of Elijah, vision of Ezekiel) with pagan conceptions and ideas (imagery of apotheosis and of imperial triumphs).[1]

The writing draws to its end. Although the disciples give

[1] On the 'chariot of the Spirit' cf. H.-Ch. Puech and G. Quispel, *Vig. Chr.* 8, 1954, pp. 15–18; on the gesture of triumphal farewell, the sign of greeting and of blessing, made by raising the right hand toward the sky, cf. H. P. L'Orange, "Sol Invictus imperator. Ein Beitrag zur Apotheose", *Symbolae Osloenses* XIV, 1935, pp. 86–114; id., *Studies on the Iconography of Cosmic Kingship in the Ancient World*, Oslo 1953, pp. 124–133 and 171–197; on the hymns which accompany the ascension into heaven cf. A. J. Festugière, *La Révélation d'Hermès Trismégiste* III, Paris 1953, pp. 133–137.

credence to the account which James has just given them, they still feel a certain bitterness. To avoid any offence (σκάνδαλον), James 'sends them separately to another place' (pp. 16. 7f.). He thus appears as leader of the Apostolic college and plays—if this refers to the sending of the disciples into the world—the rôle attributed in Mt. 28:19 to Jesus Himself; and while according to Acts 1:12 all the other apostles also returned to Jerusalem, here James is the only one to come back (pp. 16. 8f.). In conclusion, James expresses the wish that his correspondent may be the first to be enlightened by the faith which he is charged to preach, that he may have his 'part' (μέρος) among the 'beloved', the 'children' of God.

On the whole, and despite its variations from the canonical tradition, the Apocryphon does not have a thoroughly heretical character, and strictly speaking it would be permissible to see in it, with W. C. van Unnik (*art. cit.*), an offshoot of early Christian literature without any connection with Gnosticism. It would then present a case analogous to that of the *Epistula Apostolorum*, to which indeed it is akin both in form and in some of its details. Despite this, it seems preferable to consider the work as Gnostic, and to ascribe to it a Valentinian origin. This conclusion is prompted by certain features of its doctrine and vocabulary, and by the fact that the codex to which it belongs is on the whole homogeneous, and contains only writings by Valentinus or by his school.

Whatever the milieu from which it derives, the Apocryphon of James must have been composed in the second century or, if we follow van Unnik's conclusions (*Vig. Chr.* 10, 1956, p. 156), in Egypt between 125 and 150.

9. *The Gospel of Bartholomew*

On this gospel and the Gnostic origin which has been conjecturally attributed to its hypothetical primitive version, see below, pp. 484ff.

F. GOSPELS UNDER THE NAMES OF HOLY WOMEN

1. *The Questions of Mary*

Among their extensive apocryphal literature the 'Gnostics' properly so called possessed, according to Epiphanius (*Pan.* 26. 8. 1; I, pp. 284. 11f. Holl), certain books entitled 'Questions of Mary' (ἐρωτήσεις Μαρίας), in which Jesus is represented as the revealer of the obscene practices (αἰσχρουργία) which constituted the rites of redemption peculiar to the sect. The same father tells us more exactly (*Pan.* 26. 8. 2f.; I p. 284. 17–24 Holl) that two distinct works were described by this title: the 'Little Questions' (μικραὶ ἐρωτήσεις) and the 'Great Questions' of Mary; of the latter he supplies moreover two brief quotations, interpolated into the analysis of one of its episodes:

For in the Questions of Mary which are called 'Great' (for there are also 'Little' (Questions) forged by them), they assert that he (*sc. Jesus*) gave her (*sc. Mary*) a revelation, taking her aside to the mountain and praying; and he brought forth from his side a woman and began to unite with her, and so, forsooth, taking his effluent, he showed that 'we must so do, that we may live'; and how when Mary fell to the ground abashed, he raised her up again and said to her: "Why didst thou doubt, O thou of little faith?"

> (Epiphanius, *Pan.* 26. 8. 2–3; I p. 284. 17–24 Holl; for the last phrase cf. Mt. 14:31 and Apocryphon Johannis p. 21. 14–18, p. 83 Till)

It would therefore appear that the 'Great Questions of Mary' belonged to the ordinary type of Gnostic gospel: it was a revelation, an ἀποκάλυψις; a secret teaching of Christ was therein imparted to a privileged hearer, and no doubt, as the title suggests, in the form of a dialogue composed of questions and answers. The action—or at least one of its episodes—took place upon a mountain (the mount of Olives?). The other character is here probably, as in other works of the same kind, Mary Magdalene rather than Mary the mother of the Lord or Mary Salome. The procedure here ascribed to Jesus is influenced by Gen. 2:21f. (Eve, the woman, the 'mother of all living', produced from the side or from a rib of Adam, the first man). The following actions (sexual union, gathering and offering of the seed, etc.) are intended to serve as the model and first example, the prototype, for the eucharistic rites actually in use among the Nicolaitans, the Borborians and other licentious Gnostics in Egypt (Epiphanius, *Pan.* 25. 3. 2; 26. 4. 1–8; 8. 4–9. 9; 10. 8f.; Pistis Sophia c. 147; Second Book of Jeu, c. 43). Later the Manicheans also were accused of practising them.[1]

The character of the Little Questions of Mary remains more enigmatic. It has often been suggested that they are to be identified with the Pistis Sophia (above, pp. 250ff.) or, more exactly, with the first three books of that work.[2] This hypothesis finds its chief

[1] On the whole subject see L. Fendt, *Gnostische Mysterien*, Munich 1922, pp. 3–29.
[2] E. Renan, *Marc Aurèle*, 12th ed., Paris 1905, p. 120 n. 3; Harnack, *Über das gnostische Buch Pistis Sophia*, *TU* 7, 2, 1891, pp. 107–109; id., *Litg.* I, p. 172 and II, 2,

support in the fact that in the Pistis Sophia of the 46 questions addressed by the disciples to Jesus 39 are placed in the mouth of Mary Magdalene.[1] It has—it seems rightly—been criticized and rejected by Liechtenhan[2] and Bardenhewer.[3] Even Schmidt himself[4] has abandoned it. Nor is there any ground for identifying with the *Little Questions of Mary* the *Gospel according to Mary* to which we next turn.

2. *The Gospel according to Mary*

(a) Part of the text is preserved in a Coptic (Sahidic) translation at the beginning of the Papyrus Berolinensis 8502 (5th cent.) p. 7. 1–19. 5 = pp. 62–79 Till (on the manuscript see above, p. 244). The first six pages and also pages 11 to 14 are missing. Of this writing therefore, which in the original state of the manuscript extended to 18 pages only, ten pages are lost and only eight—or very little more—remain. The title of the work is given in the colophon (p. 19. 3–5; p. 79 Till): *peuaggelion kata marihamm* (written *mariham* in the body of the text).

Literature: C. Schmidt, *Ein vorirenäisches gnostisches Originalwerk in koptischer Sprache*, SB Berlin 1896, pp. 839–847. – R. Liechtenhan, "Die pseudepigraphe Litteratur der Gnostiker", *ZNW* 3, 1902, p. 228. – C. Schmidt, *Gespräche Jesu mit seinen Jüngern*, *TU* 43, 1919, p. 239. id., *Pistis Sophia*, Leipzig 1925, pp. LXXXIII–XC (with German translation of some passages). Partial translation: C. H. Roberts, *Catalogue of the Greek and Latin Papyri in the John Rylands Library* III, Manchester 1938, p. 22. – E. Hennecke, *Apokr.* 2, pp. 69f. (summary). – W. Till, "Die Berliner gnostische Handschrift", *Europäischer Wissenschafts-Dienst* 4, 1944, pp. 19–21. – id., *EΥΑΓΓΕΛΙΟΝ ΚΑΤΑ ΜΑΡΙΑΜ*, La Parola del Passato, fasc. 2, 1946, pp. 260–265. – id., "Die Gnosis in Ägypten", *La Parola del Passato*, fasc. 12, 1949, pp. 238f. (summary). – Complete Coptic text with German translation: W. C. Till, *Die gnostischen Schriften des koptischen Papyrus Berolinensis* 8502 (*TU* 60), Berlin 1955, pp. 24–32 and 62–79. English translation in *Gnosticism. An Anthology* (ed. R. M. Grant), London 1961, pp. 65ff.

(b) The text of the final pages (p. 17. 5–21 and 18. 5–19. 5 of the Coptic Ms.) is preserved in Greek, i.e. in the language of the original, in Papyrus No. 463 (beginning of 3rd cent.) of the John Rylands collection in Manchester. This is a single leaf (numbered

pp. 194f.; C. Schmidt, *Gnostische Schriften in koptischer Sprache*, *TU* 8, 1-2, 1892, p. 597; E. de Faye, *Gnostiques et Gnosticisme*, 2nd ed., Paris 1925, p. 288 n. 2; more vaguely, H. Leisegang, *Die Gnosis*, 4th ed. Leipzig 1955, p. 353; cf. Pauly-Wissowa, 1 Reihe, 40 Halbbd., 1950, col. 1820. 62–1821.11.

[1] H. Leisegang, *op. cit.* p. 353.
[2] "Untersuchungen zur koptisch-gnostischen Litteratur", *Zeitschr. f. wissenschaftl. Theol.* 44, 1901, p. 240.
[3] *Litg.* I, 2nd ed., p. 355 n. 2.
[4] *Koptisch-gnostische Schriften*, 1 Bd., Leipzig 1905, p. XVIII.

21 on the recto and 22 on the verso) of a papyrus codex brought from Oxyrhynchus and acquired in 1917. Here also the title is indicated at the end: τὸ εὐαγγέλιον κατὰ Μαριάμ (Μαριάμμη in the remainder of the extant text). The Greek version differs at some points from the Coptic, and must have been a little longer.

The papyrus was examined and published by C. H. Roberts (*Catalogue of the Greek and Latin Papyri in the John Rylands Library*, Vol. III, Manchester 1938, pp. 18–23), and in a new edition, with some notes, by G. P. Carratelli in *La Parola del Passato*, fasc. 2, 1946, pp. 266f.; cf. further G. Kapsamenos, τὸ κατὰ Μαριάμ ἀπόκρυφον Εὐαγγέλιον (P. Ryl. III 463), ᾿Αθηνᾶ 49, 1939, pp. 177–186.

Literature: G. Quispel, "Das Hebräerevangelium im gnostischen Evangelium nach Maria", *Vig. Chr.* 11, 1957, pp. 139–144; R. McL. Wilson, "The New Testament in the Gnostic Gospel of Mary", *NTS* III, 1956–7, pp. 233–243.

As it has now come down to us, the writing is composed of two distinct parts. In the first, of which the beginning is lost, we find a conversation of the risen Christ (here described exclusively as 'Saviour'—cf. Irenaeus *adv. haer.* I. 1. 1 (Harvey i, p. 12)—or 'the Blessed') with His disciples, in conformity with the usual scheme in gospels of this type. In response to a question put to Him, the Saviour describes the future destiny of matter; then, in reply to Peter, He gives instruction on the nature of sin ('the sin of the world'). Finally he takes leave of his hearers:

When the Blessed One (μακάριος) had said this, he saluted (ἀσπάζειν) them all, saying: "Peace (εἰρήνη) (be) unto you (*Lk. 24:36; Jn. 20:19, 21, 26; 1 Pet. 5:14*). Receive you my peace (εἰρήνη; cf. *Jn. 14:27*). Beware that no one lead you astray (πλανᾶν) (*Mt. 24:5; Mk. 13:5*) with the words: 'See here!' or 'See there!' (*Mt. 24:23; Mk. 13:21; Lk. 17:21, 23*). For (γάρ) the Son of man is within you (*cf. Lk. 17:21*). Follow after him! Those who seek him shall find him (*cf. Mt. 7:7*). Go then and preach the Gospel (εὐαγγέλιον) of the Kingdom (*cf. Mt. 4:23; 9:35; 28:19*). I have issued no command (ὅρος) save (παρά) that which I appointed you. Nor (οὐδέ) have I given any law (νόμος) like the lawgiver (νομοθέτης), that (μήποτε) ye may not be constrained thereby". When he had said this, he went his way.

(PBerol. p. 8. 12–9. 5; pp. 65–67 Till)

Thereupon the disciples are in great perplexity:

But (δέ) they were grieved (λυπεῖσθαι) and wept sore, saying: "How shall we go to the heathen (ἔθνος) and preach the Gospel (εὐαγγέλιον) of the Kingdom of the Son of man? If he was not spared at all, how shall we be spared?"

(PBerol. p. 9. 5–12; p. 67 Till)

Here Mary intervenes (Mary Magdalene, as is almost the rule in Gnostic literature), to comfort the disciples and draw them out of their indecision:

Then (τότε) arose Mary, saluted (ἀσπάζειν) them all, and spake to her brethren: "Weep not, be not sorrowful (λυπεῖσθαι), neither (οὐδέ) be ye undecided, for (γάρ) his grace (χάρις) will be with you all and will protect you (σκεπάζειν). Let us rather (μᾶλλον δέ) praise his greatness, for he hath made us ready, and made us to be men".

(PBerol. p. 9.12–20; p. 67 Till)

Then follows the apparent conclusion:

When Mary said this, she turned their mind to good (ἀγαθόν), and they began (ἄρχεσθαι) to discuss (γυμνάζεσθαι) the words of the [Saviour].

(PBerol. p. 9. 20–24; p. 67 Till)

The second part (p. 10. 1–19. 2 of PBerol.) begins with a question from Peter, who asks Mary to impart to him and the other disciples the revelations which she separately has received from the Saviour, who loved her above all other women. Mary consents, and relates an appearance of the Lord in a vision (ὅραμα), in which the Saviour in reply to her question informed her that what sees the vision is neither the soul (ψυχή) nor the spirit (πνεῦμα) but the understanding (νοῦς), which is in the middle between the two. In addition He described (probably, since four pages are here missing) how a soul journeying through the planetary spheres converses with five hostile powers (ἐξουσίαι), from which it frees itself in order to attain to rest (ἀνάπαυσις) "at the time (χρόνος) of the season (καιρός) of the Aeon (αἰών) in silence". The passage is thus of a different kind from that of the preceding pages; it is related to the Gnostic gospels which, like the Apocryphon of John or the Gospel of Eve (above, pp. 314ff. and 241ff.), take the form of an account of a vision in the course of which the seer and the Revealer or Saviour exchange questions and answers.

Mary's testimony meets with unbelief from Andrew and Peter: When Mary had said this, she was silent, so that (ὥστε) (thus) the Saviour (σωτήρ) had spoken with her up to this point. But (δέ) Andrew answered and said to the brethren: "Tell me, what think ye with regard to what she says? I at least (μέν) do not believe (πιστεύειν) that the Saviour (σωτήρ) said this. For (γάρ) certainly these doctrines have other meanings". Peter in answer spoke with reference to things of this kind, and asked them (sc. the disciples) about the Saviour (σωτήρ): "Did he then (μήτι) speak privily with a woman rather than with us, and not openly? Shall we turn about and all hearken unto her? Has he preferred her over against us?"

(PBerol. p. 17. 7–22; p. 75 Till = PRyl. lines 2–17)

The attitude of Andrew and Peter here corresponds more or less to that ascribed to them in the Pistis Sophia, where the former (c. 100) is rebuked for his lack of insight, while reference is made twice over (c. 36 and 72) to Peter's hostility towards women and in particular towards Mary Magdalene. Again, in the last logion of the Gospel of Thomas (logion 114; pl. 99. 18–20 Labib) Peter is made to say to the other disciples: "Let Mary (Mariham) go out from among us, because women are not worthy of the Life".

This distrust reduces Mary to despair; Levi (the son of Alphaeus, likewise mentioned with Simon Peter and Andrew in the Gospel of Peter 60?) comes to her defence:

Then (τότε) Mary wept and said to Peter: "My brother Peter, what dost thou then believe? Dost thou believe that I imagined this myself in my heart, or (ή) that I would lie about the Saviour (σωτήρ)?" Levi answered (and) said to Peter: "Peter, thou hast ever been of a hasty temper. Now I see how thou dost exercise thyself (γυμνάζεσθαι) against the woman like the adversaries (ἀντικείμενος). But (δέ) if the Saviour (σωτήρ) hath made her worthy (ἄξιος), who then (δέ) art thou, that thou reject her? Certainly (πάντως) the Saviour (σωτήρ) knows her surely (ἀσφαλῶς) enough. Therefore did he love her more than us. Let us rather (μᾶλλον) be ashamed, put on the perfect (τέλειος) Man, [form ourselves (?)] as (κατά) he charged us, and proclaim the Gospel (εὐαγγέλιον), without requiring any further command (ὅρος) or (οὐδέ) any further law (νόμος) beyond (παρά) that which the Saviour (σωτήρ) said (Gr.: neither limiting nor legislating, as the Saviour said)."

(PBerol. p. 18. 1–21; p. 77 Till = PRyl. lines 18–31)

343

We are thus brought to the conclusion of the whole work:

But [when Levi had said this,] they set about (ἄρχεσθαι) going to preach and to proclaim (Gr.: When he had thus spoken, Levi went away and began to preach).

> (PBerol. p. 18. 21–19. 2; pp. 77–79 Till = PRyl. lines 31–33)

The work therefore seems to have been put together from two small, originally independent writings, which have been more or less artificially united by the introduction, at the end of the first part, of Mary Magdalene, whose intervention is supposed to restore courage to the disciples. There is in fact a contrast between the dominant rôle which she plays in the second part and the modest place which she assumes in the first, or seems to have had in the work which lies behind it. At any rate the title 'Gospel of Mary' is strictly appropriate only to the second part of our present apocryphon.

The language and the different themes of the writing leave no doubt of its Gnostic character and origin. It is however difficult if not impossible to ascribe it to any particular Gnostic school. On the other hand we may date it fairly certainly in the 2nd century.

3. The "Genna Marias"

The apocryphal document *Genna Marias* (Birth, Genealogy or Descent of Mary?) may be included here, or mentioned by way of an appendix. It belonged to the numerous writings produced or read by the 'Gnostics' properly so called, and of its existence, its title and part of its contents we know only from a passage in the account devoted to these sectaries by Epiphanius (*Pan.* 26. 12. 1–4; I p. 290. 19–291. 13 Holl):

Among them (*sc. the 'Gnostics'*) an immense number of other forged writings are tolerated. For they say that there is a certain book, the 'Genna Marias', and when they suggest terrible and destructive things they say these are there. It was for this reason, they say, that Zacharias was slain in the Temple (*cf. Mt. 23:35; Lk. 11:51*), because, they say, he had seen a vision, and when he wished to tell the vision his mouth was stopped up (*cf. Lk. 1:22*) from fear. For he saw, they say, at the hour of the incense-offering as he was burning incense, a man standing, they say, having the form of an ass (*cf. Lk. 1:9–12*). And when he came out, they say, and wished to say "Woe unto you! Whom do ye worship?", he who appeared to him within in the Temple stopped up his mouth, that he could not speak (*cf. Lk. 1:20*). But when his mouth was opened, that he might speak (*cf. Lk. 1:64*), then he revealed it to them, and they slew him. And so, they say, died Zacharias. For it was to this end that the priest was charged by the Law-giver himself, they say, to wear bells (*cf. Exod. 28:33–35*), in order that whenever he entered in to do priestly service he who was worshipped, hearing the sound, might hide himself, that the likeness of his form might not be discovered.

(Epiphanius, *Pan.* 26. 12. 1–4; I p. 290. 19–291. 13 Holl)

This section has been specially examined by A. Berendts.[1] It may be enough to note: that the identification of the Zacharias here in question with the father of John the Baptist occurs also in the Protevangelium of James 23f. and in Origen (*Comm.* ser. 25 in Matt.)[2]; that the semblance ascribed to the figure who appeared to Zacharias in the Temple in the form of an ass (or with an ass's head?) conforms not only with the conception formed of the God of the Jews by certain pagan circles and by the polemic of antiquity,[3] but also with a conception of the same God, or of the planetary Archon identified with him, which was common among the 'Gnostics', the Ophites, and other sectaries (Origen, *c. Cels.* VI. 30, vol. II p. 100. 19–22: Θαφαβαώθ, Θαρθαραώθ or Ὀνοήλ; VI. 37, p. 106. 19 and 23; VII. 40, p. 191. 6 and 10; Epiphanius *Pan.* 26. 10. 6, I p. 287. 15: Σαβαώθ; Apocryphon of John pp. 122. 19f. Till: Eloaios = Elohim; a Coptic Gnostic fragment in C. Schmidt, *Koptisch-gnostische Schriften*, Leipzig 1905 p. 334. 8–10: *eio* = Τυφῶν; for magical gems and amulets cf. Campbell Bonner, *Studies in Magical Amulets*, Ann Arbor 1950, pp. 130–132); and more generally that if the 'Genna' thereby manifests a violent hostility towards Judaism, the title of the work appears to confirm the interest taken by the Gnostics in Mary the mother of Jesus.

The document is perhaps, as A. Meyer suggests (*Apokr.* 2, p. 82), to be ascribed to the middle of the 2nd century.

G. GOSPELS ATTRIBUTED TO AN ARCH-HERETIC

1. *The Gospel of Cerinthus*

We cannot well speak (as does e.g. Quasten I p. 128) of a *Gospel of Cerinthus*, nor can we appeal to Epiphanius (*Pan.* 51. 7. 3;

[1] *Studien über Zacharias-Apokryphen und Zacharias-Legenden*, Leipzig 1895, pp. 32–37.
[2] Cf. Zahn, *Gesch. d. ntl. Kanons* II.2, pp. 695 and 776 n. 2.
[3] Cf. among others A. Jacoby, "Der angebliche Eselskult der Juden und Christen", *Archiv f. Religionswissensch.* 25, 1927, pp. 265–282.

II pp. 257. 6f. Holl) in support of the claim that the Cerinthians, or Merinthians, composed an independent gospel of their own. As Epiphanius himself indicates elsewhere (*Pan.* 28. 5. 1, I p. 317. 10f. Holl; 30. 14. 2, I p. 351. 9f.), the gospel used by Cerinthus, and also by Carpocrates, was in fact identical with that of the Ebionites and apparently only a truncated version of Matthew; Bardy calls it a "judaizing rather than Gnostic" gospel ("Cérinthe", in *Rev. Bibl.* 30, 1921, p. 373). The heresiological tradition reckons the Cerinthians among the Gnostics, and occasionally treats them as akin to the Carpocratians; but some scholars have been led to consider them rather as Judaizers,[1] while others point to the confusion, notably in Epiphanius, between certain Jewish Christians, arbitrarily associated with a legendary Cerinthus, and the adherents of a Gnostic of the same name whose historical existence is much more probable and who worked in Asia Minor.[2]

2. *The Gospel of Basilides*

Among the non-canonical gospels which 'many' have 'undertaken' to write—or taken the liberty of writing—(Gospels of the Egyptians, of the Twelve, of Thomas, Matthias, etc.), Origen mentions (*in Luc. hom.* I, p. 5. 5–7 Rauer) that Basilides also had had the audacity to compose a work of this kind, a *Gospel according to Basilides* (κατὰ Βασιλείδην εὐαγγέλιον). This testimony is thus translated by Jerome (*op. cit.* p. 5. 4–6): "Ausus fuit et Basilides scribere euangelium et suo illud nomine titulare." Ambrose in his turn reproduces it (*Expositio euangelii Lucae* I. 2; p. 10. 19f. Schenkl): "Ausus est etiam Basilides euangelium scribere, quod dicitur secundum Basilidem". Elsewhere (*Comm. in Matth.*, prol., *PL* XXVI 17A) Jerome mentions, beside a Gospel of Apelles, the *euangelium Basilidis*. Cf. further the Venerable Bede, *In Lucae euangelium expositio* I, prol., *PL* XCII 307 C. An echo of Origen's testimony occurs in a fragment of Philip of Side's history of the Church (*TU* 5, 2, 1888, p. 169 no. 4).

It is very difficult to frame any conception of the form and content of this 'gospel', assuming that it really was an original and independent work. Hilgenfeld[3] conjectured that it was a gospel related to that of Luke. Windisch[4] saw in it a redaction of Luke, which would thus represent a counterpart to Marcion's Gospel

[1] A. Wurm, "Cerinth—ein Gnostiker oder Judaist?" *Theol. Quartal-schr.* 86, 1904, pp. 20–38.

[2] Cf. C. Schmidt–J. Wajnberg, *Gespräche Jesu mit seinen Jüngern nach der Auferstehung,* *TU* 43, 1919, pp. 403–453.

[3] *Historische-kritische Einleitung in das Neue Testament*, Leipzig 1875, pp. 46f.; *Zeitschr. f. wissensch. Theol.* 21, 1878, p. 234 note; *Die Ketzergeschichte des Urchristentums*, Leipzig 1884, p. 201.

[4] "Das Evangelium des Basilides", *ZNW* 7, 1906, pp. 236–246.

(below, pp. 348f.). According to Zahn[1] it was on the contrary a kind of Gospel-harmony, in which passages from the four canonical Gospels were arranged in a tendentious fashion.

This view was followed by Buonaiuti:[2] "The Gospel of Basilides was very probably a patchwork derived from the canonical Gospels". Hennecke for his part (*Apokr.* 2, p. 68) thought that the work made use of Matthew, as well as of a number of esoteric traditions. He writes: "But according to the text of the title this (*sc. the Gospel of Basilides*) cannot have been merely an abbreviated older Gospel (Luke, in fact, according to Windisch, *ZNW* 1906, pp. 236–246), it also very probably contained (despite Windisch pp. 239, 245) in a variant form (Clem. Alex. III. 1. 1) the independent saying Mt. 19:11f. (on its use among the early Christians cf. W. Bauer in *Ntl. Studien für Georg Heinrici* 1914, pp. 235ff.), and in addition (over and above the Synoptic character of the language) possibly some accounts which rested upon the familiar alleged relationship of Basilides to Matthias (Hippol. *Ref.* VII. 20. 1; above, p. 311) and to Glaucias, an interpreter of Peter (Clem. Alex. VII. 17. 106. 4)". Hendrix again came to the conclusion: "This 'Gospel according to Basilides' must have shown some relationship with the writing of the same name κατὰ Λουκᾶν which lies before us, and must have agreed at many points with our Fourth Gospel, since indeed at different places in Basilides' doctrine a passage from the last-named writing may already be adduced. To reconstruct the content is no longer possible. We may only here and there conjecture what may have stood therein."[3]

To judge from the list of Gospel passages quoted or employed in the extant parts of Basilides' Ἐξηγητικά—i.e. his commentary "in 24 books on the Gospel" (his own gospel?) (Agrippa Castor, in Euseb. *H.E.* IV. 7. 7; Clem. Alex., *Strom.* IV. 12. 81, who gives extracts from Book 23)—the use of Matthew beside Luke appears probable. In a fragment of Book 13 (Acta Archelai LXVII. 5) the parable of the rich man and Lazarus (peculiar to Luke 16:19–31) is expounded; the expression *natura sine radice* might perhaps be inspired by Lk. 8:13 (cf. Mt. 13:21; Mk. 4:6 and 17). Another passage, quoted by Clement of Alexandria (*Strom.* III. 1. 1), makes use of Mt. 19:11–12 (peculiar to Matthew!). A saying of Basilides reported by Epiphanius (*Pan.* 24. 5. 2; I p. 262. 8–10 Holl), which Holl believes to be derived from the Ἐξηγητικά, appeals to Mt. 7:6:

---

[1] "Basilides und die kirchliche Bibel", in *Gesch. d. ntl. Kanons* I, pp. 763–774.

[2] *Frammenti gnostici*, Rome 1923, p. 10 (ET London 1924, p. 6).

[3] *De Alexandrijnsche Haeresiarch Basilides. Een Bijdrage tot de Geschiedenis der Gnosis*, Amsterdam 1926, p. 82.

We are the men, but all the others are swine and dogs. And for this cause he said: "Cast not the pearls before the swine, neither give that which is holy to the dogs".

From the context, the passage may have been a comment on Mt. 10:33. Much less certain is Bardenhewer's conjecture (*Litg.* I, 2nd ed., p. 349) that the Basilidian theory of the μετενσωμάτωσις, based on Rom. 7:9–10 and summarized by Origen in his Commentary on Romans (V. 1; *PG* XIV 1015 A/B; add VI. 8, 1083 A/B), also belonged to the Ἐξηγητικά.

In short, it must be said that all conjectures concerning the Gospel of Basilides remain uncertain.

3. *The Gospel of Marcion*

The work of Marcion entitled Εὐαγγέλιον—of which an-Nadim as late as 987–88 writes (Fihrist al-'ulum, in G. Flügel, *Mani*, Leipzig 1862, p. 160): "Marcion composed a book which he called Evangelium"—is by no means a completely independent writing, but rather—as is almost unanimously agreed—a redaction of Luke, abridged, shorn of its first two chapters, and accommodated by changes of detail to the doctrinal views of its editor (Docetism, Encratism, hostility to Judaism and the Old Testament, etc.). On this see W. Bauer, *Apokr.* 2, pp. 71–72. The theory of Semler, Eichhorn and the Tübingen school, renewed by P. L. Couchoud,[1] asserts that Luke is dependent on Marcion's Gospel and not the reverse; that the Church expanded a Gospel narrative taken over from the heresiarch, and placed it under the authority of Luke. This view seems paradoxical and impossible to maintain; it has been refuted and rejected in particular by Loisy.[2] J. Knox[3] however refuses to admit that Marcion simply abbreviated the text of Luke as we know it; he conjectures that Marcion used an *Urlukas*, an original and shorter version of Luke which was later expanded by the Church "in the interest of anti-Marcionite apologetic". On the other hand it has been claimed that Marcion in addition also made occasional use of the other three canonical Gospels. This thesis, defended notably by Zahn (*Gesch. d. ntl. Kanons* I. 2, pp. 673–680), has been rejected by Harnack (*Marcion*, 2nd ed., Leipzig 1924, pp. 249*–255*).

Reconstructions of Marcion's εὐαγγέλιον: A. Hahn, *Das Evangelium Marcions in seiner ursprünglichen Gestalt*, Königsberg

[1] "Is Marcion's Gospel one of the Synoptics?" *The Hibbert Journal*, Jan. 1936, pp. 265–277.
[2] "Marcion's Gospel. A reply", *The Hibbert Journal*, April 1936, pp. 378–387; cf. also *Les origines du Nouveau Testament*, Paris 1936, pp. 76f.
[3] "On the Vocabulary of Marcion's Gospel", *JBL* 58, 1939, pp. 193–201, and *Marcion and the New Testament. An Essay in the early History of the Canon*, Chicago 1942, pp. 84–88 and chap. 4.

1823. – id., *Evangelium Marcionis ex autoritate veterum monumentorum* descripsit A. Hahn, in J. C. Thilo, *Codex apocryphus Novi Testamenti* I, Leipzig 1832, pp. 401–486. – A. Hilgenfeld, *Kritische Untersuchungen über die Evangelien Justin's, der clementinischen Homilien und Marcion's*, Halle 1850, pp. 389–475 ("Das Evangelium Marcions"). – G. Volckmar, *Das Evangelium Marcions*, Leipzig 1852. – Above all, Th. Zahn, *Gesch. d. ntl. Kanons* II. 2, pp. 409–529 ("Marcions Neues Testament") and A. von Harnack, *Marcion*, 2nd ed., Leipzig 1924, pp. 177*–255* ("Das Evangelium Marcions").

Literature (dealing, among other subjects, with the relation of the Marcionite Gospel to the so-called 'Western' text or a pre-canonical stage of this text): A. Hilgenfeld, "Das marcionitische Evangelium und seine neueste Bearbeitung", *Theol. Jahrbücher* 12, 1853, pp. 192–244. – id., "Die Verwerfung Jesu in Nazaret nach den kanonischen Evangelien und nach Marcion", in *Zeitschr. f. wissensch. Theol.* 45, 1902, pp. 127 144. – Th. Zahn, *Gesch. d. ntl. Kanons* I. 2, pp. 585–718 ("Marcion Neues Testament"). – A. Harnack, Tatian's Diatessaron und Marcion'.s Commentar zum Evangelium bei Ephraem Syrus, *ZKG*, 4 1881, pps 471–505. – id., *Marcion. Das Evangelium vom fremden Gott* (*TU* 45) 1st ed., Leipzig 1921; 2nd ed., 1924. – id., *Neue Studien zu Marcion* (*TU* 44, 4) Leipzig 1923. – A. Pott, "Marcions Evangelientext", *ZKG* 42, 1923, pp. 202–223. – Hans von Soden, Review of Harnack's *Marcion*, *ZKG* 40, 1922, 191–206. – R. S. Wilson, *Marcion*, London 1933. – J. Knox, *Marcion and the New Testament*, Chicago 1942. – A. F. J. Klijn, *A Survey of the Researches into the Western Text of the Gospels and Acts* (Dissert. Utrecht) 1949 (esp. pp. 61–67). – E. C. Blackman, *Marcion and his Influence*, London 1948, pp. 23–41 ("Marcion and the Canon of the New Testament"); pp. 42–60 ("Marcion and the Text of the New Testament"); p. 63 ("Tatian and Marcion"); pp. 128–168 ("Did Marcion's Text Influence the Old Latin?"); pp. 169–171 ("Did Marcion's Text influence the Old Syriac?").

4. *The Gospel of Apelles*

According to Jerome (*Comm. in Matth.*, prol., *PL* XXVI 17A), whom the Venerable Bede copies (*In Luc. ev. expos.* I, prol., *PL* XCII 307 **C**), Apelles, at first a disciple of Marcion, composed a gospel which bore his name (*Apellis euangelium*). Jerome mentions it after the Gospels of the Egyptians, of Thomas, Matthias and Bartholomew, of the Twelve Apostles and of Basilides. But in fact, as Bardenhewer notes (*Litg.* I, 2nd ed., p. 374 n. 1), Jerome when he wrote this passage had under his eyes Origen's first Homily on Luke. Such a gospel is mentioned neither in the Greek text of this homily nor in Jerome's own Latin translation (p. 5. 1– 15 Rauer), nor in a text of Ambrose (*Expositio euangelii Lucae* I. 2, pp. 10f. Schenkl) which follows Origen very closely. The testimony of Jerome, who here adds to his source, may therefore rest on his own invention or on an error. If it did exist, the Gospel of Apelles would seem to have been only "a further elaboration or a new redaction of the Gospel of Marcion".[1]

In a later work Harnack[2] advanced a more radical theory: "We cannot believe Jerome's statement that Apelles had a gospel of his own; pseudo-Tertullian attests the Marcionite canon for A. The lost sheep and Lk. 8:20 were cited by him (Tert., *de carne* 7; the same chapter presupposes that A. rejected John), and the Infancy Narrative was lacking. Certainly A. quoted (in Epiphanius, *Haer.* 44. 2. 6) the saying: 'Be good money changers' as standing in the Gospel: but that proves nothing. However, there is nothing against the view that A. altered Marcion's gospel just as much as other disciples. Hippolytus (*Ref.* VII. 38. 2) expresses himself too generally when he says of A. that he took out of the Gospels and the Apostolos whatever pleased him."

In this sense we may adduce the following testimony of Origen (*Epist. ad quosdam amicos Alexandrinos*, in Rufinus, *De adulteratione librorum Origenis*, PG XVII 625 C): "You see with what a purging he hath cleansed our disputation, such a purging indeed as that with which Marcion cleansed the Gospels and the Apostle, or his successor Apelles after him. For just as they overturned the truth of the Scriptures, so he also, subtracting the things that were truly spoken, inserted for our condemnation things that are false."

5. *The Gospel of Bardesanes*

Like Marcion, or beside Marcion, Bardesanes of Edessa is accused here and there in the heresiological tradition of having composed or possessed for his own use a special gospel. But the testimonies are so slight that nothing can be derived from them. On this subject cf. W. Bauer, *Rechtgläubigkeit und Ketzerei im ältesten Christentum*, Tübingen 1934, pp. 35–37, who is inclined to assimilate the gospel in question to the Syriac Diatessaron.

6. *The Gospel of Mani*

Here several questions must be distinguished:

(*a*) It is certain that the Manichees made use of the four canonical Gospels: very numerous exact quotations occur in their literature, especially (as is to be expected) in those works which were read in or emanated from their Western communities.[3]

---

[1] Bardenhewer, *Litg.* I, 2nd ed., p. 374, who refers to Harnack, *De Apellis gnosi monarchica*, Leipzig 1874, pp. 74f.

[2] *Marcion*, 2nd ed., Leipzig 1924, p. 190 n.1. Cf. also p. 418* n. 1.

[3] Cf. for example P. Alfaric, *L'évolution intellectuelle de saint Augustin*, Paris 1918, pp. 193–213; id., *Les écritures manichéennes* II, Paris 1919, pp. 161–169; *A Manichean Psalm-book*, Part II, ed. C. R. C. Allberry, Stuttgart 1938, pp. 47*f.: "Scriptural

Mani himself in one of his works, the *Shaburakan,* employed and cited at length Mt. 25:31–46, as is proved by two extant fragments of the original text (Turfan fragments M 475 and M 477, in *Abh. d. pr. Akad. d. Wissensch.* 1904, *Anhang, Phil.-hist. Abh., Abh.* II, pp. 11–15), and he knew also other New Testament texts.[1] Like many of his disciples however he seems to have used especially the Syriac version of Tatian's Diatessaron.[2]

(*b*) On the other hand, the Manichees received into the volume of their scriptures a certain number of apocryphal gospels borrowed from Christian or Gnostic literature: the *Gospel of Peter* (above, pp. 179ff.), the *Gospel of Philip* (above, pp. 271ff.), the *Gospel of Thomas* (above, pp. 278ff.); probably the *Memoria Apostolorum,* the *Gospel of the Twelve Apostles,* the *Gospel of the Seventy* (disciples) (see above, pp. 263–271); perhaps also the *Genna Marias* (above, pp. 344f.), or a similar work, and the *Infancy of the Lord.*[3]

From the remains of accounts of the Passion and the Resurrection preserved in the Turfan fragments M 132 and M 18 it can be established that canonical and extra-canonical Gospels were employed, and also a Gospel harmony identical with, or rather similar to, the Diatessaron.

The first fragment (*Abh. d. pr. Akad. d. Wissensch.* 1904, *Anhang, Phil.-hist. Abh., Abh.* II, pp. 36f., ed. F. W. K. Müller), the remains of a writing which cannot be more exactly identified, relating to the trial of Jesus before Pilate and the mockery, contains and combines quotations from the Gospels, especially that of John:

Jesus . . . when he . . . governor (ἡγεμών: cf. *Mt. 27:2*) and Pilate . . . asked: "[I am not] in the house of Jacob and in the race of Israel" . . . gave answer to Pilate: "My dominion is not of this world" (*Jn. 18:36*), nevertheless through the pressure of the Jews bound . . . [sent] to King Herod (cf. *Lk. 23:6–16; Diatessaron; Ev. Petri 1–5*) . . . clothing [a crown of thorns] set upon his head (*Jn. 19:2; cf. Mt. 27:27f.; Mk. 15:17*) . . . with a reed they smote him on the cheek (*Mt. 27:30; Mk. 15:19; Diatess.; Ev. Petri 9*), spat (?) upon his eyes (cf. *Ev. Petri 9*) and cried: "Our sovereign Messiah!" (*Jn. 19:3; Mt. 27:29; Mk. 15:*

Quotations and References"; for the Manicheism of Central Asia see E. Waldschmidt and W. Lentz, "Die Stellung Jesu im Manichäismus", *Abh. d. pr. Akad. d. Wissensch.* 1926, No. 4, pp. 20–40.

[1] Cf. F. C. Burkitt, *The Religion of the Manichees,* Cambridge 1925, pp. 86–91: "Mani and the Gospels".

[2] H. H. Schaeder, "Urform und Fortbildungen des manichäischen Systems", *Vorträge der Bibliothek Warburg,* 1924–1925, Leipzig–Berlin 1927, p. 72; A. Baumstark, *Or. Chr.* 3 Serie, 10, pp. 264f., and 3 Serie, 12, pp. 169–191; Curt Peters, "Das Diatessaron Tatians" = *Orientalia Christiana Analecta* 123, Rome 1939, pp. 125–132.

[3] Cf. P. Alfaric, *Les écritures manichéennes* II, pp. 169–185.

18). – Moreover three times – came, and three times they fell down (*cf. Jn. 19:4–16?*).

> (Turfan fragment M 132; *Abh. d. pr. Akad.* 1904, *Anhang, Phil.-hist. Abh., Abh.* II, pp. 36f.)

The second fragment (*Abh. d. pr. Akad.* 1904, *Anhang, Phil.-hist. Abh.* II, pp. 34–36), of which it is expressly said in the super-scription that it belonged to a cycle of Crucifixion hymns, was interpreted by Alfaric[1] as part of Mani's 'living Gospel' (below, pp. 355ff.); F. C. Burkitt[2] called it a fragment of a 'controversial writing' which combined different extracts from Christian works, perhaps in order to "show inconsistencies in the orthodox account of the Passion". In reality, as H. H. Schaeder has shown,[3] we have here a quotation drawn from a Gospel harmony which in addition to the four canonical Gospels made use of an apocryphal gospel. The beginning of the fragment is in fact influenced by the Gospel of Peter (45–48):

> "[In] truth [he] is the Son of God". And Pilate thus replied: "I have no part in the blood of this Son of God". The centurions and soldiers (*qatriyonan va istratiyotan*) received at that time from Pilate a command, namely: "Keep this secret!" and the Jews gave promises (?) (*cf. Ev. Petri 45–48*) . . . But he (*it? the gospel commented on?*) shows that on the Sunday, at the beginning of cock-crow, Maryam, Salōm (*Salome*) [and] Maryam came among many other women; they brought sweet-smelling herbs and nard (*cf. Mk. 16:1*). They had come near to the grave . . . the angel . . . See the greatness (the glory), as did Maryam, Salōm and Arsani'ah (*Arsinoe; cf. Copt. Manich. Psalter, p. 192. 24 and 194.22*), when the two angels spoke to them: "Seek not the living among the dead! (*Lk. 24:5*). Think on Jesus' words, how he taught you in Galilee: 'Me will they deliver up and crucify; on the third day will I rise again from the dead' (*Lk. 24:6f.*) On this (?) afternoon go to Galilee, and bear the news to Simon and the others" (*cf. Mk. 16:7*) . . .

> (Turfan fragment M 18; *Abh. d. pr. Akad.* 1904, *Anhang, Phil.-hist. Abh., Abh.* II, pp. 34–36)

(*c*) A special place must be reserved for the logia or Agrapha which are found in fairly large numbers here and there in Manich-ean works, but have for the most part hitherto remained un-

---

[1] *Écrit. manich.* II, p. 38.   [2] *The Religion of the Manichees*, p. 88.
[3] *Urform und Fortbildungen des manichäischen Systems*, p. 74 n. 3.

observed. Several of them are certainly drawn from apocryphal gospels, but in other cases borrowing from sources of this kind is no more than probable, and of some we cannot say whence they derive, or might derive.

Two sayings of Jesus, one concerning the essential immortality of the living substance, the other about the doom of the soul which remains a stranger to the truth, are quoted by Mani in two passages of his Book of Mysteries (or Secrets) preserved by al-Biruni (*India* I, pp. 48 and 54f., trans. Sachau). They are represented as pronounced in reply to a question of the apostles, and have been reproduced above (pp. 268f.). Whether they come, as Alfaric (*Écrit. manich.* II, p. 175) has suggested, from the Gospel of the Twelve is doubtful.

On the other hand, the following five sayings, culled from the Manichean literature, certainly have as their source the Gospel of Thomas, or at least occur in that gospel:

(He said): "The grey-haired old men, the little children instruct them. They that are six years old instruct them that are sixty years old."

> (Coptic Psalm-book II, p. 192. 2f. ed. C. R. C. Allberry = Evang. Thom., Logion 4: pl. 81. 5–10; above pp. 283f.)

On this mystery (*sc. of Light and Darkness*), which to the sects (δόγμα) is hidden, the Saviour (σωτήρ) gave a hint to his disciples: "Know what is before your face, and what is hidden from you will be revealed to you" (*cf. Mt. 10:26f.; Mk. 4:21f.; Lk. 8:16f. and 12:2f.*).

> (*Kephalaia* LXV; vol. I, p. 163. 26–29 ed. C. Schmidt-A. Böhlig = Ev. Thom., Logion 5: pl. 81. 10–14; above p. 300)

" . . . that I may redeem you from death and annihilation. I will give you what ye have not seen with the eye, nor heard with the ears, nor grasped with the hand (*cf. 1 Cor. 2:9*). He who . . . on the sinners . . .".

> (Turfan fragment M 789; *Abh. d. pr. Akad.* 1904, *Anhang, Phil.-hist. Abh., Abh.* II, p. 68; cf. M 551, *ibid.* 67f. = Ev. Thom., Logion 17: pl. 84. 5–9; above, p. 300)

"Mariam, Mariam, know me: do not touch me. Stem the tears of thy eyes and know me that I am thy master. Only touch me not, for I have not yet seen the face of my Father (*cf. Jn. 20:15–17*). Thy God was not stolen away, according to (κατά) the thoughts of thy littleness; thy God did not die, rather he mastered death. I am not the gardener (κηπουρός) (cf. Jn. 20:15). I have given, I have received the . . ., I appeared (?) [not] to thee until I saw thy tears and thy grief . . . for (?) me. Cast this sadness away from thee and do this service (λειτουργία): be a messenger for me to these wandering orphans (ὀρφανός). Make haste rejoicing, and go unto the Eleven. Thou shalt find them gathered together on the bank of the Jordan. The traitor (προδότης) persuaded (πείθειν) them to be fishermen as they were at first and to lay down their nets with which they caught men unto life (cf. Mt. 4:18f.; Jn. 21:2–8?). Say to them: 'Arise, let us go, it is your brother that calls you'. If they scorn my brotherhood, say to them: 'It is your Master'. If they disregard (ἀμελεῖν) my mastership, say to them: 'It is your Lord'. Use all skill (τέχνη) and advice until thou hast brought the sheep to the shepherd. If thou seest that their wits are gone, draw Simon Peter unto thee; say to him 'Remember what I uttered between thee and me. Remember what I said between thee and me in the Mount of Olives: I have something to say, I have none to whom to say it'."

> (Coptic Psalm-book II, p. 187. 2–29 Allberry = Ev. Thom., Logion 38: pl. 88. 2–7; on the various forms of the logion, see above, p. 301)

What the Saviour preached; he said: "Blessed are they who are persecuted, for they shall rest in light. Blessed are they who hunger and thirst, for they shall be satisfied."

> (Böhlig, *BSAC* xv (1958–60) 57 n. 5; cf. Ev. Thom., logion 69: pl. 93. 24–29; above, p. 302)

The Manichean Psalter however contains some other logia which are missing from the Gospel of Thomas, and which with two exceptions appear here for the first time:

It is Jesus, who giveth repentance (μετανοία) unto him that repents (μετανοεῖν). He stands in our midst, he winks unto us secretly, saying: "Repent (μετανοεῖν), that I may forgive you your sins" (cf. Lk. 17:3f.?).

> (Psalm CCXXXIX; II p. 39. 19–22 Allberry)

He (*sc. Jesus*) is not far from us, my brethren, even as he said in his preaching: "I am near to you, like the clothing of your body (σῶμα)" (cf. Origen, in Jerem. hom. XVIII 9; p. 163.24–27

Klostermann: "*And it is promised through the prophets (Jer. 13:11?), saying: I will be nearer to them than the tunic to their skin*").

(Psalm CCXXXIX; II p. 39. 23f. Allberry)

I gave myself up to death trusting in the . . . divine word: "He that dies shall live, he that humbles himself shall be exalted" (*cf. Mt. 16:25; 23:12 and par.*).

(Psalm CCLXXIII; II p. 93. 10f. Allberry)

. . . according to (κατά) thy word which thou (*sc. Jesus*) didst utter: "Where (?) thy (?) mind (νοῦς) . . ." (*cf. perhaps the Gospel of Mary (above, pp. 340ff.), p. 10. 13–16:* "*He (Jesus) answered and said to me (Mary): 'Well for thee, that thou didst not flinch at the sight of me, for where the mind (νοῦς) is, there is thy countenance'*" (=treasure; *cf. Mt. 6:21, Lk. 12:34*).

(Psalm CCLXXIV; II p. 94. 24f. Allberry)

As the Saviour (σωτήρ) hath said: "Where your heart is, there will your treasure be" (*cf. Mt. 6:21, Lk. 12:34*).

(*Kephalaia* LXXXIX, vol. I p. 223. 3–4 Böhlig; *cf. Kephal.* XCI, vol. I p. 234. 8–9)

A man called down unto the world (κόσμος), saying: "Blessed is he that shall know (νοεῖν) his soul" (*cf. Epist. Fundam. in Augustine, c. Felic. I 16:* "*But the love of the Holy Spirit shall open the inmost places of your heart, that with your own eyes ye may see your souls*").

(Psalms of Thomas XIII; II p. 219. 19f. Allberry)

(*d*) Up to this point we have considered only the 'gospel', or more exactly the different gospels, read, used and commented on by Mani and his adherents. But by 'Gospel of Mani' we ought, strictly speaking, to understand a work by the founder of Manicheism, the original gospel composed by Mani himself.[1] This work, generally entitled 'The Living Gospel' but also called, here and there, 'the Gospel of the Living', 'the Great Gospel', or simply 'the Gospel' (Gr. τὸ ζῶν εὐαγγέλιον, τὸ εὐαγγέλιον), is one of the four, five or seven canonical works of the master, the 'Enlightener', and as such appears regularly—most often at the head of the list—in the different canons of the Scriptures transmitted either by the Manichees themselves, by their opponents, or by neutral witnesses (*Homilies*, p. 25. 2 and 94. 18f.; *cf.* p. 43. 16;

---

[1] Cf. K. Kessler, *Mani* I, Berlin 1889, pp. 205–212; P. Alfaric, *Les écritures manichéennes* II, Paris 1919, pp. 34–43; C. Schmidt–H. J. Polotsky, "Ein Mani-fund in Ägypten", SB Berlin 1933, p. 29; 31; 35–37; H.-Ch. Puech, art. "Evangelium (Lebendiges)" in F. König, *Religionswissenschaftliches Wörterbuch*, Freiburg 1956, col. 237f.

Kephalaia, Introduction, p. 5. 23 and c. CXLVIII, SB Berlin 1933, p. 35; Coptic Psalm-book II, p. 46. 21 and 139. 56; Chinese Manichean catechism or "Compendium of the Religion of the Buddha of Light, Mani", trans. G. Haloun-W. B. Henning, *Asia Major*, New Series, vol. III, part II, 1952, p. 194: "the first: the great *ying-lun*, interpreted 'book of wisdom' which thoroughly understands the roots and origins of the entire doctrine" = unpublished translation by P. Pelliot-P. Demieville: "Ière classe: ta-ying-louen, en traduction: Livre sacré de la connaissance qui pénètre l'origine de toutes choses, ou (mot à mot) des dix mille dharma"; *Acta Archelai*, c. LXII 6; Cyril of Jerusalem, *Cat.* VI 22; Epiphanius, *Pan.* 66. 2. 9; Timotheus of Constantinople, *De recept. haer.*, PG LXXXVI, 1,21 C; first or little Greek abjuration-formula, *PG* C, 1321 B; second or great Greek abjuration-formula, *PG* I, 1465 D; Germanus of Constantinople, *De haer. et syn.* 4, *PG* XCVIII, 44 A; al-Rāzī, reproduced by al-Biruni, in *Isis V*, 1923, p. 31 (J. Ruska) = al-'Awfi, Jawami'al-Hikayat, p. 41 ed. Nizamu'd-Din; al-Ja'qubi, in Kessler, *Mani*, p. 329; al-Biruni, *Chronol.*, p. 190 Sachau).

'Living', the epithet applied to this gospel, is frequently employed in the language of Manicheism, and was inherited from Gnosticism (cf. for example, 'the living Spirit', 'the living soul', 'Jesus, the Living One', perhaps also—see H. H. Schaeder, *Urform und Fortbildungen des manichäischen Systems*, p. 88 n. 1—Mani haija, Μανιχαῖος, Mani 'the living'). The term might imply that the document was presented and considered as of divine origin or nature, as emanating from the higher world of Light, Truth and Life (cf. the tradition or legend reported by Mirkhond (in Kessler, *Mani*, p. 379), according to which, to prove his prophetic claims, Mani produced a book, the 'Gospel', and said: "This book has come down from heaven"). It means in any case that the work brought to its readers a message of regenerating truth, which could bring about and accomplish their spiritual resurrection and thus procure for them salvation: this 'Gospel of Life' or 'Living Gospel' is above all a 'life-giving Gospel' (τὸ νεκροποιὸν Εὐαγγέλιον, ὅπερ ζῶν καλοῦσι: in these words it is rejected in the second Greek abjuration-formula, *PG* I, 1465 D).

The work was divided into 22 books or λόγοι, corresponding to the 22 letters of the Syriac alphabet, each section being designated in succession by one of these letters (Epiphanius, *Pan.* 66. 13. 3–5, where this arrangement is wrongly attributed to the Book of Mysteries; al-Ja'qubi, in Kessler, *Mani*, p. 206 and 329: "twelve (read: two and twenty) gospels, of which he named each gospel after one of the letters of the alphabet"; al-Biruni, *Chronol.* p. 207 tr. Sachau, or in Kessler p. 206 and pp. 317f.). The 'Living

Gospel' is also compared in the Coptic Psalm-book (Psalm CCXLI, p. 46. 20) to an antidote (ἀντίδοτος) composed "of twenty-two ingredients (μῖγμα)", and in the fourth of the Homilies, also translated into Coptic (p. 94. 18–19), it is called "the Great Gospel from Alpha to Omega" (i.e. corresponding to the original "from Alaph to Tau"). This arrangement is confirmed and illustrated by two fragments from Turfan. One of these, S 1, published by C. Salemann ("Ein Bruchstück manichäischen Schrifttums im Asiatischen Museum", *Mémoires de l'Academié Impériale des Sciences de Saint-Pétersbourg*, 8ème série, vol. VI, no. 6, pp. 1–7), contains three successive references:
"The Gospel 'alaph is taught"
"The Gospel tau is taught"
"The Gospel of the 22 is taught".

As for fragment M 17, published by F. W. K. Müller ("Hand-schriften-Reste in Estrangelo-Schrift aus Turfan, Chinesisch-Turkistan", II Teil, *Abh. d. pr. Akad. d. Wissensch.* 1904, *Anhang, Phil.-hist. Abh., Abh.* II, pp. 25–27), it bears a superscription which in the light of the preceding document apparently ought to be interpreted:
"The Gospel 'arab ('alaph) is taught."

That a section or a book corresponded to each of these letters seems also to be confirmed by one of the volumes (still un-published) of the Manichean library discovered in 1930 in the Fayyum, where reference is made (SB Berlin 1933, pp. 30 and 37) to 'the third Logos of the Living Gospel' and (A. Böhlig, *Wissen-schaftliche Zeitschrift der Martin-Luther-Universität, Halle-Wittenberg*, 6, 1957, p. 485) to 'the first' or 'the ninth Logos'.

It is very difficult to form any very precise or exact idea of the content of the work. If we may believe Photius, or pseudo-Photius (*c. Manich.* I. 12, *PG* CII 36 A), it contained a falsified account of the life or of certain acts of Jesus (" . . . in which certain destructive and ill-omened acts of Christ our God are invented by a disposition hostile to God"). Peter of Sicily on the contrary (*Hist. Manich.* 11, *PG* CIV 1257 C) affirms that it did not touch on any such subject. The impression left by a testimony of much greater value—that of al-Biruni, who had the writing in his hands—is that it was a gospel of a special kind, and one of which the form and content contrasted strongly with those of the canonical Gospels received by the Christians. Al-Biruni writes in fact (*Chronol.* p. 23 Sachau; p. 207 Kessler): "The adherents of Mani have a gospel of a special kind, which from beginning to end contains the opposite of what the Christians hold. And they confess what stands therein, and declare that it is the genuine Gos-pel, and its demands that to which the Messiah held and which he

357

brought; everything outside this gospel is invalid, and its adherents (*sc.* of the Church's Gospel) speak lies about the Messiah".

The little that we know about the subjects there treated allows us to suppose that the writing was either, perhaps, a gospel of the Gnostic type or a commentary on the Gospel of Jesus designed to correct or supplant it, or more probably a work of didactic and dogmatic character expounding the Manichean system as a whole or at least some of its principal points. The first book was devoted to the description of the Kingdom of Light which regularly opens every exposition of the doctrinal myth. We read in fact in al-Murtada ("Das volle Meer", text and German trans. in Kessler, *Mani*, pp. 349 and 354): "Mani declares in his 'Gospel' and in the 'Shaburakan' that the King of the world of Light dwells in the navel of his earth. He declares further, in the section 'alif of his Gospel and in the first part of the Shaburakan, that he (the God of the world of Light) is present on his whole earth (i.e. not only in its inmost part), from without as from within; he has no limits, save on the side where his earth abuts on that of his enemy (*the Kingdom of Darkness*)".

Elsewhere, according to the *Kephalaia* (LXI, vol. I p. 153. 29–31), an episode belonging to a later part of the same myth was dealt with: the swallowing and absorption of water, one of the five 'elements of light', by the Archons of matter or of darkness. As the work continued a further theme—according to the witness of al-Ja'qubi (*Chronicle* I, p. 181 Houtsma; German trans. in Kessler, *Mani*, pp. 206 and 329)—was that of prayer and of "what must be employed for the liberation of the spirit". In another passage Jesus was praised and blessed before the Father, the supreme God, as is attested by the allusion in a Turfan fragment, T II D 173c, composed in Uighur (A. von Le Coq, "Türkische Manichaica aus Chotscho" III, *Abh. d. pr. Akad. d. Wissensch.* 1922, No. 2, p. 12): "And the disciples, thus speaking (their) doubts, said to their teacher: 'On what ground does one in the great Gospel-book praise and bless first the Moon-god (Jesus) and only thereafter the great princely king of the Gods, the God Zarwan?'." Finally we learn from al-Biruni (*Chronol.* p. 207 Sachau; pp. 206 and 318 Kessler) that Mani, no doubt to authenticate his gospel and guarantee its authority as superior to any other, affirmed therein that he was "the Paraclete announced by Messiah (Jn. 14:16f.; 14:26; 16:7–15), and the seal of the prophets". Unfortunately we can derive nothing from the Turfan fragment M 733 (*Abh. d. pr. Akad. d. Wissensch.* 1904, *Anhang, Phil.-hist. Abh., Abh.* II, p. 31), in which a quotation is announced: "And in the gospel 'alaph of the Living he (Mani) says . . ." The quotation has not survived.

The only text from this work which has come down to us direct is supplied by the combination of two Turfan fragments which in part coincide and more or less complete each other (cf. E. Wald-schmidt and W. Lentz, *Abh. d. pr. Akad. d. Wissensch.* 1926, No. 4, pp. 22f.): fragments M 172 and M 17. The first (*Abh. d. pr. Akad. d. Wissensch.* 1904, *Anhang, Phil.-hist. Abh., Abh.* II, pp. 100–103; 1926, No. 4, p. 23) bears the subscription: "The argument of the living Gospel of the eye and the ear is brought to an end, and the fruit of the truth is taught". The second (*Abh. d. pr. Akad.* 1904, *loc. cit.* pp. 25–27) preserves the superscription: "The gospel 'alaph is taught". The passage may be approximately restored as follows:

Praised is, and praised may he be, the dear son of Love, the life-giver Jesus, the chief of all these gifts. Praised is and praised shall be the Virgin of Light, the chief of all excellences. Praised is and praised shall be the holy religion (the pure totality of the holy religion) through the power of the Father, through the blessing of the Mother and through the goodness of the Son (Jesus). Salvation and blessing upon the sons of salvation and upon the speakers and the hearers of the renowned word (or: of the commandment of the Holy Ghost)! Praise and glory be to the Father and to the Son and to the elect Breath, the Holy Spirit, and to the creative (or: holy) Elements! The word (argument) of the 'living gospel' of the eye and ear is taught, and the fruit of truth is presented. The Blessed shall receive this offering . . . ; the wise shall know; the strong shall put on good things to him that knoweth . . . For all is, and all that is and shall be exists through his power.

Then after a considerable interval:

I, Mani, the emissary of Jesus the friend, in the love of the Father, of God the renowned (holy), every . . . was from him . . .

On the other hand, it is only with great hesitation and with express reserves that we can attach to the Living Gospel several sayings or teachings of Mani quoted in the second part of the long Turfan fragment M 801 (W. Henning, "Ein manichäisches Bet- und Beichtbuch", *Abh. d. pr. Akad. d. Wissensch.* 1936, No. 10, pp. 18–41; on the source of the quotations cf. pp. 13f.):

. . . as he taught in the scripture: "Whosoever strives to come to that world of peace, he must from henceforth collect his soul (himself) in the sign of the gods of paradise."

(M 801 §§ 476–481; p. 32)

As he taught: "He who sees himself only on the outside, not within, becomes small himself and makes others small."

(M 801 §§ 547–551; p. 34)

. . . he will have compassion on his own soul, and will weep and lament, pray and implore, and beg remission of his sins.

(M 801 §§ 594–599; p. 36)

As he taught: "Where love is little, all acts are imperfect" (cf. 1 Cor. 13:1–3).

(M 801 §§ 628–630; p. 37)

As he taught in the scripture: "What profit is it to a righteous man, who says: 'I have power in my members', when by eye, ear and the other senses ('members') he creates corruption?"

(M 801 §§ 650–656; pp. 37f.; cf. also *Abh. d. pr. Akad.* 1904, *Anhang, Phil.-hist. Abh., Abh.* II, pp. 99f.)

As he taught: "At every time shall ye come together for the remission and begging of pardon (?) for sins; forgive, and seek pardon from one another; he who does not forgive, to him it is not forgiven" (cf. *Mt. 6:15; 18:35; Ecclus. 28:2*).

(M 801 §§ 738–741; p. 40)

No doubt we shall be in a better position to know the structure and content of the work when one of the Coptic Manichean writings found in the Fayyum in 1930 has been published. 31 pages of it have been acquired by the Berlin Museum and 250 by the Chester Beatty collection in London.[1] If we may depend upon the remains of the superscriptions which it has so far been possible to read or to communicate ("the σύναξις (assembly? homily?) . . . of the ninth λόγος", "The first σύναξις of the first Logos of the living gospel", "The second σύναξις" or "the third σύναξις of the third λόγος of the living gospel"), it may be presumed that we have here a kind of commentary or else homilies (?) on the Gospel of Mani, which we owe to one of his disciples.

The Living Gospel has often been confused, or there has been a tendency to confuse it, with a work of Mani famous in the Persian tradition under the name of *Ertenk* (*Erženg*) and entitled in

[1] C. Schmidt–H. J. Polotsky, "Ein Mani-Fund in Ägypten", SB Berlin 1933, pp. 30 and 34; C. Schmidt, *Neue Originalquellen des Manichäismus aus Ägypten*, Stuttgart 1933, pp. 12f.; A. Böhlig, "Synaxis = Homilia?" *Wissenschaftl. Zeitschr. d. Martin-Luther-Univers. Halle-Wittenberg*, 6, 1957, pp. 485f.

Parthian *Ardhang*.[1] Schaeder indeed went so far as to declare that *Ardhang* (derived from Old Persian **arta-Θaⁿha* = 'message of truth') was the Persian (and not Parthian!) equivalent of εὐαγγέλιον. But it is today no longer doubtful that in reality we have here two distinct works.

The *Ardhang* was a picture-book, a kind of *Tafelband*, a collection of drawings and pictures, intended to illustrate in concrete form the essential aspects of the dualistic doctrine, perhaps as an accessory or appendix to the Living Gospel. This is shown by the following among other proofs: the title Εἰκών given to it in Greek and in Coptic; the reference to it furnished in the Chinese "Compendium of the religion of the Buddha of Light, Mani" (*Asia Major*, New Series, vol. III, part 2, 1952, p. 195), at the end of a list of the seven canonical Scriptures which begins with a mention of the 'Great Gospel' ("one drawing: *ta-men-ho-yi*, [the great *men-ho-yi*], interpreted 'the drawing of the great two principles'"); and finally the allusions to its content made by Ephraem (C. W. Mitchell, *Ephraim's Prose Refutations of Mani, Marcion and Bardaisan*, vol. I, London-Oxford 1912, p. XCIII) and the *Kephalaia* (c. XCII, p. 235. 1–17). There was even a commentary to the illustrations collected in this album, the *Ardhang Wifras*, of which fragments have been discovered in Parthian.

On the whole subject cf. E. Waldschmidt-W. Lentz, *Abh. d. pr. Akad. d. Wissensch.* 1926, no. 4, p. 23.—C. Schmidt-H. J. Polotsky, SB Berlin 1933, p. 45 n. 3.—H. J. Polotsky, *Manichäische Homilien*, Stuttgart 1934, p. 18 note a.—id., "Abriss des manichäischen Systems", Pauly-Wissowa, Supp. VI, Stuttgart 1934, col. 244. 65–68.—W. B. Henning, *Bull. SOAS* 11, 1943, p. 71 and 12, 1947, p. 310 n. 4.—id., *Asia Major*, New Series, vol. III, part 2, 1952, pp. 209–210.

H. GOSPELS UNDER THE NAME OF THEIR USERS

Two distinct works are known to us under the name of Gospel of the Egyptians. One of them was used by the Valentinians (*Exc. Theod.* 67. 2) and, if it is the same apocryphon, by the Naassenes (Hippol., *Ref.* V. 7. 9), and was very probably utilized by the compiler of the Gospel of Thomas (above, pp. 298f.). This document we need not here discuss, since it is dealt with in another section of this volume (pp. 166ff.).

The other work can only be mentioned, to be immediately set

[1] K. Kessler, *Mani*, pp. 209–212; P. Alfaric, *Les écritures manichéennes* II, pp. 40–43; H. H. Schaeder, *Gnomon* 9, 1933, p. 347.

aside. Two of the papyrus volumes discovered near Nag Hammadi contain in fact a work entitled 'the sacred Book of the Great Invisible Spirit' (*tbiblos thiera ᵉmnog ᵉnahoraton ᵉmpneuma*), but designated also in the colophon as 'Gospel of the Egyptians' (*peuaggelion ᵉnrᵉmᵉnkēme*): Codex I of my classification, where it appears as the second document on pages 40. 14–69. 21, and Codex VIII, where it stands again in second place, immediately after the Apocryphon of John.[1]

This new and so far unpublished work, despite its second title, has nothing to do with the Gospel of the Egyptians already known, and indeed nothing to do with a gospel at all. It is a dogmatic treatise, an exposition of profound Gnosis with a leaning towards ritualism, and professes to have been composed, in the immemorial past, by 'the great Seth'. He is supposed to have kept it hidden, intending that it should only be revealed in the last times to the "incorruptible and holy generation of the Great Saviour". In fact, its author was a less mythical figure, a Gnostic teacher whose double name is indicated at the end: Goggessos, mystically surnamed Εὔγνωστος ὁ ἀγαπητικός. Its ascription to Seth, the rôle played in it by Seth and by the female aeon Barbelo, the conformity of some of its statements with this passage or that of the Apocryphon of John, and many details of doctrine, all invite us to see in the document a product of the Barbelo-gnostics or the Sethians. Altogether, there is nothing to justify the title, or rather sub-title, 'Gospel' which is given to it, and it cannot by any means find a place among the Gnostic writings of the gospel type.

[1] Cf. H.-Ch. Puech and J. Doresse, *CR Acad. Inscrr. et Belles-Lettres*, 1948, pp. 87–95; J. Doresse, *Vig. Chr.* 2, 1948, pp. 139–143, 156–158 and 3, 1949, p. 136; id., *Acad. Royale de Belgique. Bull. de la classe des Lettres*, 5ème série, t. XXXV, 1949, p. 442; id., *Les livres secrets des gnostiques d'Égypte*, Paris 1958, pp. 197–198, ET 177–181; H.-Ch. Puech, *Coptic Studies in Honor of W. E. Crum*, Boston 1950, pp. 102, 107, 111; id., *Enc. Fr.* t. XIX, Paris 1957, fasc. 19. 42–7 and 19.42–10.

VIII

INFANCY GOSPELS

(*O. Cullmann*)

General Introduction. The Gospels of Mark and John say nothing of
the childhood of Jesus. The oldest gospel tradition records only
those incidents in His life of which the disciples, or at least some of
them, could be regarded as witnesses. Thus the first event in Mark
is the appearance of John as a necessary preliminary for the
baptism of Jesus. Although the Gospel of John in its prologue goes
back beyond this historical 'beginning' (Mk. 1:1) to the absolute
beginning of everything, the real story of Jesus similarly com-
mences with John the Baptist (see also Acts 1:22).

Moreover, in the earliest period it was not the birth and childhood of Jesus which were of theological interest but primarily
His death and resurrection and secondly His words and works.
It is therefore not surprising that Christmas was not observed until
the 4th century, while at first, and still comparatively late, and,
moreover, by the Gnostics it was His *baptism* which was com-
memorated as His appearing upon earth (H. Usener, *Das Weih-
nachtsfest,*[2] 1911; O. Cullmann, "The Origin of Christmas", *The
Early Church*, ed. A. J. B. Higgins, 1956, pp. 17–36).

But the need to go back beyond the information derived in general
from the apostles to the youth, infancy and birth of Jesus was felt
much earlier, and comes to expression in two of our canonical
gospels, Matthew and Luke. Of course, the material to be found
there must have circulated in the tradition in an oral and, to a
certain extent, also in a literary form, long before its incorporation
in these gospels. The following are the narratives in question.
(1) Promise and account of the birth of the Baptist, Luke 1:5–25,
57–80; (2) Promise of the birth of Jesus, Luke 1:26–38; (3) Birth
of Jesus, Luke 2:1–20; (4) Circumcision, presentation in the
temple, Symeon and Anna, Luke 2:21–38; (5) The child Jesus
in the temple, Luke 2:41–52; (6) Promise and account of the
birth of Jesus, Matthew 1:18–25; (7) The Magi, Matthew 2:1–
12; (8) Murder of the Holy Innocents at Bethlehem, flight into
Egypt, and return to Nazareth, Matthew 2:13–23.

Since the motives for the fixation of this material are partly
the same as those which gave rise to the apocryphal infancy
gospels, but on the other hand operate in the special circumstances
of an earlier stage of development in a fundamentally different

363

way, a brief discussion is necessary of, firstly, the motives which produced the canonical infancy narratives, and, secondly, the motives for the development of the material in the form it assumes in the apocryphal infancy gospels.

1. *The reasons for the formation of the infancy narratives in Matthew and Luke*

(a) In time the early Christians, out of natural curiosity, wished to learn something of that part of the life of Jesus concerning which the oldest tradition is silent. Whenever biographical literature shows gaps, legend generally springs up, in the absence of reliable information, to supply the deficiency. It is to be noted, however, that the stories about Jesus' birth and infancy in Matthew and Luke are few. They actually deal only with the nativity and the events directly connected with it. Of the long period between the return to Nazareth and the baptism of Jesus Matthew says nothing, and Luke, apart from the statement, "the child grew and became strong" (2:40), which refers only to His normal human development during this time, has only the story of Jesus at the age of twelve in the temple; a story which has extra-biblical parallels and acted as a powerful stimulus for the creation of the apocryphal infancy narratives. Even the canonical birth stories betray legendary motives which have parallels in extra-biblical literature, especially in India, Egypt and Persia (for India see especially G. A. van den Bergh van Eysinga, *Indische Einflüsse auf evangelische Erzählungen*,[2] 1909; for Egypt E. Norden, *Die Geburt des Kindes*, 1924; for Persia T. K. Cheyne, *Bible Problems*, 1904.—For a critical examination cf. Th. Boslooper, "Jesus' Virgin Birth and Non-Christian 'parallels'," *Religion in Life* 26, 1956–57, pp. 87–97).

(b) So far as the canonical infancy stories are concerned the purely narrative interest, while undoubtedly felt, is quite secondary to that theological interest which was the chief impulse to their formation. Consequently, in contrast to the apocryphal gospels, they reveal a certain sobriety and especially a close connection with christology, even where they employ extraneous material. Thus the nativity story, which Matthew and Luke give in two different and independent forms, is told in terms of a theological proposition in primitive belief, namely that God revealed Himself in Christ so directly that unity of will and being must be assumed. While the great majority of New Testament writers are content with the fact as such, the two birth stories attempt to explain the nature of this unity by means of conception by the Holy Spirit and the virgin birth, and are therefore obliged to view Joseph's paternity as adoptive.

This solution leads to a certain tension with the concern already to the forefront of theological interest, to emphasize the christological affinity of Jesus with the Old Testament. This affinity also must be proved by means of the stories of His birth. This is done in the two divergent genealogies (Mt. 1:1ff.; Lk. 3:23ff.) in which, in order to establish the Davidic descent of Jesus, already contained in an old confessional formula (Rom. 1:3), the line of His ancestors is traced back.

On the other hand there was the concern, especially in the face of Jewish polemic (Jn. 7:41f.), to remove the difficulty that Jesus came from Nazareth, whereas according to prophecy Bethlehem was to be His place of origin. Matthew deals with this by showing that the parents of Jesus fled from His birthplace Bethlehem because of the persecution of Herod and on their return from Egypt did not go there, but to Nazareth (Mt. 2:22f.). Luke in his turn resolves the difficulty by showing that it was because of the census that Jesus of Nazareth was born at Bethlehem.

Behind the story of the wise men from the east there lies the theological idea of Christ's universal kingdom, a motive which is also present in the story of the flight of His parents, which brings the child Jesus into Egypt.

Luke's Christmas story, in which Jesus first sees the light of day amidst poverty and in the company of poor shepherds, is an example of the third evangelist's theological emphasis on the ideal of poverty. The stories of the presentation of the infant Jesus in the temple, of the coming of Symeon and Anna, of Jesus at the age of twelve in the temple, are meant to point to the fulfilment of the priesthood in Christ.

Finally, the association made by Luke of the nativity story of Jesus with that of John, the latter of which was early firmly fixed, as we see, in the quite independent tradition of the later baptist sect, is intended to transpose to the time of the births of the forerunner and of him who came after him the connection of John the Baptist with the appearance of Jesus, which was regarded in Christian tradition from the outset as "the beginning of the Gospel" (Mk. 1:1). In this way the true connection between John and Jesus is brought out, in opposition to the misrepresentations of the baptist sect, which saw in John the Messiah. On the other hand, in this later combination of two originally independent traditions there are already to be seen tendencies important for the development of the apocryphal infancy gospels: the typical linking of different legends into large groups of material, a process carried out by means of secondary related elements, and especially the endeavour to make interesting in themselves figures which, in the older gospel tradition, are important solely by reason of their relation to the person of Jesus Christ.

Literature: A. Resch, *Das Kindheitsevangelium nach Lk. und Mt.* (*TU* 10, 5) 1897. L. Conrady, *Die Quelle der kanon. Kindheitsgeschichten*, 1900. H. Petersen, *Die wunderbare Geburt des Heilandes*, 1909. K. Bornhäuser, *Die Geburts- und Kindheitsgeschichte Jesu*, 1930. G. Erdmann, *Die Vorgeschichten des Lk.- und Mt.- Evangeliums*, 1932. M. Dibelius, Jungfrauensohn und Krippenkind (SHA 1932 = *Botschaft u. Geschichte* I, 1953. pp. 1–78). M. S. Enslin, "The Christian Stories of the Nativity" (*JBL* 59, 1940, pp. 317–338). E. Burrows, *The Gospel of the Infancy and other Biblical Essays*, 1945. See also commentaries.

2. *The motives for the composition of the apocryphal infancy narratives*

(*a*) In the later development of birth and infancy stories narrative interests became predominant, although theological interests are still present. The tendency to draw upon extraneous legendary material, already discernible in the infancy narratives of Matthew and Luke, is greatly increased. The further away in time we get from the roots, the more unrestrained becomes the application to Jesus of what is recounted about the birth and infancy of sons of the gods and children of supernatural origin. Mention may here be made of the exaggerations of the traditions, preserved in the (infancy) gospel of Thomas, about the playful boy Jesus who in marvellous fashion plays the most ingenious pranks. The process of the formation of the canon about the middle of the 2nd century was only able to check to a slight degree the legendary accretions which had grown up round the childhood of Jesus, since Matthew and Luke, as we have seen, say nothing about this period of His life. In the infancy narrative of Matthew itself the flight into Egypt, which is only mentioned, with no detail, supplies rich soil for the growth of fantasy and the borrowing of extraneous material. And so here full rein is given to the laws which govern the formation of legend.

In particular, the narrative interest begins to concentrate on those figures and events which in the primitive tradition remained on the periphery and played a part only in so far as they had to do directly with the work of Christ. They acquire a value of their own and, quite independently of the story of Jesus itself, become the vehicles of legendary motifs. This is especially the case with Mary and Joseph. It is true that Matthew and Luke are interested in the parents of Jesus, but only for the purpose of showing His connection with Israel and the royal house of David. But now Mary and Joseph become leading characters, whose history has an interest of its own. Details are supplied about Mary's parents, her own miraculous birth is recounted, and her perpetual virginity (which in the framework of the older tradition, concerned solely as it is with Jesus, is unknown and indeed excluded) is affirmed. Joseph the carpenter gets a biography of his own. In the apocryphal gospels, which employ all this material, it is only subsequently that a loose connection with Jesus is restored, in the Protevangelium of James for the legends about Mary and in the History of Joseph the Carpenter for those about Joseph (see IX).

(*b*) At the same time, however, apologetic-theological considerations come in. The very problems which were caused by the formation of the divergent infancy narratives in the canonical gospels awaited solution. The story in Matthew and Luke of birth without a human father raises difficulties in the face of the older demonstration of Davidic descent through Joseph. Matthew at the end (1:16) and Luke at the beginning (3:23) of the genealogy have discovered a formula permitting an adoptive view of the paternity of Joseph, and consequently of the Davidic sonship of Jesus. This solution clearly could not satisfy everybody. So another solution was proposed, that Mary also was descended from David. This tradition, already widespread in the 2nd century (Justin), found a firm foothold in the legend of Mary (Protev. James 10).

An answer had also to be given to Jewish attacks based on the older accounts of the virgin birth. The Jews had spread abroad the idea that Jesus was the illegitimate child of a soldier called Panthera (*Handb.* pp. 47ff.; H. Strack, *Jesus, die Häretiker u. die Christen nach den ältest. Jüd. Angaben*, 1910), and, in the face of such slanders, at which Matthew already seems to hint, His virgin birth of Mary had to be demonstrated more palpably by means of a special narrative. The discreet allusions in Matthew and Luke no longer sufficed.

Again, the assertion of Mary's perpetual virginity had to be reconciled with the fact that, in the primitive tradition, Jesus had brothers. As distinct from the later catholic view that these brothers were cousins, Joseph was regarded as having been a widower, and they were his sons by a former marriage.

In another direction, it was necessary to rebut gnostic-docetic notions which denied the reality of the body of Jesus, by emphasizing the reality of His birth, but at the same time maintaining that Mary remained inviolate.

(*c*) It is the Gnostics who appear to have been especially interested in infancy stories and to have encouraged the collection of all this kind of material. They were always on the look-out for details in the life of Jesus upon which to hang the speculations they attributed to Christ (see VII). Besides the appearances of

367

the risen Christ to His disciples it was especially stories like that of Jesus at the age of twelve in the temple, and all the legends which grew up from them, which provided a suitable framework for Gnostic gospels. This was the genesis of the development of Gnostic infancy narratives (see 4, pp. 404ff. below).

(d) Throughout the Middle Ages the growth of legends about the birth and childhood of Jesus and what preceded them continued apace in ever increasing profusion. New collections of such material were continually being made, its dubious nature partially disguised by borrowings from the canonical stories. Despite this, opposition was aroused against this whole type of literature, especially in the West, where Jerome's energies led to its condemnation under Popes Damasus, Innocent I and Gelasius, who in the 5th century in his famous Decree specified the infancy gospels which were to be rejected. Later, in the 16th century, under Pius V even the office of St. Joachim, the father of Mary according to the Protevangelium of James, was removed from the Roman Breviary, and the text of the Presentation of Mary in the temple was suppressed, although both were later restored.

But despite every attempt to do so, it was not possible completely to uproot this popular material, especially in its widely disseminated form in the Latin pseudo-Matthew. It had to be regarded as sufficient merely to give it a more acceptable form by means of excisions and alterations. Luther, who had become a monk at the summons of St. Anne, mother of Mary according to the Protevangelium of James, later came out strongly against the apocryphal infancy gospels.

In fact, in antiquity, in the Middle Ages and in the Renaissance these writings exercised more influence on literature and art than the Bible itself. Poets like Prudentius in antiquity, the nun Roswitha in the Middle Ages, and many others have sung the praises of Mary (see R. Reinsch, *D. Pseudo-Evangelien von Jesu u. Marias Kindheit in d. roman. u. german. Lit.*, 1879). Ancient and mediaeval Christian art showed a special interest in the infancy gospels, in the miracles performed by the child Jesus, in His birth in the cave, and above all in Mary spinning for the temple curtain. In the 9th century Leo III allowed the whole story of Joachim and Anne to be portrayed in the church of St. Paul in Rome (see E. Hennecke, *Altchristl. Malerei u. altchristl. Lit.*, 1896; J. E. Weis-Liebersdorf, *Christus-u. Apostelbilder. Der Einfluss der Apokryphen auf die ältesten Kunst-typen*, 1902). The Renaissance artists continued this tradition unbroken (see B. Kleinschmidt, *Die heil. Anna. Ihre Verehrung in Geschichte, Kunst und Volkstum*, 1930; on the whole question see also C. Cecchelli, *Mater Christi*, Bd. I–IV, 1946–1954).

Literature on the apocryphal infancy gospels in general (in addition to *Handb.*, Bauer and Findlay and the older works mentioned there): E. Amann, Art. "Apocryphes du N.T." in *Dictionn. de la Bible*, Suppl. I 1928, pp. 428ff.; G. Ghedini, "La lingua dei vangeli apocrifi greci" (*Studi in mem. P. Ubaldi*), 1937; K. L. Schmidt, "Kanon. u. apokr. Evangelien und Apostelgeschichten" (*AThANT* 5) 1944.

Complete editions of the infancy gospels: *Ea* (text); C. Michel and P. Peeters, "Évangiles apocryphes" (*Textes et documents pour l'étude historique du Christianisme* dir. par H. Hemmer et P. Lejay) I, 1924[2] and II, 1914 (text and French trans.); James pp. 38–90; G. Bonaccorsi, *Vangeli apocrifi* I, 1948 (text and Ital. trans. and notes); F. Amiot, "Évangiles apocryphes" (*La Bible apocryphe. Textes pour l'histoire sacrée*, éd. Daniel-Rops), 1952 (French; German edition 1956); Santos pp. 133–393, W. Michaelis, *Die Apokryphen Schriften zum N.T.*, 1958[2] (German). – Commentary: *Handb.*

3. *Short Survey of the Texts Referred to or Translated*

(*a*) The basis of all the vast later literature constituting the apocryphal infancy gospels is the so-called Protevangelium of James, probably of the 2nd century, particularly for the birth, childhood and motherhood of Mary, and the Gospel of Thomas, not much later in its original form, for the miracles of the child Jesus. They are both here translated in full; the second, however, only from one of the extant Greek manuscripts, with a divergent passage of some length from the Syriac version.

(*b*) From the older gnostic infancy traditions are given a fragment of the Gnostic Justin and two extracts from the Pistis Sophia.

(*c*) The exceedingly numerous later infancy gospels are almost entirely compilations made from earlier writings, with the occasional incorporation of new sources or material. Besides translations into Syriac, Latin, Armenian, Coptic, etc. of the original text, more or less expanded, of the older apocryphal infancy gospels, the most notable of these later gospels, of which some important extracts are here translated, are the following: The Arabic infancy gospel, based on a Syriac text, which contains all sorts of legends about the Holy Family's descent into Egypt, in addition to material already known; the Latin pseudo-Matthew, mistakenly regarded by Jerome as a translation of the Hebrew Matthew; a later Latin gospel (Arundel-Hereford MS.), which incorporates into otherwise known material an unknown and apparently older source; and a portion of an Arabic Life of John the Baptist probably translated from Greek.

1. THE PROTEVANGELIUM OF JAMES

1. *Texts and Literature*. From ancient times we possess only one manuscript, first known through the Bodmer papyrus collection, Papyrus Bodmer V, edited in 1958 by M. Testuz. Following the judgment of papyrologists on the palaeographical evidence, the editor assigns it to the 3rd century. The text, however, testifies to a very advanced stage of secondary expansions and sometimes also of secondary readings. The older critical editions used barely half of the Greek manuscripts previously known, amounting to over thirty; some of them, indeed, mere fragments. They differ radically from each other in details. Nearly all of them are later than 10th century; a fragment of the 5th to 6th century published by P. Grenfell in 1896 contains a scarcely better text than the later manuscripts. Enumeration of the later manuscripts in Tischendorf and in *Handb.*, pp. 106f.; A. Ehrhard (*TU* 50, 1, 1937, pp. 56f.; p. 69) deals with some papyrus fragments discovered before the Papyrus Bodmer.

Latin manuscripts have not survived because of the condemnation of the book in the West, although doubtless an old Latin edition was current. A. S. Lewis published a complete and obviously very old Syriac form of the work from two manuscripts, the older of which (with an appended Transitus Mariae) belongs to the 5th to 6th century: *Studia Sinaitica XI, Apocrypha Syriaca: The Protevangelium Jacobi and Transitus Mariae*, 1902.—An Armenian version, agreeing closely with the Greek text, in a codex in the Mechitarist library in Venice, was first published by Isaias Daietsi, Venice 1898, pp. 250–264. With this compare the form in which the same material has been worked over in the first chapters of the Armenian infancy gospel (see below, p. 405): Text in Daietsi; English: F. C. Conybeare (*The Amer. Journ. of Theol.* 1, 1897, pp. 424–442); French: P. Peeters, *Évang. apocr.* II, pp. 69ff.—A Georgian version (in *Cod. Sinait. georg.* 6, 10th century), exhibiting interesting variants, was published by G. Garitte (*Le Muséon* 70, 1957, pp. 233ff.).—The Ethiopic text forms the basis of M. Chaine's edition in *CSCO* (*scr. aethiop.*, ser. I, vol. 7), 1909, pp. 3–19.—A Sahidic fragment in J. Leipoldt (*ZNW* 6, 1905, pp. 106f.).—For old Slavonic manuscripts see N. Bonwetsch in Harnack, *Litg.* I, pp. 909f.

First edition of the basic Greek text by Michael Neander, Basel 1564, since of the projected first edition of the French Jesuit G. Postel only the Latin translation appeared (ed. Th. Bibliander, Basel 1552). Subsequently the text was often printed. Important editions: Fabricius I, pp. 66–125; Thilo, pp. 161–273. Hitherto the standard edition has been the *editio critica* in Tischendorf's *Ea*, pp. 1–50. All later editions are based on it: E. Amann, *Le Protév-angile de Jacques et ses remaniements latins*, Paris 1910 (text and French trans.; comment.); C. Michel, *Évang. apocr.* I, 1924², pp. 1–51 (text and French trans.; notes); P. Vannutelli, *Protevangelium Jacobi synoptice*, Rome 1940 (Gr. and Lat. texts); Santos pp. 145–188 (text and Spanish trans.; supplement).—More recent translations: A. Meyer in *Apokr.* 2, pp. 86–93 (German); W. Michaelis, *Apokryphen*, 1958², pp. 62–95; F. Amiot, *Évang. apocr.*, 1952, pp. 47–64 (French trans.; German edition H. Daniel-Rops, 1956, pp. 33–50): James pp. 38–49 (English trans.); E. Pistelli, *Il Protevangelo di Jacopo*, 1919 (Italian trans. and notes); C. Rotunno and E. Bartoletti, *Il Protevangelo di Giaccomo*, 1950 (Italian trans.; notes). The oldest manuscript, recently discovered, has been edited by M. Testuz with introduction and French translation, Papyrus Bodmer V, *Nativité de Marie*, 1958.

For the older literature see A. Meyer in *Handb.*, pp. 106ff. (supplemented in *Apokr.* 2, pp. 84f.), which also gives a good commentary on the whole document. All the literature is given in Santos pp. 141–144. See further the information in the Patrologies of Altaner, pp. 51f., and Quasten I, pp. 118–122; also L. M. Peretto, "La Vergine Maria nel pensiero di uno scrittore del secondo secolo" (*Marianum* 16, 1954, pp. 228–265).—All textual problems are fully dealt with in the introduction by C. Michel, *Évang. apocr.* I, 1924², pp. I–XXII, but this is now to be supplemented by M. Testuz, Papyrus Bodmer V, 1958, pp. 9–28. See also E. de Strycker, *La forme la plus ancienne du Protévangile de Jacques*, Brussels 1961.

My translation usually gives to the text of Papyrus Bodmer V the place it deserves by reason of the age assigned to it by the papyrologists. Since, however, its readings are often clearly secondary, in many places variants are added from later manuscripts, as given in C. Tischendorf's text, within square brackets or in a parallel column.

2. *Title and Contents*. The familiar title 'Protevangelium' is not old. It is to Postel and Neander that it owes its established position. It was obviously current in the East at the time, and implies that the subject-matter is earlier than the events recorded in the canonical gospels. The oldest manuscript (Papyrus Bodmer V) has: 'Birth of Mary. Revelation of James', the later Greek manuscripts usually 'Story', 'History' or 'Account' and then, either with or without mention of James, give the contents, usually described as 'Birth of Saint Mary, Mother of God'. The Syriac translation bears the title 'Birth of our Lord and our Lady Mary'. Origen refers to this document as 'Book of James'.

Although it reaches the birth of Jesus and recounts it, it is really rather an account of the miraculous birth of Mary, the daughter of the wealthy Joachim and his wife Anne, her up-bringing in the temple and her virginity, which is not impaired by the widower Joseph, to whom she is entrusted by lot, and by the birth of Jesus. Chapters 22–24 recount the murder of Zacharias, who is identified with the father of the Baptist.

3. *Author and Date.* The author purports to be James, who wrote the book after the death of Herod (the Great; or Herod Agrippa, as the necessity for the author's flight might suggest). By this James is meant the brother of the Lord, who, according to the Protev., was Joseph's son by a former marriage. This seems to have been the commonest view, although the Greek fathers, with their cautious attitude to the subject, speak of "a certain James". The Decree of Gelasius, which condemns the writing, attributes it to James the younger (cf. Mk. 15:40).

In actual fact the book cannot have been written before 150. It presupposes the canonical infancy stories, is certainly not to be regarded as their source (against Conrady), is not derived from a common written source (against Resch), and—apart perhaps from isolated passages—was not originally written in Hebrew (Resch, Conrady). It makes very free use of the narratives familiar to us from Matthew and Luke, probably to some extent following oral tradition (birth of Jesus in a cave at Bethlehem). Thus the growth of the canon had not yet finished. Since Origen certainly, and Clement of Alexandria probably, knew the document, and Justin exhibits very close contacts with its ideas (birth in the cave, Davidic descent of Mary), its roots go back to about the year 150, although several chapters must be later additions (see below). The contents do not suggest a Jewish Christian author. On the contrary, ignorance of Palestinian geography and of Jewish customs (expulsion of Joachim for childlessness, upbringing of Mary in the temple) point to a non-Jew.

4. *Unity of the Work.* Various discrepancies, which the manu-scripts attempt to harmonize, show that the original work utilized earlier materials of varying provenance and combined them. Especially important, however, are the expansions which must early have been made in this popular work. In the impressive description of the cessation of nature at the moment of Jesus' birth found in the previously known text, Joseph suddenly speaks in the first person (18:2). The view that this is a passage from another source later inserted into the narrative seems now to be confirmed by its absence from the oldest manuscript. In 20:2 the later manuscripts also have a prayer of Salome, whose addition to the midwife as a witness to the virginity of Mary is altogether second-ary, as well as unimportant details, which are lacking in the

papyrus. Although the text of this papyrus sometimes appears to show later abbreviations, these features do not actually belong to the original text. It is certain, however, that the oldest extant manuscript itself shows unmistakably clear traces of later expansion of the original work, which consisted of chapters 1–20, the story of the birth and infancy of Mary and of the birth of Jesus. Thus it is obvious that the murder of Zacharias narrated in chapters 22–24 probably did not yet form part of the book in the time of Origen, for although he cites it in referring to the first marriage of Joseph, he elsewhere gives a completely different version of the reason for the death of Zacharias from the account in chapters 22ff. (See A. Berendts, *Studien über Zacharias-Apokryphen und Zacharias-Legenden*, 1895; id., *Die handschriftliche Überlieferung der Zacharias- und Johannes-Apokryphen*, *TU* 26, 3, 1904.) The story is a later addition to the Protev. on the analogy of the combination of the John and Jesus traditions in Luke. Whether the whole of the central section (chapters 17–21) on the birth of Jesus is a later addition to the real narrative about Mary (a view which has in its favour the difference of motif), cannot be definitely decided, since here at least there is a closer connection.

5. *Literary Style and Theological Character*. In comparison with later infancy gospels the work has great merit. The borrowing of legendary details (with the exception of the story of the midwife) is comparatively restrained. The whole presentation is impressive and extremely graphic and is evidence of a sober, sincere and poetic mind. The author in using sources from oral and literary Christian tradition, besides much material from the Old Testament, especially the story of Samuel, knew how to form from them an artistic whole. Only when apologetic requires it does he not hesitate to retain crude and even distasteful features.

The whole work is written for the glorification of Mary. Not only are Jewish calumnies (see above p. 367) by implication vigorously refuted; all the themes of future Mariology are propounded: although, it is true, the 'Immaculate conception' of the mother of Jesus is not taught, her miraculous birth is recorded. The virgin birth, in contrast to the more unbiased views of Tertullian and Origen, is already understood as implying Mary's perpetual virginity. This is harmonized with the existence of brothers of Jesus in the primitive tradition by postulating a previous marriage of Joseph, an explanation which was accepted as plausible down to the time of Jerome. He, desiring that the brothers of Jesus should be regarded as really His cousins, sharply attacked the Protev. of James, an attack which was taken up by the Popes. In the Eastern church the book was popular from the beginning: first especially among the Ebionites, but also among the Greek fathers, and in the Syrian, Coptic and Armenian churches it was highly valued because of its praise of the ideal of virginity.

On the one hand we see, then, that devotion to Mary had made considerable advances even at the comparatively early date when the book was written, and that attributes reserved in the primitive tradition for Jesus were ascribed also to Mary. On the other hand, in East and West the Protev., although never regarded as canonical, being even condemned in the West, was a powerful factor in the development of Mariology. Apart from its importance for catholic devotion and art, its doctrinal importance in the narrower sense in connection with recent developments of catholicism cannot be sufficiently emphasized.

THE BOOK OF JAMES

1. 1. In 'the 'Histories of the Twelve Tribes of Israel' Joachim was a very rich (man), and he brought all his gifts for the Lord twofold; for he said in himself; What I bring in excess, shall be for the whole people, and what I bring for forgiveness [of my sins] shall be for the Lord, for a propitiation for me.

2. Now the great day of the Lord drew near, and the children of Israel were bringing their gifts. Then they stood before him, and Reubel [Reuben] also, saying: "It is not fitting for you to offer your gifts first, because you have begotten no offspring in Israel". 3. Then Joachim became very sad, and went to the record of the twelve tribes of the people [and said]: "I have searched whether I am the only one who has not begotten offspring in Israel, and I have found of all the righteous that they had raised up offspring in Israel. And I remembered the patriarch Abraham that in his last days God gave him a son, Isaac". 4. And Joachim was very sad, and did not show himself to his wife, but betook himself into the wilderness; there he pitched his tent and fasted *forty days and forty nights*[1]; and he said to himself; "I shall not go down either for food or for drink until the Lord my God visits me; prayer shall be my *food* and drink."[2]

2. 1. Meanwhile Anna his wife uttered a twofold lamentation and gave voice to a twofold bewailing:

> "I will bewail my widowhood,
> and bewail my childlessness."

---

[1] Mt. 4:2 (Lk. 4:2); cf. Exod. 24:18; 34:28; 1 Kings 19:8.   [2] Jn. 4:34.

2. Now the great day of the Lord drew near, and Euthine [Judith] her maidservant said to her: "How long do you humble your soul, since the great day of the Lord is near, and you ought not to mourn. But take this headband, which the mistress of the work gave me; it is not fitting for me to wear it, because I am [your] slave and it bears a royal mark."

3. But Anna said: "Away from me! I did not do this. It is the Lord who has greatly humbled me. Who knows whether a deceiver did not give it to you, and you have come to make me share in your sin!" Euthine [Judith] answered: "Why should I curse you because you have not listened to me? The Lord God has *shut up your womb*,[1] to give you no fruit in Israel."

4. And Anna was very sad; but she put off her mourning garments, cleansed her head, put on her bridal garments, and about the ninth hour went into her garden to walk there. And she saw a laurel tree and sat down beneath it and implored the Lord, saying: "O God of our fathers, bless me and hear my prayer, as thou didst bless the womb of Sarah [our mother Sarah] and gavest her a son, Isaac".[2]

3. 1. And Anna sighed towards heaven, and saw a nest of sparrows in the laurel tree and immediately she made lamentation within herself:

"Woe to me, who begot me,
What womb brought me forth?
For I was born as a curse before them all and before the children of Israel,
And I was reproached, and they mocked me and thrust me out of the temple of the Lord.
2. Woe is me, to what am I likened?
I am not likened to the birds of the heaven;
for even the birds of the heaven are fruitful before thee, O Lord.
Woe is me, to what am I likened?
I am not likened to the unreasoning [dumb] animals;
for even the unreasoning [dumb] animals are fruitful before thee, O Lord.
Woe is to me, to what am I likened?

1 Cf. 1 Sam. 1:6.   2 Gen. 21:1-3.

375

I am not likened to the beasts of the earth;

for even the beasts of the earth are fruitful before thee, O Lord.

3. Woe is me, to what am I likened?

I am not likened to these waters;

for even these waters gush forth merrily, and their fish praise thee, O Lord.

Woe is me, to what am I likened?

I am not likened to this earth;

for even this earth *brings forth its fruit in its season*[1] and praises thee, O Lord".

4. 1. And *behold an angel of the Lord came to her*[2] and said: "Anna, Anna, *the Lord has heard your prayer. You shall conceive and bear*,[3] and your offspring shall be spoken of in the whole world". And Anna said: "*As the Lord my God lives*,[4] if I bear a child, whether male or female, I will *bring it as a gift to the Lord my God*,[5] and it shall *serve him all the days of its life*".[6]

2. And behold there came two messengers, who said to her: "Behold, Joachim your husband is coming with his flocks; for an angel of the Lord came down to him and said to him: 'Joachim, Joachim, the Lord God has *heard your prayer*.[7] Go down; behold, your wife Anna has conceived [*shall conceive*]'."[8] 3. And Joachim went down and called his herdsmen and said: "Bring me ten lambs without blemish and without spot; they shall belong to the Lord my God. And bring me twelve [tender] calves for the priests and elders, and a hundred kids for the whole people". 4. And behold Joachim came with his flocks, and Anna stood at the gate and saw Joachim coming and ran immediately and hung on his neck, saying: "Now I know that the Lord God has greatly blessed me; for behold the widow is no longer a widow, and I, who was childless,[9] have conceived [shall conceive]".

And Joachim rested the first day in his house.

5. 1. But the next day he offered his gifts, saying in himself: "If the Lord God is gracious to me the frontlet of the priest[10] will make it clear to me".

---

[1] Cf. Ps. 1:3. [2] Cf. Lk. 2:9; Acts 12:7. [3] Lk. 1:13; Gen. 16:11; Jud. 13:3, 5, 7.
[4] Jud. 8:19; cf. 1 Sam. 1:26. [5] 1 Sam. 1:11. [6] 1 Sam. 2:11; 1:28.
[7] Lk. 1:13; See n. 3. [8] Cf. Lk. 1:31. [9] Cf. Isa. 54:1. [10] Exod. 28:36–38.

And Joachim offered his gifts, and observed the priest's frontlet when he went up to the altar of the Lord; and he saw no sin in himself. And Joachim said: "Now I know that the Lord God is gracious to me and has forgiven all my sins". And *he went down* from the temple of the Lord *justified, and went to his house*.[1]

2. And her six months [her months] were fulfilled, as (the angel) had said: in the seventh [ninth] month Anna brought forth. And she said to the midwife: "What have I brought forth?" And she said: "A female". And Anna said: "*My soul*[2] is magnified this day". And she lay down. And when the days were fulfilled, Anna purified herself from her childbed and gave suck to the child, and called her Mary.

6. 1. Day by day the child *waxed strong*[3]; when she was six months old her mother stood her on the ground to try if she could stand. And she walked [twice] seven steps and came to her bosom. And she took her up, saying: "*As the Lord my God lives,*[4] you shall walk no more upon this ground until I take you into the temple of the Lord". And she made a sanctuary in her bed-chamber, and did not permit anything common or unclean to pass through it. And she summoned the undefiled daughters of the Hebrews, and they cared for her amusement.

2. On the child's first birthday Joachim made a *great feast*,[5] and invited the chief priests and the priests and the scribes and the elders and the whole people of Israel. And Joachim brought the child to the priests, and they blessed her, saying: "O God of our fathers, bless this child and give her a name renowned for ever *among all generations*".[6] And all the people said: "So be it, [so be it,] Amen". And they brought her to the chief priests, and they blessed her, saying: "O God of the heavenly heights, look upon this child and bless her with a supreme and unsurpassable blessing". And her mother carried her into the sanctuary of her bed-chamber and gave her suck. And Anna sang this song to the Lord God:[7]

"I will sing praises to the Lord my God,
   for he has visited me and *taken away from me the reproach*[8] of my
   enemies.[9]

[1] Cf. Lk. 18:14. [2] Cf. Lk. 1:46. [3] Cf. Lk. 2:40. [4] See p. 376, n. 4.
[5] Cf. Gen. 21:8. [6] Cf. Lk. 1:48. [7] Cf. 1 Sam. 2:1.
[8] Gen. 30:23; cf. Lk. 1:25. [9] Cf. Ps. 42:10; 102:8.

And the Lord gave me the *fruit of righteousness*,[1] unique and manifold before him.

Who will proclaim to the sons of Reubel [Reuben] that Anna gives suck?[2]

[Hearken, hearken, you twelve tribes of Israel: Anna gives suck]".

And she laid the child down to rest in the bedchamber with its sanctuary, and went out and served them. When the feast was ended they went down rejoicing and glorifying the God of Israel.

7. 1. The months passed, and the child grew. When she was two years old, Joachim said to Anna: "Let us bring her up to the temple of the Lord,[3] that we may fulfil the promise which we made, lest the Lord send (some evil) upon us and our gift become unacceptable." And Anna replied: "Let us wait until the third year,[4] that the child may then no more long after her father and mother." And Joachim said: "Very well." 2. And when the child was three years old, Joachim said: "Let us call the undefiled daughters of the Hebrews, and let each one take a lamp, and let these be burning, in order that the child may not turn back and her heart be enticed away from the temple of the Lord." And he did so until they went up to the temple of the Lord. And the priest took her and kissed her and blessed her, saying: "The Lord has magnified your name among all generations; because of you the Lord at the end of the days[5] will manifest his redemption to the children of Israel." 3. And he placed her on the third step of the altar, and the Lord God put grace upon the child, and she danced for joy with her feet, and *the whole house of Israel loved her*.[6]

8. 1. And her parents went down wondering, praising and glorifying the almighty God because the child did not *turn back*[7] [to them]. And Mary was in the temple nurtured like a dove and received food from the hand of an angel. 2. When she was twelve years old, there took place a council of the priests, saying: "Behold, Mary has become twelve years old in the temple of the Lord. What then shall we do with her, that she may not pollute the temple of the Lord?" And they said to the high priest: "You stand at the altar of the Lord; enter (the sanctuary) and pray

[1] Cf. Prov. 11:30; 13:2; Am. 6:12; Jas. 3:18.   [2] Gen. 21:7.   [3] Cf. 1 Sam. 1:21ff.
[4] Cf. 1 Sam. 1:22.   [5] Cf. 1 Pet. 1:20.   [6] Cf. 1 Sam. 18:16.   [7] Cf. Gen. 19:26.

378

concerning her, and what the Lord shall reveal to you we will do".
3. And the high priest took the vestment with the twelve bells and
went into the Holy of Holies and prayed concerning her. And
behold, an angel of the Lord (suddenly) stood before him and
said to him: "Zacharias, Zacharias, go out and assemble[1] the
widowers of the people, [who *shall each bring a rod*[2]], and to whomsoever the Lord shall give a (miraculous) sign, his wife she shall
be". And the heralds went forth and spread out through all the
country round about Judaea; the trumpet of the Lord sounded,
and all ran to it.

9. 1. And Joseph threw down his axe and went out to meet
them. And when they were gathered together, they took the rods
and went to the high priest. He took the rods of all and *entered*[3]
the temple and prayed. When he had finished the prayer he took
the rods, and went out (again) and gave them to them: but there
was no sign on them. Joseph received the last rod, and behold, a
dove came out of the rod and flew on to Joseph's head.[4] And the
priest said to Joseph: "Joseph, to you has fallen the good fortune
to receive the virgin of the Lord; take her under your care".
2. (But) Joseph answered him: "I (already) have sons and am
old, but she is a girl. I fear lest I should become a laughing-stock
to the children of Israel". And the priest said to Joseph: "Fear
the Lord thy God, and remember all that God did to Dathan,
Abiram and Korah, how the earth was rent open and they were
all swallowed up because of their rebellion.[5] And now fear,
Joseph, lest this happen (also) in your house". And Joseph was
afraid, and took her under his care. And Joseph said to her:
"Mary, I have received you from the temple of the Lord, and now
I leave you in my house and go away to build my buildings;
(afterwards) I will come (again) to you; the Lord will watch
over you".

10. 1. Now there was a council of the priests, who resolved:
"Let us make a veil for the temple of the Lord". And the priest
said: "Call to me pure virgins of the tribe of David". And the
officers departed and searched, and they found seven (such)
virgins. And the priest remembered the child Mary, that she was
of the tribe of David and was pure before God. And the officers

[1] Cf. Num. 17:16–24 (1–9).   [2] Num. 17:17(2).   [3] Num. 17:23(8).
[4] Cf. Mt. 3:16.   [5] Num. 16:1, 31–33.

went and fetched her. 2. Then they brought them into the temple of the Lord, and the priest said: "Cast me lots, who shall weave the gold, the amiant, the linen, the silk, the hyacinth-blue, the scarlet and the pure purple".[1] And to Mary fell the lot of the 'pure purple' and 'scarlet'. And she took them and worked them in her house. At that time *Zacharias became dumb*,[2] and Samuel took his place until Zacharias was able to speak (again). But Mary took the scarlet and spun it.

11. 1. And she took the pitcher and went forth to draw water, and behold, a voice said: "*Hail, thou that art highly favoured, [the Lord is with thee, blessed art thou] among women*".[3] And she looked around on the right and on the left to see whence this voice came. And trembling she went to her house and put down the pitcher and took the purple and sat down on her seat and drew out (the thread). 2. And behold, an angel of the Lord (suddenly) stood before her and said: "*Do not fear, Mary; for you have found grace* before the Lord of all things *and shall conceive of his Word*".[4] When she heard this she doubted in herself and said: "Shall I conceive of the Lord, the living God, [and bear] as every woman bears?" 3. *And the angel of the Lord said:* "Not so, Mary; for a *power* of the Lord *shall overshadow you; Wherefore also that holy thing which is born of you shall be called the Son of the Highest.*[5] *And you shall call his name Jesus; for he shall save his people from their sins*".[6] And Mary said: "*Behold, (I am) the handmaid of the Lord before him: be it to me according to your word*".[7]

12. 1. And she made (ready) the purple and the scarlet and brought (them) to the priest. And the priest took (them), and blessed (Mary) and said: "Mary, the Lord God has magnified your name, and *you shall be blessed among all generations of the earth*".[8] 2. And Mary rejoiced, and went to Elizabeth her kinswoman,[9] and knocked on the door. *When Elizabeth heard it,*[10] she put down the scarlet, and ran to the door and opened it, [and when she saw Mary], she blessed her and said: "*Whence is this to me, that the mother of my Lord should come to me?*[11] *For behold, that which is in me leaped*[12] and blessed thee". But Mary forgot the mysteries which

---

[1] Cf. Exod. 35:25; 26:31, 36; 36:35, 37; 2 Chron. 3:14.   [2] Cf. Lk. 1:20–22, 64.
[3] Lk. 1:28, 42; cf. Jud. 6:12.   [4] Lk. 1:30f.   [5] Lk. 1:35, 32.   [6] Mt. 1:21; Lk. 1:31.
[7] Lk. 1:38.   [8] Gen. 12:2f.; Lk. 1:42, 48.   [9] Lk. 1:39, 36.   [10] Lk. 1:41.
[11] Lk. 1:43.   [12] Lk. 1:44, 41.

the [arch]angel Gabriel had told her, and raised a sigh towards heaven and said: "Who am I, Lord, that all the women [generations] of the earth count me blessed?"[1] 3. And she remained *three months with Elizabeth*.[2] Day by day her womb grew, and Mary was afraid and went *into her house and hid herself*[3] from the children of Israel. And Mary was sixteen years old when all these mysterious things happened.

13. 1. Now when she was in her sixth month, behold, Joseph came from his building and entered his house and found her with child. And he smote his face, threw himself down on sackcloth, and wept bitterly, saying: "With what countenance shall I look towards the Lord my God? What prayer shall I offer for her [for this maiden]? For I received her as a virgin out of the temple of the Lord my God and have not protected her. Who has deceived me? Who has done this evil in my house and defiled her [the virgin]? Has the story (of Adam) been repeated in me? For as Adam was (absent) in the hour of his prayer and *the serpent came and found Eve alone and deceived her*[4] and defiled her, so also has it happened to me". 2. And Joseph arose from the sackcloth and called Mary and said to her: "You who are cared for by God, why have you done this and forgotten the Lord your God? Why have you humiliated your soul, you who were brought up in the Holy of Holies and received food from the hand of an angel?" 3. But she wept bitterly, saying: "I am pure, and know not a man."[5] And Joseph said to her: "Whence then is this in your womb?" And she said: "*As the Lord my God lives*,[6] I do not know whence it has come to me."

14. 1. And Joseph feared greatly and parted from her, pondering what he should do with her. And Joseph said: "If I conceal her sin, I shall be found opposing the law of the Lord. If I expose her to the children of Israel, I fear lest that which is in her may have sprung from the angels and I should be found *delivering up innocent blood* to the judgment of death.[7] What then shall I do with her? *I will put her away secretly*".[8] And the night came upon him. 2. And behold, *an angel of the Lord appeared to him in a dream, saying*: "*Do not fear* because of this child. *For that which is in her is of the Holy Spirit. She shall bear a son, and you shall call his name Jesus; for*

[1] Lk. 1:48. [2] Lk. 1:56. [3] Lk. 1:56, 24. [4] Gen. 3:13; 2 Cor. 11:3; 1 Tim. 2:14.
[5] Lk. 1:34. [6] See p. 376, n. 4. [7] Cf. Mt. 27:4. [8] Mt. 1:19.

he shall save his people from their sins".[1] And *Joseph arose from sleep* and glorified the God of Israel who had bestowed his grace upon him, and he watched over her.[2]

15. 1. And Annas the scribe came to him and said to him: "Joseph, why did you not appear in our assembly?" And Joseph said to him: "I was weary from the journey, and I rested the first day". And Annas turned and saw that Mary was with child. 2. And he went hastily to the priest and said to him: "Joseph, for whom you are a witness, has grievously transgressed". And the high priest said: "In what way?" And he said: "The virgin, whom he received from the temple of the Lord, he has defiled, and has stolen marriage with her, and has not disclosed it to the children of Israel". And the high priest said to him: "Joseph! Joseph has done this?" And [Annas] said to him: "Send officers, and you will find the virgin with child." And the officers went and found her as he had said, and brought her to the temple. And she stood before the court. And the priest said: "Mary, why have you done this? Why have you humiliated your soul and forgotten the Lord your God, you who were brought up in the Holy of Holies, and received food from the hand of an angel, and heard hymns of praise, and danced before him? Why have you done this?" But she wept bitterly, saying: "*As the Lord my God lives,*[3] I am pure before him and I know not a man". And the high priest said to Joseph: "Why have you done this?" And Joseph said: "*As the Lord my God lives* I am pure concerning her". And the high priest said: "Do not give false witness, but speak the truth. You have stolen marriage with her [consummated your marriage in secret], and have not disclosed it to the children of Israel, and have not *bowed* your head *under the mighty hand*[4] in order that your seed might be blessed". And Joseph was silent.

16. 1. And the high priest said: "Give back the virgin whom you have received from the temple of the Lord". And Joseph wept bitterly. And the high priest said: "I will give you [both] to drink the water of the conviction of the Lord, and it will make manifest your sins before your eyes".[5] 2. And the high priest took (it) and gave (it) to Joseph to drink and sent him into the wilderness [into the hill-country]; and he came (back) whole. And he made

[1] Mt. 1:20f.　[2] Mt. 1:24.　[3] See p. 376, n. 4.　[4] Cf. 1 Pet. 5:6.　[5] Num. 5:11-31.

Mary also drink, and sent her into the wilderness [into the hill-country]; and she (also) returned whole. And all the people marvelled, because (the water) had not revealed any sin in them. And the high priest said: "If the Lord God has not made manifest your sins, neither do I condemn you".[1] And he released them. And Joseph took Mary and departed to his house, rejoicing and glorifying the God of Israel.

17. 1. *Now there went out a decree from* the king *Augustus that all* (inhabitants) of Bethlehem in Judaea *should be enrolled*.[2] And Joseph said: "I shall enroll my sons, but what shall I do with this child? How shall I enroll her? As my wife? I am ashamed to do that. Or as my daughter? But all the children of Israel know that she is not my daughter. The day of the Lord himself will do as [t]he [Lord] wills". 2. And he saddled his ass [his she-ass] and sat her on it; his son led it, and Samuel [Joseph] followed. And they drew near to the third mile(stone). And Joseph turned round and saw her sad, and said within himself: "Perhaps that which is within her is paining her". And again Joseph turned round and saw her laughing. And he said to her: "Mary, why is it that I see your face at one time laughing and at another sad?" And she said to him: "Joseph, I see with my eyes *two peoples*,[3] one weeping and lamenting and one rejoicing and exulting". 3. And they came half the way, and Mary said to him: "Joseph, take me down from the ass [from the she-ass], for the child within me presses me, to come forth". And he took her down there and said to her: "Where shall I take you and hide your shame? For the place is desert".

18. 1. And he found a cave there and brought her into it, and left her in the care of his sons and went out to seek for a Hebrew midwife in the region of Bethlehem. 2. [Now I, Joseph, was walking, and (yet) I did not walk, and I looked up to the air and saw the air in amazement. And I looked up at the vault of heaven, and saw it standing still and the birds of the heaven motionless. And I looked at the earth, and saw a dish placed there and workmen lying round it, with their hands in the dish. But those who chewed did not chew, and those who lifted up anything lifted up nothing, and those who put something to their mouth put nothing (to their mouth), but all had their faces turned upwards. And

---

[1] Cf. Jn. 8:11.   [2] Lk. 2:1; Mt. 2:1.   [3] Gen. 25:23; cf. Lk. 2:34.

behold, sheep were being driven and (yet) they did not come forward, but stood still; and the shepherd raised his hand to strike them with his staff, but his hand remained up. And I looked at the flow of the river, and saw the mouths of the kids over it and they did not drink. And then all at once everything went on its course (again).]

19. 1. And he found one who was just coming down from the hill country, and he took her with him, and said to the midwife: "Mary is betrothed to me; but she conceived of the Holy Spirit after she had been brought up in the temple of the Lord".

[And behold, a woman came down from the hill-country and said to me: "Man, where are you going?" And I said: "I seek a Hebrew midwife." And she answered me: "Are you from Israel?" And I said to her: "Yes." And she said: "And who is she who brings forth in the cave?" And I said: "My betrothed." And she said to me: "Is she not your wife?" And I said to her: "She is Mary, who was brought up in the temple of the Lord, and I received her by lot as my wife. And (yet) she is not my wife, but she has conceived of the Holy Spirit." And the midwife said to him: "Is this true?" And Joseph said to her: "Come and see".]

And the midwife went with him. 2. And he went to the place of the cave, and behold, *a* dark [*bright*] *cloud overshadowed*[1] the cave. And the midwife said: "My soul is magnified to-day, *for my eyes have seen* wonderful things; for salvation is born to Israel".[2] And immediately the cloud disappeared from the cave, and a great light appeared,[3] so that our eyes could not bear it. A short time afterwards that light withdrew until the child appeared, and it went and took the breast of its mother Mary. And the midwife cried: "How great is this day to me, that I have seen this new

---

[1] Cf. Mt. 17:5.   [2] Cf. Lk. 2:30, 32.   [3] Isa. 9:2.

sight". 3. And the midwife came out of the cave, and Salome met her. And she said to her: "Salome, Salome, I have a new sight to tell you; a virgin has brought forth, a thing which her nature does not allow". And Salome said: "*As the Lord my God lives,*[1] *unless I put (forward) my finger*[2] and test her condition, I will not believe that a virgin has brought forth."

20. 1. And Salome went in and made her ready [1. And the midwife went in and said to Mary: "Make yourself ready, for there is no small contention concerning you". And Salome put (forward) her finger] to test her condition. And she cried out, saying: ["Woe for my wickedness and my unbelief; for] "I have tempted the living God; and behold, my hand falls away from me, consumed by fire!"

2. And she prayed to the Lord. [2. And she bowed her knees before the Lord, saying: "O God of my fathers, remember me; for I am the seed of Abraham, Isaac and Jacob; do not make me a public example to the children of Israel, but restore me to the poor. For thou knowest, Lord, that in thy name I perform my duties and from thee I have received my hire".]

3. And behold, an angel of the Lord stood before Salome and said to her: "The Lord God has heard your prayer. Come near, touch the child, and you will be healed". 4. And she did so. [And she said: "I will worship him, for (in him) a great king has been born to Israel."] And Salome was healed as she had requested, and she went out of the cave [*iustified*[3]]. And behold, an angel of the Lord [a voice] cried: "Salome, Salome, tell [not] what marvel you have seen, before the child comes to Jerusalem."

[1] See p. 376, n. 4.   [2] Jn. 20:25.   [3] Lk. 18:14.

21. 1. And behold, Joseph prepared to go forth to Judaea. And there took place a great tumult in Bethlehem of Judaea. For there came *wise men* saying: "*Where is the [new-born] king of the Jews? For we have seen his star in the east and have come to worship him*". 2. When Herod heard this he was troubled and sent officers [to the wise men],

and sent for them and they told him about the star.

[and sent for *the high priests* and questioned them: "How is it written concerning the Messiah? *Where is he born?*" They said to him: "*In Bethlehem of Judaea; for so it is written*".[1] And he let them go. And he questioned the wise men[2] and said to them: "What sign did you see concerning the new-born king?" And the wise men said: "*We saw* how an indescribably greater *star* shone among these stars and dimmed them, so that they no longer shone; and so we knew that a king was born for Israel. *And we have come to worship him.*"[3] And Herod said: "*Go and seek, and when you have found him, tell me, that I also may come to worship him.*"[4] 3. And the wise

3. And behold, they saw stars [a star] in the east, and they [it] went before them,

men *went forth. And behold, the star which they had seen in the east, went before them,*]

until they came to the cave. And *it stood* over the head of the child [the cave].[5] And the wise men *saw the young child with Mary his mother*, and they took out of their bag gifts, *gold, and frankincense and myrrh.*[6] 4. And being warned by the angel that *they should not* go into Judaea, *they went to their own country by another way.*[7]

1 Mt. 2:1–5.   2 Mt. 2:7.   3 Mt. 2:2.   4 Mt. 2:8.
5 Mt. 2:9.   6 Mt. 2:11.   7 Mt. 2:12.

22. 1. But when *Herod* perceived *that he had been tricked by the wise men he was angry and sent* his murderers and commanded them *to kill all the children who were two years old and under.*[1] 2. When Mary heard that the children were to be killed, she was afraid and took the child and *wrapped him in swaddling clothes and laid him in an ox-manger.*[2]

3. But Elizabeth, when she heard that John was sought for, took him and went up into the hill-country. And she looked around (to see) where she could hide him, and there was no hiding-place. And Elizabeth groaned aloud and said: "O mountain of God, receive me, a mother, with my child". For Elizabeth could not go up (further) for fear. And immediately the mountain was rent asunder and received her. And that mountain made a light to gleam for her; for an angel of the Lord was with them and protected them.

23. 1. Now Herod was searching for John, and sent officers to Zacharias at the altar to ask him: "Where have you hidden your son?" And he answered and said to them: "I am a minister of God and attend continually upon his temple. How should I know where my son is?" 2. And the officers departed and told all this to Herod. Then Herod was angry and said: "Is his son to be king over Israel?" And he sent the officers to him again with the command: "Tell the truth. Where is your son? You know that your blood is under my hand". And the officers departed and told him all this. 3. And Zacharias said: "I am a martyr of God. Take my blood! But my spirit the Lord will receive,[3] for you shed innocent blood in the forecourt of the temple of the Lord".[4] And about the dawning of the day Zacharias was slain. And the children of Israel did not know that he had been slain.

24. 1. Rather, at the hour of the salutation the priests were departing, but the blessing of Zacharias did not meet them according to custom. And the priests stood *waiting for Zacharias*, to greet him with prayer and to glorify the Most High. 2. But when he *delayed to come,*[5] they were all afraid. But one of them took courage and went into the sanctuary. And he saw beside the altar[6] congealed blood; and a voice said: "Zacharias has been

---

[1] Mt. 2:16.   [2] Lk. 2:7.   [3] Cf. Acts 7:59; Lk. 23:46.
[4] Cf. 2 Chron. 24:20–22; Mt. 23:35.   [5] Cf. Lk. 1:21.   [6] Mt. 23:35.

slain, and his blood shall not be wiped away until his avenger comes." And when he heard these words, he was afraid, and went out and told the priests what he had seen. 3. And they heard and saw what had happened. And the panel-work of the ceiling of the temple wailed, and they *rent* their clothes *from the top to the bottom*.[1] And they did not find his body, but they found his blood turned into stone. And they were afraid, and went out and told all the people: "Zacharias has been slain." And all the tribes of the people heard it and mourned him and lamented[2] three days and three nights. 4. And after the three days the priests took counsel whom they should appoint in his stead. And the lot fell upon *Symeon*. Now it was he to whom *it had been revealed by the Holy Spirit that he should not see death until he had seen the Christ in the flesh*.[3]

25. 1. Now I, James, who wrote this history, when a tumult arose in Jerusalem on the death of Herod, withdrew into the wilderness until the tumult in Jerusalem ceased. And I will praise the Lord, who gave me the wisdom to write this history. Grace shall be with all those who fear the Lord.

(Nativity of Mary. Apocalypse of James. Peace be to him who wrote and to him who reads!)

2. THE INFANCY STORY OF THOMAS

1. *Texts and Literature.* For the original Greek form of the so-called Gospel of Thomas there are only a few very late and rather unreliable mss. classified, following Tischendorf, according to two recensions: 1. A longer form A with 19 chapters, undoubtedly the older, is represented by three complete mss. of the 15th–16th centuries; two of them (Bologna and Dresden) are in almost complete agreement with one another and are the basis of the edition in *Ea*, pp. 140–157 (on another ms. from Athos, cf. the notice in Lipsius, *Erg.-heft*, 1890, p. 24); also by the important Paris fragment *Bibl. nat. gr.* 239 (first edition, see below; text also in Fabricius I, pp. 159–167); after ch. 7 this gives the beginning of the story of the dyer, a passage found in no other ms., but known from the Arabic and Armenian versions. This could mean that these two later versions are considerably closer to the original form of the work than the extant Greek mss. suggest. It is not finally clear, however, whether the relationships are correctly explained by the theory proposed by the Bollandist Paul Peeters,

[1] Cf. Mt. 27:51.   [2] Cf. Zech. 12:10, 12–14.   [3] Lk. 2:25f.

that all the various forms of material on the nativity go back ultimately to a *Syriac* original. 2. A shorter form B with 11 chapters was made available by Tischendorf from a ms. from Sinai (15th century). The text is edited in *Ea*, pp. 158–163.

Of special importance are two older mss. of a shorter *Syriac* recension, which at points diverge considerably from the known Greek text (including A), but also show striking contacts with the extant Latin text. The text of the London ms. (6th century) was edited with English translation by W. Wright, *Contributions to the Apocryphal Literature of the N.T.*, 1865 (reprinted in E. A. W. Budge, *The History of the Blessed Virgin*, etc., I, 1899, pp. 217–222); the second ms. (5th–6th century) was collated by A. Meyer in Göttingen for the revision of *Apokr*. 2. The Syriac version is also found in *Cod. Vat. syr.* 159, a text to which Paul Peeters assigns very high value as standing specially close to the Syriac original which he regards as the basis of all editions of the childhood stories. The so-called Latin Thomas was first edited by Tischendorf from a late Vatican ms. (*Ea*[1], pp. 156ff.); it goes beyond the Greek and Syriac versions in having at the beginning stories of the flight into Egypt which, although only partially, agree with what is found in other writings about the infancy (especially the Arabic, Armenian, ps. Matt.). An old Latin witness at Vienna (palimpsest, 5th–6th century), seems to be very important because, in agreement with the late ms. Paris *Bibl. nat. lat.* 1652 (recension of ps. Matt.), it apparently establishes that the above-mentioned London Syriac ms. does actually preserve a very good ancient tradition.

The old Georgian version, also related to the Syriac, and hitherto hardly noticed in the West, is now available in a Latin translation in G. Garitte, "Le fragment georgien de l'"Évangile de Thomas'" (*RHE* 51, 1956, pp. 513–520).—An Ethiopic version, preserved as the eighth part of a gnostic work, 'Miracles of Jesus', was published with French translation by S. Grébaut in *Patrologia Orientalis* XII, 4, 1919, pp. 625–642; cf. also the same writer, *Rev. de l'Orient Chrétien* 16, 1911, pp. 255–265; pp. 356–367.—On Old Slavonic translations cf. N. Bonwetsch in Harnack, *Litg.* I, p. 910, and W. Lüdtke, "Die slawischen Texte des Thomas-Evang." (*Byzant.-neugr. Jahrbücher* 6, 1929, pp. 490–508); also the Russian works of M. M. N. Speranskij mentioned in Peeters, *Évang. apocr.* II, p. xviii, n. 3.—Both the Arabic infancy gospel translated from Syriac and the Armenian (see below, pp. 404ff.) are at least of importance as parallel texts.—Despite the thorough preliminary work of Paul Peeters (*Évang. apocr.* II, 1914, Introduction) which is quite indispensable for the study of the literary connections between the Gospel of Thomas and other infancy writings, there is still no comprehensive treatment and accurate analysis of the intricacies of this tradition.

The first Greek text was edited from the Paris fragment *gr.* 239 already mentioned (Cotelier 1700, reprinted in Fabricius I, pp. 159–167), and the complete text for the first time from the Bologna ms. by J. A. Mingarelli, *Nuova raccolta d'opuscoli* etc., 1764.—Important editions: Thilo, pp. 277–314; especially *Ea*, pp. 140–180. Based on this are: C. Michel, *Évang. apocr.* I, 1924², pp. 161–189 (text and French translation); Bonaccorsi I, pp. 110–152 (text and Italian translation); A. de Santos Otero, pp. 302–324 (text and Spanish translation). In 1927 A. Delatte (Bibl. de la Fac. de Philos. et Lettres de l'Univ. de Liège, Fasc. 36: *Anecdota Atheniensia I: Textes grecs inédits relatifs à l'histoire des religions*, pp. 264–271) published a Greek text from ms. Athens *Bibl. nat. gr.* 355 (15th century), related to the A form but, like the Latin version, containing at the beginning stories of the flight into Egypt.—Without the original text: W. Hayes, *The Gospel according to Thomas*, 1921 (English); A. Meyer, *Apokr.* 2, pp. 96–102 (German); E. Bock, *Die Kindheit Jesu*, 1924 (German); M. R. James, pp. 49–70 (English); W. Michaelis, pp. 96–111 (German). —Still valuable is the commentary of J. Ch. K. Hofmann, *Das Leben Jesu nach den Apokryphen in Zusammenhang aus den Quellen erzählt und wissenschaftlich untersucht*, 1851, pp. 144–265. Also A. Meyer in *Handb.*, pp. 132–142 (with older literature, supplemented in *Apokr.* 2). In addition the introduction in C. Michel, *Évang. apocr.* I, pp. xxiii–xxxii, and the discussion by M. R. James (*JTS* 30, 1928, pp. 51ff.). Cf. also the information in the Patrologies of Altaner, pp. 57f. and Quasten, pp. 123–125; comprehensive bibliography in A. de Santos Otero, p. 301.

2. *Title and Contents.* The mss. give 'Infancy of the Lord Jesus' (Syriac version), or are entitled 'Account of the Infancy of the Lord by Thomas, the philosopher of Israel' (Greek ms. A), or again 'Book of the holy apostle Thomas concerning the life of the Lord in his infancy' (Greek ms. B).

The gospel contains stories of miracles worked by the child Jesus between the ages of five and twelve years. It ends with the narrative, taken from Luke, of Jesus in the temple at the age of twelve.

3. *Date and Author.* A direct relationship with the gnostic Gospel of Thomas, of which a Coptic version has now been discovered (see above, pp. 278ff.), cannot be traced, although it has been suggested that the teaching of the boy Jesus on the allegorical meaning of the alphabet may be the narrative starting point for gnostic speculations. The choice of Thomas, who is sometimes called an apostle and sometimes an "Israelite philosopher", as

the author, may be connected with the tradition of his apostolic labours in India. Perhaps it is not accidental that it is precisely the material in this book for which parallels exist in Indian legends (see above, p. 364).

According to Irenaeus I, 13. 1 Harvey, the Marcosians possessed a document containing a portion of the Gospel of Thomas (ch. 6). It thus reaches back to the end of the 2nd century. All that can be said about the author with any certainty is that he must have been a Gentile Christian, since his book betrays no knowledge of Judaism.

There are discrepancies between the texts of the three known Greek mss., and very wide divergences between the Syriac translation and the Latin, to which it is partly related. Often they are much shorter, like the Syriac, which seems to preserve much which is primitive. It is hard to decide which of them are the older until all the material has been critically assessed, because while later editors tend to excise anything offensive, the natural tendency is always towards expansion of the text. In the absence of a critical edition it seemed advisable to translate the text of the Greek ms. A, and to supply only important variants of the Syriac version. Meyer's attempt (*Apokr.* 2), creditable though it is, to establish to some extent the original text in German translation, is premature.

4. *Nature of the material, literary style and theological motives of the book.* The main interest of the book is not the youth of Jesus from the age of twelve until his coming to be baptized in the Jordan at the age of thirty, but the years before the incident of which Luke tells us. Its purpose is to depict the boy Jesus as an infant prodigy. All the miracles he was later to perform are here patently anticipated. But there is a vast difference between these miracles and those in the canonical Gospels. The extraneous material is simply imported into the story of Jesus, without the slightest attempt to make it suit its subject. If the 'child' or 'boy' were not actually called Jesus, no one would guess that the tales of this playful divine boy were intended to supplement the traditon about him. Numerous parallels can be cited from the legends of Krishna and Buddha and from fables of all kinds. The cruder and more startling the miracle, the more the compiler is pleased with it, and he displays not the least distaste at the doubtful quality of his material. In this respect there is a vast difference between the Gospel of Thomas and the Protevangelium of James.

But not only Christ the miracle-worker but Christ the teacher must be foreshadowed in the child. The restrained account in Luke of Jesus at the age of twelve in the temple is grotesquely exaggerated. The boy not only possesses all the wisdom of the age, but baffles all human teachers by his profound and often obscure pronouncements. Here we may see contact with gnostic speculations, for the school-boy already proclaims them, and becomes the gnostic revealer. The boy already possesses all divine wisdom in its full range, and has no need whatever of that growth in wisdom of which Luke (2:40) speaks. This book displays the same docetic tendency which ultimately lies at the root of most of the infancy gospels. Although lacking in good taste, restraint and discretion, it must be admitted that the man who collected these legends and composed the Gospel of Thomas was endowed with a gift of vivid story-telling, and especially when he depicts scenes from ordinary everyday life.

5. *Dissemination of the Gospel of Thomas.* On the one hand, readers were attracted from the start by that in its material which was popular and quite free of theological bias, and so the Gospel enjoyed wide popularity, as the numerous translations and its use in later gospels testify. To be sure, the excessively crude emphasis on the miraculous, often quite devoid of ethical feeling, caused offence. (Perhaps a reaction of this kind is to be found in the History of Joseph the Carpenter, which stresses the meekness of the child Jesus; Morenz, *TU* 56, pp. 1, 43; see IX.) Moreover, the whole attempt to remove from the boy Jesus the necessity of a purely human development would have appeared questionable in some quarters. In the rejection of literature of this kind there was involved the feeling both that the true humanity of Jesus comes out in His growing up in seclusion, and that the devil would have no inkling of the coming of the Son of God.

But the Gospel of Thomas triumphed again and again over all suspicions. Not only did it spread far and wide by being translated into other languages; it was combined in popular collections with material from the favourite Protev. of James and with all kinds of popular legends about the sojourn of the child Jesus in Egypt (see pp. 404ff.).

THE ACCOUNT OF THOMAS THE ISRAELITE PHILOSOPHER CONCERNING THE CHILDHOOD OF THE LORD

1. I, Thomas the Israelite, tell and make known to you all, brethren from among the Gentiles, all the works of the childhood of our Lord Jesus Christ and his mighty deeds, which he did when he was born in our land. The beginning is as follows.

2. 1. When this boy Jesus was five years old he was playing at the ford of a brook, and he gathered together into pools the water that flowed by, and made it at once clean, and commanded it by

his word alone. 2. He made soft clay and fashioned from it twelve sparrows. And it was the sabbath when he did this. And there were also many other children playing with him. 3. Now when a certain Jew saw what Jesus was doing in his play on the sabbath, he at once went and told his father Joseph: "See, your child is at the brook, and he has taken clay and fashioned twelve birds and has profaned the sabbath". 4. And when Joseph came to the place and saw (it), he cried out to him, saying: "Why do you do on the sabbath what ought not to be done?" But Jesus clapped his hands and cried to the sparrows: "Off with you!" And the sparrows took flight and went away chirping. 5. The Jews were amazed when they saw this, and went away and told their elders what they had seen Jesus do.

3. 1. But the son of Annas the scribe was standing there with Joseph; and he took a branch of a willow and (with it) dispersed the water which Jesus had gathered together. 2. When Jesus saw what he had done he was enraged and said to him: "You insolent, godless dunderhead, what harm did the pools and the water do to you? See, now you also shall wither like a tree and shall bear neither leaves nor root nor fruit". 3. And immediately that lad withered up completely; and Jesus departed and went into Joseph's house. But the parents of him that was withered took him away, bewailing his youth, and brought him to Joseph and reproached him: "What a child you have, who does such things".

4. 1. After this again he went through the village, and a lad ran and knocked against his shoulder. Jesus was exasperated and said to him: "You shall not go further on your way", and the child immediately fell down and died. But some, who saw what took place, said: "From where does this child spring, since his every word is an accomplished deed?" 2. And the parents of the dead child came to Joseph and blamed him and said: "Since you have such a child, you cannot dwell with us in the village; or else teach him to bless and not to curse.[1] For he is slaying our children".

5. 1. And Joseph called the child aside and admonished him saying: "Why do you do such things that these people (must) suffer and hate us and persecute us?" But Jesus replied: "I know

[1] Cf. Rom. 12:14.

that these words are not yours; nevertheless for your sake I will be silent. But they shall bear their punishment". [*Syriac variant:* "If the words of my father were not wise, he would not know how to teach children." And again he said: "If these children were born in wedlock they would not be accursed. Such will see no torment."] And immediately those who had accused him became blind. 2. And those who saw it were greatly afraid and perplexed, and said concerning him: "Every word he speaks, whether good or evil, was a deed and became a marvel." And when Joseph saw that Jesus had so done, he arose and took him by the ear and pulled it hard. 3. And the child was angry and said to him: "It is sufficient for you to seek and not to find, and most unwisely have you acted. Do you not know that I am yours? Do not vex me."

6. 1. Now a certain teacher, Zacchaeus by name, who was standing there, heard in part Jesus saying these things to his father, and marvelled greatly that, being a child, he said such things. 2. And after a few days he came near to Joseph and said to him: "You have a clever child, and he has understanding. Come, hand him over to me that he may learn letters, and I will teach him with the letters all knowledge, and to salute all the older people and honour them as grandfathers and fathers, and to love those of his own age". 3. And he told him all the letters from Alpha to Omega clearly, with much questioning. But he looked at Zacchaeus the teacher and said to him: "How do you, who do not know the Alpha according to its nature, teach others the Beta? Hypocrite, first if you know it, teach the Alpha, and then we shall believe you concerning the Beta." Then he began to question the teacher about the first letter, and he was unable to answer him. 4. And in the hearing of many the child said to Zacchaeus: "Hear, teacher, the arrangement of the first letter, and pay heed to this, how it has lines and a middle mark which goes through the pair of lines which you see, (how these lines) converge, rise, turn in the dance, three signs of the same kind, subject to and supporting one another, of equal proportions; here you have the lines of the Alpha".[1]

7. 1. Now when Zacchaeus the teacher heard so many such

[1] The text appears to be corrupt. See, e.g., James p. 51, Santos p. 308.

allegorical descriptions of the first letter being expounded, he was perplexed at such a reply and such great teaching and said to those who were present: "Woe is me, I am forced into a quandary, wretch that I am; I have brought shame to myself in drawing to myself this child. 2. Take him away, therefore, I beseech you, brother Joseph. I cannot endure the severity of his look, I cannot make out his speech at all. This child is not earth-born; he can tame even fire. Perhaps he was begotten even before the creation of the world. What belly bore him, what womb nurtured him I do not know. Woe is me, my friend, he stupefies me [Tischendorf: stupefacit me], I cannot follow his understanding. I have deceived myself, thrice wretched man that I am. I strove to get a disciple, and have found myself with a teacher. 3. My friends, I think of my shame, that I, an old man, have been overcome by a child. I can only despair and die because of this child, for I cannot in this hour look him in the face. And when all say that I have been overcome by a small child, what have I to say? And what can I tell concerning the lines of the first letter of which he spoke to me? I do not know, my friends, for I know neither beginning nor end of it. 4. Therefore I ask you, brother Joseph, take him away to your house. He is something great, a god or an angel or what I should say I do not know."

8. 1. And while the Jews were trying to console Zacchaeus, the child laughed aloud and said: "Now let that which is yours bear fruit, and let the blind in heart see. I have come from above to curse them and call them to the things above, as he commanded who sent me for your sakes". 2. And when the child had ceased speaking, immediately all those were healed who had fallen under his curse. And no one after that dared to provoke him, lest he should curse him, and he should be maimed.

9. 1. Now after some days Jesus was playing in the upper story of a house, and one of the children who were playing with him fell down from the house and died. And when the other children saw it they fled, and Jesus remained alone. 2. And the parents of him that was dead came and accused him of having thrown him down. And Jesus replied: "I did not throw him down". But they continued to revile him. 3. Then Jesus leaped down from the roof and stood by the body of the child, and cried with a loud

voice: "Zenon"—for that was his name—"arise and tell me, did
I throw you down?" And he arose at once and said: "No, Lord,
you did not throw me down, but raised me up". And when they
saw it they were amazed. And the parents of the child glorified
God for the miracle that had happened and worshipped Jesus.

10. 1. After a few days a young man was cleaving wood in a
corner,[1] and the axe fell and split the sole of his foot, and he bled
so much that he was about to die. 2. And when a clamour arose
and a concourse of people took place, the child Jesus also ran there,
and forced his way through the crowd, and took the injured foot,
and it was healed immediately. And he said to the young man:
"Arise now, cleave the wood and remember me". And when the
crowd saw what happened, they worshipped the child, saying:
"Truly the spirit of God dwells in this child".

11. 1. When he was six years old, his mother gave him a pitcher
and sent him to draw water and bring it into the house. 2. But in
the crowd he stumbled, and the pitcher was broken. But Jesus
spread out the garment he was wearing, filled it with water and
brought it to his mother. And when his mother saw the miracle,
she kissed him, and kept within herself[2] the mysteries which she
had seen him do.

12. 1. Again, in the time of sowing the child went out with his
father to sow wheat in their land. And as his father sowed, the
child Jesus also sowed one corn of wheat. 2. And when he had
reaped it and threshed it, he brought in a hundred measures;[3]
and he called all the poor of the village to the threshing-floor and
gave them the wheat, and Joseph took the residue of the wheat.
He was eight years old when he worked this miracle.

13. 1. His father was a carpenter and made at that time [Syr.,
Lat. variant: only] ploughs and yokes. And he received an order
from a rich man to make a bed for him. But when one beam was
shorter than its corresponding one and they did not know what to
do, the child Jesus said to his father Joseph: "Put down the two
pieces of wood and make them even from the middle to one end".
2. And Joseph did as the child told him. And Jesus stood at the
other end and took hold of the shorter piece of wood, and stretch-
ing it made it equal with the other. And his father Joseph saw it

---

[1] Mss. γωνίᾳ; James and others read γειτονίᾳ, "in the neighbourhood".
[2] Lk. 2:19, 51.   [3] Cf. Lk. 16:7.

and was amazed, and he embraced the child and kissed him, saying: "Happy am I that God has given me this child".

14. 1. And when Joseph saw the understanding of the child and his age, that he was growing to maturity, he resolved again that he should not remain ignorant of letters; and he took him and handed him over to another teacher. And the teacher said to Joseph: "First I will teach him Greek, and then Hebrew". For the teacher knew the child's knowledge and was afraid of him. Nevertheless he wrote the alphabet and practised it with him for a long time; but he gave him no answer. 2. And Jesus said to him: "If you are indeed a teacher, and if you know the letters well, tell me the meaning of the Alpha, and I will tell you that of the Beta". And the teacher was annoyed and struck him on the head. And the child was hurt and cursed him, and he immediately fainted and fell to the ground on his face. 3. And the child returned to Joseph's house. But Joseph was grieved and commanded his mother: "Do not let him go outside the door, for all those who provoke him die".

15. 1. And after some time yet another teacher, a good friend of Joseph, said to him: "Bring the child to me to the school. Perhaps I by persuasion can teach him the letters". And Joseph said to him: "If you have the courage, brother, take him with you". And he took him with fear and anxiety, but the child went gladly. 2. And he went boldly into the school and found a book lying on the reading-desk[1] and took it, but did not read the letters in it, but opened his mouth and spoke by the Holy Spirit and taught the law to those that stood by. And a large crowd assembled and stood there listening to him, wondering at the *grace* of his teaching and the readiness of his *words*,[2] that although an infant he made such utterances. 3. But when Joseph heard it, he was afraid and ran to the school, wondering whether this teacher also was without skill (maimed). But the teacher said to Joseph: "Know, brother, that I took the child as a disciple; but he is full of great grace and wisdom; and now I beg you, brother, take him to your house". 4. And when the child heard this, he at once smiled on him and said: "Since you have spoken well and have testified rightly, for your sake shall he also that was smitten be healed". And

[1] Cf. Lk. 4:16f.   [2] Cf. Lk. 4:22.

immediately the other teacher was healed. And Joseph took the child and went away to his house.

16. 1. Joseph sent his son James to bind wood and take it into his house, and the child Jesus followed him. And while James was gathering the sticks, a viper bit the hand of James. 2. And as he lay stretched out and about to die, Jesus came near and breathed upon the bite, and immediately the pain ceased, and the creature burst, and at once James became well.

17. 1. And after these things in the neighbourhood of Joseph a little sick child[1] died, and his mother *wept* bitterly.[2] And Jesus heard that great mourning and *tumult*[3] arose, and he ran quickly, and finding the child dead, he *touched*[4] his breast and said: "*I say to you,*[5] do not die but live and be with your mother".[6] And immediately it looked up and laughed. And he said to the woman: "Take him and give him[7] milk and remember me". 2. And when the people standing round saw it, they marvelled and said:[8] "Truly, this child is either a god or an angel of God, for every word of his is an accomplished deed". And Jesus departed from there and played with other children.

18. 1. After some time a house was being built and a great disturbance arose, and Jesus arose and went there. And seeing a man lying dead he took his hand and said: "*I say to you,* man, *arise,*[9] do your work." And immediately he arose and worshipped him. 2. And when the people saw it, they were amazed and said: "This child is from heaven, for he has saved many souls from death, and is able to save them all his life long."

19. 1. *And when he was twelve years old his parents went according to the custom to Jerusalem to the feast of the passover with their company, and after the passover they returned to go to their house. And while they were returning the child Jesus went back to Jerusalem. But his parents supposed that he was in the company.* 2. *And when they had gone a day's journey, they sought him among their kinsfolk, and when they did not find him, they were troubled, and returned again to the city seeking him. And after the third day they found him in the temple sitting among the teachers, listening* to the law *and asking them questions. And all* paid attention to him and *marvelled* how he, a child, put to silence the elders and

---

[1] Cf. Mk. 5:22ff.; Lk. 7:11ff.　　[2] Cf. Mk. 5:38; Lk. 7:13.　　[3] Mk. 5:38.
[4] Lk. 7:14.　　[5] Lk. 7:14.　　[6] Cf. Lk. 7:15.　　[7] Cf. Mk. 5:43; Lk. 8:55.
[8] Cf. Lk. 7:16.　　[9] Cf. Lk. 7:14; Mk. 5:41.

teachers of the people, expounding the sections of the law and the sayings of the prophets. 3. *And his mother* Mary came near *and said to him: "Why have you done this to us, child? Behold, we have sought you sorrowing." Jesus said to them: "Why do you seek me? Do you not know that I must be in my Father's house?"*[1] 4. But the scribes and Pharisees said: "Are you the mother of this child?" And she said: "I am." And they said to her: "Blessed are you *among women,* because the Lord has *blessed the fruit of your womb.*[2] For such glory and such excellence and wisdom we have never seen nor heard." 5. And Jesus arose and followed his mother and was *subject* to his parents; *but his mother kept (in her heart) all that had taken place. And Jesus increased in wisdom and stature and grace.*[3] To him be glory for ever and ever. Amen.

VARIANT OF THE SYRIAC GOSPEL OF THOMAS TO CAP. 6–8
(The Boy Jesus and Zacchaeus the Teacher)

But a teacher, whose name was Zacchaeus, heard him speaking with his father, and said: "O wicked boy!" And he said to Joseph his father: "Till when wilt thou not choose to hand over this boy, that he may learn to be fond of children of his years, and may honour old age?" Joseph answered and said: "And who is able to teach a boy like this? Does he think that he is equal to a small cross?" Jesus answered and said to the teacher: "These words which thou hast spoken, and these names, I am strange to them; for I am apart from you, though I dwell among you. Honour in the flesh I have not. Thou art by the law, and in the law thou abidest. For when thou wast born, I was. But thou thinkest that thou art my father. Thou shalt learn from me a doctrine, which another man knows not and is not able to learn. And (as for) the cross of which thou hast spoken, he shall bear it, whose it is. For when I am greatly exalted, I shall lay aside whatever mixture I have of your race. For thou dost not know whence thou art; for I alone know truly when ye were born, and how long time ye have to remain here." But when they heard, they were astonished, and cried out and said: "O wonderful sight and hearing! Words like these we have never heard man speak, neither the priests, nor the scribes, nor the Pharisees. Whence was this (one) born, who

---

[1] Lk. 2:41–52.   [2] Lk. 1:42.   [3] Lk. 2:51f.

is five years old, and speaks such words? Man hath never seen the like of this." Jesus answered and said to them: "Ye wonder at what I have said to you, that I know when ye were; and yet I have something more to say to you." But they, when they heard, were silent, and were not able to speak. And Zacchaeus the teacher said to Joseph: "I will teach him whatever is proper for him to learn." And he made him go into the school. And he, going in, was silent. But Zacchaeus the scribe began to tell him (the letters) from Alaph, and was repeating to him many times the whole alphabet. And he says to him that he should answer and say after him; but he was silent. Then the scribe became angry, and struck him with his hand upon his head. And Jesus said: "A smith's anvil, being beaten, can learn, and it has no feeling; but I am able to say those things, which are spoken by you, with knowledge and understanding". The scribe answered and said: "This (child) is something great. He is either God, or an angel, or—what I should say I know not". Then the boy Jesus laughed and said: "Let those in whom there is no fruit, produce fruit; and let the blinded see the fruit of life of the Judge."

(Trans. W. Wright, *Contributions to the Apocryphal Literature* 1865, pp. 7–9; cf. also the Latin translation)

STORY FROM THE ARABIC INFANCY GOSPEL AND THE
PARIS MANUSCRIPT OF THE GOSPEL OF THOMAS
(The Child Jesus and the Dyer)

One day, when Jesus was running about and playing with some children, he passed by the workshop of a dyer called Salem. They had in the workshop many cloths which he had to dye. The Lord Jesus went into the dyer's workshop, took all these cloths and put them into a cauldron full of indigo. When Salem came and saw that the cloths were spoiled, he began to cry aloud and asked the Lord Jesus, saying: "What have you done to me, son of Mary? You have ruined my reputation in the eyes of all the people of the city; for everyone orders a suitable colour for himself, but you have come and spoiled everything". And the Lord Jesus replied: "I will change for you the colour of any cloth which you wish to be changed", and he immediately began to take the cloths out of the cauldron, each of them dyed in the colour the dyer wished, until he had taken them all out. When the Jews saw this miracle and wonder, they praised God.

From the Arabic Infancy Gospel c. 37, *Ea* pp. 200–201; cf. the Greek fragment Paris *Bibl. nat. gr.* 239 (see above) and the expanded form in the Armenian Infancy Gospel c. 21; see P. Peeters, *Évang. apocr.* II, 1914, pp. 232–246.

3. GNOSTIC LEGENDS

Perhaps infancy gospels were written by Gnostics at an early date. Certainly such material did not originate with them. But in order to be able to derive their speculations from Jesus Himself, they needed as a framework a setting in His life which could be fitted into the older gospel tradition, but without being controlled by its content. Besides the resurrection appearances during the forty days, there was available the whole childhood of Jesus left untouched by the older Gospels. We have seen how fruitful in this respect were the themes of Jesus at the age of twelve in the temple and of his education. What they now required, however, was a child Jesus who was only a child in appearance, but had in fact no need of development, since He possessed the full revelation in its entirety, and already had unlimited power to perform miracles.

The tendency to Docetism behind all the legends of the infancy met this need, and at the same time was greatly strengthened by it. The statements of heresiologists, and the fragments given below, show that legends in which the child Jesus stands in permanent union with the Spirit and the source of all revelation from the very beginning, and even before His baptism, were especially the ones to be adopted and developed.

Docetism, further, was bound to affect the way in which the birth of Jesus was told. The tendency is to eliminate all traces of a normal, human origin in the story of the birth of Jesus of the virgin Mary. Thus the Gnostics early wrote a 'Pre-history (Genna) of Mary', mentioned by Epiphanius, *Haer.* 26. 12, which shows that the material of the Protevangelium of James was used in gnostic circles. The apocryphal expansions of the original nativity stories all betray a more or less marked docetic tendency (see the Christian interpolation in the Ascension of Isaiah, c. 11. 5ff., and especially the fragment of the Arundel ms. given under 4).

As time went on, the narrative element in the gnostic writings faded more and more into the background. The few infancy legends still provided are completely subordinated to the scheme of the teaching of the heavenly beings. Increasingly it is regarded as sufficient to supply a merely introductory reference to the familiar framework or to mention (in the title) the traditional authority for all gnostic statements about the infancy: Thomas (see VII, above pp. 278ff.).

STORY OF THE GNOSTIC JUSTIN CONCERNING THE SENDING OF THE ANGEL BARUCH TO THE TWELVE-YEAR-OLD SHEPHERD BOY JESUS

The following story is to be found in Hippolytus' description (*Philos.* v. 26) of the system of the gnostic Justin and is closely connected with his speculations concerning the heavenly beings. The angel of Elohim, Baruch, is sent to the earth to deliver men.

Lastly in the days of King Herod Baruch is again sent down as an emissary of Elohim. When he came to Nazareth, he found Jesus (there), the son of Joseph and Mary, as a twelve-year-old boy tending sheep, and told him from the beginning everything which had happened from the time of Edem and Elohim, and what was to happen in the future, and said: "All the prophets before you[1] allowed themselves to be seized. Take heed, Jesus, son of man, that you do not allow yourself to be seized, but proclaim this word to men, and tell them what concerns God and the good, and ascend to the good and seat yourself there[2] by the side of Elohim, the father of us all". And Jesus obeyed the angel and said: "Lord, all this will I do", and he preached.

LEGENDS FROM THE PISTIS SOPHIA (THIRD CENTURY)

Translated from C. Schmidt, *Pistis Sophia. Ein gnostisches Originalwerk des 3 Jhdts. aus dem Koptischen übersetzt,* 1925.

CONCERNING THE COMMUNICATION OF HEAVENLY POWERS BY THE CHILD JESUS TO THE BAPTIST AND MARY

"And when I set out for the world, I came to the midst of the Archons of the Sphere and had the form of Gabriel, the angel of the Aeons, and the Archons of the Aeons did not recognize me, but they thought that I was the angel Gabriel. Now it happened that, when I had come to the midst of the Archons of the Aeons,

[1] Cf. Jn. 10:8.   [2] Cf. Ps. 110:1.

I looked down upon the world of mankind at the command of the first Mystery. I found Elizabeth, the mother of John the Baptist, before she had conceived him, and I sowed in her a power which I had taken from the little Jao, the Good, who was in the midst, that he might be able to proclaim before me, and prepare my way and baptize with water of the forgiveness of sins"

(Pistis Sophia c. 7, Schmidt, pp. 8f.)

Jesus again continued in his speech and said: "Now it happened afterwards, when at the command of the first Mystery I looked down upon the world of mankind and found Mary, who is called 'my mother' according to the material body, that I spoke with her in the form of Gabriel, and when she had turned upwards towards me, I thrust into her the first power, which I had taken from Barbelo, that is, the body which I have borne on high. And in the place of the soul I thrust into her the power which I have taken from the great Sabaoth the Good, who dwells in the place of the righteous ones".

(Pistis Sophia c. 8, Schmidt, pp. 9f.)

CONCERNING THE UNION OF THE CHILD JESUS WITH THE SPIRIT

[Mary declares to the risen (Jesus)]: "When you were small, before the Spirit had come upon you, while you were with Joseph in a vineyard, the Spirit came from on high and came to me in my house, resembling you, and I did not recognize him, and I thought that it was you. And the Spirit said to me: 'Where is Jesus, my brother, that I may meet him?' When he said this to me, I was perplexed and thought that it was a ghost come to tempt me. And I seized him and bound him to the foot of the bed which is in my house, until I went out to you both, to you and Joseph in the field and found you in the vineyard, while Joseph was fencing in the vineyard. Now it came to pass that, when you heard me speak the word to Joseph, you understood the word, and were glad and said: 'Where is he, that I may see him? for I await him in this place'. And it came to pass that, when Joseph heard you say these words, he was perplexed, and we went up together, entered the house, and found the Spirit bound to the bed. And we looked at you and him and found that you resembled him, and when he who was bound to the bed was freed, he embraced you and kissed you, and you kissed him and you both became one."

(Pistis Sophia c. 61, Schmidt, pp. 89f.)

4. LATER INFANCY GOSPELS

The creating of new histories of the infancy of Jesus on the basis of the two older ones, the Protevangelium of James and the (infancy) gospel of Thomas, accords with the natural law of the growth of legend. Although the prevailing tendency is towards expansion, the endeavour to eliminate legends in bad taste or dogmatically offensive makes for abbreviation. Both these tendencies are discernible and operate already in the old translations mentioned, which also represent enlarged or shortened forms. Besides these translations, however, both the older sources are deliberately combined, and the canonical accounts and much new diversified legendary material are employed, especially stories of the flight into Egypt and Jesus' stay there, concerning which there was perhaps an older written source. Sharp distinctions cannot always be drawn between expanded or abbreviated translations and compilations of this kind. On the whole question of the complicated literary-historical relationships see the discussion by Paul Peeters in the introduction to his selection of later infancy stories (*Évang. apocr.* II pp. Iff.). He assumes, of course, that all extant forms of this kind of literature go back ultimately to a Syriac base, which he assigns to a time before the 5th century —a thesis which still awaits examination.

Among these compilations special reference should be made to the Arabic infancy gospel already mentioned, extant in several mss. (Florence, Laur. orient. 32; Vat. syr. 159), and probably translated from Syriac. It combines the three cycles: birth of Jesus, miracles in Egypt (in which Mary plays a dominant rôle), and miracles of the child Jesus, most of which are borrowed from the (infancy) Gospel of Thomas. Through being translated into Arabic the legends became known to the Muslims. At any rate Mohamed was familiar with this tradition and adopted many of the legends in the Koran (see *Handb.*, pp. 165ff.). The infancy stories also probably reached India in this form.

The first edition of the Arabic infancy gospel was made by H. Sike, *Evangelium infantiae vel liber apocryphus de Infantia Servatoris*, 1697, but he had at his disposal only one ms., now lost (reprinted, as well as elsewhere, in Thilo, pp. 66–131); the text is available in *Ea*, pp. 181–209 (Latin); Peeters, *Évang. apocr.* II, pp. 1–65 (French); A. de Santos Otero, pp. 327–357 (Spanish); extracts

in F. Amiot, pp. 93–107 (French; German edn.: pp. 77–89).—
The greatest portion of the work is also contained in a "History
of the Blessed Virgin Mary and the History of the Likeness of
Christ" discovered and edited by E. A. W. Budge (2 vols., London
1899; ms. of the 13th–14th cent.), which is of special importance
for the presumed Syriac archetype. See in general on the problems
of the transmission of this work, P. Peeters, *Évang. apocr.* II, pp.
I–XXIX (supplemented in *Anal. Bolland.*, 41, 1923, pp. 132–134),
and G. Graf, *Geschichte d. christl. arab. Literatur* I (*Studi e Testi* 118),
1944, pp. 225–227. Cf. further the bibliographical note in U.
Monneret de Villard, *Le leggende orientale sui magi evangelici* (*Studi
e Testi* 163), 1952, p. 73, n. 1, and the literature in de Santos
Otero, p. 327.

Similarly, the Armenian infancy gospel, which also derives
from the Syriac (Peeters, *Évang. apocr.* II, pp. XXIXff.), embraces
all the material of the Protevangelium of James (see above, 370ff.)
but with considerable expansion. The Magi are here royal
brothers: Melqon rules over Persia, Balthasar over India, and
Gaspar over Arabia.—First edition by Isaias Daietsi (Venice 1898),
based on two mss. of the Mechitarist library in Venice; there are
other mss. in Vienna and in the Edschmiadsin monastery. The
text is available in Peeters, *Évang. apocr.* II, pp. 69–286 (French);
extracts in F. Amiot, pp. 81–93 (French; German edn.: pp. 65–77)
and de Santos Otero, pp. 380–386 (Spanish). See also on the whole
question P. Peeters, *Évang. apocr.* II, pp. XXIX–L.

At a later period there is also Coptic literature on the birth of
Mary. Its subject-matter is used in sermons of Cyril of Jerusalem,
Demetrius of Antioch, Cyril of Alexandria and others (see F.
Robinson, *Coptic Apocryphal Gospels*, 1896; E. A. W. Budge,
Miscellaneous Coptic Texts, 1915). To be included here is the gnosticizing Ethiopic "Miracles of Jesus" (edited with French translation
by S. Grébaut, *Patrol. Orientalis* XII, 4, 1919), which in the 6th–
9th miracles combines the most varied traditions about the childhood and youth of Jesus.

The further development of legends of the infancy in the West
is of particular interest. We have seen that, although we do not
possess any old Latin translation of the Protev. of James, its
content must have been known (Prudentius used it, and before
him Zeno of Verona in the 4th cent.). There is a Latin ms. of the
(infancy) Gospel of Thomas dating from the 5th to 6th century.
Opposition was, of course, directed against this whole literature
in the West, above all by Jerome, primarily for theological reasons
(sons of Joseph by a former marriage); but there was also dis-
pleasure at the bad taste of many of the legends (story of the
midwife). Then the books were condemned by the Popes (see

405

above, p. 368). Since, however, the material in the condemned
books enjoyed ever-increasing popularity among church people,
it became necessary in time, despite the rejection of certain too
crude miracles, to bring it together in a refined form in a new
collection. This was done in the so-called pseudo-Matthew, which
was written probably about the the 8th or 9th century to further
the veneration of Mary as the queen of virgins. It is a strange
irony that this work, in which the story of Joseph's first marriage
still retains its place, should have been put out as a translation
attributed to Jerome, of all people. This is due to its identification
with the Hebrew Matthew referred to by Jerome. Moreover, at
the request of bishops Chromatius and Heliodorus he had translated into Latin an allegedly Aramaic book entitled 'Tobias'.
Connected with this is the spurious correspondence according to
which Jerome is requested by these same bishops to translate the
Hebrew Matthew.

A large number of mss. of pseudo-Matt. exist, of which Tischendorf used four for his edition in *Ea*, pp. 51–112 (three of the 14th
cent.; one of the 15th cent.). The text is available in Thilo, pp.
339–400; E. Amann, *Le Protévangile de Jacques*, 1910, pp. 272–339
(text and French); C. Michel, *Évang. apocr.* I, pp. 54–159 (text
and French); Bonaccorsi I (text and Italian); de Santos Otero,
pp. 191–257 (text and Spanish); extracts also in Amiot. The
extraordinary importance of the work is that in this form the
legends from the older infancy gospels became the common
property of the people, and were thus able to exercise immense
influence on literature and art (see above, p. 368). Also pseudo-
Matt. underwent a shortened 'improved' edition, the 'Story of
the Birth of Mary', in which the first marriage of Joseph, now
rejected as heretical, was excised, together with other offensive
details, and the material was pruned and made less tedious. This
version also was provided with the fictitious correspondence of
Jerome. Through being included in the *Golden Legend* of James de
Voragine (1298) it enjoyed a very wide circulation.

From this main stream infancy legends flowed and developed
in channels of all kinds, and hitherto unknown texts are continually coming to light. Of interest is a Latin infancy gospel edited in
1927 (M. R. James, *Latin Infancy Gospels*, 1927; cf. also J. A.
Robinson, *JTS* 1928, pp. 205–207; M. J. Lagrange, *Rev. Bibl.*
1928, pp. 544–557; B. Capelle, *Rev. Bén.* 1929, pp. 79ff.; S. Ferri,
Studi Mediolatini e Volgari I, 1955, pp. 119–125), extant in two
mss.: the Hereford ms. (Library of the Chapter of Hereford
0.3.9; 13th cent.), and the Arundel ms. (Brit. Mus. 404; 14th
cent.). They diverge widely from one another. They resemble
the text of the Protev. James, but they also contain much from

pseudo-Matt. and in addition a number of peculiar features. Symeon, a son of Joseph, is named as the source of information. Since the story of the birth of Jesus, which we give in translation, is strongly docetic in character, James has raised the question whether perhaps we have here a source comparable with the docetic Gospel of Peter (see above, pp. 179ff.). Certainty in this matter, however, is unattainable without close comparison of the mss. with all the rest of the material. Extracts are to be found in Bonaccorsi I, pp. 232–259 (text and Italian); de Santos Otero, pp. 276–292 (text and Spanish).

We also give a translation of an infancy narrative from a Life of John the Baptist, which only became known comparatively late. Written in Arabic with Syriac letters ('Garshuni'), it purports, according to the testimony of the Egyptian bishop Serapion, to have been composed (in Greek) between the years 385 and 395, and is extant in two mss. of the Mingana collection (Ming. Syr. 22; 16th cent., and Ming. Syr. 183; 18th cent.); edited by A. Mingana himself: "Woodbrooke Studies, Edition and Translation of Christian Documents in Syriac and Garshuni by A. Mingana, with Introduction by Rendel Harris", (*BJRL*, Manchester 1927, pp. 329ff.).

Finally, it may be mentioned that among the multifarious modern fabrications of spurious lives of Jesus, whose authors appeal to ancient writings, infancy gospels are to be included, which have found credulous readers in Germany, France and America. There is, for instance, the *Évangile de la jeunesse de Notre-Seigneur Jésus-Christ d'après S. Pierre* by Catull Mendès (Latin text with French translation; also published in English). A still more notorious forgery, for long an object of hot dispute, was the so-called *Letter of Benan* published in 1910 under the title "A companion of the young Jesus. Letter of the Egyptian physician Benan of the time of Domitian, edited by E. Edler von der, Planitz". The letter, ostensibly translated into German from a Coptic revision of the original Greek, tells of the upbringing and youth of Jesus by an Egyptian astronomer and of his initiation into all the secret lore of the Therapeutae. The forgery was exposed by C. Schmidt, *Der Benanbrief* (*TU* 44, 1, 1921). Such recurrent undertakings (see also E. J. Goodspeed's book, *Modern Apocrypha, Famous Biblical Hoaxes*, Boston 1956) constitute a psychological rather than a literary problem. Yet one might be tempted to ask whether, at least to some extent, similar motives played a part in the production of some of the ancient infancy gospels. This is not altogether to be ruled out. But it has to be remembered that the conditions of literary activity then were quite different from those of today. The infancy gospels of antiquity and the Middle Ages belong to popular literature, and their authors were compilers whose own literary personalities were quite unimportant.

(A) EXTRACTS FROM THE ARABIC INFANCY GOSPEL
(a) *Legends of the child Jesus in Egypt*

17. . . . the woman took sweet-smelling water to wash the Lord Jesus; when she had washed him, she kept that water with which she had done that, and poured some of it upon a girl who lived there and whose body was white with leprosy, and washed her with it. Immediately the girl was cleansed of the leprosy. And the inhabitants of that town said: "There is no doubt that Joseph and Mary and this child are gods, not men." And when they prepared to depart from them, that girl who had suffered from leprosy came to them, and asked them to take her with them as a companion.

(*Ea*, pp. 188ff.)

23. From there Joseph and the lady Mary departed and came to a desert place, and when they heard that it was infested with raids by robbers, they decided to pass through this region by night. But behold, on the way they saw two robbers lying on the road, and with them a crowd of robbers who belonged to them, likewise sleeping. Now those two robbers, into whose hands they had fallen, were Titus and Dumachus. And Titus said to Dumachus: "I ask you to let these (people) go free, and in such a way that our companions do not observe them." But Dumachus refused and Titus said again: "Take from me forty drachmae and have them as a pledge." At the same time he reached him the girdle which he wore round him, that he might hold his tongue and not speak. When the noble lady Mary saw that this robber had shown kindness to them, she said to him: "The Lord God will uphold you with his right hand and grant you forgiveness of sins." And the Lord Jesus answered and said to his mother: "In thirty years, mother, the Jews will crucify me in Jerusalem, and those *two robbers* will be fastened to the cross with me, Titus *on my right hand* and Dumachus *on my left*,[1] and after that day Titus will go before me into paradise." And she said: "God preserve you from

[1] Cf. Mk. 15:27.

that,[1] my son." And they departed from there to the city of idols; and when they drew near to it, they had been changed into sand-hills. (*Ea*, pp. 192f.)

24. From there they went to that sycamore tree which today is called Matarea, and the Lord Jesus made to gush forth in Matarea a spring, in which the lady Mary washed his shirt. And from the sweat of the Lord Jesus which she wrang out there, balsam appeared in that place. (*Ea*, p. 193)

(b) *The children who were changed into goats*

40. One day the Lord Jesus went out into the street and saw children who had come together to play. He followed them, but the children hid themselves from him. Now when the Lord Jesus came to the door of a house and saw women standing there, he asked them where those children had gone. They replied that no one was there; and the Lord Jesus said: "Who are those whom you see in the furnace?" "They are three-year-old goats", they answered. And the Lord Jesus said: "Come out to your shepherd, you goats". Then the children in the form of goats came out and began to skip round him. When those women saw this, they were seized with wonder and fear, and speedily fell down before the Lord Jesus and implored him, saying: "O our Lord Jesus, son of Mary, truly you are the *good shepherd*[2] of Israel, have mercy on your handmaids who stand before you and have never doubted: for you have come, our Lord, to heal and not to destroy."[3] The Lord Jesus answered and said: "The children of Israel are like the Ethiopians among the peoples". And the women said: "You, Lord, know everything, and nothing is hidden from you; but now we beg and implore you of your mercy to restore to their former state these children, your servants". So the Lord Jesus said: "Come, children, let us go and play". And immediately in the presence of these women the goats were changed into children.

(*Ea*, pp. 202f.; cf. also the Syriac 'History of the Virgin': E. A. W. Budge, *History of the Virgin* 1899)

[1] Cf. Mt. 16:22.   [2] Jn. 10:11.   [3] Cf. Jn. 3:17.

(B) EXTRACTS FROM THE GOSPEL OF PSEUDO-MATTHEW

(a) *Ox and ass at the manger*
(first mention)

14. On the third day after the birth of our Lord Jesus Christ holy Mary went out from the cave, and went into a stable and put her child in *a manger*,[1] and an ox and an ass worshipped him. Then was fulfilled that which was said through the prophet Isaiah: "*The ox knows his owner and the ass his master's crib.*"[2] Thus the beasts, ox and ass, with him between them, unceasingly worshipped him. Then was fulfilled that which was said through the prophet Habakkuk: "*Between two beasts are you known.*"[3] And Joseph remained in the same place with Mary for three days. (*Ea*, p. 80)

(b) *Legends of the child Jesus in Egypt*

18. When they came to a cave and wished to rest (in it), holy Mary dismounted and sat down with the child Jesus in her lap. And on the journey there were with Joseph three boys and with Mary some maidens. And behold, suddenly many dragons came out of the cave. When the boys saw them they cried out in terror. Then Jesus got down from his mother's lap, and stood on his feet before the dragons; thereupon they worshipped Jesus, and then went back from them. Then was fulfilled that which was spoken through the prophet David: "*Praise the Lord,* you dragons *from the earth, you dragons and all deeps*".[4] 2. And the child Jesus himself went before the dragons and commanded them not to harm anyone. But Mary and Joseph had great fear lest the child should be hurt by the dragons. And Jesus said to them: "Have no fear, and do not think that I am a child; for I have always been and even now am perfect; all wild beasts must be docile before me."[5]

19. 1. Likewise lions and leopards worshipped him and accompanied them in the desert. Wherever Joseph and holy Mary went, they went before them, showing (them) the way and lowering their heads (in worship); they showed their servitude by wagging their tails and honoured him with great reverence. But when Mary saw the lions and leopards and all kinds of wild beasts

---

[1] Lk. 2:7.   [2] Isa. 1:3.   [3] Cf. Hab. 3:2 LXX.   [4] Ps. 148:7.   [5] Cf. Mk. 1:13.

surrounding them, she was at first gripped by violent fear. But the child Jesus looked at her face with a happy countenance, and said: "Do not fear, mother; for they do not come to harm you, but they hasten to obey you and me." With these words he removed all fear from her heart. 2. And the lions went along with them, and with the oxen and asses and the beasts of burden which carried what they needed, and they harmed no one, although they remained (with them). Rather they were docile among the sheep and rams which they had brought with them from Judaea and had with them. They walked among wolves without fear, and neither was harmed by the other. Then was fulfilled that which was said through the prophet: "*The wolves pasture with the lambs: lions and oxen eat straw together.*"[1] And the lions guided on their journey the two oxen and the wagon in which they carried what they needed.

20. 1. Now on the third day of their journey, as they went on, it happened that blessed Mary was wearied by the too great heat of the sun in the desert, and seeing a palm-tree, she said to Joseph: "I should like to rest a little in the shade of this tree." And Joseph led her quickly to the palm and let her dismount from her animal. And when blessed Mary had sat down, she looked up at the top of the palm-tree and saw that it was full of fruits, and said to Joseph: "I wish someone could fetch some of these fruits of the palm-tree." And Joseph said to her: "I wonder that you say this; for you see how high this palm-tree is, and (I wonder) that you even think about eating of the fruits of the palm. I think rather of the lack of water, which already fails us in the skins, and we have nothing with which we can refresh ourselves and the animals."

2. Then the child Jesus, who was sitting with a happy countenance in his mother's lap, said to the palm: "Bend down your branches, O tree, and refresh my mother with your fruit." And immediately at this command the palm bent its head down to the feet of blessed Mary, and they gathered from it fruits with which they all refreshed themselves. But after they had gathered all its fruits, it remained bent down and waited to raise itself again at the command of him at whose command it had bent down. Then Jesus said to it: "Raise yourself, O palm, and be

1 Isa. 11:6f.

411

strong, and join my trees which are in the paradise of my Father. And open beneath your roots a vein of water which is hidden in the earth, and let the waters flow so that we may quench our thirst from it." And immediately it raised itself, and there began to gush out by its root a fountain of water very clear, fresh, and completely bright. And when they saw the fountain of water, they rejoiced greatly, and quenched their thirst, and also all the beasts of burden and all the animals, and gave thanks to God.

21. On the next day, when they went on from there, and at the hour when they set out, Jesus turned to the palm and said to it: "O palm, I give you this privilege, that one of your branches be carried by my angels and be planted in the paradise of my Father. This blessing I will confer on you, that to all who shall be victorious in a contest it shall be said: 'you have won the palm of victory'." When he said this, behold, an *angel of the Lord*[1] appeared, standing above the palm-tree, and took one of its branches and flew to heaven with the branch in his hand. When they saw this, they fell on their faces and were as dead men. And Jesus spoke to them saying: "Why does fear grip your hearts? Do you not know that this palm, which I have caused to be carried to paradise, will stand ready for all the saints in the place of blessedness, as it has for us in the place of solitude?" And they were filled with joy, and were all strengthened and arose.

22. 1. Now when they were journeying on, Joseph said to Jesus: "Lord, we are being roasted by this heat; if you agree, let us go alongside the sea, that we may be able to rest in the coastal towns." Jesus said to him: "Do not fear, Joseph; I will shorten your journey: what you were intending to traverse in the space of thirty days, you will complete in one day." And while they were speaking, behold, they perceived already the mountains of Egypt and began to see its cities.

2. And happy and rejoicing they came to the region of Hermopolis, and entered an Egyptian city called Sotinen. And since there was in it no one they knew whom they could have asked for hospitality, they entered a temple which was called the "Capitol of Egypt". In this temple stood 365 idols, to which on appointed

---

[1] Lk. 2:9f.

days divine honour was paid in idolatrous rites. The Egyptians of this city entered the Capitol, in which the priests admonished them, to offer sacrifice on so many appointed days according to the honour of their deity.

23. But it came to pass that, when blessed Mary entered the temple with the child, all the idols fell to the ground, so that they all lay on their faces completely overturned and shattered. Thus they openly showed that they were nothing. Then was fulfilled what was said through the prophet Isaiah: *"Behold, the Lord shall come upon a swift cloud and shall enter into Egypt, and all (the idols) prepared by the hands of the Egyptians shall be removed before his face."*[1]

24. When this was told to Affrodosius, the governor of that city, he came to the temple with his whole army. And when the high priests of the temple saw that Affrodosius (Affrodosio) went to the temple with his whole army, they expected immediately to see his vengeance upon those because of whom the gods were destroyed. But when he entered the temple and saw all the idols lying prostrate on their faces, he went up to blessed Mary, who was carrying the Lord in her bosom, and worshipped him, and said to his whole army and to all his friends: "If he were not the God of our gods, our gods would not have fallen on their faces before him, and they would not lie stretched out in his presence. Thus they silently confess him as their Lord. And if we do not with prudence do all that we see our gods do, we shall perhaps be in danger of angering him and of all being destroyed, as happened to Pharaoh, king of the Egyptians, who was drowned in the sea with his whole army, because he did not believe such great wonders." Then all the people of the city believed in the Lord God through Jesus Christ.

25. After a short time the angel said to Joseph: "Return to the land of Judah; *they are dead who sought the child's life."*[2] (*Ea*, pp. 85–93)

(C) EXTRACT FROM THE LATIN INFANCY GOSPEL IN THE ARUNDEL MANUSCRIPT

THE MIDWIFE'S ACCOUNT OF THE BIRTH IN THE CAVE

73. When therefore the hour drew nearer, the might of God manifested itself. And the maiden (Mary) stood looking up to

[1] Isa. 19:1.   [2] Mt. 2:20.

heaven, and became as a grape vine[1] (?). For now the end of the
events of salvation was far advanced. And when the light had come
forth, Mary worshipped him whom she saw that she had brought
forth. And the child himself shone brightly round about like the
sun, and was pure and most beautiful to behold, since he alone
appeared as peace spreading peace everywhere. And in that hour
when he was born there was heard a voice of many invisible
beings saying with one accord "Amen".[2] And the light itself
which was born increased and darkened the light of the sun with
the brightness of its shining. And this cave was filled with bright
light together with a most sweet odour. This light was born just
as dew descends on the earth from heaven. For its odour is more
fragrant than any aroma of ointments.

74. And I stood there stupefied and amazed, and fear seized
me. For I was looking upon the intense brightness of the light
which was born. But the light itself, gradually withdrawing, became like a child, and in a moment became a child as children
are customarily born. And I took courage and bent down and
touched him, and took him up in my hands with great fear, and
was seized with terror because he had no weight like other
children who are born. And I looked at him and there was no
defilement in him, but he was in all his body shining as in the
dew of the most high God, light to carry, radiant to behold. And
while I wondered greatly because he did not cry as new-born
babes are accustomed to cry, and while I held him and looked at
his face, he smiled at me with the most sweet smile, and opened
his eyes and looked sharply on me. And suddenly there came forth
from his eyes a great light like a brilliant flash of lightning.

(From the Latin text, ed. M. R. James, *Latin Infancy Gospels*,
1927, pp. 68, 70)

(D) EXTRACT FROM THE LIFE OF JOHN ACCORDING TO SERAPION
The Child Jesus and John

(While the child Jesus is living with his parents in Egypt, the
child John wanders through the desert with his mother Elizabeth.)

After five years the pious and blessed old mother Elizabeth
passed away, and the holy John sat weeping over her, as he did

---

[1] Robinson alters *vinea* to *nivea*: 'and became snow white'.　　[2] Cf. Rev. 5:14.

not know how to shroud her and bury her, because on the day of her death he was only seven years and six months old. And Herod also died the same day as the blessed Elizabeth.

The Lord Jesus Christ who with his eyes sees heaven and earth saw his kinsman John sitting and weeping near his mother, and he also began to weep for a long time, without anyone knowing the cause of his weeping. When the mother of Jesus saw him weeping, she said to him: "Why are you weeping? Did the old man Joseph or any other one chide you?" And the mouth that was full of life answered: "No, O my mother, the real reason is that your *kinswoman*,[1] the old Elizabeth, has left my beloved John an orphan. He is now weeping over her body which is lying *in the mountain*."[2]

When the Virgin heard this she began to weep over her kinswoman, and Jesus said to her: "Do not weep, O my Virgin mother, you will see her in this very hour." And while he was still speaking with his mother, behold a luminous cloud came down and placed itself between them. And Jesus said: "Call Salome and let us take her with us." And they mounted the cloud which flew with them to the wilderness of 'Ain Kārim and to the spot where lay the body of the blessed Elizabeth, and where the holy John was sitting.

The Saviour said then to the cloud: "Leave us here at this side of the spot." And it immediately went, reached that spot, and departed. Its noise, however, reached the ears of Mar John, who, seized with fear, left the body of his mother. A voice reached him immediately and said to him: "Do not be afraid, O John. I am Jesus Christ, your master. I am your kinsman Jesus, and I came to you with my beloved mother in order to attend to the business of the burial of the blessed Elizabeth, your happy mother, because she is my mother's kinswoman." When the blessed and holy John heard this, he turned back, and Christ the Lord and his virgin mother embraced him. Then the Saviour said to his virgin mother: "Arise, you and Salome, and wash the body." And they washed the body of the blessed Elizabeth in the spring from which she used to draw water for herself and her son. Then the holy virgin Mart Mary got hold of the blessed (John) and wept over him, and cursed Herod on account of the numerous crimes which

[1] Lk. 1:36.   [2] Lk. 1:39.

he had committed. Then Michael and Gabriel came down from heaven and dug a grave; and the Saviour said to them: "Go and bring the soul of Zacharias, and the soul of the priest Simeon, in order that they may sing while you bury the body." And Michael brought immediately the souls of Zacharias[1] and Simeon[2] who shrouded the body of Elizabeth and sang for a long time over it. . . .

And Jesus Christ and his mother stayed near the blessed and the holy John seven days, and condoled with him at the death of his mother, and taught him how to live *in the desert*.[3] And the day of the death of the blessed Elizabeth was the 15th of February.

Then Jesus Christ said to his mother: "Let us now go to the place where I may proceed with my work." The Virgin Mary wept immediately over the loneliness of John, who was very young, and said: "We will take him with us, since he is an orphan without anyone." But Jesus said to her: "This is not the will of my Father who is in the heavens. He shall remain in the wilderness till the day of his showing unto Israel. Instead of a desert full of wild beasts,[4] he will walk in a desert full of angels and prophets, as if they were multitudes of people. Here is also Gabriel,[5] the head of the angels, whom I have appointed to protect him and to grant to him power from heaven. Further, I shall render the water of this spring of water as sweet and delicious to him as the milk he sucked from his mother. Who took care of him in his childhood? Is it not I, O my mother, who love him more than all the world? Zacharias also loved him, and I have ordered him to come and inquire after him, because although his body is buried in the earth, his soul is alive. . . ."

These words the Christ our Lord spoke to his mother, while John was in the desert. And they mounted the cloud, and John looked at them and wept, and Mart Mary wept also bitterly over him, saying: "Woe is me, O John, because you are alone in the desert without anyone. Where is Zacharias, your father, and where is Elizabeth, your mother? Let them come and weep with me today."

And Jesus Christ said to her: "Do not weep over this child, O my mother. I shall not forget him." And while he was uttering

[1] Lk. 1:5.   [2] Lk. 2:25.   [3] Mk. 1:4.   [4] Cf. Mk. 1:13.   [5] Lk. 1:19, 26.

these words, behold the clouds lifted them up and brought them to Nazareth. And he fulfilled there everything pertaining to humanity *except sin*.[1]

(Translation of A. Mingana in *BJRL*, Manchester, 11, 1927, pp. 446–449)

[1] Cf. Hebr. 4:15.

IX

THE RELATIVES OF JESUS

(A. Meyer—W. Bauer)

From the literature: Th. Zahn, *Brüder und Vettern Jesu (Forschungen z. Gesch. d. ntl. Kanons u. d. altk. Lit.* 6, 1900, pp. 225–364); Bauer c. I, II, VIII etc.; F. Sieffert, "Jakobus im NT", *RE* 8, pp. 571–581; E. Schwarz, "Zu Euseb. KG I. Das Martyrium Jakobus des Gerechten", *ZNW* 4 (1903) pp. 48–61; J. Blinzler, "Simon der Apostel, Simon der Herrenbruder und Bischof Symeon von Jerusalem" (*Passauer Studien, Festschr. für Bischof S. K. Landersdorfer*, 1953, pp. 25–55); F. Spitta, *Der Brief d. Julius Africanus an Aristides*, 1877; Zöckler, "Maria", *RE* 12, pp. 305–336; Th. Zahn, *Die Dormitio s. Virginis und das Haus des Johannes Marcus*, 1899; M. Jugie, *La mort et l'assomption de la Sainte Vierge, Étude historico-doctrinale (Studi e Testi* 114) 1944; R. L. P. Milburn, *Early Christian Interpretations of History* (1954) pp. 161–192.

The human nature which the Son of God took upon Himself embraced also His earthly family. This close relationship of the divine and the human confronted the Church with difficult problems, to which were added exegetical and personal questions raised by the statements in the NT. To the information provided in the NT at least one early Christian writer could still add important supplements, although they are frequently obscure; but for the rest theological construction, fantasy and sheer delight in invention have unfortunately almost completely overgrown the history.

1. Mark 3:21 records that the family of Jesus wanted to take Him home because He was out of His mind; the inhabitants of Nazareth noticed nothing remarkable in His mother and sisters (6:3); but we learn from their lips that Jesus had four brothers: James, Joses (=Joseph; in the 'Story of Joseph' c. 2 he is called Justus), Judas and Simon, and several sisters. The names of the sisters are known only to legend; according to the 'Story of Joseph' (c. 2, *Ea* pp. 122ff.) there were two: Assia and Lydia; Epiphanius (*haer.* 78, 8 and *ancor.* 60) calls them Mary and Salome; elsewhere still other names appear.

John 7:3–5 emphasizes that the brothers of Jesus did not believe in Him, but wanted Him to seek greater publicity in Jerusalem. Similarly, in the Gospel of the Nazarenes (see pp. 146f.) His mother and brothers urge Jesus to submit to the baptism of John for the forgiveness of sins.

This attitude of His brothers towards the person and mission of Jesus is not indeed cold, but betrays no understanding, and is certainly not the invention of the community, which later revered these brothers so highly. It is no less certain that soon after the death of Jesus this attitude changed. In Acts 1:14 they appear immediately after the Ascension in the circle of the apostles. Paul testifies that one of the appearances of the risen Jesus, the fourth in the sequence, was to James, His eldest brother (1 Cor. 15:7); hence he ranked among the 'pillars' of the primitive Church in Jerusalem (Gal 2:9); Paul sought contact with him (1:19); his influence was decisive for Peter and Barnabas, and extended through his emissaries as far as Antioch (2:12f.). He recognized Paul's Gentile mission, it is true (2:9), but not table-fellowship between Jewish and Gentile Christians (2:12f.). In Acts also this James appears as an authority in the primitive Church (15:13–22); later he is in fact its real representative and leader, whom Paul at once seeks out in Jerusalem and whose directions he follows (21:18–26). Here he makes a successful effort to mediate between the position of Paul and that of the Judaizers (15:13–22; 21:18–25).

About the year 180 a simple Christian from the Semitic East, Hegesippus, compiled five books of 'Memoirs' in order to demonstrate the reliability and unity of the Church's tradition over against the wild fantasies of the Gnostics (Euseb. *H.E.* IV. 8. 1f.; 22. 1; II. 23. 3); towards the end, in the fifth book, he refers to the fact that the succession (in the leadership of the community) had passed directly to James the Just, the Lord's brother, of whom he sketches the following portrait (Euseb. II. 23. 4–18): He was holy (i.e. ritually pure) from birth. He drank neither wine nor strong drink. Also he shunned the razor, anointing-oil, and baths. Since he never wore wool, but only linen, he alone was permitted to set foot in the sanctuary of the temple (otherwise forbidden to any layman). So he alone went into the temple, and there he was seen for ever on his knees imploring pardon for his people, so unremittingly indeed that his knees became calloused like those of a camel. Hence he was called 'Oblias', which was supposed to mean 'protection of the people' ('*ubla* in Aramaic is a basket-like wicker hurdle, or perhaps a palisade); he was also called 'Righteousness', or 'James the Just', to distinguish him from others of the name. Although not only the scribes and Pharisees but also other parties in Judaism attacked him, he none the less won a following among them, even among their leaders.

Because of this serious growth of faith in Jesus as the Christ, some scribes and Pharisees at a passover, where Jews and pagans came together, urged upon James that in virtue of his prestige and righteousness he should give testimony from the pinnacle of the temple to the crowds assembled in the temple court, as to what was 'the gate of Jesus the Crucified,' i.e. what was the significance of Jesus and His crucifixion. Then James declared in a loud voice: "What do you ask me with regard to Jesus, *the Son of Man*? He sits in heaven *at the right hand of the great Power*, and will one day come *on the clouds of heaven*" (Mt. 26:64 and par.). Thereupon the scribes and Pharisees hurled him down (probably outwards, into the Kidron valley), and since he was still alive began to stone him. But he prayed on his knees: "I pray thee, Lord God our *Father, forgive them, for they know not what they do*" (cf. Lk. 23:34). Then a priest of the Rechabites (cf. Jer. 35, esp. v. 19) cried out "Stop! The Just is praying for you!" Then one of them, a fuller, took the cudgel he used for beating clothes, and with it struck him on the head; and so James met with a martyr's death. It was in fact threefold, the death of a witness, just as in the Coptic Resurrection Story of Bartholomew the pious Ananias of Bethlehem dies through stoning, the furnace and the spear (James, p. 182). James was buried on the spot near the temple, and his tombstone was still there (near the site of the temple) in the time of Hegesippus. Shortly after this event Vespasian besieged the Jews. —This would therefore be a passover shortly before the siege of Jerusalem, in 68 or 69; or rather, since at that time such a passover, attended by all the tribes of Israel together with Gentiles, was hardly possible, shortly before Vespasian's campaign, i.e. probably the passover of 66 (so Zahn).

The execution of James the brother of the Lord is reported also, according to the text of our mss., by Josephus (*Ant.* XX. 9. 1): Since the procurator Festus was dead and Albinus (his successor) still on the way, the High Priest Ananus the Younger considered the time favourable (for independent action), appointed a council of judges, and brought before them the brother of Jesus the so-called Christ, a man named James, and some others, on the charge of having acted against the law, and handed them over for stoning (§ 200). The fair-minded and law-abiding people in the city took offence at this, and turned to King Agrippa, while others went to meet the governor Albinus and informed him of Ananus' arbitrary judicial proceedings. This led to the deposition of Ananus (§ 201–203). This would indicate the middle of the year 62.

Josephus gives the same text as we now read in Euseb. II. 23. 21–24; nevertheless it is possible that there is a Christian interpolation in the text of Josephus, made before Eusebius, as in the famous passage about Christ (see below, pp. 436f.). In that case, Josephus wrote only of the judicial murder of certain persons accused of violation of the Law—but thereby he would indicate just such a proceeding as the execution of James (and others). Origen indeed affirms that Josephus in his Archaeology represented the destruction of the temple as a punishment for the execution of James, the brother of Jesus the so-called Christ (*Comm. in Matt.* 13:55; cf. *c. Cels.* I. 47; II. 13; Euseb. II. 23. 20 and *Chronic. paschale* I. 463 are probably dependent on Origen). Origen may really have read such a Christian entry in the Archaeology, but the occasion must have been provided by a statement about the death of James, and so we must regard the passages about James in Josephus as surely authentic. Clement of Alexandria (*hypot.* VII, Euseb. II. 1. 5) probably drew his information from Hegesippus.

In Hegesippus' account much is improbable: the Rechabite priest (Epiphanius 78. 14 substitutes Simeon, the nephew of James (see below), but he too is borrowed from Hegesippus); the emphasis on the asceticism of James; his right to enter the Holy Place—simply because of his linen clothing; the fact that people expected of him, a Christian and a brother of Jesus, a testimony against Christ. But his confession of Christ, his fall and his stoning may well be genuine; which brings us more or less to the account in Josephus. His strict observance of the Law is also strongly attested; at that time such observance was enhanced by others also through abstinence of various kinds. We might indeed, with Schwartz, assume insertions in the text of Hegesippus; but it is simpler to ascribe to Hegesippus the repetitions and the touching up of the tradition.

In the Gospel of the Hebrews also (see p. 165) the appearance accorded to James (1 Cor. 15:7) is amplified in such a way as to emphasize the abstinence from food to which he pledged himself after the Last Supper. Here the frugality of James is so employed and presented as to prepare for the appearance of Christ, and his special devotion to Jesus, at once his brother and his Lord, is thrown into relief. This close attachment is extended backwards to the Last Supper, and the appearance which is accordingly granted to him takes place immediately after the risen Jesus has wiped away the last traces of his burial with the linen cloth. For the 'Hebrews' of this Gospel James is the first believing witness of His Resurrection. In general he would seem to have been for Jewish Christians a particularly important mediator of the truth. The Ebionites, of whom Epiphanius reports (30. 23), appealed to writings under apostolic names, including that of James. This certainly means the Lord's brother, the hero of the Ascents of James which they highly esteemed (30. 16) and in which Paul, as the opponent of circumcision, the Sabbath and the Law, is rejected, although admittedly the sacrificial worship of the temple is abandoned. James speaks "against the temple, sacrifice, and the fire on the altar". Moreover the Naassenes also (Hippol. 5. 7; 10. 9) traced their Gnosis back to James the brother of the Lord, who had transmitted it to Mariamme. Finally the Coptic Gospel of Thomas also shows the high esteem which James enjoyed in many circles in the early period (cf. logion 12 = Pahor Labib, phot. ed., pl. 82. 25–30, p. 290 above).

Hegesippus had written (Euseb. II. 23. 4): James the brother of the Lord received the Church in succession with the apostles. But in Clement of Alexandria (see vol. II, XI. 2) James is designated as Bishop even before Peter. He appears also as first Bishop of Jerusalem, appointed by the apostles immediately after the Ascension, in the lists of the Bishops of Jerusalem in Eusebius (*Chron.* 33; *H.E.* IV. 5. 3). In the pseudo-Clementines, James the brother of Jesus is installed as Bishop of Jerusalem by Christ Himself (*Rec.* I. 44), indeed he is Lord and Bishop of Holy Church and Lord and Bishop of the Bishops (in the letters of Peter and Clement to him). This literature is of later composition, but the recognition of James as chief shepherd itself derives from the oldest Jewish-Christian-Gnostic *Grundschrift*. His episcopal chair was still preserved as a precious relic in Jerusalem in the time of Eusebius (VII. 19); on it was enthroned, for example, Hermon (VII. 32. 29), the last Bishop of the see before the persecution of Diocletian (302). According to Epiphanius (78. 7) Christ entrusted His throne over the earth in the first place to James; for this he was fitted on the one hand through his holiness (see above, p. 419), on account of which he was even able, like the high priest, to enter once a year into the Holy of Holies, and on the other hand as being the brother of Jesus and son of Joseph, and therefore the heir of David and of his throne (29.4). Here the episcopal chair of James becomes the throne of David and of the world, and then it plays a further part in the legend of Mary (cf. Zahn *op. cit.*, p. 229 note, and *Die Dormitio s. Virginis*, 1899, pp. 28f.).

James and the other brothers of Jesus must in fact have been regarded by the faithful as kinsmen and earthly representatives of the true heir of David, the Messianic king who is enthroned at the right hand of God as His co-regent, the eternal king of heaven and earth, and must accordingly have been honoured in very high degree. It is thus not surprising that they should have become suspect in the eyes of the Roman state, especially when the emperors after the Jewish War had the descendants of David sought out "that none might survive among the Jews who was of the royal stock". Of this Hegesippus again informs us. It was from him that Eusebius derived the accounts of the proceedings of the emperors against the descendants of David, carried through by Vespasian (*H.E.* III. 12), Domitian (III. 19f.) and Trajan (III. 32. 3). Under Domitian certain 'heretics' denounced the descendants of Jude, who was a brother of the Saviour after the flesh, on the ground that they were descended from David, and that they boasted of a relationship to the Messiah himself. It is thus that Eusebius (III. 19) introduces Hegesippus, whom he then allows to speak in greater detail (III. 20. 1–6):

There still survived of the family of the Lord the grandchildren of Jude, who was called a brother of Christ according to the flesh. These they (the heretics already mentioned) denounced as being of the house of David. The *evocatus* (a veteran soldier) brought them before the emperor Domitian; for he was as much afraid of the advent of Christ as was Herod. He asked them if they were of the seed of David, and they admitted it. Then he asked them what property they had, or how much money they owned. They replied that together they had only 9000 denarii, of which half belonged to each of them, and this they said they had not in ready money but in the value of a piece of land extending to thirty-nine *plethra* only (about ten acres). From this they paid their taxes, and also supported themselves by their own labour. Then, relates Eusebius (still following Hegesippus), they showed their hands and, to prove that they did toil themselves, the hardness of their bodies and the calluses which from constant labour had formed upon their hands. When they were asked about Christ and His kingdom, what was its nature and where and when it was to appear, they replied that it was not of this world or earthly, but heavenly and angelic, and that it was to be at the end of time, when He came in glory to judge the living and the dead, and to render to every man according to his works.

Domitian did not condemn them in any way, but despised them as people of no importance, and set them free; moreover he put a stop, by an edict, to the persecution of the Church. Thus set at liberty, they became leaders of the Churches, as being at once confessors and of the Lord's family; and since peace had been established they lived on down to the time of Trajan. For the last statement Eusebius also (III. 32. 6) gives the more detailed text: "They come now and lead the whole Church as witnesses and of the Lord's family, and since a profound peace has been established throughout the Church they remain until the time of the emperor Trajan."

Paul already indicates that the brothers of Jesus were married (1 Cor. 9:5). According to the later legend the 'two elder', Justus and Simeon, married even during Joseph's lifetime and set up their own households, as did the two daughters (Story of

423

Joseph, c. 11). More reliable is what we hear from Hegesippus about the two grandsons of Jude; from two collections of extracts (see Zahn p. 240) it may be concluded that he also knew their names: Zōkēr and James. By 'heretics' are meant not Christian sectaries, but adherents of Jewish movements which Hegesippus has named earlier (Euseb. IV. 22. 7; II. 23. 8), and to which the Sadducees and Pharisees, among others, belong (cf. II. 23. 10, above, p. 419); some of them later were themselves arraigned as sons of David (III. 32. 4). The information is supposed to have reached the emperor in Rome, and the suspects to have been brought thither from Palestine—which is going rather far; such an investigation could have been conducted by a governor on the spot. The summons is not impossible in view of the emperor's suspicions, still less the acquittal; Domitian did not persecute the Christians as a matter of principle (but see below).

Hegesippus does not expressly say that the descendants of the family of Jesus had become bishops in particular churches; they were held in respect 'in every church'. But certainly there were bishops who came of this lineage. According to the Syrian historian Gregory Barhebraeus (13th century), three bishops from the family of Joseph followed one another as late as the 3rd century at Seleucia on the Tigris: Abrisios, Abraham and James.

The eagerness of the relatives of Jesus to prove their descent from David is reported by Julius Africanus in the passage in which he speaks of the two genealogies of Jesus (see below, pp. 431f.; Euseb. I. 7. 13f.): Herod had caused the pedigrees of the Jews to be burned; only a few particularly zealous people could boast of having preserved the memory of their noble ancestry. Among these were the relatives of Jesus, who because of their connection with the family of the Saviour were called δεσπόσυνοι (i.e. kinsmen of the Lord). From the Jewish villages of Nazareth and Kochaba (in Transjordan, where the Jewish-Christian community had later settled) they visited the rest of the country and, wherever they went, expounded the genealogies already mentioned both from the Book of Days—the Biblical Books of Chronicles—(and also from memory) so far as they were able.

The New Testament everywhere speaks without hesitation or comment of brothers of Jesus, so that we must think of full brothers; Lk. 2:7 calls Jesus Mary's first-born son, as if others followed. The same view is upheld quite frankly by Tertullian, de monog. 8 and elsewhere. But after the middle of the 2nd century the opinion prevailed that Mary both in and after the birth of Jesus remained a virgin, and bore no other children. This manner of thinking found graphic representation in the Protevangelium of James (see above, pp. 370ff.; *Handb.* pp. 99f.). Here it is presupposed as established fact that Joseph's other sons were born of an earlier marriage (8. 2 with 9; 17. 1); one of these sons indeed is supposed to be the James who wrote the Protevangelium (25. 1). This example was followed not only by all the Infancy Gospels (pp. 388ff.) but also by such fathers as Clement of Alexandria, Origen, Epiphanius, Ephraem Syrus and others (see Zahn, pp. 309ff.). But when Helvidius revived the old opinion, that the brothers of Jesus were His real brothers, Jerome in 383 introduced the theory that the brothers of Jesus were, among others, the apostles James the son of Alphaeus and 'Judas of James'. Their father thus was called Alphaeus; their mother was the 'Mary of Clopas' (Jn. 19:25), the sister of Jesus' mother, who bore the same name (Jerome, *Contra Helvidium de perpetua virginitate Mariae*; cf. Zahn pp. 316ff., 320ff.; Blinzler pp. 29f.). Dubious as this construction is, it met with great approval, and became the dominant view in the Catholic Church. Before Jerome a sharp distinction had generally been made between James the brother of the Lord and the apostles (Zahn pp. 314f., Sieffert pp. 574ff.). On the Roman Catholic point of view cf. J. Blinzler, "Zum Problem der Brüder Jesu", *Trierer Theol. Zeitschr.* 67, 1958, pp. 129–145; 224–246.

2. The brothers of Jesus are thus real brothers and not, for example, cousins of the Lord. Through Hegesippus however we make the acquaintance of a real cousin and of an uncle of Jesus.

According to Hegesippus, Joseph, the legal father of Jesus, had a brother Clopas—according to Eusebius (III. 11) the man mentioned in Jn. 19:25. The son of this Clopas, Simeon, who was thus a cousin of Jesus as of James, was appointed by a unanimous decision after the death of James to be his successor, the second Bishop of Jerusalem (IV. 22. 4). The peace which the churches and the relatives of Jesus enjoyed down to the time of Trajan (see above, p. 423) was interrupted when this Simeon was denounced by Jewish 'heretics' (see above, p. 424) before the governor Atticus as a son of David and also as a Christian. He had to suffer torture for several days, but although 120 years old bore it bravely, so that all were greatly amazed, even the governor; finally the order was given for him to be crucified (III. 32. 3–6). In the Chronicle (Helm *GCS* 47, p. 194) Eusebius assigns this martyrdom to the year 107; the governor, an earlier consul (consularis) Atticus, is either Sextus Attius Suburanus, who was *consul suffectus* in 101 and consul in 104, or Ti. Claudius Atticus, the father of Herodes Atticus, who was a teacher of Marcus Aurelius. If Simeon was a cousin of Jesus, he must under Trajan have been of considerable age; an age of 120 years nevertheless gives rise to some suspicion. May we perhaps assume some confusion, such that Jude's grandsons were prosecuted only under Trajan, but Simeon already under Domitian?—Of the two disciples at Emmaus, one is called Cleopas in Lk. 24:18, the other according to Origen and in the margin of Codex S was named Simon. It would be very appropriate if these were Clopas and Simeon, father and son, the uncle and cousin of Jesus (Zahn p. 352); Clopas is in fact an abbreviation of Cleopas, Cleopatros, and Simon is the Greek equivalent of Simeon—but it is probably a matter of conjecture; Coptic apocrypha already think of the uncle of Jesus.

3. The 'Mary of Clopas', who according to Jn. 19:25 stood with other women beneath the Cross of Jesus, may be regarded as the wife or daughter of Clopas (so in the Sahidic version); accordingly if Clopas is the brother of Joseph, she would be an aunt or cousin of Jesus. In Mt. 27:56 and Mk. 15:40 there appears at the Crucifixion an 'other Mary' (apart from Mary Magdalene; cf. Mt. 27:61; 28:1), namely Mary the mother of James the Less and Joses, and it is very natural to identify with her the 'Mary of Clopas' in John. Jerome indeed turned this to account, identifying James the Less and Joses with the brothers of Jesus, James and Joses, and so making the latter cousins of Jesus (see above). Cousins they would in fact have been, if Mary was the wife of Clopas, and Clopas the uncle of Jesus thus the father of these two. But this was not the way Jerome followed. He left the relationship of Mary to Clopas an open question; for him the two were cousins of Jesus through their mother: he considered this Mary as the 'sister of Jesus' mother', who is named in Jn. 19:25 before Mary of Clopas. Grammatically, indeed, it is quite possible that the two expressions indicate the same woman. But in that case both sisters were called Mary, which is scarcely possible (unless we think of them as step-sisters), and so probably in John the sister of Jesus' mother remains nameless, just as indeed he never calls the mother of Jesus by her name.

At any rate we hear at this point of a sister of Jesus' mother. If we would find a name for her, that of Salome offers itself; Mark (15:40; 16:1) at least names her and, beside the Maries, only her among the women who had gone out to the Crucifixion and later also went to the grave on Easter morning. Matthew (27:56) substitutes, without mentioning any name, the mother of the sons of Zebedee. According to this the apostles James and John would be cousins of Jesus, and this is why they belonged to His closest associates and wanted to sit on His right hand and on His left in the kingdom of God (Zahn p. 341). But it is not certain whether we may in such fashion illustrate the figures in John from the older Gospels, as is done by theologians ancient and modern. In antiquity possibly Joseph's first wife, of whom according to the earlier view the brothers of Jesus were born, or one of the 'sisters' of Jesus by this marriage, was called Salome, without any identification of her with the mother of the sons of Zebedee, although this also was later attempted (Zahn p. 341 n. 2).

If Mary the daughter of Clopas was really the sister of Jesus' mother, then Clopas must have been the father of the two Maries; so in Gospel fragments from Upper Egypt (Robinson *TSt* 4. 2) and in the Latin ps. Matthew (see pp. 404ff.) c. 42, where we read that the Lord God bestowed Mary of Clopas upon Clopas and Anna in consolation for their dedication of the first Mary to the temple. But since in these infancy gospels Mary's father is elsewhere called Joachim, mss. give the arrangement that Clopas became the second husband of Anna, by whom he had a daughter Mary.—This brings us to the stepsisters for Jn. 19:25 (see Bauer p. 9 note 1). The attempt has also been made by commentators to interpret the mother of Jesus as the 'other' Mary, the mother of James the Less and Joses, which indeed from the names of their sons is possible; but great as was the fame of these commentators (Gregory of Nyssa, Chrysostom), their version could not hold its ground against Jerome's construction.

Salome, Joseph's first wife, is supposed to have been related to Mary and Elizabeth. That Mary and Elizabeth were related is attested by Lk. 1:36, where the angel appearing to Mary describes Elizabeth as her kinswoman. On the basis of this passage the levitical descent of Mary has been repeatedly asserted in ancient as in modern times, since Elizabeth as the wife of a priest must have been of priestly stock—a presupposition which is not absolutely conclusive, although custom and the law of inheritance (Num. 36) prompted marriage in the father's tribe. Although the early Church readily emphasized that Christ belonged both to the royal and to the priestly stock, it for the most part, and with increasing firmness, rejected the levitical descent of Mary and based the relation of Christ to the priesthood above all on His high priestly office (Bauer pp. 9–13). Very early stress was laid on the fact that not Joseph only but Mary also was descended from David—for the virgin birth indeed completely excluded a physical descent from David through Joseph, and left only a legal membership of the royal house through the legal father (so, e.g.: Ignatius, *Eph.* 18. 2; cf. *Trall.* 9. 1; *Smyrn.* 1. 1; Justin, *Dial.* 43, 45, 101, 120; *Protevang.* 10. 1; Tert. *adv. Marc.* III. 17. 20; IV. 1; V. 8; Orig. *c. Cels.* I. 39; II. 32; Euseb. I. 7. 17); among the Syrians the Davidic descent was recorded also in the text of the Gospels (in Tatian's Diatessaron, see Zahn,

Forschungen 1, p. 118; Syr. sin. Lk. 2:4f., Aphraates *TU* 3, 3–4 pp. 388f.; cf. Zahn, *Forsch.* 6, p. 328 n. 1; Bauer pp. 13ff.). Originally the Gospels know nothing to speak of about the descent of Mary; in Lk. 1:27 clearly Joseph alone is reckoned to the house of David. At most we may assume (because of Lk. 1:36) that Luke credited her with a priestly extraction.

For Mary's parents, Joachim and his wife Anna, we must turn to the Protevangelium (above, pp. 370ff.). From this time on Anna also belongs to the holy family, and her parents' experiences are part of the Life of Mary (see *Handb.* pp. 104f.). Among the Syrians we even find the report that Anna and Elizabeth were sisters (see the creed of Jacob ⟨Bar Adai⟩ of Edessa, the founder of the Jacobites, in Bauer p. 8 n. 3).

According to Mk. 6:3 it was no title of honour on the lips of the people of Nazareth when they called Jesus 'son' of Mary; she too considered her son to be out of His mind, and wanted to take Him home (3:21, 31), and this was why Jesus renounced her (34f.); Mt. has repeated this somewhat more discreetly (13:55; 12:46–50). Lk. (4:22; 8:20) is even more considerate towards the mother of Jesus. He has a tender and thoughtful story to tell of her about the events before and after the birth (1:26–2: 52), while after the death of Jesus also he does not forget to relate that Mary was among the women who attached themselves to the first Christian community (Acts 1:14). According to John it was the mother of Jesus who was responsible for His residence in Cana and Capernaum (2:1, 12), and at the wedding she sought to influence her son (2:3–5). Later she appears also with other women at the Cross; in a kind of testament the dying Jesus entrusts her to the beloved disciple, as her son in His place (19:25–27). There is no NT account of an appearance of the risen Christ to His mother, but Ephraem Syrus claims to have read something of the sort in Tatian's Diatessaron; traces of this reading are to be found elsewhere also among the Syrians (Bauer p. 263), while apocrypha preserved in Coptic replace Mary Magdalene at the grave by Mary the mother of the Lord.

As Jewish and pagan answers to the Christian affirmation of the virgin birth, malicious reports were soon in circulation which taxed her with humble origin, unchastity and adultery, and here also there is confusion with Mary Magdalene and other women (see *Handb.* p. 50ff.). The Christians exalted her memory all the more; her birth, childhood, youth and betrothal were frequently presented and celebrated in legend and in art (see p. 368; *Handb.* pp. 95–105).—The Gnostics took a prominent share in this veneration of Mary, as is shown by the title of a document, the 'Genna Marias' (Epiph. 26. 12), and by other writings (see above, pp. 338ff.); among them she probably became, even more than we can demonstrate, the intelligent medium of profound Gnosis (see Bauer p. 448), especially after the death of Jesus.

The Church too concerned itself with the further destiny of the Mother of God after Jesus' passing. The presence of Mary with the apostles, attested in Acts 1:14, provided the initial impetus. In the Gospel of Bartholomew (see below, pp. 484ff.) she instructs them in thoroughly original fashion about the secrets of the Annunciation. Epiphanius (78. 11) turns aside the questions of the death and burial of Mary, and also the other one, whether John took her with him to Asia. Later, exact information was available concerning the very house in which she died, the Dormitio (Zahn, *Die Dormitio s. Virginis*, 1899). In general, the compilers of legend went diligently to work and produced a comprehensive description of the 'Assumption of the Virgin Mary', which has survived in Greek, Latin, Syriac, Coptic and Arabic, probably of Egyptian origin and hardly older than 400. The oldest version of the *Transitus Mariae* is probably the text which Tischendorf edited in *Apa* 124–136 (=ps. Melito; cf. B. Capelle, "Vestiges grecs et latins d'un antique 'transitus' de la Vierge": *Anal. Boll.* 67 (1949) pp. 21–48. So also M. Jugie. His book is the most comprehensive study of the problem; cf. on it the critical observations of B. Altaner in *Theol. Revue* 44 (1948) pp. 129–140; 45 (1949) pp. 129–142; 46 (1950) pp. 5–20. Cf. also B. Capelle *op. cit.*). The narrative begins after the Ascension and depicts Mary's association with the disciples, then passing to the main theme, the death and burial of the Virgin and what happened thereafter. Amid many differences of detail, all the accounts come in the end to this, that Mary, restored to life in the body, is carried off to Paradise. Cf. on this subject the festal sermon of the Jerusalem Patriarch Modestus (631–634): *PG* LXXXVI. 2, 3277–3312.— The two brief (Latin) letters (*PA* II. 299f.), which purport to contain a question from Ignatius of Antioch and the reply of Jesus' mother, need be mentioned only in passing.

4. A simpler figure is that of the foster-father Joseph, who in ancient and modern pictures for the most part sits modestly aside where Mary and the Child are saluted. In Mk. 6:3 the people of Nazareth call Jesus 'the carpenter', in Mt. 13:55 'the carpenter's son'. On this Matthaean statement, which is perhaps only a correction, is based the idea, widespread throughout Christianity, of Joseph the carpenter. He is not credited with any great skill; according to the Infancy Gospel of Thomas (c. 13; see p. 396) he could only make ploughs and yokes (on Jesus' handicraft cf. Justin, *Dial.* 88). Christendom is at one in its recognition of his Davidic descent, attested alike by Mt. 1:20 and Lk. 1:27; 2:4 and

before them already by the genealogies, which both found in existence and took over (see below). On his first marriage and the children born of it see above, pp. 424f.; at his marriage to Mary he can accordingly appear as an old man (Protevang. 9. 2, similarly ps. Mt., Story of Joseph and elsewhere); the Story of Joseph and Epiphanius (*Handb.* p. 119) offer more precise figures. Mt. and, following him, the infancy gospels (see Protevang. c. 13f.) describe his honourable conduct in Mary's pregnancy (1. 19–25), the Protevangelium his hesitation at the marriage (9. 2).

Mt. 1:18 and Lk. 1:35 both affirm that Mary conceived Jesus not of Joseph but of the Holy Spirit. Since according to the later view Mary remained a virgin even afterwards, Joseph's marriage to her constituted a special problem, upon which legend and theology frequently spent themselves (see *Handb.* p. 117; Bauer p. 29). In the Jewish and pagan account of this relationship Joseph appears as the cozened husband who repudiates the adultress (Orig. *c. Cels.* I. 28, 32, 39). According to Mt. 1:24 however Joseph takes Mary to himself as his wife and escorts her, together with the child, from Bethlehem to Egypt (2:13–15), back again (21), and then to Nazareth (23). In Lk. 2:4 he goes with her from Nazareth to Bethlehem for the census; both then return to Nazareth (2:39). Every year they go up thence to Jerusalem for the passover, once with the twelve-year-old Jesus (2:41–52); all of which the infancy gospels have richly elaborated (see pp. 363ff.). Then Joseph disappears from the story. When Jesus makes His debut, he seems to be already dead (Mk. 6:3).

The most detailed treatment is in the 'Story of Joseph the Carpenter', an Egyptian book dating from about 400 which is preserved in two forms in Coptic, completely in the Bohairic dialect (also extant in Arabic and Latin) and chapters 14–24. 1 in Sahidic (ed. P. de Lagarde, *Aegyptiaca* 1883; S. Morenz, *TU* 56), but was originally composed in Greek (Morenz 88–96). The first part (chaps. 1–11) recounts events before the birth of Jesus, then His birth and early childhood. Here the influence of the Protevangelium and of the Infancy Gospel of Thomas is unmistakable. The second part (12–32) portrays his sickness and death as a model of holy dying, and his burial, the latter corresponding to the rites of Osiris. Morenz (*Die Geschichte von Joseph dem Zimmermann übersetzt, erlautert und untersucht* (*TU* 56, 1951)) shows the strong influence from Egyptian religion (referring to G. Klameth, *Angelos* 3, 1930), and also that of Gnosis. "In the Egyptian Christianity of the late second century", he affirms, "there were no sharp lines between the Great Church and Gnostic thought". On Gnosis in Egypt cf. W. Till, "Die Gnosis in Ägypten", *La Parola del Passato* 12 (1949) 231ff.

5. For Joseph's ancestors we have two genealogies (Mt. 1:1–17; Lk. 3:23–38)—for despite the labours of ancient and modern times there is no doubt that both refer to Joseph. Admittedly they are quite different in the names from David to Joseph, and the number of the members also does not tally. This very early became a cause of concern for serious students of the Bible (Orig. *c. Cels.* II. 32; Euseb. I. 7). The faithful sought "as best they could to remove this difficulty". Julius Africanus (about 160–240) believed that he had found the best solution as follows (Euseb. I. 7. 2–10): He recalls the Jewish custom of the levirate marriage, according to which if a man dies without sons, his brother must marry the widow and raise up seed to his brother (Deut. 25:5f.). Matthan (Mt. 1:15) and Melchi (Lk. 3:24; Jul. Afr. thus did not have the two names Matthat and Levi which we read elsewhere between Eli and Melchi in Lk. 3:24) married one after the other— so he assumes—the same woman and had children by her, who were thus (step) brothers by the same mother. So by Estha, for this according to tradition was the woman's name, first Matthan, the descendant of Solomon, begot Jacob (Mt. 1:15), and then after Matthan had died Melchi, the descendant of Nathan, married the widow (the same Estha) and begot of her Eli (Lk. 3:23). (It is thus assured that Jacob and Eli were brothers, although admittedly only step-brothers.) One of these, Jacob, when his brother Eli died childless, took the latter's wife and had by her Joseph; Joseph thus was the natural son of Jacob, but the legal son of Eli —for it was to him that the seed was raised up. This is why in Lk. it is not said 'he begot', but only (going backwards) "he was a son, as was believed" (Lk. 3:23).

For this solution Africanus appeals to the relatives of the Lord, who once compiled the family pedigree (see above)—admittedly he does not say expressly that they confirmed his statements or conjectures about levirate marriage among Joseph's ancestors; rather he confesses that they noted down the names from the Chronicle (1 Chron. 1, 2, 3; Ruth 4) and from memory, as well as they could manage, and in general he seeks only to commend his solution as the best possible (Euseb. I. 7. 11–15). This is certainly the case if the two genealogies ought to be brought into agreement at all; a simpler assumption is that they represent two different attempts to establish the Davidic sonship of Jesus, when it was no longer possible fully to reach the truth.

It is equally probable that the two genealogies were composed in the opinion that Joseph was Jesus' natural father—no one would have taken the trouble to demonstrate Joseph's natural descent for the sake of a purely legal relationship. This view was long maintained by 'Ebionite' Jewish Christians, and because of it they soon ranked as heretics in the eyes of the Church (Justin, *Dial.* 48; Irenaeus I. 22.; III. 23; V. 1. 3; Euseb. III. 27; VI. 17 etc.). Finally it is probable that people believed in the Davidic sonship of Jesus not because of any family tradition but because they believed in Him as the Messiah, who of course had to be the Son of David (cf. Mk. 12:35–37). (On Panthera in the genealogy of Jesus cf. *Apokr.* 2, p. 81 and above, p. 367.)

X

THE WORK AND SUFFERINGS OF JESUS

1. JESUS' EARTHLY APPEARANCE AND CHARACTER

(*W. Bauer*)

1. In the period here under examination, understanding of the chronological structure of the life of Jesus is generally governed by the impression evoked either by the Synoptic presentation or by that of John, and here the specific statements of Lk. 3:1, 23; 4:19 in turn are still conspicuous. The reckoning of Jesus' age at 30 is in some way or other linked with the view that His public ministry lasted one year, or about a year, or even two or three years. The one-year theory is the most frequently represented: the Basilidians (in Clem. Alex. *Strom.* I. 21. 146), Valentinians (Iren. *adv. haer.* I. 1. 5; II. 32. 1, 6; 33. 1, 3), the 'Docetics' in Hippolytus (*Ref.* VIII. 10), certainly also Marcion and the Alogi, ps. Clem. *Hom.* I. 7; XVII. 19, *Rec.* IV. 35, and further Clement of Alexandria himself (I. 21. 145; V. 6. 37; VI. 11. 87) and Julius Africanus (in Euseb. *Dem. ev.* VIII. 2. 52f.; Syncellus ed. Bonn. pp. 612, 611). In the West the same view was held by Tertullian, *adv. Iud.* 8; *adv. Marc.* 1. 15; ps. Cyprian, *de pascha comp.* 18–22; Lactantius, *div. inst.* IV. 10. 18; 14. 11; *de mort. pers.* 2. 1, etc. Much less frequently was the duration of Jesus' activity reckoned at three years, or nearly three. Here must be mentioned Tatian, whose Gospel harmony was based on the Johannine version, and beside him only Melito of Sardis for certain (*frag.* 6 ed. Otto, *Corpus Apol.* vol. IX, pp. 415f.).

The two conceptions just outlined did not however remain the only theories. Irenaeus, who abhorred the one-year theory as gnostic, himself expressed the following opinion (II. 33. 1–4): Jesus sanctified all ages, in that He Himself passed through them all. He was *senior in senioribus*, and therefore qualified to be a perfect teacher. To support the view that Jesus attained to the *aetas senior*, which for Irenaeus begins with the forties, this father appeals to the old Presbyters (II. 33. 3) as well as to Jn. 8:57. That on this view the death of Jesus is set in the time of Claudius (instead of Tiberius) we know from the 'Demonstration of the Apostolic Preaching' c. 74. Thereby the 'Letter of Pilate to Claudius' (*Aa* 1, pp. 136, 196; see below, pp. 477f.) acquires increased importance for our knowledge of the chronological estimate of the life of Jesus. A very old interpolation in the text of Hippolytus' Commentary on Daniel (IV. 23. 3, *GCS* 1. 1, p. 242) likewise makes Jesus suffer in the first year of Claudius. A fragment circulating under the name of Victorinus of Pettau (*CSEL* XXXXIX pp. XXIIIf.), seconded by the *de fabrica mundi* 9, which certainly derives from Victorinus, makes the statements, which have a very ancient ring, that Jesus was born in the year 9 A.D., baptized in 46, and died in 59. Finally Jesus reaches the age of 46 also in ps. Cyprian, *de mont. Sina et Sion* 4; here we can see the influence of Jn. 2:20f.

2. *His appearance.* Portraits of Jesus first emerge among the Gnostic Carpocratians (Iren. I. 20. 4 and later writers), while according to Tertull. *de pudic.* X. 12f., He was symbolically represented as a shepherd (cf. the early Christian art of the Catacombs etc. still extant: J. Sauer, *Die ältesten Christusbilder*, 1920; W. J. A. Visser, "Die Entwicklung des Christusbildes", in *Lit. u. Kunst in der frühchristl. u. frühbyz. Zeit*, 1934; F. Gerke, *Christus in der spätantiken Plastik²*, 1941). Where anything is said about the outward appearance of Jesus, it is usually declared, with a reference to Isa. 53:2f., or less commonly Ps. 22:7, to be ill-favoured: Justin, Irenaeus, Clem. Alex., Origen, Tertullian, Cyprian, Hippolytus, Acts of Peter c. 24, Orac. Sib. VIII. 256f. Some of those mentioned, like Clem. Alex. *Strom.* II. 5. 21 or Hippol., *Comm. on Canticles, TU* 23. 2c, c. 18, p. 51, can also on occasion describe Him as handsome, in this agreeing for example with Acts of John 73f., Acts of Thomas 80; 149. Origen knows a tradition, which appears to him very plausible, according to which Jesus had at His disposal very different forms of embodiment, since He adapted Himself to the individual viewer's powers of comprehension (*Comm. in Mt.* XII. 36; *Comm. in Mt.* ser. 100; frag. *in Luc.* V. 243 Lommatzsch; *c. Cels.* II. 64; IV. 16; VI. 77). Much more peculiar and thoroughly gnostic is the description of the appearance of Jesus given in the Acts of John (c. 88–93).

3. *Calling and Manner of Life.* On Jesus' vocation as a carpenter Justin (*Dial.* 88) observes that He made ploughs and yokes, and the Infancy Gospels (see above, VIII) relate with pleasure how the boy assisted His father in the exercise of his craft. That the Lord went out as a slave upon the earth is said by many, after Paul (Phil. 2:7): Melito, Justin, Origen. This involved want and poverty (so also Hippol., *in Dan.* IV. 18; Tert. *de corona* 13), as well as shabby clothing (Tert. *de idol.* 18).

According to the Gospels Jesus felt hunger and thirst like men, and assuaged both in the same manner. Later also this was the dominant view: Ignatius, Justin, Irenaeus, Tertullian, Origen, ps. Clementines. As with the life of Jesus generally, the docetic

tendency resolved His eating and drinking also into mere sem-
blance: the opponents of Ignatius (*Trall.* 9. 1), Marcion, the
Acts of John (c. 93), also probably Heracleon (in Orig. *in Joh.*
XIII. 38). Valentinus allowed Jesus indeed to consume food, but
makes Him absorb it all (in Clem. Alex., *Strom.* III. 7. 59).
Clement of Alexandria himself denies that Jesus could have
required nourishment for the maintenance of His life (VI. 9. 71).
If the Docetic denies a real eating and drinking, so the Jesus of the
Encratites renounces the enjoyment of meat and wine, and wants
to have no knowledge of any kind of sexual intercourse. On this
point there prevailed within Christianity a belief about Jesus
from which spirits of the more extreme persuasion derived an
injunction for the sexual relationships of His people also: Encratites in Clem. Alex., *Strom.* III. 6. 45, 49f.; 13. 91; Second Book of
Jeu 45.

4. Just as widely diffused is the conviction of *His omnipotence*,
which enabled Him to perform miracles. The period of the public
ministry of Jesus was scarcely furnished any more richly than it
had already been by the canonical Gospels. The need for the
production of new miracle stories rather seized upon the period
preceding the Baptism. In addition it was a favourite practice to
represent the miraculous work of the Lord in a brief epitome,
somewhat in the style of Mt. 11:5; Lk. 7:22; Mk. 3:9–11; Lk.
6:17–19 (cf. Isa. 35:5f.; Acts 10:38); Justin, *Apol.* I. 22, 48; *Dial.*
69; *de resurr.* 4; Melito *fr.* 16; *Epist. apost.* (above, pp. 193f.);
Orig. *c. Cels.* II. 48; Tert. *Apol.* XXI. 17; *de carne Christi* 4; *de
resurr. carnis* 20; Cyprian, *de eccl. unit.* 3; ps. Cyprian, *quod idola
dii non sint* 13; Hippol. on Ps. 2.7 (*GCS* 1. 2; p. 146); ps. Clem.
Hom. I. 6; the Abgar legend in Euseb. I. 13. 6; Acts of Thomas
47; Orac. Sib. I. 351ff.; VI. 13ff.; VIII. 272ff.; Pistis Sophia c. 110f.

5. Of very similar structure are the comprehensive descriptions
of the *character of Jesus*, which now come into vogue. Starting from
the belief in the sinlessness of Jesus—which admittedly did not
remain entirely undoubted or unquestioned (cf. *Praedicatio Pauli*
in ps. Cyprian, *de rebapt.* 17; the Gospel of the Nazarenes, above,
p. 146 no. 2; Mani in the *Acta Archelai* 60, *GCS* 16, p. 88; Basilides
in Clem. Alex., *Strom.* IV. 12. 81–83; the Valentinian Alexander
in Tert., *de carne Christi* 16; the Carpocratians in Iren. I. 20. 1;
II. 49. 2; the Cainites in Hippol. *Syntagma* according to Tert.,
adv. omn. haer. 2, Epiph. 38. 3)—a more or less extensive series of
virtues was compiled which were ascribed to Jesus, and through
which He became an example for His followers: 1 Peter 2:21–24;
1 Clement 16. 2; Martyrium Apollonii 36–42 v. Gebhardt p.
55ff. (in German translation: Bauer p. 532ff.); Funk, *Didask.*
p. 97. We may add the fine testimonial in ps. Clem. *Hom.* III. 19:

That is why he rose up from his seat, and as a father for his children spared not his own blood, in order . . . to extend mercy even to the heathen, and to have compassion on the souls of all. For, elected king of the world to come, he took up the conflict against him who has received the dominion for the present according to predetermined laws. And what grieved him most deeply is this, that he was resisted, through ignorance, by those very people for whom, as for his children, he carried on the conflict. Yet did he love even those who hated him, and mourned over those who did not believe in him, blessed those who reviled him, and prayed for his enemies. And not only did he (himself) so act as a father, but taught also his disciples in their relations (towards others) to do the same as to brothers. In such manner was he a father, in such manner a prophet. And according to reasonable expectation, in such manner also will he be king over his children, that according to his fatherly love to his children, and in virtue of the child-like reverence towards their father that is in them, an eternal peace may dawn.

(Translation after German of H. Veil)

6. Brief surveys of the life of Jesus as a whole were also produced. A good example of these is the famous testimony to Jesus which a Christian inserted into the *Jewish Antiquities* of Josephus (XVIII. 63f. Niese; see below, X. 2).

2. THE ALLEGED TESTIMONY OF JOSEPHUS
(*W. Bauer*)

In the traditional text of the Jewish Antiquities of Josephus (ed. B. Niese) Jesus is mentioned twice; once quite briefly (XX. 9. 1, § 200): "Ananus summoned the Council to judgment, and brought before it the brother of Jesus, the so-called Christ, James by name". This sentence was known already to Origen as a statement of Josephus (*c. Cels.* I. 47, 2. 13; *in Matth.* tom. 10. 17, p. 22 ed. E. Klostermann), and since the author through the 'so-called' clearly stands aside from the Christian faith there is no reason for denying the words to Josephus.

The situation is then, however, all the more doubtful with regard to the other passage, the 'testimony' proper (*Ant.* XVIII. 3. 3, § 63f.):

At this time appeared Jesus, a wise man, if one may call him a man at all. For he was a doer of wonderful works, a teacher of

men, who received the truth with gladness. And he attracted
Jews as also people of the Greek sort in great number. This was
the Christ. And when on the denunciation of our leading men
Pilate had punished him with crucifixion, those who had loved
him formerly did not cease therefrom. He appeared to them alive
again on the third day, for the godly prophets had foretold this and
innumerable other wonderful things concerning him. And even
now the race of men called after him Christians has not died out.

This 'testimony' was known to Eusebius (*H.E.* I. 11. 7; *Dem.
ev.* 3. 5. 105f.), but evidently not yet to Origen, who in *c. Cels.*
I. 47 expressly denies to Josephus any belief in "Jesus as
the Christ", in direct contradiction to the words "this was the
Christ". On the whole, the 'testimony' is intelligible only as the
confession of a Christian, and for this reason even an F. C. Burkitt
(*Theol. Tidschrift* 1913, pp. 135–144) and an A. Harnack (*Inter-
nationale Monatsschrift* 1913, pp. 1037–68; most recently F.
Dornseiff, *ZNW* 46 (1955) pp. 245–250) have not succeeded in
defending its authenticity. The passage is either to be completely
rejected (so after many predecessors since the 16th century E.
Schürer, *Gesch. des jüd. Volkes* I[4], 1901, pp. 544–49; E. Norden,
Neue Jahrb. f. d. klass. Altertum 1913, pp. 637–668), or we must
assume that an original text by Josephus has been very thoroughly
transformed by a Christian hand (so among others P. Corssen,
ZNW 15 (1914) pp. 114–140; M. Goguel, *Life of Jesus* 1933, pp.
79f.). As for attempts to restore the original text (Th. Reinach,
Rev. des Études juives 35 (1897) p. 13f.; R. Eisler, Ἰησοῦς Βασιλεύς
I, 1929, pp. 1–88; F. Scheidweiler, *ZNW* 45 (1954) pp. 230–243),
the more venturesome they are, the less are they credible.

3. THE ABGAR LEGEND

(*W. Bauer*)

INTRODUCTION:

1. The theme of the Abgar legend is the correspondence between Jesus and King Abgar V Ukkama (= the Black) of Edessa
(9–46 A.D.) and the founding of the Church in Edessa which it
brought about. The king has heard of Jesus' miracles of healing,
appeals to Him by letter, acknowledges His divinity, and prays
for release from the sickness which torments him. At the same
time, in view of the hostility of the Jews, he offers to Jesus his own
city as a safe place of residence. Jesus replies likewise by a letter.
He felicitates the king, because he believes without having seen.
The invitation He must decline, since He has a vocation and an

earthly existence to fulfil in Palestine. Nevertheless after His death and ascension a disciple will come, who will heal the king and bring life to him and his. This then comes about through the mission and activity of the apostle Thaddaeus or Addai, who through his healings and preaching wins Edessa for Christianity.

2. Attestation and appraisal. We encounter this story for the first time in Eusebius (*H.E.* I. 13; II. 1. 6–8), who firmly emphasizes that he obtained it from the archives in Edessa, where it lay recorded in the Syrian tongue. The document, preserved since Abgar's reign in the archives of the city, had been made available to him, and had been incorporated by him into the Church History in a literal translation (I. 13. 5, 22; II. 1. 6ff.).

Of this report, which ostensibly rested for centuries in the custody of the record office in Edessa, there is certainly no trace in the pre-Eusebian period, even in Edessa itself. Ephraem (d. 373), who lauds the conversion of the city in rhetorical exuberance, mentions indeed the apostle Addai, but drops not a single hint about the correspondence. It is only in the *Doctrina Addai* (G. Phillips, *The Doctrine of Addai, the Apostle*, 1876), a Syriac book composed in Edessa about 400, that the material known from Eusebius again appears, now indeed considerably enlarged, among other things by a detailed description of the activity of the apostolic emissary, who in Edessa preaches, baptizes, and builds the first church. Somewhere about the same time the western pilgrim Aetheria (ed. P. Geyer, *CSEL* 39, 1898, c. 17. 1; 19. 6) testifies that the Abgar legend was known in her homeland. Cf. also the letter of Count Darius to Augustine (*PL* XXXIII, 1022). Augustine (*c. Faust. Manich.* 28. 4) and Jerome (*in Ezech.* 44. 29) affirm that Jesus left nothing in writing, and this may have led to the declaration in the Decretum Gelasianum (5. 8. 1, 2 ed. E. v. Dobschütz 1912; also p. 319) that the correspondence is apocryphal.

This did just as little harm to the legend as did the doubt expressed here and there among theologians. It enjoyed the widest dissemination in the domain of the Syriac, Armenian, Greek, Latin, Arabic, Persian, Slavonic and Coptic languages. Now it is the legend as a whole which attracts attention and further development (e.g. in the Greek Acts of Thaddaeus of the 6th century, ed. R. A. Lipsius, *Aa* I, pp. 273–278, or among the Armenians in the *Historia Armeniae*, about 700, which passes under the name of Moses of Khoren, ed. Gu. and G. Whiston, 1763, II, c. 29–32), now we meet with portions, above all the letters (careful survey of the material then known in E. v. Dobschütz, *Christusbilder*, *TU* 18, 1899, pp. 102–105, 158*–249*, 130**–156**; see also *ZwTh* 43, 1900, pp. 422–486; by way of supplement, Yassa 'abd al-Masīh, *Bull. de l'inst. franç. d'archéol. orient.* 45 (1946) pp. 65–80; 54 (1954) pp. 13–43; L. Casson and L. E. Hettich, *Excavations at Nessana* II, 1950, 143–147).

Very early, people placed themselves under the protection of the sacred document. Thus the Bishop of Edessa told Aetheria (*CSEL* 39, c. 19. 9, 13) that Abgar and many others after him, when a siege threatened, brought Jesus' letter to the gate, there read it, and immediately the enemy dispersed. Later the people of Edessa for this reason fastened the precious document in transcript on the city gates (Procop., *de bellis* 2. 12, p. 208). Probably from the same sense of need the letter—and soon outside Edessa also—was carved in stone (M. v. Oppenheim and F. Hiller von Gaertringen, "Höhleninschrift von Edessa mit dem Briefe Jesu an Abgar", SB Berlin 1914, pp. 817–828. Superscription on door in Ephesus: v. Hiller p. 823. Inscr. from Pontus: *Studia Pontica* III, 1910, No. 210, 226) and written on leaves of papyrus or on ostraca (Greek fragments from the 4th–5th century in the Bodleian: A. Ehrhard, *Die altchristliche Literatur u. ihre Erforschung von 1884–1900*, 1900, pp. 117f.; P. Gothenburg 21, ed. H. Frisk 1929, pp. 41f., from the 6th–7th century. Coptic material in Ehrhard *op. cit.* p. 118, after C. Schmidt and J. Krall, and with other Oriental versions in Yassa 'abd al-Masīh *op. cit.*). He who possessed a copy could feel secure before the judges, on a journey, or against sickness and misfortune.

3. Aim and Origin. To understand these a brief glance is necessary at the history of Edessa in the period of its turning to Christianity. That Abgar V brought this about is today no longer maintained by any serious scholar, although Protestant and Catholic scholars of repute still defended the authenticity of the letters in the 19th century. Even the view which under the guidance of A. v. Gutschmid ("Untersuchungen über die Geschichte des Königreiches Osroëne": *Mémoires de l'Académie imp. des Sciences de S. Pétersbourg*, 7 Série, Tom. 35, 1887, pp. 1–49) has come into fashion in modern study, that not Abgar V but probably a later prince of the same name—Abgar IX (179–214)—went over to Christianity and assisted it in the conversion of his city, has no ancient witness in its favour, and is untenable also on other grounds.

The 'Edessene Chronicle' (*Chronica minora*, ed. J. Guidi: *CSCO* 1 [=Script. Syr. 1] pp. 1–13 (Text) and *CSCO* 2 [=Script. Syr. 2] pp. 1–11 (Translation), re-print 1955; L. Hallier, *Untersuchungen über die Edessenische Chronik: TU* 9. 1, 1892), which belongs as a whole to the 6th century but grew up gradually and contains older material, knows nothing at all of Abgar V, and Abgar IX not as a Christian. From the period before 313 it can name as personalities significant for religious history only Marcion, Bardesanes, and Mani, and thereby clearly shows who exercised the decisive influence on the earliest history of Christianity in Edessa. Only at 313 does it note: "The Bishop Kûnê laid the foundation of the Church of Urhâi (=Edessa). And Bishop Scha'ad, his successor, built it and completed the building" (*CSCO* 2 p. 5). Thus only at that time was the orthodox Church with its succession of bishops a factor worthy of mention.

This brings us to the period in which from 311/12 to 324/25 Eusebius' Church History passed through four editions (ed. E. Schwartz III, pp. XLVIIff.), in which thus the earliest form of the Abgar legend saw the light. Now let us ask who was instrumental here. Three facts seem to me well established: (a) According to the maxim *Cui bono?* it must have originated in Edessa, and that in orthodox circles. The Marcionites or other heretics there had no occasion whatever to push back the foundation of the Church into the period before the rise of their own community. By doing so they would only have cut off their own water supply, for as soon as the documentary proof obtained that the apostolic Church in Edessa went back to Jesus Himself, they were not merely relegated to the second place but struck a mortal blow. (b) In orthodox circles in Edessa the legend was still unknown for decades after Eusebius. Proof: the silence of Ephraem in the very place where he must have spoken (see above). (c) Eusebius firmly asserts that he did not draw his information about Abgar, like so much else, from books, but used a document from the archives of Edessa.

If we compare these three facts, then the suspicion arises that the Abgar legend did indeed originate in Edessa, but was not there published for the first time. How could the orthodox minority even have hoped to prevail in Edessa, where a vigorous resistance was to be expected from all other Christians, with the statement that for nearly three hundred years past an autograph letter of Jesus in reply to a letter from the Edessene prince had been lying in the archives? On the other hand, if a way could be found of putting the 'documents' into the hands of Eusebius, who was at the time collecting material for his Church History in near-by Palestine, then the road was open to the wider world, in so far as it was Christian, and a favourable reaction upon Edessa could scarcely fail to result. It may therefore be a legitimate conjecture that Bishop Kûnê and his circle were the instigators in the formation of this legend, and that it was among them that the original form arose. For detailed presentation of the view here advanced, see W. Bauer, *Rechtgläubigkeit und Ketzerei im ältesten Christentum*, 1934, pp. 6–48.

The most important literature on the Abgar legend up to the beginning of the 20th century is to be found in v. Dobschütz (see above) and in *Handb.* p. 153. To these may be added : J. B. Aufhauser, *Antike Jesus-Zeugnisse* (=*KlT* 126) 1913, pp. 17–31; F. C. Burkitt, *Early Eastern Christianity*, 1904; Bardenhewer I², 1913, pp. 590–596; F. Haase, *Altchristliche Kirchengeschichte nach orientalischen Quellen*, 1925; Quasten I, pp. 140–143; Yassa 'abd al-Masīh, *Bull. de l'inst. franç. d'archéol. orient.* 45, 1946, pp. 65–80; 54, 1954, pp. 13–43; L. Casson and L. E. Hettich, *Excavations at Nessana* II, 1950, pp. 143–147.

The oldest form of the legend, here presented, is contained in the Church History of Eusebius (ed. E. Schwartz 1908; here is added, in Th. Mommsen's edition, the Latin translation by Rufinus of 402/3, which for our purpose is particularly important because it greatly furthered the dissemination of the legend in the West). The Church father first gives a brief report, then adduces the documents, and then returns to his narrative. After a brief summary of the contents (I. 13. 1–4) Eusebius introduces the text of the two letters in the following words (I. 13. 5):

For this there is a written testimony, taken from the public records of the city of Edessa, which at that time was governed by a king. For in the public registers there, which contain both the events of the past and also the transactions concerning Abgar, these also are found preserved from his time even until now. But there is nothing like hearing the letters themselves, which we have taken from the archives and translated literally from the Syriac tongue in the following manner.

Copy of a letter written by the toparch Abgar to Jesus, and sent to him at Jerusalem by the hand of Ananias the courier:

Abgar Uchama the toparch to Jesus the good Saviour, who has appeared in the city of Jerusalem, greeting. I have heard of thee and of thy healings, that they are done by thee without drugs and herbs. For as it is said, thou dost make blind men see again and lame walk, and dost cleanse lepers, and cast out unclean spirits and demons, and heal those tormented by long disease, and raise the dead.[1] And when I heard all these things about thee, then I concluded that either thou art God come down from heaven to do them, or thou art the son of God, who doest these things. Therefore now I write and beseech thee to visit me, and heal the

[1] Cf. Mt. 11:5,; Lk. 7:22.

affliction which I have. Moreover I have heard that the Jews murmur against thee,[1] and wish to do thee injury. Now I have a city, small indeed but noble, which is sufficient for both.

The reply sent by Jesus, by the hand of Ananias the courier, to the toparch Abgàr:

Blessed art thou, who hast believed in me without having seen me.[2] For it is written concerning me, that they who have seen me will not believe in me, and that they who have not seen me shall believe and live.[3] But concerning what thou hast written to me, that I should come to thee, it is necessary that I fulfil here all for which I was sent, and after this fulfilment be taken up again unto Him who sent me. And when I am taken up, I will send to thee one of my disciples, that he may heal thine affliction and give life to thee and them that are with thee.

To these letters there was also appended in the Syriac tongue the following:

After the Ascension of Jesus, Judas who is also called Thomas sent to him the apostle Thaddaeus, one of the seventy.[4] He came and dwelt with Tobias the son of Tobias. When the news concerning him was heard, it was reported to Abgar: "An apostle of Jesus has come hither, as he wrote to thee". Thaddaeus then began in the power of God to heal every disease and infirmity,[5] so that all were amazed. But when Abgar heard the great deeds and wonders which he wrought, and how he healed, he began to suspect that this was the very man of whom Jesus had written, saying: When I am taken up again, I will send to thee one of my disciples, who will heal thine affliction. He therefore sent for Tobias, with whom he stayed, and said: I have heard that a powerful man has come and is staying in thy house. Bring him to me. Tobias came to Thaddaeus, and said to him: The toparch Abgar sent for me, and bade me bring thee to him, that thou mightest heal him. And Thaddaeus said: I am going, since I have been sent with power to him.

On the following day Tobias rose up early, and taking Thaddaeus with him went to Abgar. But as he went up, his chief men

[1] Cf. Jn. 6:41.   [2] Cf. Jn. 20:29.
[3] Cf. Isa. 6:9; 52:15, also Mt. 13:14ff.; Jn. 12:39f.; Acts 28:25ff.
[4] Cf. Lk. 10:1.   [5] Cf. Mt. 4:23; 10.1.

were present standing, and suddenly as he entered a great vision appeared to Abgar in the face of the apostle Thaddaeus. Seeing it, Abgar did obeisance to Thaddaeus, and all who stood around were amazed; for they had not seen the vision, which appeared to Abgar alone. He asked Thaddaeus: Art thou truly a disciple of Jesus, the Son of God, who hath said[1] to me "I will send thee one of my disciples, who will heal thee and give thee life"? And Thaddaeus said: Because thou hast greatly believed in him who sent me, therefore was I sent to thee; moreover, if thou believe in him the petitions of thy heart shall be granted, as thou dost believe. And Abgar said to him: So much did I believe in him that I would have taken a force and destroyed the Jews who crucified him, had I not been prevented because of the Roman sovereignty. And Thaddaeus said: Our Lord has fulfilled the will of his Father, and having fulfilled it was taken up again to his Father. Abgar said to him: I too believe in him and in his Father. And Thaddaeus said: Therefore do I lay my hand upon thee in his name. And when he had done this, immediately he was healed of the disease and the affliction which he had. And Abgar was astonished that, even as he had heard concerning Jesus, so in very deed had he received through his disciple Thaddaeus, who healed him without drugs and herbs, and not him only but also Abdus the son of Abdus, who had the podagra. He also came and fell at his feet, and was healed through prayer and the laying on of hands. And many others of their fellow-citizens did he heal, doing great and wonderful things and proclaiming the word of God.

Thereafter Abgar said: Thaddaeus, thou dost do these things by the power of God, and we for our part are filled with wonder. But I pray thee further, tell me about the coming of Jesus, how it came to pass, and about his power, and in what manner of power he did those things whereof I have heard. And Thaddaeus said: Now shall I be silent, since I was sent to proclaim the word; but tomorrow assemble me all thy citizens, and before them will I preach, and sow in them the word of life, both concerning the coming of Jesus, how it came to pass, and concerning his mission, and for what reason he was sent by the Father; and concerning

---

[1] Of communication by letter as in 1 Cor. 6:5; 7:6; 11:22 and often in Paul.

his power and works, and the mysteries which he declared in the world, and in what manner of power he did these things; and concerning his new preaching, and his lowliness and humiliation, and how he humbled himself and laid aside his deity and made it small, and was crucified and descended into Hell, and burst asunder the barrier which had remained unbroken from eternity, and raised up the dead; alone he descended, but with a great multitude did he ascend up to his Father.

Then Abgar commanded that on the (following) morning his citizens should assemble to hear the preaching of Thaddaeus, and thereafter he ordered unminted gold to be given him. But he would not receive it, saying: If we have left our own,[1] how shall we take what belongs to others?

This took place in the year 340.[2]

The whole is brought to a conclusion by the words of Eusebius: "This story, literally translated and for good reason from the Syriac tongue, may here find its appropriate place".

4. THE GOSPEL OF NICODEMUS

ACTS OF PILATE AND CHRIST'S DESCENT INTO HELL

(F. Scheidweiler)

INTRODUCTION:

Justin in his First Apology refers twice (c. 35 and 48) to documents of the trial of Jesus before Pilate. The same author however, and in the same terms, invites us to examine the schedules of the census under Quirinius, which certainly did not exist. This prompts the suspicion that Justin's reference to the *acta* of Pilate rests solely on the fact that he assumed that such documents must have existed. A second point is this: barely 50 years after the composition of Justin's Apology, Tertullian speaks in chapters 5 and 21 of his Apologeticus about a dispatch from Pilate to Tiberius, which contained such a detailed account of the miracles of Jesus that Tertullian believed he could regard Pilate as a Christian by conviction. He must thus have known an apocryphal Christian document under Pilate's name, which must have stood in some relation not indeed to the *acta* of the trial mentioned by Justin, but probably to the Letter of Pilate presented on pp. 477f. Now Eusebius in the second chapter of the second book of his Church History, referring to Tertullian, comments at length on this forged letter of Pilate; but he makes no reference to Christian

[1] Cf. Mt. 19:27; Lk. 5:11, 28.   [2] = 28/29 A.D.

444

Acts of Pilate, although some mention of them would have been natural. This is all the more striking in that he knows pagan Acts (anti-Christian), which were fabricated under the persecutor Maximin and which at his command had to be read in the schools and committed to memory (*H.E.* I. 9 and IX. 5.1).

Accordingly the prevailing view today is that Christian Acts of Pilate were first devised and published as a counterblast to the pagan Acts just mentioned, and that previously there had been nothing of the sort. Justin's testimony is thereby set aside. Justin however also adduces these Acts to attest the miracles of Jesus, and so the question arises whether he could have assumed of purely conjectural documents that in them mention was made of the miracles. In the canonical Gospels, miracles are not once mentioned during the proceedings before Pilate. Moreover it can be shown with some probability from the Acts now before us that the work which lies behind them must have originated very early. In chapter 2 it is asserted by the mass of the Jews that Jesus was born of fornication. Some devout Jews seek to refute this by referring to the fact that they had been present (probably as witnesses to the marriage) when Mary was married to Joseph. If this reference means anything at all, then the thought behind it must be that if Mary before her marriage had entered into relations with anyone else, then even if the consequences were not yet visible in her bodily constitution there would at least have been a rumour in circulation about it, and in that case Joseph would have renounced the marriage. In this way, then, the mother of Jesus is defended against the reproach of pre-marital intercourse. When Celsus about 178 wrote his polemic against the Christians, the charge the Jews brought against Mary had already become adultery. This more extreme form of the Panthera story must however have been preceded by the milder charge of pre-marital relationships. Possibly it was already current when the list of Jesus' ancestors in the Gospel of Matthew was compiled, for the original concluding sentence, preserved in the Sinaitic Syriac, seems directed against it: "Joseph, to whom Mary was betrothed as a virgin, begat Jesus". If this is not the case, and the slanderous gossip was derived perhaps from Mt. 1:18, the conclusion drawn by a Jew who did not believe in the overshadowing by the Holy Spirit would be that Mary was guilty of pre-marital relationships, not of adultery. Our Acts of Pilate thus pre-suppose the earlier form of the Panthera story.

The situation is similar in regard to the account of the Ascension of Jesus. Anyone who reads chapters 13 and 14 in succession has the impression that the message brought by the Galileans Phineas, Addas and Angaeus about the Ascension follows in time immediately upon the report of the watchers at the grave about the Resurrection. No one would think of an interval here of forty days. Now these forty days admittedly appear in our editions at a later point. At the end of the fifteenth chapter Jesus advises Joseph of Arimathaea, whom He has delivered from the prison into which the Jews had thrown him, to remain for forty days in hiding in his house in Arimathaea. But here an important ms., the only Greek ms. also to contain the prologue, reads four days instead of forty; and this seems to me the original reading. Joseph is naturally to remain in hiding until the danger for him is past. Here there is no thought of the possibility that the Jews might seek him in his house in Arimathaea. Thus he is in danger only if he shows himself in Jerusalem, and this danger is removed at the moment when the three Galileans bring to the city the news of the Ascension; for this news makes the Jews so despondent that they dare no longer proceed against the adherents of Jesus.

But when could this news arrive? The author, who here sticks exclusively to Matthew, naturally assumes that Jesus' disciples, on hearing the news of the Resurrection from the women, set out for Galilee immediately on the Sunday morning, to meet their Lord on a mountain there—here it is called Mamilch or something similar. Being active young men, they will have covered the distance in barely $2\frac{1}{2}$ days, for they were in haste. Josephus reckons three days from Sogane, which lay fairly far to the north of Galilee, to Jerusalem, but here the people in question were already advanced in years (Life c. 52). By a forced march Sebaste (roughly in the middle of Samaria) could be reached from Jerusalem in one day (Jos. *Ant.* 15.8.5), and Galilee thus in two days. We can therefore fix the Tuesday morning for the meeting of Jesus with the disciples, and the Ascension which followed. The three Galileans, who on the way to Jerusalem became by chance witnesses of this farewell scene, will have arrived in Jerusalem in the course of the Thursday afternoon, for they too were in haste to bring their news, but not too late, for they left again on the same day. For Joseph of Arimathaea the days during which he must remain hidden extended from Sunday—for Jesus appeared to him on Saturday night—to Wednesday inclusive. If he actually set out for Jerusalem as early as the Thursday, he will scarcely have arrived there earlier than the Galileans.[1] Thus the calculation agrees with the four days of his concealment. If the Galileans had observed the Ascension only on the fortieth day, they would have reached Jerusalem at the earliest on the forty-second day, and Joseph would have had to remain in hiding for at least forty-one days.

[1] Arimathaea is 19 miles distant from Jerusalem.

This disregard of the forty days which the risen Jesus spent on earth, according to the canonical Acts, is naturally a point in favour of the early composition of the *Grundschrift* of the Acts of Pilate, unless we ascribe its authorship to an Ebionite. For this there is something to be said. We have already seen that the author adheres solely to Matthew respecting the Resurrection and Ascension. Now according to Epiphanius the Gospel of the Ebionites was a revision of this very Gospel. Further, the only alternative suggested for illegitimate birth is that Joseph was actually the father of Jesus. We shall consider this a matter of course, since it is Jews who here give their verdict; but that for a mediaeval writer it was not a matter of course is shown by the author of the second Greek version, who makes the Jews who speak in favour of Jesus actually say that Joseph under the guise of marriage simply took Mary into his protection. Among the Ebionites however one group long held fast to the physical descent of Jesus from Joseph. Be that as it may, the possibility that apocryphal Acts of Pilate were already available to Justin cannot seriously be disputed.

With Epiphanius we have really firm ground beneath our feet. When he wrote in 375 or 376 against the Quartodecimans (*Haer.* 50.1), he mentioned that these people believed that with the aid of the Acts of Pilate they could determine exactly the date of the Passion, namely that it was the eighth day before the Kalends of April. This is precisely what we read in our Acts of Pilate. At this time therefore the *Grundschrift* at any rate was in existence, but possibly already in an expanded version as compared with the original. The versions now before us are further adaptations of the text used by Epiphanius. The older of the extant Greek versions (A) goes back, according to the statements in the prologue, to the year 425. We have it also in Latin, Coptic, Syriac[1] and

---

[1] The Syriac translation was discovered by the Syrian Catholic Patriarch Ignatius Ephraim II Rahmani, under the title 'Hypomnemata of our Lord', in two mss., one in Mosul, the other at Mardin in Media. He published them with a Latin translation in *Studia Syriaca*, fasc. II (1908). This translation was rendered into German, under the title 'Neue Pilatusakten', by Jaroslav Sedláček in the *Sitzungsberichte der Kgl. Böhm. G.d.W.* 1908, No. 11.

What leads me to discuss in greater detail just this Syriac version is the assertion, made by Rahmani and repeated by Sedláček, that the Greek original of this version presented an older and more original text than A. But this is by no means the case. The prologue of Ananias stands at the end, and in it certainly original date is wanting. The Syriac translator thus undertook abridgments, and these abbreviations relate often to such charming thoughts as that Pilate's wife inclined to the Jewish faith, and to lively scenes like XIII.2. Moreover there are some thoroughly unskilful additions. In II.2 Jesus makes no reply to Pilate's questions. Whereupon Pilate says: "*Dost thou not speak? Dost thou not know that I have power to crucify thee, and to set thee free?*" *Jesus said* to him: "If thou hadst the power, yet is this power *given* thee only *from above*" (Jn. 19:10f.). For every man has the power in his mouth to speak good and evil. Yet the Jews have their lips and bring accusations". The addition from Jn. 19:10f. does not fit the context. According to II.4 the whole Jewish people was present at the

Armenian translations, and it was still not expanded by the addition of the second part of the Gospel of Nicodemus, the 'Descensus Christi ad inferos'. The addition is thoroughly out of keeping, since the work is complete and does not admit of any expansion.

The second Greek version (B) describes the mother of Jesus six times in close succession as Θεοτόκος, and thus pre-supposes the Council of Ephesus, but may indeed be considerably later. To discover in it, with Bardenhewer (*Litg.* I² p. 545 n. 3), the original recension, is impossible. B is a redaction of A. The changes made are in part by no means skilful.¹ In particular it is expanded where A left Biblical material unconsidered, thus especially in chapters 10 and 11, which deal with the crucifixion and death of Jesus. Here Simon of Cyrene, who bore the Cross, is introduced; the three words of Jesus on the Cross in A are augmented by a further two; reference is made to the breaking of the legs of the robbers crucified with Jesus, and to the thrusting of the lance into His side, etc. Also added is a lamentation for Jesus, in which one after the other His mother, Mary Magdalene and Joseph of Arimathaea give expression to their grief. Joseph's visit to Pilate to ask for the body of Jesus is developed into an extended scene. Thus these two chapters in B take up more than three times as much room as in A. But at other points we find abbreviation, particularly in the final chapter, which is reduced to less than a seventh of its extent in A. The abbreviation admittedly gives the redactor the opportunity to add the Descensus. The conclusion of

wedding of Joseph and Mary. The conclusion of II.5 runs: "And Pilate called Annas and Caiaphas and said to them: How do you defend yourselves against these? Those twelve said to him: We speak the truth when we say that it was not of adultery that he came, that man of whom all the people cry out that he was born of adultery. These are liars, and say he was a magician and made himself Son of God and a king; they do not merit any confidence." Compare the two texts! The Ascension naturally takes place on the Mount of Olives, and the command to baptize (in the name of Father, Son and Holy Spirit!), omitted probably deliberately in the original text, is added, while the words derived from the spurious ending of Mark on the other hand are omitted.

¹ This holds also for the insertion of the Mount of Olives (in Galilee!) instead of the mountain Mamilch. A. Resch admittedly has conjectured (*Ausserkanonische Paralleltexte zu den Evangelien, TU* 10, 1, 1893f., pp. 381ff.) that Galilee in the Acts of Pilate, but also in Mt. 28:16, indicates the environs of Jerusalem, so that by the mountain in Galilee it is actually the Mount of Olives that is meant. Nevertheless, even if we may put the Hebrew *galil(ah)* for *g:lilah, gilgal* (region, district), there is no support for such a form in connection with Jerusalem, and no New Testament passage knows anything of a Galilee standing in relation to the Mount of Olives, while statements like that in the Itinerary of Antonius of Cremona, compiled about 1330 ("*Prope montem Oliveti est mons collateralis, qui olim dictus est mons offensionis, eo scilicet quod rex Salamon quondam posuit ibi ydolum Moloch adorans illud. In eodem monte offensionis est locus, qui vocatur Galilaea, ubi apparuit Christus discipulis suis*"), are suspect since they are probably the result of an effort to harmonize the divergent accounts of Mt. and Lk. That communication between Galilee and Jerusalem in the Acts of Pilate presupposes only a matter of hours, as Resch declares, is false. Cf. the discussion of the four days (p. 446).

A shows the Jews resolved to reject the Divinity and Resurrection of Jesus; but previously they were at one time undecided. There were influential witnesses in Jesus' favour, and Deut. 19:15 was quoted: "*At the mouth of two or three witnesses shall a matter be decided*".

Immediately after this B breaks off, and thus it is possible for Joseph of Arimathaea to intervene and bring the story round to the sons (here still nameless) of the aged Symeon, who shared in Christ's descent into Hell and were raised again with the Lord. In this way the Descensus could be appended, but to begin with this expansion remains without result. There is no indication that the description of Christ's descent to Hell exercised any influence upon the Jews. A substantially older fragment has thus been simply added, without the redactor noticing that the real theme of the Acts of Pilate had not yet been brought to a close. This situation becomes different only in the Latin redactions, but these will be dealt with later. First of all there now follows the oldest version in each case of the Acts of Pilate proper and of the Descensus.

Editions and Literature: The standard work is still the edition of the Greek and Latin texts by Tischendorf, *Ea* pp. 210–486; the following translation is based on Tischendorf *Ea* pp. 210–286 and 323–332. – On the Syriac versions see above, p. 447. – The Coptic version was published (after a papyrus in Turin and fragments in Paris) by A. Revillout, *Les Apocryphes Coptes II, Acta Pilati* (*PO* IX. 2) 1913 (the Turin fragments were already used by Tischendorf, cf. *Ea* p. LXXIII). – The Armenian version has been edited by F. C. Conybeare with a re-translation into Greek or Latin: *Acta Pilati* (*Studia biblica et ecclesiastica* IV) 1896; this version agrees largely with Recension A. – James pp. 94–146 gives a good conspectus of the different recensions. – Santos pp. 418–569 (*Ciclo de Pilato*; pp. 501ff.: *Escritos complementarios*). – Further literature: R. A. Lipsius, *Die Pilatusakten*, 1871 (2nd ed. 1886); E. v. Dobschütz, "Der Process Jesu nach den Acta Pilati", *ZNW* 3 (1902) pp. 89–114; Th. Mommsen, "Die Pilatus-Akten", *ZNW* 3 (1902) pp. 198–205; A. Stülcken, "Pilatusakten", *Handb.* pp. 143–153; J. Kroll, *Gott und Holle. Der Mythos vom Descensuskampfe*, 1932, pp. 83ff.; P. Vannutelli, *Actorum Pilati textus synoptici*, Rome 1938.

ACTS OF PILATE

Prologue: I, Ananias, an officer of the guard, being learned in the law, came to know our Lord Jesus Christ from the sacred scriptures, which I approached with faith, and was accounted worthy of holy baptism. And having searched for the reports made at that period in the time of our Lord Jesus Christ ⟨and for that⟩,[1] which

---

[1] The Latin translation has "*et, quae Iudaei vulgarunt*".

the Jews committed to writing under Pontius Pilate, I found these acts in the Hebrew language and according to God's good pleasure I translated them into Greek for the information of all those who call upon the name of our Lord Jesus Christ, in the eighteenth year of the reign of our Emperor Flavius Theodosius and in the fifth year of the 'Nobility' of Flavius Valentinianus, in the ninth indiction.[1]

Therefore all you who read this and copy it out, remember me and pray for me that God may be gracious to me and forgive my sins which I have sinned against him. Peace be to those who read and hear it, and to their servants. Amen.

In the nineteenth year of the reign of the Roman Emperor Tiberius, when Herod was king of Galilee, in the nineteenth year of his rule, on the eighth day before the Kalends of April, that is, the 25th of March, in the consulate of Rufus and Rubellio, in the fourth year of the two hundred and second Olympiad, when Joseph Caiaphas was high priest of the Jews.[2]

What Nicodemus after the passion of the Lord upon the cross recorded and delivered concerning the conduct of the chief priests and the rest of the Jews—and the same Nicodemus drew up his records in the Hebrew language—runs approximately as follows:[3]

I. The chief priests and scribes assembled in council, Annas and Caiaphas, Semes, Dathaes and Gamaliel, Judas, Levi and Nephthalim, Alexander and Jairus and the rest of the Jews, and came to Pilate accusing Jesus of many deeds. They said: "We

---

[1] The ninth indiction extended from September 1, 425, to September 1, 426. Theodosius II ascended the throne on May 1, 408. Thus it was not the seventeenth year of his reign, as in the only Greek ms. which contains the prologue, which fell in the ninth indiction, but the eighteenth, as in the Latin version. Valentinianus III became Augustus in 425, but previously he bore the title Nobilissimus, which he probably received, according to Gutschmid, on February 8, 421. Thus the fifth year of his 'Nobility' fell in the ninth indiction. So the Coptic version, whereas the Greek ms. gives the sixth. The Latin reads 'Valentiniano Augusto'.

[2] Manuscripts and versions vary between the fifteenth, eighteenth and nineteenth year of the reign of Tiberius. The year of the Olympiad (202.4 = 32/33) supports the nineteenth, which is also given in the Armenian version of the Chronicle of Eusebius. Eusebius dates the reign of Herod Antipas from the two thousand and forty-eighth year of Abraham = A.D. 14. Rufus and Rubellio are C. Fufius Geminus and L. Rubellius Geminus, the consuls of the year 29. This would correspond to the fifteenth year of Tiberius, the date of the crucifixion according to the oldest Christian chronology based on Lk. 3:1.

[3] I read: Ὅσα μετὰ τὸν σταυρὸν καὶ τὸ πάθος τοῦ κυρίου ἱστορήσας Νικόδημος παρέδωκεν ⟨πεπραγμένα⟩ τοῖς ἀρχιερεῦσιν καὶ τοῖς ἄλλοις Ἰουδαίοις—συνέταξεν δὲ ὁ αὐτὸς Νικόδημος γράμμασιν ἐβραϊκοῖς—⟨ὧδέ πως ἔχει⟩
The last three words are found in Monac. 192(A), πεπραγμένα is supplied from Paris. 929(E) and the versions (quae summi sacerdotes . . . fecerunt, acta principibus . . .).

know that this man is the son of Joseph the carpenter and was born of Mary; but he says he is the Son of God and a king. Moreover he pollutes the Sabbath and wishes to destroy the law of our fathers." Pilate said: "And what things does he do that he wishes to destroy it?" The Jews say: "We have a law that we should not heal anyone on the Sabbath. But this man with his evil deeds has healed on the Sabbath the lame, the bent, the withered, the blind, the paralytic, and the possessed." Pilate asked them: "With what evil deeds?" They answered him: "He is a sorcerer, and by Beelzebub the prince of the devils he casts out evil spirits, and all are subject to him." Pilate said to them: "This is not to cast out demons by an unclean spirit, but by the god Asclepius."

2. The Jews said to Pilate: "We beseech your excellency to place him before your judgment-seat and to try him." And Pilate called them to him and said: "Tell me! How can I, a governor, examine a king?" They answered: "We do not say that he is a king, but he says he is." And Pilate summoned his messenger and said to him: "Let Jesus be brought with gentleness." So the messenger went out, and when he perceived him, he did him reverence, and taking the kerchief which was in his hand, he spread it upon the ground, and said to him: "Lord, walk on this and go in, for the governor calls you." But when the Jews saw what the messenger had done, they cried out against Pilate and said: "Why did you not order him to come in by a herald, but by a messenger? For as soon as he saw him the messenger reverenced him, and spread out his kerchief on the ground, and made him walk on it like a king."

3. Then Pilate called for the messenger and said to him: "Why have you done this, and spread your kerchief on the ground and made Jesus walk on it?" The messenger answered him: "Lord governor, when you sent me to Jerusalem to Alexander, I saw him sitting on an ass, and the children of the Hebrews held branches in their hands and cried out; and others spread their garments before him, saying: 'Save now, thou that art in the highest! Blessed is he that comes in the name of the Lord!'"

4. The Jews cried out to the messenger: "The children of the Hebrews cried out in Hebrew; how do you know it in Greek?" The messenger replied: "I asked one of the Jews, and said: What

is it that they cry out in Hebrew? And he interpreted it to me."
Pilate said to them: "And what did they cry out in Hebrew?"
The Jews answered: "Hosanna membrome baruchamma
adonai."[1] Pilate asked again: "And the Hosanna and the rest,
how is it translated?" The Jews replied: "Save now, thou that
art in the highest. Blessed is he that comes in the name of the
Lord." Pilate said to them: "If you testify to the words of the
children, what sin has the messenger committed?" And they were
silent. The governor said to the messenger: "Go out and bring
him in in whatever way you wish." And the messenger went out
and did as before and said to Jesus: "Enter, the governor calls
you."

5. Now when Jesus entered in, and the standard-bearers were
holding the standards, the images of the emperor on the standards
bowed and did reverence to Jesus. And when the Jews saw the
behaviour of the standards, how they bowed down and did reverence to Jesus, they cried out loudly against the standard-bearers.
But Pilate said to them: "Do you not marvel how the images
bowed and did reverence to Jesus?" The Jews said to Pilate:
"We saw how the standard-bearers lowered them and reverenced
him." And the governor summoned the standard-bearers and
asked them: "Why did you do this?" They answered: "We are
Greeks and servers of temples, and how could we reverence him?
We held the images; but they bowed down of their own accord
and reverenced him."

6. Then Pilate said to the rulers of the synagogue and the elders
of the people: "Choose strong men to carry the standards, and
let us see whether the images bow by themselves." So the elders
of the Jews took twelve strong men and made them carry the
standards by sixes, and they were placed before the judgment-
seat of the governor. And Pilate said to the messenger: "Take
him out of the praetorium and bring him in again in whatever
way you wish." And Jesus left the praetorium with the messenger.
And Pilate summoned those who before carried the images, and
said to them: "I have sworn by the safety of Caesar that, if the
standards do not bow down when Jesus enters, I will cut off your
heads." And the governor commanded Jesus to enter in the second

[1] Correctly: hōši'āh-nā' bimrōmin; barūch habbā' ‹b:šēm›'adōnāi.

time. And the messenger did as before and besought Jesus to walk upon his kerchief. He walked upon it and entered in. And when he had entered in, the standards bowed down again and did reverence to Jesus.

II. When Pilate saw this he was afraid, and sought to rise from the judgment-seat. And while he was still thinking of rising up, *his wife sent to him saying: Have nothing to do with this righteous man. For I have suffered many things because of him* by night (Mt. 27:19). And Pilate summoned all the Jews, and stood up and said to them: "You know that my wife fears God and favours rather the customs of the Jews, with you." They answered him: "Yes, we know it." Pilate said to them: "See, my wife sent to me saying: Have nothing to do with this righteous man. For I have suffered many things because of him by night." The Jews answered Pilate: "Did we not tell you that he is a sorcerer? Behold, he has sent a dream to your wife." 2. And Pilate called Jesus to him and said to him: "What do these men testify against you? Do you say nothing?" Jesus answered: "If they had no power, they would say nothing; for each man has power over his own mouth, to speak good and evil. They shall see (to it)."

3. Then the elders of the Jews answered and said to Jesus: "What should we see? Firstly, that you were born of fornication; secondly, that your birth meant the death of the children in Bethlehem; thirdly, that your father Joseph and your mother Mary fled into Egypt because they counted for nothing among the people." 4. Then declared some of the Jews that stood by, devout men: "We deny that he came of fornication, for we know that Joseph was betrothed to Mary, and he was not born of fornication." Pilate then said to the Jews who said that he came of fornication: "Your statement is not true; for there was a betrothal, as your own fellow-countrymen say." Annas and Caiaphas say to Pilate: "We, the whole multitude, cry out that he was born of fornication, and we are not believed; these are proselytes and disciples of his." And Pilate called to him Annas and Caiaphas and said to them: "What are proselytes?" They answered: "They were born children of Greeks, and now have become Jews." Then said those who said that he was not born of fornication, namely Lazarus, Asterius, Antonius, Jacob, Amnes, Zeras,

Samuel, Isaac, Phineës, Crispus, Agrippa, and Judas: "We are not proselytes, but are children of Jews and speak the truth; for we were present at the betrothal of Joseph and Mary."

5. And Pilate called to him these twelve men who denied that he was born of fornication, and said to them: "I put you on your oath, by the safety of Caesar, that your statement is true, that he was not born of fornication." They said to Pilate: "We have a law, not to swear, because it is a sin. But let *them* swear by the safety of Caesar that it is not as we have said, and we will be worthy of death." Pilate said to Annas and Caiaphas: "Do you not answer these things?" And Annas and Caiaphas said to Pilate: "These twelve men are believed (who say) that he was not born of fornication. But we, the whole multitude, cry out that he was born of fornication, and is a sorcerer, and claims to be the Son of God and a king, and we are not believed." 6. And Pilate sent out the whole multitude, except the twelve men who denied that he was born of fornication, and commanded Jesus to be set apart. And he asked them: "For what cause do they wish to kill him?" They answered Pilate: "They are incensed because he heals on the Sabbath." Pilate said: "For a good work do they wish to kill him?" They answered him: "Yes."

III. And Pilate was filled with anger and went out of the praetorium and said to them: "I call the sun to witness that I find no fault in this man." The Jews *answered and said* to the governor: "*If this man were not* an evildoer, *we would not have handed him over to you*" (Jn. 18:30). *And Pilate said: "Take him yourselves and judge him by your own law." The Jews* said to Pilate: "*It is not lawful for us to put any man to death*" (Jn. 18:31). Pilate said: "Has God forbidden you to slay, but allowed me?"

2. *And Pilate entered the praetorium again and called Jesus* apart *and asked him: "Are you the king of the Jews?" Jesus answered* Pilate: "*Do you say this of your own accord, or did others say it to you about me?" Pilate answered* Jesus: "*Am I a Jew? Your own nation and the chief priests have handed you over to me. What have you done?" Jesus answered: "My kingship is not of this world; for if my kingship were of this world, my servants would fight, that I might not be handed over to the Jews. But now is my kingship not from here." Pilate said to him: "So you are a king?" Jesus answered him: "You say that I am a king. For for this*

cause I was born and have come, that *every one who is of the truth* should hear my voice." *Pilate said* to him: *"What is truth?"* (Jn. 18:33–38). Jesus answered him: "Truth is from heaven." Pilate said: "Is there not truth upon earth?" Jesus said to Pilate: "You see how those who speak the truth are judged by those who have authority on earth."

IV. And Pilate left Jesus in the praetorium and *went out to the Jews and said to them: "I find no fault in him"* (Jn. 18:38). The Jews said to him: "He said: *I am able to destroy* this *temple and build* it *in three days"* (Mt. 26:61). Pilate said: "What temple?" The Jews said: "That which Solomon built in forty-six years; but this man says he will destroy it and build it in three days." Pilate said to them: *"I am innocent of the blood of this* righteous *man; see to it yourselves."* The Jews replied: *"His blood be on us and on our children"* (Mt. 27:24f.). 2. And Pilate called to him the elders and the priests and the Levites and said to them secretly: "Do not act thus; for nothing of which you have accused him deserves death. For your accusation concerns healing and profanation of the Sabbath." The elders and the priests and the Levites answered: "If a man blasphemes against Caesar, is he worthy of death or not?" Pilate said: "He is worthy of death." The Jews said to Pilate: "If a man blasphemes against Caesar, he is worthy of death, but this man has blasphemed against God."

3. Then the governor commanded the Jews to go out from the praetorium, and he called Jesus to him and said to him: "What shall I do with you?" Jesus answered Pilate: "As it was given to you." Pilate said: "How was it given?" Jesus said: "Moses and the prophets foretold my death and resurrection." The Jews had been eavesdropping and heard, and they said to Pilate: "What further need have you to hear of this blasphemy?" Pilate said to the Jews: "If this word is blasphemy, *take him*, bring him into your synagogue *and judge him according to your law"* (Jn. 18:31). The Jews answered Pilate: "It is contained in our law, that if a man sins against a man, he must receive forty strokes save one, but he who blasphemes against God must be stoned."

4. Pilate said to them: "Take him yourselves and punish him as you wish." The Jews said to Pilate: "We wish him to be crucified." Pilate said: "He does not deserve to be crucified." 5. The

governor looked at the multitudes of the Jews standing around, and when he saw many of the Jews weeping, he said: "Not all the multitude wishes him to die." But the elders of the Jews said: "For this purpose has the whole multitude of us come, that he should die." Pilate said to the Jews: "Why should he die?" The Jews said: "Because he called himself the Son of God and a king."

V. Now Nicodemus, a Jew, stood before the governor, and said: "I beseech you, honourable[1] (governor), to allow me a few words." Pilate said: "Speak." Nicodemus said: "I said to the elders and the priests and the Levites and to all the multitude in the synagogue: What do you intend (to do) with this man? This man does many signs and wonders, which no one has done nor will do. Let him alone and contrive no evil against him. If the signs which he does are from God, they will stand; if they are from men, they will come to nothing (Acts 5:38f.). For Moses also, when he was sent by God into Egypt, did many signs which God commanded him to do before Pharaoh, king of Egypt. And there were there servants of Pharaoh, Jannes and Jambres, and they also did signs not a few which Moses did, and the Egyptians held them as gods, Jannes and Jambres. And since the signs which they did were not from God, they perished themselves and those who believed them. And now let this man go, for he does not deserve death."

2. The Jews said to Nicodemus: "You became his disciple and speak on his behalf." Nicodemus answered them: "Has the governor also become his disciple, and speaks on his behalf? Did not Caesar appoint him to this high office?" Then the Jews raged and gnashed their teeth against Nicodemus. Pilate said to them: "Why do you gnash your teeth against him, when you hear the truth?" The Jews said to Nicodemus: "Receive his truth and his portion." Nicodemus said: "Amen, may it be as you have said."

VI. Then one of the Jews hastened forward and asked the governor that he might speak a word. The governor said: "If you wish to say anything, say it." And the Jew said: "For thirty-eight years I lay on a bed in anguish of pains, and when Jesus

---

[1] The remarkable vocative εὐσεβή is concealed by the vocative ἀσεβή in the (Infancy) Gospel of Thomas (*Ea*, pp. 142, 158). Tischendorf translates the εὐσεβής of the Coptic by 'colende praesul' (*Ea* 235 has *praeses*), taking εὐσεβής as passive. I have followed him. The 'pie' of the Syriac (Rahmani) Sedláček translates by 'merciful'.

came many demoniacs and those lying sick of diverse diseases were healed by him. And certain young men took pity on me and carried me with my bed and brought me to him. And when Jesus saw me he had compassion, and spoke a word to me: *Take up your bed and walk*. And I took up my bed and walked" (Mk. 2:1ff.; Jn. 5:1ff.). The Jews said to Pilate: "Ask him what day it was on which he was healed." He that was healed said: "On a Sabbath." The Jews said: "Did we not inform you so, that on the Sabbath he heals and casts out demons?" 2. And another Jew hastened forward and said: "I was born blind; I heard any man's voice, but did not see his face. And as Jesus passed by I cried with a loud voice: *Have mercy on me, Son of David*. And he took pity on me and put his hands on my eyes and I saw immediately" (Mk. 10:46ff.). And another Jew hastened forward and said: "I was bowed, and he made me straight with a word." And another said: "I was a leper, and he healed me with a word."

VII. And a woman called Bernice (Latin: Veronica) crying out from a distance said: "I had an issue of blood and I touched the hem of his garment, and the issue of blood, which had lasted twelve years, ceased" (Mk. 5:25ff.). The Jews said: "We have a law not to permit a woman to give testimony."

VIII. And others, a multitude of men and women, cried out: "This man is a prophet, and the demons are subject to him." Pilate said to those who said the demons were subject to him: "Why are your teachers also not subject to him?" They said to Pilate: "We do not know." Others said: "Lazarus who was dead he raised up out of the tomb after four days." Then the governor began to tremble and said to all the multitude of the Jews: "Why do you wish to shed innocent blood?"

IX. And he called to him Nicodemus and the twelve men who said he was not born of fornication and said to them: "What shall I do? The people are becoming rebellious." They answered him: "We do not know. Let them see to it." Again Pilate called all the multitude of the Jews and said: "You know the custom that at the feast of unleavened bread a prisoner is released to you. I have in the prison one condemned for murder, called Barabbas, and this Jesus who stands before you, in whom I find no fault. *Whom*

do you wish me to release to you?" But they cried out: *"Barabbas."*
Pilate said: "Then what shall I do with Jesus who is called Christ?"
The Jews cried out: *"Let him be crucified"* (Mt. 27:15ff.). But some
of the Jews answered: *"You are not Caesar's friend if you release this
man* (Jn. 19:12), for he called himself the Son of God and a king.
You wish him therefore to be king and not Caesar."

2. And Pilate was angry and said to the Jews: "Your nation is
always seditious and in rebellion against your benefactors." The
Jews asked: "What benefactors?" Pilate answered: "As I have
heard, your God brought you out of Egypt out of hard slavery,
and led you safe through the sea as if it had been dry land, and
in the wilderness nourished you and gave you manna and quails,
and gave you water to drink from a rock, and gave you the law.
And despite all this you provoked the anger of your God: you
wanted a molten calf and angered your God, and he wished to
destroy you; and Moses made supplication for you, and you
were not put to death. And now you accuse me of hating the
emperor." 3. And he rose up from the judgment-seat and sought
to go out. And the Jews cried out: "We know as king Caesar
alone and not Jesus. For indeed the wise men brought him gifts
from the east, as if he were a king. And when Herod heard from
the wise men that a king was born, he sought to slay him. But
when his father Joseph knew that, he took him and his mother,
and they fled into Egypt. And when Herod heard it, he destroyed
the children of the Hebrews who were born in Bethlehem."

4. When Pilate heard these words, he was afraid. And he silenced
the multitudes, because they were crying out, and said to them:
"So this is he whom Herod sought?" The Jews replied: "Yes,
this is he." *And* Pilate *took water and washed his hands* before the sun
*and said: "I am innocent of the blood of this righteous man. You see to
it."* Again the Jews cried out: *"His blood be on us and on our children"*
(Mt. 27:24f.). 5. Then Pilate commanded the curtain to be drawn[1]
before the judgment-seat on which he sat, and said to Jesus:

[1] The author has no knowledge of how trials were actually conducted. For him the
tribunal (βῆμα, judgment-seat) was in the praetorium; in actual fact it was never
set up there, but "under the open sky or in a covered space accessible to the public"
(Mommsen *ZNW* 3, 1902, 201), which the praetorium is not (except in the Acts of
Pilate). Correctly Jn. 19:13. A curtain was drawn only at non-public trials; when the
public was admitted, as at the pronouncement of the verdict, it was removed. Here
also the opposite takes place: the tribunal is visible during the trial, and the curtain
is drawn before it for the pronouncement of sentence.

458

"Your nation has convicted you of claiming to be a king. Therefore I have decreed that you should first be scourged according
to the law of the pious emperors, and then hanged on the cross in
the garden where you were seized. And let Dysmas and Gestas,
the two malefactors, be crucified with you."

X. And Jesus went out from the praetorium, and the two malefactors with him. And when they came to the place, they stripped
him and girded him with a linen cloth and put a crown of thorns
on his head. Likewise they hanged up also the two malefactors.[1]
But Jesus said: "Father, forgive them, for they know not what they do"
(Lk. 23:34). And the soldiers parted his garments among them.
And *the people* stood *looking* at him. And the chief priests *and the
rulers* with them *scoffed at him, saying: "He saved others, let him save
himself. If he is the Son of God, let him come down from the cross."*
And the soldiers also mocked him, coming and offering him
vinegar with gall, and they said: *"If you are the king of the Jews,
save yourself"* (Lk. 23:35ff.). And Pilate after the sentence commanded the crime brought against him to be written as a title
in Greek, Latin and Hebrew, according to the accusation of the
Jews that he was king of the Jews (Jn. 19:19f.).

2. *One of the malefactors who were crucified* said to him: "If you are
the Christ, *save yourself and us."* But Dysmas answering rebuked
him: *"Do you not at all fear God, since you are in the same condemnation?
And we indeed justly. For we are receiving the due reward of our deeds.*
But this man has done nothing wrong." And he said to Jesus:
"Lord, *remember me* in your kingdom." *And* Jesus said to him:
"Truly, I say to you, today you will be with me in paradise" (Lk.
23:39ff.).

XI. And *it was about the sixth hour, and there was darkness* over the
land *until the ninth hour*, for the sun was darkened. And *the curtain of
the temple was torn in two. And Jesus cried with a loud voice:* "Father,
baddach ephkid rouel,"[2] which means: *"Into thy hands I commit my
spirit."* And having said this he gave up the ghost. *And when the
centurion saw what had happened, he praised God, saying: "This man was
righteous." And all the multitudes who had come to this sight*, when they
saw what had taken place, *beat* their *breasts and returned* (Lk.
23:44–48).

[1] Coptic and Armenian add: Dysmas on the right, Gestas on the left.
[2] Correctly: b:jād:chā aphkidh ruachi.

2. But the centurion reported to the governor what had happened. And when the governor and his wife heard, they were greatly grieved, and they neither ate nor drank on that day. And Pilate sent for the Jews and said to them: "Did you see what happened?" But they answered: "There was an eclipse of the sun in the usual way." 3. And his acquaintances had stood far off and the women who had come with him from Galilee, and saw these things. *But a certain man named Joseph, a member of the council, from the town of Arimathaea, who also was waiting for the kingdom of God, this man went to Pilate and asked for the body of Jesus. And he took it down, and wrapped it in a clean linen cloth, and placed it in a rock-hewn tomb,* in which *no one had ever yet been laid* (Lk. 23:50–53).

XII. When the Jews heard that Joseph had asked for the body, they sought for him and the twelve men who said that Jesus was not born of fornication, and for Nicodemus and for many others, who had come forward before Pilate and made known his good works. But they all hid themselves, and only Nicodemus was seen by them, because he was a ruler of the Jews. And Nicodemus said to them: "How did you enter into the synagogue?" The Jews answered him: "How did you enter into the synagogue? You are an accomplice of his, and his portion shall be with you in the world to come." Nicodemus said: "Amen, amen." Likewise also Joseph came forth (from his concealment?) and said to them: "Why are you angry with me, because I asked for the body of Jesus? See, I have placed it in my new tomb, having wrapped it in clean linen, and I rolled a stone before the door of the cave. And you have not done well with the righteous one, for you did not repent of having crucified him, but also pierced him with a spear."

Then the Jews seized Joseph and commanded him to be secured until the first day of the week. They said to him: "Know that the hour forbids us to do anything against you, because the Sabbath dawns. But know also that you will not even be counted worthy of burial, but we shall give your flesh to the birds of the heaven." Joseph answered: "This word is like that of the boastful Goliath, who insulted the living God and the holy David. For God said by the prophet: *Vengeance is mine, I will repay, says the Lord* (Rom. 12:19; cf. Deut. 32:35). And now he who is uncircumcised in the flesh, but circumcised in heart, took water and washed his hands before the sun, saying: I am innocent of the blood of this righteous man. You see to it. And you answered Pilate: *His blood be on us and on our children* (Mt. 27:25). And now I fear lest the wrath of God come upon you and your children, as you said." When the Jews heard these words, they were embittered in their hearts, and laid hold on Joseph and seized him and shut him in a building without a window, and guards remained at the door. And they sealed the door of the place where Joseph was shut up.

2. And on the Sabbath the rulers of the synagogue and the priests and the Levites ordered that all should present themselves in the synagogue on the first day of the week. And the whole multitude rose up early and took counsel in the synagogue by what death they should kill him. And when the council was in session they commanded him to be brought with great dishonour. And when they opened the door they did not find him. And all the people were astonished and filled with consternation because they found the seals undamaged, and Caiaphas had the key. And they dared no longer to lay hands on those who had spoken before Pilate on behalf of Jesus.

XIII. And while they still sat in the synagogue and marvelled because of Joseph, there came some of the guard which the Jews had asked from Pilate to guard the tomb of Jesus, lest his disciples should come and steal him. And they told the rulers of the synagogue and the priests and the Levites what had happened: how there was a great earthquake. "And we saw an angel descend from heaven, and *he rolled away the stone* from the mouth of the cave, *and sat upon it*, and he shone *like snow and like lightning*. And we were in great fear, and lay *like dead men* (Mt. 28:2–4). And we heard the voice of the angel speaking to the women who waited at the tomb: *Do not be afraid. I know that you seek Jesus who was crucified. He is not here. He has risen, as he said. Come and see the place where* the Lord *lay. And go quickly and tell his disciples that he has risen from the dead* and is in Galilee" (Mt. 28:5–7).

2. The Jews asked: "To what women did he speak?" The members of the guard answered: "We do not know who they were." The Jews said: "At what hour was it?" The members of the guard answered: "At midnight." The Jews said: "And why

did you not seize the women?" The members of the guard said: "We were like dead men through fear, and gave up hope of seeing the light of day; how could we then have seized them?" The Jews said: "As the Lord lives, we do not believe you." The members of the guard said to the Jews: "So many signs you saw in that man and you did not believe; and how can you believe us? You rightly swore: As the Lord lives. For he *does* live." Again the members of the guard said: "We have heard that you shut up him who asked for the body of Jesus, and sealed the door, and that when you opened it you did not find him. Therefore give us Joseph and we will give you Jesus." The Jews said: "Joseph has gone to his own city." And the members of the guard said to the Jews: "And Jesus has risen, as we heard from the angel, and is in Galilee." 3. And when the Jews heard these words, they feared greatly and said: "(Take heed) lest this report be heard and all incline to Jesus." And the Jews took counsel, and offered *much money and gave it to the soldiers of the guard, saying:* "Say that when you were sleeping *his disciples* came *by night* and *stole him. And if this is heard by the governor, we will persuade* him *and keep you out of trouble*" (Mt. 28:12–14).

XIV. Now Phineës a priest and Adas a teacher and Angaeus a Levite came from Galilee to Jerusalem, and told the rulers of the synagogue and the priests and the Levites: "We saw Jesus and his disciples sitting upon the mountain which is called Mamilch. And he said to his disciples: *Go into all the world and preach the gospel to the whole creation. He who believes and is baptized will be saved; but he who does not believe will be condemned. And these signs will accompany those who believe: in my name they will cast out demons; they will speak in new tongues; they will pick up serpents; and if they drink any deadly thing, it will not hurt them; they will lay their hands on the sick, and they will recover* (Mk. 16:15–18). And while Jesus was still speaking to his disciples, we saw him taken up into heaven."

2. Then the elders and the priests and the Levites said: "Give glory to the God of Israel, and confess before him if you indeed heard and saw what you have described." Those who told them said: "As the Lord God of our fathers Abraham, Isaac and Jacob lives, we heard these things and saw him taken up to heaven." The elders and the priests and the Levites said to them: "Did you

462

come to tell us this, or did you come to offer prayer to God?"
They answered: "To offer prayer to God." The elders and the
chief priests and the Levites said to them: "If you came to offer
prayer to God, to what purpose is this idle tale which you have
babbled before all the people?" Phineës the priest and Adas the
teacher and Angaeus the Levite said to the rulers of the synagogue
and priests and Levites: "If the words which we spoke ⟨concern-
ing what we heard⟩ and saw are sin, see, we stand before you. Do
with us as it seems good in your eyes." And they took the law and
adjured them to tell this no more to any one. And they gave them
to eat and drink, and sent them out of the city, having given them
money and three men to accompany them, and ordered them to
depart as far as Galilee; and they went away in peace.

3. But when those men had departed to Galilee, the chief
priests and the rulers of the synagogue and the elders assembled in
the synagogue, and shut the gate, and raised a great lamentation,
saying: "Why has this sign happened in Israel?" But Annas and
Caiaphas said: "Why are you troubled? Why do you weep?
Do you not know that his disciples gave much money to the guards
of the tomb, ⟨took away his body[1]⟩ and taught them to say that
an angel descended from heaven and rolled away the stone from
the door of the tomb?" But the priests and the elders replied:
"Let it be that his disciples stole his body. But how did the soul
enter again into the body, so that Jesus now waits in Galilee?"
(But they, unable to give an answer, came with difficulty to say:
"It is not lawful for us to believe the uncircumcised."[2])

XV. And Nicodemus stood up and stood before the council
and said: "What you say is right. You know, people of the Lord,
that the men who came from Galilee fear God and are men of
substance, that they hate covetousness,[3] and are men of peace.
And they have declared on oath: We saw Jesus on the mountain
Mamilch with his disciples. He taught them what you have heard
from them. And we saw him (they said) taken up into heaven.

[1] Supplied from the versions (Coptic: "discipuli magnam pecuniae vim dederunt
militibus, abstulerunt corpus Jesu atque illos ita edocuerunt").

[2] What Annas and Caiaphas say makes no sense. Since the beginning of the speech
of Nicodemus: "What you say is right", relates to the preceding utterance of the priests
and elders, I have bracketed the last sentence of c. 14.

[3] As men of substance and hating covetousness they could not be bribed by the
disciples of Jesus.

And no one asked them in what manner he was taken up. Just as the holy scriptures tell us that Elijah also was taken up into heaven, and Elisha cried with a loud voice, and Elijah cast his sheepskin cloak upon Elisha, and Elisha cast his cloak upon the Jordan, and crossed over and went to Jericho. And the sons of the prophets met him and said: Elisha, where is your master Elijah? And he said that he was taken up into heaven. But they said to Elisha: Has perhaps a spirit caught him up *and cast him on one of the mountains?* But let us take our servants with us and search for him. And they persuaded Elisha, and he went with them. *And they searched* for him *for three days and did not find him,* and they knew that he had been taken up (2 Kings 2). And now listen to me, and let us send to every mountain of Israel and see whether the Christ was taken up by a spirit and cast upon a mountain." And this proposal pleased them all. And they sent to every mountain of Israel, and searched for Jesus and did not find him. But they found Joseph in Arimathaea and no one dared to seize him.

2. And they told the elders and the priests and the Levites: "We went about to every mountain of Israel, and did not find Jesus. But Joseph we found in Arimathaea." And when they heard about Joseph, they rejoiced and gave glory to the God of Israel. And the rulers of the synagogue and the priests and the Levites took counsel how they should meet with Joseph, and they took a roll of papyrus and wrote to Joseph these words. "Peace be with you. We know that we have sinned against God and against you, and we have prayed to the God of Israel that you should condescend to come to your fathers and your children, because we are all troubled. For when we opened the door we did not find you. We know that we devised an evil plan against you; but the Lord helped you, and the Lord himself has brought to nothing our plan against you, honoured father Joseph."

3. And they chose from all Israel seven men who were friends of Joseph, whom also Joseph himself acknowledged as friends, and the rulers of the synagogue and the priests and the Levites said to them: "See! If he receives our letter and reads it, know that he will come with you to us. But if he does not read it, know that he is angry with us, and salute him in peace and return to us."

And they blessed the men and dismissed them. And the men came to Joseph and greeted him with reverence, and said to him: "Peace be with you!" He replied: "Peace be with you and all Israel!" And they gave him the roll of the letter. Joseph took it and read it and kissed the letter, and blessed God and said: "Blessed be God, who has delivered the Israelites from shedding innocent blood. And blessed be the Lord, who sent his angel and sheltered me under his wings." And he set a table before them, and they ate and drank and lay down there. 4. And they rose up early in the morning and prayed. And Joseph saddled his she-ass and went with the men, and they came to the holy city Jerusalem. And all the people met Joseph and cried: "Peace be to your entering in!" And he said to all the people: "Peace be with you!" And all kissed him, and prayed with Joseph, and were beside themselves with joy at seeing him. And Nicodemus received him into his house and made a great feast, and called the elders and the priests and the Levites to his house, and they made merry, eating and drinking with Joseph. And after singing a hymn each one went to his house; but Joseph remained in the house of Nicodemus.

5. And on the next day, which was the preparation, the rulers of the synagogue and the priests and the Levites rose up early and came to the house of Nicodemus. Nicodemus met them and said: "Peace be with you!" They answered: "Peace be with you and with Joseph and with all your house and with all the house of Joseph!" And he brought them into his house. And the whole council sat down, and Joseph sat between Annas and Caiaphas. And no one dared to speak a word to him. And Joseph said: "Why have you called me?" And they beckoned to Nicodemus to speak to Joseph. Nicodemus opened his mouth and said to Joseph: "Father, you know that the honourable teachers and the priests and the Levites wish information from you." Joseph answered: "Ask me." And Annas and Caiaphas took the law and adjured Joseph, saying: "Give glory to the God of Israel and make confession to him. For Achan also, when adjured by the prophet Joshua, did not commit perjury, but told him everything and concealed nothing from him (Joshua 7). So do you also not conceal from us a single word." Joseph answered: "I will not conceal

anything from you." And they said to him: "We were very angry because you asked for the body of Jesus, and wrapped it in a clean linen cloth, and placed it in a tomb. And for this reason we secured you in a house with no window, and locked and sealed the door, and guards watched where you were shut up. And on the first day of the week we opened it, and did not find you, and were much troubled, and all the people of God were amazed until yesterday. And now tell us what happened to you."

6. And Joseph said: "On the day of preparation about the tenth hour you shut me in, and I remained the whole Sabbath. And at midnight as I stood and prayed, the house where you shut me in was raised up by the four corners, and I saw as it were a lightning flash in my eyes. Full of fear I fell to the ground. And someone took me by the hand and raised me up from the place where I had fallen, and something moist like water flowed from my head to my feet, and the smell of fragrant oil reached my nostrils. And he wiped my face and kissed me and said to me: Do not fear, Joseph. Open your eyes and see who it is who speaks with you. I looked up and saw Jesus. Trembling, I thought it was a phantom, and I said the (ten) commandments. And he said them with me. Now as you well know, a phantom immediately flees if it meets anyone and hears the commandments. And when I saw that he said them with me, I said to him: Rabbi Elijah! He said: I am not Elijah. And I said to him: Who are you, Lord? He replied: I am Jesus, whose body you asked for from Pilate, whom you clothed in clean linen, on whose face you placed a cloth, and whom you placed in your new cave, and you rolled a great stone to the door of the cave. And I asked him who spoke to me: Show me the place where I laid you. And he took me and showed me the place where I laid him. And the linen cloth lay there, and the cloth that was upon his face. Then I recognized that it was Jesus. And he took me by the hand and placed me in the middle of my house, with the doors shut, and led me to my bed and said to me: Peace be with you! Then he kissed me and said to me: Do not go out of your house for forty days. For see, I go to my brethren in Galilee."

XVI. And when the rulers of the synagogue and the priests and the Levites heard these words from Joseph, they became as dead men and fell to the ground and fasted until the ninth hour. And Nicodemus and Joseph comforted Annas and Caiaphas and the priests and Levites, saying: "Get up and stand on your feet, and taste bread and strengthen your souls. For tomorrow is the Sabbath of the Lord." And they rose up and prayed to God, and ate and drank, and went each to his own house. 2. And on the Sabbath our teachers and the priests and the Levites sat and questioned one another, saying: "What is this wrath which has come upon us? For we know his father and his mother." Levi the teacher said: "I know that his parents fear God and do not withhold their prayers and pay tithes three times a year. And when Jesus was born, his parents brought him to this place, and gave God sacrifices and burnt offerings. And the great teacher Symeon took him in his arms and said: *Lord, now lettest thou thy servant depart in peace, according to thy word; for mine eyes have seen thy salvation which thou hast prepared in the presence of all peoples, a light for revelation to the Gentiles, and for glory to thy people Israel. And Symeon blessed them and said to Mary his mother:* I give you good tidings concerning this child. And Mary said: Good, my lord? And Symeon said to her: Good. *Behold, this child is set for the fall and rising of many in Israel, and for a sign that is spoken against (and a sword will pierce through your own soul also), that thoughts out of many hearts may be revealed"* (Lk. 2:28–35).

3. They said to Levi the teacher: "How do you know this?" Levi answered them: "Do you not know that I learned the law from him?" The council said to him: "We wish to see your father." And they sent for his father. And when they questioned him, he said to them: "Why did you not believe my son? The blessed and righteous Symeon taught him the law." The council said: "Rabbi Levi, is the word true which you have spoken?" He answered: "It is true." Then the rulers of the synagogue and the priests and the Levites said among themselves: "Come, let us send to Galilee to the three men who came and told us of his teaching and of his being taken up, and let them tell us how they saw him taken up." And this word pleased them all. And they sent the three men who before had gone to Galilee with them, and said to them: "Say to Rabbi Adas and Rabbi Phineës and Rabbi Angaeus: Peace be with you and all who are with you. Since an

important inquiry is taking place in the council, we were sent to you to call you to this holy place Jerusalem." 4. And the men went to Galilee and found them sitting and studying the law, and greeted them in peace. And the men who were in Galilee said to those who had come to them: "Peace be to all Israel." They answered: "Peace be with you." And again they said to them: "Why have you come?" Those who had been sent replied: "The council calls you to the holy city Jerusalem." When the men heard that they were sought by the council, they prayed to God and sat down at table with the men and ate and drank, and then arose and came in peace to Jerusalem.

5. And on the next day the council sat in the synagogue and questioned them, saying: "Did you indeed see Jesus sitting on the mountain Mamilch, teaching his eleven disciples? And did you see him taken up?" And the men answered them and said: "As we saw him taken up, so we have told you". 6. Annas said: "Separate them from one another, and let us see if their accounts agree." And they separated them from one another. And they called Adas first and asked him: "How did you see Jesus taken up?" Adas answered: "As he sat on the mountain Mamilch and taught his disciples, we saw that a cloud overshadowed him and his disciples. And the cloud carried him up to heaven, and his disciples lay on their faces on the ground." Then they called Phineës the priest and asked him also: "How did you see Jesus taken up?" And he said the same thing. And again they asked Angaeus, and he said the same thing. Then the members of the council said: "*At the mouth of two or three witnesses shall every matter be established*" (Deut. 19:15). Abuthem the teacher said: "It is written in the law: *Enoch walked with God, and was not, for God took him*" (Gen. 5:24). Jairus the teacher said: "Also we have heard of the death of the holy Moses, and we do not know how he died.[1] For it is written in the law of the Lord: And Moses died as the mouth of the Lord determined, and no man knew *of his sepulchre to this day*" (Deut. 34:5f.). And Rabbi Levi said: "Why did Rabbi Symeon say, when he saw Jesus: *Behold, this (child) is set for the fall and rising of many in Israel, and for a sign that is spoken against?* "(Lk. 2:34). And Rabbi Isaac said: "It is written in the law: *Behold, I*

---

[1] The correct reading is οἴδαμεν, the object (αὐτόν) referring to Μωϋσέως θάνατον.

send my messenger before your face. He will go before you to guard you in every good way. In him[1] my name is named" (Exod. 23:20f.).

7. Then Annas and Caiaphas said: "You have rightly said what is written in the law of Moses, that no one knows the death of Enoch and no one has named the death of Moses. But Jesus had to give account before Pilate; we saw how he received blows and spitting on his face, that the soldiers put a crown of thorns upon him, that he was scourged and condemned by Pilate and then was crucified at the place of a skull; he was given vinegar and gall to drink, and Longinus the soldier pierced his side with a spear. Our honourable father Joseph asked for his body; and, he says, he rose again. And the three teachers declare: We saw him taken up into heaven.[2] And Rabbi Levi spoke and testified to the words of Rabbi Symeon: *Behold, this child is set for the fall and rising of many in Israel, and for a sign that is spoken against* (Lk. 2:34)." And all the teachers said to all the people of the Lord: "If this is from the Lord, and it is marvellous in your eyes, you shall surely know, O house of Jacob, that it is written: Cursed is every one who hangs on a tree (Deut. 21:23). And another passage of scripture teaches: *The gods who did not make the heaven and the earth* shall perish (Jer. 10:11)." And the priests and the Levites said to one another: "If Jesus is remembered after fifty years,[3] he will reign for ever and create for himself a new people." Then the rulers of the synagogue and the priests and the Levites admonished all Israel: "Cursed is the man who shall worship the work of man's hand,

---

[1] αὐτῇ wrongly, in agreement with the preceding ὁδῷ. It should be αὐτῷ (i.e. ἀγγέλῳ). We have here an attempt to make clear the conclusion of Exod. 23:21 τὸ γὰρ ὄνομά μου ἐστὶν ἐπ' αὐτῷ = "my own being operates in the angel" by substituting κέκληται for ἐστίν.

[2] With "ascendentem in coelum", that is, at this point, one of the two recensions of the Latin translation ends, followed by the Latin recension A of the Descensus. The other follows the Greek text a little further, taking over Levi's quotation of the words of Symeon, but remoulding the rest in a way impossible to the spirit of the Acts of Pilate: Then the teacher Didas said to all the congregation: "If everything which these men have testified came to pass in Jesus, it is of God, and let it not be marvellous in your eyes." The rulers of the synagogue and the priests and the Levites said one to another: "It is contained in our law: His name shall be blessed for ever. His place endures before the sun and his seat before the moon, and in him shall all the tribes of the earth be blessed, and all nations shall serve him; and kings shall come from afar to worship and magnify him" (after Ps. 71 LXX). The Latin recension B of the Descensus is attached to this conclusion.

[3] Greek: Εἰ ἕως τοῦ Σώμμου τοῦ λεγομένου Ἰωβήλ τὸ μνημόσυννον αὐτοῦ; Coptic: "Usque ad Sum et eum quem vocabant Jobel memoria eius permanet". Ἰωβήλ is the year of jubilee following 7 × 7 years; in Σώμμου or Sum a graecized form of šānāh (Hebrew = year) could lie concealed.

and cursed is the man who shall worship created things alongside the creator." And the people answered: "Amen, amen."

8. And all the people praised the Lord God and sang: "Blessed be the Lord who has given rest to the people of Israel according to all his promises. Not one word remains unfulfilled of all the good which he promised to his servant Moses. May the Lord our God be with us as he was with our fathers. May he not forsake us. May he not let the will die in us,[1] to turn our heart to him, and walk in all his ways, and keep his commandments and laws which he gave to our fathers. And the Lord shall be king over all the earth on that day. And there shall be one God and his name shall be one, our Lord and king. He shall save us. There is none like thee, O Lord. Great art thou, O Lord, and great is thy name. Heal us, O Lord, in thy power, and we shall be healed. Save us, Lord, and we shall be saved. For we are thy portion and inheritance. The Lord will not forsake his people for his great name's sake, for the Lord has begun to make us his people." After this hymn of praise they all departed, every man to his house, glorifying God. For his is the glory for ever and ever. Amen.

CHRIST'S DESCENT INTO HELL

I (XVII). Joseph said: "Why then do you marvel at the resurrection of Jesus? It is not this that is marvellous, but rather that he was not raised alone, but raised up many other dead men who appeared to many in Jerusalem. And if you do not know the others, yet Symeon, who took Jesus in his arms, and his two sons, whom he raised up, you do know. For we buried them a little while ago. And now their sepulchres are to be seen opened and empty, but they themselves are alive and dwelling in Arimathaea." They therefore sent men, and they found their tombs opened and empty. Joseph said: "Let us go to Arimathaea and find them." 2. Then arose the chief priests Annas and Caiaphas, and Joseph and Nicodemus and Gamaliel and others with them, and went to Arimathaea and found the men of whom Joseph spoke. So they offered prayer, and greeted one another. Then they went with

---

[1] In the Greek μὴ ἀπολέσῃ ἡμᾶς καὶ μὴ ἀπολέσῃ ἡμᾶς τοῦ κλῖναι καρδίαν ἡμῶν πρὸς αὐτόν the double ἀπολέσῃ is hardly correct. The second ἀπολέσῃ, although with a quite unusual meaning, must be retained, for the first ἀπολίπῃ is to be substituted. One ms. has ἐγκαταλίπῃς, the Coptic "ne derelinquas."

them to Jerusalem, and they brought them into the synagogue, and secured the doors, and the chief priests placed the Old Testament of the Jews in the midst and said to them: "We wish you to swear by the God of Israel and by Adonai and so speak the truth, how you arose and who raised you from the dead." 3. When the men who had arisen heard that, they signed their faces with the sign of the cross, and said to the chief priests: "Give us paper and ink and pen." So they brought these things. And they sat down and wrote as follows:

II (XVIII). "O Lord Jesus Christ, the resurrection and the life of the world, give us grace that we may tell of thy resurrection and of thy miracles which thou didst perform in Hades. We, then, were in Hades with all who have died since the beginning of the world. And at the hour of midnight there rose upon the darkness there something like the light of the sun and shone, and light fell upon us all, and we saw one another. And immediately our father Abraham, along with the patriarchs and the prophets, was filled with joy, and they said to one another: This shining comes from a great light. The prophet Isaiah, who was present there, said: This shining comes from the Father and the Son and the Holy Spirit. This I prophesied when I was still living: The land of Zabulon and the land of Nephthalim, the people that sit in darkness saw a great light (9:1, 2).

2. Then there came into the midst another, an anchorite from the wilderness. The patriarchs asked him: Who are you? He replied: I am John, the last of the prophets, who made straight the ways of the Son of God, and preached repentance to the people for the forgiveness of sins. And the Son of God came to me, and when I saw him afar off, I said to the people: *Behold, the Lamb of God, who takes away the sin of the world* (Jn. 1:29). And with my hand I baptized him in the river Jordan, and I saw the Holy Spirit like a dove coming upon him, and heard also the voice of God the Father speaking thus: *This is my beloved Son, in whom I am well pleased* (Mt. 3:16f.). And for this reason he sent me to you, to preach that the only begotten Son of God comes here, in order that whoever believes in him should be saved, and whoever does not believe in him should be condemned. Therefore I say to you all: When you see him, all of you worship him. For now only have

you opportunity for repentance because you worshipped idols in the vain world above and sinned. At another time it is impossible.

III (XIX). Now when John was thus teaching those who were in Hades, the first-created, the first father Adam heard, and said to his son Seth: My son, I wish you to tell the forefathers of the race of men and the prophets where I sent you when I fell into mortal sickness. And Seth said: Prophets and patriarchs, listen. My father Adam, the first-created, when he fell into mortal sickness, sent me to the very gate of paradise to pray to God that he might lead me by an angel to the tree of mercy, that I might take oil and anoint my father, and he arise from his sickness. This also I did. And after my prayer an angel of the Lord came and asked me: What do you desire, Seth? Do you desire, because of the sickness of your father, the oil that raises up the sick, or the tree from which flows such oil? This cannot be found now. Therefore go and tell your father that after the completion of 5,500 years from the creation of the world, the only-begotten Son of God shall become man and shall descend below the earth. And he shall anoint him with that oil. And he shall arise and wash him and his descendants with water and the Holy Spirit. And then he shall be healed of every disease. But this is impossible now. When the patriarchs and prophets heard this, they rejoiced greatly.

IV (XX). And while they were all so joyful, Satan the heir of darkness came and said to Hades: O insatiable devourer of all, listen to my words. There is one of the race of the Jews, Jesus by name, who calls himself the Son of God. But he is (only) a man, and at our instigation the Jews crucified him. And now that he is dead, be prepared that we may secure him here. For I know that he is (only) a man, and I heard him saying: *My soul is very sorrowful, even to death* (Mt. 26:38). He did me much mischief in the world above while he lived among mortal men. For wherever he found my servants, he cast them out, and all those whom I had made to be maimed or blind or lame or leprous or the like, he healed with only a word, and many whom I had made ready to be buried he also with only a word made alive again. 2. Hades said: Is he so powerful that he does such things with only a word? And if he is of such power, are you able to withstand him? It seems to me that no one will be able to withstand such as he is.

CHRIST'S DESCENT INTO HELL

But whereas you say that you heard how he feared death, he said this to mock and laugh at you, being determined to seize you with a strong hand. And woe, woe to you for all eternity. Satan answered: O all-devouring and insatiable Hades, did you fear so greatly when you heard about our common enemy? I did not fear him, but worked upon the Jews, and they crucified him and gave him gall and vinegar to drink. Therefore prepare yourself to get him firmly into your power when he comes.

3. Hades answered: O heir of darkness, son of perdition, devil, you have just told me that many whom you made ready to be buried he made alive again with only a word. If then he freed others from the grave, how and with what power will he be overcome by us? I a short time ago swallowed up a certain dead man called Lazarus, and soon afterwards one of the living snatched him up forcibly from my entrails with only a word. And I think it is the one of whom you speak. If, therefore, we receive him here, I fear lest we run the risk of losing the others also. For, behold, I see that all those whom I have swallowed up from the beginning of the world are disquieted. I have pain in the stomach. Lazarus who was snatched from me before seems to me no good sign. For not like a dead man, but like an eagle he flew away from me, so quickly did the earth cast him out. Therefore I adjure you by your gifts and mine, do not bring him here. For I believe that he comes here to raise all the dead. And I tell you this: By the darkness which surrounds us, if you bring him here, none of the dead will be left for me.

V (XXI). While Satan and Hades were speaking thus to one another, a loud voice like thunder sounded: *Lift up your gates, O rulers, and be lifted up, O everlasting doors, and the King of glory shall come in* (Ps. 23:7 LXX). When Hades heard this, he said to Satan: Go out, if you can, and withstand him. So Satan went out. Then Hades said to his demons: Make fast well and strongly the gates of brass and the bars of iron, and hold my locks, and stand upright and watch every point. For if he comes in, woe will seize us. 2. When the forefathers heard that, they all began to mock him, saying: O all-devouring and insatiable one, open, that the King of glory may come in. The prophet David said: Do you not know, blind one, that when I lived in the world, I prophesied that word: *Lift up your gates, O rulers?* (Ps. 23:7). Isaiah said: I foresaw this by the Holy Spirit and wrote: *The dead shall arise, and those •who are in the tombs shall be raised up, and those who are under the earth shall rejoice* (26:19). *O death, where is thy sting? O Hades, where is thy victory?* (I Cor. 15:55, taken as referring to Isa. 25:8). 3. Again the voice sounded: Lift up the gates. When Hades heard the voice the second time, he answered as if he did not know it and said: *Who is this King of glory?* The angels of the Lord said: *The Lord strong and mighty, the Lord mighty in battle* (Ps. 23:8 LXX). And immediately at this answer the gates of brass were broken in pieces and the bars of iron were crushed and all the dead who were bound were loosed from their chains, and we with them. And the King of glory entered in like a man, and all the dark places of Hades were illumined.

VI (XXII). Hades at once cried out: We are defeated, woe to us. But who are you, who have such authority and power? And who are you, who without sin have come here, you who appear small and can do great things, who are humble and exalted, slave and master, soldier and king, and have authority over the dead and the living? You were nailed to the cross, and laid in the sepulchre, and now you have become free and have destroyed all our power. Are you Jesus, of whom the chief ruler Satan said to us that through the cross and death you would inherit the whole world? 2. Then the King of glory seized the chief ruler Satan by the head and handed him over to the angels, saying: Bind with iron fetters his hands and his feet and his neck and his mouth. Then he gave him to Hades and said: Take him and hold him fast until my second coming.

VII (XXIII). And Hades took Satan and said to him: O Beelzebub, heir of fire and torment, enemy of the saints, through what necessity did you contrive that the King of glory should be crucified, so that he should come here and strip us naked? Turn and see that not one dead man is left in me, but that all which you gained through the tree of knowledge you have lost through the tree of the cross. All your joy is changed into sorrow. You wished to kill the King of glory, but have killed yourself. For since I have received you to hold you fast, you shall learn by experience what evils I shall inflict upon you. O arch-devil, the beginning of death, the root of sin, the summit of all evil, what evil did you find in Jesus that you went about to destroy him? How did you dare to commit such great wickedness? How were you bent on bringing down such a man into this darkness, through whom you have been deprived of all who have died since the beginning?

VIII (XXIV). While Hades was thus speaking with Satan, the King of glory stretched out his right hand, and took hold of our forefather Adam and raised him up. Then he turned also to the rest and said: Come with me, all you who have suffered death through the tree which this man touched. For behold, I raise you all up again through the tree of the cross. With that he put them all out. And our forefather Adam was seen to be full of joy, and said: I give thanks to thy majesty, O Lord, because thou hast brought me up from the lowest (depth of) Hades. Likewise also all the prophets and the saints said: We give thee thanks, O Christ, Saviour of the world, because thou hast brought up our life from destruction. 2. When they had said this, the Saviour blessed Adam with the sign of the cross on his forehead. And he did this also to the patriarchs and prophets and martyrs and forefathers, and he took them and leaped up out of Hades. And as he went the holy fathers sang praises, following him and saying: *Blessed be he who comes in the name of the Lord.* Alleluia (Ps. 118:26). To him be the glory of all the saints.

IX (XXV). Thus he went into paradise holding our forefather Adam by the hand, and he handed him over and all the righteous to Michael the archangel. And as they were entering the gate of paradise, two old men met them. The holy fathers asked them: Who are you, who have not seen death nor gone down into Hades, but dwell in paradise with your bodies and souls? One of them answered: I am Enoch, who pleased God and was removed here by him. And this is Elijah the Tishbite. We shall live until the end of the world. But then we shall be sent by God to withstand Antichrist and to be killed by him. And after three days we shall rise again and be caught up in clouds to meet the Lord.

X (XXVI). While they were saying this there came another, a humble man, carrying a cross on his shoulder. The holy fathers asked him: Who are you, who have the appearance of a robber, and what is the cross you carry on your shoulder? He answered: I was, as you say, a robber and a thief in the world, and therefore the Jews took me and delivered me to the death of the cross together with our Lord Jesus Christ. When, therefore, he hung on the cross, I saw the wonders which happened and believed in him. And I appealed to him and said: Lord, when you reign as king, do not forget me. And immediately he said to me: *Truly, truly, today, I say to you, you shall be with me in paradise* (Lk. 23:43). So I came into paradise carrying my cross, and found Michael the archangel, and said to him: Our Lord Jesus Christ, who was crucified, has sent me here. Lead me, therefore, to the gate of Eden. And when the flaming sword saw the sign of the cross, it opened to me and I went in. Then the archangel said to me: Wait a short while. For Adam also, the forefather of the race of men, comes with the righteous, that they also may enter in. And now that I have seen you, I have come to meet you. When the saints heard this, they all cried with a loud voice: Great is our Lord, and great is his power.

XI (XXVII). All this we saw and heard, we two brothers who also were sent by Michael the archangel and were appointed to preach the resurrection of the Lord, but first to go to the Jordan and be baptized. There also we went and were baptized with other dead who had risen again. Then we went to Jerusalem also and celebrated the passover of the resurrection. But now we depart, since we cannot remain here. *And the love of God* the Father and *the grace of* our *Lord Jesus Christ and the fellowship of the Holy Spirit* be with you all (2 Cor. 13:14)." When they had written this and had sealed the books, they gave half to the chief priests and half to Joseph and Nicodemus. And they immediately vanished. To the glory of our Lord Jesus Christ. Amen.

THE LATIN VERSIONS OF THE DESCENSUS
AND THE REST OF THE PILATE LITERATURE

I. The first Latin form of the Descensus (*Ea*, pp. 389–416) does not differ materially from the Greek, apart from the conclusion. The sons of Symeon are given the names Karinus and Leucius, which are somehow connected with Leukios Charinos, the Gnostic author of the Acts of John. In the speech of John the admonition to repentance, which as addressed to the righteous is inappropriate, is omitted. But otherwise the speeches are greatly expanded, and not to their advantage, so that we get the impression that the author is fascinated by his phraseology. To turn to the conclusion, in the Greek Descensus there is no description of the effect produced on the Jews by the disclosures of the sons of Symeon. But here the Jews go home in great distress, beating their breasts in fear and trembling. But Joseph of Arimathaea and Nicodemus inform Pilate of what they have heard, and he orders everything to be recorded and stored in the archives. Then he summons the chief priests and scribes of the Jews, and adjures them to tell him truthfully whether Jesus is really the promised Messiah. And behind closed doors they recount to him how in the first book of the Seventy the archangel Michael revealed to Seth that 5,500 years would pass before the advent of the Messiah, and how the same number emerges from a correct interpretation of the measurements of the ark of Noah, and how these 5,500 years have now run their full course. And they say that they have hitherto told no one this, and ask Pilate urgently not to make it known. Pilate also laid up this information in his archives. Moreover, he sent the following account to the Roman emperor Claudius:[1]

Pontius Pilate to his emperor Claudius, greeting. There happened recently something which I myself brought to light. The Jews through envy have punished themselves and their posterity with a fearful judgment. For their fathers had received the promise that God would send them from heaven his holy one, who would rightly be called their king and whom God had promised to send to earth by a virgin. But when he came to Judaea when I was governor, and they saw that he restored sight to the blind, cleansed lepers, healed paralytics, expelled evil spirits from men, and even raised the dead, and commanded the winds, and walked dry-shod upon the waves of the sea, and did many other miracles, and all the people of the Jews acknowledged him to be the Son of God, the chief priests were moved by envy against him, and they seized him and delivered him to me, and bringing forward lie after lie they accused him of being a sorcerer and transgressing their law. And I believed this was so, and ordered him to be scourged, and handed him over to their

[1] The report is included in the original Greek in the Acts of Peter and Paul §40–§42 (*Aa* I, p. 196f.). In the translation I have taken the Greek text into account. The incorrect substitution of Claudius for Tiberius is explained by R. A. Lipsius as due to the fact that the dispute between Peter and Simon Magus, in which this report was read, took place in the original legend under Claudius, who consequently became the recipient of the letter.

will. And they crucified him, and set guards at his tomb. But he rose again on the third day, while my soldiers kept watch. But the Jews were so carried away by their wickedness that they gave money to my soldiers, saying: "Say that his disciples stole his body." But although they took the money, they were unable to keep silent about what had happened. For they testified that he had arisen, and that they had seen it, and that they had received money from the Jews. I have reported this lest anyone should lie about the matter and you should think that the lies of the Jews should be believed.

(Ea, pp. 413–416)

II. More peculiar, and more interesting, is the second Latin recension (Ea, pp. 417–432). It begins with an account by the three Galilaean rabbis who had witnessed the ascension of Jesus:

When we came from Galilee to Jordan, there met us a great multitude of men clothed in white, who had died before this time. Among them we saw also Karinus and Leucius, and when they came up to us we kissed one another, for they were dear friends of ours, and asked them: "Tell us, friends and brethren, what is this soul and flesh? And who are these with whom you go? And how is it that you, who died, remain in the body?" 2. They answered: "We rose with Christ from hell, and he himself raised us from the dead. And from this you may know that the gates of death and darkness are destroyed, and the souls of the saints are set free and have ascended to heaven with Christ the Lord. But we have also been commanded by the Lord himself to walk on the banks and hills of Jordan for a set time, without being visible to all and speaking with all, except for those with whom he permits it. And even now we should not have been able to speak to you nor to be seen by you, unless we had been permitted by the Holy Spirit." 3. Then Caiaphas and Annas said to the council: "Now shall it be made plain concerning all that these men have testified, formerly and later. If it is true that Karinus and Leucius remain alive in the body, and if we can see them with our eyes, then the testimony of these men is true in all points. If we find them, they will explain everything to us. If not, then know that all is false."

(Ea, pp. 417–419)

It is next established that the graves of Karinus and Leucius are really empty. The narrative continues:

5. Then all the council was greatly troubled and distressed, and they said to one another: "What shall we do?" Annas and Caiaphas said: "Let us have recourse to the place where they are reported to be, and send to them men from among those of rank, to implore them: perhaps they will condescend to come to us." Then they directed to them Nicodemus and Joseph and the three Galilaean rabbis who had seen them, who were to entreat them to condescend to come to them. They set forth and wandered through all the region of Jordan and the mountains, but did not find them and returned home again. 6. And, behold, there suddenly appeared a very great multitude coming down from Mount Amalech, about 12,000 men, who had risen with the Lord.

(*Ea*, pp. 419f.)

Karinus and Leucius are not in this multitude, but those who were sent are ordered to seek them in their house. They are found engaged in prayer, and they are ready immediately to go with them. In the synagogue the priests put the books of the Law in their hands, and adjure them by the God Heloi and by the God Adonai, and by the Law and the prophets, to declare how they arose from the dead.

8. Then Karinus and Leucius beckoned to them with their hands to give them paper and ink. This they did because the Holy Spirit did not allow them to speak with them. They gave each of them a papyrus roll and separated them one from the other in different cells. And they made with their fingers the sign of the cross of Christ and began each one to write on his roll. And when they had finished, they cried out as with one voice each from his cell: "Amen". Then they rose, and Karinus gave his roll to Annas and Leucius to Caiaphas; and they saluted one another and went out and returned to their sepulchres.

(*Ea*, p. 421)

What they wrote is not essentially different from the account in the two other recensions. Only the order of events is changed. At the beginning the cry rings out: "Open your gates, O princes, open the everlasting doors. The King of glory, Christ the Lord, shall come in". The dialogue between Satan and Hades precedes

479

Seth's account of his fruitless mission to paradise. Then follows the reference of Isaiah to his word about the people who sit in darkness, and the coming of John the Baptist, whose call to repentance is here omitted. After David and Jeremiah have pointed to their prophecies, great joy reigns among the saints, but Satan is gripped by fear and tries to flee, but is prevented by Hades and his minions. Then chapter VII continues:

And again the voice of the Son of the most high Father sounded, like great thunder: *"Open your gates, O princes; open, ye everlasting doors. The King of glory shall come in".* Then Satan and Hades cried out: *"Who is this King of glory?"* And the Lord's voice answered them: *"The Lord strong and mighty, the Lord mighty in battle"* (Ps. 23:7f. LXX). 2. After this voice there came a man who had the appearance of a robber, carrying a cross on his shoulder and crying without: "Open to me that I may enter in." Satan opened the gate to him a little and brought him in to the house, and shut the gate after him. And all the saints saw him shining brightly, and said to him immediately: "Your appearance is that of a robber. Tell us, what is the burden you bear on your back?" He answered humbly: "Truly, I was a robber, and the Jews hanged me on a cross with my Lord Jesus Christ, the Son of the most high Father. I come thus as his forerunner, but he himself comes immediately after me." 3. Then the holy David was enraged against Satan, and cried aloud: "Open your gates, most foul one, that the King of glory may come in." Likewise also all the saints rose up against Satan and tried to seize him and tear him in pieces. And again the cry rang out within: *"Open your gates, O princes, open, ye everlasting doors. The King of glory shall come in."* Again at this clear voice Hades and Satan asked: *"Who is this King of glory?"* And that wonderful voice replied: *"The Lord of hosts, he is the King of glory"* (Ps. 23:9f. LXX).

(Ea, pp. 428f.)

Now the gates of the underworld are shattered, Christ enters in, chains Satan and hands him over to Hades. At the bidding of the saints he sets up his cross in the midst of Hades as the sign of his victory. The journey to paradise and the meeting with Enoch and Elijah are omitted. The account ends in chapter X:

Then we all went out with the Lord, and left Satan and Hades in Tartarus. And to us and many others it was commanded that we should rise again with our bodies to testify in the world to the resurrection of our Lord Jesus Christ and the things which happened in Hades. Beloved brethren, this is what we saw and do testify, being adjured by you. And our testimony is confirmed by him who died for us and rose again.

(Ea, p. 431)

The last chapter (XI) reads:

But when the roll (of Karinus) was completely read through, all who heard it fell on their faces weeping bitterly and relentlessly beating their breasts, and cried out repeatedly: "Woe to us! Why has this happened to us wretched men?" Pilate fled, Annas and Caiaphas fled, the priests and Levites fled, and all the people of the Jews, lamenting and saying: "Woe to us miserable men! We have shed innocent blood." Therefore for three days and three nights they tasted no bread or water at all, and none of them returned to the synagogue. But on the third day the council assembled again, and the second roll, that of Leucius, was read, and there was found in it neither more nor less, not even to a single letter, than what was contained in the writing of Karinus. Then the synagogue was filled with dismay, and they all mourned for 40 days and 40 nights, and expected destruction and punishment from God. But he, the gracious and merciful one, did not destroy them immediately, but gave them generously an opportunity for repentance. But they were not found worthy to turn to the Lord.

These, beloved brethren, are the testimonies of Karinus and Leucius, concerning Christ the Son of God and his holy acts in Hades. To him let us all give praise and glory always and for ever. Amen.

(Ea, pp. 431f.)

III. Most of the remaining Pilate literature is much later. It includes a forged letter of Pilate to Tiberius (Ea, pp. 433f.), a harsh reply from the emperor (cf. Santos, pp. 502ff.), a letter of Pilate to Herod and one from Herod to Pilate (cf. Santos, pp. 514ff.). More interesting are the accounts of Pilate's end. Comparatively old is the Paradosis, i.e. the handing over of Pilate (Ea, pp. 449–455), which is appended to the Anaphora (report) (Ea, pp. 435–449). Anaphora and Paradosis have been described as the genesis of the Acts of Pilate. Since the Anaphora is identical in content with the letter of Pilate to Claudius translated on pp.

477f., only more detailed (the earthquake at the death of Jesus and the darkness receive special emphasis), I confine myself to the Paradosis.

When the report (of Pilate) reached Rome and was read to Caesar, while not a few stood by, all were amazed that it was because of the lawless conduct of Pilate that the darkness and the earthquake had come upon the whole world; and Caesar, filled with anger, sent soldiers with orders to bring Pilate in chains. 2. And when he had been brought to Rome and Caesar heard that Pilate was there, he sat down in the temple of the gods in the presence of the whole senate and the whole army and all the great ones of his empire. And he commanded Pilate to come forward and said to him: "How could you dare to do such a thing, you most impious one, when you had seen such great signs concerning that man? By your wicked daring you have destroyed the whole world."

3. Pilate answered: "Almighty Caesar, I am innocent of these things; it is the multitude of the Jews who are the guilty instigators." Caesar asked: "Who are they?" Pilate said: "Herod, Archelaus, Philip, Annas and Caiaphas and all the multitude of the Jews." Caesar said: "Why did you follow their advice?" Pilate said: "This nation is rebellious and refractory, and does not submit to your power." Caesar said: "As soon as they handed him over to you, you should have kept him secure and sent him to me, and not have followed them and crucified such a man who was righteous and did such wonderful signs as you have mentioned in your report. For it is clear from these signs that Jesus was the Christ, the king of the Jews." 4. And when Caesar said this and named the name of Christ, all the gods fell down, where Caesar sat with the senate, and became as dust. And all the people who stood by Caesar trembled by reason of the naming of the name and the fall of their gods, and gripped by fear they all went away, each to his own house, marvelling at what had taken place. And Caesar commanded that Pilate should be kept in custody, in order that he might learn the truth about Jesus.

5. On the next day Caesar sat in the Capitol with all the senate with the intention of questioning Pilate. And Caesar said: "Speak the truth, you most impious man, for through your godless

behaviour against Jesus, even here the working of your crime was shown in the overthrowing of the gods. Tell me now: Who is that crucified one, that his name destroyed all the gods?" Pilate answered: "Truly, the charges made against him are true. For I myself was convinced by his deeds that he is greater than all the gods whom we worship." Caesar said: "Why then did you treat him with such wickedness, although you knew him? In doing this you must have wished to harm my kingdom." Pilate answered: "I did it because of the unlawful insubordination of the lawless and godless Jews." 6. Then Caesar, filled with anger, took counsel with all the senate and his forces, and ordered the following decree to be recorded against the Jews: "To Licianus, chief governor of the East, greeting! At the present time the Jews who live in Jerusalem and the neighbouring towns have committed a lawless crime in forcing Pilate to crucify Jesus who was acknowledged as God. Because of this crime of theirs the world was darkened and dragged down to ruin. Therefore by this decree proceed there with all speed with a strong body of troops and take them prisoner. Obey, and advance against them, and dispersing them among all the nations enslave them, and expel them from Judaea, making the nation so insignificant that it is no longer to be seen anywhere, since they are men full of evil." 7. When this decree arrived in the East, Licianus carried out its terrible instructions and destroyed the whole Jewish nation, and those who were left in Judaea he scattered as slaves among the nations, so that Caesar was pleased when he learned of the actions of Licianus against the Jews in the East.

8. And again Caesar questioned Pilate, and commanded an officer called Albius to behead him, saying: "As this man raised his hand against the righteous man called Christ, so shall he fall in the same way, and find no deliverance." 9. And when Pilate came to the place of execution, he prayed silently: "Lord, do not destroy me with the wicked Hebrews, for it was through the lawless nation of the Jews that I raised my hand against you, because they plotted a revolt against me. You know that I acted in ignorance. Therefore do not condemn me because of this sin, but pardon me, Lord, and your servant Procla, who stands with me in this hour of my death, whom you made to prophesy that you must be

nailed to the cross. Do not condemn her also because of my sin, but pardon us and number us among your righteous ones." 10. And behold, when Pilate had finished his prayer, there sounded a voice from heaven: "All generations and families of the Gentiles shall call you blessed, because in your governorship all was fulfilled which the prophets foretold about me. And you yourself shall appear as my witness at my second coming, when I shall judge the twelve tribes of Israel and those who have not confessed my name." And the prefect cut off Pilate's head, and behold, an angel of the Lord received it. And when Procla his wife saw the angel coming and receiving his head, she was filled with joy, and immediately gave up the ghost, and was buried with her husband.

Here we have Pilate regarded as a saint, as in the Coptic Church. The other accounts of his death have a totally different complexion: *Mors Pilati* (*Ea*, pp. 456–458), *Cura sanitatis Tiberii*, *Vindicta Salvatoris* (*Ea*, pp. 471–486). In all three Tiberius is very sick. He hears of the wonder-working physician Jesus and hopes to be healed by him. But his emissary Volusianus learns from Pilate that Jesus is no longer alive. But he meets Veronica, whose handkerchief had imprinted on it the wonder-working picture of Jesus, and takes her with him to Rome. So Tiberius is healed. Now punishment overtakes Pilate. In the *Mors Pilati* he protects himself from Caesar's anger for a long time by wearing the seamless robe of Jesus. But this becomes known, and Caesar forces him to commit suicide. (In the *Vindicta Salvatoris* Volusianus has already imprisoned him in Damascus, in the *Cura sanitatis Tiberii* he is sent into exile.) His body is thrown into the Tiber. There it attracts the evil spirits, which rage so fiercely that all who live near are terrified. Then the body is taken out of the Tiber and sunk in the Rhone. There also the raging of the evil spirits is repeated, so that the inhabitants of Vienne, which is interpreted via gehennae (way to hell), in allusion to Pilate, also wish to be rid of him. He then comes to the region of Lausanne, and after being removed from there also, finally finds a resting-place in a well surrounded by mountains, i.e. in an Alpine lake near the mountain named after him. There the rumbling of the spirits ceases to annoy.

5. THE GOSPEL OF BARTHOLOMEW
(*F. Scheidweiler—W. Schneemelcher*)

INTRODUCTION (*W. Schneemelcher*):

In his Commentary on Matthew Jerome mentions among other apocryphal writings an *Evangelium iuxta Bartholomaeum* (*PL* XXVI

17f.). It is uncertain whether this reference is derived from a secondary source (perhaps Origen), or is due to personal knowledge of Jerome himself. The Decretum Gelasianum also mentions among apocryphal works which are to be rejected *Evangelia nomine Bartholomaei* (cf. above, p. 47; should *evangelium* be read?). Further references to such a work are to be found in pseudo-Dionysius Areopagita (*PG* III 1000 B) and in Epiphanius the monk (*PG* CXX 213 B-D). A short quotation in the so-called Book of Hierotheos refers to a gospel of Bartholomew (cf. F. S. Marsh in *JTS* 23, 1922, pp. 400f.; on this book see Baumstark, *Gesch. d. syr. Lit.*, p. 167). The statement by the Venerable Bede (*PL* XCII 307) comes from Jerome. "We learn from Heinrich von Herford (ed. Potthast) that Ludwig the Bavarian was acquainted with the gospel of Bartholomew (comparison with Mt. and thus perhaps only in reference to Euseb., *H.E.* V. 10, 3)" (E. Hennecke, *ZKG* 45, 1927, p. 311, n. 1). No other allusions have yet been found. The late and sparse testimony, while not a proof of the lateness of the apocryphon, could well be explained in that way.

There exists a whole series of texts associated with the name of the apostle Bartholomew. These are firstly the so-called Questions of Bartholomew in Greek, Latin and Slavonic; also a Coptic text called 'Book of the Resurrection of Jesus Christ, by Bartholomew the apostle'; and in addition an abundance of Coptic fragments in various libraries, some of which have been assigned to the gospel of Bartholomew. These Coptic fragments clearly contain late texts, which hardly date from before the 5th–7th century. Nevertheless, a brief discussion of them is worth while, because these legendary narratives are in some respects descendants of older versions, and because their subject-matter provides a typical illustration of the principles of the development of apocryphal literature both in Egypt and elsewhere. The popular character, typical of these texts, never allows development to cease. This complicates considerably the question of the contents and structure of the original gospel of Bartholomew, and the history of research on the apocryphon has produced a variety of hypotheses. In particular it was long disputed whether a distinction should not be drawn between an apocalypse of Bartholomew and a gospel of Bartholomew, a view which was found to be untenable. Moreover, the problem of a 'gospel of Gamaliel' has long been connected with that of the gospel of Bartholomew, because some of the fragments have been assigned to the gospel of Gamaliel. Some mention must be made of this question. First (a) will be given an abstract of the Greek, Latin and Slavonic Questions of Bartholomew, and then (b) a brief account of the Coptic texts.

For introduction to the problem of the tradition reference may be made, among others, to A. Wilmart—E. Tisserant, "Fragments grecs et latins de l'Évangile de Barthélemy" (*Rev. Bibl.* 10, 1913, pp. 161ff.). Further literature below.

A number of references are made in the literature to the gnostic ideas in the gospel of Bartholomew (e.g. A. Baumstark, *Rev. Bibl.* 3, 1906, pp. 249ff.). Ancient Egyptian types of thought have also been pointed out (so, among others, by E. A. W. Budge, *Coptic Apocrypha*, pp. LXIff.). Now it is true that in these late witnesses of Coptic popular religion many ideas do appear which are found earlier in ancient Egyptian religion. But this does not prove much. The whole complex of relationships must be kept constantly in mind, and the problem of the survival of ancient Egyptian conceptions in the Coptic Church is very much more intricate than a mere comparison of ideas and words would suggest (cf. W. Schneemelcher, "Der Sermo 'De anima et corpore'": *Festschrift für G. Dehn*, 1957, p. 130, n. 37). The question of Gnosticism in the gospel of Bartholomew deserves serious consideration. In fact many parallels to the gnostic gospels, in content and not only in form, can be adduced (cf. the survey by H.-Ch. Puech, pp. 231ff. above; N. Bonwetsch, *NGW* Göttingen, *Phil.-Hist. Klasse* 1897, pp. 29ff., has collected a large amount of comparative material on the 'Questions of Bartholomew' which must serve as the basis of a fresh examination of the problem). But statements about the 'gnostic' character of the gospel of Bartholomew are only possible when we can say exactly what this gospel looked like, and we are still far from being able to do that. As regards dependence on gnostic ideas, the same principle applies as for dependence on ancient Egyptian types of thought.

(A) THE QUESTIONS OF BARTHOLOMEW
(F. Scheidweiler)

The document entitled in the manuscripts 'Questions of Bartholomew' is extant in five recensions, two Greek ones in Vindobonensis Gr. historicus 67 (G) and in Hierosl. sabaiticus 13 (H), two Latin ones in Vaticanus Reginensis 1050 (R) and in Casanatensis 1880 (C), and a Slavonic one in two manuscripts, one at Petersburg (P) and one in Vienna (Vindob. slav. 125 = V). The complete text is preserved only in C, but in a very corrupt form full of extensive interpolations, especially towards the end. The most valuable recension seems to be H, but it contains barely a third of the text. R contains still less, comprising but three fragments. What is essential in the textual variants is given in the notes to the translation that follows. The translation sometimes follows one recension, sometimes another. In one place I have found it necessary to place the shorter form of H alongside the longer one of CPV.

Right at the beginning it is clear that even C is not without value. The reading of H and V, "after the resurrection", is impossible, in view of the saying of Jesus: "Before I have laid aside this body of flesh." We therefore have to choose between P "before the resurrection" and C "Antequam pateretur". C undoubtedly is to be preferred. Bartholomew I 7 in H says: εἰδόν σε ἀφανὴ γεγονότα ἀπὸ τοῦ σταυροῦ· φωνῆς δὲ μόνον ἤκουον ἐν τοῖς καταχθονίοις, as against C: "Vidi te inparabilem (!, inapparabilem?) factum de cruce, voces tantum audiebam in abissum" and PV: "I saw you disappear on the cross, but I heard voices in the underworld". Here the reading of H must be accepted, and φωνῆς must be understood as "your voice", referring to σε. By φωνή can only be meant the cry of Jesus which follows in I 19: Ἔασόν με εἰσελθεῖν εἰς σεαυτόν· πρὸ γὰρ σοῦ ἐγὼ πλαστός εἰμι, which is also found in C, although this in other respects agrees with the expanded form: "Dimitte me ingredere in te ipsum, quia a (read 'ante') te plasmatus sum".

That Jesus spoke thus must, of course, be restored. The reason for the omission is obvious. But P and V have altered the text (this section is missing in G) because the cry is meaningless on the lips of Hades. P reads: "Allow me, do not oppose me; for I was created before you", V: "Allow me, interpose yourself; for I was created before you", which completely fails to fit the preceding question of Hades: "Where are we to hide ourselves from the face of the great king?" and besides would convey the remarkable information that Hades had been created before Satan. H therefore here preserves the original text. Christ was the first thing created by God. G seems to protest against this in an interpolation in IV 28: τὸ γὰρ υἱὸν αὐτοῦ πρὸ τοῦ τοὺς οὐρανοὺς καὶ τὴν γῆν ⟨καὶ⟩ ἡμᾶς (i.e the angels) πλασθῆναι εἶχεν (to be read instead of εἶχον).

Also remarkable in this connection is the prayer of Jesus in IV 70 with the twice repeated address to God: δόξα σοι, κύριε. But the cry of Jesus must be addressed to Satan. In IV 25 Satan says of himself: Εἰ θέλεις μαθεῖν τὸ ὄνομά μου, πρῶτον ἐλεγόμην Σαταναήλ, ὃ ἑρμηνεύεται ἐξάγγελος θεοῦ. ὅτε δὲ ἀπέγνων (so Bonwetsch instead of ἀγνωὸν) ἀντίτυπον τοῦ θεοῦ, ἐκλήθη τὸ ὄνομά μου Σατανᾶς, ὅ ἐστιν ἄγγελος ταρταροῦχος. This is reminiscent of the teaching of the Bogomils according to Cosmas: Christus is the elder son of God, Satan(ael) is the younger. No chronological conclusions can be deduced from this, but the lack of any influence of the gospel of Nicodemus may be significant. Doubtless H has abbreviated, so that its version is scarcely to be understood without comparing it with the complete form, and we can hardly assume that Satan granted Jesus admittance merely on the strength of his claim to have been created before him. But this is not sufficient to justify the view that H omits the expansions of the complete form derived from the gospel of Nicodemus. There appears to be no objection to assigning the original form of the Gospel of Bartholomew, which lay before H, to the 3rd century.

Literature: A. Vassiliev, *Quaestiones sancti Bartholomaei apostoli: Anecdota Graeco-Byzantina* I (1893). – N. Bonwetsch, *Die apokryphen Fragen des Bartholomäus:* Gött. Gel. Nachr. 1897 (Editions of G and PV in both these works). – André Wilmart-Eug. Tisserant, "Fragments Grecs et Latins de l'Évangile de Barthélemy": *Rev. Bibl.* 1913, pp. 161ff. (H and R). – Umberto Moricca, "Un nuovo testo dell' evangelo di Bartolomeo": *Rev. Bibl.* 1921, pp. 481ff., 1922, pp. 20ff. (R). – Felix Haase, "Zur Rekonstruktion des Bartholomäusevangeliums": *ZNW* 1915, pp. 93ff. – Jos. Kroll, *Gott und Hölle. Der Mythos vom Descensuskampfe*, 1932, pp. 71ff. – Santos, pp. 570–608.

I 1. In the time before the passion[1] of our Lord Christ all the apostles were gathered together. And they asked and besought him: Lord, show us the secrets of the heaven. 2. But Jesus answered: I can reveal nothing to you before I have put off this body of flesh. 3. But when he had suffered and risen again, all the apostles at the sight of him did not dare to ask him, because his appearance was not as it was before, but revealed the fulness of his godhead. 4. But Bartholomew went up to him and said: Lord, I wish to speak to you. 5. Jesus answered him: Beloved Bartholomew, I know what you wish to say. Ask then, and I will tell you all you wish to know. And I myself will make known to you what you do not say. 6. Bartholomew said to him: Lord, when you went to be hanged on the cross, I followed you at a distance and saw how you were hanged on the cross and how the angels descended from heaven and worshipped you. 7. And when darkness came, I looked and saw that you had vanished from the cross; only I heard your voice[2] in the underworld, and suddenly there a great wailing and gnashing of teeth arose. Tell me, Lord, where you went from the cross. 8. And Jesus answered: Blessed are you, Bartholomew, my beloved, because you saw this mystery. And now I will tell you everything you ask me. 9. When I vanished

[1] Following C (antequam pateretur); after the resurrection, H, V; before the resurrection P.

[2] φωνῆς δὲ μόνον ἤκουον H; voces tantum audiebam C; but I only heard voices PV.

488

from the cross, I went to the underworld to bring up Adam and all the patriarchs, Abraham, Isaac and Jacob. The archangel Michael had asked me to do this.[1]

H 10. Then Bartholomew said: What voice was heard? Jesus answered: Hades said to Beliar: As I perceive, God has come here. 16/17. Beliar answered Hades: Look carefully, who it is who ⟨has come here⟩, whether, as it seems to me, it is Elias or Enoch or one of the prophets. But Hades answered Beliar: The 6,000 years are not yet accomplished. From where then can these have come? I have the record of the number in my hands. 18. ⟨And Beliar said to Hades⟩: Do not fear. Secure your gates and make strong your bars. Consider, God does not come down upon the earth. 19. Hades answered: I pay no heed to your fine words. I have gripes in my belly and my entrails rumble. It cannot but be that God has come down. Woe is me! Where shall I flee before the face of the mighty great God? ⟨And

CPV: 10. When I descended with my angels to the underworld, in order to dash in pieces the iron bars and shatter the portals of the underworld, Hades said to the devil: I perceive that God has come down upon the earth. 11. And the angels cried to the mighty ones: Open your gates, you princes, for the King of glory has come down to the underworld. 12. Hades asked: Who is the King of glory who has come down to us? 13. And when I had descended 500 steps, Hades began to tremble violently and said; I believe that God has come down. His strong breath goes before him. I cannot bear it. 14. But the devil said to him: Do not submit, but make yourself strong. God has not come down. 15. But when I had descended 500 steps more, the strong angels cried out: Open, doors of your prince! Swing open, you gates! For see: the King of glory has come down. And again Hades said: Woe is me! I feel the breath of God. And yet you say: God has not come down upon the earth. 16. Beelzebub replied: Why are you afraid? It is a prophet, and you think it is God. The prophet has made himself like God. We will take him and bring him to those who think to ascend

---

[1] The last sentence is missing in the Slavonic versions.

I cried⟩: Allow me to enter into you. For I was created before you. 20. Then I entered in and scourged him and bound him with chains that cannot be loosed.

into heaven. 17. And Hades said: Which of the prophets is it? Tell me. Is it Enoch the scribe of righteousness?[1] But God has not allowed him to come down upon the earth before the end of the 6,000 years. Do you say that it is Elias the avenger? But he does not come down before the end. What am I to do, for the destruction is from God? For already our end is at hand. For I have the number ⟨of the years⟩ in my hands. 18. But when the devil perceived that the Word of the Father had come down upon the earth, he said: Do not fear, Hades; we will make fast the gates and make strong our bars. For God himself does not come down upon the earth. 19. And Hades said: Where shall we hide ourselves from the face of God, the great king? Permit me, do not resist; for I was created before you.[2] 20. And thereupon they dashed in pieces the gates of brass and he ('I'?)[3] shattered the iron bars. And I went in and smote him with a hundred blows and bound him with fetters that cannot be loosed.

And I brought out all the patriarchs and came again to the cross. 21. And Bartholomew said to him: Lord, I saw you again hanging on the cross and all the dead[4] arising and worshipping you. Tell me, Lord, who was he whom the angels carried in their arms, that exceedingly large man? And what did you say to him that he groaned so deeply? 22. It was Adam, the first created, for

---

[1] Ethiopic Enoch 12:4 and 15:1.
[2] C: Dimitte me ingredere in te ipsum, quia a te plasmatus sum.
[3] The 'I?' comes from Bonwetsch. C makes this sentence passive, but continues: Et ingressus dominus apprehendit eum, etc.
[4] S. CPV simply: the dead; cf. Mt. 27:52f. In H the first sentence of 21 is omitted.

whose sake I came down from heaven upon the earth. And I said to him: I was hanged upon the cross for your sake and for the sake of your children. And when he heard that, he groaned and said: So you were pleased to do, O Lord.

23. Again Bartholomew said: Lord, I also saw the angels ascending before Adam and singing praises. 24. But one of the angels, greater than the others, would not go up. He had in his hand a fiery sword and looked at you.[1] 25. And all the angels besought him to go up with them; but he would not. But when you commanded him, I saw a flame issuing out of his hands, which reached as far as the city of Jerusalem. 26. And Jesus said to him: Blessed are you, Bartholomew my beloved, because you saw these mysteries. This was one of the avenging angels who stand before my Father's throne. He sent this angel to me. 27. And for this reason he would not go up, because he wished to destroy the power of the world. But when I commanded him to go up, a flame issued from his hand, and after he had rent the veil of the temple, he divided it into two parts as a testimony to the children of Israel for my passion, because they crucified me.

28. And when he had said this, he said to the apostles: Wait for me in this place; for today a sacrifice is offered in paradise, that I may receive it after my arrival. 29. And Bartholomew said to him: Lord, what sacrifice is offered in paradise? Jesus answered: The souls of the righteous, when they leave the body, go to paradise, and unless I am present there they cannot enter. 30. Bartholomew asked: Lord, how many souls leave the world every day? Jesus answered: Thirty thousand. 31. And again Bartholomew asked: Lord, when you lived among us, did you receive the sacrifices in paradise? 32. Jesus answered: Verily, I say to you, my beloved, even when I taught among you, I sat at the right hand of the Father and received the sacrifices in paradise. 33. And Bartholomew said: Lord, if 30,000 souls leave this world daily, how many are admitted into paradise? Jesus answered: Only three.[2] 34. Bartholomew again asked: Lord, how many

---

[1] The archangel Michael is meant.—Paragraphs 25-28 are omitted in H, P has 25, the second part of 26 and 27 in the main. In C 26 is omitted altogether. G begins with §28.

[2] So C; PV:10, H:50. G is strange. There Bartholomew asks in §30 about the number of souls admitted into paradise and receives the answer: Three. Then come 32f.,

souls are born into the world every day? Jesus answered: Only one over and above those who leave the world. 35. And when he had said this, he gave them the peace and vanished from their sight.

II 1. Now the apostles were in the place Chritir[1] with Mary. 2. And Bartholomew came to Peter and Andrew and John, and said to them: Let us ask Mary, her who is highly favoured, how she conceived the incomprehensible or how she carried him who cannot be carried or how she bore so much greatness. But they hesitated to ask her. 3. Therefore Bartholomew said to Peter: Father Peter, do you as the chief one go to her and ask her. But Peter said to John: You are a chaste youth and blameless; you must ask her. 4. And as they all were doubtful and pondered the matter to and fro, Bartholomew came to her with a cheerful countenance and said: You who are highly favoured, tabernacle of the Most High,[2] unblemished, we, all the apostles ask you, but they have sent me to you. Tell us how you conceived the incomprehensible, or how you carried him who cannot be carried or how you bore so much greatness. 5. But Mary answered: Do not ask me concerning this mystery. If I begin to tell you, fire will come out of my mouth and consume the whole earth. 6. But they asked her still more urgently. And since she did not wish to deny the apostles a hearing, she said: Let us stand up in prayer. 7. And the apostles stood behind Mary. And she said to Peter: Peter, chief of the apostles, the greatest pillar, do you stand behind me? Did not our Lord[3] say: *The head of the man is Christ, but the head of the woman is the man?* Therefore stand in front of me to pray. 8. But they said to her: In you the Lord set his tabernacle and was pleased to be contained by you. Therefore you now[4] have more right than we to lead in the prayer. 9. But she answered them: You are shining stars, as the prophet said: *I lifted up my*

where in my view we must read: (Κύριε, εἰ) τρισμύριαι (text τρεῖς μόνον) ψυχαὶ ἐξέρχονται καθ' ἑκάστην ἡμέραν, ‹πόσαι εἰσέρχονται εἰς τὸν παράδεισον;› λέγει αὐτῷ ὁ Ἰησοῦς· Μόλις αἱ [πεντήκοντα] τρεῖς, ἀγαπητέ μου. Πάλιν Β. λέγει· Καὶ πῶς τρεῖς μόνον εἰσέρχονται εἰς τὸν παράδεισον; λέγει αὐτῷ ὁ Ἰησοῦς· Αἱ μέντοι [πεντήκοντα] τρεῖς εἰσέρχονται εἰς τὸν παράδεισον ἤτοι ἀποτίθονται εἰς τὸν κόλπον Ἀβραάμ. αἱ δὲ λοιπαὶ ἴασιν εἰς τὸν τόπον τῆς ἀναστάσεως (place where they await the resurrection), [ὅτι οὐκ εἰσὶν αἱ τρεῖς ὡς αὐταὶ αἱ πεντήκοντα].

[1] Chritir V, Ritor P, Χηλτουρά H, χερουβίμ G; C gives no name.
[2] G σκηνή περικομμένη (= κυρίου γενομένη?): become most high PV.
[3] Actually Paul, 1 Cor. 11:3.
[4] συιέναι, derived from νῦν ἰέναι?

eyes to the hills, from which comes my help (Ps. 120:1 LXX). You, then, are the hills and you must pray. 10. The apostles said to her: You ought to pray as the mother of the heavenly king. 11. Mary said to them: In your likeness God formed the sparrows and sent them to the four corners of the world.[1] 12. But they answered her: He whom the seven heavens scarcely contain was pleased to be contained in you.

13. Then Mary stood up before them, and spread out her hands to heaven and began to pray thus:[2] O God exceeding great and all-wise, king of the ages, indescribable, ineffable, who didst create the breadths of the heavens by thy word and arrange the vault of heaven in harmony,[3] who didst give form to disorderly[4] matter and didst bring together that which was separated, who didst part the gloom of the darkness from the light, who didst make the waters to flow from the same source, before whom the beings of the air tremble and the creatures of the earth fear, who didst give to the earth its place and didst not wish it to perish, in bestowing upon it abundant rain and caring for the nourishment of all things, the eternal Word (Logos) of the Father. The seven heavens could scarcely contain thee, but thou wast pleased to be contained in me, without causing me pain, thou who art the perfect Word (Logos) of the Father, through whom everything was created. Glorify thine exceedingly great name, and allow me to speak before thy holy apostles. 14. And when she had ended the prayer, she began to say to them: Let us sit down on the ground. Come, Peter, chief of the apostles, sit on my right hand and put your left hand under my shoulder. And you, Andrew, do the same on my left hand. And you, chaste John, hold my breast. And you, Bartholomew, place your knees on my shoulders and press close my back so that, when I begin to speak, my limbs are not loosed.

15. And when they had done that, she began: When I lived in the temple of God and received my food from the hand of an angel,[5] one day there appeared to me one in the form of an angel;

[1] In the Infancy Gospel of Thomas c. 2, p. 135 Tischendorf, pp. 392f. above.
[2] I have omitted the supposedly original Hebrew at the beginning.
[3] Following H; GPV are obscure; C has introduced changes.
[4] διάτριτα is to be amended to ἀδιάκριτα.
[5] According to the Protevangelium of James 8:1 (p. 378 above).

493

but his face was indescribable and in his hand he had neither bread nor cup, as had the angel who came to me before. 16. And immediately the veil of the temple was rent and there was a violent earthquake, and I fell to the earth, for I could not bear the sight of him. 17. But he took me with his hand and raised me up. And I looked toward heaven; and there came a cloud of dew on my face and sprinkled me from head to foot, and he wiped me with his robe. 18. Then he said to me: Hail, you who are highly favoured, the chosen vessel.[1] And then he struck the right side of his garment and there came forth an exceedingly large loaf, and he placed it upon the altar of the temple, and first ate of it himself and then gave to me also. 19. And again he struck his garment, on the left side, and I looked and saw a cup full of wine. And he placed it upon the altar of the temple, and drank from it first himself and gave it also to me. And I looked and saw that the bread did not diminish and the cup was full as before. 20. Then he said: Three years more, and I will send my word and you shall conceive my son, and through him the whole world shall be saved. But you will bring salvation to the world. Peace be with you, favoured one, and my peace shall be with you for ever. 21. And when he had said this, he vanished from my eyes and the temple was as before.

22. As she was saying this, fire came from her mouth, and the world was on the point of being burned up. Then came Jesus quickly and said to Mary: Say no more, or today my whole creation will come to an end. And the apostles were seized with fear lest God should be angry with them.

III 1. And he went with them to the mountain Mauria[2] and sat down in their midst. 2. But they hesitated to question him, because they were afraid. 3. And Jesus answered and said: Ask me what you wish, so that I can teach you and show you. For there are still seven days, and then I ascend to my Father and shall no more appear to you in this form. But they, hesitating, said to him: Lord, show us the abyss, as you promised us. 5. He answered: It is not good for you to see the abyss. But if you wish it, I will keep my promise. Come, follow me and see. 6. And he led them to a

[1] G has also καὶ χάρις ἀνέκλειπτε (ever favoured?), which is lacking in H and C.
[2] So PV, Μαυρεῖ H, Mambre C.

494

place called Cherubim,[1] that is, place of truth. 7. And he beckoned to the angels of the west. And the earth was rolled up like a papyrus roll, and the abyss was exposed to their eyes. 8. When the apostles saw it, they fell on their faces. 9. But Jesus said to them: Did I not say to you that it was not good for you to see the abyss? And he again beckoned to the angels, and the abyss was covered up.

IV 1. And he took them and brought them to the mount of Olives. 2. And Peter said to Mary: You who are favoured, ask the Lord to reveal to us all that is in the heavens. And Mary answered Peter: O rock hewn above,[2] did not the Lord build his church upon you? You therefore should be the first to go and ask him. 4. Peter said again: You were made the tabernacle of the most high God. You ask him. 5. Mary said: You are the image of Adam. Was not he formed first and then Eve? Look at the sun. It shines like Adam. Look at the moon. It is full of clay, because Eve transgressed the commandment. For God placed Adam in the east and Eve in the west, and he commanded the two lights to shine, so that the sun with its fiery chariot should shine on Adam in the east, and the moon in the west should shed on Eve its milk-white light. But she defiled the commandment of the Lord, and therefore the moon became soiled, and its light does not gleam. Since, therefore, you are the likeness of Adam, you ought to ask him. But in me the Lord took up his abode, that I might restore the dignity of women.

6. Now when they came to the top of the mountain, the Lord parted from them for a little while. Then Peter said to Mary: You made good the transgression of Eve, changing her shame into joy. So you ought to ask. 7. But when Jesus appeared again, Bartholomew said to him: Lord, show us the adversary of men, that we may see his form, or what his work is, or where he comes from, or what power he has that he did not even spare you, but caused you to be hanged on the cross. 8. And Jesus looked at him and said: O bold[3] heart! You ask for that which you cannot look upon. 9. But Bartholomew was frightened, and he fell at Jesus' feet and began to say: O lamp never extinguished, Lord Jesus Christ, everlasting one, who gave grace for the whole world to

---

[1] So G, Χαιρουδήκ H, Cherukt PV. This form is reminiscent of Ἀχερούσια λίμνη.
[2] ἀκρότομος 'hewn above', because on it the Church shall be built.
[3] So RC; σοὶ ἡ καρδία σκληρά H (PV), ὦ καρδία αὐστηρά G.

those who love you, and gave everlasting light through your appearing on earth, who at the command of the Father gave up your life above[1] and completed your work, who changed the dejection of Adam into joy and overcame the sorrow of Eve with gracious countenance by your birth from a virgin mother, do not be angry with me, and grant me the right to ask. 10. When he said this, Jesus raised him up and asked him: Bartholomew, do you wish to see the adversary of men? I tell you that, when you see him, not only you, but the apostles with you, and Mary will fall on your faces and will be like the dead. 11. But they all said to him: Lord, we wish to see him. 12. And he led them down from the mount of Olives, and threatened the angels of the underworld, and beckoned to Michael to sound his mighty trumpet in the height of heaven. Then the earth was shaken and Beliar came up, held by 660[2] angels and bound with fiery chains.

13. He was 1600 yards long and 40 yards broad. His face was like a lightning of fire, and his eyes like sparks,[3] and from his nostrils came a stinking smoke. His mouth was like a cleft of rock[4] and a single one of his wings was 80 yards long. 14. As soon as the apostles saw him, they fell to the ground on their faces and became like dead men. 15. But Jesus came near and raised up the apostles, and gave them the spirit of power. Then he said to Bartholomew: Come near to him, Bartholomew, and place your feet on his neck; then he will tell you what his work is, and how he deceives men. 16. And Jesus stood at a distance with the apostles. 17. And Bartholomew raised his voice and said: O womb more spacious than a city! O womb wider than the span of heaven! O womb that contained him whom the seven heavens do not contain. You contained him without pain and held in your bosom him who changed his being into the smallest of things.[5] O womb that bare, concealed in (your) body, the Christ who has been made visible to many. O womb that became more spacious than the whole creation.[6] 18. And Bartholomew was afraid, and said:

[1] ὁ τὴν ἄνω οὐσίαν λόγῳ < καταλιπὼν > πατρὸς ἔργον ἐπιτελέσας (ἐπιτελέσαι?).
[2] This and the following numbers vary in the different traditions.
[3] So PV, ζοφώδεις GH; nubilosi C.
[4] PV end here.
[5] E. Kurtz has altered the meaningless ὡσιουθέν into οὐσιωθέντα. I have added to it πρὸς βραχὺν which comes later with εὐρυχωρότερα γεναμένη but does not fit in there.
[6] The Gnostic hymn to the Μήτρα enlarged to cosmic proportions is out of place here. In H §17 reads: "And seized by fear Bartholomew raised his voice and cried:

Lord Jesus, give me a hem of your garment, that I may venture to approach him. 19. Jesus answered him: You cannot have a hem of my garment, for it is not the garment which I wore before I was crucified. 20. And Bartholomew said: Lord, I fear lest, as he did not spare your angels, he will swallow me up also. 21. Jesus answered: Were not all things made by my word and according to the plan of my Father? The spirits were made subject to Solomon himself. Go therefore, since you have been commanded to do so in my name, and ask him what you wish.

22. And Bartholomew went and trod upon his neck, and pressed down his face to the earth as far as his ears. 23. And Bartholomew asked him: Tell me who you are and what is your name. He replied: Ease me a little, and I will tell you who I am and how I came into this condition and what my work is and how great my power is. 24. Bartholomew eased him and asked him: Tell me all you have done and all you do. 25. Beliar answered and said: If you wish to know my name, I was first called Satanael, which means "angel of God". But when I rejected the image of God, I was called Satan, which means "angel of hell". 26. And again Bartholomew asked him: Reveal everything to me, and conceal nothing from me. 27. And he replied: I swear to you by the mighty glory of God that even if I wished, I can conceal nothing from you; for he who can convict me stands near me. For if I had the power, I would destroy you as I hurled one of you to destruction.[1] 28. I was the first angel to be created. For when God made the heavens, he took a handful of fire and formed me first, 29. Michael second,[2] the captain of the hosts above, Gabriel third, Uriel fourth, Raphael fifth, Nathanael sixth and 6,000 other angels, whose names I cannot tell. There are rod-bearers (lictors) of God, and these scourge me seven times a day and seven times a night and never leave me alone and break in pieces all my power.

'Praised be the name of your immortal kingdom from henceforth for ever.' When Bartholomew had said this, Jesus permitted him: 'Go and tread upon the neck of Beliar.' And Bartholomew went quickly and trod upon his neck, and Beliar trembled." At the beginning of §18 H makes Bartholomew not only fear, but weep. Then follows the same prayer as in G.—R has for §17 only: Tunc tremuit Antichristus et furore repletus est.

[1] Judas.

[2] Here G has the following insertion: "For God had his Son, before heaven and earth and we were created. For when God wished to create all things, his Son spoke the word of creation, so that we also were created by the will of the Son and the decision (or 'with the consent') of the Father."

These are the avenging angels, who stand by God's throne. All these belong to the first-created angels. 30. And after them was the whole number of the angels created: 100 myriads for the first heaven, and the same number for the second, third, fourth, fifth, sixth and seventh heavens. Outside the seven heavens there is the first sphere (the firmament); and there dwell the angels of power who influence men. 31. There are also four angels who are set over the winds. The first rules over Boreas. He is called Chairum,[1] and he has in his hand a fiery rod, and restrains the great moisture which this wind has, so that the earth should not dry up. 32. And the angel who rules over Aparktias[2] is called Oertha. He has a torch of fire in his hand, and holds it to him and to his sides and warms his coldness so that he does not freeze the earth. 33. And the angel of the south wind is called Kerkutha, and he breaks his violence so as not to shake the earth. 34. And the angel who is set over the south-west wind is called Naoutha. He has a rod of ice in his hand and puts it at his mouth, and quenches the fire which comes from his mouth. And if the angel did not quench it at his mouth, it would set the whole world on fire. 35. And another angel rules over the sea, and makes it rough with the waves.[3] 36. I will not tell you more, for he who stands near me does not permit it.

37. Then Bartholomew asked him: How do you chastise the souls of men? 38. Beliar answered: Am I to describe to you the punishment of the hypocrites, the slanderers, the jesters, the covetous, the adulterers, the sorcerers, the soothsayers, and of those who believe in us, and of all behind whom I stand? 39. Bartholomew said to him: I wish you to be brief. 40. And he gnashed his teeth together, and there came up from the abyss a wheel with a sword flashing fire, which had pipes. 41. And I asked him: What is the sword? 42. He answered: It is the sword for the gluttonous. They are put into this pipe, because in their gluttony they turn to every kind of sin. Into the second pipe come the slanderers, because they secretly slander their neighbours. Into the third pipe come the hypocrites and the rest whom I trip up with my machinations. 43. And Bartholomew said: Do you do

[1] This and the following names of the angels are different in C.
[2] Aparktis is also a north wind. E. Kurtz conjectures $\dot{a}\pi\eta\lambda\iota\dot{\omega}\tau\sigma\upsilon$ (east wind).
[3] C: "He breaks the might of the waves", which is more suitable.

this by yourself? 44. Satan replied: If I were able to go out by myself, I would destroy the whole world in three days, but neither I nor any of the 600 goes out. We have other swift servants whom we command. We equip them with a many-barbed hook, and send them out to hunt, and they catch men's souls for us, enticing them with the sweetness of various allurements, that is, drunkenness, laughter, slandering, hypocrisy, pleasures, fornications, and the other devices in their treasury which weaken men.[1] 45. I will tell you also the rest of the names of the angels. The angel of the hail is called Mermeoth. He holds the hail on his head, and my servants adjure him and send him wherever they wish. And other angels rule over the snow,[2] and others over the thunder, and others over the lightning, and when a spirit wishes to go forth from among us, either over land or over water, these angels send out fiery stones and set our limbs on fire. 46. Bartholomew said: Be silent, dragon of the abyss. 47. And Beliar said: I will tell you much about the angels. Those who run together through the heavenly and earthly regions are Mermeoth, Onomatath, Duth, Melioth, Charuth, Graphathas, Hoethra, Nephonos, and Chalkatura. Together they fly through the regions of heaven, of earth, and the underworld . . .

48. Bartholomew interrupted him and said: Be silent and powerless, so that I can entreat my Lord. 49. And Bartholomew fell on his face, and scattered earth on his head, and began: O Lord Jesus Christ, the great and glorious name. All the choirs of the angels praise you, Lord; and I also, who am unworthy in my lips,[3] praise you, Lord. Hear me, your servant, and as you called me from the custom-house[4] and did not allow me to remain to the end in my former manner of life, hear me, Lord Jesus Christ, and have mercy on the sinners. 50. When he had so prayed, the Lord said to him: Stand up, turn to him that groans. I will declare the rest to you. 51. And Bartholomew raised up Satan, and said

---

[1] For ὀλιγωρίας Bonwetsch tentatively suggests παλευτρίας, but this is too remote from the context. According to Kurtz, who cites Hesychius' explanation through ἀδημονεῖν, ὀλιγωρεῖν in 48 means something like "become weak, powerless". My rendering of ὀλιγωρίας corresponds to this. Since 45–47 incl. breaks the connection and contradicts 36, I regard it as an interpolation.

[2] χαλάζης is wrongly repeated, and some such word as above is necessary in the translation.

[3] G has κήσας (or κήσε) ὄργανον, which I am unable to emend

[4] Transferred from Matthew to Bartholomew.

to him: Go to your place with your angels,[1] but the Lord has mercy on all his world. 52. But the devil said: Allow me to tell you how I was cast down here, and how God made man. 53. I wandered to and fro in the world, and God said to Michael: Bring me earth from the four ends of the world and water out of the four rivers of paradise. And when Michael had brought them to him, he formed Adam in the east, and gave form to the shapeless earth, and stretched sinews and veins, and united everything into a harmonious whole. And he showed him reverence for his own sake, because he was his image. And Michael also worshipped him. 54. And when I came from the ends of the world, Michael said to me: Worship the image of God which he has made in his own likeness. But I said: I am fire of fire, I was the first angel to be formed, and shall I worship clay and matter? 55. And Michael said to me: Worship, lest God be angry with you. I answered: God will not be angry with me, but I will set up my throne over against his throne, and shall be as he is (Isa. 14:14f.).[2] Then God was angry with me and cast me down, after he had commanded the windows of heaven to be opened.

56. When I was thrown down, he asked the 600 angels that stood under me, whether they would worship (Adam). They replied: As we saw our leader do, we also will not worship him who is less than ourselves. 57. After our fall upon the earth we lay for forty years in deep sleep, and when the sun shone seven times more brightly than fire, I awoke. And when I looked around, I saw the 600 under me overcome by deep sleep. 58. And I awoke my son Salpsan, and took counsel with him how I could deceive the man on whose account I had been cast out of heaven. 59. And I devised the following plan. I took a bowl in my hand, and scraped the sweat from my breast and my armpits, and washed myself in the spring of water from which the four rivers flow.[3] And Eve drank of it, and desire came upon her. For if she had not drunk of that water, I should not have been able to deceive

---

[1] ἄθλων, apparently amended by James to ἀγγέλων.

[2] Of the parallel accounts of the fall of Satan which Bonwetsch has collected, that from the Latin Book of Adam is important, since Satan's threat does not begin so abruptly as it does here: si irascitur mihi (deus), ponam sedem meam super sidera caeli, et ero similis altissimo.

[3] Here he will have thrown the bowl with his sweat into the water and let it flow into paradise. C: Accipiensque folia ficus in manibus meis extersi sudorem pectoris mei et sub alarum mearum et proieci secus decursus aquarum.

her. 60. Then Bartholomew commanded him to go into Hades.
61. And he came to Jesus, and fell at his feet, and began with
tears to speak thus: Abba, Father, who cannot be discovered by
us, Word of the Father, whom the seven heavens hardly contained,
but who were pleased to be contained easily and without pain in
the body of the Virgin, without the Virgin knowing that she
carried you, while you by your thought ordained everything as it
should be, you who give us our daily bread[1] without our asking
for it. 62. You who wore a crown of thorns, in order to prepare
for us repentant sinners the precious heavenly crown, who hung
upon the cross ⟨and were given gall and vinegar to drink⟩, in
order to give us to drink the wine of contrition, and were pierced
in the side with the spear, in order to satisfy us with your body
and blood. 63. You who gave names to the four rivers, to the first
Phison because of the faith ($\pi i \sigma \tau i \varsigma$!), which you preached after
your appearance on earth, to the second Geon, because man was
formed of earth ($\gamma \hat{\eta}$!), to the third Tigris, that by you we might
be shown the consubstantial Trinity ($\tau \rho i \acute{a} \varsigma$!) in heaven, and to the
fourth Euphrates, because by your coming on earth you made
every soul to rejoice ($\epsilon \mathring{v} \phi \rho a i \nu \epsilon i \nu$!) through the message of immortality. 64. My God, great Father and King, save, Lord, the
sinners.

65. When Bartholomew had uttered this prayer, Jesus said to
him: Bartholomew, the Father named me Christ, that I might
come down on earth and anoint ($\chi \rho i \epsilon i \nu$) with the oil of life everyone who came to me. And he called me Jesus, that I might heal
($i \hat{a} \sigma \theta a i$) every sin of the ignorant and give to men the truth of
God.[2] 66. And again Bartholomew said to him: Lord, may I
reveal these mysteries to every man? 67. Jesus answered him:
Bartholomew, my beloved, entrust them to all who are faithful
and can keep them for themselves. For there are some who are
worthy[3] of them; but there are also others to whom they ought
not to be entrusted, for they are boasters, drunkards, proud,

---

[1] $\tau \grave{a}$ $\acute{e} \kappa o \acute{v} \sigma i a$ is a corruption of $\tau \grave{a}$ $\acute{e} \pi i o \acute{v} \sigma i a$, which is formed on the model of $\mathring{a} \rho \tau o \varsigma$
$\acute{e} \pi i o \acute{v} \sigma i o \varsigma$ in the Lord's Prayer. James translates "that which we need".

[2] The text is corrupt: $\tau \hat{\omega} \nu$ $\mathring{a} \gamma \nu o \acute{v} \nu \tau \omega \nu$ $\mathring{v} \pi \grave{o}$ $\theta \epsilon o \hat{v}$ $\mathring{\eta}$ $\kappa a \grave{i}$ $\theta \epsilon i \omega \nu$ $\mathring{a} \rho a i$ $\tau o \hat{i} \varsigma$ $\mathring{a} \nu \theta \rho \acute{\omega} \pi o i \varsigma$
$\delta \omega \rho \acute{\eta} \sigma o \mu a i$. In C among the mass of expansions the sentence "dei veritatem ego
omnibus donavi" may come from the original text.

[3] The text has $\mathring{a} \nu \acute{a} \xi i o i$. But since the unworthy are mentioned subsequently, I have
followed James, who translates "For some there are that be worthy of them".

merciless, idolaters, seducers to fornication, slanderers, teachers
of falsehood, and doers of all the works of the devil, and therefore
they are not worthy that they should be entrusted to them. 68.
These things are also to be kept secret because of those who cannot
contain them. For all who can contain them shall have a share in
them. As regards this, therefore, my beloved, I have spoken to
you, for you are blessed and all who are akin to you in having this
message entrusted to them, for all who contain it shall receive all
they wish in all times[1] of my judgment. 69. At that time, I,
Bartholomew, wrote this in my heart, and I took the hand of the
friend of men, and began joyfully to speak thus: Glory be to thee,
O Lord Jesus Christ, who givest to all thy grace which we have
all perceived. Alleluia. Glory be to thee, O Lord, the life of sinners.
Glory be to thee, O Lord, through whom death is put to shame.
Glory be to thee, O Lord, the treasure of righteousness. We praise
thee as God. 70. And when Bartholomew spoke thus, Jesus put
off his mantle, and took the kerchief[2] from Bartholomew's neck
and began joyfully to say: I am good to you. Alleluia. I am meek
and kind to you. Alleluia. Glory be to thee, O Lord. For I give
myself to all who desire me. Alleluia. Glory be to Thee, O Lord,
world without end. Amen. Alleluia. 71. And when he had
finished, the apostles kissed him, and he gave them the peace of
love.

V 1. Bartholomew said to him: Tell us, Lord, which sin is
more grievous than all other sins. 2. Jesus replied: Truly, I say
to you that hypocrisy and slander are more grievous than all
other sins. For because of them the prophet said in the Psalm
(1:5): *The ungodly shall not stand in the judgment nor sinners in the congregation of the righteous,* nor the godless in the judgment of my
Father. *Truly, truly, I say to you, that every sin shall be forgiven every
man, but the sin against the Holy Spirit shall not be forgiven* (Mt. 12:31).
3. And Bartholomew said: What is the sin against the Holy
Spirit? 4. Jesus answered: Everyone who decrees against any man
who serves my Father has blasphemed against the Holy Spirit.
For every man who serves God with reverence is worthy of the

---

[1] ἐν τοῖς . . . κρίσεως μου. I supply καιροῖς.
[2] The priest's stole, first used in this sense at the synod of Laodicea between 343 and
381. There the use of the kerchief is only permitted to clergy from the grade of deacon
upwards, and so not to the subdeacon, reader, and singer.

Holy Spirit, and he who speaks any evil against him shall not be forgiven. 5. Woe to him who swears by the head of God, even if he does not commit perjury, but speaks the truth.[1] For God, the Most High, has twelve heads. He is the truth, and in him is no lie and perjury. 6. Go, therefore, and preach to the whole world the word of truth, and you, Bartholomew, preach this (secret) word to everyone who wishes it, and all who believe in it shall have eternal life. 7. Bartholomew said: If any sins with lust of the flesh, how is he recompensed? 8. Jesus answered: It is good if he who is baptized preserves his baptism without blame. But the lust of the flesh will practise its allurement.[2] A single marriage belongs to chaste living. For truly I say to you: He who sins after the third marriage is unworthy of God. 9. But do you preach to all, that they must guard themselves from such things. For I do not depart from you and I give you the Holy Spirit. 10. And Bartholomew with the apostles glorified God before him exceedingly, saying: Glory be to thee, Holy Father, inextinguishable sun, incomprehensible, full of light. To thee be honour, to thee glory and worship world without end. Amen.

(B) COPTIC TEXTS OF BARTHOLOMEW

(*W. Schneemelcher*)

1. *The tradition.* Reference has already been made above (p. 485) to the fact that there is a series of Coptic texts which either themselves claim a connection with Bartholomew or are ascribed in modern research to a Gospel of Bartholomew. The problem with which we are concerned has not exactly been made any clearer by the abundance of hypotheses, and a detailed discussion of all the suggestions cannot be undertaken here. The texts are available in the following editions: "The Book of the Resurrection of Jesus Christ by Bartholomew the Apostle" was published according to the Brit. Mus. *Ms. Or.* 6804 by E. A. Wallis Budge (*Coptic Apocrypha in the dialect of Upper Egypt*, 1913, pp. 1–48 Coptic text; pp. 179–215 English translation). To this certainly belong various fragments in the National Library in Paris and one leaf in the

---

[1] This must be the meaning of the corrupt text: οὐαὶ τὸν ὀμνύοντα κατὰ τῆς κεφαλῆς τοῦ θεοῦ, οὐδὲ τῷ ἐπιορκοῦντι κατ᾽ αὐτοῦ ἀληθῶς. This is supported by the quotation of Mt. 5:36 in C at this point. James seems to alter οὐδὲ into οὐαί, but this is insufficient, and it must have continued: οὐαὶ αὐτῷ εἴτε ἐπιορκοῦντι κατ᾽ αὐτῆς εἴτε ἀληθῶς ὀμνύοντι. We must accept the change from the rare construction of οὐαί with acc. (Rev. 8:13) to the usual one with dat.

[2] ἐραστής to be altered to ἐρατή or ἐρασστή, "desired".

503

Staatsbibliothek in Berlin, published by P. Lacau ("Fragments d'apocryphes coptes": *Mémoires publiés par les membres de l'Institut français d'archéologie orientale du Caire* IX, 1904, pp. 39–77, with French translation; English translation in Budge *op. cit.* pp. 216–230). These leaves collected by Lacau present two recensions of this work, differing from one another, while the London ms. represents a third recension. A part of the leaves which Lacau printed is also to be found in E. Revillout, *Les apocryphes coptes* I (=*PO* II. 2, Paris 1904; re-printed 1946), pp. 185–194.

Now in addition to these fragments, which clearly are related to the text of the London ms. and in which Bartholomew appears as the narrator, so that they belong to the Coptic Bartholomew-literature, Revillout published a larger number of leaves (mostly from the Paris National Library, but partly from other libraries) which he declared to be the remains of a "Gospel of the Twelve Apostles". A. Baumstark (*Rev. Bibl.* 3 (1906) pp. 245–265) and P. Ladeuze (*RHE* VII (1906) pp. 245–268) have already demonstrated that both association and title are completely arbitrary (cf. also the judgment of H.-Ch. Puech, above p. 271): the texts which Revillout collected are of very diverse origin and in part do not belong to any apocryphal gospel at all, but are the remains of a homiletic work. Only for particular pieces in Revillout's collection may we consider a connection with a writing of Bartholomew, as for others we may assume a relationship with a writing of Gamaliel.

F. Haase (*ZNW* 16 (1915) pp. 93–112) endeavoured to bring a certain order into the mass of the fragments, which can indeed be achieved, above all with the aid of the London text, which was not known either to Lacau, to Revillout, or to Baumstark. James provides a survey of the fragments (James pp. 147–152: "Coptic Narratives of the Ministry and the Passion"); in an analysis of the 'Book of the Resurrection of Jesus Christ by Bartholomew the Apostle' he has further tried to summarize the text, so that the train of thought (so far as we can speak of such a thing at all) of the two (or three) recensions becomes clear (James pp. 181–186). Haase distinguished K[1] (=fragments in Lacau and Revillout) and K[2] (=British Museum ms.), but it must be observed that K[1] is extant in two recensions; at any rate for some sections the tradition contains two versions slightly different from one another, while K[2] appears rather a paraphrase than a recension of K[1].

2. *Content.* The reconstruction of the two recensions of K[1], of which of course only individual leaves are extant, can be undertaken with some probability for those sections which present manifest parallels with K[2]. On the other hand it is very difficult

to adduce texts from the fragments, as parts of K¹, for the portions which are lacking in K². Nevertheless, reference may be made to a few leaves which may possibly be considered to belong to this group of writings:

(a) *The fragments* (K¹)

(i) Revillout No. 6 (pp. 157f.)

Jesus is sitting with His disciples at the Last Supper. Matthias brings a cock which he has killed, and reports how the Jews observed that the blood of his master (*sc.* Jesus) would be shed like that of the cock. Jesus recalls the cock to life again as an indication of His Resurrection.

No cogent reasons can be produced for assigning this fragment to a document of Bartholomew. Since some pages are missing before the present beginning of the 'Book of the Resurrection', the possibility may be admitted that such a narrative of the Last Supper, developed in very legendary fashion, belonged to it—but no more. James (p. 150) refers to the Ethiopic 'Book of the Cock' and to other versions of the motif.

(ii) Revillout No. 5 (pp. 156f.) and App. No. 1 (pp. 195f.)

In these two fragments the subject is the betrayal by Judas. The first relates that Judas' wife induced her husband to treachery. The second describes how the seven-month-old child of Joseph of Arimathaea, to whom Judas' wife served as nurse, besought his father to send the woman away since she and her husband had accepted the blood-money. To this is added a short description of the incidents at the Crucifixion.

Connection with a Bartholomew-document is more than questionable. The second part of the second fragment especially points to a different relationship; in particular it is much more concise in its presentation. This argument is not however decisive, since similar summaries also occur in K².

(iii) Revillout Nos. 7–9 (pp. 159–161)

These fragments have already been discussed above (pp. 227ff.). They derive from the Strasbourg Papyrus and (against James pp. 150 and 182) can hardly be linked with the 'Book' of Bartholomew.

(iv) Revillout No. 12 (pp. 165ff.)

This tells of a man named Ananias, who hurries to the Cross and cries out to the Jews that they ought to crucify him and not Christ. A voice from the Cross promises him that his soul shall not enter into Amente, nor his body decay. The high priests seek to stone Ananias, but the attempt fails. In the fire into which he is then cast he remains three days and three nights unharmed. Finally he is slain with a spear, and Jesus takes his soul with him into heaven.

That this fragment belongs to the 'Book' of Bartholomew is

probable because there is a reference to this incident at the present beginning of the London ms.: "After they had crucified the Saviour, they laid him in a grave; on the completion of the third day he rose up from the dead; he took the soul of the holy Apa Ananias with him into heaven" (fol. 1a; Budge p. 1).

(v) Lacau IV (pp. 39–77 = Revillout pp. 185–194 and pp. 149f.; but Revillout gives a shorter text than Lacau; Lacau in his translation prints side by side the two extant versions of this passage).

The text begins with the conquest of Hell and the deliverance of the children of Adam. Then follows the cursing of Judas. After a gap it is related how Death (who previously had remained with the body of Jesus at the grave) sends his son Pestilence to secure Amente (i.e. Hell). But when Death with his six decans comes to Amente, he finds only three 'voices' left, Judas, Cain and Herod. All the rest have been set free by Christ. After a short transitional passage the narrative begins afresh: The holy women go to the grave—they are enumerated in detail—and Mary falls into conversation with Philogenes, the gardener, who relates the events at the Resurrection of Jesus. Jesus Himself now appears and speaks with Mary, whom He first favours with words of blessing and then charges to inform His disciples of His Resurrection. Mary asks for Jesus' blessing, and receives the promise that she will be with Christ in His kingdom. Here the account suddenly changes to the first person: "Believe me, my brethren, ye apostles, I Bartholomew, the apostle of the Son of God, saw the Son of God . . ." (Lacau p. 54). After the description of what Bartholomew saw, the promise to Mary is continued (have two different traditions grown together here?). Mary then goes to the apostles, who are celebrating the Eucharist on the Mount of Olives.

Some pages are now missing. The text begins again with the bringing of Adam and Eve and their children before God. "Believe me, O my brethren, ye apostles, I Bartholomew have never since my birth seen such a human form as was comparable with the form of Adam, save that of the Saviour" (Lacau p. 59). The description of the figures of Adam and Eve is followed by their acquittal by God and by the angel's song of praise. All this is given by Bartholomew as an eye-witness account, and for this he is praised by the apostles, but for his part stresses his unworthiness. A new appearance follows: Christ takes the apostles with him into heaven, where they are blessed one after the other by God. This too is the account of Bartholomew! In a new scene Christ is sent by God to comfort the apostles. He finds them in Galilee, and bestows on them the Holy Spirit. Here the fragment breaks off. There can be no doubt that these long passages represent a recension, or two recensions, of the 'Book' of Bartholomew. There are corresponding passages in the London text, which is however more detailed.

Other fragments from Revillout's collection cannot be adduced here since there are no indications of any kind that they belong to the Bartholomew literature. Perhaps a palaeographic examination of the Coptic leaves bound up together in the Paris library may yet provide a more accurate indication of where other fragments belong. From the content it is not possible, at any rate for the present, to allocate any others.

(b) *The London Text* (K²)

Despite many gaps, the London ms. presents a coherent account although the beginning is missing. Budge conjectures that five leaves have been lost. An important point is that the title of the work can be inferred from the text; in fol. 23b (Budge p. 46) we find: "This is the Book of the Resurrection of Jesus Christ our Lord in joy and exultation". Since in this text also Bartholomew frequently appears as the narrator—moreover it is reported that he committed these secrets to his son Thaddaeus (fol. 9a)—Budge has given the work the title: "The Book of the Resurrection of Jesus Christ, by Bartholomew the Apostle". Also interesting is the admonition not to let the book fall into the wrong hands, i.e. those of heretics or unbelievers (fol. 9a; cf. Puech, above pp. 328f.).

In this recension the composition of the document is even less rigorously thought out. The different items are reported in broad array, and contradictions are not lacking: scenes in the underworld, a dialogue between Death and the corpse of Jesus, the descent of Christ into Hell, the cursing of Judas, the freeing of the sons of Adam (save three, whose names however are not here mentioned), appearances of the risen Christ, the report of Philogenes, the promises to Mary, the ascent of the Redeemer and His reception in heaven, Adam and Eve in heaven, the hymns of the angels, a new epiphany of Jesus, the blessing of the apostles by God, the death and raising up of Siophanes (the son of Thomas), the story of doubting Thomas, the return of Jesus to heaven and the Eucharist of the apostles, who now separate and preach in the name of the holy and consubstantial ($\delta\mu oo\acute{v}\sigma\iota os$!) Trinity. All this is strung together, without any real logical connection between the individual episodes. The delight in broad narrative is stronger than the literary concern to produce a finished work. If we compare the corresponding parts of the London ms. with the fragments adduced above, the relationship becomes clear, but so also does the further development. Often indeed the London text seems to be a paraphrase of an older original.

3. *Assessment of the Coptic texts.* As has been shown, the Coptic texts are not a unity but reflect a development of the material with which we are concerned. So long as we do not possess texts which represent an older stage than K[1], it must admittedly be difficult to establish exactly what is original and what expansion within the Coptic field. That this literature goes back to Greek antecedents is to be assumed. The 'Questions of Bartholomew' however, in the forms in which they have come down to us, are not the direct antecedents of the Coptic recensions. Certainly there are isolated parallels (cf. for example what is said about Adam in I. 22 with fol. 11a f. in the London ms.). More important is the general tenor: in both works the descent of Christ to Hell, His Resurrection and the deliverance of Adam, and finally the figure of Bartholomew stand in the foreground. But this is certainly not enough for precise statements about the connection between the tradition in Greek, Latin and Slavonic and the Coptic texts. We can only conjecture that both streams of tradition go back to a special Bartholomew-tradition of the 3rd or 4th centuries. Possibly there was at that time a shorter Gospel of Bartholomew, which was the starting point for this literature. Even this primitive version, however, is probably not to be dated too early, since almost nothing at all is known from the first centuries about a special reverence for Bartholomew. Only in the Coptic Church does this apostle come to play a more prominent rôle. The Coptic texts are at any rate not older than the 5th–7th centuries, and for K[2] a still later date lies within the range of possibility.

The Coptic texts are however a particularly characteristic example of the growth of apocryphal literature, and especially of the survival of important cycles of narrative and motifs. In these late texts distinctive tendencies can scarcely be detected any longer. Isolated Gnostic motifs may certainly be observed, but the general tendency of the versions before us is not to be described as Gnostic.

6. THE GOSPEL OF GAMALIEL

(M.-A. van den Oudenrijn)[1]

This book is concerned with the events of Good Friday and the days which followed. The ostensible author is a contemporary of Christ, the Rabbi Gamaliel the Elder known from Acts (5:34;

---

[1] In connection with their criticism of the Coptic texts published by Revillout (cf. above, p. 504), Baumstark and Ladeuze drew attention to a lost Gospel of Gamaliel, of which we otherwise know nothing. Now Professor M.-A. van den Oudenrijn has discovered in an Ethiopic ms. a sermon in which this apocryphon has probably been worked up. Even if it is a matter of a relatively late creation, readers will be grateful for the short account which the discoverer has placed at our disposal. *W.Sch.* (See now Professor van den Oudenrijn's book: *Gamaliel: äthiopische Texte zur Pilatusliteratur*, Freiburg 1959).

22:3) and also from the Mishnah. The name 'Gospel' was bestowed on this document by Anton Baumstark (*Rev. Bibl.* 1906, 253) and Paulin Ladeuze (*RHE*, 1906, 245). The narrative was utilized by Heryäqos of Al-Bahnasâ, a bishop who is often mentioned elsewhere but cannot yet be more precisely identified, in a homily which in the Ethiopic version bears the title 'Lament of Mary' (*Lâḥa Mâryâm*), and so has come down to us. This Lament of Mary must have been a favourite work among the Copts.

Some Coptic fragments were published at the beginning of the century by Pierre Lacau ("Fragments d'apocryphes coptes", *Mémoires publiés par les membres de l'Institut français d'archéologie orientale*, IX, Cairo 1904) and E. Revillout (*Les apocryphes coptes*, I, *PO* II, 116–189, Paris 1904). There are several Arabic redactions, which in part have also appeared in print in Coptic-Arabic devotional books (Cairo 1902, 1927 and 1945; cf. Jean Simon, *Orientalia* 1940 (9), 159 and G. Giamberardini, *L'immacolata Concezione di Maria nella Chiesa Egiziana*, Cairo 1953, p. 31 n. 3). A. Mingana published in 1928 an Arabic version from two Garshūni mss. in private hands (*Woodbrooke Studies* II, 211–240; Introduction, English translation and notes, ib. 178–210 = *BJRL* 12 (1928) 411ff.). The Ethiopic version also, which is the most complete of all, was translated in the 14th century from an Arabic prototype. It was in its time very widely disseminated in Ethiopia, and was read in sections in Holy Week. Two fragments of this Ethiopic text had already been known since 1892 (cf. M. R. James, *The Apocryphal New Testament*, Oxford [5]1953, p. 152), and were recognized by Felix Haase (*Literarkr. Untersuchungen zur orient.-apokr. Evangelienliteratur*, Leipzig 1913, pp. 20–21) as detached fragments of Gamaliel.

The title 'Lament of Mary' handed down in the Ethiopic mss. is no longer appropriate for the second half of the homily; in the second part of the narrative the Virgin is not mentioned at all. In one ms., admittedly late, we find a division of the booklet into eleven chapters. In the first five it is not always clearly evident where we have to do with the original Gamaliel-narrative (G) and where with the additions of the homilist (H), but by and large the following division may be close to the mark:

I. 1–16 Exordium of the homily (H); I. 17–35 first lament of the Virgin (H); I. 36–44 Mary and the apostles (doubtful); I. 45–55 second lament of the Virgin (H, but in verses 49–51 possibly G in a shortened form); I. 56–59 John takes the place of Peter (G); I. 60 to II. 12 the Virgin betakes herself to Calvary (H); II. 13–21 the Mother beneath the Cross (G?); II. 22–26 further laments of the Virgin (H); II. 27–34 continuation of the narrative (G); II. 35–38 Mary's parting words (H); II. 39–41 earthquake and darkness at the death of Jesus (G); II. 42–51 renewed lament of the Virgin (H); II. 52–III. 25 continuation of the narrative (G); III. 26–40 insertion by the homilist (H); III. 40–IV. 4 continuation of the narrative (G); IV. 5–V. 1 homiletic developments (H). From V. 2 to XI. 11 we have the Gamaliel narrative, only rarely interrupted by some rhetorical outbursts from the homilist (e.g. VIII. 4). VI. 21–VII. 9 Pilate believes in the Resurrection of Jesus; VII. 10–21 he cross-examines the soldiers who stood guard at the grave, and unmasks their falsehoods; VII. 22–VIII. 14 healing of the captain through contact with Jesus' grave-clothes; VIII. 15–XI. 5 raising up of a dead man in Jesus' grave; XI. 6–11 explanation by the ostensible eye-witness Gamaliel. The final passage (XI. 12–50) with the exchange of letters between Pilate and Herod is probably a later continuation of the Gamaliel story, which breaks off with XI. 50.

The text as we now have it appears to be no older than the 5th or 6th century, but older elements may have been worked up in the narrative. The captain in Mt. 27:54 (Mk. 15:39), who plays a major rôle in the narrative, here bears no proper name. The document was evidently composed in Coptic by an orthodox Christian, who was however hostile to the Jews. His chief desires were first to confirm the fact of the Resurrection of Jesus by alleged new arguments, and secondly to present Pilate, who in the Coptic Church is revered as a saint, so far as possible in a favourable light.

THE GOSPEL OF THOMAS

The following is a fresh translation, made from the Coptic text published by Messrs. Brill of Leiden. In the preparation of this version the following six translations have been consulted, in addition to that published by Messrs. Brill: English by W. R. Schoedel, French by J. Doresse and R. Kasser, German by J. Leipoldt and Hans Quecke, Danish by S. Giversen. The numbering of the sayings is that of the Brill edition.

These are the secret words which the living Jesus spake, and Didymus Judas Thomas wrote them down.

(1) And he said: He who shall find the interpretation of these words shall not taste of death.

(2) Jesus said: He who seeks, let him not cease seeking until he finds; and when he finds he will be troubled, and if he is troubled he will be amazed, and he will reign over the All.

(3) Jesus said: If those who lead you say unto you: Behold, the Kingdom is in heaven, then the birds of the heaven will be before you. If they say unto you: It is in the sea, then the fish will be before you. But the Kingdom is within you, and it is outside of you. When you know yourselves, then shall you be known, and you shall know that you are the sons of the living Father. But if you do not know yourselves, then you are in poverty, and you are poverty.

(4) Jesus said: The man aged in his days will not hesitate to ask a little child of seven days about the place of life, and he shall live. For there are many first who shall be last, and they shall become a single one.

(5) Jesus said: Know what is before thy face, and what is hidden from thee shall be revealed unto thee; for there is nothing hidden which shall not be made manifest.

(6) His disciples asked him and said unto him: Wilt thou that we fast? And how shall we pray? Shall we give alms? And what rules shall we observe in eating? Jesus said: Do not lie; and that which you hate, do not do. For all things are revealed before heaven. For there is nothing hidden which shall not be manifest, and there is nothing covered which shall remain without being uncovered.

(7) Jesus said: Blessed is the lion which the man shall eat, and the lion become man; and cursed is the man whom the lion shall eat, and the lion become man.

(8) And he said: Man is like a wise fisherman, who cast his

net into the sea and drew it up from the sea full of small fish. Among them the wise fisherman found a large good fish. He threw down all the small fish into the sea; he chose the large fish without trouble. He that hath ears to hear, let him hear.

(9) Jesus said: Behold, the sower went forth, he filled his hand, he cast. Some fell upon the road; the birds came and gathered them. Others fell on the rock, and sent no root down to the earth, nor did they sprout any ear up to heaven. And others fell on the thorns; they choked the seed, and the worm ate them. And others fell on the good earth, and brought forth good fruit unto heaven, some sixty-fold and some an hundred and twenty-fold.

(10) Jesus said: I have cast fire upon the world, and behold, I guard it until it is ablaze.

(11) Jesus said: This heaven shall pass away, and that which is above it shall pass away; and they that are dead are not alive, and they that live shall not die. In the days when you were eating that which is dead, you were making it alive. When you come into the light, what will you do? On the day when you were one, you became two. But when you have become two, what will you do?

(12) The disciples said to Jesus: We know that thou wilt go from us. Who is he who shall be great over us? Jesus said to them: In the place to which you come, you shall go to James the Just, for whose sake heaven and earth came into being.

(13) Jesus said to his disciples: Make a comparison to me, and tell me whom I am like. Simon Peter said to him: Thou art like a righteous angel. Matthew said to him: Thou art like a wise man of understanding. Thomas said to him: Master, my mouth will in no wise suffer that I say whom thou art like. Jesus said: I am not thy master, because thou hast drunk, thou hast become drunk from the bubbling spring which I have measured out. And he took him, went aside, and spoke to him three words. Now when Thomas came to his companions, they asked him: What did Jesus say unto thee? Thomas said to them: If I tell you one of the words which he said to me, you will take up stones and throw them at me; and a fire will come out of the stones and burn you up.

(14) Jesus said to them: If you fast, you will beget a sin for yourselves; and if you pray, you will be condemned; and if you give alms, you will do an evil to your spirits. And if you go into any land and travel in its regions, if they receive you eat what they set before you. Heal the sick among them. For that which goes into your mouth will not defile you, but that which comes forth from your mouth, that is what will defile you.

(15) Jesus said: When you see him who was not born of woman, throw yourselves down upon your face and worship him. He is your Father.

(16) Jesus said: Perhaps men think that I am come to cast a peace upon the world, and know not that I am come to cast divisions upon the earth, fire, sword, war. For there shall be five in a house; there shall be three against two, and two against three, the father against the son and the son against the father, and they shall stand as solitaries.

(17) Jesus said: I will give you that which eye has not seen, and ear has not heard, and hand has not touched, and which has not entered into the heart of man.

(18) The disciples said to Jesus: Tell us how our end shall be. Jesus said: Have you then discovered the beginning, that you seek after the end? For where the beginning is, there shall the end be. Blessed is he who shall stand in the beginning, and he shall know the end and shall not taste of death.

(19) Jesus said: Blessed is he who was before he came into being. If you become my disciples and hear my words, these stones shall minister unto you. For you have five trees in Paradise, which do not move in summer or in winter, and their leaves do not fall. He who knows them shall not taste of death.

(20) The disciples said to Jesus: Tell us what the kingdom of heaven is like. He said to them: It is like a grain of mustard-seed, smaller than all seeds; but when it falls on the earth which is tilled, it puts forth a great branch, and becomes shelter for the birds of heaven.

(21) Mary said to Jesus: Whom are thy disciples like? He said: They are like little children dwelling in a field which is not theirs. When the owners of the field come, they will say: Yield up to us our field. They are naked before them, to yield it up to them and to give them back their field. Therefore I say: If the master of the house knows that the thief is coming, he will keep watch before he comes, and will not let him dig into his house of his kingdom to carry off his vessels. You, then, be watchful over against the world. Gird up your loins with great strength, that the brigands may not find a way to come at you, since the advantage for which you look they will find. May there be among you a man of understanding! When the fruit was ripe, he came quickly, his sickle in his hand, and reaped it. He that hath ears to hear, let him hear.

(22) Jesus saw some infants at the breast. He said to his disciples: These little ones at the breast are like those who enter into the kingdom. They said to him: If we then be children, shall we enter the kingdom? Jesus said to them: When you make the two one, and when you make the inside as the outside, and the outside as the inside, and the upper side as the lower; and when you make the male and the female into a single one, that the male be not male and the female female; when you make eyes in the

place of an eye, and a hand in place of a hand, and a foot in place of a foot, an image in place of an image, then shall you enter [the kingdom].

(23) Jesus said: I shall choose you, one out of a thousand, and two out of ten thousand, and they shall stand as a single one.

(24) His disciples said: Teach us concerning the place where thou art, for it is necessary for us to seek after it. He said to them: He that hath ears, let him hear. There is a light within a man of light, and it gives light to the whole world. If it does not give light, there is darkness.

(25) Jesus said: Love thy brother as thy soul; keep him as the apple of thine eye.

(26) Jesus said: The mote which is in thy brother's eye, thou seest; but the beam which is in thine eye, thou seest not. When thou dost cast out the beam from thine own eye, then wilt thou see to cast out the mote from thy brother's eye.

(27) ⟨Jesus said⟩: If you fast not from the world, you will not find the kingdom; if you keep not the Sabbath as Sabbath, you will not see the Father.

(28) Jesus said: I stood in the midst of the world, and I appeared to them in flesh. I found them all drunk, I found none among them thirsting; and my soul was afflicted for the sons of men, for they are blind in their heart and they do not see. For empty came they into the world, seeking also to depart empty from the world. But now they are drunk. When they have thrown off their wine, then will they repent.

(29) Jesus said: If the flesh has come into being because of the spirit, it is a marvel; but if the spirit (has come into being) because of the body, it is a marvel of marvels. But as for me, I marvel at this, how this great wealth has settled in this poverty.

(30) Jesus said: Where there are three gods, they are gods; where there are two or one, I am with him.

(31) Jesus said: No prophet is acceptable in his village; a physician does not heal those who know him.

(32) Jesus said: A city that is built on a high mountain and is fortified cannot fall, nor can it remain hidden.

(33) Jesus said: What thou shalt hear in thine ear, proclaim to the other ear[1] on your roof-tops. For no man lights a lamp and sets it under a bushel, nor does he put it in a hidden place; but he sets it upon the lamp-stand, that all who go in and come out may see its light.

(34) Jesus said: If a blind man lead a blind man, both fall into a pit.

(35) Jesus said: It is not possible for anyone to go into the strong

[1] There is possibly a dittography here in the Coptic text.

man's house and take it (*or:* him) by force, unless he bind his hands; then he will plunder his house.

(36) Jesus said: Be not anxious from morning to evening and from evening to morning about what you shall put on.

(37) His disciples said: On what day wilt thou be revealed to us, and on what day shall we see thee? Jesus said: When you unclothe yourselves and are not ashamed, and take your garments and lay them beneath your feet like little children, and tread upon them, then [shall ye see] the Son of the living One, and ye shall not fear.

(38) Jesus said: Many times have you desired to hear these words which I speak unto you, and you have none other from whom to hear them. Days will come when you will seek after me, and you will not find me.

(39) Jesus said: The Pharisees and the scribes have received the keys of knowledge; they have hidden them. They did not go in, and those who wanted to go in they did not allow. But you, be ye wise as serpents and innocent as doves.

(40) Jesus said: A vine was planted apart from the Father, and since it is not established it will be pulled up by its roots and destroyed.

(41) Jesus said: He who has in his hand, to him shall be given; and he who has not, from him shall be taken even the little that he has.

(42) Jesus said: Become passers-by.

(43) His disciples said to him: Who art thou, that thou shouldst say these things to us? ⟨Jesus said to them⟩: From what I say unto you, you do not understand who I am, but you have become as the Jews; for they love the tree and hate its fruit, and they love the fruit and hate the tree.

(44) Jesus said: He who blasphemes against the Father will be forgiven, and he who blasphemes against the Son will be forgiven, but he who blasphemes against the Holy Spirit will not be forgiven, either on earth or in heaven.

(45) Jesus said: They do not gather grapes from thorns, nor pluck figs from camel-thistles; they do not yield fruit. A good man brings forth a good thing from his treasure; a bad man brings forth evil things from his evil treasure which is in his heart, and he says evil things; for out of the abundance of his heart he brings forth evil things.

(46) Jesus said: From Adam to John the Baptist there is none born of woman who is higher than John the Baptist, so that his eyes will not be broken (?) But I have said, He who shall be among you as a little one shall know the kingdom, and shall be higher than John.

(47) Jesus said: It is not possible for a man to ride two horses or draw two bows, and it is not possible for a servant to serve two masters; or he will honour the one and insult the other. A man does not drink old wine and immediately desire to drink new wine; and they do not pour new wine into old skins, lest they burst, nor do they pour old wine into new skins, lest it spoil. They do not sew an old patch on a new garment, for a rent will come.

(48) Jesus said: If two make peace with one another in this one house, they shall say to the mountain: Be moved, and it shall be moved.

(49) Jesus said: Blessed are the solitary and the elect, for you shall find the kingdom; for you came forth thence, and shall go there again.

(50) Jesus said: If they say to you: Whence have you come?, tell them: We have come from the light, the place where the light came into being through itself alone. It [stood], and it revealed itself in their image. If they say to you: Who are you?, say: We are his sons, and we are the elect of the living Father. If they ask you: What is the sign of your Father in you?, tell them: It is a movement and a rest.

(51) His disciples said to him: On what day will the rest of the dead come into being? And on what day will the new world come? He said to them: That which ye await has come, but ye know it not.

(52) His disciples said to him: Twenty-four prophets spoke in Israel, and they all spoke concerning (*lit.:* in) thee. He said to them: You have neglected him who is alive before you, and have spoken about the dead.

(53) His disciples said to him: Is circumcision profitable or not? He said to them: Were it profitable, their father would beget them from their mother circumcised. But the true circumcision in spirit has proved entirely profitable (*lit.:* has found usefulness altogether).

(54) Jesus said: Blessed are the poor, for yours is the kingdom of heaven.

(55) Jesus said: He who shall not hate his father and his mother cannot be my disciple, and (he who does not) hate his brethren and his sisters and take up his cross like me shall not be worthy of me.

(56) Jesus said: He who has known the world has found a corpse, and he who has found a corpse, the world is not worthy of him.

(57) Jesus said: The kingdom of the Father is like a man who had [good] seed. His enemy came by night, he sowed a weed

among the good seed. The man did not allow them to pull up the weed. He said to them: Lest perhaps you go to pull up the weed, and pull up the wheat with it. For on the day of harvest the weeds will be manifest; they will be pulled up and burned.

(58) Jesus said: Blessed is the man who has suffered; he has found the life.

(59) Jesus said: Look upon the living One so long as you live, that you may not die and seek to see him, and be unable to see.

(60) ⟨They saw⟩ a Samaritan carrying a lamb going into Judaea. He said to his disciples: Why does he carry the lamb?[1] They said to him: That he may kill it and eat it. He said to them: So long as it is alive he will not eat it, but if he kill it and it become a corpse. They said: Otherwise he will not be able to do it. He said to them: You also, seek for yourselves a place within for rest, lest you become a corpse and be eaten.

(61) Jesus said: Two shall rest upon a bed; one shall die, the other live.

Salome said: Who art thou, O man? And whose son?[2] Thou hast mounted my bed, and eaten from my table. Jesus said to her: I am he who is from that which is equal; to me was given of the things of my Father. ⟨Salome said⟩: I am thy disciple. ⟨Jesus said to her⟩: Therefore I say, when it is equal it will be filled with light, but when it is divided it will be filled with darkness.

(62) Jesus said: I tell my mysteries to those [who are worthy of my] mysteries. What thy right hand shall do, let not thy left hand know what it does.

(63) Jesus said: There was a rich man who had many possessions. He said: I will use my possessions that I may sow and reap and plant, and fill my barns with fruit, that I may have need of nothing. These were his thoughts in his heart. And in that night he died. He that hath ears, let him hear.

(64) Jesus said: A man had guests, and when he had prepared the dinner he sent his servant to summon the guests. He came to the first; he said to him: My master summons thee. He said: I have money with some merchants. They are coming to me in the evening. I will go and give them orders. I pray to be excused from the dinner. He went to another; he said to him: My master has summoned thee. He said to him: I have bought a house, and they ask me for a day. I shall not have time. He came to another; he said to him: My master summons thee. He said to him: My friend is about to be married, and I am to hold a dinner. I shall not be able to come. I pray to be excused from the dinner. He went to

[1] The text appears to be corrupt, but something like this is required by the sense.
[2] This follows the editors' correction in the Brill edition. The following replies of Jesus are obscure, and several translations have been proposed.

another; he said to him: My master summons thee. He said to him: I have bought a village; I go to collect the rent. I shall not be able to come. I pray to be excused. The servant came, he said to his master: Those whom thou didst summon to the dinner have excused themselves. The master said to his servant: Go out to the roads. Bring those whom thou shalt find, that they may dine. The buyers and the merchants [shall] not [enter] the places of my Father.

(65) He said: A good man had a vineyard. He gave it to husbandmen that they might work it, and he receive its fruit at their hand. He sent his servant, that the husbandmen might give him the fruit of the vineyard. They seized his servant, they beat him, and all but killed him. The servant came (and) told his master. His master said: Perhaps they did not know him.[1] He sent another servant; the husbandmen beat the other also. Then the master sent his son. He said: Perhaps they will reverence my son. Those husbandmen, since they knew that he was the heir of the vineyard, they seized him (and) killed him. He that hath ears, let him hear.

(66) Jesus said: Teach me concerning this stone which the builders rejected; it is the corner-stone.

(67) Jesus said: He who knows the All but fails (to know) himself lacks everything.

(68) Jesus said: Blessed are you when they hate you, and persecute you, and do not find a place in the spot where they persecuted you.

(69) Jesus said: Blessed are they who have been persecuted in their heart; these are they who have known the Father in truth.

Blessed are they that hunger, that they may fill the belly of him who desires.

(70) Jesus said: When you bring forth that in yourselves, that which you have will save you. If you do not have that in yourselves, that which you do not have in you will kill you.

(71) Jesus said: I will des[troy this] house, and none shall be able to build it [again].

(72) [A man said] to him: Speak to my brethren, that they may divide my father's possessions with me. He said to him: O man, who made me a divider? He turned to his disciples (and) said to them: I am not a divider, am I?

(73) Jesus said: The harvest indeed is great, but the labourers are few; but pray the Lord, that he send forth labourers into the harvest.

(74) He said: Lord, there are many about the well, but no one in the well.

[1] This follows the editors' correction in the Brill edition.

(75) Jesus said: There are many standing at the door, but the solitary are they who shall enter the bridal chamber.

(76) Jesus said: The kingdom of the Father is like a merchant who had a load (of goods) and found a pearl. That merchant was wise. He sold the load, and bought for himself the pearl alone. You also, seek after his treasure which does not perish but endures, where moth does not enter to devour, nor does worm destroy.

(77) Jesus said: I am the light that is over them all. I am the All; the All has come forth from me, and the All has attained unto me. Cleave a (piece of) wood: I am there. Raise up the stone, and ye shall find me there.

(78) Jesus said: Why came ye forth into the field? To see a reed shaken by the wind? And to see a man clothed in soft raiment? [Behold, your] kings and your great men are they who are clothed in soft [raiment], and they [shall] not be able to know the truth.

(79) A woman in the crowd said to him: Blessed is the womb which bore thee, and the breasts which nourished thee. He said to her: Blessed are they who have heard the word of the Father, and have kept it in truth. For there shall be days when you will say: Blessed is that womb which has not conceived, and those breasts which have not given suck.

(80) Jesus said: He who has known the world has found the body, and he who has found the body, the world is not worthy of him.

(81) Jesus said: He who has become rich, let him become king; and he who has power let him deny.

(82) Jesus said: He who is near to me is near the fire, and he who is far from me is far from the kingdom.

(83) Jesus said: The images are revealed to the man, and the light which is in them is hidden in the image of the light of the Father. He shall be revealed, and his image is hidden by his light.

(84) Jesus said: When you see your likeness, you rejoice; but when you see your images which came into being before you— they neither die nor are made manifest—how much will you bear?

(85) Jesus said: Adam came into being out of a great power and a great wealth, and yet he was not worthy of you. For if he had been worthy, he would not have tasted of death.

(86) Jesus said: [The foxes have] the[ir holes] and the birds have [their] nest, but the Son of Man has no place to lay his head and rest.

(87) Jesus said: Wretched is the body which depends upon a body, and wretched is the soul which depends on these two.

(88) Jesus said: The angels come to you, and the prophets, and

they shall give you what belongs to you; and you also, give them what is in your hands, and say to yourselves: On what day do they come and take what is theirs?

(89) Jesus said: Why do you wash the outside of the cup? Do you not understand that he who made the inside is also he who made the outside?

(90) Jesus said: Come unto me, for easy is my yoke and my lordship is gentle, and you shall find rest for yourselves.

(91) They said to him: Tell us who thou art, that we may believe in thee. He said to them: You test the face of the heaven and the earth, and him who is before you you do not know, and you know not to test this moment.

(92) Jesus said: Seek, and ye shall find; but those things concerning which ye asked me in those days, I did not tell you then. Now I wish to tell them, and ye seek not after them.

(93) ⟨Jesus said⟩: Give not that which is holy to the dogs, lest they cast them on the dung-heap; cast not the pearls to the swine, lest they make it [. . .]

(94) Jesus [said]: He who seeks shall find, and he who knocks, to him it shall be opened.

(95) [Jesus said]: If you have money, do not lend at interest, but give [. . .] to him from whom you will not receive them back.

(96) Jesus [said]: The kingdom of the Father is like a woman who took a little leaven and [hid] it in meal; she made large loaves of it. He that hath ears, let him hear.

(97) Jesus said: The kingdom of the [Father] is like a woman carrying a jar full of meal and walking a long way. The handle of the jar broke; the meal poured out behind her on the road. She was unaware, she knew not her loss.[1] When she came into her house, she put down the jar (and) found it empty.

(98) Jesus said: The kingdom of the Father is like a man who wanted to kill a great man. He drew the sword in his house and drove it into the wall, that he might know that his hand would be strong. Then he slew the great man.

(99) The disciples said to him: Thy brethren and thy mother are standing outside. He said to them: Those here who do the will of my Father, these are my brethren and my mother; these are they who shall enter into the kingdom of my Father.

(100) They showed Jesus a gold piece and said to him: They who belong to Caesar demand tribute from us. He said to them: What belongs to Caesar give to Caesar, what belongs to God give to God, and what is mine give unto me.

(101) ⟨Jesus said⟩: He who shall not hate his father and his mother like me cannot be my [disciple], and he who shall

[1] These words are variously rendered.

[not] love [his father] and his mother like me cannot be my [disciple]; for my mother [. . .] but my true [mother] gave me life.

(102) And Jesus said: Woe to them, the Pharisees! For they are like a dog sleeping in the manger of the cattle; for he neither eats, nor does he let the cattle eat.

(103) Jesus said: Blessed is the man who knows in what part the robbers are coming, that he may rise and gather his [. . .] and gird up his loins before they come in.

(104) They said [to him]: Come, let us pray today and fast. Jesus said: What then is the sin that I have done, or wherein have I been vanquished? But when the bridegroom comes forth from the bridal chamber, then let them fast and pray.

(105) Jesus said: He who shall know father and mother shall be called the son of a harlot.[1]

(106) Jesus said: When you make the two one, you shall become sons of man, and when you say: Mountain, be moved, it shall be moved.

(107) Jesus said: The kingdom is like a shepherd who had a hundred sheep. One of them, the biggest, went astray. He left the ninety-nine and sought after the one till he found it. When he had laboured, he said to the sheep: I love thee more than the ninety-nine.

(108) Jesus said: He who shall drink from my mouth shall become like me; I myself will become he, and the hidden things shall be revealed to him.

(109) Jesus said: The kingdom is like a man who had in his field a [hidden] treasure about which he did not know; and [after] he died he left it to his [son. The] son also did not know; he took (possession of) that field and sold it. The man who bought it came to plough, and [found] the treasure. He began to lend money at interest to whomsoever he chose.

(110) Jesus said: He who has found the world and become rich, let him deny the world.

(111) Jesus said: The heavens shall be rolled up and the earth before your face, and he who lives in the living One shall neither see death nor ⟨fear⟩; because Jesus says: He who shall find himself, of him the world is not worthy.

(112) Jesus said: Woe to the flesh which depends upon the soul; woe to the soul which depends upon the flesh.

(113) His disciples said to him: On what day will the kingdom come? ⟨Jesus said⟩: It cometh not with observation. They will not say: Lo, here! or: Lo, there! But the kingdom of the Father is spread out upon the earth, and men do not see it.

1 "Will they call him the son of a harlot?" (Quecke).

(114) Simon Peter said to them: Let Mary go forth from among us, for women are not worthy of the life. Jesus said: Behold, I shall lead her, that I may make her male, in order that she also may become a living spirit like you males. For every woman who makes herself male shall enter into the kingdom of heaven.

The Gospel according to Thomas.

THE GOSPEL OF TRUTH

Much of the Gospel of Thomas consists of sayings already long familiar through their occurrence in the canonical Gospels, and on the whole there is a fairly large measure of agreement among translators as to the meaning of the text. Only a few passages remain obscure. With the Gospel of Truth however it is another matter. This text is entirely new, and at some points is extremely difficult. To think of a definitive translation would at this stage be altogether premature, nor is it possible here to enter into discussion of the various alternative renderings which have been proposed at different points; for these reference must be made to the commentaries mentioned below. For this and other reasons the following pages present only a series of further extracts, where the translation is fairly certain, linked by summaries of the intervening sections; in short, a paraphrase or summary rather than a complete translation. The extracts are from the second (revised) edition published by Messrs. Rascher of Zürich, and are included here by their permission. Other English versions of the complete text have been published by Kendrick Grobel (*The Gospel of Truth. A Valentinian Meditation on the Gospel. Translation from the Coptic and Commentary*, London 1960) and by W. W. Isenberg (in Grant: *Gnosticism: An Anthology*, London 1961, pp. 146–161). The Rascher version is shortly to be made available in a cheap English edition, with introduction and commentary.

The text begins with the words from which it derives its name:

The Gospel of Truth is joy for those who have received from the Father of Truth the grace of knowing Him through the power of the Word, which has come forth from the Pleroma, (the Word) which is in the thought and mind of the Father (and) which is he whom they call 'the Saviour', for that is the name of the work which he is to accomplish for the salvation of those who were ignorant of the Father; for this name 'the Gospel' is the revelation of hope, since it is a discovery for those who seek Him. (16.31–17.4)

This theme is now elaborated and explained:

. . . this ignorance concerning the Father produced anguish and terror. And the anguish became dense like a mist, so that no one could see. For this reason Error waxed strong. (17.9–15)

The works of Error, designed to "lead astray those of the Midst and take them captive", involve no humiliation for the Father, nor do they come from Him. They are as nothing, whereas the truth is "unalterable, unshakable, and of a beauty which cannot be improved upon". What did come from the Father was knowledge, "which was manifested in order that oblivion might be done away and that (men) might know the Father". As soon as men come to this knowledge, 'oblivion' (which is ignorance of God) will no longer exist, and this is the Gospel revealed to the perfect. Here the author refers to the ministry of Jesus, who

enlightened those who were in darkness by reason of oblivion. He enlightened them. He gave them a way. And the way is the truth which he taught them. Because of this Error was wroth with him, persecuted him, oppressed him, brought him to naught. He was nailed to a tree, and became a fruit of the knowledge of the Father. (18.17–26)

After a brief digression on the relation between 'the All' and the Father, the theme is resumed:

In the place of instruction he came in the midst, he spake the word as a master. There came to him those who were wise in their own estimation, putting him to the proof; but he confounded them, for they were foolish. They hated him, for they were not truly wise men. After all these there came to him the little children, those to whom belongs the knowledge of the Father. (19.18–30)

These both knew and were known, were glorified and gave glory.

There was manifested in their heart the living Book of the living, which is written in the thought and (in) the mind of the Father and which from before the foundation of the All was in that part of Him which is incomprehensible, this (Book) which none has power to take, since that is reserved for him who shall take it and shall be slain. No one could become manifest of those who believed in the salvation, so long as that Book had not made its appearance. For this reason the merciful and faithful Jesus was compassionate, he accepted the sufferings until he took that Book, since he knew that his death is life for many. (19.34–20.14)

He was nailed to a tree (and) he affixed the ordinance of the Father to the Cross. O, what a great teaching! He humbles himself even unto death though clothed with immortal life. Having divested himself of these perishable rags, he clothed himself with incorruptibility, which it is impossible for anyone to take away from him. (20.25–34)

The next section speaks of a teaching received by "the living who are inscribed in the Book of the living", a teaching which relates to themselves, their own true nature and origin. It has already been said (in the digression mentioned above) that the Father had retained in Himself the perfection of the All, and this theme is now developed.

Therefore if anyone possesses knowledge, he receives that which is his own and draws it back to himself. For he who is ignorant is deficient, and it is a great thing which he lacks, since he lacks what will make him perfect. Since the perfection of the All is in the Father, it is necessary that the All ascend to Him, and that each one receive that which is his own, (the things) which He has written down beforehand, having prepared them to be given to those who came forth from Him. Those whose names He knew beforehand are called at the end, so that he who knows is he whose name the Father has pronounced. For he whose name has not been pronounced is ignorant. Indeed, how should anyone hear, if his name has not been called? For he who remains ignorant to the end is a creature of oblivion, and will be destroyed with it. (21.11–37)

In contrast,

If anyone possesses knowledge, he is a being from on high. If he is called, he hears, replies, and turns towards Him who calls him in order to ascend to Him, and he knows in what way he is called. Since he knows, he performs the will of Him who called him. He desires to please Him (and) receives rest. (22.3–12)

He who thus possesses knowledge knows whence he is come and whither he is going. He knows even as a person who, having been intoxicated, has recovered from his intoxication, and having come to himself sets in order the things that belong to him. (22.13–19)

In the following section the author again digresses, to discuss the 'letters' written by the Father in order that the aeons might thereby come to know Him. The passage culminates in lines which appear to be in the nature of a hymn in honour of the Word. Then the text proceeds:

Thus the Word of the Father proceeds forth into the All, being the fruit of His heart and a form of His will. It upholds the All, it chooses it, and also takes (upon itself) the form of the All, purifying it and causing it to return to the Father and to the

Mother, Jesus of the infinite gentleness. The Father reveals His breast; but His breast is the Holy Spirit. He reveals that of Himself which was hidden (that of Himself which was hidden was His Son) in order that through the compassion of the Father the aeons might know Him, and cease to torment themselves in search of the Father, resting in Him since they know that this is rest. When he had filled up the deficiency he abolished the form. His form is the world, that wherein he served. For where there is envy and dissension, there is deficiency; but where there is unity, there is perfection. Since deficiency came into existence because they did not know the Father, so when they know the Father deficiency from that moment will no longer exist. Just as in the case of anyone's ignorance, at the moment when he comes to know his ignorance disappears of its own accord; just as the darkness dissolves when the light appears, so also the deficiency is dissolved by the perfection. (23.33–25.3)

By means of knowledge each

will purify himself from diversity into unity, devouring the matter within him like a fire, darkness by light, death by life. If then these things have happened to each one of us, it is fitting for us to take thought above all that the house may be holy and silent for the Unity. (25.13–25)

Here the author introduces an analogy of unsound vessels which are smashed by their owners and replaced by sound ones. This, he says,

is the judgment come from above, which has judged every man, a drawn sword with double edge which cuts on one side and on the other. When the Word appeared . . . a great confusion arose among the vessels, for some had been emptied, others filled; for lo, some were provided for, others were overturned; some were purified, others were broken to pieces. (25.35–26.15)

Then follows a description of the agitation of Error at the manifestation of the Word. This, then, is the manifestation of the Father, His revelation to the aeons. He alone is perfect, and knows all things, bringing them to pass in His own time. This somewhat obscure passage leads up to the question:

What then is that which He desires that (man) should think? This: "I am become like the shadows and the phantoms of the night". When the light dawns upon the terror which had laid hold of him, that man knows that it is nothing. (28.24–31)

The state of the 'ignorant' is vividly portrayed, "as if they were sunk in sleep and found themselves a prey to troubled dreams":

Either it is a place to which they are fleeing, or they are powerless when they have been in pursuit of someone; or they are involved in brawls, or they are themselves receiving blows; or they are falling from great heights, or they fly off into the air, even though they have no wings. At other times again it is as if someone were trying to kill them, although there is no one pursuing them, or they themselves were killing those near to them, for they are defiled with their blood. Up to the time when those who pass through all these things wake up, they see nothing, those who were in all these confusions, for they were nothing. So it is with those who have cast ignorance away from them, like sleep, because they reckon (it) as nothing. (29.8–35)

The works of ignorance are abandoned "like a dream in the night". The knowledge of the Father, on the other hand, "they esteem as the light". To receive *gnosis* is like awaking from sleep. The Spirit gives to men the possibility of knowing "the knowledge of the Father and the revelation of His Son".

For when they had seen and heard him, he allowed them to taste him and to smell him, and to lay hold of the beloved Son. He appeared, instructing them about the Father, the incomprehensible. He breathed into them that which is in the thought, accomplishing His will. Many received the light and turned to him. (30.27–31.1)

Here the author appears to return to the ministry of Jesus. Material men were alien to Him, and did not recognize Him, for He came "in a likeness of flesh".

The Light spoke through his mouth, and his voice engendered life. He gave them thought and understanding, compassion and deliverance and the Spirit of power from the boundlessness and sweetness of the Father. He caused the punishments and torments to cease, for it was they which caused many in need of mercy to wander from Him in error and in chains; and with power he destroyed them, and he put them to shame through knowledge. He became a way for those who erred, and knowledge for those

527

who were ignorant; a discovery for those who sought, and strength for those who wavered; spotlessness for those who were defiled. He is the Shepherd who abandoned the ninety-nine sheep which had not gone astray. He went in search of that one which had strayed. He rejoiced when he found it. For ninety-nine is a number which is in the left hand, which encompasses it. But as soon as the one is found the whole number passes over to the right (hand). Thus it is with him who lacks the one, that is to say, the entire right hand, which attracts that which is lacking and takes it away from the left side, and passes over to the right; and in this way the number becomes a hundred . . . Even on the Sabbath he laboured for the sheep, which he found fallen into a pit. He preserved the sheep alive by bringing it out of the pit, that you may understand—you, the children of understanding—what is that Sabbath on which it is not fitting that redemption remain inactive; that you may speak of that day which is above, wherein there is no night; and of the light which does not pass away, because it is perfect. Speak, then, from your hearts, for you are this perfect day, and in you dwells the light which has no end. (31.13–32.35)

The following passage consists of exhortations, but the meaning of some lines is still obscure. The readers are urged: "Do you then the will of the Father, for you are of Him". The next section seems to introduce a new theme:

For the children of the Father, they are His fragrance, since they are from the grace of His countenance. Because of this the Father loves His fragrance, and makes it manifest in every place; and if it be mixed with matter, He gives His fragrance to the light and in His silence He causes it to rise above every form and every sound. For it is not the ears which smell the fragrance, but it is the spirit which has the (faculty of) smelling, and it draws it itself, and plunges down into the fragrance of the Father. (33.39–34.14)

The original fragrance however is cold, the result (34.27) of the 'separation'.

Because of this, faith came. It destroyed the separation and brought the warm fulness of love; in order that the cold might not come again into existence, but the unity of the perfect thought.

This is the word of the glad tidings of the coming of the fulness for those who are awaiting the salvation that comes from above.[1] (34.28–35.2)

The following lines speak of the hope of those "whose likeness is the light in which there is no shadow", and of the return to the Father which is called conversion.

For this reason Imperishability breathed forth. It followed after him who had sinned, that he might find rest . . . For the physician hastens to the place where there is a sick (man), for that is the desire that is in him. He then who suffers lack hides it not, for he (the physician) has what he (the sick man) needs. Thus the pleroma, which does not lack, fills up the deficiency, (the pleroma) which He (the Father) gave of Himself to fill up what he needs, in order that he might receive grace; for at the time when he was deficient he did not possess grace. (35.23–36.5)

Another obscure passage, which has been variously rendered, leads to a reference to anointing with the chrism.

This chrism is the mercy of the Father, who will have mercy upon them. But those whom he anointed, these are those who are perfect. (36.17–20)

Here the author introduces an analogy, which again has been variously understood. The section ends with a reference to the paradise of the Father, which is His place of rest, and to "the words of His meditation", each of which "is the work of His unique will, in the revelation of His Word". The following lines refer to the beginning of things, when the Logos was the first to come forth "at the moment pleasing to the will of Him who willed".

But the will is that in which the Father rests and which pleases Him. Nothing comes to pass without Him, nor does anything occur without the will of the Father. But incomprehensible is His will. (37.19–25)

It is the Father

from whom the beginning came forth and to whom shall return all those who came forth from Him. But they were manifested for the glory and the joy of His name. But the name of the Father is the Son. He it is who in the beginning gave a name to him who came forth from Him, and who was Himself, and whom He

[1] The word here rendered 'fulness' is the Greek πλήρωμα.

engendered as a Son. He gave him His name which belonged to Him, since He it is, even the Father, to whom belong all things which are with Him. He has the name, He has the Son. It is possible for them to see him. But the name, on the contrary, is invisible, since it alone is the mystery of the Invisible, which comes to ears which are all filled with it. For indeed one does not pronounce the name of the Father, but He is revealed in a Son. (38.1–24)

This theme of the Name is developed at length, and is evidently one on which the author laid great stress:

The first thing we must do, then, is to understand this point: "What is the Name?" For it is the true name. It is indeed the name which came from the Father, for it is He who is Lord of the name. Now he received the name not by way of loan, like others, according to the manner in which every one is equipped. But He is Lord of the name. There is no other to whom He has given it. But it is unnameable (and) ineffable until the moment when He alone who is perfect pronounced it; and He it is who has power to pronounce His name and to see it. When it pleased Him, then, that His Son should be His name . . . he spoke of His secrets, knowing that the Father is absolute Goodness. For that reason also He brought him forth, that he might speak of that place and about His place of rest from which he had come, and that he might glorify the Pleroma, the greatness of His name and the gentleness of the Father. (40.2–41.3)

The final section deals with the destiny of the blessed:

He will speak about the place from which each one has come, and (each) will hasten to return once more to the region from which he derived his true condition, and to be delivered from that place, the place wherein he has been, since he tastes of that place and receives nourishment and growth (therein). And his own place of rest is his pleroma. All the emanations of the Father, then, are pleromas, and all His emanations have their root in Him who caused them all to grow from Himself and gave to them their destiny. (41.4–20)

The place to which they direct their thoughts, that place is

their root, which lifts them up through all the heights to the
Father. (41.24–28)

Of such people the writer says:

Neither did they disparage the glory of the Father, nor did
they think of Him as small; nor that He is harsh, nor that He is
wrathful; but He is absolutely good, unshakable, mild, knowing
all the spaces even before they have come into existence, and
having no need of instruction. This is the manner of those who
have something from on high, through this immeasurable greatness, in that they strain towards that unique One who is perfect
and who is there for their sakes. And they do not descend into
Hades, nor have they any jealousy or sighing, nor is there any
death among them, but they rest in Him who rests. They labour
not, neither are they entangled in the search for the truth, but
they are themselves the truth. And the Father is in them, and they
are in the Father, perfect and inseparable from that truly good
(Being). (42.3–30)

This is the place of the blessed; this is their place. As for the
rest, let them consider in their places that it is not befitting for
me, after I have been in the place of rest, to speak of anything
else. But therein shall I be, and devote myself at all times to the
Father of the All, and to the true brethren, upon whom the love
of the Father is poured out, and in whose midst nothing of Him
is lacking. These are they who are manifest in truth, since they
are in that true and eternal life, and speak of the light that is
perfect and filled with the seed of the Father, and which is in
His heart and in the pleroma, while His Spirit rejoices in Him and
glorifies Him in whom it was, for He is good. And His children
are perfect, and worthy of His name, for it is children of this kind
that He, the Father, loves. (42.37–43.23)

On this note the document ends.